Sylvia Wilson's Bovee Files

(Descendants of Mathieu Boifils of France)

By Sylvia E Wilson
1912-2006

Printed in the
United States of America

ISBN: 9781449537982

FORWORD

While researching her grandmother's Dutch Huyck family, the author learned that Huyck family members had married into the French Bovee family, both families having settled in Albany County, New York in pre-Revolutionary days. The earliest documentation of the Bovee family came from church baptism records and court records for Albany County as early as 1681.

The reader should note that the descendants of the Huyck family carried on the Dutch tradition of naming the first-born son for the paternal grandfather, the second son for the maternal grandfather, and the third son after the father. This practice has proved to be an invaluable clue for the author in developing the lineage, particularly where baptismal or other records were missing or otherwise unavailable to the author or her fellow contributors.

In Acknowledgement:

The author's expanded interest into the Bovee family genealogy has culminated with this book, a product of 40 years of research and correspondence with many interested parties. The principal ones are listed below and their contributions are deeply appreciated by the author.

The late Nina Bovee whose research collection resides in the Montgomery County Dept of History and Archives in Fonda, NY.,

Richard Atkinson
Robert Clare Bovee
Irene Ferguson Bovee
Constance Reed Diamond
Bill Filgate
Ila Bovee Kraft
Patricia Hayes Smith
Shirley Woodward.

Ruth Bovee Beecher
Robert Frederick Bovee
Linda Currie
Lawrence T. Fadner
Robert Gedlinske
Doris Martin
William R Strouse

See also: Historians as noted by their families.

This text was prepared for publication by me at the request of Sylvia A. Wilson, a wonderful friend with a memory and knowledge of this material of unbelievable proportions. Though documentation is not included herein nothing was placed in the file until she was satisfied that in was correct to the best of her ability to determine.
With deep admiration and love I dedicate this work to her memory.

William R Strouse

While this book is extensive in it's listing of **Bovee**, (The spelling we have chosen to use for the book) lines of descent it contains only the lines we have researched. It is certain that many other lines do exist as evidenced by the last section containing what we have labeled "unknown". In addition there are lines of **Bovie** which are not included though a few families included used that variation at one time or another. We hope that this book will aid others who may be interested in their ancestry. Information included has been carefully checked for accuracy and is believed to be correct. However, as with all such compilations, nothing here is considered absolute and further research could prove facts included to be in error.

The lines of descent start with **Mathew Bovee**, the first we know of to enter the United States in this line. "While absolute proof is not available, it may well be that Mathieu Bovie of New York is the same as the Mathieu Boifils, a laborer from the Ile de Ré who signed on as an engagé (indentured servant) at La Rochelle, France, on 17 April 1678 to work for three years at a wage of 90 1. a year for the Montreal merchant and trader, Jacques Leber". (Gabriel Debien, "Liste des Engagés pour le Canada" in *Revue d'histoire de l'Amerique Francaise 6* [1952];

399). Jacque Leber was a great uncle of **Catherine Barrois** who married **Mathew Bovee**.

The earliest knowledge of Bovee in America is in 1860's court records of Albany and Rensselaer counties of New York, followed by baptism and marriage records of the Dutch Reformed Church. French Bovees married into Dutch families and carried on the Dutch naming program which carried on family names. Census records helped to place families and military pension records provided much additional family information. Three or four generations were furnished by several family historians.

Individual documentation is not provided for all records since it would consume many pages. For those instances where baptisms, marriages or other events are reported to have occurred in churches, the church records are considered to be the documentation. Other examples are wills, land records, census records, bible records, letters, history reports and obituaries. In addition several documents authored by persons included in this book provided valuable information not otherwise available.

INTRODUCTION

"It may well be that Mathew Bovee of New York is the same as the Mathieu Boifils, a laborer from the Ile de Ré who signed on as an engagé (indentured servant) at La Rochelle, France, on 17 April 1678 to work for three years at a wage of 90 1. a year for the Montreal merchant and trader, Jacques Leber".

Jacque Leber was a great uncle of **Catherine Barrois** who married **Mathew Bovee**.

(Gabriel Debien, "Liste des Engagés pour le Canada" in *Revue d'histoire de l'Amerique Francaise 6* [1952]; 399).

Mathew Bovee first appears in New York as "Matthys, a Frenchman" while he was being sued by Barent Myndertse in 1683.

Myndertse had fl 79 in seawan (wampum) of Matthys, then being held by Pieter van Wuggelum, attached for payment of debt and requested the court to validate the attachment. In a related suit, Cornelis Corn Viele attached two beavers in the hands of Pieter van Wuggelum belonging to Matthys. Both cases were held over until the next court day. On Sept 11, 1683 a number of attachments were levied on merchandise held at the house of Pieter van Wuggelum by Duplicee, Tardivet, and Matthys, a Frenchman, apparent partners in a fur trading venture that soured, leaving the three owing more that they had the resources to pay. In each suit, as in the case of Cornelis Corn Viele vs Matthys the Frenchman, the court found that "the beavers and goods of the defendant and his partners have been attached by several creditors; (the court) adjudge and decide that all the attachments shall have equal effect and that each person shall be paid in proportion to the amount due to him and, if the property is not sufficient, the defendant is ordered to pay the remainder of his debt to the plaintiff cum expensis".

The following year Matthew was in more serious trouble.

Jacob Sanders, constable, informs the court that a certain Frenchman, named Matthys, threatens to poison his Negress and he offers to prove it.

The Frenchman, Matthys Boffie, appearing before the court, acknowledges that he has slept for 2 years with the Negress and that he has 2 children by her and that he would like to buy her.

Matthys, the Frenchman, being summoned to appear in court, the examination of Francyn, the Negress of Jacob Staets, and the examination of various Negroes and Negresses of Schenectady are read to him, in which they unanimously charge him with having employed every means to entice her to run away to Canada, saying that he would show her the way and make her free.

The honorable court order Matthys, the Frenchman, to give security in the sum of 100 lbs. to answer the charge of having endeavored to allure away some Negroes and Negresses before the next Court of Oyer and Terminer to be held for this county and in May and, if he can not furnish any security, the sheriff is ordered to confine him and to produce him before the Court of Oyer and Terminer aforesaid.

(Minutes of the Court of Albany, Rensselaerswyck, and Schenectady 1680-1685, Volume 3: 381 – 383, 390 – 394, 480, 526 – 527).

Matthew is probably the "Mattias Boose Snor" listed as a freeholder at Canistignione in 1720 in :A list of the Freeholders of the City and County of Albany, 1720" in "The Documentary History of the State of New York" 1 (Albany 1849) : 373, by Edmund Bailey O'Callaghan.

Descendants of
Mathieu Bovee and Catherine Barrois

1. Mathieu[1] **Bovee**, born in France; died aft 1720 in Albany Co, NY. He married abt 1688 Catherine Barrois, christened 26 May 1674 in la Prairie,Quebec, Canada, daughter of Antonie Barrois and Anne LeBer.

Children of Mathieu Bovee and Catherine Barrois were as follows:

+	2	i	Mathieu[2] **Bovee** Jr, born abt 1688. He married (1) **Maria Van Vranken**; (2) **Eleanor Bennewe**.
	3	ii	Catarina[2] **Bovee**, christened 12 Feb 1689/90 in DRC, Albany, Albany Co., NY.
+	4	iii	Nicholas[2] **Bovee**, christened 18 Apr 1692 in Stonebridge, Bergen Co., NJ. He married **Cornelia Brouwer**.
	5	iv	Anthony[2] **Bovee**, christened 18 May 1696 in New York Co., NY.
+	6	v	Maria[2] **Bovee**, christened 8 Sep 1699 in DRC, Albany, Albany Co., NY. She married **Jacob Brouwer**.
	7	vi	Anna[2] **Bovee**, christened 18 Jan 1701/02 in DRC, Schenectady, Schenectady Co., NY.
+	8	vii	Catarina[2] **Bovee**, christened 7 Jan 1704/05 in DRC, Schenectady, Schenectady Co., NY. She married **Jacobus Radcliff**.
+	9	viii	Anthony[2] **Bovee**, christened 2 Nov 1707 in DRC, Albany, Albany Co., NY. He married **Catharine Van Dewerken**.
	10	ix	Philip[2] **Bovee**, christened 30 Oct 1710 in DRC, Albany, Albany Co., NY.
+	11	x	Francois[2] **Bovee**, born in Wonende, Rensselaerwyck, Albany Co., NY.; christened 25 May 1713 in DRC, Albany, Albany Co., NY. He married **Machtelt Van Vranken**.

Generation 2

2. Mathieu[2] **Bovee** Jr (Mathieu[1]), born abt 1688. He married (1) abt 1715 Maria Van Vranken, daughter of Garrit Van Vranken and Ariantje Uldricks Kleyn; (2) on 21 Jun 1744 in DRC, Albany, NY Eleanor Bennewe.

Children of Mathieu Bovee Jr and Maria Van Vranken were as follows:

	12	i	Gerrit[3] **Bovee**, christened 23 Sep 1716 in RDC, Albany, Albany Co., NY, died abt 1716.
+	13	ii	Catharine[3] **Bovee**, christened 25 Oct 1719 in RDC, Albany, Albany Co., NY. She married **Abraham Vin Hagen**.
	14	iii	Gerrit[3] **Bovee**, christened 3 May 1722 in RDC, Albany, Albany Co., NY.
	15	iv	Uldrick[3] **Bovee**, christened 8 Jan 1723/24 in RDC, Albany,

Albany Co., NY.

16   v   Margaret ^{3} **Bovee**, christened 24 Oct 1725 in RDC, Albany, Albany Co., NY. She married in Nov 1754 in Albany, Albany Co., NY **John Carr**.

+ 17   vi   Anna ^{3} **Bovee**, christened 4 Jun 1727 in DRC, Albany, Albany Co., NY. She married **Vincent Bennewe**.

18   vii   Claas ^{3} **Bovee**, christened 15 Jan 1728/29 in RDC, Albany, Albany Co., NY.

+ 19   viii   Ariantje ^{3} **Bovee**, born abt 1731. She married **Robert Crannell**.

+ 20   ix   Philip ^{3} **Bovee**, christened 13 Oct 1732 in RDC, Albany, Albany Co., NY, died 24 Sep 1788 in Albany Co, NY. He married (1) **Gertrude Vanden Berg**; (2) **Eva Sharp**.

4. Nicholas ^{2} **Bovee** (Mathieu ^{1}), christened 18 Apr 1692 in Stonebridge, Bergen Co., NJ. He married on 24 Sep 1714 in RDC, Albany, Albany Co., NY Cornelia Brouwer, born 13 Mar 1691; christened 1692 in DRC, Brooklyn, Kings Co., NY, daughter of Pieter Adam Brouwer and Peternelle Uldricks Kleyn.

Children of Nicholas Bovee and Cornelia Brouwer were as follows:

+ 21   i   Neeltje ^{3} **Bovee**, christened Mar 1716 in DRC, Albany, Albany Co., NY. She married **Andries Cornelius Huyck**.

22   ii   Peter ^{3} **Bovee**, christened 31 Mar 1717 in Albany, Albany Co., NY, died Oct 1747 in Fort Massachusetts.

+ 23   iii   Catharine ^{3} **Bovee**, christened 8 Mar 1718/19 in Albany, Albany Co., NY. She married **John Cornelius Huyck**.

+ 24   iv   Rykert ^{3} **Bovee**, christened 11 Jan 1720/21 in Albany, Albany Co., NY, died aft 1768. He married **Marytie Huyck**.

25   v   Hendrik ^{3} **Bovee**, christened 3 Mar 1722/23 in Albany, Albany Co., NY.

+ 26   vi   Matthew ^{3} **Bovee**, christened 16 Aug 1725 in DRC, Albany, Albany Co., NY. He married **Maria Cole**.

+ 27   vii   Abraham ^{3} **Bovee**, born in NY; christened 20 Oct 1728 in DRC, Albany, Albany Co., NY; died 1800. He married (1) **Sarah Cool**; (2) **Anna (---)**.

+ 28   viii   Philip ^{3} **Bovee**, christened 2 Aug 1730 in DRC, Albany, Albany Co., NY. He married unknown.

+ 29   ix   Jacob ^{3} **Bovee**, born in NY; christened 2 Jul 1732 in Albany, Albany Co., NY. He married (1) **Anna Cole**; (2) **Bata De Graaf**.

6. Maria ^{2} **Bovee** (Mathieu ^{1}), christened 8 Sep 1699 in DRC, Albany, Albany Co., NY. She married on 6 Apr 1717 in RDC, Albany, Albany Co., NY Jacob Brouwer, born 13 Nov 1694, son of Pieter Adam Brouwer and Peternelle Uldricks Kleyn.

Children of Maria Bovee and Jacob Brouwer were as follows:

30	i	Catryna[3] **Brouwer**, born 29 Dec 1717; christened in Albany, Albany Co., NY.
31	ii	Neeltje[3] **Brouwer**, born 13 Mar 1719/20.
32	iii	Petrus[3] **Brouwer**, born 29 Apr 1722; christened in Albany, Albany Co., NY.
33	iv	Anna[3] **Brouwer**, born 7 Jun 1724.
34	v	Mathew[3] **Brouwer**, born 15 Jun 1727; christened in Albany, Albany Co., NY.
35	vi	Lena[3] **Brouwer**, born 30 Mar 1729; christened in Albany, Albany Co., NY.
36	vii	Lena[3] **Brouwer**, born 9 May 1731.
37	viii	Maria[3] **Brouwer**, born 7 Oct 1733.
38	ix	Ariantje[3] **Brouwer**, born 8 Mar 1737/38; died 1818. She married on 7 Sep 1754 in Albany, Albany Co., NY **Gerrit Bovee** (see 52), born 1730 in Halfmoon, Saratoga Co., NY; christened 3 Feb 1730 in Albany, Albany Co., NY; died 2 Feb 1804, son of Anthony Bovee and Catharine Van Dewerken.
39	x	Catarina[3] **Brouwer**, born 28 Sep 1740.
40	xi	Mathew[3] **Brouwer**, born 7 Aug 1743.

8. Catarina[2] **Bovee** (Mathieu[1]), christened 7 Jan 1704/05 in DRC, Schenectady, Schenectady Co., NY. She married Jacobus Radcliff, son of Jan Radcliff and Rachel Van Valkenburg.

Children of Catarina Bovee and Jacobus Radcliff were as follows:

41	i	Rachel[3] **Radcliff**, born 19 Feb 1728/29; christened in Albany, Albany Co., NY.
42	ii	Mathew[3] **Radcliff**, born 3 Oct 1730; christened in Albany, Albany Co., NY.
43	iii	Catherine[3] **Radcliff**, born 21 Nov 1731; christened in Albany, Albany Co., NY.
44	iv	Johannes[3] **Radcliff**, born 6 Jan 1733/34; christened in Albany, Albany Co., NY.
45	v	Philip[3] **Radcliff**, born 26 Oct 1735; christened in Albany, Albany Co., NY.
46	vi	William[3] **Radcliff**, born 16 Apr 1738; christened in Albany, Albany Co., NY.
47	vii	William[3] **Radcliff**, born 23 Dec 1739; christened in Albany, Albany Co., NY.
48	viii	William[3] **Radcliff**, born 12 Jul 1741; christened in Albany, Albany Co., NY.
49	ix	Maria[3] **Radcliff**, born 26 Feb 1743/44; christened in Albany, Albany Co., NY.
50	x	Elizabeth[3] **Radcliff**, born 16 Aug 1747; christened in Albany, Albany Co., NY.

9. Anthony[2] **Bovee** (Mathieu[1]), christened 2 Nov 1707 in DRC, Albany, Albany Co., NY. He married abt 1727 Catharine Van Dewerken, christened 6 May 1705 in RDC, Albany, Albany Co., NY, daughter of Gerrit Van Dewerken and Marytie Jans DeVoe.

Children of Anthony Bovee and Catharine Van Dewerken were as follows:

+ 51   i   Catherine[3] **Bovee**, christened 23 Aug 1729 in Albany, Albany Co., NY. She married **Ruloff Mackerie**.

+ 52   ii   Gerrit[3] **Bovee**, born 1730 in Halfmoon, Saratoga Co., NY; christened 3 Feb 1730 in Albany, Albany Co., NY; died 2 Feb 1804. He married **Ariantje Brouwer** (see 38).

53   iii   Maria[3] **Bovee**, christened 20 May 1733 in Albany, Albany Co., NY.

54   iv   Antje[3] **Bovee**, christened 13 Apr 1735 in Albany, Albany Co., NY.

55   v   Jannetje[3] **Bovee**, christened 23 Dec 1737 in Albany, Albany Co., NY.

+ 56   vi   Matthew[3] **Bovee**, christened 9 Sep 1739 in Albany, Albany Co., NY. He married **Maria Wendell**.

57   vii   Ariantje[3] **Bovee**, christened 14 Jun 1741 in Albany, Albany Co., NY.

58   viii   Anneke[3] **Bovee**, christened 29 May 1743 in Albany, Albany Co., NY.

59   ix   Marytie[3] **Bovee**, christened 8 Nov 1747 in Albany, Albany Co., NY. She married **Nicholas Huyck** (see 79), christened 29 May 1743 in DRC, Albany, Albany Co., NY, son of Andries Cornelius Huyck and Neeltje Bovee.

+ 60   x   Philip[3] **Bovee**, christened 20 Jan 1749/50 in Coxsackie, Greene Co., NY. He married **Catherine Westfall**.

11. Francois[2] **Bovee** (Mathieu[1]), born in Wonende, Rensselaerwyck, Albany Co., NY.; christened 25 May 1713 in DRC, Albany, Albany Co., NY. He married on 7 Feb 1734/35 in Schenectady, Schenectady Co., NY Machtelt Van Vranken, born 3 Apr 1712; christened 20 Apr 1712, daughter of Nicholas Van Vranken and Gertrude Quackenbush.

Children of Francois Bovee and Machtelt Van Vranken were as follows:

+ 61   i   Elizabeth[3] **Bovee**, christened 13 Jun 1736 in Schenectady, Schenectady Co., NY. She married **Johannes Heemstradt Jr.**

+ 62   ii   Mathew[3] **Bovee**, christened 22 Oct 1738 in Albany, Albany Co., NY. He married **Bata Van Der Heyden**.

63   iii   Gertrude[3] **Bovee**, christened 24 Jun 1741. She married on 3 Dec 1759 **Vincent Bennewe**, son of Guert Bennewe and Peternelle de la Montagne.

64   iv   Carel[3] **Bovee**, c 24 Jun 1744 in Albany, Albany Co., NY.

13. Catharine³ **Bovee** (Mathieu², Mathieu¹), christened 25 Oct 1719 in RDC, Albany, Albany Co., NY. She married abt 1756 Abraham Vin Hagen, son of Johannes Vin Hagen and Maria Van Tricht.

Children of Catharine Bovee and Abraham Vin Hagen were as follows:

65　　i　　　　Maria⁴ **Vin Hagen**, christened 13 Sep 1757.

17. Anna³ **Bovee** (Mathieu², Mathieu¹), christened 4 Jun 1727 in DRC, Albany, Albany Co., NY. She married abt 1755 Vincent Bennewe, son of Guert Bennewe and Peternelle de la Montagne.

Children of Anna Bovee and Vincent Bennewe were as follows:

66　　i　　　　Guert⁴ **Bennewe**, born 25 Jan 1756.

67　　ii　　　Peternelle⁴ **Bennewe**, born 14 Aug 1757.

19. Ariantje³ **Bovee** (Mathieu², Mathieu¹), born abt 1731. She married on 13 Nov 1748 in Albany, Albany Co., NY Robert Crannell, son of William Crannell and Margaret Bennewe.

Children of Ariantje Bovee and Robert Crannell were as follows:

68　　i　　　　William⁴ **Crannell**, born 1749 in NY.

69　　ii　　　Mathew⁴ **Crannell**, born 14 Aug 1751; christened in Albany, Albany Co., NY.

70　　iii　　Mary⁴ **Crannell**, christened 10 Mar 1754 in Albany, Albany Co., NY.

71　　iv　　Petrus⁴ **Crannell**, born 14 Nov 1756.

72　　v　　　Petrus⁴ **Crannell**, born 11 Mar 1759.

73　　vi　　Nicholas⁴ **Crannell**, born 20 Apr 1760.

20. Philip³ **Bovee** (Mathieu², Mathieu¹), christened 13 Oct 1732 in RDC, Albany, Albany Co., NY, died 24 Sep 1788 in Albany Co, NY. He married (1) on 3 Nov 1764 in Albany, Albany Co., NY Gertrude Vanden Berg, born 9 Jan 1736/37 in Albany, Albany Co., NY; died in Rensselaer Co., NY, daughter of Andries Vanden Berg and Maria Vin Hagen; (2) on 15 Dec 1775 in Albany, Albany Co., NY Eva Sharp.

Children of Philip Bovee and Gertrude Vanden Berg were as follows:

74　　i　　　　Mathew⁴ **Bovee**, christened 15 Sep 1765 in RDC, Albany, Albany Co., NY.

+ 75　　ii　　　Mathew⁴ **Bovee**, christened 11 Sep 1768 in DRC, Albany, Albany Co., NY. He married **Elizabeth Lansing**.

+ 76　　iii　　Andrew⁴ **Bovee**, born abt 1770. He married **Aaltje Bradt**.

Children of Philip Bovee and Eva Sharp were as follows:

77   i   Abraham[4] **Bovee**, born abt 1776.

21. Neeltje[3] **Bovee** (Nicholas[2], Mathieu[1]), christened Mar 1716 in DRC, Albany, Albany Co., NY. She married on 24 Nov 1739 Andries Cornelius Huyck, born abt 1713, son of Cornelius Huyck and Gertrude Vosburgh.

Children of Neeltje Bovee and Andries Cornelius Huyck were as follows:

     78   i   Peter **Huyck**, christened 11 Jan 1740/41 in DRC, Albany, Albany Co., NY.

+   79   ii   Nicholas[4] **Huyck**, christened 29 May 1743 in DRC, Albany, Albany Co., NY. He married **Marytie Bovee** (see 59).

+   80   iii   Cornelius A[4] **Huyck**, born 13 Dec 1747; christened 17 Jun 1748 in Zion Luth Ch, Louvenburg, Greene Co., NY. He married **Hester Gardinier**.

     81   iv   Hendrick[4] **Huyck**, christened 5 Apr 1751 in Claverack, Columbia Co., NY, died 1828.

     82   v   Cornelia[4] **Huyck**, christened 19 Jul 1752 in DRC, Albany, Albany Co., NY.

23. Catharine[3] **Bovee** (Nicholas[2], Mathieu[1]), christened 8 Mar 1718/19 in Albany, Albany Co., NY. She married on 24 Nov 1739 in Albany, Albany Co., NY John Cornelius Huyck, son of Cornelius Huyck and Gertrude Vosburgh.

Children of Catharine Bovee and John Cornelius Huyck were as follows:

     83   i   Cornelius J[4] **Huyck**, christened 29 Jun 1740 in Albany, Albany Co., NY.

     84   ii   Nicholas[4] **Huyck**, christened 14 Feb 1741/42 in Albany, Albany Co., NY.

     85   iii   Andries[4] **Huyck**, christened 20 May 1744 in Albany, Albany Co., NY.

     86   iv   Cornelia[4] **Huyck**, christened 5 Apr 1746 in Albany, Albany Co., NY.

     87   v   Isaac[4] **Huyck**, christened 24 Apr 1748 in Loonenburg, Greene Co., NY.

     88   vi   Gertrude[4] **Huyck**, born 5 Apr 1751; christened in Albany, Albany Co., NY.

     89   vii   Catherine[4] **Huyck**, born 31 Dec 1752; christened in Albany, Albany Co., NY.

     90   viii   Maria[4] **Huyck**, christened 27 Oct 1764 in Albany, Albany Co., NY.

     91   ix   Elizabeth[4] **Huyck**, christened 25 Dec 1756 in Coxsackie, Green Co., NY.

     92   x   Johannes[4] **Huyck**, christened 8 Apr 1757 in Coxsackie, Green Co., NY.

93 xi Peter[4] **Huyck**, christened 2 May 1761 in Albany, Albany Co., NY.

24. Rykert[3] **Bovee** (Nicholas[2], Mathieu[1]), christened 11 Jan 1720/21 in Albany, Albany Co., NY, died aft 1768. He married on 5 Sep 1743 in Albany, Albany Co., NY Marytie Huyck, christened 24 Sep 1727 in Kinderhoock, Columbia Co,. NY, daughter of Cornelius Huyck and Gertrude Vosburgh.

Children of Rykert Bovee and Marytie Huyck were as follows:

94 i Nicholas[4] **Bovee**, born in NY; christened 26 Aug 1744 in RDC, Schenectady, Schenectady Co., NY.

95 ii Gertrude[4] **Bovee**, born in NY; christened 31 Jan 1747/48 in Albany, Albany Co., NY.

+ 96 iii Sarah[4] **Bovee**, born 12 May 1750 in NY; christened 30 Jun 1750 in Albany, Albany Co., NY; died 2 May 1827. She married **Peter Ostrander**.

+ 97 iv Cornelia[4] **Bovee**, born 27 Feb 1754 in NY; christened 7 Apr 1754 in Albany, Albany Co., NY. She married **Christopher Snyder**.

98 v Hendrick[4] **Bovee**, born 4 Oct 1757 in NY; christened 30 Oct 1757 in Coxsackie, Greene co., NY; died 1784.

+ 99 vi John[4] **Bovee**, born 3 Oct 1759; died 22 Dec 1830 in Hoosick, Renssalaer Co., NY. He married (1) **Keziah Wells**; (2) **Susanna Hallenbeck Heller**.

+ 100 vii Maria[4] **Bovee**, born 15 May 1762 in Albany, Albany Co., NY; christened 18 Jun 1762 in Albany, Albany Co., NY. She married **Abraham Ostrander**.

+ 101 viii Cornelius[4] **Bovee**, born 11 Jul 1765 in Albany, Albany Co., NY; died 15 Mar 1847 in Kellogsville, Ashtabula Co., OH. He married **Lucretia Bailey**.

102 ix Annatie[4] **Bovee**, born 24 Jan 1768 in Albany, Albany Co., NY; christened 27 May 1768 in Albany, Albany Co., NY.

26. Matthew[3] **Bovee** (Nicholas[2], Mathieu[1]), christened 16 Aug 1725 in DRC, Albany, Albany Co., NY. He married Maria Cole, christened abt 1734 in Pompton Plains, Morris Co, NJ, daughter of Jacobus L Cool and Sarah Davenport.

Children of Matthew Bovee and Maria Cole were as follows:

+ 103 i Cornelia[4] **Bovee**, born abt 1756 in NY; died bef 1786. She married **Teunis Barheyt**.

104 ii Sarah[4] **Bovee**, born abt 1758; died aft 1810. She married **Nicholas Jacob Bovee** (see 127), christened 15 Aug 1754 in (as Hendrickus) Pompton Plains, Morris Co., NJ, died aft 1810, son of Jacob Bovee and Anna Cole.

+ 105 iii Nicholas M[4] **Bovee**, born 17 Mar 1760 in New Bruswick, Middlesex co., NJ; died 12 Feb 1843 in Villenova,

7

Chautauqua Co., NY. He married **Nancy Baptist**.

106	iv	Maria[4] **Bovee**, born 12 Mar 1761; christened 19 Dec 1761 in Coxsackie, Greene co., NY; died abt 1761.
+ 107	v	Maria[4] **Bovee**, christened 8 Apr 1763 in Catskill, Greene Co., NY. She married **Jacobus Barheyt**.
+ 108	vi	Jacob Mathias[4] **Bovee**, born 17 Mar 1766; christened 3 Aug 1766 in Coxsackie, Green Co., NY; died 17 Sep 1807 in Amsterdam, Montgomery Co., NY. He married **Jane Dods**.
+ 109	vii	Abraham[4] **Bovee**, born 29 Oct 1768 in NY; christened 6 Nov 1768 in DRC, Schenectady, Schenectady Co., NY; died 21 Oct 1830 in Berne, Albany Co., NY. He married (1) **Anna Warner**; (2) **Catherine Van Yveren**.
+ 110	viii	John[4] **Bovee**, born abt 1770 in Montgomery Co., NY. He married **Magdelena Schermerhorn**.
+ 111	ix	John Henry[4] **Bovee**, born 1772 in Saratoga Co., NY; died 28 Mar 1846 in Hudson, Lenawee Co., MI. He married **Aaltje Sutphin**.

27. Abraham[3] **Bovee** (Nicholas[2], Mathieu[1]), born in NY; christened 20 Oct 1728 in DRC, Albany, Albany Co., NY; died 1800. He married (1) abt 1761 Sarah Cool, christened 13 Jun 1742 in Kingston, Ulster Co., NY, daughter of Jacobus L Cool and Sarah Davenport; (2) Anna (---), born abt 1763; died 1 May 1815.

Children of Abraham Bovee and Sarah Cool were as follows:

+ 112	i	Jacob[4] **Bovee**, born 5 Jul 1763 in Hoosick, Rensselaer Co., NY; died 21 Aug 1853 in Hoosick, Rensselaer Co., NY. He married **Lydia Hall**.
+ 113	ii	Matthew[4] **Bovee**, born 19 Jan 1765 in Hoosick, Rensselaer Co., NY; christened 9 Jun 1765 in St. Pauls's Luth Ch., Schoharie, Schoharie Co., NY. He married **Elizabeth Wilson**.
+ 114	iii	John[4] **Bovee**, born abt 1770 in NY. He married (1) **Elizabeth Primmer**; (2) **Elizabeth Whitaker**.
+ 115	iv	Abraham[4] **Bovee**, born abt 1772 in NY; died 10 May 1838 in T/Lenox, Madison Co., NY. He married **Eleanor Huyck** (see 179).
116	v	Sarah[4] **Bovee**, born 14 Apr 1775 in NY; christened in DRC, Schaghticoke, Rensselaer Co., NY.
117	vi	Cornelia[4] **Bovee**, born 4 Jan 1779 in NY; christened 7 Feb 1779 in Gilead Luth Ch., Centre Brunswick, Rensselaer Co., NY.
+ 118	vii	Henry[4] **Bovee**, born 23 Aug 1781; christened 26 Aug 1781 in Gilead Luth Ch., Centre Brunswick, Rensselaer Co., NY; died 6 Nov 1864 in Union Town, Broome Co., NY. He married **Betsy Brimmer**.

Children of Abraham Bovee and Anna (---) were as follows:

+ 119 i Peter[4] **Bovee**, born 25 Jul 1787; christened 23 Feb 1788 in Centre Brunswick, Rensselaer Co., NY. He married **Catherine Holbrook**.

120 ii Charles E[4] **Bovee**, died 27 Feb 1865.

121 iii Louise[4] **Bovee**, born 16 Mar 1796; christened 17 Jul 1796; buried in Ouquaga Cem., Colesville, Broome Co., NY.

28. Philip[3] **Bovee** (Nicholas[2], Mathieu[1]), christened 2 Aug 1730 in DRC, Albany, Albany Co., NY. He married unknown.

Children of Philip Bovee were as follows:

+ 122 i Jacob Philip[4] **Bovee**, born abt 1750. He married (1) **Rebecca Cronke**; (2) **Jacomyntje Marcellus**.

123 ii Elizabeth[4] **Bovee**, born abt 1754. She married **(---) Eldridge**.

+ 124 iii Nicholas P[4] **Bovee**, born abt 1757 in Hoosick, Rensselaer Co., NY; died 11 Mar 1796 in Schenectady, Schenectady Co., NY. He married **Polly Cotrell**.

125 iv Philip[4] **Bovee**, christened 18 Oct 1761 in 1st Presb Ch., Morristown, Morris Co., NJ.

+ 126 v Catherine[4] **Bovee**, born abt 1768. She married **Joseph Kemp**.

29. Jacob[3] **Bovee** (Nicholas[2], Mathieu[1]), born in NY; christened 2 Jul 1732 in Albany, Albany Co., NY. He married (1) on 1 Jan 1754 in Morris Co., NJ Anna Cole, daughter of Jacobus L Cool and Sarah Davenport; (2) aft 1771 Bata De Graaf, christened 19 Oct 1735 in DRC, Schenectady, Schenectady Co., NY, daughter of John Quackenbush and Helena Clute.

Children of Jacob Bovee and Anna Cole were as follows:

+ 127 i Nicholas Jacob[4] **Bovee**, christened 15 Aug 1754 in (as Hendrickus) Pompton Plains, Morris Co., NJ, died aft 1810. He married **Sarah Bovee** (see 104).

+ 128 ii Jacob[4] **Bovee** Jr, born 24 Nov 1756 in Outcalt, Middlesex Co., NJ; died 24 Sep 1837. He married **Elizabeth Beth**.

+ 129 iii Isaac[4] **Bovee**, born 10 Dec 1762; died 20 Sep 1821 in Schenectady, Schenectady Co., NY. He married **Rebecca Vedder**.

+ 130 iv Abraham[4] **Bovee**, died Oct 1823 in Amsterdam, Montgomery Co., NY. He married **Elizabeth Vedder**.

+ 131 v Matthew[4] **Bovee**, born abt 1765; died abt 1830 in Genesee Co., NY. He married **Maria Schermerhorn**.

+ 132 vi Sara[4] **Bovee**, born 20 Aug 1768; christened 11 Sep 1768 in Coxsackie, Greene Co., NY; died 1 Sep 1855 in Burnt Hills, Saratoga Co., NY. She married **Jacobus A Van Vorst**.

133 vii Cornelia[4] **Bovee**, christened 14 Oct 1770 in Schodack,

Renssalaer Co., NY, died bef 1805.

51. Catherine[3] **Bovee** (Anthony[2], Mathieu[1]), christened 23 Aug 1729 in Albany, Albany Co., NY. She married on 29 Mar 1755 in Albany, Albany Co., NY Ruloff Mackerie.

    Children of Catherine Bovee and Ruloff Mackerie were as follows:

    134   i   Anthony[4] **Mackerie**, christened 30 Sep 1758 in Katsbaan, Ulster Co., NY.
    135   ii   Antje[4] **Mackerie**, born 9 Aug 1756; christened 8 Sep 1756 in Albany, Albany Co., NY.
    136   iii   Ariantje[4] **Mackerie**, born 4 Feb 1767; christened in Schaghticoke, Rensselaer Co., NY.

52. Gerrit[3] **Bovee** (Anthony[2], Mathieu[1]), born 1730 in Halfmoon, Saratoga Co., NY; christened 3 Feb 1730 in Albany, Albany Co., NY; died 2 Feb 1804. He married on 7 Sep 1754 in Albany, Albany Co., NY Ariantje Brouwer (see 38), born 8 Mar 1737/38; died 1818, daughter of Jacob Brouwer and Maria Bovee.

    Children of Gerrit Bovee and Ariantje Brouwer were as follows:

    +   137   i   Anthony[4] **Bovee**, christened 21 Dec 1755 in DRC, Albany, Albany Co., NY, died 26 Jul 1822. He married **Maria Barnhart**.
    +   138   ii   Maria[4] **Bovee**, christened 30 Dec 1761 in Albany, Albany Co., NY. She married **Thomas Powell**.
    +   139   iii   Peter[4] **Bovee**, born 16 Jan 1764 in Halfmoon, Saratoga Co., NY; christened 15 Apr 1764 in Albany, Albany Co., NY; died 13 Apr 1837 in Belcher, Hebron,Washington Co., NY. He married **Jane Wygant**.
         140   iv   Catrina[4] **Bovee**, born 12 Mar 1765.
         141   v   David[4] **Bovee**, born Mar 1767; christened in Schaghticoke, Rensselaer Co., NY.
         142   vi   Antje[4] **Bovee**, born 1 Apr 1769; christened in Schaghticoke, Rensselaer Co., NY.
         143   vii   Ariantje[4] **Bovee**, born 2 Apr 1772; christened in Schaghticoke, Rensselaer Co., NY.
    +   144   viii   Jacob[4] **Bovee**, born abt 1774 in NY; died 2 Jan 1842 in West Barnet, Caledonia Co., VT. He married **Elizabeth Redding**.
         145   ix   Elizabeth[4] **Bovee**, born 14 Jan 1776; christened in Schaghticoke, Rensselaer Co., NY.

56. Matthew[3] **Bovee** (Anthony[2], Mathieu[1]), christened 9 Sep 1739 in Albany, Albany Co., NY. He married abt 1762 Maria Wendell.

    Children of Matthew Bovee and Maria Wendell were as follows:

146	i	Catharina[4] **Bovee**, born 31 Oct 1764; christened 4 Feb 1765 in Albany, Albany Co., NY.
147	ii	Annatie[4] **Bovee**, born 29 Oct 1765; christened 18 Jan 1766 in Albany, Albany Co., NY.
+ 148	iii	Anthony[4] **Bovee**, born Sep 1767 in Hoosick, Renssalaer Co., NY; christened 11 Oct 1767 in St. Paul's Luth Ch., Schoharie, Schoharie Co., NY. He married **Catherine Huyck** (see 178).

60. Philip[3] **Bovee** (Anthony[2], Mathieu[1]), christened 20 Jan 1749/50 in Coxsackie, Greene Co., NY. He married Catherine Westfall.

Children of Philip Bovee and Catherine Westfall were as follows:

149	i	Anna[4] **Bovee**, born 15 Jun 1778; christened 7 Sep 1779 in Gilead Lutheran Ch, Centre Brunswick, Rensselaer Co., NY.
150	ii	Elizabeth[4] **Bovee**, born 7 Aug 1782; christened in Schaghticoke, Rensselaer Co., NY.
151	iii	Anthony[4] **Bovee**, born abt 1784.
152	iv	Peter[4] **Bovee**, born abt 1786.

61. Elizabeth[3] **Bovee** (Francois[2], Mathieu[1]), christened 13 Jun 1736 in Schenectady, Schenectady Co., NY. She married on 30 Dec 1757 in Albany, Albany Co., NY Johannes Heemstradt Jr, born 19 Nov 1732, son of John Heemstradt and Beta Quackenbush.

Children of Elizabeth Bovee and Johannes Heemstradt Jr were as follows:

153	i	Macheldt[4] **Heemstradt**, born 15 Oct 1758.
154	ii	Bata[4] **Heemstradt**, born 20 Jul 1764.
155	iii	Catherine[4] **Heemstradt**, born 3 Mar 1767.
156	iv	Frans[4] **Heemstradt**, born 23 Aug 1769.
157	v	Annatje[4] **Heemstradt**, christened 4 Nov 1773 in Schenectady, Schenectady Co., NY.
158	vi	Johannes[4] **Heemstradt**, born 24 May 1779.

62. Mathew[3] **Bovee** (Francois[2], Mathieu[1]), christened 22 Oct 1738 in Albany, Albany Co., NY. He married on 11 Oct 1760 in Schenectady, Schenectady Co., NY Bata Van Der Heyden.

Children of Mathew Bovee and Bata Van Der Heyden were as follows:

+ 159	i	Bata[4] **Bovee**, born 31 May 1761. She married **Gerrit Clute**.
+ 160	ii	Gertrude[4] **Bovee**, born 2 Feb 1766; christened in Albany, Albany Co., NY. She married **Nicholas S Fort**.
+ 161	iii	Catharina[4] **Bovee**, born 11 Sep 1768; died 10 Apr 1810.

She married **Evert Van Vranken**.

162	iv	Rachel[4] **Bovee**, born 1772 in Schenectady Co., NY; christened 6 Sep 1772 in 1st Reformed Church, Schenectady, Schenectady Co., NY.
+ 163	v	Rachel[4] **Bovee**, born 15 Nov 1776. She married **Daniel Van Antwerp**.
+ 164	vi	Elizabeth[4] **Bovee**, born 8 Jul 1784; christened 16 Jul 1784 in DRC Schenectady, Albany Co., NY. She married **David Chambers**.

Generation 4

75. Mathew[4] **Bovee** (Philip[3], Mathieu[2], Mathieu[1]), christened 11 Sep 1768 in DRC, Albany, Albany Co., NY. He married on 6 Mar 1790 in DRC, Albany, Albany Co., NY Elizabeth Lansing, born 3 Dec 1771 in NY, daughter of Jacob H Lansing and Maria Ouderkerk.

Children of Mathew Bovee and Elizabeth Lansing were as follows:

+ 165	i	Philip[5] **Bovee**, born 16 Sep 1790. He married **Elizabeth Van Olinda**.
166	ii	Maria[5] **Bovee**, born 4 Aug 1796; christened in DRC, Schenectady, Schenectady Co., NY.
+ 167	iii	Jacob[5] **Bovee**, born 11 Sep 1798. He married **Mary Thompson**.
168	iv	Gertrude[5] **Bovee**, born 6 Mar 1800; christened in Albany, Albany Co., NY.
169	v	Ann[5] **Bovee**, born 18 Aug 1802; christened in Albany, Albany Co., NY.
170	vi	Catherine[5] **Bovee**, born 18 Aug 1802; christened in Albany, Albany Co., NY. She married on 24 Nov 1824 **John Cutter**.
171	vii	William Ouderkerk[5] **Bovee**, christened 22 Aug 1806 in DRC, Boght Corners, Albany Co., NY.

76. Andrew[4] **Bovee** (Philip[3], Mathieu[2], Mathieu[1]), born abt 1770. He married on 19 Apr 1794 in DRC ,Bought Corners, Albany Co., NY Aaltje Bradt, born 4 Nov 1773; christened in Albany, Albany Co., NY, daughter of John A Bradt and Maicke Fonda.

Children of Andrew Bovee and Aaltje Bradt were as follows:

| 172 | i | Gertrude[5] **Bovee**, christened 25 Apr 1795 in DRC ,Bought Corners, Albany Co., NY. |
| 173 | ii | (---)[5] **Bovee**. |

79. Nicholas[4] **Huyck** (Neeltje[3] Bovee, Nicholas[2], Mathieu[1]), christened 29 May 1743 in DRC, Albany, Albany Co., NY. He married Marytie Bovee (see 59), christened 8 Nov 1747 in Albany, Albany Co., NY, daughter of Anthony Bovee

and Catharine Van Dewerken.

Children of Nicholas Huyck and Marytie Bovee were as follows:

174   i   Jurgen^5 **Huyck**, born 1765 in Hoosick, Rensselaer Co., NY; christened in St Paul's Luth Ch, Schoharie, Schoharie Co., NY; died 1819.

175   ii   Anthony^5 **Huyck**, born abt 1770.

176   iii   Garrit^5 **Huyck**, born 4 May 1774 in Schaghticoke, Rensselaer Co., NY.

177   iv   Jane^5 **Huyck**, born 1791; christened 18 Jun 1814 in DRC, Fort Plain, Montgomery Co., NY.

178   v   Catherine^5 **Huyck**, christened 10 Oct 1767 in Schaghticoke, Rensselaer Co., NY. She married **Anthony Bovee** (see 148), born Sep 1767 in Hoosick, Rensselaer Co., NY; christened 11 Oct 1767 in St. Paul's Luth Ch., Schoharie, Schoharie Co., NY, son of Matthew Bovee and Maria Wendell.

80. Cornelius A^4 **Huyck** (Neeltje^3 Bovee, Nicholas^2, Mathieu^1), born 13 Dec 1747; christened 17 Jun 1748 in Zion Luth Ch, Louvenburg, Greene Co., NY. He married Hester Gardinier.

Children of Cornelius A Huyck and Hester Gardinier were as follows:

179   i   Eleanor^5 **Huyck**, christened 6 Jun 1779 in Coxackie, Green Co., NY. She married **Abraham Bovee** (see 115), born abt 1772 in NY; died 10 May 1838 in T/Lenox, Madison Co., NY, son of Abraham Bovee and Sarah Cool.

96. Sarah^4 **Bovee** (Rykert^3, Nicholas^2, Mathieu^1), born 12 May 1750 in NY; christened 30 Jun 1750 in Albany, Albany Co., NY; died 2 May 1827. She married on 21 Oct 1766 in Albany, Albany Co., NY Peter Ostrander, son of Peter Ostrander and Maria Pier.

Children of Sarah Bovee and Peter Ostrander were as follows:

180   i   Peter^5 **Ostrander**, born 6 Apr 1767; christened 21 Jun 1767 in Schaghticoke, Rensselaer Co., NY.

181   ii   Richard^5 **Ostrander**, born 11 Jan 1780; christened 27 Feb 1780 in Gilead LuCh,Centre Brunswick, Rensselear Co., NY.

182   iii   Annatje^5 **Ostrander**, born 14 Jan 1785; christened 16 Oct 1785 in Gilead LuCh,Centre Brunswick, Rensselear Co., NY; died 15 Mar 1858.

183   iv   Child^5 **Ostrander**, born 30 Oct 1789 in Schaghticoke, Rensselaer Co., NY.

184   v   Richard^5 **Ostrander**, born 29 Sep 1792 in Schaghticoke, Rensselaer Co., NY; died 12 May 1869 in Hoosick, Rensselear Co., NY.

185   vi   Catherine^5 **Ostrander**.

186   vii   John[5] **Ostrander**.

97. Cornelia[4] **Bovee** (Rykert[3], Nicholas[2], Mathieu[1]), born 27 Feb 1754 in NY; christened 7 Apr 1754 in Albany, Albany Co., NY. She married Christopher Snyder.

Children of Cornelia Bovee and Christopher Snyder were as follows:

187   i   John[5] **Snyder**, born 6 May 1774; christened in Schaghticoke, Rensselaer Co., NY.

188   ii   Abraham[5] **Snyder**, born 12 Jul 1776; christened in Schaghticoke, Rensselaer Co., NY.

189   iii   Nicholas[5] **Snyder**, born 12 Feb 1779; christened in Schaghticoke, Rensselaer Co., NY.

190   iv   Sara[5] **Snyder**, born 18 Mar 1781; christened in Schaghticoke, Rensselaer Co., NY.

99. John[4] **Bovee** (Rykert[3], Nicholas[2], Mathieu[1]), born 3 Oct 1759; died 22 Dec 1830 in Hoosick, Renssalaer Co., NY. He married (1) abt 1779 Keziah Wells, daughter of Nathanial Wells; (2) Susanna Hallenbeck Heller, born 16 Dec 1759; died 6 Feb 1823.

Children of John Bovee and Keziah Wells were as follows:

+   191   i   Sarah[5] **Bovee**, born 25 Oct 1780; christened 4 Feb 1781 in Centre Brunswick, Renssalaer Co., NY; died 1861. She married **Col David Wiltse**.

    192   ii   Polly[5] **Bovee**, born 1782 in Renssalaer Co., NY; died 3 Sep 1868.

+   193   iii   Henry[5] **Bovee**, born 12 Apr 1785 in Breese Hollow, Rensselaer Co., NY; died 8 May 1863 in Hoosick, Rensselaer Co., NY. He married **Hannah Hewitt**.

+   194   iv   John[5] **Bovee** Jr, born 15 Dec 1786 in NY. He married (1) **Tabitha Parker**; (2) **Maria Deal**.

    195   v   Hannah[5] **Bovee**, born 14 Mar 1790 in Renssalaer Co., NY; died 12 Feb 1868. She married **Daniel D Bradt**, son of Daniel D Bradt and Hannah Best.

+   196   vi   Susanna[5] **Bovee**, born 22 Mar 1793 in Renssalaer Co., NY; died 19 Jan 1872. She married **Daniel B Bradt**.

    197   vii   Elsie[5] **Bovee**, born 4 Mar 1794 in Hoosick, Renssalaer Co., NY. She married bef 1820 **John Corbett**.

+   198   viii   Keziah[5] **Bovee**, born 18 Jun 1796 in Hoosick, Renssalaer Co., NY. She married **(---) Vaughn**.

    199   ix   Richard[5] **Bovee**, born 4 Feb 1798.

100. Maria[4] **Bovee** (Rykert[3], Nicholas[2], Mathieu[1]), born 15 May 1762 in Albany, Albany Co., NY; christened 18 Jun 1762 in Albany, Albany Co., NY. She married Abraham Ostrander, son of Peter Ostrander and Maria Pier.

Children of Maria Bovee and Abraham Ostrander were as follows:

200   i   Maria[5] **Ostrander**, born 31 May 1779; christened in Schaghticoke, Rensselaer Co., NY.

201   ii   Peter[5] **Ostrander**, born 28 Oct 1781; christened 1 Jan 1782 in Gilead LuCh,Centre Brunswick, Rensselaer Co., NY.

202   iii   Cornelius[5] **Ostrander**, born 4 Oct 1783; christened 5 Jun 1784 in Gilead LuCh,Centre Brunswick, Rensselaer Co., NY.

203   iv   Sarah[5] **Ostrander**, born 3 May 1789; christened 6 Sep 1789 in Gilead LuCh,Centre Brunswick, Rensselaer Co., NY.

204   v   Henry[5] **Ostrander**, born 15 Jun 1794; christened 30 Jun 1797 in Gilead LuCh,Centre Brunswick, Rensselaer Co., NY.

205   vi   Catherine[5] **Ostrander**, born 15 Nov 1796; christened 21 May 1797 in Hoosick, Rensselaer Co., NY.

101. Cornelius[4] **Bovee** (Rykert[3], Nicholas[2], Mathieu[1]), born 11 Jul 1765 in Albany, Albany Co., NY; died 15 Mar 1847 in Kellogsville, Ashtabula Co., OH. He married abt 1786 Lucretia Bailey, born 3 Sep 1767 in New London, New London Co., CT; died 9 Apr 1831 in Kellogsville, Ashtabula Co., OH, daughter of Elisha Bailey and Freelove (---).

Children of Cornelius Bovee and Lucretia Bailey were as follows:

206   i   Richard[5] **Bovee**, born 1 Oct 1787 in Hoosick, Renssalaer Co., NY; died abt 1787.

+ 207   ii   Elisha[5] **Bovee**, born 26 Nov 1788 in Hoosick, Rensselaer Co., NY; died 27 Apr 1864 in Richland Center, Orion Twp, Richland Co.,WI. He married (1) **Mary Springer**; (2) **Sally Smith**.

+ 208   iii   Nicholas[5] **Bovee**, born 11 Jan 1790 in Hoosick, Rensselaer Co., NY; died 16 Apr 1868 in WI. He married **Mercy (---)**.

+ 209   iv   Sarah[5] **Bovee**, born 19 Sep 1791 in Hoosick, Renssalaer Co., NY; died 6 Apr 1881 in Evansville, Rock Co., WI. She married **Allen Springer**.

210   v   Mary[5] **Bovee**, born 10 Jan 1793 in Hoosick, Renssalaer Co., NY; died abt 1793.

+ 211   vi   Mary[5] **Bovee**, born 27 Jan 1796 in Hoosick, Renssalaer Co., NY; died May 1877 in Kingsville, Ashtabula Co., OH. She married **Alanson Colegrove**.

+ 212   vii   Elizabeth[5] **Bovee**, born 20 Oct 1797 in Hoosick, Renssalaer Co., NY; died 12 Jan 1886. She married **Elnathan Wetmore**.

+ 213   viii   Cornelius[5] **Bovee** Jr, born 7 Nov 1799 in Hoosick, Rensselaer Co., NY; died aft 1870. He married **Harriet**

Kellogg.

+	214	ix	Frederick[5] **Bovie**, born 26 May 1801 in Hoosick, Rensselaer Co., NY; christened 23 Aug 1801 in Tioshoke Protestant Reformed Dutch Church; died 9 May 1872 in Gallipolis, Gallia Co., OH. He married **Mercy Maria Clark**.
+	215	x	John E[5] **Bovee**, born 31 Jul 1802 in Hoosick, Rensselaer Co., NY; died 27 Feb 1850. He married **Mary Palmer**.
+	216	xi	Catherine[5] **Bovee**, born 25 Nov 1803 in Hoosick, Renssalaer Co., NY. She married **Richard Stoughton**.
+	217	xii	Peter[5] **Bovee**, born 13 Mar 1806 in Hoosick, Rensselaer Co., NY; died 6 Nov 1890 in Kingsville, Ashtabula Co., OH. He married **Margaret Amelia Wetmore**.
	218	xiii	Henrietta[5] **Bovee**, born 12 Dec 1808 in Hoosick, Renssalaer Co., NY; died 22 Sep 1845.
	219	xiv	Joshua[5] **Bovee**, born 30 Jun 1811 in Hoosick, Renssalaer Co., NY. He married on 25 Mar 1835 in Ashtabula Co., OH **Emily Dun**.

103. Cornelia[4] **Bovee** (Matthew[3], Nicholas[2], Mathieu[1]), born abt 1756 in NY; died bef 1786. She married on 7 May 1775 Teunis Barheyt, son of John Barheyt and Cornelia Putman.

Children of Cornelia Bovee and Teunis Barheyt were as follows:

	220	i	Mathew[5] **Barheyt**, christened 4 Aug 1776 in Schenectady, Schenectady Co., NY..
	221	ii	Cornelius[5] **Barheyt**, christened 1 Nov 1778 in Schenectady, Schenectady Co., NY..
	222	iii	Nicholas[5] **Barheyt**, born abt 1781; christened 4 Mar 1781 in Schenectady, Schenectady Co., NY.; died 1861.

105. Nicholas M[4] **Bovee** (Matthew[3], Nicholas[2], Mathieu[1]), born 17 Mar 1760 in New Bruswick, Middlesex co., NJ; died 12 Feb 1843 in Villenova, Chautauqua Co., NY. He married on 6 Dec 1785 in Schenectady, Schenectady Co., NY Nancy Baptist, born 18 Jun 1766; died 1 Nov 1832 in Villenova, Chautauqua Co., NY.

Children of Nicholas M Bovee and Nancy Baptist were as follows:

+	223	i	Maria[5] **Bovee**, born 22 Sep 1786 in Amsterdam, Montgomery Co., NY; died 28 Apr 1873 in Salt Lake City, Salt Lake Co., UT. She married **Harmon Bogardus Groesbeck**.
+	224	ii	John[5] **Bovee**, born 11 Sep 1788 in Schenectady, Schenectady Co., NY; christened 21 Jan 1789 in DRC, Schenectady, Schenectady Co., NY; died 21 Jan 1868 in Fairfield, Wayne Co., IL. He married (1) **Mary Burt**; (2) **Phoebe Gardner**; (3) **Jane Catherine Gaston**.
+	225	iii	Cornelia[5] **Bovee**, born 10 Mar 1791; christened 6 Jan 1792 in DRC, Schenectady, Schenectady Co., NY; died

16 Sep 1874 in Sheridan, Chautauqua Co., NY. She married **Steven Bush Jr.**

+ 226   iv   Mathew[5] **Bovee**, born 19 Oct 1794 in Charleston, Montgomery Co., NY; died 15 Sep 1846 in Nauvoo, Hancock co., IL. He married (1) **Waitstill Hill**; (2) **Julia Allen**; (3) **Sarah Ester Mecham**.

227   v   Nicholas[5] **Bovee**, born 19 Mar 1796; christened in Cobleskill, Schoharie Co., NY; died 20 May 1817 in Chautauqua Co., NY.

228   vi   Jacob[5] **Bovee**, born 6 Sep 1799 in NY; christened 16 Feb 1800 in DRC, Schenectady, Schenectady Co., NY; died 7 Jun 1825 in Chautauqua Co., NY.

229   vii   Michael Benson[5] **Bovee**, born 20 Aug 1801 in NY; christened 29 Jul 1802 in Woestina Ref Ch., Rotterdam, Schenectady Co., NY; died 15 Mar 1823 in Chautauqua Co., NY.

230   viii   Elizabeth[5] **Bovee**, born 4 Nov 1803; christened 9 Sep 1804 in Woestina Ref Ch., Rotterdam, Schenectady Co., NY; died in Nauvoo, Hanock Co., IL. She married abt 1825 **Ebenezer Baldwin**.

231   ix   Sarah[5] **Bovee**, born 13 Jun 1806 in NY; christened 26 Feb 1807 in Amsterdam, Montgomery Co., NY; died 10 Jun 1851. She married **(---) Stewart**.

232   x   Margaret Ann[5] **Bovee**, born 2 Aug 1811 in Amsterdam, Montgomery Co., NY; died 27 Jun 1830.

In this duly sworn statement Nicholas of Chautauqua, aged eighty-four years, does depose and say he is the son of Mathias Bovee and Polly Bovee, late of Florida, in the county of Montgomery and the State of New York, now deceased. His mother's maiden name was Polly Cole, the daughter of Jacob and Sarah Cole, both now deceased. This deponent further sayith that Mathias Bovee and Polly Bovee, had eight children who's names are as follows; Sarah, Nicholas, Polly, Jacob, Abraham, John, Henry, and Cornelia. That Sarah married her cousin Nicholas Bovee and died leaving one child Jacob Bovee. That Polly married Cobus Barheyt and died leaving only two children Polly, and a son, name forgotten. That Jacob died leaving Polly, Mathias, Philip, Sarah, John and Salia, his children. That Abraham Died leaving Katherine Maria and several others names forgotten. That John Bovee now lives in Erie County, New York. That Henry Bovee now lives in Gates, Monroe County, NY. That Cornelia Married Tunnis Barheit leaving Cornelia, Towas, Cornelius, her children, and further saith not.

107. Maria[4] **Bovee** (Matthew[3], Nicholas[2], Mathieu[1]), christened 8 Apr 1763 in Catskill, Greene Co., NY. She married Jacobus Barheyt, son of John Barheyt and Cornelia Putman.

Children of Maria Bovee and Jacobus Barheyt were as follows:

233   i   Cornelia[5] **Barheyt**, christened 20 May 1781 in DRC, Schenectady, Schenectady Co., NY.

234   ii   Mathew[5] **Barheyt**, christened 20 Mar 1783, died 1850.

235   iii   Marytie[5] **Barheyt**, born 22 Jun 1785; christened in DRC,

Schenectady, Schenectady Co., NY.

236   iv   Cornelia[5] **Barheyt**, born 11 Jan 1795; christened in DRC, Schenectady, Schenectady Co., NY.

108. Jacob Mathias[4] **Bovee** (Matthew[3], Nicholas[2], Mathieu[1]), born 17 Mar 1766; christened 3 Aug 1766 in Coxsackie, Green Co., NY; died 17 Sep 1807 in Amsterdam, Montgomery Co., NY. He married Jane Dods, born 29 Jan 1770 in Florida, Montgomery Co., NY; died 16 Jan 1844 in Eagle, Waukesha Co., WI.

Children of Jacob Mathias Bovee and Jane Dods were as follows:

+   237   i   Mary[5] **Bovee**, born 25 Oct 1789; christened 15 Nov 1789 in DRC, Schenectady, Schenectady Co., NY; died 28 Apr 1869. She married **Benedict Arnold**.

+   238   ii   Selia[5] **Bovee**, born 21 May 1791; christened in DRC, Schenectady, Schenectady Co., NY. She married **(---) Brooks**.

+   239   iii   Mathias Jacob[5] **Bovee**, born 24 Jul 1793 in Amsterdam, Montgomery Co., NY; christened in DRC, Schenectady, Schenectady Co., NY; died 12 Sep 1872 in Eagle, Waukesha Co.,WI. He married **Elizabeth Maria Bovee** (see 346).

+   240   iv   John[5] **Bovee**, born 26 Sep 1795 in Amsterdam, Montgomery Co., NY; christened in DRC, Schenectady, Schenectady Co., NY; died 23 Mar 1872 in Brooklyn, Kings Co., NY. He married (1) **Mercy A Hodson**; (2) **Julia A Holden**; (3) **Phoebe C Reybert**.

241   v   Sarah[5] **Bovee**, born 19 Oct 1797; christened in DRC, Schenectady, Schenectady Co., NY; died 14 Aug 1881.

+   242   vi   Catherine[5] **Bovee**, born 22 Feb 1800; christened in DRC, Schenectady, Schenectady Co., NY. She married **Jonathan Sedgewick**.

+   243   vii   Philip Vedder[5] **Bovee**, born 12 Jun 1802 in NY; christened 18 Jul 1802 in Woetina Ref Ch, Rotterdam, Schenectady Co., NY; died 21 Nov 1873 in Eagle, Waukesha Co., WI. He married **Charlotte Ann Pittman**.

244   viii   Elizabeth[5] **Bovee**, born 18 Sep 1804.

109. Abraham[4] **Bovee** (Matthew[3], Nicholas[2], Mathieu[1]), born 29 Oct 1768 in NY; christened 6 Nov 1768 in DRC, Schenectady, Schenectady Co., NY; died 21 Oct 1830 in Berne, Albany Co., NY. He married (1) abt 1796 Anna Warner, born 28 Oct 1776 in NY; died bef 1824 in NY, daughter of Phillip Warner and Elizabeth Schaeffer; (2) on 5 Sep 1824 in Lutheran Church, Albany, Albany Co., NY Catherine Van Yveren.

Children of Abraham Bovee and Anna Warner were as follows:

245   i   Maria[5] **Bovee**, born 22 Nov 1798; christened 13 Jan 1799 in Schenectady Co., NY.

+   246   ii   Catharine[5] **Bovee**, born 2 May 1802; christened 26 Jun

1802 in St Paul Lutheran Evan Ch, Berne, Albany Co., NY; died 11 Jan 1865. She married **Robert C Van Deusen**.

+ 247   iii   Elizabeth[5] **Bovee**, born Jul 1804 in South Berne, Albany Co., NY; christened 27 Jul 1804 in DRC, Schoharie, Schoharie Co., NY. She married **Michael Decker**.

+ 248   iv   Sarah[5] **Bovee**, born 9 Dec 1806 in NY; christened in DRC, Schoharie, Schoharie Co., NY; died 9 Jan 1887. She married **Jacob P Decker**.

    249   v   Cornelia[5] **Bovee**, born 17 Apr 1813. She married aft 1830 **Peter Palmetier**.

110. John[4] **Bovee** (Matthew[3], Nicholas[2], Mathieu[1]), born abt 1770 in Montgomery Co., NY. He married abt 1798 Magdelena Schermerhorn, born in Pompton, NJ.; christened 26 Feb 1776, daughter of John Schermerhorn and Anna (---).

Children of John Bovee and Magdelena Schermerhorn were as follows:

+ 250   i   Mathew J[5] **Bovee**, born 11 Sep 1799; christened 3 Nov 1799 in Schenectady, Albany Co., NY; died 7 Apr 1863 in Sugar Creek, Walworth Co., WI. He married **Emily Harris**.

+ 251   ii   John Grant[5] **Bovee**, born 29 Oct 1802; christened in DRC, Amsterdam, Montgomery Co., NY; died abt 1884 in Redfield, Oswego Co., NY. He married **Emeline Baird**.

+ 252   iii   Nicholas[5] **Bovee**, born 1 Jul 1804; christened 6 Jan 1805 in DRC, Amsterdam, Montgomery Co., NY; died Sep 1873. He married **Jane (---)**.

    253   iv   Jane[5] **Bovee**, born aft 1806.

    254   v   Catherine[5] **Bovee**, born abt 1806.

111. John Henry[4] **Bovee** (Matthew[3], Nicholas[2], Mathieu[1]), born 1772 in Saratoga Co., NY; died 28 Mar 1846 in Hudson, Lenawee Co., MI. He married abt 1797 Aaltje Sutphin, born 29 Oct 1774 in NY; died 11 Sep 1828 in Yates,Orleans Co., NY, daughter of John Sutphin and Charity Lott.

Children of John Henry Bovee and Aaltje Sutphin were as follows:

+ 255   i   Mary[5] **Bovee**, born 31 Mar 1798 in NY; christened in DRC, Schenectady, Schenectady Co., NY; died 17 Sep 1831 in Orleans Co, NY. She married **Philip Harmon Vedder**.

+ 256   ii   John Henry[5] **Bovee**, born 22 Aug 1799 in NY; christened 27 Aug 1799 in DRC, Schenectady, Schenectady Co., NY; died 10 Jul 1860 in Lenawee Co., MI. He married **Electa Hamlin**.

+ 257   iii   Charity[5] **Bovee**, born 24 Mar 1801 in NY; christened 17 May 1801 in Woestina Ref Ch., Rotterdam, Schenectady Co., NY; died 1824. She married **William Hart**.

+ 258   iv   Mathew[5] **Bovee**, born 31 Jan 1803 in NY; christened 12

Aug 1804 in Woestina Ref Ch, Rotterdam, Schenectady Co., NY; died 25 Nov 1879 in Lenawee Co., MI. He married **Maria Louisa Marlatt**.

+ 259 v Anna[5] **Bovee**, born 10 Feb 1805 in NY; christened in DRC, Amsterdam, Montgomery Co., NY; died 5 May 1879. She married (1) **Obediah H Marlatt**; (2) **Benjamin T Marlatt**.

+ 260 vi Jacob[5] **Bovee**, born 27 Nov 1806 in Montgomery Co., NY; christened 18 Oct 1807 in DRC, Amsterdam, Mongomery Co., NY; died 15 Jan 1885 in Dover Twp, Lenawee Co., MI. He married (1) **Ester Marlatt**; (2) **Fanny Bovee**.

+ 261 vii Sally[5] **Bovee**, born 25 Dec 1808 in Charleston, Montgomery Co., NY; died 29 Jan 1849 in Dover, Lenawee co., MI. She married **Isaac Deline**.

+ 262 viii Ester[5] **Bovee**, born 20 Mar 1811 in Montgomery Co., NY; died 12 May 1887. She married **William Deline**.

+ 263 ix Abraham[5] **Bovee**, born 22 Apr 1813 in NY; died 13 Apr 1873 in Hudson Twp , Lenawee Co., MI. He married **Sarah Grattan**.

+ 264 x Peter[5] **Bovee**, born 13 Dec 1815 in NY; died 16 Sep 1853. He married **Mary Millens**.

+ 265 xi Elsie[5] **Bovee**, born 11 Sep 1817 in NY; died 7 Jul 1897. She married **Aaron Johnson**.

112. Jacob[4] **Bovee** (Abraham[3], Nicholas[2], Mathieu[1]), born 5 Jul 1763 in Hoosick, Rensselaer Co., NY; died 21 Aug 1853 in Hoosick, Rensselaer Co., NY. He married on 25 Dec 1786 Lydia Hall, born 3 Jul 1763 in RI; died 12 Feb 1846 in NY, daughter of (---) Hall and Mary Gardiner.

Children of Jacob Bovee and Lydia Hall were as follows:

266 i Nathaniel[5] **Bovee**, born 2 Feb 1788; christened 30 Jun 1788 in Gilead Luth Ch., Centre Brunswick, Rensselaer Co., NY; died 1813.

+ 267 ii John E[5] **Bovie**, born 17 Feb 1790 in Hoosick, Rensselaer Co., NY. He married **Amy Gardner**.

+ 268 iii Abraham[5] **Bovee**, born 3 Feb 1792 in Hoosick, Rensselaer Co., NY; died 21 Jun 1849 in Hoosick, Rensselaer Co., NY. He married **Sally Shaw**.

+ 269 iv Isaac[5] **Bovee**, born 22 May 1794 in Hoosick, Rensselaer Co., NY; died 21 Jun 1862 in Hoosick, Rensselaer Co., NY. He married (1) **Annie Allen**; (2) **Phebe Wilson**.

+ 270 v Jacob[5] **Bovee** Jr, born 12 Aug 1796. He married **Mary Ann Stanton**.

+ 271 vi William G[5] **Bovee**, born 17 May 1801 in Rensselaer Co., NY. He married **Mary Ann Carpenter**.

+ 272 vii Asa[5] **Bovee**, born 20 Apr 1805 in Hoosick, Rensselaer Co., NY; died 1 Aug 1872 in Riceville, Fulton Co., NY. He married **Weltha Marie Gooding**.

113. Matthew[4] **Bovee** (Abraham[3], Nicholas[2], Mathieu[1]), born 19 Jan 1765 in Hoosick, Rensselaer Co., NY; christened 9 Jun 1765 in St. Pauls's Luth Ch., Schoharie, Schoharie Co., NY. He married Elizabeth Wilson.

Children of Matthew Bovee and Elizabeth Wilson were as follows:

	273	i	Betsey[5] **Bovee**, born 26 Jan 1791 in Hoosick, Rensselaer Co., NY. She married **(---) Edrick**.
	274	ii	Matilda[5] **Bovee**, born abt 1795 in Hoosick, Rensselaer Co., NY. She married **William Shemes**.
+	275	iii	Sally[5] **Bovee**, born 30 Apr 1798 in NY; christened 7 Feb 1799 in Gilead Luth Ch., Centre Brunswick, Rensselaer Co., NY; died 10 Jul 1868 in Otsego Co., NY. She married **Jacob Quackenbush**.
+	276	iv	Lucinda[5] **Bovee**, born 27 Jun 1805 in East Sydney, Delaware Co., NY; died 20 Oct 1882 in East Sydney, Delaware Co., NY. She married **Hiram Smith Whitney**.
+	277	v	Rodney.[5] **Bovee**, born 1807 in Rensselaer Co., NY; died in Unadilla, Otsego Co., NY. He married (1) **Cynthia Youmans**; (2) **Mary (---)**.
+	278	vi	Peter[5] **Bovee**, born 11 Aug 1811 in Schoharie Co., NY; died 9 Dec 1894 in Williamsport, Lycoming Co., PA. He married **Nancy Wiles**.
	279	vii	John[5] **Bovee**, born aft 1811; died in Otsego, Otsego Co., NY.

114. John[4] **Bovee** (Abraham[3], Nicholas[2], Mathieu[1]), born abt 1770 in NY. He married (1) Elizabeth Primmer; (2) Elizabeth Whitaker, born 21 Apr 1786; died 11 Jan 1854.

Children of John Bovee and Elizabeth Primmer were as follows:

+	280	i	Susan[5] **Bovee**, born 1806 in Hoosick, Rensselaer Co., NY; died 1843 in St Joseph Co., MI. She married **Luther Rawson**.
+	281	ii	Aurelia[5] **Bovee**, born 13 Dec 1807 in Hoosick, Rensselaer Co., NY; died 21 Aug 1854. She married **Nathaniel Reynolds**.
+	282	iii	Eliza[5] **Bovee**, born abt 1809 in NY; died bef 1875. She married **Gabriel Langdon**.
+	283	iv	Emily A[5] **Bovee**, born 17 Apr 1811 in NY; died 19 Jun 1895 in Mendon, St Joseph Co., MI. She married **William A Langdon**.
	284	v	Harriet[5] **Bovee**, born abt 1813.
+	285	vi	Orrin Primmer[5] **Bovee**, born 1814 in Hoosick, Rensselaer Co., NY; died 22 Oct 1883 in Kalamazoo, Kalamazoo Co., MI. He married (1) **Maria Snow**; (2) **Eliza Jane Waggoner**.

+ 286   vii   Permelia[5] **Bovee**, born 10 Sep 1817 in NY; died 14 Mar 1906 in Lisbon, Ransom Co., ND. She married **John Laughlin**.

Children of John Bovee and Elizabeth Whitaker were as follows:

+ 287   i   Sarah Matilda[5] **Bovee**, born 1826 in Lyons, Wayne Co., NY; died 27 Jan 1903 in Fargo, Cass Co., ND. She married (1) **George Leonard Lincoln**; (2) **Benjamin Ayer Lowell**.

115. Abraham[4] **Bovee** (Abraham[3], Nicholas[2], Mathieu[1]), born abt 1772 in NY; died 10 May 1838 in T/Lenox, Madison Co., NY. He married Eleanor Huyck (see 179), christened 6 Jun 1779 in Coxackie, Green Co., NY, daughter of Cornelius A Huyck and Hester Gardinier.

Children of Abraham Bovee and Eleanor Huyck were as follows:

+ 288   i   Cornelius[5] **Bovee**, born 1800 in Delaware Co., NY. He married **Margaret Helmer**.

289   ii   William[5] **Bovee**, born 7 Feb 1802 in Milford, Otsego Co., NY; christened 22 Jun 1802 in 2nd Presb Ch., Milford, Otsego Co., NY; died 15 May 1836 in T/Lenox, Madison Co., NY. He married **Sarah Helmer**.

+ 290   iii   Abraham[5] **Bovee**, born abt 1807 in Milford, Ostego Co., NY; died 15 Jan 1882 in Manawa, Waupaca Co., WI. He married (1) **Unknown (---)**; (2) **Abigail Oscott**.

291   iv   Sally Mary[5] **Bovee**, born abt 1810 in Otsego Co., NY. She married **Alexander Dunlap**.

+ 292   v   Frederick Brown[5] **Bovee**, born 2 Feb 1812 in Lebenon, Madison Co., NY; died 19 Jul 1904 in Stockbridge, Calumet Co., WI. He married **Olive Babcock**.

+ 293   vi   Ester Ann[5] **Bovee**, born 17 Aug 1816 in T/Lenox, Madison Co., NY; died 6 Sep 1849 in Boltonville, Washington Co., WI. She married **Elijah Alvin Duncan**.

+ 294   vii   Henry[5] **Bovee**, born 9 Aug 1818 in T/Lenox, Madison Co., NY; died 1 Jan 1870 in Stockbridge, Calumet Co., WI. He married **Lucy Evelyn Wilson**.

+ 295   viii   Rebecca[5] **Bovee**, born 16 Mar 1824 in Madison Co., NY; died 1 May 1892 in Christie, Clark Co., WI. She married **Martin Victor Fadner**.

118. Henry[4] **Bovee** (Abraham[3], Nicholas[2], Mathieu[1]), born 23 Aug 1781; christened 26 Aug 1781 in Gilead Luth Ch., Centre Brunswick, Rensselaer Co., NY; died 6 Nov 1864 in Union Town,Broome Co., NY. He married on 14 May 1809 Betsy Brimmer, born 1791 in Rensselaer Co., NY; died 29 Sep 1862 in Union Town,Broome Co., NY.

Children of Henry Bovee and Betsy Brimmer were as follows:

+ 296   i   Hiram[5] **Bovee**, born 22 Jun 1814 in NY; died 18 Oct 1881.

He married **Lucy Ann Northrup**.

+ 297 ii Betsey[5] **Bovee**, born 18 Feb 1817; died 1905. She married **Franklin Gibson**.

+ 298 iii Ira[5] **Bovee**, born 5 Jun 1819 in Ostego Co., NY; died 3 Oct 1888. He married **Amanda O'Brien**.

+ 299 iv Aaron[5] **Bovee**, born 11 Feb 1822 in Otsego, Ostego Co., NY; died 17 Feb 1856 in Union Town, Broome Co., NY. He married **Frances Lyman**.

+ 300 v John[5] **Bovee**, born 11 May 1824 in Broome Co., NY; died 29 Jul 1881 in Groton, Brown Co., SD. He married **Ann Eliza LeBaron**.

301 vi Rachel[5] **Bovee**, born 17 Sep 1826; died 2 Dec 1869. She married on 26 Jul 1846 **Joseph Lyman**.

302 vii Anna M[5] **Bovee**, born abt 1828. She married on 20 Jan 1849 **Edward B Edwards**.

303 viii James[5] **Bovee**, born 14 Nov 1830.

304 ix Henry[5] **Bovee**, born 11 Jul 1833.

119. Peter[4] **Bovee** (Abraham[3], Nicholas[2], Mathieu[1]), born 25 Jul 1787; christened 23 Feb 1788 in Centre Brunswick, Rensselaer Co., NY. He married abt 1810 Catherine Holbrook, born abt 1790 in NY.

Children of Peter Bovee and Catherine Holbrook were as follows:

+ 305 i Peter[5] **Bovee**, born 1821; died bef 1900. He married **Angeline (---)**.

306 ii Lydia Ann[5] **Bovee**, born abt 1826 in NY; died 20 Sep 1848.

+ 307 iii Cornelius[5] **Bovee**, born 27 Nov 1832 in Madison Co., NY; died 30 Nov 1914 in Alvin, Brazoria Co., TX. He married (1) **Rebecca H Higbee**; (2) **Caroline Bowen**.

308 iv Adeline[5] **Bovee**, born abt 1838.

122. Jacob Philip[4] **Bovee** (Philip[3], Nicholas[2], Mathieu[1]), born abt 1750. He married (1) on 29 Oct 1774 in Albany, Albany Co., NY Rebecca Cronke; (2) on 14 Sep 1789 in 1st Presb Ch., Ballston, Saratoga Co., NY Jacomyntje Marcellus, christened 22 Dec 1771 in Schenectady, Schenectady Co., NY, daughter of John T Marcellus and Anna Van Antwerp.

Children of Jacob Philip Bovee and Rebecca Cronke were as follows:

309 i Anna[5] **Bovee**, born 15 Oct 1775; christened in St. George Ep Ch., Schenectady, Schenectady Co., NY.

Children of Jacob Philip Bovee and Jacomyntje Marcellus were as follows:

+ 310 i Philip[5] **Bovee**, born 26 Mar 1790 in Charleston, Montgomery Co., NY; christened 9 May 1790 in DRC, Schenectady, Schenectady Co., NY; died 30 May 1865 in New Lyme, Ashtabula Co., OH. He married **Hannah**

Dolph.

311	ii	Annatje[5] **Bovee**, born 5 Nov 1791; christened 15 Feb 1792 in DRC Schenectady, Schenectady Co., NY.
+ 312	iii	John[5] **Bovee**, born 28 May 1793 in Schenectady Co., NY; christened 6 Oct 1793 in DRC, Schenectady, Schenectady Co., NY; died abt 1872 in MI. He married **Samantha Hedden.**
+ 313	iv	Nicholas[5] **Bovee**, born 11 Feb 1796 in Montgomery Co., NY; died 10 Feb 1865 in Seneca Twp, Lenawee Co., MI. He married **Phebe (---).**

124. Nicholas P[4] **Bovee** (Philip[3], Nicholas[2], Mathieu[1]), born abt 1757 in Hoosick, Rensselaer Co., NY; died 11 Mar 1796 in Schenectady, Schenectady Co., NY. He married on 15 Mar 1779 in White Creek,Washington Co., NY Polly Cotrell, died 25 May 1843 in Gainesville, Wyoming Co., NY.

Children of Nicholas P Bovee and Polly Cotrell were as follows:

314	i	Philip[5] **Bovee**, born 11 Dec 1781; christened in Schaghticoke, Rensselaer Co., NY; died abt 1781.
+ 315	ii	Elizabeth[5] **Bovee**, born 12 Apr 1783; died 15 Jun 1842 in Gainesville, Wyoming Co., NY. She married **Daniel Cargill.**
+ 316	iii	Daniel R[5] **Bovee**, born abt 1784; died abt 1825 in Perry, Wyoming Co., NY. He married **Sarah (---).**
+ 317	iv	Jacob[5] **Bovee**, born abt 1786 in NY; died Jan 1842. He married **Rachel (---).**
+ 318	v	Catherine[5] **Bovee**, born 22 Feb 1787; died 30 Apr 1842. She married (1) **James Moffitt**; (2) **Alinos Matthews.**
+ 319	vi	Sarah (Sally)[5] **Bovee**, born 15 Aug 1789 in NY; christened in Broadalbin, Montgomery Co., NY. She married **John Moffitt.**
320	vii	John[5] **Bovee**, born 1791.
+ 321	viii	Harper[5] **Bovee**, born abt 1793; died abt 1852 in St Louis, MO. He married **Lydia Nichols.**
+ 322	ix	Ester[5] **Bovee**, born abt 1795 in Montgomery Co., NY; died 1831. She married **Ezekiel Perkins.**
+ 323	x	Isabel[5] **Bovee**, born 1796. She married **John Foote.**

126. Catherine[4] **Bovee** (Philip[3], Nicholas[2], Mathieu[1]), born abt 1768. She married on 3 Dec 1787 in 1st Presb Ch., Ballston, Saratoga Co., NY Joseph Kemp, born 20 Jul 1761 in Schenectady, Albany Co., NY, son of John Kemp and Anna Van Vorst.

Children of Catherine Bovee and Joseph Kemp were as follows:

324	i	John[5] **Kemp**, born 4 Oct 1788 in Canada; christened 20 Nov 1788.
325	ii	Jacob[5] **Kemp**, born 15 May 1791 in Canada.

326	iii	James[5] **Kemp**, born 3 Mar 1793 in Canada.
327	iv	Philip[5] **Kemp**, born 31 May 1795 in Canada.
328	v	Henry Bertskey[5] **Kemp**, born 23 Jul 1797 in Canada.
329	vi	Anne[5] **Kemp**, born 10 Nov 1799 in Canada.
330	vii	Joseph[5] **Kemp**, born 19 Apr 1805 in Canada.

127. Nicholas Jacob[4] **Bovee** (Jacob[3], Nicholas[2], Mathieu[1]), christened 15 Aug 1754 in (as Hendrickus) Pompton Plains, Morris Co., NJ, died aft 1810. He married Sarah Bovee (see 104), born abt 1758; died aft 1810, daughter of Matthew Bovee and Maria Cole.

Children of Nicholas Jacob Bovee and Sarah Bovee were as follows:

331	i	Annatje[5] **Bovee**, christened 18 Mar 1783 in DRC Schenectady, Schenectady Co., NY.
332	ii	Mathew[5] **Bovee**, born 5 Jul 1784; christened 11 Jul 1784 in DRC Schenectady, Schenectady Co., NY.
+ 333	iii	Jacob Nicholas[5] **Bovee**, born 5 Jul 1790; christened 11 Jul 1790 in DRC, Schenectady, Schenectady Co., NY. He married **Catherine Slingerland**.

128. Jacob[4] **Bovee** Jr (Jacob[3], Nicholas[2], Mathieu[1]), born 24 Nov 1756 in Outcalt, Middlesex Co., NJ; died 24 Sep 1837. He married in DRC Schenectady, Schenectady Co., NY Elizabeth Beth, born 25 Nov 1756; christened 28 Nov 1756 in DRC Schenectady, Albany Co., NY, daughter of William Beth and Maris Bosie.

Children of Jacob Bovee Jr and Elizabeth Beth were as follows:

+ 334	i	Anna[5] **Bovee**, born 16 Jul 1777; christened 11 Aug 1777 in DRC Schenectady, Schenectady Co., NY. She married **Izacc P Truax**.
335	ii	William[5] **Bovee**, christened 14 Mar 1779 in DRC Schenectady, Schenectady Co., NY.
336	iii	Maria[5] **Bovee**, born 23 Oct 1780; christened 26 Nov 1780 in DRC Schenectady, Schenectady Co., NY.
+ 337	iv	John[5] **Bovee**, christened 11 Sep 1783 in DRC, Schenectady, Schenectady Co., NY, died bef 1829. He married unknown.
+ 338	v	Peter[5] **Bovee**, born 4 Mar 1785 in NY; christened in DRC, Schenectady, Schenectady Co., NY; died aft 1840. He married (1) **Anna Lighthall**; (2) **Sarah Truax**.
339	vi	Jacob[5] **Bovee**, born 7 Apr 1787; christened 27 May 1787 in DRC Schenectady, Schenectady Co., NY; died bef 1829.
+ 340	vii	Maria[5] **Bovee**, born 15 Jan 1789; christened 8 Feb 1789 in DRC Schenectady, Schenectady Co., NY; died 11 May 1865. She married (1) **Philip P Van Patten**; (2) **Nicholas S Van Patten**.
+ 341	viii	Isaac[5] **Bovee**, born 1 Mar 1791; christened 25 Apr 1791 in

DRC, Schenectady, Schenectady Co., NY; died 13 Aug 1865. He married **Hannah (---)**.

+ 342   ix   Philip[5] **Bovee**, born 18 Sep 1792; died abt 1854. He married **Ruth Shepherd**.

+ 343   x   Sarah[5] **Bovee**, born 26 Sep 1794; christened 2 Nov 1794 in DRC Schenectady, Schenectady Co., NY. She married **Ahaserous W Van Patten**.

   344   xi   Elisabeth[5] **Bovee**, born 6 Mar 1797; christened in DRC Schenectady, Schenectady Co., NY; died abt 1798.

+ 345   xii   Henry[5] **Bovee**, born 20 Feb 1801; christened in DRC, Schenectady, Schenectady Co., NY; died 19 May 1888 in Broadalbin, Fulton Co., NY. He married **Abigail Whitlock**.

129. Isaac[4] **Bovee** (Jacob[3], Nicholas[2], Mathieu[1]), born 10 Dec 1762; died 20 Sep 1821 in Schenectady, Schenectady Co., NY. He married on 19 Apr 1789 in Schenectady, Schenectady Co., NY Rebecca Vedder, born 24 Jan 1763; christened 29 Jan 1763 in DRC Schenectady, Schenectady Co., NY; died 2 Mar 1842, daughter of Albert Vedder and Anna Quackenbush.

Children of Isaac Bovee and Rebecca Vedder were as follows:

   346   i   Elizabeth Maria[5] **Bovee**, born 16 Apr 1793 in NY; christened 19 May 1793 in DRC, Schenectady, Schenectady Co., NY; died 12 Jun 1884 in Whitewater, Walworth Co., WI. She married on 19 Mar 1817 in Amsterdam, Montgomery Co., NY **Mathias Jacob Bovee** (see 239), born 24 Jul 1793 in Amsterdam, Montgomery Co., NY; christened in DRC, Schenectady, Schenectady Co., NY; died 12 Sep 1872 in Eagle, Waukesha Co.,WI, son of Jacob Mathias Bovee and Jane Dods.

+ 347   ii   Annatje[5] **Bovee**, born 18 Feb 1797; christened 25 Jun 1797 in DRC Schenectady, Schenectady Co., NY. She married **(---) Haswell**.

+ 348   iii   Albert[5] **Bovee** Sr, born 24 May 1799 in Albany Co., NY; christened 7 Jul 1799 in DRC, Schenectady, Schenectady Co., NY; died 1894 in Arena, Iowa Co., WI. He married (1) **Mary Van Dyke**; (2) **Valerie Stout DuBois**; (3) **Sophronia Benedict Dowd**.

+ 349   iv   Jacob I[5] **Bovee**, born 9 Mar 1801 in NY; christened 26 Apr 1801 in DRC, Schenectady, Schenectady Co., NY; died 1876. He married (1) **Maria Van Eps**; (2) **Mary Clark**.

130. Abraham[4] **Bovee** (Jacob[3], Nicholas[2], Mathieu[1]), died Oct 1823 in Amsterdam, Montgomery Co., NY. He married on 3 Feb 1793 in DRC Schenectady, Schenectady Co., NY Elizabeth Vedder, born 17 Aug 1768; christened 21 Aug 1768 in Schenectady, Schenectady Co., NY, daughter of Albert Vedder and Anna Quackenbush.

Children of Abraham Bovee and Elizabeth Vedder were as follows:

| 350 | i | Antje[5] **Bovee**, born 11 Feb 1794; christened 9 Mar 1794 in DRC Schenectady, Schenectady Co., NY. |

350   i   Antje[5] **Bovee**, born 11 Feb 1794; christened 9 Mar 1794 in DRC Schenectady, Schenectady Co., NY.

351   ii   Annatje[5] **Bovee**, born 28 Jan 1795; christened 8 Mar 1795 in DRC Schenectady, Schenectady Co., NY; died abt 1795.

+ 352   iii   Annatje[5] **Bovee**, born 29 Jan 1796; christened 6 Mar 1796 in DRC Schenectady, Schenectady Co., NY. She married **Peter Van Dyke**.

+ 353   iv   John A[5] **Bovee**, born 5 Feb 1800; christened 11 Mar 1800 in Amsterdam, Montgomery Co., NY. He married **Catherine Van Eps**.

+ 354   v   Albert[5] **Bovee**, born 1808. He married **Elizabeth (---)**.

355   vi   Davis[5] **Bovee**.

131. Matthew[4] **Bovee** (Jacob[3], Nicholas[2], Mathieu[1]), born abt 1765; died abt 1830 in Genesee Co., NY. He married on 25 May 1788 in Kinderhook, Columbia Co., NY Maria Schermerhorn, christened 24 Sep 1769 in Kinderhook, Columbia Co., NY, died 6 Oct 1843 in Riga, Monroe Co., NY, daughter of Daniel C Schermerhorn and Maria Van Derpool.

Children of Matthew Bovee and Maria Schermerhorn were as follows:

356   i   Daniel[5] **Bovee**, born 27 Jan 1789; christened in Schodack, Rensselaer Co., NY.

+ 357   ii   Anatje[5] **Bovee**, born Dec 1790; christened 9 Jan 1791 in Schodack, Rensselaer Co., NY; died 27 Oct 1861 in Medina Co., OH. She married **Nicholas Spitzer**.

+ 358   iii   Daniel[5] **Bovee**, born 23 Jan 1794 in Rensselaer Co., NY; christened in Shodack, Rensselaer Co., NY; died 27 Nov 1860 in Monmouth, Warren Co., IL. He married (1) **Clarissa Schermerhorn**; (2) **Charlotte Van Yveren**.

+ 359   iv   Maria[5] **Bovee**, born 20 Mar 1795; christened 16 Aug 1795 in Kinderhook, Columbia Co., NY; died 30 Mar 1876. She married **Ryer B Springsteen**.

+ 360   v   Jacob[5] **Bovee**, born abt 1797 in Schoharie, Schoharie Co., NY; died 24 Nov 1865 in Riga, Monroe Co., NY. He married (1) **Susanna Schermerhorn**; (2) **Lucinda Hubbard**.

+ 361   vi   Sarah[5] **Bovee**, born 22 Nov 1799; christened 23 Feb 1800 in DRC Schenectady, Schenectady Co., NY; died 2 Dec 1828 in Monroe Co., NY. She married **Joseph Spitzer**.

+ 362   vii   Bata[5] **Bovee**, born 1 Mar 1802; christened 25 Mar 1802 in DRC Schenectady, Schenectady Co., NY; died 15 Sep 1881 in Bergen, Genesee Co., NY. She married **John C Moore**.

+ 363   viii   Isaac[5] **Bovee**, born 31 Aug 1804 in NY; christened 18 Nov 1804 in DRC, Schenectady, Schenectady Co., NY; died abt 1856 in Delaware Co., OH. He married (1) **Sarah Williams**; (2) **Hannah A Hays**.

+ 364 ix Cornelius Schermerhorn[5] **Bovee**, born 3 Mar 1807; christened 21 Jun 1807 in Amsterdam, Montgomery Co., NY; died 25 May 1839 in Riga, Monroe Co., NY. He married **Eliza Sparks**.

+ 365 x Caty Ann[5] **Bovee**, born 25 Apr 1810 in NY; christened 30 Sep 1810 in St. George Ep Ch., Schenectady, Schenectady Co., NY; died 9 Dec 1890 in Williamsville, Deleware Co., OH. She married **Jerrad Sanford Williams**.

132. Sara[4] Bovee (Jacob[3], Nicholas[2], Mathieu[1]), born 20 Aug 1768; christened 11 Sep 1768 in Coxsackie, Greene Co., NY; died 1 Sep 1855 in Burnt Hills, Saratoga Co., NY. She married Jacobus A Van Vorst, son of Abraham Van Vorst and Maria Heemstradt.

Children of Sara Bovee and Jacobus A Van Vorst were as follows:

366 i Abram[5] **Van Vorst**, born 3 Jan 1792 in Schenectady, Schenectady Co., NY..

367 ii Jacob Bovee[5] **Van Vorst**, born 9 Oct 1794 in Schenectady, Schenectady Co., NY..

368 iii Maria[5] **Van Vorst**, born 27 Oct 1796 in Schenectady, Schenectady Co., NY..

369 iv Antje[5] **Van Vorst**, born 2 Sep 1799 in Schenectady, Schenectady Co., NY..

370 v Nicholas[5] **Van Vorst**, born 15 Dec 1801 in Schenectady, Schenectady Co., NY..

371 vi Jacob[5] **Van Vorst**, born 1 Jun 1804 in Schenectady, Schenectady Co., NY..

372 vii Rebecca[5] **Van Vorst**, born 8 Dec 1806.

373 viii Isaac[5] **Van Vorst**, born 21 May 1809 in Schenectady, Schenectady Co., NY..

374 ix Esther[5] **Van Vorst**, born 24 Jul 1812 in Schenectady, Schenectady Co., NY..

137. Anthony[4] Bovee (Gerrit[3], Anthony[2], Mathieu[1]), christened 21 Dec 1755 in DRC, Albany, Albany Co., NY, died 26 Jul 1822. He married Maria Barnhart, born 24 Jun 1764, daughter of Henry Barnhart and Elizabeth Van Curler.

Children of Anthony Bovee and Maria Barnhart were as follows:

375 i Henry[5] **Bovee**, born 15 Apr 1784; christened 5 Jun 1784 in Gilead Luth Ch., Centre Brunswick, Rensselaer Co, NY.

376 ii Elizabeth[5] **Bovee**, born 11 Aug 1785; christened 16 Oct 1785 in Gilead Luth Ch., Centre Brunswick, Rensselaer Co, NY.

+ 377 iii Walter[5] **Bovee**, born abt 1790. He married **Hannah (---)**.

+ 378 iv John[5] **Bovee**, born abt 1795 in Hartford, Washington Co., NY; died 1831. He married **Sarah Stearns**.

+ 379   v   Jacob[5] **Bovee**, born Dec 1798 in Washington Co., NY; died 26 Sep 1876 in Day, Saratoga Co., NY. He married **Eunice Howard**.

+ 380   vi   Joseph[5] **Bovee**, born abt 1821; died bef 1860. He married **Lucinda Crissey**.

138. Maria[4] **Bovee** (Gerrit[3], Anthony[2], Mathieu[1]), christened 30 Dec 1761 in Albany, Albany Co., NY. She married in Hartford, Washington Co., NY. Thomas Powell.

Children of Maria Bovee and Thomas Powell were as follows:

381   i   Isaac[5] **Powell**, born 28 Apr 1783; christened in Schaghticoke, Rensselaer Co., NY.

382   ii   Ariantje[5] **Powell**, born 26 Dec 1784; christened in Brunswick, Rensselaer Co., NY.

383   iii   Garritt[5] **Powell**, born abt 1785.

384   iv   Thomas[5] **Powell**, born abt 1788.

385   v   Mary[5] **Powell**, born 23 Jul 1791; christened 1791 in Saratoga Co., NY.

386   vi   Margaret[5] **Powell**, born 14 Apr 1793; christened in Schaghticoke, Rensselaer Co., NY.

139. Peter[4] **Bovee** (Gerrit[3], Anthony[2], Mathieu[1]), born 16 Jan 1764 in Halfmoon, Saratoga Co., NY; christened 15 Apr 1764 in Albany, Albany Co., NY; died 13 Apr 1837 in Belcher, Hebron,Washington Co., NY. He married on 22 Aug 1784 in Rensselaer Co., NY Jane Wygant, born 24 Jan 1764; christened 16 Aug 1770 in 1st Presb. Ch., Marlborough, Ulster Co., NY; died 9 Nov 1842 in Belcher, Hebron,Washington Co., NY, daughter of John Wygant and Catherine Powell.

Children of Peter Bovee and Jane Wygant were as follows:

+ 387   i   Orra[5] **Bovee**, born 17 Nov 1785 in NY; died 1 May 1850 in Adams Center, Jefferson Co., NY. She married **Timothy Heath Jr.**

+ 388   ii   John W[5] **Bovee**, born 16 Jan 1788 in Rensselaer Co., NY; christened 6 Sep 1789 in Centre Brunswick, Rensselaer Co., NY; died 5 Jul 1844. He married (1) **Elizabeth Earl**; (2) **Nancy B Stone**.

+ 389   iii   Catherine[5] **Bovee**, born 1 Feb 1790. She married **John Powell**.

+ 390   iv   Gerrit[5] **Bovee**, born 5 Sep 1792; died 2 Apr 1879 in Adams, Jefferson Co., NY. He married **Hannah Wigant**.

+ 391   v   Sarah[5] **Bovee**, born 24 Sep 1794; died 27 Sep 1870 in Algansee, Branch Co., MI. She married **Samuel Chapman**.

+ 392   vi   Jonathan[5] **Bovee**, born 12 Oct 1796 in Hartford, Washington Co., NY; died 31 Mar 1881 in Algansee, Branch Co., MI. He married **Lucy Smith**.

| 393 | vii | Margaret Ann[5] **Bovee**, born 6 Aug 1800. |

393 vii Margaret Ann[5] **Bovee**, born 6 Aug 1800.

394 viii Jacob[5] **Bovee**, born 26 Aug 1802 in Washington Co., NY.

+ 395 ix William W[5] **Bovee**, born 3 Nov 1803 in Hartford Washington Co., NY; died 5 Nov 1882. He married **Charlotte Davison**.

396 x Betsey[5] **Bovee**, born 8 Apr 1808 in Washington Co., NY. She married on 1 Nov 1832 **Abraham Ouderkerk**.

144. Jacob[4] **Bovee** (Gerrit[3], Anthony[2], Mathieu[1]), born abt 1774 in NY; died 2 Jan 1842 in West Barnet, Caledonia Co., VT. He married Elizabeth Redding, born 22 Feb 1778; died 11 Jul 1857 in West Barnet, Caledonia Co., VT, daughter of Moses Redding and Priscilla Rider.

Children of Jacob Bovee and Elizabeth Redding were as follows:

397 i (---)[5] **Bovee**, born bef 1800.

398 ii (---)[5] **Bovee**, born bef 1800.

+ 399 iii Peter[5] **Bovee**, born 21 Jun 1797 in Rensselaer Co., NY; died 1873. He married **Margaret McLeron**.

+ 400 iv Moses R[5] **Bovee**, born 10 Nov 1799 in Rensselaer Co., NY; died 19 Jan 1879 in Green Mountain, Marshall Co., IA. He married **Helen Warden**.

+ 401 v Courtland[5] **Bovee**, born 10 Oct 1800 in Rensselaer Co., NY; died 10 Jul 1872. He married **Eliza J Blood**.

+ 402 vi Elvira Priscilla[5] **Bovee**, born abt 1809 in NY; died 17 Mar 1882 in Page Co., IA. She married **John F Nelson**.

+ 403 vii Elizabeth R[5] **Bovee**, born Jun 1812. She married **William B Ouderkerk**.

404 viii (---)[5] **Bovee**, born bef 1815.

405 ix (---)[5] **Bovee**, born bef 1815 in VT.

148. Anthony[4] **Bovee** (Matthew[3], Anthony[2], Mathieu[1]), born Sep 1767 in Hoosick, Renssalaer Co., NY; christened 11 Oct 1767 in St. Paul's Luth Ch., Schoharie, Schoharie Co., NY. He married Catherine Huyck (see 178), christened 10 Oct 1767 in Schaghticoke, Rensselaer Co., NY, daughter of Nicholas Huyck and Marytie Bovee.

Children of Anthony Bovee and Catherine Huyck were as follows:

406 i Maria[5] **Bovee**, born 3 Sep 1787; christened 20 Oct 1787 in Gilead Lutheran Church, Centre Brunswick, Rensselear Co., NY.

407 ii Jannetje[5] **Bovee**, born 15 May 1790; christened 14 Mar 1791 in Fonda, Montgomery Co., NY.

159. Bata[4] **Bovee** (Mathew[3], Francois[2], Mathieu[1]), born 31 May 1761. She married on 13 Jun 1779 in DR Church, Schaghticoke, Rensselaer Co., NY Gerrit Clute, christened 8 Mar 1761 in DRC Albany, Albany Co., NY, son of Frederick

Clute and Maria De Ridder.

Children of Bata Bovee and Gerrit Clute were as follows:

408   i   Maria[5] **Clute**, christened 25 Jan 1783 in DRC, Schenectady, Schenectady Co., NY.

409   ii   Gertrude[5] **Clute**, born 9 Jan 1785.

410   iii   Annatie[5] **Clute**, christened 15 Jun 1788 in DRC, Schenectady, Schenectady Co., NY.

411   iv   William[5] **Clute**, born 22 Dec 1790; christened 16 Jan 1791.

412   v   Catherine[5] **Clute**, born 23 Jul 1793; christened 11 Aug 1793 in Cohoes, Albany Co., NY.

413   vi   Mathew[5] **Clute**, born 15 Dec 1795; christened 10 Jan 1796 in Cohoes, Albany Co., NY.

414   vii   Frederick[5] **Clute**, born 6 Apr 1798; christened 12 Apr 1798.

415   viii   Rachel[5] **Clute**, born 20 Mar 1799; christened 14 Apr 1799 in Cohoes, Albany Co., NY.

416   ix   Hendrick[5] **Clute**, born 24 Aug 1801; christened 18 Sep 1801 in Cohoes, Albany Co., NY.

417   x   Charles[5] **Clute**, christened 21 Oct 1804.

160. Gertrude[4] **Bovee** (Mathew[3], Francois[2], Mathieu[1]), born 2 Feb 1766; christened in Albany, Albany Co., NY. She married on 15 Jan 1786 in DRC Schenectady, Albany Co., NY Nicholas S Fort.

Children of Gertrude Bovee and Nicholas S Fort were as follows:

418   i   Simon[5] **Fort**, born 30 Aug 1786 in NY; christened in Niskayuna, Schenectady Co., NY.

419   ii   Mathew[5] **Fort**, born 24 Jan 1795 in NY; christened in Niskayuna, Schenectady Co., NY.

420   iii   Annatje[5] **Fort**, born 12 Sep 1800; christened in Niskayuna, Schenectady Co., NY.

421   iv   Elizabeth[5] **Fort**, born 2 Apr 1806 in NY; christened in Niskayuna, Schenectady Co., NY.

161. Catharina[4] **Bovee** (Mathew[3], Francois[2], Mathieu[1]), born 11 Sep 1768; died 10 Apr 1810. She married on 16 Nov 1793 Evert Van Vranken.

Children of Catharina Bovee and Evert Van Vranken were as follows:

422   i   Nicholas[5] **Van Vranken**, born 12 Mar 1795; christened 19 Apr 1795.

423   ii   Mathew[5] **Van Vranken**, born abt 1795; christened 2 Apr 1795; died abt 1795.

424   iii   Janette[5] **Van Vranken**, christened 10 Oct 1797.

425   iv   Gerrit[5] **Van Vranken**, christened 30 Jul 1799.

| 426 | v | Mathew[5] **Van Vranken**, christened 18 Sep 1801. |

| 427 | vi | Elizabeth[5] **Van Vranken**, born 9 Jul 1806; christened 24 Aug 1806 in Amity Ref Ch, Vischers Ferry, Saratoga Co., NY. |

| 428 | vii | Abraham[5] **Van Vranken**, christened 5 May 1813. |

| 429 | viii | Harmon[5] **Van Vranken**. |

163. Rachel[4] **Bovee** (Mathew[3], Francois[2], Mathieu[1]), born 15 Nov 1776. She married Daniel Van Antwerp, christened 26 Aug 1774 in DRC Schenectady, Albany Co., NY, son of Abraham Van Antwerp and Sarah (---).

Children of Rachel Bovee and Daniel Van Antwerp were as follows:

| 430 | i | Abram[5] **Van Antwerp**, christened 21 Jul 1800 in Schenectady, Schenectady Co., NY.. |

| 431 | ii | Katherine[5] **Van Antwerp**, born 23 Apr 1810 in Niskayuna, Schenectady Co., NY; died 6 Jan 1888. |

164. Elizabeth[4] **Bovee** (Mathew[3], Francois[2], Mathieu[1]), born 8 Jul 1784; christened 16 Jul 1784 in DRC Schenectady, Albany Co., NY. She married on 24 Dec 1808 in Colonie, Albany Co., NY David Chambers.

Children of Elizabeth Bovee and David Chambers were as follows:

| 432 | i | Margaret[5] **Chambers**, born 1809 in NY; christened in Niskayuna, Schenectady Co., NY. |

| 433 | ii | Margaret[5] **Chambers**, christened 7 Apr 1811 in Niskayuna, Schenectady Co., NY. |

| 434 | iii | Mathew[5] **Chambers**, christened 19 Dec 1813 in Niskayuna, Schenectady Co., NY. |

| 435 | iv | David[5] **Chambers** Jr., born 1817 in NY; christened in Niskayuna, Schenectady Co., NY. |

| 436 | v | Getty Maria[5] **Chambers**, christened 4 Jun 1820 in Niskayuna, Schenectady Co., NY. |

Generation 5

165. Philip[5] **Bovee** (Mathew[4], Philip[3], Mathieu[2], Mathieu[1]), born 16 Sep 1790. He married Elizabeth Van Olinda, born Apr 1789; christened 26 Apr 1789 in DRC, Albany, Albany Co., NY; died 13 Nov 1837 in T/Colonie, Albany Co., NY, daughter of Peter Van Olinda and Sussana Anthony.

Children of Philip Bovee and Elizabeth Van Olinda were as follows:

| 437 | i | Peter[6] **Bovee**, christened 12 Aug 1810 in DRC, Boght Corners, Albany Co., NY. |

| + 438 | ii | Stephen[6] **Bovee**, born abt 1814 in Cohoes, Albany Co., NY. He married **Sally Caroline Calhoun**. |

167. Jacob[5] **Bovee** (Mathew[4], Philip[3], Mathieu[2], Mathieu[1]), born 11 Sep 1798. He married Mary Thompson.

Children of Jacob Bovee and Mary Thompson were as follows:

439   i   Anna Maria[6] **Bovee**, born 1822. She married on 28 Oct 1845 in Troy, Rensselaer Co., NY **Henry Brumhall**.

191. Sarah[5] **Bovee** (John[4], Rykert[3], Nicholas[2], Mathieu[1]), born 25 Oct 1780; christened 4 Feb 1781 in Centre Brunswick, Renssalaer Co., NY; died 1861. She married on 22 Feb 1798 Col David Wiltse.

Children of Sarah Bovee and Col David Wiltse were as follows:

440   i   William[6] **Wiltse**, born 6 Oct 1798 in Burlington, Chittenden Co., VT.

441   ii   Hiram[6] **Wiltse**, born 5 Sep 1800 in Burlington, Chittenden Co., VT.

442   iii   Betsey[6] **Wiltse**, born 22 Aug 1802 in Burlington, Chittenden Co., VT.

443   iv   Pamela[6] **Wiltse**, born 3 May 1805 in Burlington, Chittenden Co., VT.

444   v   Keziah[6] **Wiltse**, born 9 Nov 1807 in Burlington, Chittenden Co., VT.

445   vi   John B[6] **Wiltse**, born 9 May 1810 in Burlington, Chittenden Co., VT.

446   vii   David C[6] **Wiltse**, born 10 Oct 1812 in Burlington, Chittenden Co., VT.

447   viii   Sally A[6] **Wiltse**, born 3 Sep 1815 in Burlington, Chittenden Co., VT.

448   ix   Malinda[6] **Wiltse**, born 3 Jun 1817 in Burlington, Chittenden Co., VT.

449   x   Polly[6] **Wiltse**, born 14 Mar 1821 in Burlington, Chittenden Co., VT.

450   xi   Laffayette[6] **Wiltse**, born 19 Aug 1824 in Burlington, Chittenden Co., VT.

193. Henry[5] **Bovee** (John[4], Rykert[3], Nicholas[2], Mathieu[1]), born 12 Apr 1785 in Breese Hollow, Rensselaer Co., NY; died 8 May 1863 in Hoosick, Rensselaer Co., NY. He married in Feb 1809 in Hoosick, Rensselaer Co., NY Hannah Hewitt, born 7 Apr 1787 in Petersburg, Rensselaer Co., NY; died 1 Apr 1864, daughter of Starry Hewitt.

Children of Henry Bovee and Hannah Hewitt were as follows:

451   i   Heman[6] **Bovee**, born 12 Nov 1810; died 20 Aug 1836.

+ 452   ii   Henry[6] **Bovee** Jr., born 29 Sep 1815; died 21 Aug 1872. He married **Amity G Lake**.

453   iii   Hewitt[6] **Bovee**, born 31 Dec 1817; died 15 Jul 1900. He married on 11 Feb 1841 **Eunice Wylie**.

+ 454   iv   Richard H[6] **Bovee**, born 6 Nov 1819 in Rensselaer Co., NY; died 2 Nov 1860 in Hoosick, Rensselaer Co., NY. He married **Sarah M Bovee** (see 721).

+ 455   v   Sanford S[6] **Bovee**, born 5 Dec 1821 in Breese Hollow, Rensselaer Co., NY; died 15 Nov 1875. He married (1) **Jane Pine**; (2) **Jane C Stover**.

456   vi   Israel[6] **Bovee**, born 5 Feb 1824 in Hoosick, Rensselaer Co., NY; died 1 Apr 1897. He married (1) on 26 Mar 1846 in Hoosick, Rensselaer Co., NY **Ruby LeBarron**; (2) **Frances E LeBarron**.

194. John[5] **Bovee** Jr (John[4], Rykert[3], Nicholas[2], Mathieu[1]), born 15 Dec 1786 in NY. He married (1) in 1809 in Pownal, Bennington Co., VT Tabitha Parker, born abt 1791; died 12 Aug 1818 in Pownal, Bennington Co., VT; (2) abt 1823 Maria Deal, born 30 Jun 1799; died 30 Jan 1873 in Pownal, Bennington Co., VT, daughter of Peter Deal.

Children of John Bovee Jr and Tabitha Parker were as follows:

+ 457   i   Sarah[6] **Bovee**, born 22 Feb 1815 in Pownal, Bennington Co., VT. She married **Charles Stearns**.

+ 458   ii   Parker R.[6] **Bovee**, born 1816 in VT; died 1848 in Pownal, Bennington Co., VT. He married **Caroline Palmer**.

459   iii   Teresa[6] **Bovee**, born abt 1818. She married **David Gardner**.

Children of John Bovee Jr and Maria Deal were as follows:

460   i   John S[6] **Bovee**, born 1824; died 2 Oct 1834 in Pownal, Bennington Co., VT.

+ 461   ii   Maria Antoinette[6] **Bovee**, born abt 1819; died 25 Feb 1848. She married **Benjamin R Green**.

196. Susanna[5] **Bovee** (John[4], Rykert[3], Nicholas[2], Mathieu[1]), born 22 Mar 1793 in Renssalaer Co., NY; died 19 Jan 1872. She married on 11 Jun 1811 Daniel B Bradt, son of Barnabus Bradt and Hannah Martin.

Children of Susanna Bovee and Daniel B Bradt were as follows:

462   i   Caroline[6] **Bradt**, born abt 1811.

463   ii   Barnabus[6] **Bradt**, born abt 1814.

464   iii   John[6] **Bradt**, born abt 1817.

465   iv   Keziah[6] **Bradt**, born abt 1819.

466   v   William W[6] **Bradt**, born abt 1822.

467   vi   Hannah Elizabeth[6] **Bradt**, born aft 1822.

468   vii   Richard O[6] **Bradt**.

469   viii   James M[6] **Bradt**, born abt 1833.

470   ix   Aurelius[6] **Bradt**, born abt 1835.

198. Keziah[5] **Bovee** (John[4], Rykert[3], Nicholas[2], Mathieu[1]), born 18 Jun 1796 in Hoosick, Renssalaer Co., NY. She married aft 1820 (---) Vaughn.

Children of Keziah Bovee and (---) Vaughn were as follows:

471	i	Hiram[6] **Vaughn**.
472	ii	Herman[6] **Vaughn**.
473	iii	Sylvester[6] **Vaughn**.

207. Elisha[5] **Bovee** (Cornelius[4], Rykert[3], Nicholas[2], Mathieu[1]), born 26 Nov 1788 in Hoosick, Rensselaer Co., NY; died 27 Apr 1864 in Richland Center, Orion Twp, Richland Co.,WI. He married (1) Mary Springer; (2) on 27 Jan 1850 in Boone Co., IN Sally Smith, born 10 Apr 1802 in KY.

Children of Elisha Bovee and Mary Springer were as follows:

+	474	i	Richard[6] **Bovee**, born 9 Jun 1810 in Petersburg, Rensselaer Co., NY; died 11 Mar 1879. He married **Orpha Zelpha Parke**.
+	475	ii	Durfee[6] **Bovee**, born 17 Feb 1812 in Rensselaer Co., NY; died 16 Oct 1887. He married **Anna B Duncan**.
+	476	iii	Erastus[6] **Bovee**, born bef 1815 in NY; died 1862. He married **Elizabeth Hill**.
+	477	iv	David[6] **Bovee**, born 27 Apr 1822 in Rensselaer Co., NY; died 10 Sep 1871 in Richland Center, Richland Co., WI. He married **Frances A (---)**.

208. Nicholas[5] **Bovee** (Cornelius[4], Rykert[3], Nicholas[2], Mathieu[1]), born 11 Jan 1790 in Hoosick, Rensselaer Co., NY; died 16 Apr 1868 in WI. He married Mercy (---), born 17 Apr 1792 in NY; died 29 May 1864.

Children of Nicholas Bovee and Mercy (---) were as follows:

+	478	i	Jonas Nicholas[6] **Bovee**, born abt 1816; died 12 Aug 1868. He married (1) **Orinda Green**; (2) **Ellen Soper**.
	479	ii	Jane[6] **Bovee**, born abt 1818. She married **John Hull**.
+	480	iii	Silas Lewis[6] **Bovee**, born 27 Nov 1821 in Rensselaer Co., NY; died 17 Jul 1909. He married **Sara Jane Morris**.
+	481	iv	Zebulon[6] **Bovee**, born 1824 in Pinckney, Lewis Co., NY; died 9 May 1891. He married **Waity Brundige**.
+	482	v	Lucretia M[6] **Bovee**, born 21 Sep 1827; died 12 Dec 1886. She married **Hosea Cobb Hoisington**.

209. Sarah[5] **Bovee** (Cornelius[4], Rykert[3], Nicholas[2], Mathieu[1]), born 19 Sep 1791 in Hoosick, Renssalaer Co., NY; died 6 Apr 1881 in Evansville, Rock Co., WI. She married on 8 Aug 1813 in NY Allen Springer.

Children of Sarah Bovee and Allen Springer were as follows:

483	i	Mariah[6] **Springer**, born 12 Jan 1815.
484	ii	Matilda[6] **Springer**, born 29 Jul 1817.
485	iii	Louisa[6] **Springer**, born 14 Mar 1820.
486	iv	Leroy[6] **Springer**, born 7 Nov 1822 in NY.
487	v	Mary Jane[6] **Springer**, born 2 Mar 1837.

211. Mary[5] **Bovee** (Cornelius[4], Rykert[3], Nicholas[2], Mathieu[1]), born 27 Jan 1796 in Hoosick, Renssalaer Co., NY; died May 1877 in Kingsville, Ashtabula Co., OH. She married abt 1818 in Petersburg, Renssalaer Co., NY Alanson Colegrove, son of Christopher Colegrove and Ellen Lewis.

Children of Mary Bovee and Alanson Colegrove were as follows:

488	i	Lewis[6] **Colegrove**, born 29 Apr 1819 in Petersburg, Rensselear Co., NY.
489	ii	Joshua[6] **Colegrove**, born 11 Jul 1820 in OH.
490	iii	Sarah[6] **Colegrove**, born 8 Feb 1822 in OH.
491	iv	Louisa[6] **Colegrove**, born 27 Sep 1824 in OH.
492	v	Lucretia Ellen[6] **Colegrove**, born 10 Jun 1827.
493	vi	Richard[6] **Colegrove**, born 17 Feb 1829 in OH.
494	vii	(Mary) Harriet[6] **Colegrove**, born 20 Mar 1832 in OH.
495	viii	Maria[6] **Colegrove**, born 3 Aug 1835.
496	ix	Benjamin[6] **Colegrove**, born 4 Jun 1840.
497	x	Child[6] **Colegrove**, born aft 1840 in OH.
498	xi	Child[6] **Colegrove**, born aft 1840.

212. Elizabeth[5] **Bovee** (Cornelius[4], Rykert[3], Nicholas[2], Mathieu[1]), born 20 Oct 1797 in Hoosick, Renssalaer Co., NY; died 12 Jan 1886. She married on 25 Apr 1843 in Monroe Twp., Ashtabula Co., OH Elnathan Wetmore, son of Benjamin Wetmore and Thankful Griswold Lucas.

Children of Elizabeth Bovee and Elnathan Wetmore were as follows:

| 499 | i | Edwin Bovie[6] **Wetmore**, born abt 1836. |

213. Cornelius[5] **Bovee** Jr (Cornelius[4], Rykert[3], Nicholas[2], Mathieu[1]), born 7 Nov 1799 in Hoosick, Rensselaer Co., NY; died aft 1870. He married Harriet Kellogg, born 1805 in NY; died 29 Aug 1874 in Ionia Co., MI, daughter of Stephen Kellogg and Sarah (---).

Children of Cornelius Bovee Jr and Harriet Kellogg were as follows:

| + | 500 | i | James R[6] **Bovee**, born abt 1825 in Onondaga Co., NY; died 7 Mar 1909 in Milesgrove, Erie Co., PA. He married **Caroline Maria Hill**. |
| + | 501 | ii | Lucretia M[6] **Bovee**, born abt 1833 in NY. She married **Loren J Mosher**. |

502	iii		Cornelius[6] **Bovee**, born abt 1839 in OH. He married on 4 Jul 1860 in Ionia Co., MI **Charity M Hayward**.
+ 503	iv		Sylvester A[6] **Bovee**, born abt 1841 in OH; died bef 1864. He married **Olive J Hayward**.

214. Frederick[5] **Bovie** (Cornelius[4], Rykert[3], Nicholas[2], Mathieu[1]), born 26 May 1801 in Hoosick, Rensselaer Co., NY; christened 23 Aug 1801 in Tioshoke Protestant Reformed Dutch Church; died 9 May 1872 in Gallipolis, Gallia Co., OH. He married Mercy Maria Clark, born 27 Nov 1806 in Hartford Co., CT; died 1869.

Children of Frederick Bovie and Mercy Maria Clark were as follows:

504	i		Lucretia[6] **Bovie**, born 1831. She married on 6 Sep 1855 **Lewis Curry**, son of Lewis Curry and Susanna Sprague.
+ 505	ii		Elizabeth[6] **Bovie**, born abt 1833 in Gallipolis,Gallia Co., OH; died 19 May 1866. She married **Lewis Curry**.
506	iii		Hannah[6] **Bovie**, born 1836.
507	iv		Marilla[6] **Bovie**, born 1838.
+ 508	v		Frederick Morgan[6] **Bovie**, born 23 Oct 1846 in Gallipolis,Gallia Co., OH; died 29 Oct 1930 in Gallipolis,Gallia Co., OH. He married **Lucy Vernon Alexander**.

215. John E[5] **Bovee** (Cornelius[4], Rykert[3], Nicholas[2], Mathieu[1]), born 31 Jul 1802 in Hoosick, Rensselaer Co., NY; died 27 Feb 1850. He married on 1 Feb 1832 in Medina Co., OH Mary Palmer, born 25 Apr 1808; died abt 1888, daughter of Ephriam Palmer and Margaret Force.

Children of John E Bovee and Mary Palmer were as follows:

509	i		John Leslie[6] **Bovee**, born Dec 1845 in OH; died 12 Aug 1851.
+ 510	ii		Andrew Elliott[6] **Bovee**, born 18 Jul 1847 in Monroe Twp, Ashtabula Co., OH; died Mar 1908 in Kelloggsville, Ashtabula Co., OH. He married **Ermina Lucinda Ruland**.

216. Catherine[5] **Bovee** (Cornelius[4], Rykert[3], Nicholas[2], Mathieu[1]), born 25 Nov 1803 in Hoosick, Renssalaer Co., NY. She married on 5 Jun 1825 in Ashtabula Co., OH Richard Stoughton.

Children of Catherine Bovee and Richard Stoughton were as follows:

511	i		Richard[6] **Stoughton**.
512	ii		Chester[6] **Stoughton**, born 17 Jul 1830 in Kingsville Ashtabula Co., OH.
513	iii		Elizabeth[6] **Stoughton**.
514	iv		Caroline[6] **Stoughton**.
515	v		Emily[6] **Stoughton**.

516	vi	William[6] **Stoughton**.
517	vii	John[6] **Stoughton**.
518	viii	Porter[6] **Stoughton**.
519	ix	Gilbert[6] **Stoughton**.
520	x	Child[6] **Stoughton**.
521	xi	Child[6] **Stoughton**.

217. Peter[5] Bovee (Cornelius[4], Rykert[3], Nicholas[2], Mathieu[1]), born 13 Mar 1806 in Hoosick, Rensselaer Co., NY; died 6 Nov 1890 in Kingsville, Ashtabula Co., OH. He married on 17 Sep 1833 in Ashtabula Co., OH Margaret Amelia Wetmore, daughter of Benjamin Wetmore and Thankful Griswold Lucas.

Children of Peter Bovee and Margaret Amelia Wetmore were as follows:

	522	i	Helen[6] **Bovee**, born abt 1835.
+	523	ii	Emory John[6] **Bovee**, born 24 May 1836 in Ashtabula Co., OH. He married **Emmeline L Fox**.
	524	iii	Margaret[6] **Bovee**, born 1839; buried in Oak Ridge Cem, Eagle, Waukesha Co., WI. She married on 25 Aug 1866 in Ashtabula, Ashtabula Co., OH **Gilbert Kingsley**.

223. Maria[5] Bovee (Nicholas M[4], Matthew[3], Nicholas[2], Mathieu[1]), born 22 Sep 1786 in Amsterdam, Montgomery Co., NY; died 28 Apr 1873 in Salt Lake City, Salt Lake Co., UT. She married in 1807 Harmon Bogardus Groesbeck, son of Nicholas W Groesbeck and Sarah Becker.

Children of Maria Bovee and Harmon Bogardus Groesbeck were as follows:

525	i	Sarah[6] **Groesbeck**, born abt 1809 in NY.
526	ii	David[6] **Groesbeck**, born abt 1811 in NY.
527	iii	Hannah[6] **Groesbeck**, born abt 1813.
528	iv	Maria[6] **Groesbeck**, born abt 1815 in NY.
529	v	Cornelius[6] **Groesbeck**, born abt 1817 in NY.
530	vi	Nicholas Harmon[6] **Groesbeck**, born 5 Sep 1819 in Buskirk Bridge, Rensselaer Co., NY.
531	vii	James[6] **Groesbeck**.
532	viii	Stephen[6] **Groesbeck**.

224. John[5] Bovee (Nicholas M[4], Matthew[3], Nicholas[2], Mathieu[1]), born 11 Sep 1788 in Schenectady, Schenectady Co., NY; christened 21 Jan 1789 in DRC, Schenectady, Schenectady Co., NY; died 21 Jan 1868 in Fairfield, Wayne Co., IL. He married (1) abt 1806 Mary Burt; (2) abt 1812 in Chautauqua Co., NY Phoebe Gardner, born abt 1792 in NY; died Apr 1821 in Wayne Co., IL; (3) abt 1826 Jane Catherine Gaston, born 11 Jul 1785 in SC; died 1 Sep 1865 in Wayne Co., IL, daughter of James Gaston and Catherine Crieghton.

Children of John Bovee and Mary Burt were as follows:

	533	i	Nathan[6] **Bovee**.
+	534	ii	Mary[6] **Bovee**, born 4 Oct 1809 in Hanover,Chautauqua Co., NY; died 17 Sep 1883 in Wayne Co., IL. She married **Dr. Nathan Elliott Roberts Sr**.
+	535	iii	Sarah[6] **Bovee**, born 9 Jun 1811 in Sheridan, Chautauqua Co., NY. She married **George Clinton McMackin**.

Children of John Bovee and Phoebe Gardner were as follows:

+	536	i	John[6] **Bovee** Jr, born 12 Feb 1813 in Chautauqua Co., NY; died 2 Apr 1903 in Blair, Washington Co., NE. He married **Sarah Harlan**.
+	537	ii	Hannah[6] **Bovee**, born 10 Aug 1814 in NY; died 25 Nov 1856 in Wayne Co., IL. She married **John Gaston**.
	538	iii	Russell[6] **Bovee**, born abt 1817 in NY; died abt 1820.
+	539	iv	Aaron Milton[6] **Bovee**, born 15 Jul 1817 in NY; died 29 Sep 1880 in IA. He married **Mary Jay**.
+	540	v	Wesley[6] **Bovee**, born 19 Apr 1821 in Wayne Co., IL; died 29 May 1905 in Panther Creek, Dallas Co., IA. He married **Nancy Caroline Bailey**.
+	541	vi	Phoebe[6] **Bovee**, born 19 Apr 1821 in NY; died abt 1863. She married (1) **John Burch**; (2) **Moses Ellis**.

Children of John Bovee and Jane Catherine Gaston were as follows:

	542	i	Catherine[6] **Bovee**, born abt 1826 in Wayne Co., IL. She married **(---) Edgings**.
+	543	ii	Nelson John[6] **Bovee**, born 24 Jan 1828 in Wayne Co., IL; died 27 Aug 1881 in Herman, Washington Co., NE. He married **Nancy Walton**.

225. Cornelia[5] **Bovee** (Nicholas M[4], Matthew[3], Nicholas[2], Mathieu[1]), born 10 Mar 1791; christened 6 Jan 1792 in DRC, Schenectady, Schenectady Co., NY; died 16 Sep 1874 in Sheridan, Chautauqua Co., NY. She married in 1815 in Pomfret, Chautauqua Co., NY Steven Bush Jr.

Children of Cornelia Bovee and Steven Bush Jr were as follows:

544	i	Zelpha[6] **Bush**, born 14 Nov 1815.
545	ii	Nicholas[6] **Bush**, born 15 May 1818 in Sheridan Twp., Chatauqua Co., NY.
546	iii	Hannah A[6] **Bush**, born 17 Aug 1819.
547	iv	Mary Elizabeth[6] **Bush**, born 25 May 1822.
548	v	Sally[6] **Bush**, born 2 Apr 1824.
549	vi	John Almus[6] **Bush**, born 15 May 1826.
550	vii	Albert Jacob[6] **Bush**, born 4 Jul 1828.
551	viii	Squire White[6] **Bush**, born 20 Oct 1830.
552	ix	Andrew Jackson[6] **Bush**, born 18 Dec 1832 in Sheridan Twp., Chatauqua Co., NY.

553	x	Sarah A[6] **Bush**, born 28 Sep 1834.
554	xi	Joseph Henry[6] **Bush**, born 20 Jul 1836.
555	xii	Benjamin Emery[6] **Bush**, born 20 Jul 1836.

226. Mathew[5] **Bovee** (Nicholas M[4], Matthew[3], Nicholas[2], Mathieu[1]), born 19 Oct 1794 in Charleston, Montgomery Co., NY; died 15 Sep 1846 in Nauvoo, Hancock co., IL. He married (1) abt 1826 Waitstill Hill, died abt 1841 in Springfield, Sangamon Co., IL; (2) on 26 Nov 1842 in Sangamon Co., IL Julia Allen, born in Sangamon Co., IL; (3) on 30 Dec 1844 in Nauvoo, Hancock co., IL Sarah Ester Mecham, born in Nauvoo, Hancock co., IL.

Children of Mathew Bovee and Waitstill Hill were as follows:

+ 556   i   Ann Elizabeth[6] **Bovee**, born 18 Apr 1827 in Hanover, Chautauqua Co., NY; died 17 Oct 1869 in Milton, Morgan Co., UT. She married **Joseph Mecham**.

+ 557   ii   Sarah Ann[6] **Bovee**, born 6 Apr 1831 in Fredonia, Chautauqua Co., NY; died in UT. She married **Jeremiah Stringham**.

558   iii   Hannah Waitstill[6] **Bovee**, born abt 1833 in Hanover, Chautauqua Co., NY. She married on 10 Nov 1852 in Springfield, Sangamon Co., IL **Elisha House**.

+ 559   iv   Joseph Smith[6] **Bovee**, born 25 Dec 1840 in Springfield, Sangamon Co., IL; died 27 Jan 1911 in Cheyenne, Laramie Co., WY. He married **Elizabeth Sampson**.

237. Mary[5] **Bovee** (Jacob Mathias[4], Matthew[3], Nicholas[2], Mathieu[1]), born 25 Oct 1789; christened 15 Nov 1789 in DRC, Schenectady, Schenectady Co., NY; died 28 Apr 1869. She married on 21 Aug 1806 in Amsterdam, Montgomery Co., NY Benedict Arnold, born 5 Oct 1780; christened in Schagticoke, Rensselaer Co., NY; died 3 Mar 1849, son of Elisha Arnold and Sarah Francisco.

Children of Mary Bovee and Benedict Arnold were as follows:

560   i   Hiram[6] **Arnold**, born 20 Sep 1806; christened in Amsterdam, Montgomery Co., NY.

561   ii   Jane[6] **Arnold**, born 1 Mar 1808; christened in Amsterdam, Montgomery Co., NY.

562   iii   William[6] **Arnold**, born 31 Aug 1811; christened in Amsterdam, Montgomery Co., NY.

563   iv   Maria[6] **Arnold**, born 6 Feb 1813; christened in Amsterdam, Montgomery Co., NY.

564   v   James Mansfield[6] **Arnold**, born 15 May 1815; christened in Amsterdam, Montgomery Co., NY.

565   vi   Charlotte[6] **Arnold**, born 3 Jan 1817; christened in Amsterdam, Montgomery Co., NY.

566   vii   Lorenzo Meigs[6] **Arnold**, born 26 Sep 1818; christened in Amsterdam, Montgomery Co., NY.

567   viii   Benedict[6] **Arnold**, born 8 Apr 1820; christened in

Amsterdam, Montgomery Co., NY.

568	ix	Halsey Wood[6] **Arnold**, born 9 Jun 1822; christened in Amsterdam, Montgomery Co., NY.
569	x	Sarah B[6] **Arnold**, born 2 Nov 1824.

238. Selia[5] **Bovee** (Jacob Mathias[4], Matthew[3], Nicholas[2], Mathieu[1]), born 21 May 1791; christened in DRC, Schenectady, Schenectady Co., NY. She married abt 1811 (---) Brooks.

Children of Selia Bovee and (---) Brooks were as follows:

570	i	Mary Ann[6] **Brooks**, born 11 Mar 1814.
571	ii	Jane[6] **Brooks**, born 9 Dec 1815.

239. Mathias Jacob[5] **Bovee** (Jacob Mathias[4], Matthew[3], Nicholas[2], Mathieu[1]), born 24 Jul 1793 in Amsterdam, Montgomery Co., NY; christened in DRC, Schenectady, Schenectady Co., NY; died 12 Sep 1872 in Eagle, Waukesha Co.,WI. He married on 19 Mar 1817 in Amsterdam, Montgomery Co., NY Elizabeth Maria Bovee (see 346), born 16 Apr 1793 in NY; christened 19 May 1793 in DRC, Schenectady, Schenectady Co., NY; died 12 Jun 1884 in Whitewater, Walworth Co., WI, daughter of Isaac Bovee and Rebecca Vedder.

Children of Mathias Jacob Bovee and Elizabeth Maria Bovee were as follows:

+	572	i	Sarah Jane[6] **Bovee**, born 20 Mar 1818 in DRC, Amsterdam, Montgomery Co., NY; died 5 Oct 1882. She married **Thomas W Pittman**.
+	573	ii	Emily Maria[6] **Bovee**, born 31 Jan 1820; christened 12 Mar 1820 in DRC, Amsterdam, Montgomery Co., NY; died 22 Jun 1848 in Jericho, Waukesha Co., WI. She married **Jerry Parsons**.
+	574	iii	Benedict Arnold[6] **Bovee**, born 20 Feb 1822 in NY; christened 22 Apr 1822 in DRC, Amsterdam, Montgomery Co., NY; died 3 Oct 1875 in Eagle, Waukesha Co.,WI. He married **Catharine A Cramer**.
+	575	iv	William Reid[6] **Bovee**, born 11 Oct 1823 in NY; christened in DRC, Amsterdam, Montgomery Co., NY; died 18 Mar 1874. He married **Sarah Ann Snover**.
+	576	v	Marvin Henry[6] **Bovee**, born 5 Jan 1827 in Amsterdam, Montgomery Co., NY; christened in DRC, Amsterdam, Montgomery Co., NY; died 7 May 1888 in Whitewater, Walworth Co., WI. He married **Laura Doud**.
+	577	vi	Anna Elizabeth[6] **Bovee**, born 20 Feb 1829; christened in DRC, Amsterdam, Montgomery Co., NY; died 10 Oct 1875. She married **Joseph Sprague**.
+	578	vii	Halsey Wood[6] **Bovee**, born 18 Apr 1831 in Amsterdam, Montgomery Co., NY; christened in DRC, Amsterdam, Mongomery Co., NY; died 1 Oct 1879 in Chicago, Cook Co., IL. He married **Mary Henrietta Kinder**.

+ 579 viii Edward Livingston[6] **Bovee**, born 20 Jun 1833 in Amsterdam, Montgomery Co., NY; christened in DRC, Amsterdam, Montgomery Co., NY; died 5 Jul 1892 in Waukesha, Waukesha Co., WI. He married **Elizabeth B Hellier**.

580 ix Harriet Minerva[6] **Bovee**, born 20 Oct 1835 in Amsterdam, Montgomery Co., NY; christened in DRC, Amsterdam, Montgomery Co., NY; died 18 Dec 1927 in Los Angeles, Los Angeles Co., CA. She married on 10 Aug 1862 **Michael McHugh**.

240. John[5] **Bovee** (Jacob Mathias[4], Matthew[3], Nicholas[2], Mathieu[1]), born 26 Sep 1795 in Amsterdam, Montgomery Co., NY; christened in DRC, Schenectady, Schenectady Co., NY; died 23 Mar 1872 in Brooklyn, Kings Co., NY. He married (1) on 6 Aug 1820 in Levant, Penobscot Co., ME Mercy A Hodson, born 4 Oct 1795; died 13 May 1831 in Levant, Penobscot Co., ME, daughter of Moses Hodson and Mercy (---); (2) on 15 Jan 1834 Julia A Holden, born 10 Mar 1812 in Charlestown, Suffolk Co., MA; died 12 Oct 1844 in Boston, Suffolk Co., MA, daughter of Life Holden and Abigail Hearsey; (3) on 25 Sep 1861 in Ney York, New York Co., NY Phoebe C Reybert, born 1841 in Islip, Suffolk Co., NY; died 6 Mar 1922 in Brooklyn, Kings Co., NY.

Children of John Bovee and Mercy A Hodson were as follows:

581 i Amanda Matilda[6] **Bovee**, born 27 Nov 1820. She married **Elijah Smith**.

582 ii Marinda[6] **Bovee**, born 5 Nov 1822. She married **Simeon Gifford**.

583 iii Moses Frederick[6] **Bovee**, born 3 Sep 1824; died 25 Aug 1825.

584 iv Amelia Jane[6] **Bovee**, born abt 1826. She married **Walter S Tarbox**.

585 v William[6] **Bovee**. He married (1) **Charlotte Rogers**; (2) **Emily (---)**.

Children of John Bovee and Julia A Holden were as follows:

+ 586 i Romania[6] **Bovee**, born 5 Apr 1840 in Provincetown, Barnstable Co., MA; died 31 Oct 1898 in Troy, Rensselaer Co., NY. She married **Louis Younglove Schermerhorn**.

242. Catherine[5] **Bovee** (Jacob Mathias[4], Matthew[3], Nicholas[2], Mathieu[1]), born 22 Feb 1800; christened in DRC, Schenectady, Schenectady Co., NY. She married on 21 Dec 1831 in Amsterdam, Montgomery Co., NY Jonathan Sedgewick.

Children of Catherine Bovee and Jonathan Sedgewick were as follows:

587 i Mary Jane[6] **Sedgewick**, born 27 Oct 1833 in Kingsborough, Fulton Co., NY.

243. Philip Vedder[5] **Bovee** (Jacob Mathias[4], Matthew[3], Nicholas[2], Mathieu[1]), born 12 Jun 1802 in NY; christened 18 Jul 1802 in Woetina Ref Ch, Rotterdam, Schenectady Co., NY; died 21 Nov 1873 in Eagle, Waukesha Co., WI. He married on 27 Jun 1827 in Amsterdam, Montgomery Co., NY Charlotte Ann Pittman, born 23 Feb 1805 in New York, New York Co., NY; died 14 Apr 1879 in Eagle, Waukesha Co., WI.

Children of Philip Vedder Bovee and Charlotte Ann Pittman were as follows:

+ 588 i Eliza Ann[6] **Bovee**, born 1 Mar 1830 in Amsterdam, Montgomery Co., NY; died 28 Sep 1884. She married **Lucian Weeks Robinson**.

+ 589 ii Thomas Pittman[6] **Bovee**, born 11 Jul 1832 in Amsterdam, Montgomery Co., NY; died 26 Oct 1906 in Plainfield, Waushara Co., WI. He married **Susan M Walker**.

+ 590 iii Sharina[6] **Bovee**, born 25 Apr 1834 in Amsterdam, Montgomery Co., NY; died 2 Mar 1887 in KS. She married **John Batrell**.

+ 591 iv Lemuel Jacob[6] **Bovee**, born 21 Sep 1835 in Amsterdam, Montgomery Co., NY; died May 1910. He married **Susan A Betts**.

+ 592 v Katherine Elizabeth[6] **Bovee**, born 11 Feb 1839 in Amsterdam, Montgomery Co., NY; died 3 Apr 1925. She married (1) **Henry L Jaycox**; (2) **Edward Button Parsons**.

+ 593 vi Mary Arnold[6] **Bovee**, born 4 Nov 1840 in Amsterdam, Montgomery Co., NY; died 2 Apr 1891 in Eagle, Waukesha Co., WI. She married **John William Hubbard**.

+ 594 vii John Isaac[6] **Bovee**, born 9 Jan 1844 in Eagle, Waukesha Co., WI; died 10 Sep 1916 in Gould City, Mackinac Co., MI. He married (1) **Frances L Lumb**; (2) **Marion A Morrison**; (3) **Kate Louella Morrison**.

  595 viii Eugene[6] **Bovee**, born 8 Jul 1846; died 17 Nov 1849.

+ 596 ix Eugene Charles[6] **Bovee**, born 8 Jul 1850; died 24 Aug 1909. He married (1) **Martha H Betts**; (2) **Marge Parsons**.

246. Catharine[5] **Bovee** (Abraham[4], Matthew[3], Nicholas[2], Mathieu[1]), born 2 May 1802; christened 26 Jun 1802 in St Paul Lutheran Evan Ch, Berne, Albany Co., NY; died 11 Jan 1865. She married Robert C Van Deusen, born 5 Nov 1797 in New Salem, Albany Co., NY; christened 23 Nov 1797; died 17 May 1853, son of Cornelius Van Deusen and Tryntje Bradt.

Children of Catharine Bovee and Robert C Van Deusen were as follows:

  597 i Abraham[6] **Van Deusen**, born 13 May 1831 in Albany Co., NY.

  598 ii Daniel[6] **Van Deusen**, born abt 1837.

  599 iii William H H[6] **Van Deusen**, born abt 1840.

247. Elizabeth^5 **Bovee** (Abraham^4, Matthew^3, Nicholas^2, Mathieu^1), born Jul 1804 in South Berne, Albany Co., NY; christened 27 Jul 1804 in DRC, Schoharie, Schoharie Co., NY. She married Michael Decker, born 1793 in NY.

Children of Elizabeth Bovee and Michael Decker were as follows:

600	i	Samuel I^6 **Decker**, born abt 1827 in South Berne, Albany Co., NY.
601	ii	Lucius^6 **Decker**, born abt 1831 in South Berne, Albany Co., NY.
602	iii	Wesley^6 **Decker**, born abt 1836 in South Berne, Albany Co., NY.
603	iv	Elizabeth^6 **Decker**, born abt 1839 in South Berne, Albany Co., NY.
604	v	Lodena^6 **Decker**, born abt 1842 in South Berne, Albany Co., NY.
605	vi	Angeline^6 **Decker**, born abt 1845 in South Berne, Albany Co., NY.
606	vii	William^6 **Decker**, born abt 1847 in South Berne, Albany Co., NY.

248. Sarah^5 **Bovee** (Abraham^4, Matthew^3, Nicholas^2, Mathieu^1), born 9 Dec 1806 in NY; christened in DRC, Schoharie, Schoharie Co., NY; died 9 Jan 1887. She married Jacob P Decker, born abt 1794 in NY; died 9 Jan 1840.

Children of Sarah Bovee and Jacob P Decker were as follows:

607	i	Jacob E^6 **Decker**, born abt 1824.
608	ii	Phebe^6 **Decker**, born 12 Nov 1836 in NY.
609	iii	Juston^6 **Decker**, born abt 1837.
610	iv	Rachel W^6 **Decker**, born 21 May 1840 in Berne, Albany Co., NY.

250. Mathew J^5 **Bovee** (John^4, Matthew^3, Nicholas^2, Mathieu^1), born 11 Sep 1799; christened 3 Nov 1799 in Schenectady, Albany Co., NY; died 7 Apr 1863 in Sugar Creek, Walworth Co., WI. He married on 21 Sep 1825 in Alden, Erie Co., NY Emily Harris, born 1812 in MA; died aft 1870.

Children of Mathew J Bovee and Emily Harris were as follows:

	611	i	Andrew D^6 **Bovee**, born 1837 in NY; died 24 Jun 1864 in Murfreesboro,Rutherfoed Co., TN.
+	612	ii	Martha Sprague^6 **Bovee**, born 3 Dec 1838 in Plainville, Adams Co., IL; died 14 Feb 1911 in Jacksonport, Door Co., WI. She married **William Robert Brabazon**.
	613	iii	Harriet^6 **Bovee**, born abt 1841 in IL.
	614	iv	James^6 **Bovee**, born 18 Apr 1853 in WI; died 11 Nov 1911 in Lake City, Calhoun Co., IA..

251. John Grant[5] **Bovee** (John[4], Matthew[3], Nicholas[2], Mathieu[1]), born 29 Oct 1802; christened in DRC, Amsterdam, Montgomery Co., NY; died abt 1884 in Redfield, Oswego Co., NY. He married in Jul 1826 Emeline Baird, died in Fulton Co., NY, daughter of Beriah Baird and Martha Scott.

Children of John Grant Bovee and Emeline Baird were as follows:

+ 615   i   William Henry[6] **Bovee**, born 20 Feb 1827 in Gloversville, Fulton Co., NY. He married **Sarah Elizabeth Roat**.

   616   ii   George Mathew[6] **Bovee**, born 15 May 1828. He married **Mary H Brooks**.

   617   iii   Emily[6] **Bovee**, born 6 Jul 1830. She married **David Dana**.

+ 618   iv   Almira[6] **Bovee**, born 17 May 1832; died 18 Mar 1911. She married **Dennis A Wilson**.

   619   v   Mary Ann[6] **Bovee**, born 12 Nov 1833. She married **Henry Stayley**.

+ 620   vi   Harriet[6] **Bovee**, born 12 Nov 1835. She married (1) **Charles Hayes**; (2) **Joseph Burnett**.

+ 621   vii   Katherine[6] **Bovee**, born 7 Jul 1838 in Clayton, Jefferson Co., NY; died 3 Feb 1897. She married **Henry Paddock**.

+ 622   viii   John Wesley[6] **Bovee**, born 17 Jul 1840; died 26 Aug 1924 in Redfield, Oswego Co., NY. He married (1) **Amelia Miller**; (2) **Mary Packard**.

   623   ix   Beriah[6] **Bovee**, born 9 Jul 1841; died 1850 in Clayton, Jefferson Co., NY.

+ 624   x   Martha Eleanor[6] **Bovee**, born 9 Jul 1843 in NY; died 3 Sep 1900. She married **George Kenyon Palmer**.

252. Nicholas[5] **Bovee** (John[4], Matthew[3], Nicholas[2], Mathieu[1]), born 1 Jul 1804; christened 6 Jan 1805 in DRC, Amsterdam, Montgomery Co., NY; died Sep 1873. He married Jane (---), born abt 1807; died 1890.

Children of Nicholas Bovee and Jane (---) were as follows:

   625   i   Geraldine[6] **Bovee**, born abt 1843.

255. Mary[5] **Bovee** (John Henry[4], Matthew[3], Nicholas[2], Mathieu[1]), born 31 Mar 1798 in NY; christened in DRC, Schenectady, Schenectady Co., NY; died 17 Sep 1831 in Orleans Co, NY. She married on 7 Sep 1816 Philip Harmon Vedder, son of Harmanus S Vedder and Annatje (---).

Children of Mary Bovee and Philip Harmon Vedder were as follows:

   626   i   Lavina[6] **Vedder**, born 17 Jul 1822 in Orleans Co., NY.

   627   ii   Henry[6] **Vedder**, born 23 Jul 1825 in Orleans Co., NY.

   628   iii   Herman[6] **Vedder**, born 3 Jun 1828 in Orleans Co., NY.

256. John Henry[5] **Bovee** (John Henry[4], Matthew[3], Nicholas[2], Mathieu[1]), born 22 Aug 1799 in NY; christened 27 Aug 1799 in DRC, Schenectady, Schenectady

Co., NY; died 10 Jul 1860 in Lenawee Co., MI. He married on 1 Jan 1823 Electa Hamlin, born 19 Jul 1808 in Canada; died 12 Apr 1874.

Children of John Henry Bovee and Electa Hamlin were as follows:

629   i   Henry[6] **Bovee**, born 3 Aug 1825 in NY; died 20 Apr 1910 in Chelsea,Washtenaw Co., MI. He married **Amanda Catherine Robb**, born Aug 1833; died 1912 in Chelsea,Washtenaw Co., MI.

+ 630   ii   Aaron[6] **Bovee**, born 21 Apr 1827 in NY; died 18 Jan 1856 in Hudson, Lenawee Co., MI. He married **Fanny Johnson**.

+ 631   iii   Levi[6] **Bovee**, born 14 Nov 1829 in Orleans Co., NY; died 23 Apr 1903 in IN. He married (1) **Laura Jane Silsbee**; (2) **Minerva Bovee** (see 642).

+ 632   iv   Hiram[6] **Bovee**, born 27 Oct 1831 in Yates, Orleans Co., NY; died 18 Jan 1902 in North Star Twp, Gratiot Co., MI. He married **Adaline A Austin**.

633   v   Ira[6] **Bovee**, born 25 Jan 1833 in NY; died 12 Mar 1858.

+ 634   vi   Lorenzo J[6] **Bovee**, born 30 Jun 1837 in NY; died 3 Jun 1862 in Dover Twp, Lenawee Co., MI. He married **Clara J (---)**.

+ 635   vii   David[6] **Bovee**, born 29 Jun 1839 in Orleans Co., NY; died 24 Sep 1904. He married **Elma Jane Bordine**.

636   viii   Charles[6] **Bovee**, born 25 Jun 1844 in NY; died 17 Oct 1928. He married on 8 Dec 1869 in Lenawee Co., MI **Lydia Mullins**, born 1846; died 1924.

257. Charity[5] Bovee (John Henry[4], Matthew[3], Nicholas[2], Mathieu[1]), born 24 Mar 1801 in NY; christened 17 May 1801 in Woestina Ref Ch., Rotterdam, Schenectady Co., NY; died 1824. She married William Hart.

Children of Charity Bovee and William Hart were as follows:

637   i   Asa[6] **Hart**.

638   ii   Ester[6] **Hart**.

258. Mathew[5] Bovee (John Henry[4], Matthew[3], Nicholas[2], Mathieu[1]), born 31 Jan 1803 in NY; christened 12 Aug 1804 in Woestina Ref Ch, Rotterdam, Schenectady Co., NY; died 25 Nov 1879 in Lenawee Co., MI. He married on 14 Sep 1828 Maria Louisa Marlatt, born 30 Jun 1810; died 14 May 1887, daughter of Enoch Marlatt and Anna Sutphin.

Children of Mathew Bovee and Maria Louisa Marlatt were as follows:

639   i   Melissa S[6] **Bovee**, born 17 Mar 1830 in NY; died 10 Jun 1895.

640   ii   Oscar F[6] **Bovee**, born 5 May 1832; died 10 Mar 1849.

641   iii   Martha[6] **Bovee**, born abt 1832 in NY. She married **Leander Johnson**.

+	642	iv	Minerva^6 **Bovee**, born 15 Feb 1833 in Yates, Orleans Co., NY; died 11 Apr 1905 in IN. She married (1) **Darius S Grant**; (2) **Levi Bovee** (see 631).
+	643	v	Andrew J^6 **Bovee**, born 7 Sep 1837 in Hudson, Lenawee Co., MI. He married (1) **Melissa Eliza Smith**; (2) **Sarah Maria Frier**.
+	644	vi	Grosvenor D^6 **Bovee**, born Nov 1839 in MI. He married **Adaline Hanbiel**.

259. Anna^5 **Bovee** (John Henry^4, Matthew^3, Nicholas^2, Mathieu^1), born 10 Feb 1805 in NY; christened in DRC, Amsterdam, Montgomery Co., NY; died 5 May 1879. She married (1) in 1824 Obediah H Marlatt, son of Enoch Marlatt and Anna Sutphin; (2) on 14 Oct 1838 Benjamin T Marlatt, son of Enoch Marlatt and Anna Sutphin.

Children of Anna Bovee and Obediah H Marlatt were as follows:

	645	i	Eliza Ann^6 **Marlatt**, born 10 Aug 1824.
	646	ii	Silas^6 **Marlatt**, born 8 Jul 1826.
	647	iii	Eli^6 **Marlatt**, born 28 Dec 1828.

Children of Anna Bovee and Benjamin T Marlatt were as follows:

	648	i	Child^6 **Marlatt**, born Stillborn in Stillborn.
	649	ii	Angeline^6 **Marlatt**, born 28 Jul 1840.
	650	iii	Salome^6 **Marlatt**, born 1847.

260. Jacob^5 **Bovee** (John Henry^4, Matthew^3, Nicholas^2, Mathieu^1), born 27 Nov 1806 in Montgomery Co., NY; christened 18 Oct 1807 in DRC, Amsterdam, Mongomery Co., NY; died 15 Jan 1885 in Dover Twp, Lenawee Co., MI. He married (1) in 1827 in Yates, Orleans Co., NY Ester Marlatt, born 4 Nov 1808; died 24 Sep 1856 in Dover Twp, Lenawee Co., MI, daughter of Enoch Marlatt and Anna Sutphin; (2) on 19 Apr 1857 Fanny Bovee, born 25 Sep 1830; died 4 Feb 1912.

Children of Jacob Bovee and Ester Marlatt were as follows:

+	651	i	Elisha H^6 **Bovee**, born 17 Aug 1829 in NY; died 1 Feb 1889. He married **Susannah R Hamilton**.
+	652	ii	Elijah^6 **Bovee**, born 16 Apr 1831 in NY; died 11 Sep 1914. He married **Phelina Meyers**.
+	653	iii	Ezra^6 **Bovee**, born 27 Oct 1832 in Cayuga Co., NY; died 16 Nov 1913 in Cheppewa Twp, Isabella Co., MI. He married **Elizabeth Hamilton**.
+	654	iv	Albert^6 **Bovee**, born 7 Mar 1835 in Dover, Lenawee Co., MI; died 11 Jul 1907 in Ithaca,Gratiot Co., MI. He married **Eliza Jane Meyers**.
+	655	v	Milo^6 **Bovee**, born 13 Jan 1837 in Dover, Lenawee Co., MI; died 17 Nov 1903. He married **Harriet Lucinda Warren**.

+ 656 vi Arthur[6] **Bovee**, born 10 Oct 1838 in Dover, Lenawee Co., MI; died 18 Feb 1915. He married **Ester A Cross**.

+ 657 vii Hamilton[6] **Bovee**, born 23 Oct 1840 in Dover, Lenawee Co., MI; died 4 Apr 1919. He married **Lucina Hamlin**.

+ 658 viii Lucy Ann[6] **Bovee**, born 3 Dec 1842; died 6 Jan 1914. She married **William Steadman**.

+ 659 ix Myron[6] **Bovee**, born Dec 1844 in Dover Twp, Lenawee Co., MI; died 8 Nov 1908 in Ithaca,Gratiot Co., MI. He married **Jane Elizabeth Cleveland**.

+ 660 x Ester[6] **Bovee**, born 1 Jul 1847; died 23 Feb 1932. She married (1) **John Wise**; (2) **Jacob Hathaway**; (3) **Joseph Duerr**.

+ 661 xi Hulda[6] **Bovee**, born 28 Sep 1848; died 8 May 1936. She married **David Bordine**.

+ 662 xii Elsie[6] **Bovee**, born 28 Feb 1851; died 21 Jan 1875. She married **Jerry Thompson**.

Children of Jacob Bovee and Fanny Bovee were as follows:

+ 663 i Flora Zarepha[6] **Bovee**, born 18 Mar 1858 in Tecumseh, Lewanee Co., MI; died 2 Nov 1948. She married **David Connor**.

664 ii Alta[6] **Bovee**, born 2 Apr 1860; died 19 Feb 1891. She married in 1876 **Jerry Thompson**.

+ 665 iii Lodica[6] **Bovee**, born 8 Jun 1862; died 10 May 1899. She married **Edward Decker**.

+ 666 iv Alda[6] **Bovee**, born 17 Sep 1864; died 17 May 1939 in Dover Twp, Lenawee Co., MI. He married (1) **Eliza Hawkins**; (2) **Helen A Lord**.

+ 667 v Oma[6] **Bovee**, born 16 Oct 1866; died 20 Sep 1935. He married **Harriet Wood**.

+ 668 vi Devillow[6] **Bovee**, born 8 Nov 1868 in Lenawee Co., MI; died 16 Nov 1964 in CA. He married **Mary Ethel Mayfield**.

669 vii Victoria[6] **Bovee**, born 3 Aug 1870 in Dover Twp, Lenawee Co., MI; died 11 Apr 1964. She married on 12 Sep 1887 in Hillsdale, Hillsdale Co., MI **Harvey A Wise**.

670 viii Jasper[6] **Bovee**, born 24 Jul 1872 in MI; died 20 Feb 1873 in Dover Twp, Lenawee Co., MI.

671 ix Lulu Belle[6] **Bovee**, born 20 Oct 1876; died 14 Oct 1900. She married on 9 Feb 1897 in Clayton, Lenawee Co., MI **Robert Deline**.

261. Sally[5] **Bovee** (John Henry[4], Matthew[3], Nicholas[2], Mathieu[1]), born 25 Dec 1808 in Charleston, Montgomery Co., NY; died 29 Jan 1849 in Dover, Lenawee co., MI. She married on 12 Apr 1827 Isaac Deline, born 6 Jun 1806 in Charleston, Montgomery Co., NY; died 29 Jan 1888 in Adrian, Lenawee Co., MI, son of John Deline and Verne Mary Hogaboom.

Children of Sally Bovee and Isaac Deline were as follows:

672   i   George W[6] **Deline**, born 20 Jul 1828 in Charleston, Montgomery Co., NY.

673   ii   John Henry[6] **Deline**, born 25 Oct 1829 in Ridgeway, Orleans Co., NY.

674   iii   Isaac Marshall[6] **Deline**, born 25 Mar 1831 in Ridgeway, Orleans Co., NY.

675   iv   George[6] **Deline**, born 17 Oct 1832 in Ridgeway, Orleans Co., NY.

676   v   Albert[6] **Deline**, born 14 Oct 1834 in Ridgeway, Orleans Co., NY.

677   vi   Orville[6] **Deline**, born 10 Mar 1836 in Ridgeway, Orleans Co., NY.

678   vii   Juliana[6] **Deline**, born 19 Feb 1838 in Adrian, Lenawee Co., MI.

679   viii   William H[6] **Deline**, born 26 Oct 1840 in Adrian, Lenawee Co., MI.

680   ix   Ester A[6] **Deline**, born 16 Nov 1841 in Adrian, Lenawee Co., MI.

681   x   Edgar[6] **Deline**, born 27 Aug 1843 in Adrian, Lenawee Co., MI.

682   xi   Miles Wesley[6] **Deline**, born 24 Mar 1846 in Adrian, Lenawee Co., MI.

683   xii   Elsie Ann[6] **Deline**, born 17 Sep 1847 in Adrian, Lenawee Co., MI.

684   xiii   Sarrah Ann[6] **Deline**, born 1848 in Adrian, Lenawee Co., MI.

262. Ester[5] **Bovee** (John Henry[4], Matthew[3], Nicholas[2], Mathieu[1]), born 20 Mar 1811 in Montgomery Co., NY; died 12 May 1887. She married on 19 Sep 1830 William Deline, born 6 Feb 1808; died 7 Apr 1892, son of John Deline and Verne Mary Hogaboom.

Children of Ester Bovee and William Deline were as follows:

685   i   Alonzo[6] **Deline**, born 31 Jul 1831 in Orleans Co., NY.

686   ii   John (Daniel)[6] **Deline**, born 5 Jan 1833 in Orleans Co., NY.

687   iii   Andrew[6] **Deline**, born 16 Nov 1834 in Orleans Co., NY.

688   iv   Cyrenius[6] **Deline**, born 29 Aug 1836 in Lenawee Co., MI.

689   v   John Edward[6] **Deline**, born 29 May 1838 in Lenawee Co., MI.

690   vi   Edwin[6] **Deline**, born 1 Dec 1839 in Lenawee Co., MI.

691   vii   William Henry[6] **Deline**, born 29 Aug 1841 in MI.

692   viii   Cynthia[6] **Deline**, born 3 May 1843.

693   ix   Eliza[6] **Deline**, born 22 Sep 1846 in Lenawee Co., MI.

694   x   Wellington[6] **Deline**, born 19 Mar 1848 in Lenawee Co., MI.

695   xi   Irving[6] **Deline**, born 6 Jul 1849 in Lenawee Co., MI.

263. Abraham[5] **Bovee** (John Henry[4], Matthew[3], Nicholas[2], Mathieu[1]), born 22 Apr 1813 in NY; died 13 Apr 1873 in Hudson Twp , Lenawee Co., MI. He married on 22 Oct 1837 in Hudson, Lenawee Co., MI Sarah Grattan, born 6 May 1817, daughter of Jason Grattan and Betsey (---).

Children of Abraham Bovee and Sarah Grattan were as follows:

+   696   i   Mary Elizabeth[6] **Bovee**, born abt 1840 in Hudson, Lenawee Co., MI. She married **Edward Hyatt**.

    697   ii   David F[6] **Bovee**, born abt 1843 in MI; died 3 Dec 1864.

    698   iii   Francis H[6] **Bovee**, born abt 1846 in Hudson, Lenawee Co., MI. He married on 22 Feb 1865 **Sarah Ann Jewel**.

    699   iv   Chauncey G[6] **Bovee**, born 30 Oct 1851 in Hudson, Lenawee Co., MI; died 9 Mar 1897 in IN. He married on 26 Feb 1884 in Clayton, Lenawee Co., MI **Martha Robbins**, born 1862; died 1925 in IN.

+   700   v   Harrison C[6] **Bovee**, born 22 Jan 1854. He married **Almina A Deline**.

    701   vi   Harriet[6] **Bovee**, born 22 Jan 1854 in Hudson, Lenawee Co., MI.

    702   vii   Alvira[6] **Bovee**, born 2 May 1857 in Hudson, Lenawee Co., MI; died Nov 1938. She married **Moses Dillon**.

264. Peter[5] **Bovee** (John Henry[4], Matthew[3], Nicholas[2], Mathieu[1]), born 13 Dec 1815 in NY; died 16 Sep 1853. He married on 6 Nov 1838 in Lenawee Co., MI Mary Millens, born 9 Aug 1823 in Bridgewater, Oneida Co., NY, daughter of Jacob Millens and Polly Ries.

Children of Peter Bovee and Mary Millens were as follows:

    703   i   Eliza Jane[6] **Bovee**, born 5 Sep 1840 in Dover, Lenawee Co., MI. She married on 5 Jan 1860 in Lenawee Co., MI **Burret Graves**.

+   704   ii   James H[6] **Bovee**, born 5 Nov 1849 in Dover, Lenawee Co., MI. He married **Laura Van Pelt**.

265. Elsie[5] **Bovee** (John Henry[4], Matthew[3], Nicholas[2], Mathieu[1]), born 11 Sep 1817 in NY; died 7 Jul 1897. She married on 21 Oct 1837 Aaron Johnson, born 24 Nov 1812; died 11 Mar 1901.

Children of Elsie Bovee and Aaron Johnson were as follows:

    705   i   Stephen[6] **Johnson**, born 1838; died 29 Nov 1845.

    706   ii   Lorinda[6] **Johnson**, born 6 Mar 1840; died 26 Feb 1872.

    707   iii   Chloe Ann[6] **Johnson**, born 1854; died 3 May 1858.

267. John E[5] **Bovie** (Jacob[4], Abraham[3], Nicholas[2], Mathieu[1]), born 17 Feb 1790 in Hoosick, Rensselaer Co., NY. He married Amy Gardner.

  Children of John E Bovie and Amy Gardner were as follows:

	708	i	John Edward[6] **Bovie**, born 9 Jan 1815; died 13 Nov 1893 in Martin, Allegan Co., MI.
+	709	ii	Anna Elizabeth[6] **Bovie**, born aft 1817. She married **Thomas Hall**.
+	710	iii	Chester A[6] **Bovie**, born abt 1822 in NY. He married **Julia Ann Chase**.
	711	iv	Asa Rial[6] **Bovie**, born abt 1823; died 17 Oct 1847 in Rush, Monroe Co., NY. He married on 1 Oct 1845 **Sarah M Davis**, daughter of Ethan Davis.
	712	v	Stephen G[6] **Bovie**, born 21 Nov 1827 in Livingston Co., NY; died 30 Nov 1888 in Watseka, Iroquois Co., IL. He married on 20 Feb 1852 **Julia Symson**.
+	713	vi	William T[6] **Bovie**, born abt 1829 in NY; died 25 Apr 1901 in Kalamazoo, Kalamazoo Co., MI. He married (1) **Susan Pack**; (2) **Henrietta Barnes**.

268. Abraham[5] **Bovee** (Jacob[4], Abraham[3], Nicholas[2], Mathieu[1]), born 3 Feb 1792 in Hoosick, Rensselaer Co., NY; died 21 Jun 1849 in Hoosick, Rensselaer Co., NY. He married abt 1814 Sally Shaw, born abt 1800 in NY.

  Children of Abraham Bovee and Sally Shaw were as follows:

714	i	Lydia Ann[6] **Bovee**, born 18 Mar 1815 in Hoosick, Rensselaer Co., NY; died 2 Jun 1840.
715	ii	Jane[6] **Bovee**, born abt 1816 in Hoosick, Rensselaer Co., NY. She married on 22 Sep 1836 **Squire Lorenzo Allen**.
716	iii	Matilda[6] **Bovee**, born abt 1818 in Hoosick, Rensselaer Co., NY. She married on 5 Jul 1839 in Rensselaer Co., NY **William H Thomas**.
717	iv	Henry[6] **Bovee**, born abt 1822 in Rensselaer Co., NY.
718	v	Charles[6] **Bovee**, born abt 1824 in Rensselaer Co., NY.

269. Isaac[5] **Bovee** (Jacob[4], Abraham[3], Nicholas[2], Mathieu[1]), born 22 May 1794 in Hoosick, Rensselaer Co., NY; died 21 Jun 1862 in Hoosick, Rensselaer Co., NY. He married (1) Annie Allen, born 28 Aug 1790; died 11 Nov 1851 in Hoosick, Rensselaer Co., NY; (2) on 4 Mar 1857 in Hoosick, Rensselaer Co., NY Phebe Wilson, born 1816.

  Children of Isaac Bovee and Annie Allen were as follows:

	719	i	Mary Ann[6] **Bovee**, born 20 Nov 1817 in Hoosick, Rensselaer Co., NY; died 14 Aug 1908. She married **Thomas Davis**.
+	720	ii	George Washington[6] **Bovee**, born 4 Oct 1819 in Hoosick, Rensselaer Co., NY; died 28 Apr 1865. He married

Martha A Weaver.

721   iii   Sarah M^6 **Bovee**, born 7 Nov 1821 in Hoosick, Rensselaer Co., NY; died 16 Dec 1885. She married on 27 May 1847 **Richard H Bovee** (see 454), born 6 Nov 1819 in Rensselaer Co., NY; died 2 Nov 1860 in Hoosick, Rensselaer Co., NY, son of Henry Bovee and Hannah Hewitt.

+ 722   iv   Isaac Warren I^6 **Bovee**, born 17 Jan 1824 in Hoosick, Rensselaer Co., NY; died 25 Oct 1891 in Hoosick, Rensselaer Co., NY. He married **Sarah Minerva Jones**.

Children of Isaac Bovee and Phebe Wilson were as follows:

723   i   Joseph^6 **Bovee**, born 18 Jun 1860 in Hoosick, Rensselaer Co., NY.

270. Jacob^5 **Bovee** Jr (Jacob^4, Abraham^3, Nicholas^2, Mathieu^1), born 12 Aug 1796. He married on 17 Jul 1819 in New York, New York Co., NY Mary Ann Stanton.

Children of Jacob Bovee Jr and Mary Ann Stanton were as follows:

724   i   William Henry^6 **Bovee**, born 1820 in New York, New York Co., NY; christened 2 Dec 1820 in DRC, New York, New York Co., NY. He married on 3 Oct 1849 in New York, New York Co., NY **Catherine Frazer**.

725   ii   Jacob^6 **Bovee** III, born 1822.

726   iii   John^6 **Bovee**, born abt 1826.

727   iv   Charles^6 **Bovee**, born abt 1827.

+ 728   v   Alfred^6 **Bovee**, born 1830. He married **Marian F Gray**.

729   vi   Abraham^6 **Bovee**, born abt 1830.

271. William G^5 **Bovee** (Jacob^4, Abraham^3, Nicholas^2, Mathieu^1), born 17 May 1801 in Rensselaer Co., NY. He married Mary Ann Carpenter, born 1812; died abt 1890.

Children of William G Bovee and Mary Ann Carpenter were as follows:

+ 730   i   Maria Isabella Louise^6 **Bovee**, born 9 Oct 1832 in Rensselaer Co., NY. She married **John Agan**.

+ 731   ii   Jacob F W^6 **Bovie**, born 3 May 1836 in Hoosick, Rensselaer Co., NY. He married **Margaret Fox**.

272. Asa^5 **Bovee** (Jacob^4, Abraham^3, Nicholas^2, Mathieu^1), born 20 Apr 1805 in Hoosick, Rensselaer Co., NY; died 1 Aug 1872 in Riceville, Fulton Co., NY. He married on 21 Jul 1839 in Bannington, Bennington Co., VT Weltha Marie Gooding, born 16 Dec 1813; died 4 Mar 1887.

Children of Asa Bovee and Weltha Marie Gooding were as follows:

+	732	i	Mehitable[6] **Bovee**, born 2 Oct 1853. She married **Sanford Carpenter Plass**.
+	733	ii	Culver Nathaniel[6] **Bovee**, born 1855; died Sep 1913 in Johnstown, Fulton Co., NY. He married **Mary Jane Wells**.

275. Sally[5] **Bovee** (Matthew[4], Abraham[3], Nicholas[2], Mathieu[1]), born 30 Apr 1798 in NY; christened 7 Feb 1799 in Gilead Luth Ch., Centre Brunswick, Rensselaer Co., NY; died 10 Jul 1868 in Otsego Co., NY. She married in Otsego Co., NY Jacob Quackenbush, born 18 Jan 1793; christened 3 Feb 1793 in DRC, Albany, Albany Co., NY; died 26 Aug 1846 in Ostego Co., NY, son of Isaac Quackenbush and Katherine Gardinier.

Children of Sally Bovee and Jacob Quackenbush were as follows:

734	i	David[6] **Quackenbush**, born abt 1820.
735	ii	Catherine[6] **Quackenbush**, born abt 1822.
736	iii	Betsey[6] **Quackenbush**, born abt 1823.
737	iv	Orlando[6] **Quackenbush**, born Feb 1824.
738	v	Nancy Maria[6] **Quackenbush**, born abt 1828.
739	vi	Caroline[6] **Quackenbush**, born 18 Aug 1829.
740	vii	Peter[6] **Quackenbush**, born abt 1832.
741	viii	Jacob[6] **Quackenbush**, born 28 Dec 1833.
742	ix	John[6] **Quackenbush**, born Oct 1838.
743	x	Rachel[6] **Quackenbush**, born 1841.

276. Lucinda[5] **Bovee** (Matthew[4], Abraham[3], Nicholas[2], Mathieu[1]), born 27 Jun 1805 in East Sydney, Delaware Co., NY; died 20 Oct 1882 in East Sydney, Delaware Co., NY. She married on 3 Mar 1831 in Otsego, Otsego Co., NY Hiram Smith Whitney, born 24 Jun 1807 in Fairfield, Franklin Co., VT; died 2 Feb 1896 in East Sidney, Delaware Co., NY, son of Henry Whitney and Ruth St John.

Children of Lucinda Bovee and Hiram Smith Whitney were as follows:

744	i	Warren Winslow Westler[6] **Whitney**, born 23 Mar 1832 in Unadilla, Delaware Co., NY.
745	ii	Theodore Legrand[6] **Whitney**, born 13 Aug 1833 in Sidney, Delaware Co., NY.
746	iii	Harriet Minerva[6] **Whitney**, born 17 Mar 1835 in Sidney, Delaware Co., NY.
747	iv	Phebe Lavinia[6] **Whitney**, born 26 Jul 1837 in Sidney, Delaware Co., NY.
748	v	Caroline[6] **Whitney**, born 26 Aug 1839.
749	vi	Eliza Ann[6] **Whitney**, born 13 Apr 1841.
750	vii	Henry Delos[6] **Whitney**, born 14 Aug 1846 in Sidney, Delaware Co., NY.

277. Rodney.^{5} **Bovee** (Matthew^4, Abraham^3, Nicholas^2, Mathieu^1), born 1807 in Rensselaer Co., NY; died in Unadilla, Otsego Co., NY. He married (1) abt 1824 Cynthia Youmans, born 23 Jan 1803; died 25 May 1860, daughter of John Youmans and Polly Birdsall; (2) bef 1870 Mary (---), born abt 1808.

Children of Rodney. Bovee and Cynthia Youmans were as follows:

751   i   Unknown^6 **Bovee**.

752   ii   Edwin^6 **Bovee**, born Jan 1834 in Sidny, Delaware Co., NY; died Jun 1834.

753   iii   Ellen D^6 **Bovee**, born Dec 1836; died 16 Apr 1841.

754   iv   Eugene^6 **Bovee**, born Aug 1839 in Sidny, Delaware Co., NY; died 14 Apr 1841.

755   v   Charlotte^6 **Bovee**, born abt 1842 in Sidny, Delaware Co., NY; buried in East Sidney Cem, Sidney, Delaware Co., NY. She married in Unadilla, Ostego Co., NY **William Harlan Brooks**.

278. Peter^5 **Bovee** (Matthew^4, Abraham^3, Nicholas^2, Mathieu^1), born 11 Aug 1811 in Schoharie Co., NY; died 9 Dec 1894 in Williamsport, Lycoming Co., PA. He married in 1833 Nancy Wiles, born 1813 in Broome Co., NY; died 24 Nov 1893 in Williamsport, Lycoming Co., PA.

Children of Peter Bovee and Nancy Wiles were as follows:

756   i   Adeline^6 **Bovee**, born 19 Mar 1834 in Colesville, Broome Co., NY; died 2 Feb 1840.

+ 757   ii   Sarah Livonia^6 **Bovee**, born 4 Mar 1836 in Harpursville, Broome Co., NY; died 6 May 1895. She married **Abram Good**.

758   iii   Dolly Ann^6 **Bovee**, born 10 May 1838 in Colesville, Broome Co., NY; died 11 Feb 1840.

+ 759   iv   Rodney Mathias^6 **Bovee**, born 24 Apr 1840 in Colesville, Broome Co., NY; died 19 Jan 1890. He married **Loeva Matilda Bovee**.

+ 760   v   John Oscar^6 **Bovee**, born 14 Mar 1842 in Colesville, Broome Co., NY; died 28 Jan 1916 in Buffalo, Erie Co., NY. He married (1) **Catharine Fredericka Fisher**; (2) **Arvilla Jane Bussler**.

+ 761   vi   George Burton^6 **Bovee**, born 15 Jun 1844 in Barton, Tioga Co., NY; died 14 Dec 1912 in Hepburn Town, Lycoming Co., PA. He married **Sarah Elizabeth Ball**.

+ 762   vii   Perry Henry^6 **Bovee**, born 27 Apr 1848 in Owego, Tioga Co., NY; died 22 Oct 1928 in Newberry, Lycoming Co., PA. He married **Ann Elizabeth Patterson**.

+ 763   viii   Walter Haywood^6 **Bovee**, born 13 Feb 1853 in Tioga, Tioga Co., NY. He married **Emma Frances Morris**.

280. Susan^5 **Bovee** (John^4, Abraham^3, Nicholas^2, Mathieu^1), born 1806 in

Hoosick, Rensselaer Co., NY; died 1843 in St Joseph Co., MI. She married abt 1837 Luther Rawson, born 14 Mar 1786 in Buckland, Hampshire Co., MA; died Aug 1861 in St Joseph Co., MI, son of Moses Rawson.

Children of Susan Bovee and Luther Rawson were as follows:

764　　i　　　Emily M A ^{6} **Rawson**, born 19 Jun 1838 in MI.

765　　ii　　　Sarah Arrilla ^{6} **Rawson**, born May 1840.

281. Aurelia ^{5} **Bovee** (John ^{4}, Abraham ^{3}, Nicholas ^{2}, Mathieu ^{1}), born 13 Dec 1807 in Hoosick, Rensselaer Co., NY; died 21 Aug 1854. She married Nathaniel Reynolds, born 1791 in NY; buried in Scott-Doane Cem, W Mendon St. Joseph Co., MI.

Children of Aurelia Bovee and Nathaniel Reynolds were as follows:

766　　i　　　Susan ^{6} **Reynolds**, born 20 Nov 1826 in Troy, Rensselaer Co., NY.

767　　ii　　　Hiram ^{6} **Reynolds**, born 17 Sep 1827 in NY.

768　　iii　　　Child ^{6} **Reynolds**, born abt 1828 in NY.

769　　iv　　　George W ^{6} **Reynolds**, born 30 Oct 1832 in NY.

770　　v　　　Mark ^{6} **Reynolds**, born abt 1835 in NY.

771　　vi　　　Deborah ^{6} **Reynolds**, born 7 Jan 1836 in NY.

772　　vii　　　Eliza ^{6} **Reynolds**, born 17 Feb 1839 in NY.

773　　viii　　Margaret ^{6} **Reynolds**, born 1844 in MI.

774　　ix　　　William L ^{6} **Reynolds**, born 25 Mar 1848 in MI.

282. Eliza ^{5} **Bovee** (John ^{4}, Abraham ^{3}, Nicholas ^{2}, Mathieu ^{1}), born abt 1809 in NY; died bef 1875. She married on 18 Nov 1832 in Crawford Co., OH Gabriel Langdon, born 4 Sep 1809 in NY; died 7 Feb 1875 in Mendon St. Joseph Co., MI, son of William Langdon Jr..

Children of Eliza Bovee and Gabriel Langdon were as follows:

775　　i　　　Elizabeth ^{6} **Langdon**, born 11 Jan 1834 in OH.

776　　ii　　　Child ^{6} **Langdon**, born Dec 1838 in Mendon St. Joseph Co., MI.

777　　iii　　　William ^{6} **Langdon**, born 1839 in Mendon St. Joseph Co., MI.

778　　iv　　　Mortimer ^{6} **Langdon**, born Feb 1844 in Mendon St. Joseph Co., MI.

283. Emily A ^{5} **Bovee** (John ^{4}, Abraham ^{3}, Nicholas ^{2}, Mathieu ^{1}), born 17 Apr 1811 in NY; died 19 Jun 1895 in Mendon, St Joseph Co., MI. She married abt 1828 William A Langdon, born 16 Sep 1803 in NY; died 11 Oct 1888 in Mendon St. Joseph Co., MI, son of William Langdon Jr..

Children of Emily A Bovee and William A Langdon were as follows:

779	i	John [6] **Langdon**, born 10 Jan 1829 in NY.
780	ii	Hannah [6] **Langdon**, born 1831 in OH.
781	iii	Charles Gabriel [6] **Langdon**, born 2 Jun 1834 in OH.
782	iv	Martin Luther [6] **Langdon**, born 2 Aug 1840 in Mendon St. Joseph Co., MI.
783	v	William A [6] **Langdon**, born 28 Sep 1844 in Mendon St. Joseph Co., MI.
784	vi	Frances [6] **Langdon**, born 16 Nov 1849 in Mendon St. Joseph Co., MI.

285. Orrin Primmer [5] **Bovee** (John [4], Abraham [3], Nicholas [2], Mathieu [1]), born 1814 in Hoosick, Rennselaer Co., NY; died 22 Oct 1883 in Kalamazoo, Kalamazoo Co., MI. He married (1) on 27 Nov 1840 in At home of John Laughlin,Bucks Twp, St Joseph Co., MI Maria Snow, born abt 1823 in MA; died 1861 in MI; (2) on 7 Oct 1862 in Monterey, Allegan Co., MI Eliza Jane Waggoner, born 4 Aug 1832 in OH; died 13 Mar 1908 in Battle Creek, Calhoun Co., MI, daughter of George Walker Waggoner and Elizabeth Jane Guise.

Children of Orrin Primmer Bovee and Maria Snow were as follows:

+	785	i	Melissa [6] **Bovee**, born abt 1842 in MI. She married (1) **Lock V Mosher**; (2) **(---) Emery**.
	786	ii	Orrin J [6] **Bovee**, born abt 1848 in MI; died bef 1860.

Children of Orrin Primmer Bovee and Eliza Jane Waggoner were as follows:

	787	i	Estella [6] **Bovee**, born Dec 1863 in MI; died 1927.
+	788	ii	George Walker [6] **Bovee**, born 5 Jan 1866 in MI; died 18 May 1964. He married **Anna Smith**.
+	789	iii	Mark Orin [6] **Bovee**, born 18 Jul 1868 in MI; died 15 Jul 1960 in Los Angeles Co., CA. He married **Minnie Standen**.
+	790	iv	Wright Ingraham [6] **Bovee**, born 18 Aug 1871 in MI; died 11 Feb 1966 in Stanislaus Co., CA. He married **Ethel Paulina Harrison**.
	791	v	Mary Isabella [6] **Bovee**, born Jan 1876 in MI.

286. Permelia [5] **Bovee** (John [4], Abraham [3], Nicholas [2], Mathieu [1]), born 10 Sep 1817 in NY; died 14 Mar 1906 in Lisbon, Ransom Co., ND. She married on 15 Apr 1839 in Mendon, St Joseph Co., MI John Laughlin, born 10 Mar 1809 in Ryegate, Caledonia Co., VT; died 8 Jul 1861 in Markesan, Green Lake Co., WI, son of Hugh Laughlin and Elizabeth Clark.

Children of Permelia Bovee and John Laughlin were as follows:

792	i	Elizabeth Ann [6] **Laughlin**, born 2 Jun 1840 in Three Rivers, St Joseph Co., MI.
793	ii	Julia Amanda [6] **Laughlin**, born 4 Dec 1841 in St Joseph Co., MI.
794	iii	William John [6] **Laughlin**, born abt 1842 in St Joseph Co.,

MI.

795	iv	John William[6] **Laughlin**, born 1 Mar 1844 in St Joseph Co., MI.
796	v	Lucy Jane[6] **Laughlin**, born 25 Oct 1846 in Ripon, Fon du Lac Co., WI.
797	vi	Andrew Hugh[6] **Laughlin**, born 11 Nov 1848 in Markesan, Green Lake Co., WI.
798	vii	George[6] **Laughlin**, born Dec 1850 in Markesan, Green Lake Co., WI.

287. Sarah Matilda[5] **Bovee** (John[4], Abraham[3], Nicholas[2], Mathieu[1]), born 1826 in Lyons, Wayne Co., NY; died 27 Jan 1903 in Fargo, Cass Co., ND. She married (1) on 1 Mar 1840 in Sandusky, Erie Co., OH George Leonard Lincoln; (2) on 14 Nov 1859 in St. Peter, Nicollet Co., MN Benjamin Ayer Lowell, died 12 May 1893 in Jamestown, Stutsman Co., ND.

Children of Sarah Matilda Bovee and George Leonard Lincoln were as follows:

799	i	Elizabeth Maria[6] **Lincoln**, born 9 Apr 1846.
800	ii	Lucius George[6] **Lincoln**, born 3 Mar 1847 in Rome Twp., Lenawee Co., MI.
801	iii	Eliza Almira[6] **Lincoln**, born 8 Sep 1849.
802	iv	Edwin Herbert[6] **Lincoln**, born 24 Dec 1851 in Adrian, Lenawee Co., MI.
803	v	Willard Hopkins[6] **Lincoln**, born 13 Apr 1852 in Almena Twp., VanBuren Co., MI.

Children of Sarah Matilda Bovee and Benjamin Ayer Lowell were as follows:

804	i	Benjamin Ayer[6] **Lowell** Jr., born 12 Sep 1861 in Otisco, Waseca Co., MN.
805	ii	Child[6] **Lowell**.
806	iii	Child[6] **Lowell**.
807	iv	Martha Belle[6] **Lowell**, born 20 Apr 1866.
808	v	Bertha L[6] **Lowell**, born Jul 1869.

288. Cornelius[5] **Bovee** (Abraham[4], Abraham[3], Nicholas[2], Mathieu[1]), born 1800 in Delaware Co., NY. He married abt 1832 in T/Lenox, Madison Co., NY Margaret Helmer, born 1 Jan 1817 in Steuben Co., NY; died aft 1880, daughter of John Helmer and Urana (---).

Children of Cornelius Bovee and Margaret Helmer were as follows:

| + | 809 | i | George C[6] **Bovee**, born 22 May 1833 in Madison Co., NY; died 20 Sep 1915 in Bath, Steuben Co., NY. He married **Lavina Jackson**. |
| + | 810 | ii | Lucinda[6] **Bovee**, born 1835 in Steuben Co., NY. She married (1) **Solomon Brownell**; (2) **Harry J Vaughn**. |

+ 811 iii John W[6] **Bovee**, born 18 Oct 1836 in Canisteo, Steuben Co., NY; died 4 Apr 1915 in Addison, Steuben Co., NY. He married (1) **Margaret Lucina Jackson**; (2) **Amanda Jackson**.

+ 812 iv Lydia E[6] **Bovee**, born 6 Sep 1840 in Addison, Steuben Co., NY. She married **William Paul Barker**.

813 v Ann E[6] **Bovee**, born 1843 in Steuben Co., NY.

+ 814 vi Henry M[6] **Bovee**, born 1847 in Canisteo, Steuben Co., NY; christened 27 Apr 1895 in St Peter's Episcopal Ch, Dansville, Steuben Co., NY; died 11 Oct 1901 in Oakland, Livingston Co., NY. He married **Laura Ann Barker**.

290. Abraham[5] **Bovee** (Abraham[4], Abraham[3], Nicholas[2], Mathieu[1]), born abt 1807 in Milford, Ostego Co., NY; died 15 Jan 1882 in Manawa, Waupaca Co., WI. He married (1) abt 1833 Unknown (---); (2) abt 1841 in T/Lenox, Madison Co., NY Abigail Oscott, born 1819 in NY; died 1890 in Manawa, Waupaca Co., WI.

Children of Abraham Bovee and Unknown (---) were as follows:

815 i Henry[6] **Bovee**, born 1835 in Madison Co., NY. He married **Ellen (---)**.

+ 816 ii William R[6] **Bovee**, born 18 Dec 1840 in Madison Co., NY; died 4 Dec 1908 in Manawa, Waupaca Co., WI. He married **Mary Louisa Bruyette**.

Children of Abraham Bovee and Abigail Oscott were as follows:

817 i Caroline[6] **Bovee**, born 1842 in Madison Co., NY. She married on 1 May 1859 in Stockbridge, Calumet Co., WI **Lorenzo D Coan**.

818 ii Eleanor[6] **Bovee**, born abt 1844 in Lenox, Madison Co., NY.

+ 819 iii Rachel Mary[6] **Bovee**, born 1846 in Madison Co., NY. She married **Benneryer Fry Rice**.

+ 820 iv Marsha[6] **Bovee**, born 18 Dec 1846 in Lenox, Madison Co., NY; died aft 1924. She married **John Hubbard**.

+ 821 v Sarah Jane[6] **Bovee**, born 1849 in Madison Co., NY. She married **Soloman Youmans**.

+ 822 vi Minard[6] **Bovee**, born 1851 in Lenox, Madison Co., NY; died 24 Mar 1929 in New London,Waupaca Co., WI. He married **Mararetha Ann Martin**.

+ 823 vii Abraham[6] **Bovee**, born 15 Sep 1852 in Stockbridge, Calumet Co., WI; died 24 Feb 1911 in Antigo, Langlade Co., WI. He married **Mary A Corrigan**.

+ 824 viii Erastus[6] **Bovee**, born 23 Jul 1854 in Stockbridge, Calumet Co., WI; died 2 Feb 1938 in Appleton, Outagamie Co., WI. He married (1) **Joanna Corrigan**; (2) **Corina Jergenson**.

+ 825 ix Frances[6] **Bovee**, born abt 1859 in WI. She married **Melbourne Bessey**.

292. Frederick Brown[5] **Bovee** (Abraham[4], Abraham[3], Nicholas[2], Mathieu[1]), born 2 Feb 1812 in Lebenon, Madison Co., NY; died 19 Jul 1904 in Stockbridge, Calumet Co., WI. He married in 1833 in T/Lenox, Madison Co., NY Olive Babcock, born 1815 in Madison Co., NY; died 1882 in Stockbridge, Calumet Co., WI.

Children of Frederick Brown Bovee and Olive Babcock were as follows:

+ 826   i   Adelia[6] **Bovee**, born 2 Oct 1837 in NY; died 9 Apr 1871 in Stockbridge, Calumet Co., WI. She married **Lewis Solomon Myrick**.

  827   ii   Almira[6] **Bovee**, born abt 1840 in NY.

+ 828   iii   William Edgar[6] **Bovee**, born 17 Jun 1844 in Madison Co., NY; died 14 Apr 1914 in Fond du Lac, Fond du Lac Co., WI. He married **Mary Elizabeth Leathart**.

+ 829   iv   Angelica[6] **Bovee**, born 1849 in Madison Co., NY; died in Stockbridge, Calumet Co., WI. She married **Seth Stone**.

+ 830   v   Ervin[6] **Bovee**, born 26 Feb 1851 in Madison Co., NY; died 12 Jun 1928 in Stockbridge, Calumet Co., WI. He married (1) **Rose Griffith**; (2) **Antionette Dailey**.

  831   vi   Hannah[6] **Bovee**, born 1852 in Madison Co., NY.

  832   vii   Georgie[6] **Bovee**, born abt 1854; died abt 1854.

293. Ester Ann[5] **Bovee** (Abraham[4], Abraham[3], Nicholas[2], Mathieu[1]), born 17 Aug 1816 in T/Lenox, Madison Co., NY; died 6 Sep 1849 in Boltonville, Washington Co., WI. She married on 24 May 1835 Elijah Alvin Duncan, born 1815 in VT; died 18 Dec 1887 in Boltinville, Washington Co., WI, son of John Duncan.

Children of Ester Ann Bovee and Elijah Alvin Duncan were as follows:

  833   i   Adelia Ann[6] **Duncan**, born 10 Jun 1836 in NY.

  834   ii   Adelia Ann[6] **Duncan**, born 21 Feb 1841 in NY.

  835   iii   John[6] **Duncan**, born 30 Jun 1843.

  836   iv   Albert[6] **Duncan**, born 18 Dec 1844 in Ashippun, Dodge Co., WI.

  837   v   Mary Louise[6] **Duncan**, born 27 Jun 1846 in Wauwatosa, Milwaukee Co., WI.

  838   vi   Alvin[6] **Duncan**, born 4 Nov 1848 in Ashippun, Dodge Co., WI.

294. Henry[5] **Bovee** (Abraham[4], Abraham[3], Nicholas[2], Mathieu[1]), born 9 Aug 1818 in T/Lenox, Madison Co., NY; died 1 Jan 1870 in Stockbridge, Calumet Co., WI. He married abt 1845 Lucy Evelyn Wilson, born 24 Feb 1823 in Pa; died 17 Apr 1900 in Chilton, Calumet Co., WI, daughter of Asa Wilson and Esther (---).

Children of Henry Bovee and Lucy Evelyn Wilson were as follows:

  839   i   Emily[6] **Bovee**, born 26 Jan 1846 in Madison Co., NY. She

married on 3 Mar 1869 in Chilton, Calumet Co., WI **Edward LaLonde**, son of William LaLonde and Susannah (---).

+ 840 ii Andrew Jackson[6] **Bovee**, born 26 Jul 1848 in Madison Co., NY; died 14 Oct 1912 in Lawrence, Whatcom Co., WA. He married (1) **Sevilla R Baldock**; (2) **Sophia Minor**; (3) **Phoebe Tenney**.

841 iii Myron[6] **Bovee**, born 19 Sep 1850.

+ 842 iv Matilda E[6] **Bovee**, born 16 Sep 1854 in Stockbridge, Calumet Co., WI; died aft 1936 in Battle Creek, Calhoun Co., MI. She married (1) **Calvin U Tracy**; (2) **Nathan DeMoss**.

+ 843 v Warren Henry[6] **Bovee**, born 20 Mar 1858 in Calumet Co., WI; died 22 Aug 1922 in Spooner, Washburn Co., WI. He married **Rosalie Katherine Gleason Chapman**.

295. Rebecca[5] **Bovee** (Abraham[4], Abraham[3], Nicholas[2], Mathieu[1]), born 16 Mar 1824 in Madison Co., NY; died 1 May 1892 in Christie, Clark Co., WI. She married on 4 Jun 1843 in T/Lenox, Madison Co., NY Martin Victor Fadner, born 20 Jun 1819 in AlsaceLorraine, Strinseltz, France; died 21 Apr 1898 in Berlin, Green Lake Co., WI, son of Martin George Fadner and Elizabeth Marie Haas.

Children of Rebecca Bovee and Martin Victor Fadner were as follows:

844 i Ellen Marie[6] **Fadner**, born 10 Jan 1844 in Madison Co., NY.

845 ii Eliza Anne[6] **Fadner**, born 21 Jan 1845 in Oneida Co., NY.

296. Hiram[5] **Bovee** (Henry[4], Abraham[3], Nicholas[2], Mathieu[1]), born 22 Jun 1814 in NY; died 18 Oct 1881. He married on 29 Oct 1839 in T/Woodhull, Steuben Co., NY Lucy Ann Northrup, daughter of George Northrup and Wealthy Tracy.

Children of Hiram Bovee and Lucy Ann Northrup were as follows:

846 i Rosaltha[6] **(---)**, born abt 1842 in Steuben Co., NY.

297. Betsey[5] **Bovee** (Henry[4], Abraham[3], Nicholas[2], Mathieu[1]), born 18 Feb 1817; died 1905. She married Franklin Gibson.

Children of Betsey Bovee and Franklin Gibson were as follows:

847 i Lucy J[6] **Gibson**, born 1842.

298. Ira[5] **Bovee** (Henry[4], Abraham[3], Nicholas[2], Mathieu[1]), born 5 Jun 1819 in Ostego Co., NY; died 3 Oct 1888. He married Amanda O'Brien, born Jan 1829; died 1917 in Union Center, Broome Co., NY.

Children of Ira Bovee and Amanda O'Brien were as follows:

848 i Frederick[6] **Bovee**, born Aug 1866 in Union Town, Broome

Co., NY; died 1943.

299. Aaron[5] **Bovee** (Henry[4], Abraham[3], Nicholas[2], Mathieu[1]), born 11 Feb 1822 in Otsego, Ostego Co., NY; died 17 Feb 1856 in Union Town, Broome Co., NY. He married on 25 Jan 1843 in E Orange, NY Frances Lyman, born abt 1823; died 1862.

Children of Aaron Bovee and Frances Lyman were as follows:

849   i   Joseph[6] **Bovee**, born 15 Feb 1844 in Broome Co., NY; died 18 Jul 1894 in Broome Co., NY. He married bef 1865 **Roxanna J (---)**.

850   ii   James M[6] **Bovee**, born abt 1846 in Broome Co., NY; died 5 Nov 1909 in Bexar Co., TX. He married **Sarah (---)**, died 10 Jan 1906 in Bexar Co., TX.

+   851   iii   Franklin Gibson[6] **Bovee**, born Jun 1855; died 25 Oct 1918 in Binghamton, Broome Co., NY. He married (1) **Mary Harris**; (2) **Julie E (---)**.

300. John[5] **Bovee** (Henry[4], Abraham[3], Nicholas[2], Mathieu[1]), born 11 May 1824 in Broome Co., NY; died 29 Jul 1881 in Groton, Brown Co., SD. He married on 1 Jan 1849 in Main, Broome Co., NY Ann Eliza LeBaron, born 12 May 1830 in Union Center, Broome Co., NY; died 7 Nov 1921 in Hector,Renville Co., MN.

Children of John Bovee and Ann Eliza LeBaron were as follows:

852   i   Henry DeLoss[6] **Bovee**, born 2 May 1851 in Main, Broome Co., NY; died 25 Apr 1856 in Union Center, Broome Co., NY.

853   ii   Mary Roselia[6] **Bovee**, born 19 Aug 1856 in Union Center, Broome Co., NY. She married **Delford H Halloway**.

854   iii   Cora Bell[6] **Bovee**, born 2 Apr 1859 in Chesterfield, Macoupin Co., IL; died in Hector,Renville Co., MN. She married **William Dodge**.

855   iv   Libbie E[6] **Bovee**, born 25 Dec 1860 in Green Co., IL; died 31 Mar 1861 in Green Co., IL.

856   v   Hattie May[6] **Bovee**, born 29 Apr 1863 in Union Center, Broome Co., NY. She married **William Clark**.

857   vi   Henry Burr[6] **Bovee**, born 25 Jun 1865 in Union Center, Broome Co., NY; died in St Paul, Ramsey Co., MN. He married **Amelia Thirley**.

858   vii   Rachel Elizabeth[6] **Bovee**, born 14 Jun 1866 in Union Center, Broome Co., NY; died 27 Sep 1915 in Hector,Renville Co., MN. She married (1) **Lebe Lanon**; (2) **Frank Hooker**.

+   859   viii   John Ira[6] **Bovee**, born 4 Mar 1870 in Union Center, Broome Co., NY; died 15 Dec 1923. He married **Mary Elizabeth Norton**.

860   ix   Ina Mae[6] **Bovee**, born 4 Mar 1870 in Union Center, Broome Co., NY; died in St Paul, Ramsey Co., MN.

<table>
<tr><td>861</td><td>x</td><td>William[6] Bovee, born 2 May 1872 in Union Center, Broome Co., NY; died 9 Mar 1915 in Hector,Renville Co., MN.</td></tr>
<tr><td>+ 862</td><td>xi</td><td>Charles J[6] Bovee, born 18 Oct 1876 in Rochester, Olmsted Co., MN; died 11 Oct 1949 in St Paul, Ramsey Co., MN. He married Cassie Fay Oothoutdt.</td></tr>
</table>

305. Peter[5] **Bovee** (Peter[4], Abraham[3], Nicholas[2], Mathieu[1]), born 1821; died bef 1900. He married Angeline (---), born 1835 in NY.

Children of Peter Bovee and Angeline (---) were as follows:

| 863 | i | Cornelius Harvey[6] **Bovee**, born Jan 1857 in NY. |
| 864 | ii | William[6] **Bovee**, born abt 1860. |

307. Cornelius[5] **Bovee** (Peter[4], Abraham[3], Nicholas[2], Mathieu[1]), born 27 Nov 1832 in Madison Co., NY; died 30 Nov 1914 in Alvin, Brazoria Co., TX. He married (1) in 1867 in Richmond, Wallworth Co., WI Rebecca H Higbee, born in Keene, Ionia Co., MI; died 9 Feb 1871; (2) on 27 Sep 1871 in Fallasburgh, Kent Co., MI Caroline Bowen, born 24 Dec 1838 in Pontiac, Oakland Co., MI; died 12 Jul 1928 in Alvin, Brazoria Co., TX.

Children of Cornelius Bovee and Caroline Bowen were as follows:

+ 865	i	Myron Edgar[6] **Bovee**, born 10 Apr 1876 in Kalamazoo, Kalamazoo Co., MI; died 1941 in Alvin, Brazoria Co., TX. He married **Florence Bessie Flexman**.
866	ii	Vern Wheeler[6] **Bovee**, born 7 Nov 1877 in Keene, Ionia Co., MI; died in TX. He married **Martie E Jackson**.
867	iii	Glen Roy[6] **Bovee**, born 22 Dec 1878 in Keene, Ionia Co., MI; died 1913 in TX.

310. Philip[5] **Bovee** (Jacob Philip[4], Philip[3], Nicholas[2], Mathieu[1]), born 26 Mar 1790 in Charleston, Montgomery Co., NY; christened 9 May 1790 in DRC, Schenectady, Schenectady Co., NY; died 30 May 1865 in New Lyme, Ashtabula Co., OH. He married on 4 Jun 1816 Hannah Dolph, born 18 Feb 1800; died 7 Apr 1865 in New Lyme, Ashtabula Co., OH.

Children of Philip Bovee and Hannah Dolph were as follows:

868	i	Judith[6] **Bovee**, born 14 Dec 1817; died 3 May 1819 in Murray, Orleans Co., NY.
869	ii	Clarissa[6] **Bovee**, born 5 Jan 1819; died 3 May 1819 in Murray, Orleans Co., NY.
+ 870	iii	Jacob[6] **Bovee**, born 16 Mar 1820 in NY; died 10 Nov 1890 in Ashtabula, Ashtabula Co., OH. He married **Isabelle Ainslie**.
+ 871	iv	Aaron[6] **Bovee**, born 20 Jul 1822 in Monroe Co., NY; died 27 Oct 1906. He married **Lucy Ann Gunn**.

+ 872 v Philip[6] **Bovee** Jr, born 29 Mar 1825 in Monroe Co., NY; died 26 Feb 1889 in Gordon, Sheridan Co., NE. He married **Mary Crowell**.

873 vi Julia Jane[6] **Bovee**, born 18 Feb 1827 in NY. She married on 3 May 1858 in Barry Co., MI **Charles C Hunn**.

874 vii John[6] **Bovee**, born 13 Mar 1829 in NY; died 5 Aug 1855.

+ 875 viii George[6] **Bovee**, born 27 Nov 1830 in NY; died 4 Jul 1862 in Independence Rock, WY. He married (1) **Mary Clark**; (2) **Harriet G Groves**.

+ 876 ix Catherine[6] **Bovee**, born 1 Jul 1833 in Monroe Co., NY; died 1906 in Ann Arbor, Washtenaw Co., MI. She married (1) **William Wilder**; (2) **Christopher C Deuress**.

877 x Emily[6] **Bovee**, born 23 Aug 1835. She married on 14 Jan 1858 in Ashtabula Co., OH **D C Gunn**.

878 xi Ira[6] **Bovee**, born 21 Oct 1837; died 21 May 1866.

+ 879 xii Byron E[6] **Bovee**, born 27 Sep 1839 in Ashtabula Co., OH; died 27 Dec 1911 in New Lyme, Ashtabula Co., OH. He married **Maria C Regal**.

312. John[5] **Bovee** (Jacob Philip[4], Philip[3], Nicholas[2], Mathieu[1]), born 28 May 1793 in Schenectady Co., NY; christened 6 Oct 1793 in DRC, Schenectady, Schenectady Co., NY; died abt 1872 in MI. He married on 25 Oct 1815 in Schenectady, Schenectady Co., NY Samantha Hedden, born 15 Jan 1798 in Montgomery Co., NY; died 10 Mar 1868 in OH, daughter of Job Hedden and Phebe Ogden.

Children of John Bovee and Samantha Hedden were as follows:

+ 880 i Jemina[6] **Bovee**, born 11 Nov 1816; died bef 1902 in Herndon, Fairfax Co., VA. She married **Stephen Killion**.

881 ii Letitia[6] **Bovee**, born 25 Oct 1818. She married on 21 Mar 1841 **Ross Ball**.

+ 882 iii Job Hedden[6] **Bovee**, born 25 Sep 1820 in East Bloomfield, Ontario Co., NY; died 10 Dec 1894. He married **Mary A Welch**.

883 iv John Smith[6] **Bovee**, born 29 Jun 1822 in Ontario Co., NY; died 3 Jul 1863.

+ 884 v Nicholas[6] **Bovee**, born 15 Aug 1824; died 9 Jan 1901 in Ypsilanti, Washtnaw Co., MI. He married **Julia Sherwood**.

885 vi Nancy J[6] **Bovee**, born 22 Jun 1828; died 20 Sep 1829.

886 vii Frederick D[6] **Bovee**, born 7 Jun 1830. He married on 15 Feb 1870 **Maggie Alyea**.

+ 887 viii Edwin Henry[6] **Bovee**, born 6 Oct 1832 in Monroe Co., NY; died 11 May 1903 in Washington, Washington Co., IA. He married **Rachel Anna Huskins**.

888 ix Phoebe Orissa[6] **Bovee**, born 19 May 1834 in Monroe Co., NY. She married on 4 Jul 1866 **Nathan Coonrod**.

| + | 889 | x | Joseph W[6] **Bovee**, born 18 Jul 1840 in Monroe Co., NY; died 26 Mar 1911 in Three Rivers, St Joseph Co., MI. He married **Irene Mary Randolph**. |
| + | 890 | xi | Francis M[6] **Bovee**, born 2 Aug 1843 in Clarkson, Monroe Co., NY. He married **Zeoba Elester**. |

Excerpts from letter by Mrs. E. H. Bovee, Washington, Iowa. Feb 6,1902.

John Bovee, my husbands father was born in France, May 28th 1796, came to New York, when a small boy, and on October 25th ,1815 was married to Samantha Hedden of Schenectady, NY. His father died, and his wife married again, a man by name of Smith. My husband only remembers two uncles – brothers to his father. Their names were Jacob and Nicholas. He has visited his Uncle Nicholas, who then lived in Michigan, but never remembers seeing his Uncle Jacob. My husband's mother died in Ohio in 1868. His father died a few years after, but we do not have the date, as he lived with some of his sons, and they were careless about informing us.

My husband came west when quite young, and was only back to N. Y. twice afterwards. So as is too often the case, they drifted away from each other. He had three living sisters, and five brothers, at the time he left home. All the sisters are dead, and several of his brothers. John Bovee, his father, was a Stone Mason by trade, and built some of the first houses and bridges about Rochester, N. Y.

313. Nicholas[5] **Bovee** (Jacob Philip[4], Philip[3], Nicholas[2], Mathieu[1]), born 11 Feb 1796 in Montgomery Co., NY; died 10 Feb 1865 in Seneca Twp, Lenawee Co., MI. He married on 24 Feb 1822 in Courtland Co., NY Phebe (---), born 4 Sep 1796 in Cortland Co., NY; died 31 Jan 1890 in Seneca Twp, Lenawee Co., MI.

Children of Nicholas Bovee and Phebe (---) were as follows:

	891	i	Annis P[6] **Bovee**, born 22 Dec 1822. She married on 20 Apr 1843 in Trumbull Co., OH **Eber M Conant**.
+	892	ii	John C[6] **Bovee**, born 5 Sep 1824; died 1897 in Devils Lake, MI. He married **Cynthia Ann Eddy**.
	893	iii	Margaret C[6] **Bovee**, born 20 Aug 1826; died 1907. She married (1) on 24 Feb 1847 **Aaron Seward**; (2) **James Nichols**.
	894	iv	George W[6] **Bovee**, born 10 Jan 1829; died in Sailor barracks, Detroit, Wayne Co., MI..
+	895	v	Charles P[6] **Bovee**, born 26 Jul 1831 in NY; died 14 Apr 1910 in Village Cem, Weston, Lenawee Co., MI. He married **Nancy H Southworth**.
+	896	vi	Nelson H[6] **Bovee**, born 20 Feb 1834 in NY; died 17 Mar 1907 in Whitehouse, Lucas Co., OH. He married **Sally Ann Merritt**.
	897	vii	Horace M[6] **Bovee**, born 9 Jun 1839; died 5 May 1864 in Chattanooga, Hamilton Co., TN.

315. Elizabeth[5] **Bovee** (Nicholas P[4], Philip[3], Nicholas[2], Mathieu[1]), born 12 Apr

1783; died 15 Jun 1842 in Gainesville, Wyoming Co., NY. She married Daniel Cargill, born 17 Dec 1773 in Cumberland, Providence Co., RI; died 22 Oct 1853 in Gainesville, Wyoming Co., NY.

Children of Elizabeth Bovee and Daniel Cargill were as follows:

898	i	Elizabeth^6 **Cargill**, born 4 Apr 1802.
899	ii	Daniel^6 **Cargill** Jr., born 25 Jun 1803.
900	iii	Mary^6 **Cargill**, born 24 Apr 1805.
901	iv	Polly^6 **Cargill**, born 7 Apr 1806.
902	v	Sally^6 **Cargill**, born 25 Mar 1808.
903	vi	Preston^6 **Cargill**, born 6 Jan 1810.

316. Daniel R^5 **Bovee** (Nicholas P^4, Philip^3, Nicholas^2, Mathieu^1), born abt 1784; died abt 1825 in Perry, Wyoming Co., NY. He married on 6 Oct 1806 Sarah (---), born abt 1786.

Children of Daniel R Bovee and Sarah (---) were as follows:

+	904	i	Alvah C^6 **Bovee**, born 28 Aug 1807 in NY; died abt 1854. He married (1) **Catherine Row**; (2) **Mary E (---)**.
+	905	ii	William R^6 **Bovee**, born 21 Jul 1809 in NY; died 18 Jan 1857 in Spartansburg, Crawford Co., PA. He married **Maria Quackenbush**.
	906	iii	Ruby^6 **Bovee**, born 13 Mar 1812 in NY.
	907	iv	Polly Almira^6 **Bovee**, born May 1814 in NY.

317. Jacob^5 **Bovee** (Nicholas P^4, Philip^3, Nicholas^2, Mathieu^1), born abt 1786 in NY; died Jan 1842. He married abt 1807 Rachel (---), born abt 1786.

Children of Jacob Bovee and Rachel (---) were as follows:

+	908	i	Nicholas^6 **Bovee**, born 29 Feb 1808; died 26 Jun 1888. He married **Polly Selfidge**.
	909	ii	Rebecca Jane^6 **Bovee**, born abt 1810.
+	910	iii	Harper R^6 **Bovee**, born 25 Oct 1812 in NY; died 27 Nov 1893 in Big Rapids, Mecosta Co., MI. He married **Sarah Jane Hills**.
+	911	iv	Abraham^6 **Bovee**, born abt 1814 in NY; died 4 Apr 1872 in Nunda, Livingston Co., NY. He married (1) **Hulda (---)**; (2) **Tryphena (---)**.
+	912	v	John C^6 **Bovee**, born 1816 in NY; died 9 May 1894 in Amy, Oakland Co., MI. He married (1) **Lovena Barnard**; (2) **Sarah A Verney**.
	913	vi	Nelson^6 **Bovee**, born abt 1817; died bef 1880. He married **Sabra (---)**.
+	914	vii	Daniel^6 **Bovee**, born abt 1818 in NY. He married **Elizabeth Bliss**.

318. Catherine [5] **Bovee** (Nicholas P [4], Philip [3], Nicholas [2], Mathieu [1]), born 22 Feb 1787; died 30 Apr 1842. She married (1) abt 1810 James Moffitt; (2) on 19 Dec 1820 in St. John's Ep Ch., Johnstown,Fulton Co., NY Alinos Matthews, born 31 Mar 1780 in Chesire, New Haven Co., CT; died 5 Apr 1859, son of Eliada Matthews and Lucy Curtis.

Children of Catherine Bovee and James Moffitt were as follows:

915 i Sarah [6] **Moffitt**, born abt 1808; christened 6 Jun 1833 in Broadalbin Bap Ch, Montgomery Co., NY.

916 ii William Henry [6] **Moffitt**, born abt 1810.

917 iii Mary Jane [6] **Moffitt**, born abt 1812.

918 iv Nancy [6] **Moffitt**, born abt 1814; christened 6 Nov 1831 in Broadalbin Bap Ch, Montgomery Co., NY.

Children of Catherine Bovee and Alinos Matthews were as follows:

919 i Ruth Foote [6] **Matthews**, born 27 Aug 1821; christened 27 Aug 1821 in St John's Ep Ch, Johnstown, Fulton Co., NY.

920 ii Octavia R [6] **Matthews**, born 6 Jul 1823 in Mayfield, Fulton Co., NY.

921 iii James M [6] **Matthews**, born 1827 in Mayfield, Fulton Co., NY.

922 iv Elvira [6] **Matthews**, born 13 May 1829 in Mayfield, Fulton Co., NY.

923 v Alinus Curtis [6] **Matthews**, born 1 Feb 1832 in Mayfield, Fulton Co., NY.

319. Sarah (Sally) [5] **Bovee** (Nicholas P [4], Philip [3], Nicholas [2], Mathieu [1]), born 15 Aug 1789 in NY; christened in Broadalbin, Montgomery Co., NY. She married John Moffitt, born abt 1789 in England.

Children of Sarah (Sally) Bovee and John Moffitt were as follows:

924 i William B [6] **Moffitt**, born 17 Mar 1816 in Montgomery Co., NY.

925 ii Catherine [6] **Moffitt**, born 21 Feb 1821; christened 17 Sep 1821 in United Presb Ch, Broadalbin, Montgomery Co., NY.

926 iii Maria [6] **Moffitt**, born 21 Feb 1821; christened 17 Sep 1821 in United Presb Ch, Broadalbin, Montgomery Co., NY.

927 iv John [6] **Moffitt**, born 14 Nov 1822; christened 8 May 1823 in United Presb Ch, Broadalbin, Montgomery Co., NY.

928 v Isabel [6] **Moffitt**, born 16 Jul 1824; christened 3 Oct 1824 in United Presb Ch, Broadalbin, Montgomery Co., NY.

929 vi Elizabeth [6] **Moffitt**, born 17 Feb 1826; christened Apr 1826 in United Presb Ch, Broadalbin, Montgomery Co., NY.

930 vii Margaret [6] **Moffitt**, born 22 Feb 1828; christened 1 Jun 1828 in United Presb Ch, Broadalbin, Montgomery Co., NY.

931   viii   Ellen Jennett[6] **Moffitt**, born 20 Feb 1830; christened Oct 1830 in United Presb Ch, Broadalbin, Montgomery Co., NY.

932   ix   Lydia Ann[6] **Moffitt**, born 21 Nov 1835 in Mayfield, Fulton Co., NY.

321. Harper[5] **Bovee** (Nicholas P[4], Philip[3], Nicholas[2], Mathieu[1]), born abt 1793; died abt 1852 in St Louis, MO. He married Lydia Nichols, born 10 Nov 1793 in RI; died 15 Mar 1879 in Peoria, Peoria Co., IL, daughter of Stephen Nichols and Roby Kinnecut.

Children of Harper Bovee and Lydia Nichols were as follows:

933   i   Roby[6] **Bovee**, born abt 1814.

934   ii   Olivia[6] **Bovee**, born abt 1816; died bef 1820.

+ 935   iii   Mary[6] **Bovee**, born abt 1818. She married **Solon Billings**.

+ 936   iv   Norman[6] **Bovee**, born abt 1820 in Gainesville, Wyoming Co., NY. He married **Permelia Loucks**.

+ 937   v   Harmon[6] **Bovee**, born 9 Aug 1825 in Genesee Co., NY; died 9 Jan 1898 in Carlton, Carlton Co., MN. He married **Lydia Jane Wright**.

+ 938   vi   Harper[6] **Bovee** Jr, born 25 Jun 1827 in Gainesville, Wyoming Co., NY. He married (1) **Marietta Linn**; (2) **Lora Tilden**.

+ 939   vii   John[6] **Bovee**, born 19 Feb 1831 in Gainesville, Wyoming Co., NY; died 18 Feb 1893 in Wilmington, Will Co., IL. He married **Sarah A Frazer**.

+ 940   viii   Alexander[6] **Bovee**, born 1835. He married **Sally Gray**.

+ 941   ix   Charles[6] **Bovee**, born 1838 in Cattaraugus Co., NY; died 5 May 1887 in Peoria, Peoria Co., IL. He married **Laura Phenix**.

322. Ester[5] **Bovee** (Nicholas P[4], Philip[3], Nicholas[2], Mathieu[1]), born abt 1795 in Montgomery Co., NY; died 1831. She married abt 1810 Ezekiel Perkins, born 1788 in NY, son of Nathaniel Perkins and Martha Johnson.

Children of Ester Bovee and Ezekiel Perkins were as follows:

942   i   Edward Barker[6] **Perkins**.

943   ii   Thomas[6] **Perkins**.

944   iii   Elmer Crimble[6] **Perkins**.

945   iv   James[6] **Perkins**.

946   v   Sarah[6] **Perkins**.

947   vi   Johnson[6] **Perkins**.

948   vii   Myra[6] **Perkins**.

949   viii   Martha[6] **Perkins**.

950	ix	Mary^6 **Perkins**.
951	x	Hezekia^6 **Perkins**.
952	xi	Galosia^6 **Perkins**.
953	xii	Erbana^6 **Perkins**.

323. Isabel^5 **Bovee** (Nicholas P^4, Philip^3, Nicholas^2, Mathieu^1), born 1796. She married in 1814 John Foote.

Children of Isabel Bovee and John Foote were as follows:

954	i	Sarah^6 **Foote**, born abt 1822.
955	ii	John James^6 **Foote**, born 22 Dec 1825 in Castile, Wyoming Co., NY.
956	iii	Anganette^6 **Foote**, born abt 1833.

333. Jacob Nicholas^5 **Bovee** (Nicholas Jacob^4, Jacob^3, Nicholas^2, Mathieu^1), born 5 Jul 1790; christened 11 Jul 1790 in DRC, Schenectady, Schenectady Co., NY. He married on 25 Dec 1811 in DRC, Schenectady, Schenectady Co., NY Catherine Slingerland, born 14 Oct 1795; christened 1 Nov 1795 in DRC, Albany, Albany Co., NY; died 20 Mar 1886, daughter of Jacob Slingerland and Catherine Van Yveran.

Children of Jacob Nicholas Bovee and Catherine Slingerland were as follows:

	957	i	Nicholas^6 **Bovee**, born 1 Jan 1814 in Charlton, Saratoga Co., NY; died 15 Oct 1889. He married on 12 Apr 1880 **Mary Bovee**, born 14 Sep 1830 in NY; died 31 Aug 1888.
+	958	ii	Eliad E^6 **Bovee**, born 1817 in NY. He married (1) **Jane Burch**; (2) **Eva Ann Bovee**.
	959	iii	Sophia^6 **Bovee**, born 15 Jun 1820; died 13 Jul 1881.
+	960	iv	Mathew J^6 **Bovee**, born 4 Sep 1823 in NY; died 12 Dec 1882. He married **Susan Swits**.
+	961	v	Isaac^6 **Bovee**, born 1828 in NY; died bef 1880 in Ionia Co., MI. He married **Mary Cromwell**.
	962	vi	Martha^6 **Bovee**, born 1832.
+	963	vii	Marvin^6 **Bovee**, born Sep 1836; died 1913. He married **Lucy Ambler**.

334. Anna^5 **Bovee** (Jacob^4, Jacob^3, Nicholas^2, Mathieu^1), born 16 Jul 1777; christened 11 Aug 1777 in DRC Schenectady, Schenectady Co., NY. She married on 17 Jan 1805 in 1st Presb Ch., Ballston, Saratoga Co., NY Izacc P Truax, born 5 May 1771, son of Peter Truax and Jacoba Van Santvoord.

Children of Anna Bovee and Izacc P Truax were as follows:

| 964 | i | Sarah Ann^6 **Truax**, born 24 Oct 1805; christened 26 Jan 1807. |

965 ii Isaac VanSanford[6] **Truax**, born 17 Apr 1808; christened 24 Sep 1808.

966 iii Cornelius VanSanford[6] **Truax**, born 17 Apr 1810.

967 iv Ezekiel VanSanford[6] **Truax**, born 4 Jan 1812.

968 v Elizabeth Maria[6] **Truax**.

969 vi Alid Mead[6] **Truax**, born 1819.

970 vii George Mead[6] **Truax**, born 1819.

337. John[5] **Bovee** (Jacob[4], Jacob[3], Nicholas[2], Mathieu[1]), christened 11 Sep 1783 in DRC, Schenectady, Schenectady Co., NY, died bef 1829. He married unknown.

Children of John Bovee were as follows:

971 i Betsey[6] **Bovee**, born abt 1810.

338. Peter[5] **Bovee** (Jacob[4], Jacob[3], Nicholas[2], Mathieu[1]), born 4 Mar 1785 in NY; christened in DRC, Schenectady, Schenectady Co., NY; died aft 1840. He married (1) abt 1808 in NY Anna Lighthall, born 13 Mar 1790 in Schenectady, Schenectady Co., NY, daughter of Abraham Lighthall and Catherine Cuyler; (2) Sarah Truax, born 1788.

Children of Peter Bovee and Anna Lighthall were as follows:

+ 972 i Peter[6] **Bovee**, born 1809. He married **Eliza Dayton**.

973 ii (---)[6] **Bovee**, born aft 1812.

+ 974 iii Jacob Clayton[6] **Bovee**, born abt 1814 in Montgomery Co., NY. He married **Sophia Barton**.

975 iv Eliza[6] **Bovee**.

976 v Hannah[6] **Bovee**.

977 vi Catherine[6] **Bovee**.

340. Maria[5] **Bovee** (Jacob[4], Jacob[3], Nicholas[2], Mathieu[1]), born 15 Jan 1789; christened 8 Feb 1789 in DRC Schenectady, Schenectady Co., NY; died 11 May 1865. She married (1) abt 1808 in Schenectady, Schenectady Co., NY Philip P Van Patten, born 18 Jun 1780, son of Simon F Van Patten and Maria Wendell; (2) on 8 May 1817 Nicholas S Van Patten, born 23 May 1796 in Schenectady, Schenectady Co., NY, son of Simon F Van Patten and Maria Wendell.

Children of Maria Bovee and Philip P Van Patten were as follows:

978 i Deborah[6] **Van Patten**, born 1 Aug 1809 in NY.

979 ii Elizabeth[6] **Van Patten**, born abt 1812.

980 iii Clarissa[6] **Van Patten**, born 2 Jan 1815.

Children of Maria Bovee and Nicholas S Van Patten were as follows:

981 i Maria[6] **Van Patten**, born 6 Dec 1818.

982 ii Philip[6] **Van Patten**, born 1820.

983   iii   Rebecca A[6] **Van Patten**, born 1824.

984   iv   Sarah[6] **Van Patten**, born abt 1826.

985   v   Philip V[6] **Van Patten**, born 4 Nov 1827.

986   vi   Catherine Ann[6] **Van Patten**, born 17 Feb 1833.

341. Isaac[5] **Bovee** (Jacob[4], Jacob[3], Nicholas[2], Mathieu[1]), born 1 Mar 1791; christened 25 Apr 1791 in DRC, Schenectady, Schenectady Co., NY; died 13 Aug 1865. He married Hannah (---), born 7 Oct 1794; died 14 Mar 1866.

Children of Isaac Bovee and Hannah (---) were as follows:

987   i   (---)[6] **Bovee**, born abt 1820.

+ 988   ii   Isaac[6] **Bovee** Jr, born 22 Nov 1822 in Montgomery Co., NY; died 11 Jul 1886 in MI. He married (1) **Minerva Ruth Eastman**; (2) **Elizabeth Peck**.

342. Philip[5] **Bovee** (Jacob[4], Jacob[3], Nicholas[2], Mathieu[1]), born 18 Sep 1792; died abt 1854. He married in Dec 1817 Ruth Shepherd, born abt 1797; died abt 1856, daughter of Benjamin Shepherd and Ruth Mosher.

Children of Philip Bovee and Ruth Shepherd were as follows:

+ 989   i   Benjamin[6] **Bovee**, born abt 1818 in Fulton Co., NY; died 5 Apr 1897 in Union Twp., Black Hawk Co., IA. He married (1) **Sarah (---)**; (2) **Caroline P Sent**.

+ 990   ii   Jacob[6] **Bovee**, born Mar 1822 in NY; died 6 Jun 1902. He married (1) **Nancy Lappin**; (2) **Sarah A (---)**.

+ 991   iii   Ruth M[6] **Bovee**, born 19 Jul 1824 in Broadalbin, Fulton Co., NY; died 4 Aug 1870. She married **David H Chase**.

992   iv   Isaac M[6] **Bovee**, born 6 Mar 1836 in Fulton Co., NY.

+ 993   v   Lydia Carrie[6] **Bovee**, born abt 1840 in NY. She married **William A Crandall**.

994   vi   Henry[6] **Bovee**.

995   vii   William[6] **Bovee**.

996   viii   Louise[6] **Bovee**.

343. Sarah[5] **Bovee** (Jacob[4], Jacob[3], Nicholas[2], Mathieu[1]), born 26 Sep 1794; christened 2 Nov 1794 in DRC Schenectady, Schenectady Co., NY. She married Ahaserous W Van Patten, born 23 Jan 1789 in Schenectady, Schenectady Co., NY, son of Simon F Van Patten and Maria Wendell.

Children of Sarah Bovee and Ahaserous W Van Patten were as follows:

997   i   Mary Ann[6] **Van Patten**, born abt 1814.

998   ii   Jacob[6] **Van Patten**, born abt 1816.

999   iii   Simon A[6] **Van Patten**, born 27 Mar 1819.

1000   iv   Elizabeth R[6] **Van Patten**.

1001	v	Ahaserous[6] **Van Patten**.
1002	vi	Jemima[6] **Van Patten**.
1003	vii	William[6] **Van Patten**.
1004	viii	Cornelius[6] **Van Patten**.
1005	ix	James VanDyk[6] **Van Patten**.
1006	x	Staats Ezekiel V S[6] **Van Patten**.

345. Henry[5] **Bovee** (Jacob[4], Jacob[3], Nicholas[2], Mathieu[1]), born 20 Feb 1801; christened in DRC, Schenectady, Schenectady Co., NY; died 19 May 1888 in Broadalbin, Fulton Co., NY. He married Abigail Whitlock, born 1806; died 13 Jul 1888.

Children of Henry Bovee and Abigail Whitlock were as follows:

+ 1007   i   Abel W[6] **Bovee**, born abt 1827 in Fulton Co., NY; died 12 Dec 1891 in Gloversville, Fulton Co., NY. He married **Mary A Lasher**.

   1008   ii   Mary E[6] **Bovee**, born 1831. She married on 15 Sep 1884 **Asa Woodcock**.

   1009   iii   Emily[6] **Bovee**, born 1833. She married **(---) Ellsworth**.

   1010   iv   Eliza C[6] **Bovee**, born 1838; died 1907. She married **Abraham Manchester**.

   1011   v   William H[6] **Bovee**, born 1839; died 1899.

   1012   vi   Harriet[6] **Bovee**, born 1844. She married **Oscar Eaton**.

347. Annatje[5] **Bovee** (Isaac[4], Jacob[3], Nicholas[2], Mathieu[1]), born 18 Feb 1797; christened 25 Jun 1797 in DRC Schenectady, Schenectady Co., NY. She married (---) Haswell.

Children of Annatje Bovee and (---) Haswell were as follows:

   1013   i   Ida[6] **Haswell**.

   1014   ii   William[6] **Haswell**.

   1015   iii   Lizzie[6] **Haswell**.

348. Albert[5] **Bovee** Sr (Isaac[4], Jacob[3], Nicholas[2], Mathieu[1]), born 24 May 1799 in Albany Co., NY; christened 7 Jul 1799 in DRC, Schenectady, Schenectady Co., NY; died 1894 in Arena, Iowa Co., WI. He married (1) on 4 Mar 1824 in Coxsackie, Green Co., NY Mary Van Dyke, born 21 Nov 1803 in Coxsackie, Green Co., NY; died aft 1842 in WI; (2) on 13 Nov 1843 in Waukesha, Waukesha Co., WI Valerie Stout DuBois; (3) in 1860 Sophronia Benedict Dowd.

Children of Albert Bovee Sr and Mary Van Dyke were as follows:

+ 1016   i   Edwin Ruthven[6] **Bovee**, born 22 Jan 1825 in Amsterdam, Montgomery Co., NY; died 23 Dec 1896 in Arena, Iowa Co., WI. He married **Anne Bird**.

   1017   ii   Theodore[6] **Bovee**, born Sep 1827 in Amsterdam,

Montgomery Co., NY.

+ 1018 iii George E[6] **Bovee**, born 1834 in Amsterdam, Montgomery Co., NY. He married **Della S Laughlin**.

+ 1019 iv Clara M[6] **Bovee**, born abt 1836 in NY. She married **John Wilson**.

1020 v Mary[6] **Bovee**, born abt 1837 in Amsterdam, Montgomery Co., NY; died abt 1914 in Arena, Iowa Co., WI. She married **Augustus Barber**.

1021 vi Albert[6] **Bovee** Jr, born 27 Feb 1842 in Amsterdam, Montgomery Co., NY; died 17 Oct 1914 in Palmyra, Jefferson Co., WI. He married on 21 Feb 1875 in Jefferson Co., WI **Cordelia Pool**, born abt 1828 in NY; died bef 1898.

349. Jacob I[5] **Bovee** (Isaac[4], Jacob[3], Nicholas[2], Mathieu[1]), born 9 Mar 1801 in NY; christened 26 Apr 1801 in DRC, Schenectady, Schenectady Co., NY; died 1876. He married (1) on 25 Dec 1821 in DRC, Schenectady, Schenectady Co., NY Maria Van Eps, born 1802 in Glenville Twp, Schenectady Co., NY, daughter of Alexander Van Eps and Clara Van Slyk; (2) Mary Clark, born in NY.

Children of Jacob I Bovee and Mary Clark were as follows:

+ 1022 i Marquis[6] **Bovee**, born abt 1828 in NY; died 5 Apr 1893 in Chicago, Cook Co., IL. He married **Margaret Scott**.

352. Annatje[5] **Bovee** (Abraham[4], Jacob[3], Nicholas[2], Mathieu[1]), born 29 Jan 1796; christened 6 Mar 1796 in DRC Schenectady, Schenectady Co., NY. She married Peter Van Dyke.

Children of Annatje Bovee and Peter Van Dyke were as follows:

1023 i Emily[6] **Van Dyke**, born 1822.

353. John A[5] **Bovee** (Abraham[4], Jacob[3], Nicholas[2], Mathieu[1]), born 5 Feb 1800; christened 11 Mar 1800 in Amsterdam, Montgomery Co., NY. He married on 12 Feb 1823 in DRC, Schenectady, Schenectady Co., NY Catherine Van Eps, born 24 Oct 1799, daughter of Alexander Van Eps and Clara Van Slyk.

Children of John A Bovee and Catherine Van Eps were as follows:

1024 i (---)[6] **Bovee**, born abt 1824.

1025 ii (---)[6] **Bovee**, born abt 1826.

354. Albert[5] **Bovee** (Abraham[4], Jacob[3], Nicholas[2], Mathieu[1]), born 1808. He married Elizabeth (---).

Children of Albert Bovee and Elizabeth (---) were as follows:

1026 i Delavan[6] **Bovee**, born abt 1830.

1027 ii Sanford[6] **Bovee**, born abt 1837.

+ 1028 iii Sarah Jane[6] **Bovee**, born abt 1844. She married **John Coppernol**.

357. Anatje[5] **Bovee** (Matthew[4], Jacob[3], Nicholas[2], Mathieu[1]), born Dec 1790; christened 9 Jan 1791 in Schodack, Rensselaer Co., NY; died 27 Oct 1861 in Medina Co., OH. She married on 13 Nov 1813 Nicholas Spitzer, born 26 Nov 1783 in Schenectady, Schenectady Co., NY; christened Dec 1783.

Children of Anatje Bovee and Nicholas Spitzer were as follows:

1029 i Ann Maria[6] **Spitzer**, born 13 Aug 1814; christened 30 Oct 1814 in St Geo Ep Ch, Schenectady, Schenectady Co., NY.

1030 ii Susanna[6] **Spitzer**, born 8 Feb 1816; christened 6 May 1816 in Glenville Ref Ch, Schenectady, Schenectady Co., NY.

1031 iii Garritt[6] **Spitzer**, born 7 Nov 1817; christened 12 Apr 1818 in Glenville Ref Ch, Schenectady, Schenectady Co., NY.

1032 iv Sally[6] **Spitzer**, born 3 Dec 1819; christened 9 Jan 1820 in Woestina Ref Ch, Schenectady Co., NY.

1033 v Matthew S[6] **Spitzer**, born 11 May 1822.

1034 vi Aaron B[6] **Spitzer**, born 16 Jul 1824 in Schenectady, Schenectady Co., NY; christened 12 Aug 1824 in Woestina Ref Ch, Schenectady Co., NY.

1035 vii Jacob Bovee[6] **Spitzer**, born 13 Oct 1827 in NY.

1036 viii Sarah[6] **Spitzer**, born 13 May 1829 in NY.

1037 ix Mary E[6] **Spitzer**, born 20 Aug 1836 in NY.

358. Daniel[5] **Bovee** (Matthew[4], Jacob[3], Nicholas[2], Mathieu[1]), born 23 Jan 1794 in Rensselaer Co., NY; christened in Shodack, Rensselaer Co., NY; died 27 Nov 1860 in Monmouth, Warren Co., IL. He married (1) on 16 Oct 1813 in Schenectady, Schenectady Co., NY Clarissa Schermerhorn, born 24 Dec 1794; christened in Schenectady, Schenectady Co., NY; (2) on 16 Nov 1816 Charlotte Van Yveren, born 4 Jul 1793 in Charlton, Saratoga Co., NY; died Aug 1875 in Monmouth, Warren Co., IL.

Children of Daniel Bovee and Clarissa Schermerhorn were as follows:

1038 i Mathew[6] **Bovee**, born 23 Oct 1814; christened 15 Jan 1815 in St George Epis Ch, Schenectady, Schenectady Co., NY. He married unknown.

Children of Daniel Bovee and Charlotte Van Yveren were as follows:

+ 1039 i Myndert[6] **Bovee**, born 7 May 1818 in NY; died 8 Jun 1894 in Greenville, Montcalm Co., MI. He married (1) **Julia C Denmark**; (2) **Elizabeth Swan Tasher**.

+ 1040 ii Harriet T[6] **Bovee**, born 10 Mar 1821 in Brookfield, Madison Co., NY; christened 8 Mar 1832 in St Paul's Luth Ch, Schoharie, Schoharie Co., NY; died 21 Aug 1883.

73

She married **Franklin Parker**.

+ 1041   iii   Cornelius[6] **Bovee**, born 23 Jan 1824 in Schoharie, Schoharie Co., NY; christened 8 Mar 1832 in St Paul's Luth Ch, Schoharie, Schoharie Co., NY; died 27 Jan 1853 in Schoharie, Schoharie Co., NY. He married **Eva Ann Livingston**.

1042   iv   Maria[6] **Bovee**, born 1 Feb 1827; christened 8 Mar 1832 in St Paul's Luth Ch, Schoharie, Schoharie Co., NY.

1043   v   Abraham Lawyer Snyder[6] **Bovee**, born 22 Sep 1829 in Schoharie, Schoharie Co., NY; christened 8 Mar 1832 in St Paul's Luth Ch, Schoharie, Schoharie Co., NY; died 9 Mar 1832 in Schoharie, Schoharie Co., NY.

+ 1044   vi   Daniel D[6] **Bovee**, born 1 Jan 1833; died 29 Dec 1913. He married **Mary Van Vorst**.

359. Maria[5] **Bovee** (Matthew[4], Jacob[3], Nicholas[2], Mathieu[1]), born 20 Mar 1795; christened 16 Aug 1795 in Kinderhook, Columbia Co., NY; died 30 Mar 1876. She married in Schaghticoke, Rensselaer Co., NY Ryer B Springsteen, born 30 Apr 1790 in Schodack, Rensselaer Co., NY, son of Bastiaan Springsteen and Annatje Schermerhorn.

Children of Maria Bovee and Ryer B Springsteen were as follows:

1045   i   Benjamin R[6] **Springsteen**, born abt 1817 in NY.

1046   ii   Mary Magdalena[6] **Springsteen**, born 10 Oct 1819 in Schodack, Rensselaer Co., NY.

1047   iii   John[6] **Springsteen**, born 24 Jul 1821 in Schodack, Rensselaer Co., NY.

1048   iv   Asa Bennett[6] **Springsteen**, born 18 Nov 1824 in Schodack, Rensselaer Co., NY.

1049   v   Anna Catherine[6] **Springsteen**, born 27 Feb 1827 in Schodack, Rensselaer Co., NY.

360. Jacob[5] **Bovee** (Matthew[4], Jacob[3], Nicholas[2], Mathieu[1]), born abt 1797 in Schoharie, Schoharie Co., NY; died 24 Nov 1865 in Riga, Monroe Co., NY. He married (1) on 28 Dec 1816 in Schenectady, Schenectady Co., NY Susanna Schermerhorn, born 4 Dec 1792; christened 6 Jan 1793 in DRC, Schenectady, Schenectady Co., NY; died 6 Mar 1834 in Riga, Monroe Co., NY, daughter of Abraham Schermerhorn and Maria Sixberry; (2) on 23 Mar 1836 in Stone Church, Genesee Co., NY Lucinda Hubbard, born abt 1794 in Glastonbury, Hartford Co., CT; died 25 Dec 1865 in Riga, Monroe Co., NY, daughter of David Hubbard and Jemima Chamberlin.

Children of Jacob Bovee and Susanna Schermerhorn were as follows:

+ 1050   i   Mary Ann[6] **Bovee**, born 26 Mar 1813; christened in Schenectady, Schenectady Co., NY; died 8 Dec 1902 in LeRoy, Genesee Co., NY. She married **Lewis S Davis**.

+ 1051   ii   Abraham[6] **Bovee**, born 22 Dec 1817 in Schenectady, Schenectady Co., NY; christened 1 May 1818 in St

George Epis Ch, Schenectady, Schenectady Co., NY; died 9 Jan 1861 in Stone Church Rural Cem, Stone Church, Genesee Co., NY. He married **Catherine More** (see 1058).

+ 1052 iii Maria[6] **Bovee**, born 15 Jan 1820 in NY; christened 14 May 1820 in Woestina Ref Ch, Rotterdam, Schenectady Co.; died 9 Mar 1887 in Litchfield, Hillsdale Co., MI. She married **Stephen Canniff**.

Children of Jacob Bovee and Lucinda Hubbard were as follows:

+ 1053 i Henry Jacob[6] **Bovee**, born 27 Nov 1837 in NY; christened 6 May 1838 in Congregational, Ch, Riga, Monroe Co., NY; died 29 Sep 1924 in Los Angeles Co., CA. He married **Sabrina Emogene Fordham**.

361. Sarah[5] **Bovee** (Matthew[4], Jacob[3], Nicholas[2], Mathieu[1]), born 22 Nov 1799; christened 23 Feb 1800 in DRC Schenectady, Schenectady Co., NY; died 2 Dec 1828 in Monroe Co., NY. She married in 1820 in Glenville Ref Ch., Schenectady Co., NY Joseph Spitzer, son of Garrit Spitzer and Annatje Sixberry.

Children of Sarah Bovee and Joseph Spitzer were as follows:

1054 i Garritt J[6] **Spitzer**, born 5 Oct 1820; christened 31 Dec 1820 in Woestina Ref Ch, Schenectady Co., NY.

1055 ii Mathew[6] **Spitzer**, born abt 1825.

362. Bata[5] **Bovee** (Matthew[4], Jacob[3], Nicholas[2], Mathieu[1]), born 1 Mar 1802; christened 25 Mar 1802 in DRC Schenectady, Schenectady Co., NY; died 15 Sep 1881 in Bergen, Genesee Co., NY. She married on 24 May 1821 in Bergen, Genesee Co., NY John C Moore, born 30 Dec 1796 in NJ, son of John Moore and Catherine (---).

Children of Bata Bovee and John C Moore were as follows:

1056 i Maria[6] **More**, born 2 Apr 1822 in LeRoy, Genesee Co., NY.

1057 ii Rachel Ann[6] **More**, born abt 1824 in LeRoy, Genesee Co., NY.

1058 iii Catherine[6] **More**, born 4 Sep 1826 in LeRoy, Genesee Co., NY. She married on 9 Apr 1844 in Congregational, Ch, Riga, Monroe Co., NY **Abraham Bovee** (see 1051), born 22 Dec 1817 in Schenectady, Schenectady Co., NY; christened 1 May 1818 in St George Epis Ch, Schenectady, Schenectady Co., NY; died 9 Jan 1861 in Stone Church Rural Cem, Stone Church, Genesee Co., NY, son of Jacob Bovee and Susanna Schermerhorn.

1059 iv Daniel B[6] **More**, born 7 Jan 1829 in LeRoy, Genesee Co., NY.

1060 v Jane[6] **More**, born abt 1831 in LeRoy, Genesee Co., NY.

1061 vi Sarah[6] **More**, born 6 Aug 1834 in Riga, Monroe Co., NY.

1062	vii	Jacob Bovee[6] **More**, born 31 Mar 1837 in LeRoy, Genesee Co., NY.
1063	viii	Matthew[6] **More**, born 11 Jan 1840 in LeRoy, Genesee Co., NY.
1064	ix	Mary Elizabeth[6] **More**, born 21 Mar 1844 in Riga, Monroe Co., NY.

363. Isaac[5] **Bovee** (Matthew[4], Jacob[3], Nicholas[2], Mathieu[1]), born 31 Aug 1804 in NY; christened 18 Nov 1804 in DRC, Schenectady, Schenectady Co., NY; died abt 1856 in Delaware Co., OH. He married (1) abt 1823 Sarah Williams, born 23 Jan 1806 in Ovid, Seneca Co., NY; died 3 Nov 1852 in Williamsville, Orange Twp Delaware Co., OH, daughter of Anson Williams and Mary More; (2) on 11 Aug 1854 in Franklin Co., OH Hannah A Hays, born 1 Mar 1812 in OH; died 22 Apr 1903 in Elmer, Reno Co., KS.

Children of Isaac Bovee and Sarah Williams were as follows:

+	1065	i	Mary[6] **Bovee**, born abt 1824 in NY. She married **Cleophus R Seely**.
+	1066	ii	Catherine Ann[6] **Bovee**, born 1828. She married **Nathan Gardner**.
+	1067	iii	Susan[6] **Bovee**, born 15 Aug 1829 in OH; died 22 Mar 1901 in Delaware Co., OH. She married **Lorenzo Dow Farnsworth**.
	1068	iv	Clarissa Eliza[6] **Bovee**, born 1844 in Medina Co., OH. She married on 3 Mar 1863 in Medina Co., OH **Henry W Collins**.
+	1069	v	Sarah Elizabeth[6] **Bovee**, born 1846 in OH. She married **John Wesley Dyer**.

Children of Isaac Bovee and Hannah A Hays were as follows:

| | 1070 | i | David P[6] **Bovee**, born Sep 1854 in Delaware Co., OH; died 18 Nov 1875. |

364. Cornelius Schermerhorn[5] **Bovee** (Matthew[4], Jacob[3], Nicholas[2], Mathieu[1]), born 3 Mar 1807; christened 21 Jun 1807 in Amsterdam, Montgomery Co., NY; died 25 May 1839 in Riga, Monroe Co., NY. He married on 1 Jul 1833 Eliza Sparks, born 12 Feb 1812; died 6 May 1894.

Children of Cornelius Schermerhorn Bovee and Eliza Sparks were as follows:

| | 1071 | i | Herriet Eliza[6] **Bovee**, born 20 Mar 1834 in Riga, Monroe Co., NY; christened 16 May 1839 in Congregational, Ch, Riga, Monroe Co., NY; died 28 Nov 1916 in NY. She married (1) **(---) Starkweather**; (2) **(---) Birdsall**. |
| + | 1072 | ii | Lorenzo Jacob[6] **Bovee**, born 18 May 1835 in Riga, Monroe Co., NY; christened 16 May 1839 in Congregational, Ch, Riga, Monroe Co., NY; died 20 Aug 1893 in LeRoy,Genesee Co., NY. He married **Sarah** |

Adelia Kelsey.

| + | 1073 | iii | Cornelius Elihu **Bovee**[6], born 23 Jun 1836 in Riga, Monroe Co., NY; christened 16 May 1839 in Congregational, Ch, Riga, Monroe Co., NY; died 22 Mar 1911 in Stone Church, Genesee Co., NY. He married **Harriet M Ludington**. |
| | 1074 | iv | Frances Maria **Bovee**[6], born 5 Apr 1838 in Riga, Monroe Co., NY; christened 16 May 1839 in Congregational, Ch, Riga, Monroe Co., NY; died 5 Mar 1857. |

365. Caty Ann[5] **Bovee** (Matthew[4], Jacob[3], Nicholas[2], Mathieu[1]), born 25 Apr 1810 in NY; christened 30 Sep 1810 in St. George Ep Ch., Schenectady, Schenectady Co., NY; died 9 Dec 1890 in Williamsville, Deleware Co., OH. She married on 8 Feb 1830 in Leroy, Genesee Co., NY Jerrad Sanford Williams, born 21 Jul 1809, son of Anson Williams and Mary More.

Children of Caty Ann Bovee and Jerrad Sanford Williams were as follows:

	1075	i	Mary Abbie **Williams**[6], born 12 Feb 1833 in NY.
	1076	ii	Sally J **Williams**[6], born 15 Apr 1835 in NY.
	1077	iii	Martha (Patty) **Williams**[6], born 20 Dec 1837 in OH.
	1078	iv	George M **Williams**[6], born 1840 in OH.
	1079	v	Cornelius Sanford **Williams**[6], born 20 Jul 1842 in OH.
	1080	vi	Cornelia M **Williams**[6], born 24 Sep 1844.
	1081	vii	Russell B **Williams**[6], born abt 1847 in OH.

377. Walter[5] **Bovee** (Anthony[4], Gerrit[3], Anthony[2], Mathieu[1]), born abt 1790. He married Hannah (---).

Children of Walter Bovee and Hannah (---) were as follows:

+	1082	i	Anthony **Bovee**[6], born 1816; died 26 Aug 1858. He married **Pamela (---)**.
+	1083	ii	Walter **Bovee**[6], born 1819. He married **Lenora Van Willer**.
	1084	iii	John **Bovee**[6], born abt 1825.
	1085	iv	Almeda **Bovee**[6], born 1835.
	1086	v	Amos **Bovee**[6], born 1837.

378. John[5] **Bovee** (Anthony[4], Gerrit[3], Anthony[2], Mathieu[1]), born abt 1795 in Hartford, Washington Co., NY; died 1831. He married Sarah Stearns, born abt 1799 in VT.

Children of John Bovee and Sarah Stearns were as follows:

| | 1087 | i | John **Bovee**[6], born 3 Apr 1825 in Hebron, Washington Co., NY; died 29 Aug 1899 in Indian Lake, Hamilton Co., NY. He married (1) bef 1854, divorced **Eunice A (---)**; (2) on 7 Jan 1857 **Angenette Lucinda Heath**. |

379. Jacob[5] **Bovee** (Anthony[4], Gerrit[3], Anthony[2], Mathieu[1]), born Dec 1798 in Washington Co., NY; died 26 Sep 1876 in Day, Saratoga Co., NY. He married on 29 Jul 1820 in Luzerne, Warren Co., NY Eunice Howard, born 20 Mar 1798; died 11 Dec 1894 in Lake Luzerne, Warren Co., NY.

    Children of Jacob Bovee and Eunice Howard were as follows:

	1088	i	Julia[6] **Bovee**, born abt 1821. She married **David Duff**.
	1089	ii	Phebe[6] **Bovee**, born abt 1823; died 2 Aug 1886. She married in 1849 in Lake Luzerne, Warren Co., NY **Nathan Wells**.
	1090	iii	Louise[6] **Bovee**, born 23 Apr 1824; died 2 Dec 1910 in Hadley, Saratoga Co., NY. She married **Charles Jeffers**.
+	1091	iv	Luther[6] **Bovee**, born Jun 1827 in Warren Co., NY; died 22 Aug 1910. He married **Mary Ann Scoville**.
	1092	v	Mary[6] **Bovee**, born 1830; died 20 Jan 1910 in Luzerne, Warren Co., NY. She married **Henry McMasters**.
+	1093	vi	Orra[6] **Bovee**, born 30 May 1831 in Luzerne, Warren Co., NY; died 13 Nov 1913 in Saranac, Clinton Co., NY. He married (1) **Louise Daniels**; (2) **Julia A Goodsoe**.
	1094	vii	Helen[6] **Bovee**, born abt 1835. She married **David Taber**.
+	1095	viii	Norman[6] **Bovee**, born Jul 1839; died 5 Aug 1928. He married **Nancy White**.
+	1096	ix	Wallace[6] **Bovee**, born 13 Aug 1840; died 14 Oct 1907. He married **Sarah Jane Clute**.

380. Joseph[5] **Bovee** (Anthony[4], Gerrit[3], Anthony[2], Mathieu[1]), born abt 1821; died bef 1860. He married abt 1840 Lucinda Crissey, born abt 1828 in England.

    Children of Joseph Bovee and Lucinda Crissey were as follows:

+	1097	i	William Halsey[6] **Bovee**, born Jun 1843 in Fort Edward, Washington Co., NY; died 15 Aug 1909 in Kensington, Smith Co., KS. He married (1) **Emma Hardee Glidden**; (2) **Delissia P Donophon**.
	1098	ii	Mary[6] **Bovee**, born abt 1844 in NY.
	1099	iii	Henry[6] **Bovee**, born abt 1847 in Fort Edward, Washington Co., NY; died 12 Jan 1849.
+	1100	iv	Henry Joseph[6] **Bovee**, born 18 Apr 1854 in Fort Edward, Washington Co., NY; died 10 Nov 1903 in Cozad, Dawson Co., NE. He married **Mary J Hubbard** (see 1406).
+	1101	v	Eugene M[6] **Bovee**, born 27 Oct 1855 in Fort Edward, Washington Co., NY; died 30 Sep 1931. He married **Mary Elizabeth Osbourne**.

387. Orra[5] **Bovee** (Peter[4], Gerrit[3], Anthony[2], Mathieu[1]), born 17 Nov 1785 in NY; died 1 May 1850 in Adams Center, Jefferson Co., NY. She married on 24 May

1803 Timothy Heath Jr, born 1780; died Nov 1854, son of Timothy Heath and Lydia Smith.

Children of Orra Bovee and Timothy Heath Jr were as follows:

	1102	i	Jane[6] **Heath**, born in Jefferson Co, NY..
+	1103	ii	Peter[6] **Heath**, born in Jefferson Co, NY.. He married **Ruth Richards**.
	1104	iii	Betsey[6] **Heath**, born in Jefferson Co, NY..
	1105	iv	John[6] **Heath**, born in Jefferson Co, NY..
	1106	v	Paulina[6] **Heath**, born in Jefferson Co, NY..
	1107	vi	Albert Galiton Pool[6] **Heath**, born abt 1822 in Adams. Jefferson Co., NY..
	1108	vii	Maria[6] **Heath**, born in Jefferson Co, NY..
	1109	viii	Hiram[6] **Heath**, born 1827 in Jefferson Co, NY..

388. John W[5] **Bovee** (Peter[4], Gerrit[3], Anthony[2], Mathieu[1]), born 16 Jan 1788 in Rensselaer Co., NY; christened 6 Sep 1789 in Centre Brunswick, Rensselaer Co., NY; died 5 Jul 1844. He married (1) on 11 Sep 1817 Elizabeth Earl; born 13 Aug 1798; died 8 Aug 1825; (2) on 3 Jul 1828 Nancy B Stone.

Children of John W Bovee and Elizabeth Earl were as follows:

+	1110	i	Alvin Earl[6] **Bovay**, born 12 Jul 1818 in Adams, Jefferson Co., NY; died 29 Jan 1903 in Los Angeles, Los Angeles Co., CA. He married **Caroline Elizabeth Smith**.
	1111	ii	Fanny Rosette[6] **Bovee**, born 18 Jun 1820; died 4 Feb 1821.
	1112	iii	Hortentia Dianna[6] **Bovee**, born 28 Jun 1823; died 12 Nov 1897. She married on 31 May 1841 **Chandler Davis**, died 24 Jun 1874.
	1113	iv	Cordelia Annete[6] **Bovee**, born 27 Jul 1825; died 20 Oct 1825.

Children of John W Bovee and Nancy B Stone were as follows:

1114	i	Warren Polaski[6] **Bovee**, born 23 Feb 1830; died 26 Jul 1906. He married on 3 Mar 1851 **Harriet Dodd**.
1115	ii	Frances Maria[6] **Bovee**, born 2 Sep 1838; died 25 Apr 1864. She married on 16 Feb 1856 **William Rozell Steele**.

389. Catherine[5] **Bovee** (Peter[4], Gerrit[3], Anthony[2], Mathieu[1]), born 1 Feb 1790. She married in 1806 in Hoosick, Rensselaer Co., NY John Powell, born 20 Jul 1783; died 15 Jun 1860 in Sheldon, Iroquois Co., IL.

Children of Catherine Bovee and John Powell were as follows:

1116	i	Jane[6] **Powell**, born 19 Mar 1810.
1117	ii	Peter B[6] **Powell**, born 11 Feb 1817.

1118   iii   Hulda[6] **Powell**, born 2 Jun 1821.

390. Gerrit[5] **Bovee** (Peter[4], Gerrit[3], Anthony[2], Mathieu[1]), born 5 Sep 1792; died 2 Apr 1879 in Adams, Jefferson Co., NY. He married on 3 Feb 1819 Hannah Wigant, born 1794; died 1868 in Adams, Jefferson Co., NY.

Children of Gerrit Bovee and Hannah Wigant were as follows:

+   1119   i   Ervin Washington[6] **Bovee**, born 22 Mar 1821 in Adams, Jefferson Co., NY; died 1852. He married **Evalena Felt**.
+   1120   ii   Peter B[6] **Bovee**, born 13 Jan 1824 in Adams, Jefferson Co., NY; died 24 Nov 1880. He married (1) **Lucy (---)**; (2) **Nancy Sodin**.
    1121   iii   William W[6] **Bovee**, born 23 Jul 1825; died 1891.
    1122   iv   Margaret[6] **Bovee**, born 1829 in Adams, Jefferson Co., NY; died 1872.
+   1123   v   Seymour C[6] **Bovee**, born Jul 1829 in CT; died 3 Dec 1913 in Allegan Co., MI.. He married (1) **Louisa C Lewis**; (2) **Rosanah S (---)**.
+   1124   vi   Jane[6] **Bovee**, born 25 Mar 1831; died 13 Jan 1895 in Jefferson Co., NY. She married **Joseph A Brownell**.

391. Sarah[5] **Bovee** (Peter[4], Gerrit[3], Anthony[2], Mathieu[1]), born 24 Sep 1794; died 27 Sep 1870 in Algansee, Branch Co., MI. She married on 24 Feb 1819 Samuel Chapman, born abt 1789; died 15 Apr 1874 in Northumberland, NY.

Children of Sarah Bovee and Samuel Chapman were as follows:

    1125   i   John[6] **Chapman**, born abt 1823.
    1126   ii   Francis[6] **Chapman**, born 1828.
    1127   iii   Sara[6] **Chapman**, born abt 1834.
    1128   iv   Henry[6] **Chapman**, born abt 1837.
    1129   v   Eliza A[6] **Chapman**, born abt 1842.

392. Jonathan[5] **Bovee** (Peter[4], Gerrit[3], Anthony[2], Mathieu[1]), born 12 Oct 1796 in Hartford, Washington Co., NY; died 31 Mar 1881 in Algansee, Branch Co., MI. He married on 22 Oct 1818 in Hertford, Washington Co., NY Lucy Smith, born 3 Jul 1800 in Hartford Washington Co., NY; died 21 Oct 1859 in Algansee, Branch Co., MI.

Children of Jonathan Bovee and Lucy Smith were as follows:

+   1130   i   David[6] **Bovee**, born 11 Nov 1819 in Hartford, Washington Co., NY; died 19 Jul 1900 in Coldwater, Branch Co., MI. He married **Cynthia Ann Goodman**.
+   1131   ii   Eli William[6] **Bovee**, born 1 Nov 1821 in Adams, Jefferson Co., NY; died 25 Oct 1906 in Benton Harbor, Berrien Co., MI. He married (1) **Ann Amelia Cook**; (2) **Mary H Hall**; (3) **Lorinda Gregg Horton**.

+ 1132 iii Hannah[6] **Bovee**, born 31 Jan 1826 in Washington Co., NY; died 30 Jan 1914 in Branch Co.,MI. She married (1) **Rueben J Miller**; (2) **J M Rodenbaugh**.

+ 1133 iv Caleb Drake[6] **Bovee**, born 8 Mar 1829 in Hartford Washington Co., NY; died 15 Apr 1854 in Coldwater, Branch Co., MI. He married (1) **Maria Murdock**; (2) **Hester A Estice**.

+ 1134 v Clark[6] **Bovee**, born 8 May 1831 in Hartford, Washington Co., NY; christened 5 Oct 1831; died 17 Jul 1908 in Algansee, Branch Co., MI. He married **Aurelia Randall**.

395. William W[5] **Bovee** (Peter[4], Gerrit[3], Anthony[2], Mathieu[1]), born 3 Nov 1803 in Hartford Washington Co., NY; died 5 Nov 1882. He married on 22 Sep 1829 Charlotte Davison, born abt 1811 in Washington Co., NY; died 3 Jan 1884.

Children of William W Bovee and Charlotte Davison were as follows:

1135 i Seymore K[6] **Bovee**, born Aug 1830 in Washington Co., NY; died 20 Nov 1911. He married **Am Clove**, born 1830 in Ireland; died 11 Jun 1921.

1136 ii Orlando[6] **Bovee**, born abt 1833 in Washington Co., NY; died 18 Jan 1835.

1137 iii Daisy[6] **Bovee**, born 1835 in Washington Co., NY.

1138 iv Betty[6] **Bovee**, born abt 1837 in Washington Co., NY.

1139 v Mary[6] **Bovee**, born abt 1839 in Washington Co., NY.

+ 1140 vi Abraham[6] **Bovee**, born aft 1842 in Washington Co., NY; died 14 Apr 1903 in Fabius, Onondaga Co., NY. He married **Mary E (---)**.

+ 1141 vii Orlando A[6] **Bovee**, born Mar 1844 in Washington Co., NY; died 15 Mar 1926 in Syracuse, Onondaga Co., NY. He married **Frances G (---)**.

1142 viii Jane[6] **Bovee**, born abt 1848 in Washington Co., NY. She married **(---) Bran**.

399. Peter[5] **Bovee** (Jacob[4], Gerrit[3], Anthony[2], Mathieu[1]), born 21 Jun 1797 in Rensselaer Co., NY; died 1873. He married on 21 Feb 1828 in Ryegate, Caledonia Co.,VT Margaret McLeron.

Children of Peter Bovee and Margaret McLeron were as follows:

+ 1143 i Maria R[6] **Bovee**, born abt 1829; died 10 Jul 1864 in West Farmington, Trumbull Co., OH. She married **Henry Martin Kibbe**.

+ 1144 ii Moses S[6] **Bovee**, born 24 Feb 1834 in VT. He married **Adeline Ouderkerk** (see 1180).

+ 1145 iii Lydia[6] **Bovee**, born 1839. She married **Moses F Hunt**.

1146 iv Mary Ann[6] **Bovee**, born abt 1842. She married on 26 Jul 1862 unknown.

1147 v Rhoda[6] **Bovee**, born Dec 1847; died 1863.

400. Moses R[5] **Bovee** (Jacob[4], Gerrit[3], Anthony[2], Mathieu[1]), born 10 Nov 1799 in Rensselaer Co., NY; died 19 Jan 1879 in Green Mountain, Marshall Co., IA. He married on 22 Feb 1827 Helen Warden, born 8 Aug 1804; died 1881.

Children of Moses R Bovee and Helen Warden were as follows:

+ 1148 i William W[6] **Bovee**, born 18 Nov 1827 in Barnet, Caledonia Co., VT; died 1902 in CA. He married **Johanna Hussey**.

  1149 ii Elizabeth[6] **Bovee**, born 1830; died Mar 1902 in Pasadena, Los Angeles Co., CA. She married **James Lang**.

+ 1150 iii Moses C[6] **Bovee**, born 23 Aug 1831 in Barnet, Caledonia Co., VT; died 23 Dec 1907 in Marshall Co., IA. He married **Eliza A Ferguson**.

+ 1151 iv James B[6] **Bovee**, born 19 Feb 1834 in Caledonia Co., VT. He married **Eliza A Morris**.

+ 1152 v Mark[6] **Bovee**, born 1836 in Peacham, Caledonia Co., VT; died 1909 in Marshall Co., IA. He married **Jane N Varnum**.

  1153 vi Florence B[6] **Bovee**, born abt 1840 in Peacham, Caledonia Co., VT. She married **William J Evans**.

  1154 vii Margaret A[6] **Bovee**, born Mar 1841 in Barnet, Caledonia Co., VT; died 6 Apr 1841 in Barnet, Caledonia Co., VT.

  1155 viii Azro[6] **Bovee**, born 1844; died 18 Jan 1864 in Green Mountain, Marshall Co., IA.

+ 1156 ix Cassius J C[6] **Bovee**, born 1846 in Peacham, Caledonia Co., VT; died abt 1914 in Eugene, Lane Co., OR. He married **Sarah A (---)**.

  1157 x Mary Selina[6] **Bovee**, born 1849; died 11 Oct 1869 in Green Mountain, Marshall Co., IA. She married **Abel Woodward**.

401. Courtland[5] **Bovee** (Jacob[4], Gerrit[3], Anthony[2], Mathieu[1]), born 10 Oct 1800 in Rensselaer Co., NY; died 10 Jul 1872. He married Eliza J Blood, born 16 Feb 1808 in Rumney, Grafton Co., NH, daughter of William Earl Blood and Sarah Townsend.

Children of Courtland Bovee and Eliza J Blood were as follows:

  1158 i Jane L[6] **Bovee**, born 11 May 1827 in Danville, Caledonia Co., VT. She married on 13 Mar 1849 **Rufus Ingerson**.

  1159 ii Elizabeth Redding[6] **Bovee**, born 2 Jan 1829 in Danville, Caledonia Co., VT. She married on 18 Aug 1857 **Joseph A Bixby**.

  1160 iii John[6] **Bovee**, born 28 Dec 1830 in Danville, Caledonia Co., VT.

  1161 iv William R[6] **Bovee**, born 4 Jan 1833 in Danville, Caledonia Co., VT.

  1162 v Lucy R[6] **Bovee**, born 7 Jan 1835 in Danville, Caledonia

		Co., VT; died 12 Jul 1854.
1163	vi	Lyman^6 **Bovee**, born 1 Jan 1837 in Danville, Caledonia Co., VT.
1164	vii	Dianne P^6 **Bovee**, born 28 Dec 1838 in Danville, Caledonia Co., VT.
+ 1165	viii	Clark G^6 **Bovee**, born 1 Dec 1840 in Danville, Caledonia Co., VT; died 5 Feb 1905 in Madison, Somerset Co., ME. He married (1) **Addie A Locke**; (2) **Alice G chipman**.
1166	ix	Harriet^6 **Bovee**, born 13 Jul 1842 in Danville, Caledonia Co., VT. She married on 1 Jan 1863 **Thomas W Taylor**.
+ 1167	x	Otis M^6 **Bovee**, born 26 Jul 1845 in Danville, Caledonia Co., VT. He married **Ella S Robinson**.

402. Elvira Priscilla^5 **Bovee** (Jacob^4, Gerrit^3, Anthony^2, Mathieu^1), born abt 1809 in NY; died 17 Mar 1882 in Page Co., IA. She married in VT John F Nelson, born abt 1799 in Scotland; died abt 1865.

Children of Elvira Priscilla Bovee and John F Nelson were as follows:

1168	i	Robert^6 **Nelson**, born 8 Jul 1836 in VT.
1169	ii	Frederick Calvin^6 **Nelson**, born 12 Apr 1838 in VT.
1170	iii	Jacob Bovee^6 **Nelson**, born 13 Apr 1839 in VT.
1171	iv	John^6 **Nelson**, born 5 Aug 1840.
1172	v	William^6 **Nelson**.
1173	vi	Courtland^6 **Nelson**.
1174	vii	Jane^6 **Nelson**.
1175	viii	Mary Elizabeth^6 **Nelson**.
1176	ix	Lydia^6 **Nelson**.
1177	x	Child^6 **Nelson**.
1178	xi	Samuel W^6 **Nelson**.

403. Elizabeth R^5 **Bovee** (Jacob^4, Gerrit^3, Anthony^2, Mathieu^1), born Jun 1812. She married abt 1838 William B Ouderkerk.

Children of Elizabeth R Bovee and William B Ouderkerk were as follows:

1179	i	Mary A^6 **Ouderkerk**, born 22 Oct 1843 in Hoosick, Rensselaer Co., NY; died 24 Nov 1925. She married **Silas K Bovee**.
1180	ii	Adeline^6 **Ouderkerk**, born 8 Dec 1846; died 3 Feb 1896. She married on 23 May 1864 **Moses S Bovee** (see 1144), born 24 Feb 1834 in VT, son of Peter Bovee and Margaret McLeron.

Generation 6

438. Stephen^6 **Bovee** (Philip^5, Mathew^4, Philip^3, Mathieu^2, Mathieu^1), born abt 1814 in Cohoes, Albany Co., NY. He married abt 1840 Sally Caroline Calhoun,

born 1815 in MA; died 19 Jan 1901 in Rose, Wayne Co., NY, daughter of Herman Calhoun and Mary (---).

Children of Stephen Bovee and Sally Caroline Calhoun were as follows:

1181	i	William H[7] **Bovee**, born 1839; died 28 Aug 1874 in Rose, Wayne Co., NY.
+ 1182	ii	Herman[7] **Bovee**, born Dec 1840 in Lyons, Wayne Co., NY. He married **Sophia L Winchell**.
+ 1183	iii	George E[7] **Bovee**, born abt 1841 in NY; died 4 Oct 1901 in Lyons, Wayne Co., NY. He married **Angeline L Reynolds**.
+ 1184	iv	Edward H[7] **Bovee**, born 3 Jan 1843 in Lyons, Wayne Co., NY; died 4 Mar 1899 in Walcott, Wayne Co., NY. He married (1) **Theresa Hampson**; (2) **Amelia Wraight Wager**.
1185	v	Mary[7] **Bovee**, born abt 1845.
+ 1186	vi	Elizabeth[7] **Bovee**, born 15 Aug 1847 in Lyons, Wayne Co., NY. She married **Jay Dickerson**.
1187	vii	Alice[7] **Bovee**, born abt 1851 in Lyons, Wayne Co., NY.
+ 1188	viii	Caroline[7] **Bovee**, born abt 1855 in Lyons, Wayne Co., NY. She married **(---) Finney**.

452. Henry[6] **Bovee** Jr. (Henry[5], John[4], Rykert[3], Nicholas[2], Mathieu[1]), born 29 Sep 1815; died 21 Aug 1872. He married on 10 Nov 1842 Amity G Lake, born 8 Nov 1820; died 12 Oct 1906, daughter of James Lake and Lydia Cross.

Children of Henry Bovee Jr. and Amity G Lake were as follows:

1189	i	Marvin S[7] **Bovee**, born abt 1849; died abt 1850 in White Creek, Washington Co., NY.
1190	ii	Ervin K[7] **Bovee**, born abt 1852; died abt 1852.

454. Richard H[6] **Bovee** (Henry[5], John[4], Rykert[3], Nicholas[2], Mathieu[1]), born 6 Nov 1819 in Rensselaer Co., NY; died 2 Nov 1860 in Hoosick, Rensselaer Co., NY. He married on 27 May 1847 Sarah M Bovee (see 721), born 7 Nov 1821 in Hoosick, Rensselaer Co., NY; died 16 Dec 1885, daughter of Isaac Bovee and Annie Allen.

Children of Richard H Bovee and Sarah M Bovee were as follows:

1191	i	Isaac Henry[7] **Bovie**, born 24 Jan 1852; died 21 Nov 1917 in Hoosick, Rensselaer Co., NY. He married on 9 Nov 1880 **Charlotte Kelly**, daughter of Joseph Kelly and Mary Furman.
+ 1192	ii	Richard Heman[7] **Bovie**, born 24 Dec 1854 in Hoosick Falls, Rensselaer Co., NY; died 24 Mar 1940 in Cambridge, Washington Co., NY. He married **Rose Abby Curtis**.

455. Sanford S[6] **Bovee** (Henry[5], John[4], Rykert[3], Nicholas[2], Mathieu[1]), born 5 Dec 1821 in Breese Hollow, Rensselaer Co., NY; died 15 Nov 1875. He married (1) bef 1856 Jane Pine, born 1825; died 15 Feb 1856, daughter of Joshua Pine and Betsey Cotrell; (2) on 16 Dec 1857 Jane C Stover, born 17 Dec 1821 in Pittstown, Rensselaer Co., NY; died 2 Oct 1898, daughter of Jacob M Stover and Christina Wetzell.

Children of Sanford S Bovee and Jane C Stover were as follows:

+ 1193 i Charles S[7] **Bovee**, born 23 Jan 1861; died 28 Apr 1933 in Hoosick, Rensselaer Co., NY. He married **Anna Julia Smith**.

457. Sarah[6] **Bovee** (John[5], John[4], Rykert[3], Nicholas[2], Mathieu[1]), born 22 Feb 1815 in Pownal, Bennington Co., VT. She married on 20 Sep 1834 Charles Stearns, born 3 Apr 1813.

Children of Sarah Bovee and Charles Stearns were as follows:

1194 i Sarah[7] **Stearns**, born 4 Aug 1837.
1195 ii Elvira[7] **Stearns**, born 29 Nov 1839.

458. Parker R.[6] **Bovee** (John[5], John[4], Rykert[3], Nicholas[2], Mathieu[1]), born 1816 in VT; died 1848 in Pownal, Bennington Co., VT. He married Caroline Palmer, born in Troy, Rensselaer Co., NY.

Children of Parker R. Bovee and Caroline Palmer were as follows:

1196 i John W[7] **Bovee**, born abt 1840.
+ 1197 ii William H[7] **Bovee**, born 4 Jun 1842 in Pownal, Bennington Co., VT. He married **Anna M Whitbeck**.

461. Maria Antoinette[6] **Bovee** (John[5], John[4], Rykert[3], Nicholas[2], Mathieu[1]), born abt 1819; died 25 Feb 1848. She married on 21 Jan 1836 Benjamin R Green.

Children of Maria Antoinette Bovee and Benjamin R Green were as follows:

1198 i Niles C[7] **Green**, born abt 1839.
1199 ii Warren C[7] **Green**, born abt 1841.
1200 iii Benjamin[7] **Green**, born 1846.

474. Richard[6] **Bovee** (Elisha[5], Cornelius[4], Rykert[3], Nicholas[2], Mathieu[1]), born 9 Jun 1810 in Petersburg, Rensselaer Co., NY; died 11 Mar 1879. He married Orpha Zelpha Parke, born 14 May 1811 in Greene Co., NY; died 16 Jan 1913 in Brians Plains, Dawson Co., MT, daughter of Ruben Parke and Elizabeth Lord.

Children of Richard Bovee and Orpha Zelpha Parke were as follows:

1201 i Candace E[7] **Bovee**, born abt 1836. She married on 2 Jul 1865 in De Kalb Co., IL **Elijah Curtis**.

1202	ii	Mary[7] **Bovee**, born 9 Oct 1838 in Eagle Town, Boone Co., IN; died 14 Jul 1855. She married on 14 Jun 1855 in De Kalb, De Kalb Co., IL **Morris Willey**, born abt 1828 in NY.
1203	iii	Sarah[7] **Bovee**, born abt 1842 in IN. She married in 1872 in Boone Co., IN **Nicholas Davis**.
1204	iv	Emily W[7] **Bovee**, born Sep 1844 in IN; died aft 1920 in Spokane, Spokane Co., WA. She married on 29 Apr 1866 in Richland Co., WI **Samuel D Bovee** (see 1209), born Feb 1847 in Boone Co., IN; died in SD, son of Durfee Bovee and Anna B Duncan.
+ 1205	v	Eleanor Parke[7] **Bovee**, born 16 Sep 1849 in Eagletown, IN; died 23 Aug 1927. She married **Edwin Wallace Lewis**.
+ 1206	vi	John Nelson[7] **Bovee**, born 27 Oct 1851 in Cortland, De Kalb Co., IL; died 10 Jul 1918 in Penrose, Freemont Co., CO. He married (1) **Althea Ann Burt**; (2) **Mary Ann Needham**.

475. Durfee[6] **Bovee** (Elisha[5], Cornelius[4], Rykert[3], Nicholas[2], Mathieu[1]), born 17 Feb 1812 in Rensselaer Co., NY; died 16 Oct 1887. He married Anna B Duncan, born 11 Nov 1820 in IN; died 26 Aug 1911.

Children of Durfee Bovee and Anna B Duncan were as follows:

1207	i	Rev Elisha[7] **Bovee**, born 13 Mar 1840 in Boone Co., IN; died 18 Oct 1913 in Waterloo, Black Hawk Co., IA. He married on 1 Oct 1862 **Victoria Potter**, born abt 1845 in Canada; died 16 Apr 1930 in Waterloo, Black Hawk Co., IA.
+ 1208	ii	Mary[7] **Bovee**, born abt 1843 in Boone Co., IN; died abt 1939. She married **Clinton Dewitt Wood**.
+ 1209	iii	Samuel D[7] **Bovee**, born Feb 1847 in Boone Co., IN; died in SD. He married **Emily W Bovee** (see 1204).
+ 1210	iv	David William[7] **Bovee**, born Aug 1853 in Orion, Richland Co., WI; died 6 Apr 1924 in Waterloo, Black Hawk Co., IA. He married **Anna Caroline Palmer**.

476. Erastus[6] **Bovee** (Elisha[5], Cornelius[4], Rykert[3], Nicholas[2], Mathieu[1]), born bef 1815 in NY; died 1862. He married on 11 Oct 1838 in Marion Co., IN Elizabeth Hill.

Children of Erastus Bovee and Elizabeth Hill were as follows:

+ 1211	i	Martha E[7] **Bovee**, born 27 Apr 1841 in Clinton Co., IN; died 24 Feb 1913. She married **David Crose**.
1212	ii	Angeline[7] **Bovee**. She married on 10 Mar 1857 in Clinton Co., IN **Isaac Crose**.

477. David[6] **Bovee** (Elisha[5], Cornelius[4], Rykert[3], Nicholas[2], Mathieu[1]), born 27

Apr 1822 in Rensselaer Co., NY; died 10 Sep 1871 in Richland Center, Richland Co., WI. He married Frances A (---), born 7 Jul 1824 in VA; died 1 Dec 1893 in Richland Center, Richland Co., WI.

Children of David Bovee and Frances A (---) were as follows:

+ 1213 i Esther[7] **Bovee**, born 1844 in Boone Co., IN. She married **Thomas Bass**.

+ 1214 ii John Sylvester[7] **Bovee**, born Jul 1849 in Boone Co., IN. He married (1) **Hattie Woodman**; (2) **Ethel Z Dillon**.

+ 1215 iii Jacob Newton[7] **Bovee**, born 2 Feb 1854 in Richland Co., WI; died 2 Dec 1916 in Shevlin, Clearwater Co., MN. He married **Martha A Davis**.

478. Jonas Nicholas[6] **Bovee** (Nicholas[5], Cornelius[4], Rykert[3], Nicholas[2], Mathieu[1]), born abt 1816; died 12 Aug 1868. He married (1) Orinda Green, born 19 Jan 1815 in Pinckney, Lewis Co., NY, daughter of Ethan Green and Mercy Chase; (2) on 13 Aug 1866 Ellen Soper.

Children of Jonas Nicholas Bovee and Orinda Green were as follows:

+ 1216 i Cornelius[7] **Bovee**, born 1840 in Pinckney, Lewis Co., NY; died 17 Dec 1899 in Fairchild, Eau Claire Co., WI. He married (1) **Mary Hindman**; (2) **Hannah M Pettis**.

+ 1217 ii Julia[7] **Bovee**, born abt 1842 in Pinckney, Lewis Co., NY. She married **Truman A Hoisington**.

+ 1218 iii Truman Andrew[7] **Bovee**, born abt 1845 in Pinckney, Lewis Co., NY; died 9 Oct 1897 in Clayton, Polk Co., WI. He married (1) **Eliza Hamlin**; (2) **Eliza Jane Hamlin**; (3) **Julia Pettis Peysen**.

1219 iv Mercy Rosella[7] **Bovee**, born abt 1847 in Pinckney, Lewis Co., NY.

+ 1220 v Celestia[7] **Bovee**, born 26 Apr 1852 in NY. She married **Calvin W Letson**.

1221 vi Mary[7] **Bovee**, born abt 1854 in NY.

+ 1222 vii Silas N[7] **Bovee**, born Oct 1855 in NY; died 12 Jan 1933 in Eau Claire Co., WI. He married **Caroline W Bovee** (see 1235).

480. Silas Lewis[6] **Bovee** (Nicholas[5], Cornelius[4], Rykert[3], Nicholas[2], Mathieu[1]), born 27 Nov 1821 in Rensselaer Co., NY; died 17 Jul 1909. He married on 10 Mar 1842 in Pinckney, Lewis Co., NY Sara Jane Morris, born 5 Nov 1818 in NY; died 21 Jan 1891 in Jackson Co., WI.

Children of Silas Lewis Bovee and Sara Jane Morris were as follows:

+ 1223 i Annie Malvina[7] **Bovee**, born abt 1843 in Lewis Co., NY. She married **Joseph Olver**.

+ 1224 ii Sarah Jane[7] **Bovee**, born 23 Jan 1845 in Pinckney, Lewis Co., NY; died 11 Feb 1921 in Long Beach, Los Angeles

Co., CA. She married **Isaac Shoemaker Hallenbeck**.

1225	iii	Doan Elisha[7] **Bovee**, born 13 Oct 1848 in Lewis Co., NY; died 10 Apr 1867 in T/Garden Valley, Jackson Co., NY.
+ 1226	iv	Mary Josephine[7] **Bovee**, born 25 Feb 1850 in Pinckney, Lewis Co., NY; died 15 Jan 1925 in Minneapolis, Hennepin Co., MN. She married **Henry Olver**.
+ 1227	v	Electa[7] **Bovee**, born 1852. She married **Alexander Meek**.
1228	vi	Ida A[7] **Bovee**, born 22 Jun 1855 in NY; died 23 Apr 1905.
1229	vii	Florence[7] **Bovee**, born 1856; died abt 1864.
+ 1230	viii	Gilbert Humphrey[7] **Bovee**, born Apr 1862 in WI. He married **Jessie L Warren**.
+ 1231	ix	Silas Lewis[7] **Bovee** Jr, born Sep 1864 in WI. He married **Della A Warren**.

481. Zebulon[6] Bovee (Nicholas[5], Cornelius[4], Rykert[3], Nicholas[2], Mathieu[1]), born 1824 in Pinckney, Lewis Co., NY; died 9 May 1891. He married Waity Brundige, born 2 Feb 1835 in Pinckney, , NY, daughter of Joseph Brundige and Charolotte Green.

Children of Zebulon Bovee and Waity Brundige were as follows:

+ 1232	i	Joseph Milford[7] **Bovee**, born 18 Jun 1855 in Alma, Buffalo Co., WI. He married **Mary Christensen**.
+ 1233	ii	Charlotte Melissa[7] **Bovee**, born abt 1858 in Jackson Co., WI. She married **Andrew J Stafford**.
1234	iii	Cora M[7] **Bovee**, born Nov 1860.
1235	iv	Caroline W[7] **Bovee**, born 1862 in WI. She married on 7 Oct 1877 in Jackson Co., WI **Silas N Bovee** (see 1222), born Oct 1855 in NY; died 12 Jan 1933 in Eau Claire Co., WI, son of Jonas Nicholas Bovee and Orinda Green.
+ 1236	v	Lucretia M[7] **Bovee**, born 1863 in WI. She married **Charles Edward Burnett**.
1237	vi	Jerome M[7] **Bovee**, born Feb 1868 in WI.
1238	vii	John F[7] **Bovee**, born Dec 1869 in WI.
1239	viii	David S[7] **Bovee**, born Aug 1874 in WI.

482. Lucretia M[6] Bovee (Nicholas[5], Cornelius[4], Rykert[3], Nicholas[2], Mathieu[1]), born 21 Sep 1827; died 12 Dec 1886. She married on 30 Dec 1843 in NY Hosea Cobb Hoisington, born 5 Aug 1820 in VT, son of Hosea Hoisington and Chloe Davis.

Children of Lucretia M Bovee and Hosea Cobb Hoisington were as follows:

1240	i	Helen Elizabeth[7] **Hoisington**, born 1 Dec 1846.
1241	ii	Jenison Franklin[7] **Hoisington**, born 6 Apr 1849.
1242	iii	Alice Melissa[7] **Hoisington**, born 4 Apr 1853.
1243	iv	Artimishia Jane[7] **Hoisington**, born 6 Jan 1856 in Garden Valley, Jackson Co., WI.

1244   v   Margaret Alvina[7] **Hoisington**, born 9 Feb 1861.

1245   vi   Emily Matilda[7] **Hoisington**, born 23 Nov 1865.

500. James R[6] **Bovee** (Cornelius[5], Cornelius[4], Rykert[3], Nicholas[2], Mathieu[1]), born abt 1825 in Onondaga Co., NY; died 7 Mar 1909 in Milesgrove,Erie Co., PA. He married Caroline Maria Hill.

Children of James R Bovee and Caroline Maria Hill were as follows:

+   1246   i   Harriet[7] **Bovee**, born abt 1856. She married **George A Graves**.

+   1247   ii   Edmund L[7] **Bovee**, born abt 1860 in Elk Creek, Erie Co., PA. He married **Ada E Campbell**.

+   1248   iii   Alice[7] **Bovee**, born 14 Feb 1863. She married **Henry Billet**.

+   1249   iv   James Elmer[7] **Bovee**, born abt 1864. He married **Susan Beard**.

    1250   v   William C[7] **Bovee**, born abt 1868 in PA.

501. Lucretia M[6] **Bovee** (Cornelius[5], Cornelius[4], Rykert[3], Nicholas[2], Mathieu[1]), born abt 1833 in NY. She married on 13 Nov 1848 in Ionia Co., MI Loren J Mosher, born 4 Nov 1824, son of William Mosher and Samantha Laurence.

Children of Lucretia M Bovee and Loren J Mosher were as follows:

    1251   i   William M[7] **Mosher**, born 1850.

    1252   ii   Chloe Marilla[7] **Mosher**, born abt 1852.

    1253   iii   Alice Salome[7] **Mosher**, born abt 1854.

    1254   iv   Harriet E[7] **Mosher**, born abt 1856.

503. Sylvester A[6] **Bovee** (Cornelius[5], Cornelius[4], Rykert[3], Nicholas[2], Mathieu[1]), born abt 1841 in OH; died bef 1864. He married on 13 Mar 1861 in Eaton Co., MI Olive J Hayward.

Children of Sylvester A Bovee and Olive J Hayward were as follows:

    1255   i   Hattie[7] **Bovee**, born 1862 in MI.

505. Elizabeth[6] **Bovie** (Frederick[5], Cornelius[4], Rykert[3], Nicholas[2], Mathieu[1]), born abt 1833 in Gallipolis,Gallia Co., OH; died 19 May 1866. She married on 3 Oct 1858 in Gallia Co., OH Lewis Curry, born 18 May 1831 in Gallipolis, Gallia Co., OH; died 2 Sep 1908 in Springfield, Clark Co., OH, son of James Curry and Susanna Sprague.

Children of Elizabeth Bovie and Lewis Curry were as follows:

    1256   i   Harry Mortimer[7] **Curry**, born 5 May 1860 in Gallipolis, Gallia Co., OH.

    1257   ii   Lulu May[7] **Curry**, born abt 1865 in Gallipolis, Gallia Co.,

508. Frederick Morgan[6] **Bovie** (Frederick[5], Cornelius[4], Rykert[3], Nicholas[2], Mathieu[1]), born 23 Oct 1846 in Gallipolis,Gallia Co., OH; died 29 Oct 1930 in Gallipolis,Gallia Co., OH. He married on 24 Nov 1870 Lucy Vernon Alexander, born 1850 in Butler Co., OH; died 1927 in Gallia Co., OH, daughter of Joseph Alexander and Martha White.

Children of Frederick Morgan Bovie and Lucy Vernon Alexander were as follows:

+   1258   i   George Frederick[7] **Bovie**, born 21 Dec 1872 in Gallia Co., OH; died 25 Sep 1943. He married (1) **Nellie Gatewood**; (2) **Gladys Carpenter**.

+   1259   ii   Joseph Harley Clark[7] **Bovie**, born 9 Nov 1874 in Gallipolis, Gallia Co., OH; died 1959. He married **Emma G Geissler**.

+   1260   iii   Vernon Morgan[7] **Bovie**, born 10 Mar 1878 in Gallipolis, Gallia Co., OH; died 9 Mar 1926 in San Francisco, San Francisco Co., CA. He married **Mary Roland Tinker**.

+   1261   iv   Elizabeth[7] **Bovie**, born 8 Mar 1879 in Gallia Co., OH; died 1951. She married **Everette Humphrey Morgan**.

+   1262   v   Marilla[7] **Bovie**, born Jul 1882 in Gallia Co., OH; died 1960. She married **Dr. Ira J Kail**.

510. Andrew Elliott[6] **Bovee** (John E[5], Cornelius[4], Rykert[3], Nicholas[2], Mathieu[1]), born 18 Jul 1847 in Monroe Twp, Ashtabula Co., OH; died Mar 1908 in Kelloggsville, Ashtabula Co., OH. He married on 7 Sep 1867 in Ashtabula Co., OH Ermina Lucinda Ruland.

Children of Andrew Elliott Bovee and Ermina Lucinda Ruland were as follows:

     1263   i   William T[7] **Bovee**, born 1 Oct 1899; died Oct 1978. He married **Rachel Adams**.

523. Emory John[6] **Bovee** (Peter[5], Cornelius[4], Rykert[3], Nicholas[2], Mathieu[1]), born 24 May 1836 in Ashtabula Co., OH. He married Emmeline L Fox, born Nov 1840 in OH.

Children of Emory John Bovee and Emmeline L Fox were as follows:

+   1264   i   Frank Merton[7] **Bovee**, born 29 Mar 1868 in Kingsville Twp, Ashtabula Co., OH; died 29 Nov 1950 in Kingsville Twp, Ashtabula Co., OH. He married **Eleanor Camham**.

     1265   ii   Hulbert[7] **Bovee**, born abt 1871 in OH.

534. Mary[6] **Bovee** (John[5], Nicholas M[4], Matthew[3], Nicholas[2], Mathieu[1]), born 4 Oct 1809 in Hanover,Chautauqua Co., NY; died 17 Sep 1883 in Wayne Co., IL.

She married on 1 Mar 1827 in Wayne Co., IL Dr. Nathan Elliott Roberts Sr, born 9 Aug 1808 in Cumberland Co., KY; died abt 1874 in Coffeyville. Montgomery Co., KY, son of Archibald Roberts and Sarah Pennington.

Children of Mary Bovee and Dr. Nathan Elliott Roberts Sr were as follows:

1266   i   Hester Ann[7] **Roberts**, born 3 Mar 1829 in Wayne Co., IL.

1267   ii   Jane[7] **Roberts**, born 16 Nov 1830 in Wayne Co., IL.

1268   iii   Zadok Casey[7] **Roberts**, born 13 Aug 1832 in Jasper Twp., Wayne Co., IL.

1269   iv   John Wesley[7] **Roberts**, born 25 Jun 1834 in Wayne Co., IL.

1270   v   Archibald Hezekiah[7] **Roberts**, born 29 Jun 1836 in Wayne Co., IL.

1271   vi   Sally[7] **Roberts**, born 30 May 1838 in Wayne Co., IL.

1272   vii   Ebenezer Baldwin[7] **Roberts**, born 6 Jun 1840 in Fairfield, Wayne Co., IL.

1273   viii   Mary Elizabeth[7] **Roberts**, born 31 Jul 1846 in Wayne Co., IL.

1274   ix   Nathan Elliot[7] **Roberts** Jr, born 26 Apr 1849 in Wayne Co., IL.

1275   x   Daniel Fletcher[7] **Roberts**, born 12 Aug 1851 in Wayne Co., IL.

1276   xi   Emma[7] **Roberts**.

535. Sarah[6] **Bovee** (John[5], Nicholas M[4], Matthew[3], Nicholas[2], Mathieu[1]), born 9 Jun 1811 in Sheridan, Chautauqua Co., NY. She married on 28 Dec 1828 in Wayne Co., IL George Clinton McMackin, born 18 May 1807 in Butler Co., KY.

Children of Sarah Bovee and George Clinton McMackin were as follows:

1277   i   L[7] **McMackin**, born abt 1835.

1278   ii   Mary Temperance[7] **McMackin**.

1279   iii   Child[7] **McMackin**.

1280   iv   Matilda[7] **McMackin**, born abt 1842.

1281   v   Eliza J[7] **McMackin**, born abt 1844.

1282   vi   John W[7] **McMackin**, born abt 1845.

1283   vii   Thomas C[7] **McMackin**, born 8 May 1848 in Jasper Twp., Wayne Co., IL.

1284   viii   Catherine[7] **McMackin**, born abt 1850.

1285   ix   Tabitha[7] **McMackin**.

1286   x   William B[7] **McMackin**, born abt 1853.

536. John[6] **Bovee** Jr (John[5], Nicholas M[4], Matthew[3], Nicholas[2], Mathieu[1]), born 12 Feb 1813 in Chautauqua Co., NY; died 2 Apr 1903 in Blair, Washington Co., NE. He married on 27 Mar 1833 Sarah Harlan, born 7 Jun 1812 in Butler Co., KY; died 9 Nov 1896 in Conrad Grove, Grundy Co., IA, daughter of John Harlan

and Mary Dunn.

Children of John Bovee Jr and Sarah Harlan were as follows:

+ 1287   i   Archibald Melrose[7] **Bovee**, born 25 Jul 1838 in Wayne Co., IL; died 25 Dec 1900 in Blair, Washington Co., NE. He married **Evaline C Gossard**.

+ 1288   ii   Nicholas Aaron[7] **Bovee**, born 17 Jan 1841 in Fairfield, Wayne Co., IL; died 20 Mar 1916 in IA. He married **Anna Maria Betzer**.

+ 1289   iii   John Wesley[7] **Bovee**, born 16 Aug 1843 in Wayne Co., IL; died 15 Jan 1914 in Salem, Marion Co., OR. He married **Margaret Critchfield**.

+ 1290   iv   Jacob Nelson[7] **Bovee**, born 5 Sep 1845 in Wayne Co., IL; died 10 Jun 1904 in Vashon Island, King Co., WA. He married **Mary Jennie Heron**.

1291   v   Sarah Jane[7] **Bovee**, born 28 Mar 1848 in Wayne Co., IL; died 29 Aug 1934 in Evansville, Rock Co., WI. She married on 23 Jan 1868 in McClean Co, IL **Albert Crichfield**.

1292   vi   Richard Baxter[7] **Bovee**, born 3 Jun 1853 in Wayne Co., IL. He married **Mary Ellen Story**.

537. Hannah[6] **Bovee** (John[5], Nicholas M[4], Matthew[3], Nicholas[2], Mathieu[1]), born 10 Aug 1814 in NY; died 25 Nov 1856 in Wayne Co., IL. She married in 1834 John Gaston.

Children of Hannah Bovee and John Gaston were as follows:

1293   i   Eli[7] **Gaston**, born 18 Sep 1835.

1294   ii   Caleb[7] **Gaston**, born 1 Jun 1837.

1295   iii   Cynthia[7] **Gaston**, born 4 Apr 1839.

1296   iv   George[7] **Gaston**, born 14 Jul 1840.

1297   v   Jane C[7] **Gaston**, born 22 Feb 1844.

1298   vi   Mary[7] **Gaston**, born 1846.

1299   vii   Rodira[7] **Gaston**, born 22 Aug 1849.

539. Aaron Milton[6] **Bovee** (John[5], Nicholas M[4], Matthew[3], Nicholas[2], Mathieu[1]), born 15 Jul 1817 in NY; died 29 Sep 1880 in IA. He married on 9 Oct 1845 in Jo Davies Co., IL Mary Jay, born 22 May 1827; died 6 Mar 1880.

Children of Aaron Milton Bovee and Mary Jay were as follows:

+ 1300   i   Nelson LeGrande[7] **Bovee**, born 5 Aug 1846 in IL. He married **Martha Jane Kuison**.

1301   ii   Lavinia[7] **Bovee**, born 20 Sep 1848; died 29 Jun 1913. She married on 30 Jan 1866 in Cassville, Grant Co., WI **Charles White**.

1302   iii   Ursula Lenora[7] **Bovee**, born 1851 in IL; died 1852.

+ 1303 iv Charles Franklin Leroy[7] **Bovee**, born 24 Feb 1853 in WI; died 6 Apr 1905. He married **Josephine Amidon**.

+ 1304 v Ida Ann[7] **Bovee**, born 29 Mar 1855; died 27 Jan 1942. She married **David Jackson DeVoe**.

+ 1305 vi William Levant[7] **Bovee**, born 4 Aug 1857 in WI; died 1936. He married **Pauline M Minerta**.

540. Wesley[6] **Bovee** (John[5], Nicholas M[4], Matthew[3], Nicholas[2], Mathieu[1]), born 19 Apr 1821 in Wayne Co., IL; died 29 May 1905 in Panther Creek, Dallas Co., IA. He married in Oct 1853 in Bollinger Co., MO Nancy Caroline Bailey, born 24 Jan 1837 in MO, daughter of (---) Bailey and Margaret Peuterbaugh.

Children of Wesley Bovee and Nancy Caroline Bailey were as follows:

1306 i Mary Susan[7] **Bovee**, born abt 1854 in Bollinger Co., MO; died 17 Feb 1884 in Calhoun Co., IL.

1307 ii Sarah Margaret[7] **Bovee**, born 4 Dec 1856; died 6 Aug 1935. She married on 17 Jun 1896 **Gottlieb Quiller**.

1308 iii Julia[7] **Bovee**, born abt 1858; died 9 Sep 1908. She married **Frank Calvin**.

1309 iv Verna[7] **Bovee**, born 7 Apr 1862 in Calhoun Co., IL; died 12 Feb 1884.

+ 1310 v John McClellan[7] **Bovee**, born 6 Jun 1863 in IL; died 1 Jul 1932 in Los Angeles, Los Angeles Co., CA. He married **Laura May Mosely**.

1311 vi Emma Alice[7] **Bovee**, born 24 Sep 1866 in IL. She married **John Foiles**.

1312 vii William[7] **Bovee**, born 28 Jan 1869 in Calhoun Co., IL; died 23 Jun 1884.

1313 viii Ida Bell[7] **Bovee**, born 6 Aug 1871 in IL; died 8 Dec 1943. She married **John M Freesmeyer**.

541. Phoebe[6] **Bovee** (John[5], Nicholas M[4], Matthew[3], Nicholas[2], Mathieu[1]), born 19 Apr 1821 in NY; died abt 1863. She married (1) John Burch; (2) Moses Ellis.

Children of Phoebe Bovee and Moses Ellis were as follows:

1314 i Frances Marion[7] **Ellis**.

543. Nelson John[6] **Bovee** (John[5], Nicholas M[4], Matthew[3], Nicholas[2], Mathieu[1]), born 24 Jan 1828 in Wayne Co., IL; died 27 Aug 1881 in Herman, Washington Co., NE. He married on 28 Sep 1848 in Fairfield, Wayne Co., IL Nancy Walton, born 13 May 1828 in IL; died 13 Jan 1887 in Fletcher, Washington Co., NE, daughter of George Walton and Nancy J McClellan.

Children of Nelson John Bovee and Nancy Walton were as follows:

+ 1315 i Nancy Jane[7] **Bovee**, born 9 Jul 1849 in Wayne Co., IL; died 25 Nov 1909 in Randolph, Cedar Co., NE. She married **Thomas Jefferson Howarth**.

+	1316	ii	Mary Elizabeth[7] **Bovee**, born 11 Dec 1850 in IL; died 5 Apr 1901. She married **Caleb Loftus**.
	1317	iii	George Nicholas[7] **Bovee**, born 22 Jan 1852 in Wayne Co., IL; died 6 Sep 1853 in IL.
+	1318	iv	John Milton[7] **Bovee**, born 25 Oct 1853 in IL; died 2 Apr 1940. He married **Clara Dulceina Hancock**.
+	1319	v	Sarah Catherine[7] **Bovee**, born 20 Jan 1855 in Wayne Co., IL; died 2 Apr 1881 in Tekama, Burt Co., NB. She married **George Calvin Geary**.
	1320	vi	William Mazey[7] **Bovee**, born 17 Feb 1858 in IL; died 20 Jul 1938. He married **Permilla Mildred Brown**.
+	1321	vii	James Massey[7] **Bovee**, born 3 Mar 1860 in Fairfield, Wayne Co., IL; died 10 Apr 1938 in Laramie, Albany Co., WY. He married **Sarah Ann Flanagan**.
+	1322	viii	Emma Louise[7] **Bovee**, born 10 Feb 1862 in Wayne Co., IL; died 17 Nov 1948. She married **Jefferson H Gossard**.
+	1323	ix	Margaret Olive[7] **Bovee**, born 17 Apr 1864 in Wayne Co., IL; died 20 Nov 1955 in Wayne, Wayne Co., NE. She married **Amzi Phillip Gossard**.
	1324	x	Richard Wilbur[7] **Bovee**, born 16 May 1866 in IL; died 6 Aug 1928 in Canton, Fulton Co., IL.
	1325	xi	Ira Nelson[7] **Bovee**, born 9 Nov 1868 in IL; died 31 May 1914 in Hulsey. Thomas Co., NE.
	1326	xii	Leon A[7] **Bovee**, born Nov 1869 in Wayne Co., IL.
	1327	xiii	Nettie Belle[7] **Bovee**, born 23 Dec 1870 in Wayne Co., IL; died 7 Sep 1933. She married **Ernest C McConnahay**.
	1328	xiv	Minnie Luella[7] **Bovee**, born 5 Jun 1872 in Wayne Co., IL; died 1962. She married in Burt Co, NE **Howard C Hancock**, born May 1867 in PA; died 1932 in NE.
	1329	xv	Cora May[7] **Bovee**, born 5 Mar 1874 in Washington Co., NE; died 9 Apr 1959. She married **Arthur George Clark**.

556. Ann Elizabeth[6] **Bovee** (Mathew[5], Nicholas M[4], Matthew[3], Nicholas[2], Mathieu[1]), born 18 Apr 1827 in Hanover, Chautauqua Co., NY; died 17 Oct 1869 in Milton, Morgan Co., UT. She married on 22 Jan 1846 in Nauvoo, Hancock co., IL Joseph Mecham, born 1 Feb 1806 in Thornton, Grafton Co., IL; died 6 Mar 1894 in St George, Washington Co., UT, son of Joseph Mecham and Sarah Basford.

Children of Ann Elizabeth Bovee and Joseph Mecham were as follows:

1330	i	Josephine[7] **Mecham**, born 1847 in Council Bluffs, Potawattamie Co., IA.
1331	ii	Arianiah[7] **Mecham**, born 18 Apr 1849 in Council Bluffs, Potawattamie Co., IA.
1332	iii	Joseph[7] **Mecham**, born 16 Feb 1851 in Woodbine, Harrison Co., IA.

1333	iv	Ammon Earth^7 **Mecham**, born 1853 in Salt Lake City, Salt Lake Co., UT.
1334	v	Amaron^7 **Mecham**, born 6 Dec 1855 in Salt Lake City, Salt Lake Co., UT.
1335	vi	Emma Waitstill^7 **Mecham**, born 18 Oct 1858 in East Tooele, Tooele Co., UT.
1336	vii	Brigham Bovee^7 **Mecham**, born 18 Feb 1860 in Salt Lake City, Salt Lake Co., UT.
1337	viii	Lucian Mormon^7 **Mecham**, born 16 Feb 1862 in Milton Morgan Co., UT.
1338	ix	Seymour Brunson^7 **Mecham**, born 14 Dec 1864 in Milton Morgan Co., UT.
1339	x	Deseret^7 **Mecham**, born 5 Nov 1865 in Milton Morgan Co., UT.
1340	xi	Elizabeth Vilate^7 **Mecham**, born 7 Nov 1867 in Milton Morgan Co., UT.

557. Sarah Ann^6 **Bovee** (Mathew^5, Nicholas M^4, Matthew^3, Nicholas^2, Mathieu^1), born 6 Apr 1831 in Fredonia, Chautauqua Co., NY; died in UT. She married on 1 Sep 1849 in Sangamon Co., IL Jeremiah Stringham, born 5 Feb 1828, son of George Stringham and Polly Hendrickson.

Children of Sarah Ann Bovee and Jeremiah Stringham were as follows:

1341	i	Benjamin Franklin^7 **Stringham**, born 24 Mar 1851 in Springfield, Sangamon Co., IL.
1342	ii	George Walter^7 **Stringham**, born 5 Oct 1852 in Springfield, Sangamon Co., IL.
1343	iii	William Elisha^7 **Stringham**, born 12 Nov 1856 in Eddyville, Wapello Co., IA.
1344	iv	Mary Ellen^7 **Stringham**, born 13 Oct 1859 in St Joseph, Buchanan Co., MO.
1345	v	Jeremiah^7 **Stringham**, born 7 Feb 1865 in Salt Lake City, Salt Lake Co., UT.

559. Joseph Smith^6 **Bovee** (Mathew^5, Nicholas M^4, Matthew^3, Nicholas^2, Mathieu^1), born 25 Dec 1840 in Springfield, Sangamon Co., IL; died 27 Jan 1911 in Cheyenne, Laramie Co., WY. He married on 22 Jan 1865 in Denver, Denver Co., CO Elizabeth Sampson, born Nov 1844 in Clay Co., MO; died 28 Sep 1928 in Wheatland, Platte Co., WY.

Children of Joseph Smith Bovee and Elizabeth Sampson were as follows:

+	1346	i	Jasper Lincoln^7 **Bovee**, born 21 May 1866 in Denver Denver Co., CO; died 25 Jun 1941 in Wheatland, Platte Co., WY. He married **Rosa Quincy Shanks**.
	1347	ii	Minnie Alice^7 **Bovee**, born 27 Apr 1871.
	1348	iii	Olive Jannett^7 **Bovee**, born 16 Feb 1873.

1349   iv   Aaron Australia[7] **Bovee**, born 8 Jan 1875.

\+ 1350   v   Lester La Grand[7] **Bovee**, born 22 Feb 1878. He married
                        Nellie Bollin.

572. Sarah Jane[6] **Bovee** (Mathias Jacob[5], Jacob Mathias[4], Matthew[3], Nicholas[2], Mathieu[1]), born 20 Mar 1818 in DRC, Amsterdam, Montgomery Co., NY; died 5 Oct 1882. She married Thomas W Pittman, born 12 Dec 1798 in New York, New York Co., NY; died 19 Sep 1882.

Children of Sarah Jane Bovee and Thomas W Pittman were as follows:

1351   i   Mathew B[7] **Pittman**, born 18 May 1837.

1352   ii   Anna[7] **Pittman**. She married **(---) Hiney**.

1353   iii   Emma J[7] **Pittman**, born abt 1840 in NY. She married in
                       1969 in Eagle, Waukesha Co., WI **J Warren Wallace**.

1354   iv   Elnora[7] **Pittman**, born abt 1846 in WI. She married
                       Harvey Clemons.

1355   v   Sarah[7] **Pittman**, born abt 1849 in WI. She married
                       William McWilliams.

573. Emily Maria[6] **Bovee** (Mathias Jacob[5], Jacob Mathias[4], Matthew[3], Nicholas[2], Mathieu[1]), born 31 Jan 1820; christened 12 Mar 1820 in DRC, Amsterdam, Montgomery Co., NY; died 22 Jun 1848 in Jericho, Waukesha Co., WI. She married on 11 Nov 1845 in Milwaukee, Milwaukee Co., WI Jerry Parsons, born 1 Jun 1815 in Colebrook, Coos Co., NH; died 24 Dec 1866 in Yuba Co., CA, son of Jonathan Parsons and Lovyse Booth.

Children of Emily Maria Bovee and Jerry Parsons were as follows:

1356   i   Hector[7] **Parsons**, born 30 Sep 1846; died 2 Apr 1847.

1357   ii   Emily Louise[7] **Parsons**, born 16 Jun 1848.

574. Benedict Arnold[6] **Bovee** (Mathias Jacob[5], Jacob Mathias[4], Matthew[3], Nicholas[2], Mathieu[1]), born 20 Feb 1822 in NY; christened 22 Apr 1822 in DRC, Amsterdam, Montgomery Co., NY; died 3 Oct 1875 in Eagle, Waukesha Co.,WI. He married on 30 Mar 1843 Catharine A Cramer, born 25 Jan 1823 in NY; died 6 Dec 1893 in Eagle, Waukesha Co.,WI.

Children of Benedict Arnold Bovee and Catharine A Cramer were as follows:

1358   i   Mathew Jacob[7] **Bovee**, born 7 Jan 1844 in NY; died 6 Aug
                       1905 in Palmyra, Jefferson Co., WI. He married on 24
                       Nov 1869 in Waukesha, Waukesha Co., WI **Mary S
                       Perkins**, daughter of Daniel Perkins and Olive Satridge.

1359   ii   Frank A[7] **Bovee**, born 2 Dec 1849 in Eagle, Waukesha
                       Co., WI.

\+ 1360   iii   Marvin W[7] **Bovee**, born 31 Jan 1859 in Eagle, Waukesha
                       Co., WI; died 25 Nov 1947 in Eagle, Waukesha Co., WI.
                       He married **Mararet Robinson**.

575. William Reid[6] **Bovee** (Mathias Jacob[5], Jacob Mathias[4], Matthew[3], Nicholas[2], Mathieu[1]), born 11 Oct 1823 in NY; christened in DRC, Amsterdam, Montgomery Co., NY; died 18 Mar 1874. He married on 1 May 1848 Sarah Ann Snover, born 15 Mar 1825 in NJ; died 16 Mar 1906 in WI.

Children of William Reid Bovee and Sarah Ann Snover were as follows:

+ 1361　i　　Manley W[7] **Bovee**, born 25 Feb 1849 in Eagle, Waukesha Co., WI; died 7 Feb 1919 in Bartlesville, Washington Co., OK. He married **Elizabeth Ford McCool**.

　 1362　ii　　Ella E[7] **Bovee**, born 1 Oct 1855 in WI; died 26 Oct 1857 in Eagle, Waukesha Co., WI.

　 1363　iii　　Edna E[7] **Bovee**, born Aug 1858 in WI; died Mar 1919 in Eagle, Waukesha Co., WI. She married **Ezra Clemons**.

576. Marvin Henry[6] **Bovee** (Mathias Jacob[5], Jacob Mathias[4], Matthew[3], Nicholas[2], Mathieu[1]), born 5 Jan 1827 in Amsterdam, Montgomery Co., NY; christened in DRC, Amsterdam, Montgomery Co., NY; died 7 May 1888 in Whitewater, Walworth Co., WI. He married on 13 Oct 1862 in Milwaukee, Milwaukee Co., WI Laura Doud, born Oct 1843 in NY, daughter of Capt John Doud and Saphonia Benedict.

Children of Marvin Henry Bovee and Laura Doud were as follows:

+ 1364　i　　Maude[7] **Bovee**. She married **Halbert L Halverson**.

　 1365　ii　　Rollin J[7] **Bovee**, born 15 Sep 1874 in Chicago, Cook Co., IL. He married **Irene (---)**.

577. Anna Elizabeth[6] **Bovee** (Mathias Jacob[5], Jacob Mathias[4], Matthew[3], Nicholas[2], Mathieu[1]), born 20 Feb 1829; christened in DRC, Amsterdam, Montgomery Co., NY; died 10 Oct 1875. She married on 15 Mar 1848 Joseph Sprague, born 30 Jan 1825 in Summit Co., OH.; died 28 Jun 1896.

Children of Anna Elizabeth Bovee and Joseph Sprague were as follows:

　 1366　i　　Theodore Joseph[7] **Sprague**.

　 1367　ii　　Ambrose B[7] **Sprague**, born Apr 1851.

　 1368　iii　　Alice[7] **Sprague**.

　 1369　iv　　Jesse B[7] **Sprague**.

　 1370　v　　Sidney[7] **Sprague**.

　 1371　vi　　Owen[7] **Sprague**.

　 1372　vii　　Delia[7] **Sprague**.

578. Halsey Wood[6] **Bovee** (Mathias Jacob[5], Jacob Mathias[4], Matthew[3], Nicholas[2], Mathieu[1]), born 18 Apr 1831 in Amsterdam, Montgomery Co., NY; christened in DRC, Amsterdam, Mongomery Co., NY; died 1 Oct 1879 in

Chicago, Cook Co., IL. He married in Feb 1853 Mary Henrietta Kinder.

Children of Halsey Wood Bovee and Mary Henrietta Kinder were as follows:

1373 i Ada Estelle[7] **Bovee**, born abt 1858; died abt 1944. She married **Thomas Coddington Ketcham**.

1374 ii Dora May[7] **Bovee**, born 10 Feb 1872; died 28 Nov 1948 in Los Angeles, Los Angeles Co., CA. She married on 15 Dec 1892 **William Arthur Burch**.

579. Edward Livingston[6] **Bovee** (Mathias Jacob[5], Jacob Mathias[4], Matthew[3], Nicholas[2], Mathieu[1]), born 20 Jun 1833 in Amsterdam, Montgomery Co., NY; christened in DRC, Amsterdam, Montgomery Co., NY; died 5 Jul 1892 in Waukesha, Waukesha Co., WI. He married on 4 Nov 1859 in Eagle, Waukesha Co., WI Elizabeth B Hellier, born 22 May 1840 in Bradford, England; died 10 Sep 1894 in PA.

Children of Edward Livingston Bovee and Elizabeth B Hellier were as follows:

+ 1375 i Dewitt Clinton[7] **Bovee**, born 21 Jan 1861 in WI; died 17 Sep 1908 in Chicago, Cook Co., IL. He married **Nettie (---)**.

+ 1376 ii Herbert Stephen[7] **Bovee**, born 17 Sep 1863 in WI. He married **Edith F Burgit**.

 1377 iii Halsey Wood[7] **Bovee**, born 17 Sep 1863 in WI; died 1918 in Eagle, Waukesha Co., WI. He married **Emma M Brokaw**, born 1862; died 1918.

+ 1378 iv Marvin W[7] **Bovee**, born 27 Jan 1868 in WI. He married **Mabel Gilman**.

+ 1379 v Emily L[7] **Bovee**, born 17 Oct 1869 in WI; died 15 May 1958. She married **Jonathan Malin Jones**.

586. Romania[6] **Bovee** (John[5], Jacob Mathias[4], Matthew[3], Nicholas[2], Mathieu[1]), born 5 Apr 1840 in Provincetown, Barnstable Co., MA; died 31 Oct 1898 in Troy, Rensselaer Co., NY. She married on 4 Dec 1866 in NY Louis Younglove Schermerhorn, born 18 Nov 1840 in Greenwich, Washington Co., NY; died 3 Apr 1908, son of Barent C Schermerhorn and Catherine Witbeck.

Children of Romania Bovee and Louis Younglove Schermerhorn were as follows:

1380 i Holden[7] **Schermerhorn**, born 18 Jul 1868.

1381 ii Rene[7] **Schermerhorn**, born 21 Feb 1870.

1382 iii Louis W[7] **Schermerhorn**, born 16 Nov 1871.

1383 iv Alfred R[7] **Schermerhorn**, born 8 Feb 1876.

588. Eliza Ann[6] **Bovee** (Philip Vedder[5], Jacob Mathias[4], Matthew[3], Nicholas[2], Mathieu[1]), born 1 Mar 1830 in Amsterdam, Montgomery Co., NY; died 28 Sep

1884. She married on 19 Jul 1849 in Eagle, Waukesha Co., WI Lucian Weeks Robinson, born abt 1823 in CT; died Feb 1863 in Springfield, Green Co., IL, son of Ebenezer Robinson and Harriet Pierce.

Children of Eliza Ann Bovee and Lucian Weeks Robinson were as follows:

1384	i	Frank[7] **Robinson**, born abt 1851.
1385	ii	Philip W[7] **Robinson**, born abt 1853.
1386	iii	Lottie E[7] **Robinson**, born abt 1857.
1387	iv	Harriet E[7] **Robinson**, born abt 1858.
1388	v	Mabel A[7] **Robinson**.

589. Thomas Pittman[6] **Bovee** (Philip Vedder[5], Jacob Mathias[4], Matthew[3], Nicholas[2], Mathieu[1]), born 11 Jul 1832 in Amsterdam, Montgomery Co., NY; died 26 Oct 1906 in Plainfield, Waushara Co., WI. He married in WI Susan M Walker, born 21 Feb 1839 in England; died 27 Sep 1913 in Plainfield, Waushara Co., WI.

Children of Thomas Pittman Bovee and Susan M Walker were as follows:

	1389	i	Susie Adela[7] **Bovee**, born 7 Dec 1862; died 21 Sep 1863.
+	1390	ii	John Walker[7] **Bovee**, born May 1865; died 1933 in Plainfield, Waushara Co., WI. He married **Mary A Margeson**.

590. Sharina[6] **Bovee** (Philip Vedder[5], Jacob Mathias[4], Matthew[3], Nicholas[2], Mathieu[1]), born 25 Apr 1834 in Amsterdam, Montgomery Co., NY; died 2 Mar 1887 in KS. She married John Batrell.

Children of Sharina Bovee and John Batrell were as follows:

1391	i	Phil[7] **Batrell**.
1392	ii	John[7] **Batrell**.
1393	iii	Grace[7] **Batrell**.
1394	iv	Guy[7] **Batrell**.
1395	v	Richard[7] **Batrell**.

591. Lemuel Jacob[6] **Bovee** (Philip Vedder[5], Jacob Mathias[4], Matthew[3], Nicholas[2], Mathieu[1]), born 21 Sep 1835 in Amsterdam, Montgomery Co., NY; died May 1910. He married in 1867 Susan A Betts, born abt 1847 in WI, daughter of Jonathan Betts and Lucinda Ewer.

Children of Lemuel Jacob Bovee and Susan A Betts were as follows:

+	1396	i	Wilbert Lemuel[7] **Bovee**, born abt 1869 in WI; died 24 Jun 1938. He married **Anna Betts**.
+	1397	ii	Jonathan Betts[7] **Bovee**, born 26 Feb 1871 in WI. He married **Addie Belle Lamphere**.
	1398	iii	Amy[7] **Bovee**, born 1872; died 1872.

+ 1399 iv Minnie Susan[7] **Bovee**, born 11 Dec 1874 in WI; died 30 Aug 1894. She married **Charles Tuttle**.

+ 1400 v Elmer Ford[7] **Bovee**, born 22 Feb 1882. He married **Helen Ione Harland**.

   1401 vi Bessie Leona[7] **Bovee**, born 7 May 1889. She married on 26 Jul 1910 **Walter Malchow**.

+ 1402 vii Charles Eugene[7] **Bovee**, born 15 Aug 1892. He married **Pansy Van Clive**.

592. Katherine Elizabeth[6] **Bovee** (Philip Vedder[5], Jacob Mathias[4], Matthew[3], Nicholas[2], Mathieu[1]), born 11 Feb 1839 in Amsterdam, Montgomery Co., NY; died 3 Apr 1925. She married (1) on 4 Nov 1857 in Eagle, Waukesha Co., WI Henry L Jaycox, born abt 1835 in Rushville, Yates Co., NY; died bef 1870; (2) aft 1870 Edward Button Parsons, born 2 Nov 1847; died 23 Dec 1922.

   Children of Katherine Elizabeth Bovee and Henry L Jaycox were as follows:

   1403 i Henry[7] **Jaycox** Jr, born 13 May 1859 in Eagle, Waukesha Co., WI.

   Children of Katherine Elizabeth Bovee and Edward Button Parsons were as follows:

   1404 i Myrtle Eugenia[7] **Parsons**, born 13 Sep 1873 in Eagle, Waukesha Co., WI.

   1405 ii Charlotte Elizabeth[7] **Parsons**, born 22 May 1879 in Eagle, Waukesha Co., WI.

593. Mary Arnold[6] **Bovee** (Philip Vedder[5], Jacob Mathias[4], Matthew[3], Nicholas[2], Mathieu[1]), born 4 Nov 1840 in Amsterdam, Montgomery Co., NY; died 2 Apr 1891 in Eagle, Waukesha Co., WI. She married on 30 May 1858 in Troy Center, Walworth Co., WI John William Hubbard, born 1 Aug 1836 in Milwaukee, Milwaukee Co., WI; died 19 Jan 1873 in Lanesboro, Fillmore Co., MN, son of Henry M Hubbard and Mary Jane Alcutt.

   Children of Mary Arnold Bovee and John William Hubbard were as follows:

   1406 i Mary J[7] **Hubbard**, born 28 Sep 1859 in Mukwonago, Waukesha Co., WI. She married on 3 Jul 1880 in Milton, Rock Co., WI **Henry Joseph Bovee** (see 1100), born 18 Apr 1854 in Fort Edward, Washington Co., NY; died 10 Nov 1903 in Cozad, Dawson Co., NE, son of Joseph Bovee and Lucinda Crissey.

   1407 ii Lottie M[7] **Hubbard**, born 2 Aug 1861 in Eagle, Waukesha Co., WI.

   1408 iii William Eugene[7] **Hubbard**, born 3 Aug 1868 in La Crosse, La Crosse Co., WI.

594. John Isaac[6] **Bovee** (Philip Vedder[5], Jacob Mathias[4], Matthew[3], Nicholas[2],

Mathieu[1]), born 9 Jan 1844 in Eagle, Waukesha Co., WI; died 10 Sep 1916 in Gould City,Mackinac Co., MI. He married (1) on 24 Nov 1867 in Oconto Co., WI Frances L Lumb, died 27 Dec 1871; (2) on 2 Sep 1873 Marion A Morrison, born abt 1854 in NY; died 1904; (3) on 14 Nov 1906 in Cleae Lake, Cerro Gordo Co., IA Kate Louella Morrison.

Children of John Isaac Bovee and Marion A Morrison were as follows:

+ 1409 i Grace M[7] **Bovee**, born 4 Feb 1879; died Aug 1916. She married **Dr. Frank Markey**.

596. Eugene Charles[6] **Bovee** (Philip Vedder[5], Jacob Mathias[4], Matthew[3], Nicholas[2], Mathieu[1]), born 8 Jul 1850; died 24 Aug 1909. He married (1) Martha H Betts, died 10 Jul 1893 in Denver, Denver Co., CO; (2) abt 1893 Marge Parsons.

Children of Eugene Charles Bovee and Martha H Betts were as follows:

+ 1410 i Philip LaRue[7] **Bovee**, born 14 Jul 1875 in Denver, Denver Co., CO; died 1924. He married **Ava Graves**.
  1411 ii Lionel[7] **Bovee**, born aft 1875.

612. Martha Sprague[6] **Bovee** (Mathew J[5], John[4], Matthew[3], Nicholas[2], Mathieu[1]), born 3 Dec 1838 in Plainville, Adams Co., IL; died 14 Feb 1911 in Jacksonport, Door Co., WI. She married on 4 Jul 1860 in Racine, Racine Co., WI. William Robert Brabazon, born 1832 in England; died 23 Aug 1919 in Oshkosh, Winnebago Co., WI..

Children of Martha Sprague Bovee and William Robert Brabazon were as follows:

1412 i Eva May[7] **Brabazon**, born 10 May 1861.
1413 ii Elbert William[7] **Brabazon**, born 7 Jun 1863.
1414 iii Rosella[7] **Brabazon**, born 17 Jun 1864.
1415 iv Emilie Edora[7] **Brabazon**, born in Hilbert, Calumet Co., WI..
1416 v Martha M[7] **Brabazon**, born 11 Dec 1866.
1417 vi Effie V[7] **Brabazon**, born 10 Feb 1870.
1418 vii Jennie E[7] **Brabazon**, born 10 Feb 1875.
1419 viii Ermine E[7] **Brabazon**, born 10 Feb 1875.
1420 ix Myron J[7] **Brabazon**, born 22 Dec 1876.

615. William Henry[6] **Bovee** (John Grant[5], John[4], Matthew[3], Nicholas[2], Mathieu[1]), born 20 Feb 1827 in Gloversville, Fulton Co., NY. He married aft 1850 Sarah Elizabeth Roat, born bef 1830, daughter of John Wesley Roat.

Children of William Henry Bovee and Sarah Elizabeth Roat were as follows:

1421 i ?[7] **Bovee**, born bef 1853.

+	1422	ii	George Willard[7] **Bovee**, born 4 Jun 1853 in Clayton, Jefferson Co., NY; died 11 Dec 1944. He married (1) **Jessie W Harris**; (2) **Mattie McIvor**; (3) **Eleanor Carpenter**.
	1423	iii	William Henry[7] **Bovee** Jr, born May 1856; died bef 1927. He married **Ettie M (---)**.
+	1424	iv	Frederick Charles[7] **Bovee**, born 20 Aug 1859 in Jefferson Co., NY; died 15 Jun 1929 in Watertown, Jefferson Co., NY. He married (1) **Elizabeth McKeever**; (2) **Ida May Juby**.
	1425	v	Dr John Wesley[7] **Bovee**, born 31 Dec 1861 in Clayton, Jefferson Co., NY; died 3 Sep 1927 in Washington, DC. He married (1) bef 1914 **Katherine Seager**, died in CA; (2) **Caroline Copley**.
	1426	vi	Frank McClellan[7] **Bovee**, born abt 1864; died bef 1927.
+	1427	vii	Hiram David[7] **Bovee**, born abt 1866; died 1944 in Clayton, Jefferson Co., NY. He married **Lana M Jondrew**.
	1428	viii	Charles L[7] **Bovee**, born Jul 1869.
	1429	ix	Lulu S[7] **Bovee**, born aft 1870; died aft 1927. She married **A F Vanderwater**.
+	1430	x	Bruce[7] **Bovee**, born Oct 1873 in NY; died bef 1927. He married **Martha I Wakefield**.
+	1431	xi	Burton G[7] **Bovee**, born abt 1874; died 7 Jan 1912 in Depauville, Clayton Twp., Jefferson Co., NY. He married (1) **Grace M Walrath**; (2) **L Maude De Rosia**.

618. Almira[6] **Bovee** (John Grant[5], John[4], Matthew[3], Nicholas[2], Mathieu[1]), born 17 May 1832; died 18 Mar 1911. She married Dennis A Wilson, born 1833; died 3 Oct 1885.

Children of Almira Bovee and Dennis A Wilson were as follows:

1432	i	Lydia[7] **Wilson**, born abt 1855.
1433	ii	Leman[7] **Wilson**, born Mar 1858; died 1925.
1434	iii	Henrietta[7] **Wilson**, born abt 1859.
1435	iv	Louisa[7] **Wilson**, born abt 1860.
1436	v	Arvilla[7] **Wilson**, born abt 1862.
1437	vi	Daniel Edward[7] **Wilson**, born abt 1864.
1438	vii	Mary A[7] **Wilson**, born abt 1866.
1439	viii	Jennie[7] **Wilson**, born abt 1867; died 1869.
1440	ix	John Seymour[7] **Wilson**, born abt 1868.

620. Harriet[6] **Bovee** (John Grant[5], John[4], Matthew[3], Nicholas[2], Mathieu[1]), born 12 Nov 1835. She married (1) abt 1860 Charles Hayes; (2) on 12 Jan 1886 in Redfield, Oswego Co., NY Joseph Burnett.

Children of Harriet Bovee and Charles Hayes were as follows:

1441   i   William[7] **Hayes**, born abt 1859; died 3 Dec 1910.

621. Katherine[6] **Bovee** (John Grant[5], John[4], Matthew[3], Nicholas[2], Mathieu[1]), born 7 Jul 1838 in Clayton, Jefferson Co., NY; died 3 Feb 1897. She married Henry Paddock, born abt 1817; died 6 Jun 1877.

Children of Katherine Bovee and Henry Paddock were as follows:

1442   i   Jane[7] **Paddock**, born abt 1856 in Three Mile Bay, Jefferson CO, NY.

1443   ii   Elmira[7] **Paddock**, born 1859.

622. John Wesley[6] **Bovee** (John Grant[5], John[4], Matthew[3], Nicholas[2], Mathieu[1]), born 17 Jul 1840; died 26 Aug 1924 in Redfield, Oswego Co., NY. He married (1) abt 1860 Amelia Miller, born abt 1838; died 9 Mar 1887 in Redfield, Oswego Co., NY; (2) on 15 Apr 1888 in Camden, Oneida Co., NY Mary Packard, born Mar 1855 in NY; died 22 Feb 1922 in Redfield, Oswego Co., NY.

Children of John Wesley Bovee and Amelia Miller were as follows:

\+   1444   i   Franklin E[7] **Bovee**, born 26 Aug 1865 in Springfield, Sangamon Co., IL; buried in Forest Cem, Camden, Oneida Co., NY. He married **Helen L Flagg**.

\+   1445   ii   Milton H[7] **Bovee**, born Jun 1871 in Redfield, Oswego Co., NY. He married **Minnie Redman**.

Children of John Wesley Bovee and Mary Packard were as follows:

1446   i   Charlotte M[7] **Bovee**, born 22 Dec 1891 in NY. She married in Redfield, Oswego Co., NY **John E Secor**.

624. Martha Eleanor[6] **Bovee** (John Grant[5], John[4], Matthew[3], Nicholas[2], Mathieu[1]), born 9 Jul 1843 in NY; died 3 Sep 1900. She married George Kenyon Palmer.

Children of Martha Eleanor Bovee and George Kenyon Palmer were as follows:

1447   i   Frederick Charles[7] **Palmer**, born 10 Jul 1870.

1448   ii   Hattie[7] **Palmer**.

1449   iii   George[7] **Palmer**.

1450   iv   William[7] **Palmer**.

1451   v   Clarence[7] **Palmer**.

1452   vi   Howard[7] **Palmer**.

1453   vii   Helen[7] **Palmer**.

1454   viii   Orpha[7] **Palmer**.

1455   ix   Lena[7] **Palmer**.

630. Aaron[6] **Bovee** (John Henry[5], John Henry[4], Matthew[3], Nicholas[2], Mathieu[1]), born 21 Apr 1827 in NY; died 18 Jan 1856 in Hudson, Lenawee Co., MI. He married abt 1851 Fanny Johnson, born 25 Sep 1830; died 4 Feb 1912.

Children of Aaron Bovee and Fanny Johnson were as follows:

1456	i	Harvey[7] **Bovee**, born 7 Sep 1848; died 7 Jan 1861.
1457	ii	Alvy[7] **Bovee**, born 5 Oct 1853; died 10 Jan 1854.
1458	iii	Alby[7] **Bovee**, born 5 Oct 1853; died 30 Nov 1855.
1459	iv	Abigail[7] **Bovee**, born abt 1856.

631. Levi[6] **Bovee** (John Henry[5], John Henry[4], Matthew[3], Nicholas[2], Mathieu[1]), born 14 Nov 1829 in Orleans Co., NY; died 23 Apr 1903 in IN. He married (1) on 6 Nov 1851 Laura Jane Silsbee, born abt 1832 in NY; died 19 Mar 1867; (2) on 25 Sep 1868 Minerva Bovee (see 642), born 15 Feb 1833 in Yates, Orleans Co., NY; died 11 Apr 1905 in IN, daughter of Mathew Bovee and Maria Louisa Marlatt.

Children of Levi Bovee and Laura Jane Silsbee were as follows:

1460	i	Augusta E[7] **Bovee**, born 17 Oct 1852; died 8 Nov 1860.
1461	ii	Hiram[7] **Bovee**, born 1 Aug 1854; died 5 Aug 1854.
1462	iii	John H[7] **Bovee**, born 1 Jun 1856; died 3 Jan 1857.
1463	iv	Lillian[7] **Bovee**, born 1860.
1464	v	George[7] **Bovee**, born abt 1862.
1465	vi	Lorenzo John[7] **Bovee**, born May 1865 in MI. He married on 21 Jun 1887 in Lake Co., MI **Arizona Hoisington**.
+ 1466	vii	Jennie[7] **Bovee**, born abt 1867. She married **James E Marvin**.

Children of Levi Bovee and Minerva Bovee were as follows:

| 1467 | i | Lucy[7] **Bovee**, born 14 Jul 1869; died 16 Aug 1869. |
| + 1468 | ii | Grosvenor A[7] **Bovee**, born 4 Apr 1871 in Lake Co., MI. He married **Viola E Boren**. |

632. Hiram[6] **Bovee** (John Henry[5], John Henry[4], Matthew[3], Nicholas[2], Mathieu[1]), born 27 Oct 1831 in Yates, Orleans Co., NY; died 18 Jan 1902 in North Star Twp, Gratiot Co., MI. He married on 8 Jan 1857 Adaline A Austin, born 30 Sep 1833 in Bradford, Orange Co., VT; died 27 Nov 1899 in North Star Twp, Gratiot Co., MI.

Children of Hiram Bovee and Adaline A Austin were as follows:

| + 1469 | i | Woodbury H[7] **Bovee**, born 15 Oct 1859 in North Star Twp., Gratiot Co., MI; died 12 Jul 1917. He married **Jeanette Vedder**. |
| + 1470 | ii | Clara A[7] **Bovee**, born 25 Jan 1864 in North Star Twp., Gratiot Co., MI; died 1 Dec 1910 in St Johns, Clinton Co., MI. She married **Calvin A Crandell**. |

634. Lorenzo J[6] **Bovee** (John Henry[5], John Henry[4], Matthew[3], Nicholas[2], Mathieu[1]), born 30 Jun 1837 in NY; died 3 Jun 1862 in Dover Twp, Lenawee Co., MI. He married Clara J (---), born abt 1842; buried in S Dover Cem, Dover Twp, Lenawee Co., MI.

Children of Lorenzo J Bovee and Clara J (---) were as follows:

1471   i   Hiram[7] **Bovee**, died 6 Aug 1860.

635. David[6] **Bovee** (John Henry[5], John Henry[4], Matthew[3], Nicholas[2], Mathieu[1]), born 29 Jun 1839 in Orleans Co., NY; died 24 Sep 1904. He married abt 1864 Elma Jane Bordine, born 23 Oct 1844 in MI; died 9 Jan 1918.

Children of David Bovee and Elma Jane Bordine were as follows:

1472   i   Mary[7] **Bovee**, born 1867; died 21 Nov 1935. She married **Henry Wallworth**.

1473   ii   Jay Bordine[7] **Bovee**.

642. Minerva[6] **Bovee** (Mathew[5], John Henry[4], Matthew[3], Nicholas[2], Mathieu[1]), born 15 Feb 1833 in Yates, Orleans Co., NY; died 11 Apr 1905 in IN. She married (1) Darius S Grant, son of John C Grant and Phebe Covert; (2) on 25 Sep 1868 Levi Bovee (see 631), born 14 Nov 1829 in Orleans Co., NY; died 23 Apr 1903 in IN, son of John Henry Bovee and Electa Hamlin.

Children of Minerva Bovee and Darius S Grant were as follows:

1474   i   Almon Henry[7] **Grant**, born 3 Feb 1853.

1475   ii   Byron Mathias[7] **Grant**, born 27 Mar 1854 in IN.

1476   iii   Lora Adelia[7] **Grant**, born 7 Oct 1857 in IN.

643. Andrew J[6] **Bovee** (Mathew[5], John Henry[4], Matthew[3], Nicholas[2], Mathieu[1]), born 7 Sep 1837 in Hudson, Lenawee Co., MI. He married (1) on 6 Aug 1858 in Washington Twp, Gratiot Co., MI Melissa Eliza Smith, born Oct 1839 in NY; (2) on 1 Oct 1879 in Rapid River, Delta Co., MI Sarah Maria Frier, born Jun 1843.

Children of Andrew J Bovee and Melissa Eliza Smith were as follows:

+   1477   i   Ida A[7] **Bovee**, born Apr 1863; died 22 Mar 1924 in Minneapolis, Hennepin Co., MN.. She married **Myron Stearns**.

+   1478   ii   Edward Hill[7] **Bovee**, born 18 Sep 1864 in Flint, Genesee Co., MI; died 18 Jun 1960 in Girard, Erie Co. PA. He married **Adelia Ann Schutte**.

+   1479   iii   Selden Martin[7] **Bovee**, born 19 Sep 1872 in Hudson, Lenawee Co., MI; died 28 Apr 1950 in Sonoma, Sonoma Co., CA. He married (1) **Ethel Bates**; (2) **Elizabeth (---)**.

+   1480   iv   Daisy Mae[7] **Bovee**, born 30 Jan 1876 in Hudson, Lenawee Co., MI. She married (1) **William T Dalton**; (2) **Richard W Schoonmaker**.

644. Grosvenor D[6] **Bovee** (Mathew[5], John Henry[4], Matthew[3], Nicholas[2], Mathieu[1]), born Nov 1839 in MI. He married on 21 Oct 1863 in Lenawee Co., MI Adaline Hanbiel, born 1845; died 1 Aug 1932 in Chelsea,Washtenaw Co., MI.

Children of Grosvenor D Bovee and Adaline Hanbiel were as follows:

+ 1481   i   Calvin O[7] **Bovee**, born Sep 1867 in Woodstock Twp., Lenawee Co., MI; died 27 Oct 1929. He married **Olcea Owen**.

651. Elisha H[6] **Bovee** (Jacob[5], John Henry[4], Matthew[3], Nicholas[2], Mathieu[1]), born 17 Aug 1829 in NY; died 1 Feb 1889. He married on 9 Jul 1854 in Dover Twp, Lenawee Co., MI Susannah R Hamilton, born 13 Jul 1831; died 4 Oct 1919 in Clayton, Lenawee Co., MI.

Children of Elisha H Bovee and Susannah R Hamilton were as follows:

1482   i   Liona[7] **Bovee**, born 15 Sep 1859.

1483   ii   Warren[7] **Bovee**, born 18 Aug 1862.

1484   iii   Lorenzo A[7] **Bovee**, born 7 Sep 1868. He married **Christine (---)**.

1485   iv   Edward N[7] **Bovee**.

652. Elijah[6] **Bovee** (Jacob[5], John Henry[4], Matthew[3], Nicholas[2], Mathieu[1]), born 16 Apr 1831 in NY; died 11 Sep 1914. He married on 28 May 1854 in Lenawee, Dover Twp, Lenawee Co., MI Phelina Meyers, born 10 Feb 1838 in Dover Twp, Lenawee Co., MI; died 25 Feb 1904 in Ithaca,Gratiot Co., MI, daughter of John William Meyers and Philena Baker.

Children of Elijah Bovee and Phelina Meyers were as follows:

+ 1486   i   Marion Lysander[7] **Bovee**, born 14 Mar 1855 in MI; died 1 Dec 1913. He married **Lucy M Chalker**.

653. Ezra[6] **Bovee** (Jacob[5], John Henry[4], Matthew[3], Nicholas[2], Mathieu[1]), born 27 Oct 1832 in Cayuga Co., NY; died 16 Nov 1913 in Cheppewa Twp, Isabella Co., MI. He married on 24 Jul 1859 Elizabeth Hamilton, born 25 May 1841; died 9 Nov 1903.

Children of Ezra Bovee and Elizabeth Hamilton were as follows:

1487   i   Leroy Joseph[7] **Bovee**, born 15 May 1860. He married on 4 Jul 1883 in Clayton, Lenawee Co., MI **Lily Ludlum**.

1488   ii   Clarence J[7] **Bovee**, born 20 Apr 1864. He married on 28 Jan 1899 in Marion Co., IN **Flora B West**.

+ 1489   iii   Elmore Mary[7] **Bovee**, born 24 Dec 1867; died 8 Jun 1910. She married **George N Smith**.

1490   iv   Louise[7] **Bovee**, born 18 Dec 1870. She married (1) **Henry**

Chatfield; (2) **Ira Van Doren**.

1491   v   Laura A^7 **Bovee**, born 12 Aug 1873. She married **(---) Grubb**.

654. Albert^6 **Bovee** (Jacob^5, John Henry^4, Matthew^3, Nicholas^2, Mathieu^1), born 7 Mar 1835 in Dover, Lenawee Co., MI; died 11 Jul 1907 in Ithaca,Gratiot Co., MI. He married on 2 Jul 1854 in Dover, Lenawee Co., MI Eliza Jane Meyers, born 18 Oct 1834 in Dover Twp, Lenawee Co., MI; died 15 Jul 1915 in Ashley, Washington Twp, Gratior Co., MI, daughter of John William Meyers and Philena Baker.

Children of Albert Bovee and Eliza Jane Meyers were as follows:

+   1492   i   Lillian^7 **Bovee**, born 25 Jul 1855 in MI; died 1 Mar 1937. She married **Francis Leroy Cook**.

+   1493   ii   Fremont^7 **Bovee**, born 9 Dec 1856 in MI; died 8 Nov 1933. He married **Martha Older**.

+   1494   iii   Virgil Albert^7 **Bovee**, born 27 Sep 1861 in MI; died 1 Aug 1943 in San Diego Co., CA. He married **Bertha Jane Cook**.

   1495   iv   Rubyline^7 **Bovee**, born 8 Feb 1871; died 1938. She married **Lorenzo N Parmenter**.

655. Milo^6 **Bovee** (Jacob^5, John Henry^4, Matthew^3, Nicholas^2, Mathieu^1), born 13 Jan 1837 in Dover, Lenawee Co., MI; died 17 Nov 1903. He married on 27 Apr 1862 in Dover, Lenawee Co., MI Harriet Lucinda Warren, born 15 Aug 1842; died 23 Dec 1905 in Sand Creek, Lenawee Co., MI.

Children of Milo Bovee and Harriet Lucinda Warren were as follows:

+   1496   i   Herbert Warren^7 **Bovee**, born 27 Jul 1867 in Dover, Lenawee Co., MI; died 22 Nov 1936. He married **Mary McFetridge**.

+   1497   ii   Dora Arvilla^7 **Bovee**, born 10 Nov 1868 in Dover, Lenawee Co., MI; died 1944. She married **Frank Bryant**.

+   1498   iii   Cornelius Anson^7 **Bovee**, born 15 Apr 1872 in Dover, Lenawee Co., MI; died 25 Sep 1961. He married **Gertrude Seton Chapelle**.

656. Arthur^6 **Bovee** (Jacob^5, John Henry^4, Matthew^3, Nicholas^2, Mathieu^1), born 10 Oct 1838 in Dover, Lenawee Co., MI; died 18 Feb 1915. He married on 17 Sep 1862 Ester A Cross, born 31 Mar 1841; died 21 Mar 1927.

Children of Arthur Bovee and Ester A Cross were as follows:

+   1499   i   Emma^7 **Bovee**, born 13 Jul 1863 in Dover, Lenawee Co., MI; died 24 Jul 1942. She married **William Shepherd**.

+   1500   ii   Ella L^7 **Bovee**, born 15 Nov 1865 in Dover, Lenawee Co., MI. She married **George H Deline**.

   1501   iii   Carrie Amelia^7 **Bovee**, born 11 Mar 1880; died 23 Apr

1928. She married **Lozell Whaley**.

657. Hamilton[6] **Bovee** (Jacob[5], John Henry[4], Matthew[3], Nicholas[2], Mathieu[1]), born 23 Oct 1840 in Dover, Lenawee Co., MI; died 4 Apr 1919. He married on 12 Sep 1865 Lucina Hamlin, born 14 Jul 1844; died 5 Dec 1926, daughter of Aaron S Hamlin and Maria Rose.

Children of Hamilton Bovee and Lucina Hamlin were as follows:

1502	i	Almond[7] **Bovee**, born 4 Sep 1866; died 22 Jul 1875.
1503	ii	Roswell[7] **Bovee**, born 12 Nov 1869; died 7 Mar 1870.
1504	iii	Hervey[7] **Bovee**, born 3 Feb 1871; died 19 Jul 1875.
1505	iv	Leon[7] **Bovee**, born 9 Jun 1874; died 22 May 1875.
+ 1506	v	Aurilla[7] **Bovee**, born 3 Dec 1876; died 16 Dec 1954. She married **Willis Tracey**.
1507	vi	Ada Marie[7] **Bovee**, born 12 Jan 1880; died 3 Feb 1939. She married on 29 Sep 1901 **Edwin C Belding**.
1508	vii	Child[7] **Bovee**, born 3 Sep 1882; died 12 Dec 1882.
+ 1509	viii	Archie Dell[7] **Bovee**, born 8 Apr 1884 in Gratiot Co., MI; died Jan 1969 in Ithaca, Gratiot Co., MI. He married **Hazel Ellen Greenlee**.
+ 1510	ix	Carl Aaron[7] **Bovee**, born 7 Feb 1888 in Gratiot Co., MI; died 22 Feb 1956. He married **Zora Palmer**.

658. Lucy Ann[6] **Bovee** (Jacob[5], John Henry[4], Matthew[3], Nicholas[2], Mathieu[1]), born 3 Dec 1842; died 6 Jan 1914. She married on 28 Feb 1866 William Steadman, born 29 Mar 1841.

Children of Lucy Ann Bovee and William Steadman were as follows:

1511	i	Vinnie[7] **Steadman**, born 12 Mar 1867.
1512	ii	Marvin[7] **Steadman**, born 20 Oct 1869.
1513	iii	William[7] **Steadman**, born 25 Feb 1879.

659. Myron[6] **Bovee** (Jacob[5], John Henry[4], Matthew[3], Nicholas[2], Mathieu[1]), born Dec 1844 in Dover Twp, Lenawee Co., MI; died 8 Nov 1908 in Ithaca, Gratiot Co., MI. He married on 29 May 1870 in Waverly, Van Buren Co., MI Jane Elizabeth Cleveland, born 19 Nov 1853 in Hannibal, Oswego Co., MI; died 29 Oct 1897 in Ithaca, Gratiot Co., MI, daughter of Henry Cleveland and Elizabeth Bessey.

Children of Myron Bovee and Jane Elizabeth Cleveland were as follows:

+ 1514	i	Earl Eugene[7] **Bovee**, born 19 Jun 1872 in Clinton Co., MI; died 4 Feb 1951 in San Luis Obispo, San Luis Obispo Co., CA. He married (1) **Martha Nora Johnson**; (2) **Maude Fair**.
+ 1515	ii	Cora May[7] **Bovee**, born 29 Oct 1874 in Clayton, Lenawee Co., MI; died Feb 1956. She married **Franklin Delmore Powell**.

+	1516	iii	Orlin Henry[7] **Bovee**, born 1 Aug 1876 in Lenawee Co., MI; died 25 Nov 1973. He married (1) **Elnora Stearns**; (2) **Mazell Stearns**.
	1517	iv	Homer Myron[7] **Bovee**, born 1 Feb 1878 in Lenawee Co., MI; died 29 Oct 1891 in Fulton Twp., Gratiot Co., MI.
+	1518	v	Arthur Jewett[7] **Bovee**, born 30 Jun 1880; died 17 Aug 1953. He married **Marian Christina McInnis**.
+	1519	vi	Addie Elizabeth[7] **Bovee**, born 27 Oct 1882 in Gratiot Co., MI; died 24 Feb 1965 in Gratiot Co., MI. She married **Charles Misenhelder**.
+	1520	vii	Harlow[7] **Bovee**, born 30 Nov 1885 in North Star Twp., Gratiot Co., MI; died 27 Sep 1951. He married (1) **Cora Edna Munson**; (2) **Jessie Murray Sarich**.
+	1521	viii	Ethel Alta[7] **Bovee**, born 21 Nov 1889 in Fulton Center, Gratiot Co., MI; died 5 Nov 1984. She married **Earnest Sorrell**.
+	1522	ix	Vena Imis[7] **Bovee**, born 16 Dec 1893 in Fulton Center, Gratiot Co., MI; died 13 May 1986. She married **John Wesley Ritz**.

660. Ester[6] **Bovee** (Jacob[5], John Henry[4], Matthew[3], Nicholas[2], Mathieu[1]), born 1 Jul 1847; died 23 Feb 1932. She married (1) abt 1866 John Wise, died abt 1968; (2) on 31 Dec 1869 Jacob Hathaway, born 1833; (3) on 12 Aug 1885 Joseph Duerr, born 3 May 1837.

Children of Ester Bovee and John Wise were as follows:

| | 1523 | i | Harvey A[7] **Wise**, born 25 Sep 1867 in Dover, Lenawee Co., MI. |

Children of Ester Bovee and Jacob Hathaway were as follows:

	1524	i	Richard[7] **Hathaway**, born 13 Jul 1869.
	1525	ii	Jeanette[7] **Hathaway**, born 1 Mar 1872.
	1526	iii	Jesse Elwood[7] **Hathaway**, born 13 Mar 1874.
	1527	iv	Ella May[7] **Hathaway**, born 27 Aug 1876.
	1528	v	Lillian[7] **Hathaway**, born 3 Mar 1879.

Children of Ester Bovee and Joseph Duerr were as follows:

| | 1529 | i | Alda[7] **Duerr**, born 16 Jul 1886. |
| | 1530 | ii | Bessie[7] **Duerr**, born 6 Dec 1887. |

661. Hulda[6] **Bovee** (Jacob[5], John Henry[4], Matthew[3], Nicholas[2], Mathieu[1]), born 28 Sep 1848; died 8 May 1936. She married on 6 Jul 1866 David Bordine, born 17 May 1846; died 9 Dec 1929.

Children of Hulda Bovee and David Bordine were as follows:

| | 1531 | i | Flora[7] **Bordine**, born 5 Oct 1867. |

1532   ii   William[7] **Bordine**, born 28 Jan 1869.

1533   iii   Vanora[7] **Bordine**, born 6 Feb 1871.

1534   iv   Effie[7] **Bordine**, born 16 Feb 1874.

1535   v   Allen R[7] **Bordine**, born 7 Jan 1877 in North Star, Gratiot Co., MI.

1536   vi   Martha E[7] **Bordine**, born 20 Feb 1879.

1537   vii   Peter Clyde[7] **Bordine**, born 18 Feb 1882 in North Star, Gratiot Co., MI.

1538   viii   Harry[7] **Bordine**, born 15 Feb 1884.

1539   ix   Child[7] **Bordine**, born 1886; died 1886.

1540   x   Hazel[7] **Bordine**, born 28 Jul 1888.

1541   xi   Donald Merle[7] **Bordine**, born 17 Mar 1891.

662. Elsie[6] **Bovee** (Jacob[5], John Henry[4], Matthew[3], Nicholas[2], Mathieu[1]), born 28 Feb 1851; died 21 Jan 1875. She married on 9 Feb 1869 in Lenawee Co., MI Jerry Thompson, died 1932.

    Children of Elsie Bovee and Jerry Thompson were as follows:

1542   i   Alfred[7] **Thompson**, born abt 1872.

663. Flora Zarepha[6] **Bovee** (Jacob[5], John Henry[4], Matthew[3], Nicholas[2], Mathieu[1]), born 18 Mar 1858 in Tecumseh, Lewanee Co., MI; died 2 Nov 1948. She married on 5 Jan 1877 in Dover Twp, Lenawee Co., MI David Connor, born 25 Dec 1856; died 25 Nov 1940.

    Children of Flora Zarepha Bovee and David Connor were as follows:

1543   i   Florence[7] **Connor**, born 4 Mar 1878.

1544   ii   Fannie[7] **Connor**, born 30 Jul 1879.

1545   iii   Alfred[7] **Connor**.

665. Lodica[6] **Bovee** (Jacob[5], John Henry[4], Matthew[3], Nicholas[2], Mathieu[1]), born 8 Jun 1862; died 10 May 1899. She married on 31 Dec 1881 Edward Decker, born 30 Aug 1856.

    Children of Lodica Bovee and Edward Decker were as follows:

1546   i   Fern Alice[7] **Decker**, born 12 Jul 1885.

1547   ii   Marvel[7] **Decker**.

666. Alda[6] **Bovee** (Jacob[5], John Henry[4], Matthew[3], Nicholas[2], Mathieu[1]), born 17 Sep 1864; died 17 May 1939 in Dover Twp, Lenawee Co., MI. He married (1) on 19 Dec 1889 in Dover Twp, Lenawee Co., MI Eliza Hawkins, born 5 Apr 1869; died 15 Apr 1892; (2) abt 1898 Helen A Lord, born 27 Sep 1867; died 15 Jun 1939.

Children of Alda Bovee and Eliza Hawkins were as follows:

+ 1548 i Echo H[7] **Bovee**, born 15 Apr 1892 in Dover, Lenawee Co., MI; died 29 Oct 1954 in Mt Carmel Hosp, Detroit, Wayne Co., MI. He married **Florence Shattuck**.

Children of Alda Bovee and Helen A Lord were as follows:

+ 1549 i Harold L[7] **Bovee**, born 17 Jan 1900 in Dover Twp., Lenawee Co., MI; died 24 Sep 1953 in Adrian, Lenawee Co., MI. He married **Ruth Barnes**.

667. Oma[6] **Bovee** (Jacob[5], John Henry[4], Matthew[3], Nicholas[2], Mathieu[1]), born 16 Oct 1866; died 20 Sep 1935. He married abt 1890 Harriet Wood, born May 1869 in MI.

Children of Oma Bovee and Harriet Wood were as follows:

1550 i Lena[7] **Bovee**, born Apr 1891.

668. Devillow[6] **Bovee** (Jacob[5], John Henry[4], Matthew[3], Nicholas[2], Mathieu[1]), born 8 Nov 1868 in Lenawee Co., MI; died 16 Nov 1964 in CA. He married abt 1893 Mary Ethel Mayfield.

Children of Devillow Bovee and Mary Ethel Mayfield were as follows:

+ 1551 i Fred Mayfield[7] **Bovee**, born 18 Nov 1895 in Cambria, San Luis Obispo Co., CA; died 4 Jan 1981. He married **Lydia Maxine Dominguez**.

1552 ii Everett Milton[7] **Bovee**, born 8 Aug 1901 in Cambria, San Luis Obispo Co., CA; died Dec 1976 in Atascardero, San Luis Obispo Co., CA.

696. Mary Elizabeth[6] **Bovee** (Abraham[5], John Henry[4], Matthew[3], Nicholas[2], Mathieu[1]), born abt 1840 in Hudson, Lenawee Co., MI. She married on 27 Apr 1859 Edward Hyatt.

Children of Mary Elizabeth Bovee and Edward Hyatt were as follows:

1553 i Arthur[7] **Hyatt**, born abt 1860.

700. Harrison C[6] **Bovee** (Abraham[5], John Henry[4], Matthew[3], Nicholas[2], Mathieu[1]), born 22 Jan 1854. He married on 22 Nov 1883 in Medina Twp , Lenawee Co., MI Almina A Deline, born 1860; died 5 Jan 1887 in Hudson, Lenawee Co., MI.

Children of Harrison C Bovee and Almina A Deline were as follows:

1554 i Ward[7] **Bovee**, born 1885; died 11 Oct 1885 in Clayton, Lenawee Co., MI.

704. James H[6] **Bovee** (Peter[5], John Henry[4], Matthew[3], Nicholas[2], Mathieu[1]), born 5 Nov 1849 in Dover, Lenawee Co., MI. He married Laura Van Pelt, born abt 1858 in IN.

Children of James H Bovee and Laura Van Pelt were as follows:

+ 1555   i   James Byron[7] **Bovee**, born 1879 in Steuben Co., IN; died 1954. He married **Myrtle Mae Collins**.

709. Anna Elizabeth[6] **Bovie** (John E[5], Jacob[4], Abraham[3], Nicholas[2], Mathieu[1]), born aft 1817. She married Thomas Hall.

Children of Anna Elizabeth Bovie and Thomas Hall were as follows:

1556   i   Frances[7] **Hall**, born abt 1845.
1557   ii   Eugene[7] **Hall**, born abt 1846.

710. Chester A[6] **Bovie** (John E[5], Jacob[4], Abraham[3], Nicholas[2], Mathieu[1]), born abt 1822 in NY. He married Julia Ann Chase, born abt 1825, daughter of Edward S Chase and Isabel (---).

Children of Chester A Bovie and Julia Ann Chase were as follows:

+ 1558   i   Edward E[7] **Bovie**, born 1844 in MI; died 15 Sep 1879. He married **Marcie E Richards**.
+ 1559   ii   Clare Byron[7] **Bovie**, born abt 1857 in Kalamazoo, Kalamazoo Co., MI; died 5 Sep 1921 in Milford, Iroquois Co., IL. He married **Jessie Rebecca Merriam**.

713. William T[6] **Bovie** (John E[5], Jacob[4], Abraham[3], Nicholas[2], Mathieu[1]), born abt 1829 in NY; died 25 Apr 1901 in Kalamazoo, Kalamazoo Co., MI. He married (1) Susan Pack; (2) Henrietta Barnes, born Mar 1854 in MI.

Children of William T Bovie and Henrietta Barnes were as follows:

1560   i   Grace[7] **Bovie**, born Aug 1877 in MI; died 1904 in Vicksburg, Kalamazoo Co., MI.
1561   ii   Zella[7] **Bovie**, born 1879 in MI.
+ 1562   iii   William T[7] **Bovie**, born 11 Sep 1882 in Augusta, Kalamazoo Co., MI; died 1 Jan 1958 in Fairfield, Somerset Co., ME. He married **Martha Adams**.
1563   iv   Addie[7] **Bovie**, born 1885 in MI.
1564   v   Clarence A[7] **Bovie**, born 1892; died 22 Sep 1928.

720. George Washington[6] **Bovee** (Isaac[5], Jacob[4], Abraham[3], Nicholas[2], Mathieu[1]), born 4 Oct 1819 in Hoosick, Rensselaer Co., NY; died 28 Apr 1865. He married Martha A Weaver, born abt 1825, daughter of Benjamin Weaver and Sophia (---).

Children of George Washington Bovee and Martha A Weaver were as follows:

1565   i   George Franklin[7] **Bovee**, born 24 Mar 1853; died 21 Sep 1856.

1566   ii   Mary A[7] **Bovee**, born 14 Dec 1854. She married **John Daniel Keefe**.

722. Isaac Warren I[6] **Bovee** (Isaac[5], Jacob[4], Abraham[3], Nicholas[2], Mathieu[1]), born 17 Jan 1824 in Hoosick, Rensselaer Co., NY; died 25 Oct 1891 in Hoosick, Rensselaer Co., NY. He married on 30 Nov 1849 Sarah Minerva Jones, born 7 Jan 1827 in Chester, Warren Co., NY; died 7 Mar 1899, daughter of Lindell J W Jones and Mary Biglow White.

Children of Isaac Warren I Bovee and Sarah Minerva Jones were as follows:

1567   i   Anna Maria[7] **Bovee**, born 1852. She married **John J Brimmer**.

+ 1568   ii   Isaac Warren[7] **Bovee** II, born 26 Jun 1855. He married **Cora Slade**.

1569   iii   Thomas Lindell[7] **Bovee**, born 27 Jul 1858; died bef 1937. He married **Jennie Rising**.

1570   iv   George McClellan[7] **Bovee**, born 17 Dec 1864 in Hoosick, Rensselaer Co., NY.

1571   v   Frank Allen[7] **Bovee**, born 21 Aug 1870; died 21 Jun 1893.

728. Alfred[6] **Bovee** (Jacob[5], Jacob[4], Abraham[3], Nicholas[2], Mathieu[1]), born 1830. He married on 11 Apr 1858 in Bedford St. Meth Ch, New York, New York Co., NY Marian F Gray.

Children of Alfred Bovee and Marian F Gray were as follows:

1572   i   Susie[7] **Bovee**.

+ 1573   ii   Alfred[7] **Bovee** II, born in Hoosick, Rensselaer Co., NY. He married unknown.

1574   iii   Nellie[7] **Bovee**.

1575   iv   Walter[7] **Bovee**.

1576   v   Mabel[7] **Bovee**.

730. Maria Isabella Louise[6] **Bovee** (William G[5], Jacob[4], Abraham[3], Nicholas[2], Mathieu[1]), born 9 Oct 1832 in Rensselaer Co., NY. She married on 7 Jun 1855 John Agan, born 1834 in Hoosick, Rensselaer Co., NY.

Children of Maria Isabella Louise Bovee and John Agan were as follows:

1577   i   Anna Maria[7] **Agan**, born 1857.

1578   ii   Lizzie M[7] **Agan**.

1579   iii   Minnie[7] **Agan**.

1580   iv   Frank[7] **Agan**.

1581　　v　　　James[7] **Agan**.

731. Jacob F W[6] **Bovie** (William G[5], Jacob[4], Abraham[3], Nicholas[2], Mathieu[1]), born 3 May 1836 in Hoosick, Rensselaer Co., NY. He married Margaret Fox, born abt 1840 in Pittstown, Rensselaer Co., NY.

Children of Jacob F W Bovie and Margaret Fox were as follows:

+　1582　i　　　John Jacob[7] **Bovie**, born 28 Apr 1878 in Pittstown, Rensselaer Co, NY; died 12 Nov 1941 in Spokane, Spokane Co., WA. He married **Gertrude Jones**.

　　1583　ii　　WilliamFrancis[7] **Bovie**, born 19 May 1879.

　　1584　iii　　James Thomas[7] **Bovie**, born 10 Aug 1883 in Pittstown, Rensselaer Co, NY; died 28 Aug 1958. He married **Lena M Losey**.

732. Mehitable[6] **Bovee** (Asa[5], Jacob[4], Abraham[3], Nicholas[2], Mathieu[1]), born 2 Oct 1853. She married on 6 Aug 1871 Sanford Carpenter Plass, born 12 Mar 1852; died 28 Oct 1905.

Children of Mehitable Bovee and Sanford Carpenter Plass were as follows:

　　1585　i　　　Cora Mahala[7] **Plass**, born abt 1872 in Mayfield, Fulton Co., NY.

733. Culver Nathaniel[6] **Bovee** (Asa[5], Jacob[4], Abraham[3], Nicholas[2], Mathieu[1]), born 1855; died Sep 1913 in Johnstown, Fulton Co., NY. He married on 27 Oct 1878, divorced Mary Jane Wells, born 1861.

Children of Culver Nathaniel Bovee and Mary Jane Wells were as follows:

　　1586　i　　　William A[7] **Bovee**, born 1880.

　　1587　ii　　Eva[7] **Bovee**. She married **James Orlando Tasbrook**.

　　1588　iii　　Jacob Alexander[7] **Bovee**, born Mar 1884; died 1 Nov 1966. He married (1) on 2 Jun 1907 **Florence Smith**; (2) **Pauline (---)**.

　　1589　iv　　Hazel[7] **Bovee**, born Dec 1891. She married **Mace Evans**.

757. Sarah Livonia[6] **Bovee** (Peter[5], Matthew[4], Abraham[3], Nicholas[2], Mathieu[1]), born 4 Mar 1836 in Harpursville, Broome Co., NY; died 6 May 1895. She married on 5 Aug 1861 Abram Good, born 30 Jan 1835 in Northampton Co., PA; died 1 Feb 1918 in Newberry, Lycoming Co., PA.

Children of Sarah Livonia Bovee and Abram Good were as follows:

　　1590　i　　　Edward Burton[7] **Good**, born 9 Jul 1862 in Newberry, Lycoming Co., PA.

　　1591　ii　　George Grant[7] **Good**, born Nov 1863 in Newberry, Lycoming Co., PA.

1592   iii   Wallace Thomas[7] **Good**, born 11 Jan 1865 in Newberry, Lycoming Co., PA.

1593   iv   Jesse Pearl[7] **Good**, born abt 1870 in Newberry, Lycoming Co., PA.

759. Rodney Mathias[6] **Bovee** (Peter[5], Matthew[4], Abraham[3], Nicholas[2], Mathieu[1]), born 24 Apr 1840 in Colesville, Broome Co., NY; died 19 Jan 1890. He married Loeva Matilda Bovee, born 18 Jul 1850 in NY; died 12 Feb 1928 in Troy, Rensselaer Co., NY.

Children of Rodney Mathias Bovee and Loeva Matilda Bovee were as follows:

1594   i   Bertha[7] **Bovee**, born 9 Dec 1868; died 1929. She married on 11 Aug 1892 **Rollin Judson Hurd**.

1595   ii   Carl G[7] **Bovee**, born 9 Sep 1869 in NY; died 24 Aug 1892.

1596   iii   Walter[7] **Bovee**, born 8 Mar 1871; died 8 Jan 1890.

760. John Oscar[6] **Bovee** (Peter[5], Matthew[4], Abraham[3], Nicholas[2], Mathieu[1]), born 14 Mar 1842 in Colesville, Broome Co., NY; died 28 Jan 1916 in Buffalo, Erie Co., NY. He married (1) on 20 Jun 1867 Catharine Fredericka Fisher, born 8 Mar 1850; died 28 Jan 1874 in Williamsport, Lycoming Co., PA; (2) on 11 Mar 1875 Arvilla Jane Bussler, born 20 Jan 1857 in Newberry, Lycoming Co., PA; died in Williamsport, Lycoming Co., PA.

Children of John Oscar Bovee and Catharine Fredericka Fisher were as follows:

+   1597   i   Grace Gertrude[7] **Bovee**, born 14 Mar 1868 in PA; died 7 Oct 1909. She married **John Lawrence Herman**.

Children of John Oscar Bovee and Arvilla Jane Bussler were as follows:

+   1598   i   David Bussler[7] **Bovee**, born 5 Oct 1876 in Newberry, Lycoming Co., PA; died 1940 in Bolivar, Allegany Co., NY. He married (1) **May Sloan**; (2) **Burdette Fish**.

+   1599   ii   Pearl Lorena[7] **Bovee**, born 8 Jun 1883 in Olean, Cattaraugus Co., NY; died in Berwyn, Cook Co., IL. She married **Raymond Uriah Meyers**.

+   1600   iii   Charles Oscar[7] **Bovee** Sr, born 7 Mar 1891 in Newberry, Lycoming Co., PA; died 3 Feb 1964 in Houston, Harris Co., TX. He married **Lucy Elizabeth Yxera**.

761. George Burton[6] **Bovee** (Peter[5], Matthew[4], Abraham[3], Nicholas[2], Mathieu[1]), born 15 Jun 1844 in Barton, Tioga Co., NY; died 14 Dec 1912 in Hepburn Town, Lycoming Co., PA. He married on 5 Jun 1866 in Williamsport, Lycoming Co., PA Sarah Elizabeth Ball, born 16 Dec 1846 in Hepburnville, Lycoming Co., PA; died 15 Jan 1928 in Hepburnville, Lycoming Co., PA.

Children of George Burton Bovee and Sarah Elizabeth Ball were as follows:

+ 1601 i Alice Estella[7] **Bovee**, born 31 Mar 1867 in Hepburnville, Lycoming Co., PA. She married **David Augustus Edler**.

+ 1602 ii Samuel Ball[7] **Bovee**, born 29 Jul 1869 in Hepburnville, Lycoming Co., PA; died 2 Jan 1916. He married **Sarah Catherine Blair**.

+ 1603 iii Burton Raymond[7] **Bovee**, born 28 Jun 1872 in Hepburnville, Lycoming Co., PA. He married **Katherine Jane Snyder**.

+ 1604 iv Ervin Emerson Edward[7] **Bovee**, born 20 Jun 1878 in PA; died 17 Aug 1945 in San Bernardino, San Bernardino Co., CA. He married **Edna E Litz**.

762. Perry Henry[6] **Bovee** (Peter[5], Matthew[4], Abraham[3], Nicholas[2], Mathieu[1]), born 27 Apr 1848 in Owego, Tioga Co., NY; died 22 Oct 1928 in Newberry, Lycoming Co., PA. He married on 12 Jan 1871 in Hepburnville, Lycoming Co., PA Ann Elizabeth Patterson, born 5 Jan 1851 in Selinsgrove, Snyder Co., PA.

Children of Perry Henry Bovee and Ann Elizabeth Patterson were as follows:

+ 1605 i Lemon Peter[7] **Bovee**, born 28 Oct 1871 in Newberry, Lycoming Co., PA; died 1928. He married (1) **Mildred Kyler**; (2) **Catherine Louise Owens**.

1606 ii Josephine Good[7] **Bovee**, born 29 Aug 1873 in PA; died 1 Jun 1895.

+ 1607 iii George Gregg[7] **Bovee**, born 16 Jun 1875 in Newberry, Lycoming Co., PA. He married **Maud Delilah Love**.

+ 1608 iv Gertrude Grace[7] **Bovee**, born 27 Sep 1877 in Newberry, Lycoming Co., PA. She married **Charles Eugene Alden**.

+ 1609 v Blanche[7] **Bovee**, born 2 Jan 1880 in PA. She married **Archibald Miller Hoagland**.

1610 vi Guy Patterson[7] **Bovee**, born 9 Sep 1881 in Newberry, Lycoming Co., PA; died 5 Aug 1883.

+ 1611 vii Luther Martin[7] **Bovee**, born 18 Oct 1883 in Newberry, Lycoming Co., PA. He married **Elsie May Grimsley**.

1612 viii Ruth[7] **Bovee**, born 30 Apr 1886 in Newberry, Lycoming Co., PA; died 18 Sep 1891.

+ 1613 ix Perry Graham[7] **Bovee**, born 29 Apr 1889 in Newberry, Lycoming Co., PA; died 25 Jul 1917. He married (1) **Mabel (---)**; (2) **Grace (---)**.

763. Walter Haywood[6] **Bovee** (Peter[5], Matthew[4], Abraham[3], Nicholas[2], Mathieu[1]), born 13 Feb 1853 in Tioga, Tioga Co., NY. He married Emma Frances Morris, born 4 Jul 1858.

Children of Walter Haywood Bovee and Emma Frances Morris were as follows:

1614 i Oscar L[7] **Bovee**, born 8 Apr 1877 in Sundbury, Northumberland Co., PA; died 10 Jul 1878.

+ 1615 ii Lottie May[7] **Bovee**, born 31 Aug 1879 in Sundbury, Northumberland Co., PA. She married **Harry James Lincoln**.

+ 1616 iii Eva Lee[7] **Bovee**, born 2 Apr 1881 in Sundbury, Northumberland Co., PA. She married **Lionelle Hornberger**.

+ 1617 iv Alva Davis[7] **Bovee**, born 21 Jun 1886 in Newberry, Lycoming Co., PA. He married **Florence Wheeler**.

+ 1618 v Lulu Hartman[7] **Bovee**, born 25 Nov 1889 in Newberry, Lycoming Co., PA. She married **William Edward Young**.

1619 vi Chester Peter[7] **Bovee**, born 18 Feb 1891 in Williamsport, Lycoming Co., PA; died 18 Jul 1900.

+ 1620 vii LeRoy George[7] **Bovee**, born 1 Dec 1895; died in Phoenix, Maricopa Co., AZ. He married (1) **Rita E Smith**; (2) **Oleta Alberta Kern**.

785. Melissa[6] **Bovee** (Orrin Primmer[5], John[4], Abraham[3], Nicholas[2], Mathieu[1]), born abt 1842 in MI. She married (1) on 19 Sep 1863 in Ionia Co., MI Lock V Mosher, born abt 1833 in MI; (2) (---) Emery.

Children of Melissa Bovee and Lock V Mosher were as follows:

1621 i Walter[7] **Mosher**, born abt 1866 in MI.

1622 ii Belle[7] **Mosher**, born abt 1872 in MI.

788. George Walker[6] **Bovee** (Orrin Primmer[5], John[4], Abraham[3], Nicholas[2], Mathieu[1]), born 5 Jan 1866 in MI; died 18 May 1964. He married in 1899 Anna Smith, born 15 Dec 1868 in MI; died 19 Aug 1952.

Children of George Walker Bovee and Anna Smith were as follows:

1623 i Mark Leon[7] **Bovee**, born 20 Dec 1899 in Newton Twp., Calhoun Co., MI; died 17 Aug 1990 in Bedford, Calhoun Co., MI. He married **Eva Olena Nelson**, born 1902; died 1974 in MI.

789. Mark Orin[6] **Bovee** (Orrin Primmer[5], John[4], Abraham[3], Nicholas[2], Mathieu[1]), born 18 Jul 1868 in MI; died 15 Jul 1960 in Los Angeles Co., CA. He married Minnie Standen, born 29 Apr 1868 in OH; died 23 Nov 1951 in Los Angeles, Los Angeles Co., CA.

Children of Mark Orin Bovee and Minnie Standen were as follows:

1624 i Lois[7] **Bovee**, born 17 Apr 1901 in IN; died 10 May 1982 in Santa Barbara, Santa Barbara Co., CA. She married **(---) Proud**.

1625 ii Robert Standen[7] **Bovee**, born 13 Jun 1905 in OH; died 30 Jul 1986 in Seal Beach, Orange Co., CA. He married **Olivia (---)**.

1626   iii   Mark[7] **Bovee**, born abt 1916 in OH.

790. Wright Ingraham[6] **Bovee** (Orrin Primmer[5], John[4], Abraham[3], Nicholas[2], Mathieu[1]), born 18 Aug 1871 in MI; died 11 Feb 1966 in Stanislaus Co., CA. He married Ethel Paulina Harrison, born 12 Sep 1875 in MN; died 6 Jun 1958 in Modesto, Stanislaus Co., CA.

Children of Wright Ingraham Bovee and Ethel Paulina Harrison were as follows:

+   1627   i   Donald Wright[7] **Bovee**, born Mar 1900 in Calhoun Co., MI. He married **(---) Wortinger**.
     1628   ii   Dorothy M[7] **Bovee**, born 16 May 1913 in CA; died 15 Jun 1981 in Stanislau Co., CA. She married **(---) Hopcraft**.

809. George C[6] **Bovee** (Cornelius[5], Abraham[4], Abraham[3], Nicholas[2], Mathieu[1]), born 22 May 1833 in Madison Co., NY; died 20 Sep 1915 in Bath, Steuben Co., NY. He married abt 1855 in Jasper, Steuben Co., NY Lavina Jackson, born 1829; died 15 Jul 1886 in Groveland, Livingston Co., NY, daughter of Isaac Jackson and Mary Ann (---).

Children of George C Bovee and Lavina Jackson were as follows:

     1629   i   Mary[7] **Bovee**, born 1857. She married **(---) Bell**.
     1630   ii   William[7] **Bovee**, born 1859; died abt 1859.
     1631   iii   Orro[7] **Bovee**, born abt 1864; died aft 1870.
     1632   iv   Henry[7] **Bovee**, born Mar 1866 in NY; died 9 Feb 1908 in Groveland, Livingston Co., NY.
     1633   v   Margaret[7] **Bovee**, born Jun 1870; died abt 1870.
     1634   vi   Edna[7] **Bovee**, born 1873. She married **(---) Yodey**.
     1635   vii   Frances E[7] **Bovee**, born May 1876. She married **Harry Penney**.
     1636   viii   Cornelia[7] **Bovee**, born Nov 1878 in NY. She married **(---) Henry**.
     1637   ix   Child[7] **Bovee**, died bef 1900.

810. Lucinda[6] **Bovee** (Cornelius[5], Abraham[4], Abraham[3], Nicholas[2], Mathieu[1]), born 1835 in Steuben Co., NY. She married (1) in Steuben Co., NY Solomon Brownell; (2) in Steuben Co., NY Harry J Vaughn, born 1816 in RI.

Children of Lucinda Bovee and Solomon Brownell were as follows:

     1638   i   Dellu[7] **Brownell**, born 1855.
     1639   ii   Cornelius[7] **Brownell**, born 1857.
     1640   iii   James[7] **Brownell**, born 1860.

811. John W[6] **Bovee** (Cornelius[5], Abraham[4], Abraham[3], Nicholas[2], Mathieu[1]),

born 18 Oct 1836 in Canisteo, Steuben Co., NY; died 4 Apr 1915 in Addison, Steuben Co., NY. He married (1) abt 1857 in Steuben Co., NY Margaret Lucina Jackson, born 1841 in NY; died 8 Apr 1864 in Groveland, Livingston Co., NY, daughter of Isaac Jackson and Mary Ann (---); (2) on 10 Aug 1865 in Bath, Steuben Co., NY Amanda Jackson, born 16 May 1842 in NY; died 30 May 1923 in Mt Morris, Livingston Co., NY, daughter of Isaac Jackson and Mary Ann (---).

Children of John W Bovee and Margaret Lucina Jackson were as follows:

1641	i	Ida **Bovee**[7], born 1858.
1642	ii	Lydia **Bovee**[7], born Jun 1860 in NY.
1643	iii	Josephine **Bovee**[7], born abt 1860 in NY. She married **Samuel Stewart**.
+ 1644	iv	John W **Bovee**[7], born 16 Dec 1861 in Groveland, Livingston Co., NY; died 1943 in NY. He married **Martha Fleck**.

Children of John W Bovee and Amanda Jackson were as follows:

1645	i	Victor **Bovee**[7], born Apr 1867 in NY; died 30 May 1922 in NY.
+ 1646	ii	Frederick **Bovee**[7], born Apr 1867 in NY; died 1934 in NY. He married **Jennie Van Valkenberg**.
1647	iii	Sylvenis **Bovee**[7], born 1869 in NY; died bef 1880 in NY.
1648	iv	Ella **Bovee**[7], born Nov 1872 in Groveland, Livingston Co., NY; died 21 May 1875 in Groveland, Livingston Co., NY.
1649	v	Emmett **Bovee**[7], born Nov 1872 in Groveland, Livingston Co., NY.
1650	vi	Orvilla **Bovee**[7], born Aug 1874 in NY. She married in Nov 1900 in Groveland, Livingston Co., NY **Daniel Coleman**.
1651	vii	Charles **Bovee**[7], born 1877 in Groveland, Livingston Co., NY.
1652	viii	Ann **Bovee**[7], born 1879 in Groveland, Livingston Co., NY. She married on 12 Oct 1899 in Mt Morris, Livingston Co., NY ? (---).
1653	ix	Scott **Bovee**[7], born Aug 1880 in Groveland, Livingston Co., NY.
1654	x	Franklin **Bovee**[7], born Apr 1883 in Groveland, Livingston Co., NY.
1655	xi	Charlotte **Bovee**[7], born May 1884 in NY.

812. Lydia E[6] **Bovee** (Cornelius[5], Abraham[4], Abraham[3], Nicholas[2], Mathieu[1]), born 6 Sep 1840 in Addison, Steuben Co., NY. She married William Paul Barker, born 22 Aug 1837 in Thurston, Steuben Co., NY, son of John Barker and Sarah Ann Watts.

Children of Lydia E Bovee and William Paul Barker were as follows:

1656	i	Charles H **Barker**[7].
1657	ii	William L **Barker**[7].

119

1658	iii	Fannie J[7] **Barker**.

1658	iii	Fannie J[7] **Barker**.
1659	iv	John W[7] **Barker**.
1660	v	Margaret E[7] **Barker**.
1661	vi	Sarah L[7] **Barker**.

814. Henry M[6] **Bovee** (Cornelius[5], Abraham[4], Abraham[3], Nicholas[2], Mathieu[1]), born 1847 in Canisteo, Steuben Co., NY; christened 27 Apr 1895 in St Peter's Episcopal Ch, Dansville, Steuben Co., NY; died 11 Oct 1901 in Oakland, Livingston Co., NY. He married on 3 May 1871 in Addison, Steuben Co., NY Laura Ann Barker, born 7 Jan 1854 in T/Thurston, Steuben Co., NY; christened 27 Apr 1895 in St Peter's Episcopal Ch, Dansville, Steuben Co., NY; died 9 Jul 1932 in Hornell, Steuben Co., NY, daughter of John Barker and Sarah Ann Watts.

Children of Henry M Bovee and Laura Ann Barker were as follows:

	1662	i	Oscar Milton[7] **Bovee**, born 19 Nov 1872 in Cameron, Steuben Co., NY; died 18 Jul 1932 in Hornell, Steuben Co., NY. He married in Steuben Co., NY **Elizabeth IOne**.
+	1663	ii	Clara Leone[7] **Bovee**, born 31 Jan 1874 in Rathbone, Steuben Co., NY; christened 27 Apr 1895 in St Peter's Episcopal Ch, Dansville, Steuben Co., NY. She married **William James Jackson**.
	1664	iii	George Otto[7] **Bovee**, born 25 Apr 1876 in Rathbone, Steuben Co., NY; christened 1 Feb 1891 in St Peter's Episcopal Ch, Dansville, Steuben Co., NY; died Dec 1910. He married on 1 Dec 1906 in Painted Post, Steuben Co., NY **Mabel Chart**.
	1665	iv	Henry M[7] **Bovee**, born abt 1879 in NY.
	1666	v	Charles Clinton[7] **Bovee**, born 22 Mar 1881; christened 27 Apr 1895 in St Peter's Episcopal Ch, Dansville, Steuben Co., NY.
+	1667	vi	Jesse Clayton[7] **Bovee**, born 29 Nov 1882 in Portville, Cattaraugus Co., NY; christened 27 Apr 1895 in St Peter's Episcopal Ch, Dansville, Steuben Co., NY; died 3 Aug 1962 in Hornell, Steuben Co., NY. He married **Dora Elva Welch**.
+	1668	vii	Mabel Melvina[7] **Bovee**, born 17 Jul 1888 in Rathbone, Steuben Co., NY; christened 27 Apr 1895 in St Peter's Episcopal Ch, Dansville, Steuben Co., NY; died 1962 in Hornell, Steuben Co., NY. She married (1) **Bert Angel**; (2) **Samuel L Bickford**.
+	1669	viii	Laura Bonabel[7] **Bovee**, born 7 Jan 1890 in Groveland, Livingston Co., NY; christened 27 Apr 1895 in St Peter's Episcopal Ch, Dansville, Steuben Co., NY. She married **Dorr Lieb**.
	1670	ix	Margaret Ethel[7] **Bovee**, born 27 May 1892 in Dansville, Steuben Co., NY; christened 27 Apr 1895 in St Peter's Episcopal Ch, Dansville, Steuben Co., NY; died 1925 in Hornell, Steuben Co., NY. She married (1) in Hornell,

Steuben Co., NY **Lewis Turck**; (2) in Hornell, Steuben Co., NY **Harry Conover**.

+ 1671 x Edith Mildred[7] **Bovee**, born 29 Dec 1894 in Dansville, Steuben Co., NY; christened 27 Apr 1895 in St Peter's Episcopal Ch, Dansville, Steuben Co., NY; died 1948 in Portville, Cattaraugus Co., NY. She married **Clyde G Bridenbaker**.

+ 1672 xi Earl Erwin[7] **Bovee**, born 22 Nov 1898 in Short Tract, Allegany Co., NY; died in Hornell, Steuben Co., NY. He married **Minnie Smith**.

816. William R[6] **Bovee** (Abraham[5], Abraham[4], Abraham[3], Nicholas[2], Mathieu[1]), born 18 Dec 1840 in Madison Co., NY; died 4 Dec 1908 in Manawa, Waupaca Co., WI. He married Mary Louisa Bruyette, born 1 Jul 1847 in Canada; died 3 Jun 1891 in Manawa, Waupaca Co., WI, daughter of William Bruyette.

Children of William R Bovee and Mary Louisa Bruyette were as follows:

1673 i Frederick[7] **Bovee**, born 1865 in Calumet Co., WI; died 6 Dec 1934.

+ 1674 ii George William[7] **Bovee**, born 17 Feb 1868 in Oshkosh, Winnebago Co., WI; died 6 Dec 1934 in Manawa, Waupaca Co., WI. He married **Olive M Bozile**.

+ 1675 iii Arthur Vernon[7] **Bovee**, born 13 Feb 1871 in Oshkosh, Winnebago Co., WI; died 13 Apr 1939 in Manawa, Waupaca Co., WI. He married **Augusta Ernestina Ferg**.

1676 iv Lester W[7] **Bovee**, born 1876 in WI; died 31 Jan 1958 in Manawa, Waupaca Co., WI.

1677 v Cora[7] **Bovee**, born 1878 in WI.

+ 1678 vi Maude[7] **Bovee**, born 7 Jun 1881 in Manawa, Waupaca Co., WI. She married **Avery J Baldwin**.

1679 vii Blanche[7] **Bovee**, born 7 Jun 1881 in Manawa, Waupaca Co., WI. She married **William Kashur**.

819. Rachel Mary[6] **Bovee** (Abraham[5], Abraham[4], Abraham[3], Nicholas[2], Mathieu[1]), born 1846 in Madison Co., NY. She married on 27 Mar 1869 in Calumet Co., WI Benneryer Fry Rice, born abt 1828 in VT, son of Amos Rice and Lovena (---).

Children of Rachel Mary Bovee and Benneryer Fry Rice were as follows:

1680 i Otto[7] **Rice**, born abt 1870 in WI.

1681 ii Rufus[7] **Rice**, born abt 1871 in WI.

1682 iii Lovina[7] **Rice**, born abt 1873 in WI.

1683 iv Guy[7] **Rice**, born abt 1876 in WI.

1684 v Peter[7] **Rice**, born abt 1878.

1685 vi Truman[7] **Rice**, born abt 1879 in WI.

820. Marsha[6] **Bovee** (Abraham[5], Abraham[4], Abraham[3], Nicholas[2], Mathieu[1]), born 18 Dec 1846 in Lenox, Madison Co., NY; died aft 1924. She married on 21 Nov 1865 in Stockbridge, Calumet Co., WI John Hubbard, born abt 1843 in NY.

Children of Marsha Bovee and John Hubbard were as follows:

1686   i   Viola[7] **Hubbard**, born abt 1867 in Calumet Co., WI.

1687   ii   Carrie[7] **Hubbard**, born abt 1870 in Calumet Co., WI.

1688   iii   Charles Minard[7] **Hubbard**, born 20 Sep 1871 in Calumet Co., WI.

1689   iv   Pearl[7] **Hubbard**, born abt 1873 in Calumet Co., WI.

1690   v   Orrin[7] **Hubbard**, born abt 1876 in Calumet Co., WI.

1691   vi   John[7] **Hubbard**, born abt 1879 in Calumet Co., WI.

1692   vii   Matilda Violet[7] **Hubbard**, born 15 Jul 1885 in Deerbrook, Langlade Co., WI; died 25 Jul 1965 in Doering, Lincoln Co., WI.

1693   viii   Bernice[7] **Hubbard**.

1694   ix   Marsha[7] **Hubbard**, born 10 Jan 1892 in WI.

821. Sarah Jane[6] **Bovee** (Abraham[5], Abraham[4], Abraham[3], Nicholas[2], Mathieu[1]), born 1849 in Madison Co., NY. She married on 20 Feb 1866 in Stockbridge, Calumet Co., WI Soloman Youmans, son of John Youmans and Olive (---).

Children of Sarah Jane Bovee and Soloman Youmans were as follows:

1695   i   Ida[7] **Youmans**, born 1866 in WI; died 1866 in WI (stillborn).

1696   ii   Olive[7] **Youmans**, born 1867 in WI.

1697   iii   Adolph[7] **Youmans**, born 1869 in WI.

822. Minard[6] **Bovee** (Abraham[5], Abraham[4], Abraham[3], Nicholas[2], Mathieu[1]), born 1851 in Lenox, Madison Co., NY; died 24 Mar 1929 in New London, Waupaca Co., WI. He married on 1 Jan 1877 in Stockbridge, Calumet Co., WI Mararetha Ann Martin, born 8 Dec 1859 in Sheboygan Co., WI; died 3 Jan 1922 in Manawa, Waupaca Co., WI, daughter of John Martin and Maggie (---).

Children of Minard Bovee and Mararetha Ann Martin were as follows:

+ 1698   i   George Lewis[7] **Bovee**, born 9 May 1879 in Stockbridge, Calumet Co., WI; died Jul 1963. He married **Mabel A Mallory**.

1699   ii   Ethyle Mary[7] **Bovee**, born 1882 in Waupaca Co., WI; died bef 1974 in New London, Waupaca Co., WI. She married on 25 Nov 1909 in New London, Waupaca Co., WI **Levi C Larson**.

1700   iii   John William Edward[7] **Bovee**, born 9 Oct 1883 in Manawa, Waupaca Co., WI; died bef 1974 in Oshkosh, Winnebago Co., WI. He married on 20 Apr 1906 in Oshkosh, Winnebago Co., WI **Emma Rasmussen**, daughter of Peter Rasmussen and Annie Knudson.

1701   iv   Edwith Walker[7] **Bovee**, born 23 Oct 1885 in Manawa, Waupaca Co., WI; died 31 Jan 1887 in Waupaca Co., WI.

1702   v   Anna Laura[7] **Bovee**, born 23 Mar 1888 in T/Union, Waupaca Co., WI; died bef 1974 in Clintonville, Waupaca Co., WI. She married on 22 Mar 1922 in Clintonville, Waupaca Co., WI **Austin H Decker**.

1703   vi   Mary Florence[7] **Bovee**, born 9 May 1890 in Manawa, Waupaca Co., WI; died 3 Nov 1890 in Manawa, Waupaca Co., WI.

1704   vii   Herbert H[7] **Bovee**, born 20 Dec 1891 in Manawa, Waupaca Co., WI; died 16 Dec 1957 in Waukesha Co., WI. He married in 1923 in Gogebic Co., MI **Ella Ann Frederick**.

+   1705   viii   Howard Norman[7] **Bovee**, born 7 Jan 1898 in Manawa, Waupaca Co., WI; died 1974 in Clintonville, Waupaca Co., WI. He married **Linda Henrietta Helms**.

1706   ix   Clyde M[7] **Bovee**, born 15 Sep 1900 in WI; died Jun 1976 in Milwaukee, Milwaukee Co., WI.

823. Abraham[6] **Bovee** (Abraham[5], Abraham[4], Abraham[3], Nicholas[2], Mathieu[1]), born 15 Sep 1852 in Stockbridge, Calumet Co., WI; died 24 Feb 1911 in Antigo, Langlade Co., WI. He married on 1 Nov 1880 in M E Church, Brant, Calumet Co., WI Mary A Corrigan, born 27 Apr 1857 in Antigo, Langlade Co., WI; died 25 May 1928 in Antigo, Langlade Co., WI, daughter of James Corrigan and Ellen (---).

Children of Abraham Bovee and Mary A Corrigan were as follows:

+   1707   i   Ella Rose[7] **Bovee**, born 26 Aug 1881 in New London, Waupaca Co., WI; died 18 Mar 1965. She married **Martin Elliot**.

+   1708   ii   Michael James[7] **Bovee**, born 27 Apr 1883; died 23 Mar 1976 in Antigo, Langlade Co., WI. He married **Frances Marciniak**.

+   1709   iii   John Byron[7] **Bovee**, born 18 Feb 1885 in Langlade Co., WI; died 3 Oct 1960 in Antigo, Langlade Co., WI. He married **Mabel J Gould**.

1710   iv   Alford[7] **Bovee**, born 1889; died 1891.

1711   v   Ethel[7] **Bovee**, born 1892; died 1892.

+   1712   vi   Marie Pearl[7] **Bovee**, born 27 Apr 1897 in Antigo, Langlade Co., WI; died 31 Jul 1983. She married **Thomas J McGoff**.

824. Erastus[6] **Bovee** (Abraham[5], Abraham[4], Abraham[3], Nicholas[2], Mathieu[1]), born 23 Jul 1854 in Stockbridge, Calumet Co., WI; died 2 Feb 1938 in Appleton, Outagamie Co., WI. He married (1) on 23 Apr 1878 in Hilbert Junction, Calumet Co., WI Joanna Corrigan, born 20 Mar 1857 in Quebec, Canda; died 23 Mar 1902, daughter of James Corrigan and Ellen (---); (2) on 21 Oct 1903 in Antigo

Evangelic Ch, Antigo, Langlade Co., WI Corina Jergenson.

Children of Erastus Bovee and Joanna Corrigan were as follows:

+   1713   i   William H^7 **Bovee**, born May 1880 in WI; died abt 1908. He married **Emma (---)**.

     1714   ii   John C^7 **Bovee**, born Nov 1881 in WI. He married **Wilda E (---)**, born abt 1886.

+   1715   iii   Clarence Abraham^7 **Bovee**, born 28 Sep 1883 in WI; died 5 Jul 1960. He married **Odela Luckow**.

+   1716   iv   Edward C^7 **Bovee**, born 25 Dec 1890 in Antigo, Langlade Co., WI; died 28 Aug 1961. He married **Hazel Thisdale**.

     1717   v   Chester J^7 **Bovee**, born 21 Jan 1892 in WI; died Aug 1963.

     1718   vi   Child^7 **Bovee**.

     1719   vii   Child^7 **Bovee**.

825. Frances^6 **Bovee** (Abraham^5, Abraham^4, Abraham^3, Nicholas^2, Mathieu^1), born abt 1859 in WI. She married Melbourne Bessey, born abt 1858 in Clinton Co., NY.

Children of Frances Bovee and Melbourne Bessey were as follows:

     1720   i   Evelyn J^7 **Bessey**, born 24 Nov 1897 in Lincoln Co., WI..

826. Adelia^6 **Bovee** (Frederick Brown^5, Abraham^4, Abraham^3, Nicholas^2, Mathieu^1), born 2 Oct 1837 in NY; died 9 Apr 1871 in Stockbridge, Calumet Co., WI. She married on 16 Nov 1857 in Stockbridge, Calumet Co., WI Lewis Solomon Myrick, born 24 Nov 1832 in Adams, Jefferson Co., NY; died 22 Oct 1905 in West Bend, Washington Co., WI, son of Soloman Myrick.

Children of Adelia Bovee and Lewis Solomon Myrick were as follows:

     1721   i   Willis E^7 **Myrick**, born 24 Dec 1859 in Stockbridge,Calumet Co., WI.

     1722   ii   Eva A^7 **Myrick**, born 22 Oct 1864 in Stockbridge,Calumet Co., WI; died 27 Sep 1938 in Chilton, Calumet Co., WI.

     1723   iii   Lulu N^7 **Myrick**, born 24 Dec 1868 in Stockbridge,Calumet Co., WI.

828. William Edgar^6 **Bovee** (Frederick Brown^5, Abraham^4, Abraham^3, Nicholas^2, Mathieu^1), born 17 Jun 1844 in Madison Co., NY; died 14 Apr 1914 in Fond du Lac, Fond du Lac Co., WI. He married on 24 Dec 1867 in Stockbridge, Calumet Co., WI Mary Elizabeth Leathart, born 26 Oct 1847 in Brooklyn, Kings Co., NY; died 31 Aug 1913 in Stockbridge, Calumet Co., WI, daughter of William Leathart and Catherine King.

Children of William Edgar Bovee and Mary Elizabeth Leathart were as follows:

+	1724	i	Bertha Antionete[7] **Bovee**, born 22 Dec 1872 in Stockbridge, Calumet Co., WI; died 22 Sep 1971 in Stockbridge, Calumet Co., WI. She married **Warren Bruce Millar**.
	1725	ii	George Frederick[7] **Bovee**, born Oct 1874 in Stockbridge, Calumet Co., WI; died 1879 in Stockbridge, Calumet Co., WI.
+	1726	iii	Lotta May[7] **Bovee**, born 25 Jun 1876 in Stockbridge, Calumet Co., WI; died abt 1962. She married **Arthur Floyd Dutcher**.
	1727	iv	Zaidee Isabel[7] **Bovee**, born 9 Feb 1881 in Stockbridge, Calumet Co., WI; died 1912 in Stockbridge, Calumet Co., WI.

829. Angelica[6] **Bovee** (Frederick Brown[5], Abraham[4], Abraham[3], Nicholas[2], Mathieu[1]), born 1849 in Madison Co., NY; died in Stockbridge, Calumet Co., WI. She married on 6 Jul 1866 in Stockbridge, Calumet Co., WI Seth Stone, born Jan 1843 in Stockbridge,Calumet Co., WI; died in Stockbridge,Calumet Co., WI.

Children of Angelica Bovee and Seth Stone were as follows:

	1728	i	Irving G[7] **Stone**, born abt 1867 in WI.
	1729	ii	Mabel[7] **Stone**, born Sep 1878 in WI.

830. Ervin[6] **Bovee** (Frederick Brown[5], Abraham[4], Abraham[3], Nicholas[2], Mathieu[1]), born 26 Feb 1851 in Madison Co., NY; died 12 Jun 1928 in Stockbridge, Calumet Co., WI. He married (1) on 17 Jun 1875 in Stockbridge, Calumet Co., WI, divorced Rose Griffith, died in Stockbridge, Calumet Co., WI; (2) in Stockbridge, Calumet Co., WI Antionette Dailey, born 24 Apr 1851 in Charles City, Floyd Co., IA; died 30 Mar 1915 in Stockbridge, Calumet Co., WI.

Children of Ervin Bovee and Rose Griffith were as follows:

+	1730	i	Albert[7] **Bovee**, born 4 Dec 1892 in MO; died May 1971 in Concord, Merrimac Co., NH. He married **Elizabeth Heberlein**.
	1731	ii	Olive A[7] **Bovee**, born abt 1902 in WI; died in Chilton, Calumet Co., WI. She married on 14 Apr 1925 in Chilton, Calumet Co., WI **Paul F Schneider**, son of John Schneider and Johanna Weisbriegh.

840. Andrew Jackson[6] **Bovee** (Henry[5], Abraham[4], Abraham[3], Nicholas[2], Mathieu[1]), born 26 Jul 1848 in Madison Co., NY; died 14 Oct 1912 in Lawrence, Whatcom Co., WA. He married (1) on 12 Mar 1869 in Chilton, Calumet Co., WI Sevilla R Baldock, born abt 1850 in Calumet Co., WI; died Apr 1876 in Calumet Co., WI, daughter of Edward Baldock and Rose (---); (2) on 11 Feb 1877 in T/Union, Dodge Co., WI Sophia Minor, born 4 Jul 1842 in Milwaukee, Milwaukee Co., WI; died 13 Dec 1885 in Waupac Co., WI, daughter of John Minor and Frances (---); (3) on 13 Sep 1886 in Antigo, Langlade Co., WI Phoebe Tenney,

born 27 Jan 1866 in Buckhannon, Upshur Co.,WV; died 9 Apr 1934 in Buchanan, Berrien Co., MI, daughter of John Nicholas Tenney and Rachel DeMoss.

Children of Andrew Jackson Bovee and Sevilla R Baldock were as follows:

1732　i　Della[7] **Bovee**, born abt 1870 in Stockbridge, Calumet Co., WI; died abt 1960. She married **Carl Landis**.

Children of Andrew Jackson Bovee and Phoebe Tenney were as follows:

+ 1733　i　Andrew Jackson[7] **Bovee** Jr, born 23 Jul 1887 in Antigo, Langlade Co., WI; died 5 Nov 1918 in St Paul, Ramsey Co., MN. He married **Edith Tenney**.

+ 1734　ii　Jesse Arthur[7] **Bovee**, born 9 Oct 1889 in Antigo, Langlade Co., WI; died 18 Sep 1946 in St Paul, Ramsey Co., MN. He married (1) **Attie Anne Victoria Nelson**; (2) **Gertrude Caroline Fitzpatrick**.

+ 1735　iii　Nellie Elizabeth[7] **Bovee**, born 9 Oct 1892 in Antigo, Langlade Co., WI; died 13 Jun 1965. She married (1) **Clarence J Leen**; (2) unknown.

1736　iv　Henry Gordon[7] **Bovee**, born 6 Apr 1894 in Antigo, Langlade Co., WI; died 5 Feb 1973 in Helena, Lewis & Clark Co., MT. He married in Nov 1934 **Lela King**.

+ 1737　v　Isabel Louise[7] **Bovee**, born 3 Jun 1897 in Antigo, Langlade Co., WI; died 1 Jul 1986 in Olympia, Thurston Co., WA. She married (1) **Jesse P Gooding**; (2) **Frank George Starring**.

842. Matilda E[6] **Bovee** (Henry[5], Abraham[4], Abraham[3], Nicholas[2], Mathieu[1]), born 16 Sep 1854 in Stockbridge, Calumet Co., WI; died aft 1936 in Battle Creek, Calhoun Co., MI. She married (1) on 30 Nov 1876 in Chilton, Calumet Co., WI Calvin U Tracy, son of Charles F Tracy and Nancy L (---); (2) on 8 May 1887 in Ackley Twp, Langlade Co., WI Nathan DeMoss, born Dec 1847 in Buckhannon, Upshur Co., WV, son of Charles DeMoss and Elizabeth Spurgeon.

Children of Matilda E Bovee and Calvin U Tracy were as follows:

1738　i　Helen[7] **Tracy**, died in Owosso, Shiawassee Co., MI.

Children of Matilda E Bovee and Nathan DeMoss were as follows:

1739　i　George Arthur[7] **DeMoss**, born 6 Oct 1889; died in Ackley Twp., Langlade Co., WI.

1740　ii　Myrtle Ione[7] **DeMoss**, born 1 Aug 1892.

843. Warren Henry[6] **Bovee** (Henry[5], Abraham[4], Abraham[3], Nicholas[2], Mathieu[1]), born 20 Mar 1858 in Calumet Co., WI; died 22 Aug 1922 in Spooner, Washburn Co., WI. He married on 5 Nov 1878 in Stockbridge, Calumet Co., WI Rosalie Katherine Gleason Chapman, born 5 Nov 1841 in Jasper, Pike Co., OH; died 11 Oct 1929 in Stockbridge, Calumet Co., WI, daughter of Henry Gleason Sr. and Charlotte (---).

Children of Warren Henry Bovee and Rosalie Katherine Gleason Chapman were as follows:

+ 1741 i Grace Evelyn[7] **Bovee**, born 24 Jun 1879 in Chilton, Calumet Co., WI; died in Appleton, Outagamie Co., WI. She married **Clifford Bishop**.

+ 1742 ii Robert Clare[7] **Bovee**, born 30 Mar 1881 in Calumet Co., WI; died bef 1963 in Fairfax,VA. He married **Catherine (---)**.

1743 iii Edna May[7] **Bovee**, born 18 Jul 1883; died in Milwaukee, Milwaukee Co., WI. She married **Robert Albert Summerfield**.

+ 1744 iv John Henry[7] **Bovee**, born 19 Jul 1887; died 21 Aug 1944 in Calumet Co., WI. He married **Rose Winkle**.

851. Franklin Gibson[6] **Bovee** (Aaron[5], Henry[4], Abraham[3], Nicholas[2], Mathieu[1]), born Jun 1855; died 25 Oct 1918 in Binghamton, Broome Co., NY. He married (1) on 30 Jun 1876 in Brooktondale, Tompkins Co., NY Mary Harris, born 29 May 1857 in Brooktondale, Tompkins Co., NY, daughter of Elisha Harris and Mary Lelly; (2) on 5 Aug 1892 Julie E (---), born Oct 1873 in PA; died 23 Oct 1918.

Children of Franklin Gibson Bovee and Mary Harris were as follows:

+ 1745 i Lyman George[7] **Bovee**, born Apr 1878 in Danby, Thomkins Co., NY. He married **Evaleen Elizabeth Thomas**.

+ 1746 ii Charles W[7] **Bovee**, born Sep 1879 in Tomkins Co., NY. He married **Louise Davis**.

859. John Ira[6] **Bovee** (John[5], Henry[4], Abraham[3], Nicholas[2], Mathieu[1]), born 4 Mar 1870 in Union Center, Broome Co., NY; died 15 Dec 1923. He married on 19 Jul 1898 Mary Elizabeth Norton, born 4 Aug 1875; died 22 Feb 1960.

Children of John Ira Bovee and Mary Elizabeth Norton were as follows:

1747 i James F[7] **Bovee**, born 12 Jul 1899 in St Paul, Ramsey Co., MN; died Dec 1968 in St. Paul, Ramsey Co., MN. He married **Louise Bongee**, born 21 Sep 1894; died Oct 1970.

1748 ii Eugene[7] **Bovee**, born 1902.

1749 iii John Ira[7] **Bovee** Jr, born 2 Jan 1907 in Olmsted Co., MN.

+ 1750 iv Lucille Monica[7] **Bovee**, born 1910. She married **Oswald Ronald Gravelle**.

+ 1751 v Gerald P[7] **Bovee**, born 10 Jun 1915; died 20 Jan 1990 in St. Paul, Ramsey Co., MN. He married **Florence M Neitje**.

+ 1752 vi Mary Helen[7] **Bovee**, died 6 Dec 2000 in Saint Paul, Ramsey Co., MN. She married **William Anthony Cassen**.

862. Charles J[6] **Bovee** (John[5], Henry[4], Abraham[3], Nicholas[2], Mathieu[1]), born 18 Oct 1876 in Rochester, Olmsted Co., MN; died 11 Oct 1949 in St Paul, Ramsey Co., MN. He married on 27 Oct 1908 Cassie Fay Oothoutdt, born 31 Jul 1890 in Huntley, Faribault Co., MN; died 23 Dec 1971 in Bismark, Burleigh Co., ND, daughter of Addison Charles Oothoutdt and Margaret Jane Burgess.

Children of Charles J Bovee and Cassie Fay Oothoutdt were as follows:

1753	i	John Addison[7] **Bovee**, born 4 May 1910 in Enderlin, Ransom Co., ND; died 10 Nov 1992 in Hettinger. Adams Co., ND. He married on 2 Jun 1937 **Lois Spencer**, born abt 1915.
1754	ii	Ina Vera[7] **Bovee**, born 10 Jan 1913 in Bowbells, Burke Co., ND. She married on 10 Jun 1937 **Ralph L Werner**.
+ 1755	iii	Rachel Eliza[7] **Bovee**, born 18 Oct 1915 in Plaza, Mountrail Co., ND; died 27 Jun 1992 in Portland, Multnoma Co., OR. She married **Lloyd Jacob Walters**.
+ 1756	iv	Charles Avery[7] **Bovee**, born in Jamestown, Stutsman Co., ND. He married **Mary Jane Parkhouse**.

865. Myron Edgar[6] **Bovee** (Cornelius[5], Peter[4], Abraham[3], Nicholas[2], Mathieu[1]), born 10 Apr 1876 in Kalamazoo, Kalamazoo Co., MI; died 1941 in Alvin, Brazoria Co., TX. He married on 14 Apr 1897 Florence Bessie Flexman, born 1 Apr 1879 in McGregor, Clayton Co., IA, daughter of Arthur Flexman.

Children of Myron Edgar Bovee and Florence Bessie Flexman were as follows:

+ 1757	i	Florence Marie[7] **Bovee**, born 1 Apr 1898 in Mendon. Clayton Co., IA; died 16 Aug 1979 in St Petersburg, Pinellas Co., FL. She married **Charles Sawvell**.
1758	ii	Child[7] **Bovee**, born bef 1900.
+ 1759	iii	Edward Wheeler[7] **Bovee**, born 12 Dec 1900 in Mendon. Clayton Co., IA; died Jul 1987 in Cottonwood, Yavapai Co., AZ. He married **Amy Bass**.
+ 1760	iv	Roy Alvin[7] **Bovee**, born 5 Aug 1902 in Mendon. Clayton Co., IA; died 20 Feb 1983 in S Beloit, Winnebego Co., IL. He married **Ellen A Taylor**.
+ 1761	v	Arthur Cornelius[7] **Bovee**, born 24 Mar 1904 in Mendon. Clayton Co., IA; died Oct 1970 in McGregor, Clayton Co., IA. He married **Emma Schultz**.
1762	vi	Leonard[7] **Bovee**, born abt 1906; died 4 Sep 1907.
1763	vii	Mabel[7] **Bovee**, born abt 1908.
+ 1764	viii	Marie Ellen[7] **Bovee**, born 8 Feb 1911 in Mendon. Clayton Co., IA; died 11 Jun 1977 in McGregor, Clayton Co., IA. She married **Mark Daniel Wilson**.
+ 1765	ix	Raymond Ralph[7] **Bovee**, born 14 Jan 1916; died 17 Nov 1984 in McGregor, Clayton Co., IA. He married **Arlene Kruse**.
+ 1766	x	Ethel May[7] **Bovee**, born 21 Mar 1918. She married (1)

870. Jacob[6] **Bovee** (Philip[5], Jacob Philip[4], Philip[3], Nicholas[2], Mathieu[1]), born 16 Mar 1820 in NY; died 10 Nov 1890 in Ashtabula, Ashtabula Co., OH. He married on 29 Jan 1843 in Parkman, Geauga Co., OH Isabelle Ainslie, born 11 Feb 1818 in Chardon, Geauga Co., OH; died 24 May 1891 in New Lyme, Ashtabula Co., OH, daughter of Thomas Ainslie.

Children of Jacob Bovee and Isabelle Ainslie were as follows:

	1767	i	Tryphena[7] **Bovee**, born 7 Jan 1844 in Cherry Valley, Ashtabula Co., OH; died 9 Aug 1858 in Cherry Valley, Ashtabula Co., OH.
	1768	ii	Mary[7] **Bovee**, born 28 May 1846 in Cherry Valley, Ashtabula Co., OH; died 30 Dec 1861 in Cherry Valley, Ashtabula Co., OH.
	1769	iii	Juliette H[7] **Bovee**, born Nov 1852 in Cherry Valley, Ashtabula Co., OH. She married abt 1877 **John Lamont**.
+	1770	iv	Delila Sarah[7] **Bovee**, born 7 Nov 1853 in Cherry Valley, Ashtabula Co., OH; died 20 Feb 1926 in Los Angeles, Los Angeles Co., CA. She married **Henry D Miner**.
	1771	v	Tryphena[7] **Bovee**, born abt 1858 in Cherry Valley, Ashtabula Co., OH; died 3 May 1908. She married in 1876 **John R Beckwith**.
	1772	vi	Mary[7] **Bovee**, born Mar 1862 in Cherry Valley, Ashtabula Co., OH. She married abt 1885 **Stephen Lamont**.

871. Aaron[6] **Bovee** (Philip[5], Jacob Philip[4], Philip[3], Nicholas[2], Mathieu[1]), born 20 Jul 1822 in Monroe Co., NY; died 27 Oct 1906. He married on 29 Oct 1848 in Ashtabula, Ashtabula Co., OH Lucy Ann Gunn, born Feb 1830 in OH; died 9 Mar 1903 in Portland, Multnomah Co., OR.

Children of Aaron Bovee and Lucy Ann Gunn were as follows:

1773	i	Emily[7] **Bovee**, born 1849; died 18 Dec 1856.
1774	ii	Seymour[7] **Bovee**, born 12 Aug 1850.
1775	iii	Lottie F[7] **Bovee**, born abt 1853. She married **O A Darling**.
1776	iv	Hattie[7] **Bovee**, born 1859; died 10 Sep 1863.
1777	v	Aaron K[7] **Bovee**, born 1863 in MI; died 13 May 1885.
1778	vi	Emma D[7] **Bovee**, born May 1864 in MI. She married abt 1890 **George Myers**.
1779	vii	Miron F[7] **Bovee**, born 1866; died 29 Sep 1877.
1780	viii	Frederick L[7] **Bovee**, born 1870 in MI.

872. Philip[6] **Bovee** Jr (Philip[5], Jacob Philip[4], Philip[3], Nicholas[2], Mathieu[1]), born 29 Mar 1825 in Monroe Co., NY; died 26 Feb 1889 in Gordon, Sheridan Co., NE. He married on 17 Aug 1847 in Orwell, Ashtabula Co., OH Mary Crowell, born

Nov 1824; died 8 Sep 1906 in Sheridan Co., NE, daughter of Obadiah Crowell and Amy Osborn.

Children of Philip Bovee Jr and Mary Crowell were as follows:

+ 1781   i   Julia Jane[7] **Bovee**, born Jun 1850 in Ashtabula Co., OH. She married **George Washington Frost**.

   1782   ii   Mary Arminda[7] **Bovee**, born abt 1852 in OH.

   1783   iii   Florence[7] **Bovee**, born abt 1854 in OH. She married on 11 Oct 1870 in Milford Center, Portage Co., OH **William H Reed**, son of Harlow Reed and Fidellia Griffin.

+ 1784   iv   Hannah[7] **Bovee**, born 19 Oct 1856 in Grand Rapids, Kent Co., MI; died 2 Dec 1923. She married **Henry Roswell Reed**.

+ 1785   v   Emily Melvina[7] **Bovee**, born 19 Jan 1859 in Dorr, Allegan Co., MI; died 3 May 1930 in Central City, Merrick Co., NE. She married **William Moss Clark**.

   1786   vi   Sarah[7] **Bovee**, born abt 1861 in MI.

+ 1787   vii   Byron J[7] **Bovee**, born 26 Jan 1868 in Allegan Co., MI. He married (1) **Florence (---)**; (2) **Laura (---)**.

+ 1788   viii   Arthur E[7] **Bovee**, born 10 Aug 1873 in NE. He married **Melinda (---)**.

875. George[6] **Bovee** (Philip[5], Jacob Philip[4], Philip[3], Nicholas[2], Mathieu[1]), born 27 Nov 1830 in NY; died 4 Jul 1862 in Independence Rock, WY. He married (1) on 14 Nov 1847 in Ashtabula Co., OH Mary Clark; (2) on 20 Jul 1854 in Delaware Co., OH Harriet G Groves, born 30 Mar 1839 in Delaware Co., OH.

Children of George Bovee and Harriet G Groves were as follows:

   1789   i   Florence M[7] **Bovee**, born 18 Feb 1856 in Knox Co., IL. She married on 25 Nov 1879 in Umatilla Co., OR **Melzer W Coon**.

+ 1790   ii   Manfred[7] **Bovee**, born Aug 1858 in Jefferson Co., IA. He married **Martha Parker**.

+ 1791   iii   Orbie O[7] **Bovee**, born 23 Jan 1862 in Jefferson Co., IA; died 3 Jun 1930 in Wenatchee. Chelan Co., WA. He married **May Florence Parker**.

876. Catherine[6] **Bovee** (Philip[5], Jacob Philip[4], Philip[3], Nicholas[2], Mathieu[1]), born 1 Jul 1833 in Monroe Co., NY; died 1906 in Ann Arbor, Washtenaw Co., MI. She married (1) on 8 Jun 1856 in Ashtabula Co., OH William Wilder; (2) bef 1866 Christopher C Deuress, died 22 Oct 1911 in Ann Arbor, Washtenaw, son of Peter Deuress and Mary Killen.

Children of Catherine Bovee and William Wilder were as follows:

   1792   i   Emma[7] **Wilder**, born Oct 1857.

Children of Catherine Bovee and Christopher C Deuress were as follows:

1793	i	Clyde William[7] **Deuress**, born 1868 in OH.
1794	ii	Viola B[7] **Deuress**, born 10 Jul 1870 in Ypsilanti, Washtenaw Co., MI.

879. Byron E[6] **Bovee** (Philip[5], Jacob Philip[4], Philip[3], Nicholas[2], Mathieu[1]), born 27 Sep 1839 in Ashtabula Co., OH; died 27 Dec 1911 in New Lyme, Ashtabula Co., OH. He married on 4 Jul 1870 in New Lyme, Ashtabula Co., OH Maria C Regal.

Children of Byron E Bovee and Maria C Regal were as follows:

1795	i	Edna Valera[7] **Bovee**, born 4 Jan 1872 in Ashtabula Co., OH. She married in 1893 in OH **Edward Way**.
1796	ii	Inez[7] **Bovee**, born Feb 1874.
1797	iii	Frank C[7] **Bovee**, born Jan 1882.
+ 1798	iv	Vida A[7] **Bovee**, born Oct 1884; died 3 Oct 1964 in Adrian, Lewanee Co., MI. She married **Ray Fachman**.

880. Jemina[6] **Bovee** (John[5], Jacob Philip[4], Philip[3], Nicholas[2], Mathieu[1]), born 11 Nov 1816; died bef 1902 in Herndon, Fairfax Co., VA. She married on 4 Jul 1839 Stephen Killion, died bef 1902 in Herndon, Fairfax Co., VA.

Children of Jemina Bovee and Stephen Killion were as follows:

1799	i	Child 1[7] **Killion**.
1800	ii	Child 2[7] **Killion**.
1801	iii	Child 3[7] **Killion**.

882. Job Hedden[6] **Bovee** (John[5], Jacob Philip[4], Philip[3], Nicholas[2], Mathieu[1]), born 25 Sep 1820 in East Bloomfield, Ontario Co., NY; died 10 Dec 1894. He married on 2 Jun 1855 Mary A Welch, born 4 May 1836 in Hoosick, Rensselaer Co., NY; died 1 Mar 1917 in Rochester, Monroe Co., NY.

Children of Job Hedden Bovee and Mary A Welch were as follows:

1802	i	Alice L[7] **Bovee**, born 1856 in Orleans Co., NY.
1803	ii	Ella L[7] **Bovee**, born 1858 in Orleans Co., NY. She married **(---) McKenna**.
1804	iii	Mary[7] **Bovee**, born 28 May 1860 in Clarkson, Monroe Co., NY; died 7 Apr 1934 in Rochester, Monroe Co., NY. She married **Charles J Hull**, born 16 Dec 1856 in Rochester, Monroe Co., NY; died 13 Jun 1939 in Westernville, Oneida Co., NY.
1805	iv	Mina A[7] **Bovee**, born 1862 in Orleans Co., NY. She married **John Snooks**.
1806	v	Hattie G[7] **Bovee**, born 1865 in Orleans Co., NY. She married **(---) Groom**.
1807	vi	Sarah[7] **Bovee**, born 1867. She married **(---) Kinsella**.

1808	vii	Julia Teresa[7] **Bovee**, born 1869 in Monroe Co., NY. She married on 21 Apr 1897 in Monroe Co., NY **Jeremiah Halicy**.
1809	viii	Carrie E[7] **Bovee**, born 1872 in NY; died 10 Nov 1887.
+ 1810	ix	Charles H[7] **Bovee**, born Apr 1878. He married **Elizabeth Morrison**.

884. Nicholas[6] **Bovee** (John[5], Jacob Philip[4], Philip[3], Nicholas[2], Mathieu[1]), born 15 Aug 1824; died 9 Jan 1901 in Ypsilanti, Washtnaw Co., MI. He married on 7 Aug 1853 Julia Sherwood, born 6 Dec 1833 in NY; died 15 Jan 1914, daughter of Germond Sherwood and Edeth (---).

Children of Nicholas Bovee and Julia Sherwood were as follows:

1811	i	George[7] **Bovee**, born abt 1854. He married on 7 Sep 1879 in Washtenaw Co., MI **Etta J Fuller**.
+ 1812	ii	Frederick Germond[7] **Bovee**, born abt 1855 in Rawsonville, Wayne Co., MI; died 25 Apr 1935 in Plymouth, Wayne Co., MI. He married **Elsie L Bridger**.
+ 1813	iii	Alfretta[7] **Bovee**, born 12 Aug 1861 in Ypsilanti, Washtenaw Co., MI; died 21 Mar 1943 in Wayne Co., MI. She married **Frederick Forsythe**.

887. Edwin Henry[6] **Bovee** (John[5], Jacob Philip[4], Philip[3], Nicholas[2], Mathieu[1]), born 6 Oct 1832 in Monroe Co., NY; died 11 May 1903 in Washington, Washington Co., IA. He married on 26 Nov 1861 in Johnson Co., IA Rachel Anna Huskins, born 1841 in Uniontown, Fayette Co., PA; died 25 Nov 1907 in Washington, Washington Co., IA.

Children of Edwin Henry Bovee and Rachel Anna Huskins were as follows:

1814	i	Charlotte Huskins[7] **Bovee**, born 14 Jan 1863; died 20 Aug 1931 in Trinidad, Las Animas Co., CO. She married on 7 Oct 1885 **George S Norton**.
+ 1815	ii	John Edwin[7] **Bovee**, born 16 Jul 1866 in Johnson Co., IA; died 11 Jun 1955. He married **Bessie A Babcock**.

889. Joseph W[6] **Bovee** (John[5], Jacob Philip[4], Philip[3], Nicholas[2], Mathieu[1]), born 18 Jul 1840 in Monroe Co., NY; died 26 Mar 1911 in Three Rivers, St Joseph Co., MI. He married on 4 Jul 1869 Irene Mary Randolph, born 18 Aug 1845 in MI; died 2 Nov 1908 in Three Rivers, St Joseph Co., MI, daughter of Abel Randolph and Fannie Cusic.

Children of Joseph W Bovee and Irene Mary Randolph were as follows:

1816	i	Gordon H[7] **Bovee**, born 6 May 1870 in Morenci, Lewanee Co., MI; died Feb 1928.
1817	ii	Fanny L[7] **Bovee**, born abt 1872; died 26 Nov 1878 in Morenci, Lewanee Co., MI.
+ 1818	iii	Beatrice Ann[7] **Bovee**, born 10 Apr 1874 in Morenci,

Lewanee Co., MI. She married **Byron Silvernail**.

1819   iv   Ernest R[7] **Bovee**, born 6 Apr 1875; died 27 Nov 1876 in Oak Grove Cem, Morenci, Lewanee Co., MI.

1820   v   Nellie A[7] **Bovee**, born 15 Sep 1876; died 3 Dec 1878 in Morenci, Lewanee Co., MI.

1821   vi   Elizabeth[7] **Bovee**, born abt 1882 in OH.

1822   vii   Josia A **Bovee**, born abt 1886 in OH.

1823   viii   Charles E[7] **Bovee**, born abt 1890 in OH.

890. Francis M[6] **Bovee** (John[5], Jacob Philip[4], Philip[3], Nicholas[2], Mathieu[1]), born 2 Aug 1843 in Clarkson, Monroe Co., NY. He married on 3 Nov 1867 Zeoba Elester, born 2 Mar 1840 in Dutchess Co., NY; died 18 Jan 1885 in Springville, Lenawee Co., MI.

Children of Francis M Bovee and Zeoba Elester were as follows:

+   1824   i   Frank J[7] **Bovee**, born Jan 1868 in MI. He married **Clara Bartholomew**.

892. John C[6] **Bovee** (Nicholas[5], Jacob Philip[4], Philip[3], Nicholas[2], Mathieu[1]), born 5 Sep 1824; died 1897 in Devils Lake, MI. He married on 29 Mar 1859 Cynthia Ann Eddy.

Children of John C Bovee and Cynthia Ann Eddy were as follows:

1825   i   Ella S[7] **Bovee**, born abt 1861. She married on 28 Nov 1880 in Seneca, Lenawee Co., MI **George A Camburn**.

1826   ii   Louise[7] **Bovee**, born abt 1863. She married **Addison Farmer**.

895. Charles P[6] **Bovee** (Nicholas[5], Jacob Philip[4], Philip[3], Nicholas[2], Mathieu[1]), born 26 Jul 1831 in NY; died 14 Apr 1910 in Village Cem, Weston, Lenawee Co., MI. He married on 2 Aug 1849 Nancy H Southworth, born 12 Apr 1832 in Shelby, Orleans Co., NY; died 15 Jan 1899, daughter of Thomas F Southworth and Althea W Aldrich.

Children of Charles P Bovee and Nancy H Southworth were as follows:

1827   i   Evaline[7] **Bovee**, born 25 Mar 1858; died 9 Nov 1874.

+   1828   ii   Freeman[7] **Bovee**, born Jul 1864 in MI. He married **Abbie Terry**.

896. Nelson H[6] **Bovee** (Nicholas[5], Jacob Philip[4], Philip[3], Nicholas[2], Mathieu[1]), born 20 Feb 1834 in NY; died 17 Mar 1907 in Whitehouse, Lucas Co., OH. He married on 4 Jul 1865 Sally Ann Merritt, born Apr 1837 in MI; died 1922.

Children of Nelson H Bovee and Sally Ann Merritt were as follows:

1829   i   Luette L[7] **Bovee**, born abt 1867 in MI.

+ 1830 ii Seymour Nelson[7] **Bovee**, born 25 Jun 1868 in Lenawee Co., MI; died 28 Dec 1953 in Detroit, Wayne Co., MI. He married **Bertha H Votzka**.

  1831 iii Mina May[7] **Bovee**, born abt 1873 in MI.

+ 1832 iv Cora Bell[7] **Bovee**, born 11 Oct 1876 in Seneca, Lenawee Co., MI; died 1960. She married **Clyde L Onweller**.

  1833 v Willard F[7] **Bovee**, born 20 May 1878 in Lenawee Co., MI; died 12 Aug 1907.

  1834 vi Child[7] **Bovee**, born abt 1880.

+ 1835 vii Floyd B[7] **Bovee**, born Apr 1884 in MI; died 1948. He married (1) **Mable Darling**; (2) **Effie Humble**.

+ 1836 viii Charles Henry[7] **Bovee**, born May 1885 in MI; died 1 Oct 1940. He married (1) **Verlie Seevey**; (2) **Effie Roop**.

904. Alvah C[6] **Bovee** (Daniel R[5], Nicholas P[4], Philip[3], Nicholas[2], Mathieu[1]), born 28 Aug 1807 in NY; died abt 1854. He married (1) abt 1834 Catherine Row, born abt 1811 in NY; died bef 1852; (2) aft 1850 Mary E (---).

Children of Alvah C Bovee and Catherine Row were as follows:

  1837 i Harriet[7] **Bovee**, born abt 1835 in NY.

  1838 ii Elizabeth[7] **Bovee**.

  1839 iii Clarissa M[7] **Bovee**, born abt 1841 in Canada; died 1907 in Dearborn, Wayne Co., MI. She married on 4 Dec 1860 in Detroit, Wayne Co., MI **John R Forsythe**.

  1840 iv Alvah C[7] **Bovee** Jr, born 7 Aug 1849 in MI; died 2 May 1851.

Children of Alvah C Bovee and Mary E (---) were as follows:

  1841 i Catherine Mary[7] **Bovee**, born 23 Mar 1852 in Trenton, Wayne Co., MI; christened 5 Jun 1864 in St Paul Cath Ch, Trenton, Wayne co., MI. She married on 10 Nov 1867 in Romulus, Wayne Co., MI **Abram Compton**.

905. William R[6] **Bovee** (Daniel R[5], Nicholas P[4], Philip[3], Nicholas[2], Mathieu[1]), born 21 Jul 1809 in NY; died 18 Jan 1857 in Spartansburg, Crawford Co., PA. He married on 8 Apr 1838 in Morgan Co., KY Maria Quackenbush, born 5 Feb 1820 in NY; died 29 Apr 1900, daughter of (---) Quackenbush.

Children of William R Bovee and Maria Quackenbush were as follows:

+ 1842 i Jeremiah W[7] **Bovee**, born 22 Apr 1839 in NY. He married **Maria Hungerford**.

+ 1843 ii Daniel Reynolds[7] **Bovee**, born 10 Feb 1840 in Gainesville, Wyoming Co., NY; died 21 Jun 1926 in Lowville, Erie Co., PA. He married **Lucina Raymond**.

  1844 iii Ruby[7] **Bovee**, born 25 Dec 1842 in Springville, Erie Co., NY.

  1845 iv Margaret[7] **Bovee**, born 22 Aug 1844 in Pike, Wyoming

Co., NY.

+ 1846 v Charles Dexter[7] **Bovee**, born 12 Oct 1846 in Springville, Erie Co., NY; died 6 Dec 1923 in Erie, Erie Co., PA. He married **Almira E Smith**.

1847 vi Sarah[7] **Bovee**, born 26 Feb 1848 in Springville, Erie Co., NY.

908. Nicholas[6] **Bovee** (Jacob[5], Nicholas P[4], Philip[3], Nicholas[2], Mathieu[1]), born 29 Feb 1808; died 26 Jun 1888. He married on 18 Apr 1830 Polly Selfidge, born 11 Oct 1806; died 10 Mar 1886 in IL.

Children of Nicholas Bovee and Polly Selfidge were as follows:

+ 1848 i Mary Jane[7] **Bovee**, born 9 Sep 1830 in Chautauqua Co., NY; died 28 Sep 1861. She married **Amos Benton**.

+ 1849 ii Harper W[7] **Bovee**, born 21 Feb 1832 in Chautauqua Co., NY; died 30 Nov 1916. He married **Susan Benton**.

+ 1850 iii Lorenzo Dow[7] **Bovee**, born 17 Jan 1834 in Edmeston, Otsego Co., NY; died 25 Apr 1911 in Miami, Dade Co., FL. He married **Ellen G Goodrich**.

+ 1851 iv Eunice S[7] **Bovee**, born 10 Dec 1835 in Ashtabula Co., OH; died 18 Sep 1883. She married **Alex Loucks**.

+ 1852 v Hannah Marie[7] **Bovee**, born 23 Sep 1837 in Ashtabula Co., OH; died 12 Jan 1918. She married **Benjamin Cahoon**.

+ 1853 vi Emily E[7] **Bovee**, born 11 Jun 1840 in Ashtabula Co., OH; died 3 Feb 1923. She married (1) **Antone Lahmar**; (2) **Abner Loucks**; (3) **Charles Wilkins**; (4) **John Kanagy**.

+ 1854 vii Harriet Augusta[7] **Bovee**, born 24 Jun 1845 in Ashtabula Co., OH; died 3 Apr 1925 in Morris, Grundy Co., IL. She married **George Wickes**.

+ 1855 viii Harmon E[7] **Bovee**, born 8 Oct 1847 in Kingsville, Ashtabula Co., OH; died 15 May 1910. He married **Marietta Wickes**.

910. Harper R[6] **Bovee** (Jacob[5], Nicholas P[4], Philip[3], Nicholas[2], Mathieu[1]), born 25 Oct 1812 in NY; died 27 Nov 1893 in Big Rapids, Mecosta Co., MI. He married on 24 May 1834 in Utica, Macomb Co., MI Sarah Jane Hills, born 12 Apr 1816 in Antrim Co, NH; died 18 Apr 1910 in Big Rapids, Mecosta Co., MI.

Children of Harper R Bovee and Sarah Jane Hills were as follows:

1856 i George A[7] **Bovee**, born abt 1836; died 14 Mar 1846.

1857 ii Mary E[7] **Bovee**, born 1838 in NY.

1858 iii Charles D W[7] **Bovee**, born abt 1840 in MI.

1859 iv James M[7] **Bovee**, born abt 1844 in MI.

1860 v Adelia[7] **Bovee**, born abt 1847 in MI.

1861 vi Alta[7] **Bovee**, born abt 1849 in MI.

1862	vii	Luther[7] **Bovee**, born 1852 in MI.
+ 1863	viii	Viola[7] **Bovee**, born 1854 in MI; died Mar 1929. She married **Paris Banfield**.
+ 1864	ix	Eva Rachel[7] **Bovee**, born 6 Jun 1858 in Wayne Co., MI; died 1931. She married **George Willard Trowbridge**.

911. Abraham[6] **Bovee** (Jacob[5], Nicholas P[4], Philip[3], Nicholas[2], Mathieu[1]), born abt 1814 in NY; died 4 Apr 1872 in Nunda, Livingston Co., NY. He married (1) Hulda (---), born abt 1815; (2) bef 1860 Tryphena (---).

Children of Abraham Bovee and Hulda (---) were as follows:

1865	i	Alvira[7] **Bovee**, born abt 1852.
1866	ii	Jenette[7] **Bovee**, born 1846.
1867	iii	Mary[7] **Bovee**, born abt 1848.
1868	iv	Jacob Monroe[7] **Bovee**, born 5 Aug 1850; died 25 Mar 1881.

912. John C[6] **Bovee** (Jacob[5], Nicholas P[4], Philip[3], Nicholas[2], Mathieu[1]), born 1816 in NY; died 9 May 1894 in Amy, Oakland Co., MI. He married (1) on 4 Jul 1838 in Gainesville, Wyoming Co., NY Lovena Barnard, born 1814 in NY; died 5 Apr 1850 in Delavan, Walworth Co., WI, daughter of Thomas Barnard and Polly (---); (2) aft 1850 Sarah A Verney, born 1826 in PA; died bef 1894.

Children of John C Bovee and Lovena Barnard were as follows:

1869	i	William P[7] **Bovee**, born abt 1841.
1870	ii	Adelbert[7] **Bovee**, born abt 1847 in Delavan, Walworth Co., WI; died 13 Aug 1864 in Troy Twp., Oakland Co., MI.

Children of John C Bovee and Sarah A Verney were as follows:

+ 1871	i	Frank[7] **Bovee**, born 11 Mar 1857 in Howard Co., IA. He married **Mary E Strator**.

914. Daniel[6] **Bovee** (Jacob[5], Nicholas P[4], Philip[3], Nicholas[2], Mathieu[1]), born abt 1818 in NY. He married abt 1845 Elizabeth Bliss, born abt 1825 in NY.

Children of Daniel Bovee and Elizabeth Bliss were as follows:

+ 1872	i	Frank E[7] **Bovee**, born 2 Nov 1847 in WI; died 9 Jun 1917 in Rochester, Monroe Co., NY. He married **Flora Cole**.
1873	ii	Emma Susan[7] **Bovee**, born 17 Nov 1849 in Genesee Falls, Wyoming co., NY. She married **G R Wyllie**.
1874	iii	Carrie[7] **Bovee**, born abt 1859. She married **(---) Pritchard**.
1875	iv	William[7] **Bovee**, born 1862.

935. Mary[6] **Bovee** (Harper[5], Nicholas P[4], Philip[3], Nicholas[2], Mathieu[1]), born abt

1818. She married Solon Billings, born 1812 in VT.

Children of Mary Bovee and Solon Billings were as follows:

1876 i Frances[7] **Billings**, born abt 1838 in PA.

1877 ii Ellen[7] **Billings**, born abt 1842 in PA.

936. Norman[6] **Bovee** (Harper[5], Nicholas P[4], Philip[3], Nicholas[2], Mathieu[1]), born abt 1820 in Gainesville, Wyoming Co., NY. He married Permelia Loucks, born abt 1820 in NY.

Children of Norman Bovee and Permelia Loucks were as follows:

+ 1878 i Norman[7] **Bovee** Jr, born abt 1845 in NY; died abt 1899. He married **Addie S Green**.

+ 1879 ii Alson L[7] **Bovee**, born 1847 in NY. He married **Sarah Jane Stebbins**.

937. Harmon[6] **Bovee** (Harper[5], Nicholas P[4], Philip[3], Nicholas[2], Mathieu[1]), born 9 Aug 1825 in Genesee Co., NY; died 9 Jan 1898 in Carlton, Carlton Co., MN. He married on 23 Dec 1848 in Pierpont, Ashtabula Co., OH Lydia Jane Wright, born 14 Aug 1825 in Allegheny Co., PA; died 22 Aug 1903 in Elk Point, Union Co., SD.

Children of Harmon Bovee and Lydia Jane Wright were as follows:

+ 1880 i Charles Elliott[7] **Bovee**, born 23 Apr 1851 in Pennline, Crawford Co., PA. He married **Clara (---)**.

+ 1881 ii Lydia Jane[7] **Bovee**, born 7 Aug 1854 in Pennline, Crawford Co., PA. She married (1) **(---) Winslow**; (2) **Hugh McMillan**.

+ 1882 iii George Edmond[7] **Bovee**, born 21 Apr 1857 in Rockville, Kankakee Co., IL. He married **Verna M (---)**.

+ 1883 iv William Harmon[7] **Bovee**, born 16 Apr 1863 in Hammond, St Croix Co., WI. He married **Nellie B (---)**.

1884 v Clarence[7] **Bovee**, born 31 Mar 1867 in Fayetteville, Franklin Co., PA. He married on 3 Nov 1885 in Douglas Co., WI **? (---)**.

938. Harper[6] **Bovee** Jr (Harper[5], Nicholas P[4], Philip[3], Nicholas[2], Mathieu[1]), born 25 Jun 1827 in Gainesville, Wyoming Co., NY. He married (1) in Crawford Co., PA Marietta Linn, born in Crawford Co., PA; died abt 1856; (2) Lora Tilden, born 5 Mar 1839 in Williamsport, Orange Co., VT.

Children of Harper Bovee Jr and Marietta Linn were as follows:

1885 i Odel[7] **Bovee**.

939. John[6] **Bovee** (Harper[5], Nicholas P[4], Philip[3], Nicholas[2], Mathieu[1]), born 19 Feb 1831 in Gainesville, Wyoming Co., NY; died 18 Feb 1893 in Wilmington, Will

Co., IL. He married in 1861 in Kankakee Co., IL Sarah A Frazer, born in Wesley Twp, Kankakee Co., IL.

Children of John Bovee and Sarah A Frazer were as follows:

1886   i   Mary[7] **Bovee**.
1887   ii   Frank[7] **Bovee**, born abt 1868.

940. Alexander[6] **Bovee** (Harper[5], Nicholas P[4], Philip[3], Nicholas[2], Mathieu[1]), born 1835. He married on 4 Mar 1861 Sally Gray.

Children of Alexander Bovee and Sally Gray were as follows:

1888   i   Charles[7] **Bovee**, born abt 1862.
1889   ii   Minnie[7] **Bovee**, born abt 1868.

941. Charles[6] **Bovee** (Harper[5], Nicholas P[4], Philip[3], Nicholas[2], Mathieu[1]), born 1838 in Cattaraugus Co., NY; died 5 May 1887 in Peoria, Peoria Co., IL. He married Laura Phenix, born Jul 1849 in LA; died 11 Oct 1913 in Stockton, San Joaquin Co., CA.

Children of Charles Bovee and Laura Phenix were as follows:

1890   i   Eva L M[7] **Bovee**, born 18 Aug 1873 in IL.
1891   ii   Ethel May[7] **Bovee**, born 22 Sep 1875 in IL. She married **Noel H Jack**.
1892   iii   Leroy H[7] **Bovee**, born 28 Dec 1882 in IL; died 5 Sep 1930 in San Francisco, San Francisco Co., CA.

958. Eliad E[6] **Bovee** (Jacob Nicholas[5], Nicholas Jacob[4], Jacob[3], Nicholas[2], Mathieu[1]), born 1817 in NY. He married (1) on 15 Mar 1837 in Charlton, Saratoga Co., NY Jane Burch, born abt 1820 in NY; (2) abt 1864 Eva Ann Bovee, born abt 1828 in Schoharie, Schoharie Co., NY.

Children of Eliad E Bovee and Jane Burch were as follows:

+   1893   i   Catherine[7] **Bovee**, born abt 1837 in Saratoga Co., NY. She married **Edward Pelton**.
     1894   ii   Halsey L[7] **Bovee**, born Jun 1841 in Saratoga Co., NY; died aft 1904.
+   1895   iii   John N[7] **Bovee**, born abt 1843 in Charlton, Saratoga Co., NY; died bef 1915. He married **Ann Elizabeth Shivley**.
     1896   iv   Charlotte[7] **Bovee**, born abt 1846 in NY.
+   1897   v   Eliad A[7] **Bovee**, born 3 Jul 1848 in Glenville Twp., Schenectady Co., NY; died 23 Jan 1917 in Ypsilanti, Washtenaw Co., MI. He married **Jennie L Cady**.
     1898   vi   Jane L[7] **Bovee**, born abt 1850 in Schenectady Co., NY.
     1899   vii   Ira[7] **Bovee**, born 2 Jun 1852 in NY. He married (1) abt 1875 **Carry Taft**; (2) on 23 Nov 1902 **Rosella Sell**.

Children of Eliad E Bovee and Eva Ann Bovee were as follows:

1900   i   Lucy^7 **Bovee**, born abt 1856 in NY.

1901   ii   Ira^7 **Bovee**, born abt 1858.

1902   iii Anna^7 **Bovee**, born 1 Oct 1860 in NY; died 15 Sep 1951 in Los Angeles, Los Angeles Co., CA.

1903   iv   Edward^7 **Bovee**, born abt 1863 in NY.

1904   v   Cora^7 **Bovee**, born abt 1868 in MI.

+ 1905 vi   Howard L^7 **Bovee**, born Jul 1869 in MI. He married **Nettie Blanch Farwell**.

960. Mathew J^6 **Bovee** (Jacob Nicholas^5, Nicholas Jacob^4, Jacob^3, Nicholas^2, Mathieu^1), born 4 Sep 1823 in NY; died 12 Dec 1882. He married abt 1847 Susan Swits, born abt 1824; died Dec 1874.

Children of Mathew J Bovee and Susan Swits were as follows:

1906   i   Sarah A^7 **Bovee**, born abt 1848 in NY; buried in Rural Hill Cem, Northville Twp., Wayne Co., MI. She married on 8 Feb 1866 in At Farmington Hotel. **William H Ambler**.

+ 1907 ii   Stillman^7 **Bovee**, born Mar 1850 in Saratoga Co., NY. He married **Josephine (---)**.

1908   iii Eva^7 **Bovee**, born abt 1853.

961. Isaac^6 **Bovee** (Jacob Nicholas^5, Nicholas Jacob^4, Jacob^3, Nicholas^2, Mathieu^1), born 1828 in NY; died bef 1880 in Ionia Co., MI. He married in 1847 Mary Cromwell, born 14 Sep 1830 in NY; died 31 Aug 1888.

Children of Isaac Bovee and Mary Cromwell were as follows:

1909   i   Rosana^7 **Bovee**, born 17 Jul 1848 in Charlton, Saratoga Co., NY.

+ 1910 ii   John M^7 **Bovee**, born Apr 1850 in Charlton, Saratoga Co., NY. He married **Ida M Houghton**.

1911   iii Mary J^7 **Bovee**, born 1853 in NY.

1912   iv   Augusta^7 **Bovee**, born 1855 in NY.

+ 1913 v   Jacob^7 **Bovee**, born 1858 in Plynouth, Wayne co., MI; died abt 1886. He married **Cora A Hotchkiss**.

1914   vi   Dolly^7 **Bovee**, born 1860 in Wayne Co., MI.

1915   vii Lucy^7 **Bovee**, born 1862 in MI.

1916   viii Alice ^{7} **Bovee**, born 1863 in MI.

1917   ix   Isaac^7 **Bovee**, born abt 1867; died 1885 in Jackson Co., MI.

1918   x   Minnie^7 **Bovee**, born 1869 in MI.

1919   xi   Pearl^7 **Bovee**, born 1872 in Ionia Co., MI.

963. Marvin^6 **Bovee** (Jacob Nicholas^5, Nicholas Jacob^4, Jacob^3, Nicholas^2,

Mathieu[1]), born Sep 1836; died 1913. He married abt 1865 Lucy Ambler, born Apr 1840; died 1912.

Children of Marvin Bovee and Lucy Ambler were as follows:

1920   i   Harry A[7] **Bovee**, born Apr 1867 in Plynouth, Wayne co., MI. He married **Fanny Perry**, daughter of Robert Perry.

1921   ii   Leafy[7] **Bovee**, born 1868 in Plynouth, Wayne co., MI; died 27 Feb 1869.

1922   iii   May[7] **Bovee**, born Aug 1869 in Wayne Co., MI; died 26 May 1948. She married **Byron G Filkins**.

1923   iv   Carrie **Bovee**, born Dec 1879 in Plynouth, Wayne co., MI; died 1959. She married **Perry Woodworth**.

972. Peter[6] **Bovee** (Peter[5], Jacob[4], Jacob[3], Nicholas[2], Mathieu[1]), born 1809. He married Eliza Dayton, born 1811.

Children of Peter Bovee and Eliza Dayton were as follows:

1924   i   Elizabeth[7] **Bovee**, born 1832.

1925   ii   John[7] **Bovee**, born 1838.

1926   iii   James[7] **Bovee**, born 1841. He married **Marianne (---)**.

\+ 1927   iv   Christian[7] **Bovee**, born 18 Aug 1843 in Kingston, Ulster Co., NY; died 18 Mar 1908 in Dayton, Montgomery Co., OH. He married **Jane Jay**.

1928   v   Hiram[7] **Bovee**, born 1845.

1929   vi   Mary[7] **Bovee**, born 1845.

1930   vii   George[7] **Bovee**, born Apr 1851.

\+ 1931   viii Lorenzo[7] **Bovee**, born Oct 1854. He married **Jennie Wood**.

\+ 1932   ix   Samuel[7] **Bovee**, born Mar 1857. He married **Nina J (---)**.

974. Jacob Clayton[6] **Bovee** (Peter[5], Jacob[4], Jacob[3], Nicholas[2], Mathieu[1]), born abt 1814 in Montgomery Co., NY. He married Sophia Barton, born 1812 in MA.

Children of Jacob Clayton Bovee and Sophia Barton were as follows:

\+ 1933   i   George A[7] **Bovee**, born 15 Apr 1837 in Greene Co., NY. He married **Mary Geddes**.

\+ 1934   ii   Pliny L[7] **Bovee**, born 2 Apr 1841 in Ulster Co., NY. He married **Melissa Longendyke**.

\+ 1935   iii   Jacob Henry[7] **Bovee**, born 1843 in Ulster Co., NY; died 22 Jun 1919 in Saugerties, Ulster Co., NY.. He married **Sarah Brink**.

\+ 1936   iv   Elijah[7] **Bovee**, born May 1846. He married **Anna Dederick**.

\+ 1937   v   Edgar[7] **Bovee**, born 1849 in Saugerties, Ulster Co., NY; died 9 Oct 1896 in Kingston, Ulster Co., NY. He married **Alice Russel**.

+   1938   vi   Hiram[7] **Bovee**, born abt 1851; died 1 Nov 1919 in Woodstock, Ulster Co., NY.. He married **Martha Kierstede**.

988. Isaac[6] **Bovee** Jr (Isaac[5], Jacob[4], Jacob[3], Nicholas[2], Mathieu[1]), born 22 Nov 1822 in Montgomery Co., NY; died 11 Jul 1886 in MI. He married (1) on 7 Dec 1843 Minerva Ruth Eastman, born 17 May 1818; (2) aft 1883 Elizabeth Peck.

Children of Isaac Bovee Jr and Minerva Ruth Eastman were as follows:

+   1939   i   Aldo Harris[7] **Bovee**, born 22 Jan 1845 in OH. He married **Harriet Lucetta Mugg**.

        1940   ii   Alicia[7] **Bovee**, born 18 Oct 1846 in OH. She married **Carl Brown**.

        1941   iii   Joanna Corsine[7] **Bovee**, born 24 Jul 1848 in Seneca Co., OH. She married on 25 Dec 1868 **Calvin C Coleman**, born 26 Jan 1847; died 19 Mar 1871 in MI.

        1942   iv   Mary Ellen[7] **Bovee**, born 13 Oct 1849 in Cass Co., MI.

        1943   v   James Ashley[7] **Bovee**, born 18 Jul 1852 in OH; died 1874.

+   1944   vi   William Irvin[7] **Bovee**, born 28 Mar 1854 in Cayahoga Co., OH; died 4 Apr 1928 in Los Angeles, Los Angeles Co., CA. He married **Mary Etta Young**.

989. Benjamin[6] **Bovee** (Philip[5], Jacob[4], Jacob[3], Nicholas[2], Mathieu[1]), born abt 1818 in Fulton Co., NY; died 5 Apr 1897 in Union Twp., Black Hawk Co., IA. He married (1) on 17 Jul 1842 in Montgomery Co., NY Sarah (---), died 9 Aug 1866 in Butler Co., IA; (2) on 21 Oct 1869 in Black Hawk Co., IA Caroline P Sent.

Children of Benjamin Bovee and Sarah (---) were as follows:

        1945   i   William M[7] **Bovee**, born 1843 in NY; died 3 Jul 1865 in Butler Co., IA. He married on 6 Sep 1863 in Butler Co., IA **S E Overacker**.

Children of Benjamin Bovee and Caroline P Sent were as follows:

+   1946   i   Edwin Orville[7] **Bovee**, born Jan 1847 in NY. He married **Almira R Eggleston**.

990. Jacob[6] **Bovee** (Philip[5], Jacob[4], Jacob[3], Nicholas[2], Mathieu[1]), born Mar 1822 in NY; died 6 Jun 1902. He married (1), divorced Nancy Lappin, born Sep 1834 in PA; died 1915, daughter of Stephen Lappin and Polly Slater; (2) Sarah A (---), born Jan 1846 in IA.

Children of Jacob Bovee and Nancy Lappin were as follows:

        1947   i   Philip[7] **Bovee**, born abt 1860 in IL.

        1948   ii   Ruth[7] **Bovee**, born 13 May 1861 in IL; died 7 Feb 1905. She married on 21 Oct 1878 in Shell Rock, Butler Co., IA **William Thompson**.

+	1949	iii	Ezra[7] **Bovee**, born 20 Oct 1865 in Kane, Kane Co., IL; died 18 Nov 1956 in Sturgis, Meade Co., SD. He married **Lois Lomeda Baker**.
	1950	iv	Sarah[7] **Bovee**, born abt 1868.
	1951	v	Benjamin[7] **Bovee**, born Jan 1870 in IA; died 13 Jul 1904.

991. Ruth M[6] **Bovee** (Philip[5], Jacob[4], Jacob[3], Nicholas[2], Mathieu[1]), born 19 Jul 1824 in Broadalbin, Fulton Co., NY; died 4 Aug 1870. She married on 19 Jul 1842 David H Chase, born 4 Jun 1818 in Providence, Saratoga Co., NY, son of Wing Chase and Cynthia Howland Wilson.

Children of Ruth M Bovee and David H Chase were as follows:

1952	i	Mary[7] **Chase**, born 8 Nov 1844 in Providence, Saratoga Co., NY.
1953	ii	Philip B[7] **Chase**, born 15 Mar 1847 in Providence, Saratoga Co., NY.
1954	iii	Cynthia[7] **Chase**, born 29 Dec 1848.
1955	iv	Wing[7] **Chase**, born 22 Feb 1851 in Raisin, Lenawee Co., MI.
1956	v	David[7] **Chase**, born 6 Jul 1852.
1957	vi	William[7] **Chase**, born 29 May 1855.
1958	vii	Peleg[7] **Chase**, born 18 Jan 1858.
1959	viii	Mosher[7] **Chase**, born 6 Oct 1859.
1960	ix	Jacob H[7] **Chase**, born 22 Nov 1861.
1961	x	Benjamin[7] **Chase**, born 6 Jun 1864.
1962	xi	Lorenzo[7] **Chase**, born 27 Feb 1866.

993. Lydia Carrie[6] **Bovee** (Philip[5], Jacob[4], Jacob[3], Nicholas[2], Mathieu[1]), born abt 1840 in NY. She married on 2 Dec 1856 in Black Hawk Co., IA William A Crandall, born abt 1837 in NY, son of (---) Crandall and Mary (---).

Children of Lydia Carrie Bovee and William A Crandall were as follows:

1963	i	Edwin[7] **Crandall**, born abt 1858 in IA.
1964	ii	Edson[7] **Crandall**, born abt 1859 in IA.
1965	iii	Cora[7] **Crandall**, born abt 1862.
1966	iv	William[7] **Crandall**, born abt 1863.
1967	v	Alysus[7] **Crandall**, born abt 1866.
1968	vi	Nora A[7] **Crandall**, born abt 1868.
1969	vii	Bert[7] **Crandall**, born abt 1871.

1007. Abel W[6] **Bovee** (Henry[5], Jacob[4], Jacob[3], Nicholas[2], Mathieu[1]), born abt 1827 in Fulton Co., NY; died 12 Dec 1891 in Gloversville, Fulton Co., NY. He married Mary A Lasher, born 12 Jul 1834 in Mayfield, Fulton Co., NY; died 4 Jan 1915 in Gloversville, Fulton Co., NY, daughter of James Lasher and Anna Maria

Thurston.

Children of Abel W Bovee and Mary A Lasher were as follows:

- 1970   i   Olive C[7] **Bovee**, born Dec 1851; died 16 Jan 1859.
- 1971   ii   Helen I[7] **Bovee**, born Mar 1860 in NY.
- + 1972   iii   James V[7] **Bovee**, born Feb 1861 in NY. He married (1) **Ella Bentley**; (2) **Marian (---)**.

1016. Edwin Ruthven[6] **Bovee** (Albert[5], Isaac[4], Jacob[3], Nicholas[2], Mathieu[1]), born 22 Jan 1825 in Amsterdam, Montgomery Co., NY; died 23 Dec 1896 in Arena, Iowa Co., WI. He married on 29 Apr 1855 in Ft Atkinson, Jefferson Co., WI Anne Bird, born 26 Aug 1838 in England; died aft 1893, daughter of William Bird.

Children of Edwin Ruthven Bovee and Anne Bird were as follows:

- 1973   i   Willie R[7] **Bovee**, born abt 1860; died 1861.
- 1974   ii   Lourette[7] **Bovee**, born Dec 1867 in WI.
- 1975   iii   John R[7] **Bovee**, born abt 1873; died 1891.

1018. George E[6] **Bovee** (Albert[5], Isaac[4], Jacob[3], Nicholas[2], Mathieu[1]), born 1834 in Amsterdam, Montgomery Co., NY. He married on 11 Mar 1857 in Barton, Washington Co., WI Della S Laughlin, born abt 1845 in Canada.

Children of George E Bovee and Della S Laughlin were as follows:

- 1976   i   James[7] **Bovee**, born abt 1865 in LA.
- 1977   ii   Sheldon[7] **Bovee**, born abt 1871 in LA.
- 1978   iii   Field[7] **Bovee**, born abt 1874 in LA.
- 1979   iv   George[7] **Bovee**, born abt 1876 in LA.

1019. Clara M[6] **Bovee** (Albert[5], Isaac[4], Jacob[3], Nicholas[2], Mathieu[1]), born abt 1836 in NY. She married abt 1855 John Wilson, born Apr 1836.

Children of Clara M Bovee and John Wilson were as follows:

- 1980   i   Lenette W (Nettie)[7] **Wilson**, born 28 Dec 1856 in Whitewater, Walworth Co., WI.
- 1981   ii   Harry[7] **Wilson**, born abt 1870 in Whitewater, Walworth Co., WI.

1022. Marquis[6] **Bovee** (Jacob I[5], Isaac[4], Jacob[3], Nicholas[2], Mathieu[1]), born abt 1828 in NY; died 5 Apr 1893 in Chicago, Cook Co., IL. He married Margaret Scott, born Mar 1839 in England, daughter of Robert Scott.

Children of Marquis Bovee and Margaret Scott were as follows:

- 1982   i   Clarence F[7] **Bovee**, born Sep 1859 in WI; died 10 Jun 1931 in San Francisco, San Francisco Co., CA. He married **Frances O**.

+   1983   ii   Manley S[7] **Bovee**, born Oct 1869 in WI. He married (1)
                        Mary W (---); (2) **Martha (---)**.
+   1984   iii   Charles A[7] **Bovee**, born Nov 1872 in WI. He married
                        Amanda (---).

1028. Sarah Jane[6] **Bovee** (Albert[5], Abraham[4], Jacob[3], Nicholas[2], Mathieu[1]), born
abt 1844. She married abt 1866 John Coppernol.

Children of Sarah Jane Bovee and John Coppernol were as follows:
      1985   i   Albert[7] **Coppernol**.

1039. Myndert[6] **Bovee** (Daniel[5], Matthew[4], Jacob[3], Nicholas[2], Mathieu[1]), born 7
May 1818 in NY; died 8 Jun 1894 in Greenville, Montcalm Co., MI. He married
(1) on 10 Nov 1837 in Congregational Ch, Riga, Monroe Co., NY Julia C
Denmark, born 15 May 1817 in NY; died 8 Feb 1889; (2) Elizabeth Swan Tasher,
born 1825 in Charlotte, Washington Co., ME.

Children of Myndert Bovee and Julia C Denmark were as follows:
      1986   i   Mary J[7] **Bovee**, born 1838.
      1987   ii   Alma G[7] **Bovee**, born 1839.
+   1988   iii   Selena Viola[7] **Bovee**, born 1842 in Lenawee Co., MI. She
                        married (1) **Nathan E Stoughton**; (2) **John C Stoughton**.
      1989   iv   Servila A[7] **Bovee**, born 1845.
+   1990   v   Selinda H[7] **Bovee**, born 1847. She married **James J
                        Norris**.
      1991   vi   Symantha M[7] **Bovee**, born 1848.
      1992   vii   Alida Lovina[7] **Bovee**, born Aug 1850. She married on 22
                        Dec 1869 **George Claycomb**.
      1993   viii   Carrie[7] **Bovee**, born 1856 in MI. She married **Peter
                        McDermand**.

1040. Harriet T[6] **Bovee** (Daniel[5], Matthew[4], Jacob[3], Nicholas[2], Mathieu[1]), born 10
Mar 1821 in Brookfield, Madison Co., NY; christened 8 Mar 1832 in St Paul's
Luth Ch, Schoharie, Schoharie Co., NY; died 21 Aug 1883. She married on 8
Jun 1839 in DRC, Schoharie, Schoharie Co., NY. Franklin Parker, born 1819 in
MA.

Children of Harriet T Bovee and Franklin Parker were as follows:
      1994   i   Daniel W[7] **Parker**, born 1840 in NY.
      1995   ii   Almira[7] **Parker**, born 1842.
      1996   iii   Charles H[7] **Parker**, born 1844 in NY.
      1997   iv   Charlotte N[7] **Parker**, born 1846 in NY.
      1998   v   Anna Melissa[7] **Parker**, born 6 Jul 1862 in Oquawka,
                        Henderson Co., IL; died 6 Apr 1890 in Macedonia,
                        Pottawattamie Co., IA.

144

1041. Cornelius[6] **Bovee** (Daniel[5], Matthew[4], Jacob[3], Nicholas[2], Mathieu[1]), born 23 Jan 1824 in Schoharie, Schoharie Co., NY; christened 8 Mar 1832 in St Paul's Luth Ch, Schoharie, Schoharie Co., NY; died 27 Jan 1853 in Schoharie, Schoharie Co., NY. He married on 4 Jul 1843 in Schoharie, Schoharie Co., NY Eva Ann Livingston, born abt 1828 in Schoharie, Schoharie Co., NY, daughter of John J Livingston and Alida Borst.

Children of Cornelius Bovee and Eva Ann Livingston were as follows:

+ 1999   i   John Livingston[7] **Bovee**, born 3 Jul 1846 in NY; died 2 Apr 1917 in Seward, Seward Co., NB. He married **Elizabeth Bell Andrews**.

    2000   ii   Catherine[7] **Bovee**, born abt 1849 in Schoharie Co., NY. She married on 29 Sep 1870 in Oakland Co., MI **William H Chilson**.

+ 2001   iii   Jacob C[7] **Bovee**, born Feb 1850 in MI. He married **Jenevieve Fox**.

    2002   iv   Cornelius[7] **Bovee**, born 19 Jun 1853.

1044. Daniel D[6] **Bovee** (Daniel[5], Matthew[4], Jacob[3], Nicholas[2], Mathieu[1]), born 1 Jan 1833; died 29 Dec 1913. He married on 23 Jun 1857 Mary Van Vorst, born 24 Dec 1838 in Glennville Twp, Schnectady Co., NY; died 12 Oct 1914 in Winfield, Cowley Co., KS.

Children of Daniel D Bovee and Mary Van Vorst were as follows:

+ 2003   i   Sarah E[7] **Bovee**, born 1859 in IL. She married **Wesley McEwen**.

    2004   ii   Julia J[7] **Bovee**, born abt 1862 in IL. She married abt 1884 **James C McClelland**.

    2005   iii   William Theodore[7] **Bovee**, born 31 Dec 1874 in New Salem, KS; died 3 Jul 1897.

1050. Mary Ann[6] **Bovee** (Jacob[5], Matthew[4], Jacob[3], Nicholas[2], Mathieu[1]), born 26 Mar 1813; christened in Schenectady, Schenectady Co., NY; died 8 Dec 1902 in LeRoy,Genesee Co., NY. She married on 15 Oct 1840 in Cong Ch, Riga, Monroe Co., NY Lewis S Davis, born 9 Apr 1800 in CT; died 17 Feb 1879 in NY.

Children of Mary Ann Bovee and Lewis S Davis were as follows:

    2006   i   Lewis S[7] **Davis** Jr, born 1843 in NY.

    2007   ii   Monroe[7] **Davis**, born Aug 1850 in NY.

    2008   iii   Alfred[7] **Davis**.

1051. Abraham[6] **Bovee** (Jacob[5], Matthew[4], Jacob[3], Nicholas[2], Mathieu[1]), born 22 Dec 1817 in Schenectady, Schenectady Co., NY; christened 1 May 1818 in St George Epis Ch, Schenectady, Schenectady Co., NY; died 9 Jan 1861 in Stone Church Rural Cem, Stone Church, Genesee Co., NY. He married on 9 Apr 1844 in Congregational, Ch, Riga, Monroe Co., NY Catherine More (see 1058), born 4 Sep 1826 in LeRoy,Genesee Co., NY, daughter of John C Moore and Bata Bovee.

Children of Abraham Bovee and Catherine More were as follows:

+ 2009 i Jacob Lorenzo[7] **Bovee**, born 9 May 1845 in NY; died 18 Oct 1921 in Richford, Tioga Co., NY. He married (1) **Malona A (---)**; (2) **Catherine (---)**; (3) **Frances H Belden**.

2010 ii Susan L[7] **Bovee**, born 1847 in Riga, Monroe Co., NY; died 16 Sep 1866. She married **Thomas McPherson**, son of James McPherson and Christy Gordon.

2011 iii Frances C[7] **Bovee**, born abt 1848 in Monroe Co., NY; died 29 Nov 1925 in Berkshire, Tioga Co., NY. She married **Howard Carmell**, son of John Carmell and Fanny (---).

2012 iv Julia M[7] **Bovee**, born 7 Nov 1853 in Riga, Monroe Co., NY; died 12 Jun 1934 in Bergen, Genesee Co., NY. She married **William H Johnson**.

2013 v Dellie[7] **Bovee**, born Sep 1855 in Riga, Monroe Co., NY; died 16 Mar 1858.

2014 vi Estella[7] **Bovee**, born abt 1857 in Monroe Co., NY; died 1936. She married **Henry Cooper**.

2015 vii Hattie[7] **Bovee**, born 1859 in NY; died 1889. She married **George C Woodworth**.

2016 viii Mary Ann[7] **Bovee**, born abt 1860 in Monroe Co., NY.

1052. Maria[6] **Bovee** (Jacob[5], Matthew[4], Jacob[3], Nicholas[2], Mathieu[1]), born 15 Jan 1820 in NY; christened 14 May 1820 in Woestina Ref Ch, Rotterdam, Schenectady Co.; died 9 Mar 1887 in Litchfield, Hillsdale Co., MI. She married on 30 Apr 1839 Stephen Canniff, born 30 Apr 1816 in Knowlesville, Orleans Co., NY; died 22 Nov 1876 in Litchfield, Hillsdale Co., MI.

Children of Maria Bovee and Stephen Canniff were as follows:

2017 i Susan M[7] **Canniff**, born 15 Apr 1841 in NY.

2018 ii Helen S[7] **Canniff**, born 13 Sep 1843 in NY.

2019 iii Chauncey Bird[7] **Canniff**, born 7 Apr 1846 in Litchfield, Hillsdale Co., MI.

2020 iv Harlan A[7] **Canniff**, born 19 Mar 1848 in Litchfield, Hillsdale Co., MI.

2021 v Charles B[7] **Canniff**, born 20 May 1850 in Litchfield, Hillsdale Co., MI.

2022 vi Julia L[7] **Canniff**, born 26 Jul 1856 in MI.

1053. Henry Jacob[6] **Bovee** (Jacob[5], Matthew[4], Jacob[3], Nicholas[2], Mathieu[1]), born 27 Nov 1837 in NY; christened 6 May 1838 in Congregational, Ch, Riga, Monroe Co., NY; died 29 Sep 1924 in Los Angeles Co., CA. He married on 6 Nov 1856, divorced Sabrina Emogene Fordham, born 26 May 1840 in Genesee Co., NY; died 23 Dec 1910 in San Diego, San Diego Co., CA, daughter of

Francis Fordham and Caroline Woodward.

Children of Henry Jacob Bovee and Sabrina Emogene Fordham were as follows:

2023   i   Caroline Lucinda[7] **Bovee**, born 22 Dec 1857 in Riga, Monroe Co., NY; christened 1 May 1858 in Congregational Ch, Riga, Monroe Co., NY; died 12 Mar 1940. She married on 22 Dec 1884 in Burlingame, Osage Co., KS **Dr. Edmind Longley**, son of Edmund Longley and Annis Kilbourn.

+   2024   ii   Wayland Henry[7] **Bovee**, born 24 Oct 1860 in Riga, Monroe Co., NY; christened 10 May 1862 in Congregational Ch, Riga, Monroe Co., NY; died 9 Jun 1919 in Oakland, Alameda Co., CA. He married (1) **Ida May Bartlett Shibley**; (2) **Pauline Morton Houk**; (3) **Florence L Houk**.

2025   iii   Metta Lunette[7] **Bovee**, born 29 Oct 1863 in Monroe Co., NY. She married on 31 Dec 1892 **James G Chapman**.

1065. Mary[6] **Bovee** (Isaac[5], Matthew[4], Jacob[3], Nicholas[2], Mathieu[1]), born abt 1824 in NY. She married on 3 Oct 1852 in Delaware Co., OH Cleophus R Seely, born abt 1802 in NY.

Children of Mary Bovee and Cleophus R Seely were as follows:

2026   i   Mary[7] **Seely**, born abt 1855 in OH.

1066. Catherine Ann[6] **Bovee** (Isaac[5], Matthew[4], Jacob[3], Nicholas[2], Mathieu[1]), born 1828. She married on 24 Sep 1845 in Delaware Co., OH Nathan Gardner, born 30 Jan 1822 in OH; died 23 Jun 1853.

Children of Catherine Ann Bovee and Nathan Gardner were as follows:

2027   i   Nancy R[7] **Gardner**, born 25 Jan 1846.

2028   ii   George W[7] **Gardner**, born abt 1848.

2029   iii   Aaron Mason[7] **Gardner**, born abt 1851.

2030   iv   Nathan[7] **Gardner**, born abt 1853 in OH.

1067. Susan[6] **Bovee** (Isaac[5], Matthew[4], Jacob[3], Nicholas[2], Mathieu[1]), born 15 Aug 1829 in OH; died 22 Mar 1901 in Delaware Co., OH. She married on 29 Mar 1849 in Delaware Co., OH Lorenzo Dow Farnsworth, born 10 Jun 1828 in New York, New York Co, NY; died 25 Mar 1909.

Children of Susan Bovee and Lorenzo Dow Farnsworth were as follows:

2031   i   James B[7] **Farnsworth**, born 20 Aug 1850 in Delaware Co., OH.

2032   ii   Melvin S[7] **Farnsworth**, born 22 Mar 1853 in Delaware Co., OH.

2033   iii   William Henry[7] **Farnsworth**, born 25 Aug 1855 in

Delaware Co., OH.

2034   iv   James Elmus[7] **Farnsworth**, born 14 Mar 1858.

1069. Sarah Elizabeth[6] **Bovee** (Isaac[5], Matthew[4], Jacob[3], Nicholas[2], Mathieu[1]), born 1846 in OH. She married on 2 Apr 1867 in Franklin Co., OH John Wesley Dyer, born 27 Jan 1824 in OH; died 11 Aug 1907 in Labette Co., KS.

Children of Sarah Elizabeth Bovee and John Wesley Dyer were as follows:

2035   i   William Addison[7] **Dyer**, born 25 Sep 1875 in IL.

2036   ii   Ida A[7] **Dyer**, born 24 Dec 1879 in KS.

2037   iii   Charles Eugene[7] **Dyer**, born 24 May 1885 in Wilsonton, Labrette Twp., Labrette Co., KS.

1072. Lorenzo Jacob[6] **Bovee** (Cornelius Schermerhorn[5], Matthew[4], Jacob[3], Nicholas[2], Mathieu[1]), born 18 May 1835 in Riga, Monroe Co., NY; christened 16 May 1839 in Congregational, Ch, Riga, Monroe Co., NY; died 20 Aug 1893 in LeRoy,Genesee Co., NY. He married on 25 Sep 1860 Sarah Adelia Kelsey, died 20 Aug 1893 in LeRoy, Genesee Co., NY.

Children of Lorenzo Jacob Bovee and Sarah Adelia Kelsey were as follows:

2038   i   Ola E[7] **Bovee**, died 20 Aug 1893 in LeRoy, Genesee Co., NY.

1073. Cornelius Elihu[6] **Bovee** (Cornelius Schermerhorn[5], Matthew[4], Jacob[3], Nicholas[2], Mathieu[1]), born 23 Jun 1836 in Riga, Monroe Co., NY; christened 16 May 1839 in Congregational, Ch, Riga, Monroe Co., NY; died 22 Mar 1911 in Stone Church, Genesee Co., NY. He married on 24 Nov 1859 Harriet M Ludington, born 1837 in Ostego Co., NY; died 31 Mar 1898.

Children of Cornelius Elihu Bovee and Harriet M Ludington were as follows:

2039   i   Frances L[7] **Bovee**, born 30 Sep 1860 in Stone Church, Genesee Co., NY; died 29 Jul 1938 in Leroy, Genesee Co., NY. She married on 6 Feb 1882 **Charles B Mortimer**, son of John Mortimer and Ann Price.

2040   ii   Charles[7] **Bovee**, born abt 1863 in Genesee Co., NY; died 1903.

2041   iii   Minnie L[7] **Bovee**, born abt 1864 in Genesee Co., NY; died 3 May 1940 in Byron, Genesee Co., NY. She married **John WAtson**.

+   2042   iv   William Ludington[7] **Bovee**, born Apr 1867 in Genesee Co., NY; died 20 Dec 1926 in Riga, Monroe Co., NY. He married **Lottie May Bovee** (see 3124).

+   2043   v   George W[7] **Bovee**, born Nov 1868 in Genesee Co., NY; died 30 Jan 1925 in Stone Church, Genesee Co., NY. He married **Matilda (---)**.

2044   vi   Armanell E[7] **Bovee**, born 26 Mar 1881 in Genesee Co.,

NY; died 3 Apr 1962. She married on 18 Apr 1916 in Stone Church, Genesee Co., NY **Clifford J Davy**, son of James Davy and Mary Watson.

1082. Anthony[6] **Bovee** (Walter[5], Anthony[4], Gerrit[3], Anthony[2], Mathieu[1]), born 1816; died 26 Aug 1858. He married Pamela (---), born abt 1817.

Children of Anthony Bovee and Pamela (---) were as follows:

| 2045 | i | Alice[7] **Bovee**, born 11 Sep 1843; died 13 Jan 1846. |
| 2046 | ii | Frank H[7] **Bovee**, born 1 Dec 1849; died 1 Dec 1853. |

1083. Walter[6] **Bovee** (Walter[5], Anthony[4], Gerrit[3], Anthony[2], Mathieu[1]), born 1819. He married Lenora Van Willer.

Children of Walter Bovee and Lenora Van Willer were as follows:

2047	i	Alfred Purvee[7] **Bovee**, born 1839.
2048	ii	George Y[7] **Bovee**, born 1843.
2049	iii	William D[7] **Bovee**, born 1845.
2050	iv	Malinda A[7] **Bovee**, born 1848.
2051	v	Allen[7] **Bovee**, born abt 1852.
2052	vi	Leland[7] **Bovee**, born abt 1858.

1091. Luther[6] **Bovee** (Jacob[5], Anthony[4], Gerrit[3], Anthony[2], Mathieu[1]), born Jun 1827 in Warren Co., NY; died 22 Aug 1910. He married on 18 Jul 1852 in Black Brook, Clinton Co., NY Mary Ann Scoville, born 17 Jul 1830; died 14 Aug 1908.

Children of Luther Bovee and Mary Ann Scoville were as follows:

+	2053	i	George[7] **Bovee**, born 13 Jun 1853 in Saratoga Co., NY; died 29 Sep 1924 in Utica Oneida Co., NY. He married (1) **Endora Austin**; (2) **Frances Lindsey**.
+	2054	ii	Hiram[7] **Bovee**, born 10 Sep 1855 in Saratoga Co., NY; died bef 1900. He married **Emile Daniels**.
	2055	iii	Lewis[7] **Bovee**, born 23 Dec 1857 in Saratoga Co., NY; died 4 Sep 1858.
+	2056	iv	Henry L[7] **Bovee**, born 14 Aug 1859 in Saratoga Co., NY; died 1928 in Glens Falls, Warren Co., NY. He married **Mary Noonan**.
	2057	v	Eunice[7] **Bovee**, born 9 Sep 1861 in Saratoga Co., NY; died 20 Dec 1889.
+	2058	vi	Orra Martin[7] **Bovee**, born 27 Feb 1864 in Saratoga Co., NY; died 10 Jul 1936 in Lake Luzerne, Warren Co., NY. He married **Agnes Mary Reed**.
	2059	vii	Harriet[7] **Bovee**, born 6 Jun 1865 in Saratoga Co., NY; died 6 Sep 1865.
+	2060	viii	Fred[7] **Bovee**, born 26 Jun 1867 in Saratoga Co., NY; died

19 Nov 1934 in Conklinville, Saratoga Co., NY. He married **Lydia Ann Ovitt**.

2061   ix   Nathan[7] **Bovee**, born Aug 1869 in Saratoga Co., NY; died 11 Nov 1869.

2062   x   Wallace[7] **Bovee**, born 14 Apr 1872 in Saratoga Co., NY; died 22 Jul 1872.

1093. Orra[6] **Bovee** (Jacob[5], Anthony[4], Gerrit[3], Anthony[2], Mathieu[1]), born 30 May 1831 in Luzerne, Warren Co., NY; died 13 Nov 1913 in Saranac, Clinton Co., NY. He married (1) Louise Daniels, born abt 1836; died 28 Oct 1873 in Saranac, Clinton Co., NY; (2) on 30 May 1884 in Redford, Clinton Co., NY Julia A Goodsoe, daughter of John Goodsoe and Charlotte Shinville.

Children of Orra Bovee and Louise Daniels were as follows:

2063   i   Emma[7] **Bovee**, born 17 Feb 1853; died 13 Jul 1948. She married (1) on 7 Nov 1878 **Elmore L Lyons**, son of Louis Lyons and Johanna Ryan; (2) on 29 Jun 1916 **Nelson Raymond**.

2064   ii   Anna[7] **Bovee**, born abt 1857.

2065   iii   Fred[7] **Bovee**, born abt 1859.

2066   iv   Lincoln[7] **Bovee**, born 20 Apr 1861 in NY. He married on 4 May 1889 in Plattsburg, Clinton Co., NY **Nellie DeYoung**.

2067   v   Wallace[7] **Bovee**, born abt 1868.

2068   vi   Alice May[7] **Bovee**, born Jul 1870 in NY; died 1920. She married **Frank Bovee** (see 2073), born Sep 1863; died 1940, son of Norman Bovee and Nancy White.

Children of Orra Bovee and Julia A Goodsoe were as follows:

2069   i   Catherine[7] **Bovee**, born 6 Aug 1885 in Saranac, Clinton Co., NY.

+   2070   ii   Henry Harrison[7] **Bovee**, born 18 Apr 1888 in Saranac, Clinton Co., NY. He married **Mary A (---)**.

2071   iii   Frances[7] **Bovee**, born 18 Apr 1888; died 21 Sep 1888.

2072   iv   Charlotte L[7] **Bovee**, born 14 Jul 1892 in Saranac, Clinton Co., NY. She married **Ardin Hutchins**.

1095. Norman[6] **Bovee** (Jacob[5], Anthony[4], Gerrit[3], Anthony[2], Mathieu[1]), born Jul 1839; died 5 Aug 1928. He married Nancy White, born Feb 1845 in NY; died 15 Jun 1912.

Children of Norman Bovee and Nancy White were as follows:

+   2073   i   Frank[7] **Bovee**, born Sep 1863; died 1940. He married **Alice May Bovee** (see 2068).

2074   ii   Orrie[7] **Bovee**, born 1864; died 8 Dec 1870.

+   2075   iii   Charles[7] **Bovee**. He married **Ada Carel**.

+   2076   iv   Cora L[7] **Bovee**, born 24 Mar 1857; died 5 Jan 1915. She married **Charles L Frasier**.

+ 2077   v   Rosalie[7] **Bovee**, born 1872. She married **Ulysses Grant Frasier**.

2078   vi   Mary Jane[7] **Bovee**, born Mar 1874; died 4 Apr 1874.

+ 2079   vii   Mary Ardell[7] **Bovee**, born 28 Jul 1875; died 1959. She married **Truman E Frasier**.

2080   viii   Ormand E[7] **Bovee**, born Aug 1877; died 9 Dec 1877.

+ 2081   ix   Orange[7] **Bovee**, born 22 Dec 1878; died Jan 1968. He married **Emma Wells Orton**.

+ 2082   x   Lester[7] **Bovee**, born Mar 1881. He married **Carrie Carleton**.

+ 2083   xi   Anna Lorra[7] **Bovee**, born 30 Jul 1882; died 1962 in Gloversville, Fulton Co., NY. She married **Roscoe White**.

2084   xii   Lincoln[7] **Bovee**, born 1884; died 5 May 1886.

2085   xiii   LeRoy[7] **Bovee**, born May 1887; died 1961. He married **Anna Handy**, daughter of George Handy and Frances (---).

1096. Wallace[6] **Bovee** (Jacob[5], Anthony[4], Gerrit[3], Anthony[2], Mathieu[1]), born 13 Aug 1840; died 14 Oct 1907. He married Sarah Jane Clute, born 19 Jul 1842; died 11 May 1916.

Children of Wallace Bovee and Sarah Jane Clute were as follows:

+ 2086   i   Luther E[7] **Bovee**, born Apr 1865 in NY; died 4 May 1939. He married (1) **Mary Jane Swart**; (2) **Mayme J Morris**.

+ 2087   ii   Jacob H[7] **Bovee**, born Jan 1868 in NY; died 1945. He married **Ida May Stewart**.

2088   iii   Henry[7] **Bovee**, born Sep 1873 in NY; died 1930.

2089   iv   Lemuel[7] **Bovee**, born Sep 1876 in NY; died 11 Sep 1933 in NY.

+ 2090   v   David Duff[7] **Bovee**, born Mar 1877. He married **Sarah M Davidson**.

2091   vi   Marvin[7] **Bovee**, born Mar 1879 in NY; died 1942. He married on 23 Jun 1900 **Minnie Herschfield**.

+ 2092   vii   Marshall[7] **Bovee**, born Feb 1881 in NY. He married **Mable Tissue**.

2093   viii   Harvey G[7] **Bovee**, born May 1884 in NY.

1097. William Halsey[6] **Bovee** (Joseph[5], Anthony[4], Gerrit[3], Anthony[2], Mathieu[1]), born Jun 1843 in Fort Edward, Washington Co., NY; died 15 Aug 1909 in Kensington, Smith Co., KS. He married (1) abt 1869 Emma Hardee Glidden, born 1847; died 1894, daughter of Calvin Selden Glidden and Olive Steward; (2) on 29 Mar 1899 in Bloomington, Franklin Co., NE Delissia P Donophon, daughter of Philip Donophon.

Children of William Halsey Bovee and Emma Hardee Glidden were as follows:

2094   i   Lucia Maryette[7] **Bovee**, born 7 Aug 1879 in Spring Valley
                Twp., Fillmore Co., MN; died 13 Feb 1951 in Los Angeles
                Co., CA.

1100. Henry Joseph[6] **Bovee** (Joseph[5], Anthony[4], Gerrit[3], Anthony[2], Mathieu[1]),
born 18 Apr 1854 in Fort Edward, Washington Co., NY; died 10 Nov 1903 in
Cozad, Dawson Co., NE. He married on 3 Jul 1880 in Milton, Rock Co., WI Mary
J Hubbard (see 1406), born 28 Sep 1859 in Mukwonago, Waukesha Co., WI,
daughter of John William Hubbard and Mary Arnold Bovee.

Children of Henry Joseph Bovee and Mary J Hubbard were as follows:

2095   i   Edith[7] **Bovee**, born 23 Jul 1881; died May 1971. She
                married **George O'Brien**, born abt 1878.
2096   ii   Philip Arthur[7] **Bovee**, born 26 Jan 1889; died 6 Feb 1951
                in CA. He married **E B (---)**.
2097   iii   Sidney[7] **Bovee**, born Jun 1896.
+ 2098 iv   Mac Henry[7] **Bovee**, born 8 Oct 1903 in Cozad, Dawson
                Co., NE; died 20 Aug 1951. He married **E Blandena
                Johnson**.

1101. Eugene M[6] **Bovee** (Joseph[5], Anthony[4], Gerrit[3], Anthony[2], Mathieu[1]), born
27 Oct 1855 in Fort Edward, Washington Co., NY; died 30 Sep 1931. He
married on 4 Apr 1876 Mary Elizabeth Osbourne, born 29 Nov 1856; died 28 Oct
1918 in Reedpoint, Stillwater Co. MT.

Children of Eugene M Bovee and Mary Elizabeth Osbourne were as follows:

2099   i   Eugene Roy[7] **Bovee**, born abt 1878 in IA.
2100   ii   Earl Steven[7] **Bovee**, born 8 Jan 1882 in IA; died Nov 1964
                in Grants Pass, Josephine Co.,OR. He married **Eve
                Reed**.
2101   iii   L[7] **Bovee**, born 20 Sep 1885 in IA; died 24 Nov 1920 in
                Reed Point, Stillwater Co., MT. She married on 12 Apr
                1904 in Burr Oak, Winneshiek Co., IA **George M Price**,
                born Dec 1878; died 7 Feb 1944 in Reed Point, Stillwater
                Co., MT, son of Daniel Price and Nancy (---).
+ 2102 iv   Guy Harrison[7] **Bovee**, born 1 Jan 1889 in Burr Oak,
                Winneshiek Co., IA; died May 1964 in CA. He married
                Mary Isabel Fillipe.
+ 2103 v   Claude Alva[7] **Bovee**, born 5 Feb 1898 in MT; died Jun
                1969 in Reedpoint, Stillwater Co. MT. He married (1)
                Mamie (---); (2) **Catherine Lannen**.

1103. Peter[6] **Heath** (Orra[5] Bovee, Peter[4], Gerrit[3], Anthony[2], Mathieu[1]), born in
Jefferson Co, NY.. He married Ruth Richards.

Children of Peter Heath and Ruth Richards were as follows:

2104   i   Hiram[7] **Heath**, born 18 Jul 1849 in Adams, Jefferson Co.,

152

1110. Alvin Earl[6] **Bovay** (John W[5], Peter[4], Gerrit[3], Anthony[2], Mathieu[1]), born 12 Jul 1818 in Adams, Jefferson Co., NY; died 29 Jan 1903 in Los Angeles, Los Angeles Co., CA. He married on 25 Nov 1846 in St. Lukes Ch., New York, New York Co., NY Caroline Elizabeth Smith, died 1896 in Los Angeles, Los Angeles Co., CA, daughter of Ransom Smith.

Children of Alvin Earl Bovay and Caroline Elizabeth Smith were as follows:

2105   i   Child[7] **Bovee**, born abt 1848; died abt 1865 in New York, New York Co., NY.

1119. Ervin Washington[6] **Bovee** (Gerrit[5], Peter[4], Gerrit[3], Anthony[2], Mathieu[1]), born 22 Mar 1821 in Adams, Jefferson Co., NY; died 1852. He married on 26 Sep 1849 in Adams, Jefferson Co., NY Evalena Felt, born abt 1826, daughter of Henry Felt and Melinda (---).

Children of Ervin Washington Bovee and Evalena Felt were as follows:

2106   i   Hennry James[7] **Bovee**, born 26 Nov 1850 in Adams, Jefferson Co., NY. He married on 9 Mar 1881 in Lacona, Oswego Co., NY **Caroline Chorley**.

2107   ii   Berthana Melinda[7] **Bovee**, died 20 Sep 1954 in Oswegatchie, St Lawrence Co., NY. She married on 21 Nov 1869 in Fine, St Lawrence Co., NY **Albert Marsh**.

1120. Peter B[6] **Bovee** (Gerrit[5], Peter[4], Gerrit[3], Anthony[2], Mathieu[1]), born 13 Jan 1824 in Adams, Jefferson Co., NY; died 24 Nov 1880. He married (1) Lucy (---), born abt 1840 in NY; (2) on 20 Nov 1875 in Nelson Twp., Kent Co., MI Nancy Sodin, born abt 1828 in PA.

Children of Peter B Bovee and Lucy (---) were as follows:

2108   i   Harriet M[7] **Bovee**, born abt 1858 in MI.
+   2109   ii   U N[7] **Bovee**. He married **Melissa (---)**.

1123. Seymour C[6] **Bovee** (Gerrit[5], Peter[4], Gerrit[3], Anthony[2], Mathieu[1]), born Jul 1829 in CT; died 3 Dec 1913 in Allegan Co., MI.. He married (1) on 1 Jan 1854 Louisa C Lewis, born 17 Jan 1836 in PA; died 14 Sep 1876, daughter of Jonah Rogers Lewis and Caroline Bogardus; (2) Rosanah S (---), born 4 Jul 1837 in Canada; died 23 Feb 1928.

Children of Seymour C Bovee and Louisa C Lewis were as follows:

2110   i   Linnie K[7] **Bovee**, born abt 1857. She married on 3 Nov 1877 in Allegan Co., MI. **Francis M Huntley**.

Children of Seymour C Bovee and Rosanah S (---) were as follows:

2111   i   Mina[7] **Bovee**, born Oct 1883 in MI. She married on 1 Oct 1907 **Clarence J McCune**, son of John McCune and

Emerilda A Dailey.

1124. Jane^6 **Bovee** (Gerrit^5, Peter^4, Gerrit^3, Anthony^2, Mathieu^1), born 25 Mar 1831; died 13 Jan 1895 in Jefferson Co., NY. She married on 6 Mar 1852 Joseph A Brownell.

Children of Jane Bovee and Joseph A Brownell were as follows:

2112	i	Perry A^7 **Brownell**, born 16 Sep 1855.
2113	ii	Ellen^7 **Brownell**, born 24 Nov 1860. She married **William Fairbanks**.
2114	iii	Jefferson L^7 **Brownell**, born 20 Nov 1864.
2115	iv	Jennie^7 **Brownell**, born 14 Oct 1868.

1130. David^6 **Bovee** (Jonathan^5, Peter^4, Gerrit^3, Anthony^2, Mathieu^1), born 11 Nov 1819 in Hartford, Washington Co., NY; died 19 Jul 1900 in Coldwater, Branch Co., MI. He married on 3 Feb 1842 Cynthia Ann Goodman, born 24 Nov 1821 in Bainbridge,Chenango Co., NY; died 5 Feb 1899 in Coldwater, Branch Co., MI, daughter of Thomas Goodman and Roxy Upson.

Children of David Bovee and Cynthia Ann Goodman were as follows:

2116	i	Helen Salina^7 **Bovee**, born 6 Apr 1843; died 19 Feb 1900. She married **George Melvin Dumond**, born Apr 1844 in NY.
2117	ii	Child^7 **Bovee**, born 27 Jul 1845; died 27 Jul 1845.
2118	iii	Edward Raphael^7 **Bovee**, born 31 Aug 1848; died 1865 in Civil War.
2119	iv	Eva Alvira^7 **Bovee**, born 16 Apr 1850 in MI; died 1934. She married (1) on 24 Oct 1867 in Branch Co., MI **Eugene Vaughn**; (2) aft 1867 **Frank Dart**.
2120	v	George Washington^7 **Bovee**, born 13 Aug 1853 in Coldwater, Branch Co., MI; died 24 Oct 1862 in Coldwater, Branch Co., MI.
+ 2121	vi	Charles Howard^7 **Bovee**, born 14 Jul 1861 in Coldwater, Branch Co., MI; died 2 May 1906 in Reno, Washo Co., NV. He married **Bessie Grosvenor**.

1131. Eli William^6 **Bovee** (Jonathan^5, Peter^4, Gerrit^3, Anthony^2, Mathieu^1), born 1 Nov 1821 in Adams, Jefferson Co., NY; died 25 Oct 1906 in Benton Harbor, Berrien Co., MI. He married (1) on 2 Nov 1848 in Jonesville, Hillsdale Co., MI Ann Amelia Cook, born 25 Nov 1827 in Greenwood, Steuben Co., NY; died 22 Sep 1865 in Coldwater, Branch Co., MI, daughter of Anson Cook and Anna Wheeler; (2) on 29 Jul 1866 Mary H Hall, born 3 May 1834 in NY; died 3 May 1872 in Algansee, Branch Co.,MI; (3) on 26 Oct 1879 Lorinda Gregg Horton, born Sep 1839 in OH.

Children of Eli William Bovee and Ann Amelia Cook were as follows:

2122	i	Georgia Anna^7 **Bovee**, born 7 Aug 1850 in Hillsdale Co.,

154

MI; died 13 Sep 1850 in Hillsdale Co., MI.

+ 2123 ii Edwin Anson[7] **Bovee**, born 30 Sep 1851 in Litchfield, Hillsdale Co., MI; died 16 Dec 1910 in Grand Rapids, Kent Co., MI. He married (1) **Jullia A Session**; (2) **Adeline Elizabeth Stevens**.

+ 2124 iii Ella Jane[7] **Bovee**, born 29 Jan 1854 in Coldwater, Branch Co., MI; died Nov 1936 in Benton Harbor, Berrien Co., MI. She married **Henry W Kent**.

  2125 iv Jay[7] **Bovee**, born 3 Nov 1856 in Coldwater, Branch Co., MI; died 16 Nov 1856.

+ 2126 v Carolyn Amelia[7] **Bovee**, born 29 Jan 1858 in Coldwater, Branch Co., MI; died 11 Jun 1936 in St Joseph, Berrien Co., MI. She married **Henry Joseph Lewis**.

In a very long letter written by Eli William Bovee in 1904 he describes in great detail and flourish how his father Jonathan, his wife, Lucy Smith and five children emigrated to the state of Michigan in the summer of 1838 when it was all a vast wilderness. They settled in an area of the forest where they cleared the land to grow crops and build a cabin for shelter. The hardships were many but the rewards plentiful as their homestead grew and more settlers arrived. He continued to live there until nearly the time of his death in 1906.

1132. Hannah[6] **Bovee** (Jonathan[5], Peter[4], Gerrit[3], Anthony[2], Mathieu[1]), born 31 Jan 1826 in Washington Co., NY; died 30 Jan 1914 in Branch Co.,MI. She married (1) on 28 Oct 1846 in Rochester, Monroe Co., NY Rueben J Miller, born abt 1827; died 4 Jan 1877 in Toledo, Lucas Co., OH; (2) aft 1877 in Coldwater, Branch Co., MI J M Rodenbaugh, died 1890 in Coldwater, Branch Co., MI.

Children of Hannah Bovee and Rueben J Miller were as follows:

  2127 i Child[7] **Miller**.
  2128 ii Fayette[7] **Miller**.

1133. Caleb Drake[6] **Bovee** (Jonathan[5], Peter[4], Gerrit[3], Anthony[2], Mathieu[1]), born 8 Mar 1829 in Hartford Washington Co., NY; died 15 Apr 1854 in Coldwater, Branch Co., MI. He married (1) on 8 Mar 1849 Maria Murdock; (2) Hester A Estice.

Children of Caleb Drake Bovee and Maria Murdock were as follows:

  2129 i Perry E[7] **Bovee**, born 9 Dec 1849 in Coldwater, Branch Co., MI; died 1 Sep 1850 in Coldwater, Branch Co., MI.

Children of Caleb Drake Bovee and Hester A Estice were as follows:

  2130 i Herbert O[7] **Bovee**.

1134. Clark[6] **Bovee** (Jonathan[5], Peter[4], Gerrit[3], Anthony[2], Mathieu[1]), born 8 May 1831 in Hartford, Washington Co., NY; christened 5 Oct 1831; died 17 Jul 1908 in Algansee, Branch Co., MI. He married Aurelia Randall, born 13 May 1832 in Fairfield, Hamilton Co., OH; died 14 Feb 1911 in Algansee Twp., Branch Co., MI.

Children of Clark Bovee and Aurelia Randall were as follows:

+ 2131 i Jonathan Orly[7] **Bovee**, born 4 Jul 1858 in Algansee Twp., Branch Co., MI; died 9 Dec 1925. He married (1) **Ida M Camp**; (2) **Ada W Pruce**.

+ 2132 ii Elmer Ellsworth[7] **Bovee**, born 30 Aug 1859 in Algansee Twp., Branch Co.,MI; died 11 Jul 1938 in Algansee Twp., Branch Co., MI. He married **Nettie Follette**.

+ 2133 iii Lucy Lovina[7] **Bovee**, born 30 Aug 1862 in Algansee, Branch Co.,MI. She married **Walter Frank**.

  2134 iv Minnie[7] **Bovee**, born 5 Mar 1865 in MI; died 16 Jun 1940. She married on 27 Nov 1884 in Branch Co., MI **Charles E Hall**.

+ 2135 v Henry Orgo[7] **Bovee**, born 14 Sep 1867 in Algansee Twp., Branch Co., MI; died 4 Apr 1938 in Coldwater, Branch Co., MI. He married **Dora Quimby**.

  2136 vi Lillie May[7] **Bovee**, born 4 May 1870 in MI.

+ 2137 vii Edward Clark[7] **Bovee**, born 16 Jul 1872 in Algansee, Branch Co.,MI; died aft 1938. He married **Inez Mae Brainard**.

1140. Abraham[6] Bovee (William W[5], Peter[4], Gerrit[3], Anthony[2], Mathieu[1]), born aft 1842 in Washington Co., NY; died 14 Apr 1903 in Fabius, Onondaga Co., NY. He married Mary E (---), born abt 1838 in OH; died 1 Nov 1909 in Fabius, Onondaga Co., NY.

Children of Abraham Bovee and Mary E (---) were as follows:

+ 2138 i Charles A[7] **Bovee**, born abt 1873 in NY. He married **Clara K Jones**.

1141. Orlando A[6] Bovee (William W[5], Peter[4], Gerrit[3], Anthony[2], Mathieu[1]), born Mar 1844 in Washington Co., NY; died 15 Mar 1926 in Syracuse, Onondaga Co., NY. He married abt 1868 Frances G (---), born Jun 1848 in NY; died 7 Dec 1921 in Syracuse, Onondaga Co., NY.

Children of Orlando A Bovee and Frances G (---) were as follows:

  2139 i Franklin O[7] **Bovee**, born abt 1866 in Onondaga Co., NY.; died 25 Dec 1924.

  2140 ii Merton S[7] **Bovee**, born Mar 1867 in Onondaga Co., NY.; died 23 Oct 1908 in Syracuse, Onondaga Co., NY..

  2141 iii Kittie E[7] **Bovee**, born abt 1868. She married **(---) Priest**.

  2142 iv Walter C[7] **Bovee**, born in Onondaga Co., NY.; died 25 Dec 1925 in Syracuse, Onondaga Co., NY.. He married **Cora (---)**.

1143. Maria R[6] Bovee (Peter[5], Jacob[4], Gerrit[3], Anthony[2], Mathieu[1]), born abt 1829; died 10 Jul 1864 in West Farmington, Trumbull Co., OH. She married

Henry Martin Kibbe, born 12 Oct 1826 in Hardwick, Caledonia Co., VT; died 15 Nov 1908 in West Farmington, Trumbull Co., OH, son of Martin Kibbe.

Children of Maria R Bovee and Henry Martin Kibbe were as follows:

2143　i　　Sophonia[7] **Kibbe**, born abt 1848 in Hartwick, Caledonia Co., VT.

2144　ii　　Alvin[7] **Kibbe**, born abt 1858. He married **May Ford**.

2145　iii　　Henry[7] **Kibbe**.

1144. Moses S[6] **Bovee** (Peter[5], Jacob[4], Gerrit[3], Anthony[2], Mathieu[1]), born 24 Feb 1834 in VT. He married on 23 May 1864 Adeline Ouderkerk (see 1180), born 8 Dec 1846; died 3 Feb 1896, daughter of William B Ouderkerk and Elizabeth R Bovee.

Children of Moses S Bovee and Adeline Ouderkerk were as follows:

2146　i　　Alice B[7] **Bovee**, born 22 Mar 1864 in Danville, Caledonia Co., VT.

+　2147　ii　　Frank[7] **Bovee**, born 9 Apr 1865 in VT; died 17 Dec 1904. He married **Elsie Freeman**.

1145. Lydia[6] **Bovee** (Peter[5], Jacob[4], Gerrit[3], Anthony[2], Mathieu[1]), born 1839. She married on 15 May 1858 Moses F Hunt.

Children of Lydia Bovee and Moses F Hunt were as follows:

2148　i　　Frank Hubert[7] **Hunt**, born 14 Oct 1859 in Walden Twp., Caledonia Co., VT.

1148. William W[6] **Bovee** (Moses R[5], Jacob[4], Gerrit[3], Anthony[2], Mathieu[1]), born 18 Nov 1827 in Barnet, Caledonia Co., VT; died 1902 in CA. He married in 1857 Johanna Hussey, born Dec 1833 in Ireland; died 19 Dec 1913.

Children of William W Bovee and Johanna Hussey were as follows:

+　2149　i　　William Francis[7] **Bovee**, born abt 1869 in Australia; died 16 Sep 1931 in Santa Barbara Co., CA. He married **Minnie May Isenhart**.

2150　ii　　Charles A[7] **Bovee**, born abt 1861 in Australia; died 6 Apr 1877 in Marshall Co., IA.

+　2151　iii　　Henry M[7] **Bovee**, born 10 Jan 1862 in Australia; died 29 Jul 1942 in Monrovia, Los Angeles Co., CA. He married **Georgia V Cooper**.

2152　iv　　Elizabeth M[7] **Bovee**, born 1865 in Australia; died 1882 in Marshall Co., IA.

2153　v　　Jessie[7] **Bovee**, born 6 Oct 1869 in Marshall Co., IA; died Aug 1870.

+　2154　vi　　Ernest A[7] **Bovee**, born 5 Oct 1871 in Marshall Co., IA; died 17 Dec 1945 in Los Angeles, Los Angeles Co., CA.

He married **WinnieA Valentine**.

1150. Moses C[6] **Bovee** (Moses R[5], Jacob[4], Gerrit[3], Anthony[2], Mathieu[1]), born 23 Aug 1831 in Barnet, Caledonia Co., VT; died 23 Dec 1907 in Marshall Co., IA. He married on 26 Apr 1860 in Marshall Co., IA Eliza A Ferguson, born 28 Nov 1838 in Decatur, Co., IN; died 1916 in Marshall Co., IA.

Children of Moses C Bovee and Eliza A Ferguson were as follows:

	2155	i	Loretta Selina[7] **Bovee**, born 5 Apr 1861 in Marshall Co., IA; died 10 Jan 1864.
	2156	ii	William Hanford[7] **Bovee**, born 19 May 1863 in Marshall Co., IA; died 13 Jan 1864.
+	2157	iii	Frank Luther[7] **Bovee**, born 4 Jul 1865 in Marshall Co., IA; died 30 Dec 1949. He married **Jessie Elizabeth Isenhart**.
	2158	iv	Helen Isabel[7] **Bovee**, born 30 Sep 1867 in Marshall Co., IA; died 23 Oct 1899. She married **Henry Bruett**.
	2159	v	Mary Ada[7] **Bovee**, born 15 Feb 1870 in Marshall Co., IA. She married **Bert Brock**.
	2160	vi	Katy Darling[7] **Bovee**, born 11 Apr 1873 in Marshall Co., IA; died 17 Jan 1958. She married **Frank Thomas**.
	2161	vii	Josephine[7] **Bovee**, born 24 Jun 1875 in Marshall Co., IA; died 26 Jul 1954. She married **Thomas Young**.
+	2162	viii	Charles Edward[7] **Bovee**, born 13 May 1878 in Marshall Co., IA; died 17 Oct 1963 in Marshall Co., IA. He married **Bertha Harriet Lampman**.
	2163	ix	Benjamin Lewis[7] **Bovee**, born 28 Mar 1883 in Marshall Co., IA; died 18 Jan 1884.

1151. James B[6] **Bovee** (Moses R[5], Jacob[4], Gerrit[3], Anthony[2], Mathieu[1]), born 19 Feb 1834 in Caledonia Co., VT. He married in Jan 1864 Eliza A Morris, born 1844 in IL.

Children of James B Bovee and Eliza A Morris were as follows:

+	2164	i	Clyde Charles[7] **Bovee**, born 18 Nov 1864 in Marshall Co., IA; died 1956. He married **Alice C Shearer**.
	2165	ii	Maude[7] **Bovee**, born abt 1872 in Marshal Co., IA.
	2166	iii	Minnie[7] **Bovee**, born 1874; died 1874.
	2167	iv	Morris[7] **Bovee**, born abt 1877 in Marshal Co., IA.

1152. Mark[6] **Bovee** (Moses R[5], Jacob[4], Gerrit[3], Anthony[2], Mathieu[1]), born 1836 in Peacham, Caledonia Co., VT; died 1909 in Marshall Co., IA. He married on 23 Jan 1862 in Peacham, Caledonia Co., VT Jane N Varnum, born 1837 in Peacham, Caledonia Co., VT; died 15 Jan 1904 in Marshall Co., IA, daughter of Simon B Varnum and Mary Cahill.

Children of Mark Bovee and Jane N Varnum were as follows:

+ 2168   i   George M[7] **Bovee**, born 10 Nov 1862; died 13 Aug 1893 in Laurens, Pocahontas Co., IA. He married **Minnie M Kahley**.

+ 2169   ii   Phineas Arno[7] **Bovee**, born 27 Jul 1864 in Peacham, Caledonia Co., VT; died 17 Jan 1917 in Marshal Co., IA. He married **Lucinda Owen**.

   2170   iii   Luella Jane[7] **Bovee**, born 1867 in IA. She married **Frederio W Hopkins**.

   2171   iv   Flora Etta[7] **Bovee**, born 7 Sep 1870 in Marshal Co., IA; died 22 Jun 1956. She married **Edward G Wallace**.

+ 2172   v   Thaddeus Fairbanks[7] **Bovee**, born 9 Jun 1873 in Marshall Co., IA; died 3 Mar 1952. He married (1) **Elizabeth Wilson**; (2) **Mabel C Hayes**.

   2173   vi   Mary S[7] **Bovee**, born 1875 in Marshal Co., IA. She married (1) **(---) Stewart**; (2) **Will Miller**.

1156. Cassius J C[6] **Bovee** (Moses R[5], Jacob[4], Gerrit[3], Anthony[2], Mathieu[1]), born 1846 in Peacham, Caledonia Co., VT; died abt 1914 in Eugene, Lane Co., OR. He married Sarah A (---), born abt 1856 in IA.

Children of Cassius J C Bovee and Sarah A (---) were as follows:

   2174   i   Daniel W[7] **Bovee**, born abt 1879 in Marion Twp., Marshall Co., IA; died 1 Jan 1921 in Los Angeles, Los Angeles Co., CA.

1165. Clark G[6] **Bovee** (Courtland[5], Jacob[4], Gerrit[3], Anthony[2], Mathieu[1]), born 1 Dec 1840 in Danville, Caledonia Co., VT; died 5 Feb 1905 in Madison, Somerset Co., ME. He married (1) on 5 Dec 1865, divorced Addie A Locke, born 1847 in Davison, Genesee Co., MI; (2) on 21 Jul 1898 Alice G chipman, born 1857.

Children of Clark G Bovee and Addie A Locke were as follows:

   2175   i   Leon A[7] **Bovee**, born 2 Sep 1870 in Monroe, Grafton Co., NH.

1167. Otis M[6] **Bovee** (Courtland[5], Jacob[4], Gerrit[3], Anthony[2], Mathieu[1]), born 26 Jul 1845 in Danville, Caledonia Co., VT. He married on 27 May 1869 in VT Ella S Robinson, born Jul 1853 in VT.

Children of Otis M Bovee and Ella S Robinson were as follows:

   2176   i   Luella[7] **Bovee**, born 1871 in VT; died 1965. She married **Oral C Van Slyke**.

   2177   ii   Hattie B[7] **Bovee**, born 1879 in Adair Co., IA.

+ 2178   iii   Harry W[7] **Bovee**, born 12 Feb 1884 in IA; died 1959. He married **Ruth Mercedes Findlay**.

+ 2179   iv   William Courtland[7] **Bovee**, born 25 Jul 1885 in IA; died 10

Jul 1966 in Red Bluff, Tehama Co., CA. He married **Pearl Lorraine Van Hoesen**.

Generation 7

1182. Herman[7] **Bovee** (Stephen[6], Philip[5], Mathew[4], Philip[3], Mathieu[2], Mathieu[1]), born Dec 1840 in Lyons, Wayne Co., NY. He married on 18 Oct 1866 in Wayne Co., NY Sophia L Winchell, born Jun 1850 in T/Gallen, Wayne Co., NY.

Children of Herman Bovee and Sophia L Winchell were as follows:

2180　　i　　　　Frank H[8] **Bovee**, born Apr 1872 in NY.

1183. George E[7] **Bovee** (Stephen[6], Philip[5], Mathew[4], Philip[3], Mathieu[2], Mathieu[1]), born abt 1841 in NY; died 4 Oct 1901 in Lyons, Wayne Co., NY. He married on 31 Oct 1868 in Lyons, Wayne Co., NY Angeline L Reynolds, born in NY; died 25 Sep 1928 in Lyons, Wayne Co., NY.

Children of George E Bovee and Angeline L Reynolds were as follows:

2181　　i　　　　Benjamin F[8] **Bovee**, born 28 Dec 1869; died 25 Nov 1925 in Lyons, Wayne Co., NY. He married on 15 Nov 1901 in NY **Jennie Warren Tinney**, born 28 Dec 1869 in NY; died 25 Nov 1925 in Lyons, Wayne Co., NY.

1184. Edward H[7] **Bovee** (Stephen[6], Philip[5], Mathew[4], Philip[3], Mathieu[2], Mathieu[1]), born 3 Jan 1843 in Lyons, Wayne Co., NY; died 4 Mar 1899 in Walcott, Wayne Co., NY. He married (1) bef 1868 Theresa Hampson, born 10 Nov 1842; died 27 Aug 1868 in Newark, Wayne Co., NY, daughter of Henry Hampson and Julia (---); (2) on 25 Sep 1874 in Butler, Wayne Co., NY Amelia Wraight Wager, born 8 Jan 1846 in Rose, Wayne Co., NY; died 12 Mar 1929 in Walcott, Wayne Co., NY, daughter of James Wager and Frances (---).

Children of Edward H Bovee and Amelia Wraight Wager were as follows:

+　2182　　i　　　　Bert[8] **Bovee**, born 24 Mar 1883 in NY; died Sep 1962 in NY. He married **Lila (---)**.
　　2183　　ii　　　Grace[8] **Bovee**, born 28 Feb 1886 in NY.

1186. Elizabeth[7] **Bovee** (Stephen[6], Philip[5], Mathew[4], Philip[3], Mathieu[2], Mathieu[1]), born 15 Aug 1847 in Lyons, Wayne Co., NY. She married Jay Dickerson.

Children of Elizabeth Bovee and Jay Dickerson were as follows:

2184　　i　　　　William[8] **Dickerson**.
2185　　ii　　　Robert D[8] **Dickerson**.
2186　　iii　　Charles A[8] **Dickerson**.
2187　　iv　　　Stephen[8] **Dickerson**.
2188　　v　　　George[8] **Dickerson**.

2189 vi John[8] **Dickerson**.
2190 vii Minnie[8] **Dickerson**.

1188. Caroline[7] **Bovee** (Stephen[6], Philip[5], Mathew[4], Philip[3], Mathieu[2], Mathieu[1]), born abt 1855 in Lyons, Wayne Co., NY. She married abt 1873 (---) Finney.

Children of Caroline Bovee and (---) Finney were as follows:

2191 i Sarah[8] **Finney**, born abt 1874 in Wayne Co., NY.
2192 ii Harriet[8] **Finney**, born abt 1875 in Wayne Co., NY.

1192. Richard Heman[7] **Bovie** (Richard H[6], Henry[5], John[4], Rykert[3], Nicholas[2], Mathieu[1]), born 24 Dec 1854 in Hoosick Falls, Rensselaer Co., NY; died 24 Mar 1940 in Cambridge, Washington Co., NY. He married on 9 Apr 1890 Rose Abby Curtis, born 21 Sep 1857; died 22 Oct 1908 in Cambridge, Washington Co., NY, daughter of William M Curtis and Freelove Warner.

Children of Richard Heman Bovie and Rose Abby Curtis were as follows:

2193 i Sarah Freelove[8] **Bovie**, born 8 Aug 1890; died 22 Jan 1918.
+ 2194 ii Richard Curtis[8] **Bovie**, born 30 Apr 1896 in Cambridge, Washington Co., NY; died 18 May 1976 in Bennington, Bennington Co., VT. He married **Orpha Anna Cain**.

1193. Charles S[7] **Bovee** (Sanford S[6], Henry[5], John[4], Rykert[3], Nicholas[2], Mathieu[1]), born 23 Jan 1861; died 28 Apr 1933 in Hoosick, Rensselaer Co., NY. He married on 27 Feb 1889 Anna Julia Smith, born 12 Dec 1863 in Schuylerville, Saratoga Co., NY; died 28 Aug 1947 in Hoosick, Rensselaer Co., NY, daughter of Stephen Smith and Mary Robinson.

Children of Charles S Bovee and Anna Julia Smith were as follows:

+ 2195 i Sanford Harold[8] **Bovie**, born 13 Oct 1892; died 2 Jul 1969 in Hoosick, Rensselaer Co., NY. He married **Sarah Albertine Turner**.
2196 ii Mary A[8] **Bovee**, born 26 Mar 1897.
2197 iii Helen May[8] **Bovee**, born 1 May 1900; died 8 Nov 1969.

1197. William H[7] **Bovee** (Parker R.[6], John[5], John[4], Rykert[3], Nicholas[2], Mathieu[1]), born 4 Jun 1842 in Pownal, Bennington Co., VT. He married in 1861 Anna M Whitbeck, born abt 1844; died 17 Jul 1878, daughter of John Whitbeck and Annie (---).

Children of William H Bovee and Anna M Whitbeck were as follows:

+ 2198 i George P[8] **Bovie**, born May 1862 in NY; died abt 1920 in Chicago, Cook Co., IL. He married **Elizabeth (---)**.
2199 ii John E[8] **Bovee**, born Dec 1864; died Jan 1944. He

married (1) on 30 Apr 1889 in N Greenbush Twp., Rensselaer Co., NY **Fannie L Phillips**, daughter of David Phillips and Emmeline DeFreest; (2) aft 1890 **Grace Denison**.

1205. Eleanor Parke[7] **Bovee** (Richard[6], Elisha[5], Cornelius[4], Rykert[3], Nicholas[2], Mathieu[1]), born 16 Sep 1849 in Eagletown, IN; died 23 Aug 1927. She married on 28 Nov 1869 in DeKalb Co., IL Edwin Wallace Lewis, born 5 Jun 1837; died 7 Jul 1904.

Children of Eleanor Parke Bovee and Edwin Wallace Lewis were as follows:

2200   i   Jessie Matilda[8] **Lewis**, born 22 Oct 1871; died Jan 1872.

2201   ii   Bassie May[8] **Lewis**, born 23 Dec 1873 in CT; died 11 Mar 1959.

1206. John Nelson[7] **Bovee** (Richard[6], Elisha[5], Cornelius[4], Rykert[3], Nicholas[2], Mathieu[1]), born 27 Oct 1851 in Cortland, De Kalb Co., IL; died 10 Jul 1918 in Penrose, Freemont Co., CO. He married (1) on 18 Mar 1872 in Afton Center, De Kalb Co., IL Althea Ann Burt, born 1 Mar 1854 in Big Rock, Kane Co., IL; died 17 Oct 1895 in La Junta, Otero Co., CO; (2) on 4 Jul 1896 Mary Ann Needham, born Aug 1851 in IA; died 15 Jul 1923.

Children of John Nelson Bovee and Althea Ann Burt were as follows:

+   2202   i   Richard Harrison[8] **Bovee**, born 24 May 1875 in Pilla Twp., Ford Co., IL; died 28 Apr 1957. He married **Jennie O Towne**.

2203   ii   Sarah Emma[8] **Bovee**, born 20 Feb 1877 in Afton Twp., De Kalb Co., IL; died 18 Feb 1948. She married on 9 Mar 1898 **Jefferson Davis Herring**.

+   2204   iii   John Earl LeRoy[8] **Bovee**, born 22 Jun 1879 in WI; died 2 Nov 1967 in Anaheim, Orange Co., CA. He married **Daisy L McFie**.

2205   iv   Chester Willey Grant[8] **Bovee**, born 9 Nov 1882 in Richland Center, Richland Co., WI.

+   2206   v   Manley Glenn[8] **Bovee**, born 31 Dec 1884 in Richland Center, Richland Co., WI; died 20 Dec 1953 in San Diego, San Diego Co., CA. He married **Anna Frances Taylor**.

+   2207   vi   Ira Burt[8] **Bovee**, born 15 Jan 1891 in Otero Co., CO; died 6 Jun 1948 in Lawson, Clay Co., MO. He married **Blanche Christine Atterbury**.

2208   vii   Mabel Pearle[8] **Bovee**, born 10 Dec 1894 in Fairmont, Otero Co., CO. She married on 6 Jun 1923 **Arthur C Prey**.

Children of John Nelson Bovee and Mary Ann Needham were as follows:

+   2209   i   Jesse Morris[8] **Bovee**, born 3 Oct 1897 in La Junta, Otero Co., CO; died 22 Jun 1956 in Santa Clara, Santa Clara Co., CA. He married **Mary Jane Spearman**.

1208. Mary[7] **Bovee** (Durfee[6], Elisha[5], Cornelius[4], Rykert[3], Nicholas[2], Mathieu[1]), born abt 1843 in Boone Co., IN; died abt 1939. She married on 25 Oct 1860 in Richland Co., WI Clinton Dewitt Wood, born abt 1837 in MI, son of David Wood and Ruth Naomi Warden.

Children of Mary Bovee and Clinton Dewitt Wood were as follows:

2210	i	Bertha[8] **Wood**, born abt 1862.
2211	ii	Annette[8] **Wood**.
2212	iii	Ezra[8] **Wood**, born abt 1864.
2213	iv	Milton Durfee[8] **Wood**, born 7 Dec 1867 in Avoca, Steuben Co., NY.
2214	v	Asa[8] **Wood**.
2215	vi	Bertha[8] **Wood**.
2216	vii	Naomi[8] **Wood**, born 1879.

1209. Samuel D[7] **Bovee** (Durfee[6], Elisha[5], Cornelius[4], Rykert[3], Nicholas[2], Mathieu[1]), born Feb 1847 in Boone Co., IN; died in SD. He married on 29 Apr 1866 in Richland Co., WI Emily W Bovee (see 1204), born Sep 1844 in IN; died aft 1920 in Spokane, Spokane Co., WA, daughter of Richard Bovee and Orpha Zelpha Parke.

Children of Samuel D Bovee and Emily W Bovee were as follows:

2217	i	Orpha Annie[8] **Bovee**, born 27 Feb 1873; died 13 Jul 1874.
2218	ii	Emma Estella[8] **Bovee**, born May 1879 in WI.
2219	iii	Cora[8] **Bovee**, born Feb 1881 in WI.

1210. David William[7] **Bovee** (Durfee[6], Elisha[5], Cornelius[4], Rykert[3], Nicholas[2], Mathieu[1]), born Aug 1853 in Orion, Richland Co., WI; died 6 Apr 1924 in Waterloo, Black Hawk Co., IA. He married on 19 Apr 1874 in Monroe Co., WI Anna Caroline Palmer, born Apr 1856 in WI; died aft 1936.

Children of David William Bovee and Anna Caroline Palmer were as follows:

+	2220	i	Lulu Victoria[8] **Bovee**, born Mar 1879 in WI. She married **Bert Lincoln Morrow**.
+	2221	ii	Helen A[8] **Bovee**, born 6 Jul 1897 in IA; died Oct 1987. She married **Rillmond W Schear**.

1211. Martha E[7] **Bovee** (Erastus[6], Elisha[5], Cornelius[4], Rykert[3], Nicholas[2], Mathieu[1]), born 27 Apr 1841 in Clinton Co., IN; died 24 Feb 1913. She married on 10 Sep 1857 David Crose, born 27 Apr 1835 in Tippecanoe Co., IN, son of Benjamin F Crose and Cynthia Martin.

Children of Martha E Bovee and David Crose were as follows:

2222	i	Marion[8] **Crose**, born 20 Aug 1858 in Thornton, Boone Co., IN; died 11 Nov 1858.
2223	ii	Francis[8] **Crose**, born 20 Aug 1858 in Thornton, Boone Co., IN; died 11 Nov 1858.
2224	iii	William Butler[8] **Crose**, born 2 Feb 1860 in Thornton, Boone Co., IN; died 26 Jul 1939 in Zionsville, Boone Co., IN.
2225	iv	Clement L[8] **Crose**, born 8 May 1863 in Thornton, Boone Co., IN; died 4 Oct 1887 in Thornton, Boone Co., IN.
2226	v	Cynthia Ella[8] **Crose**, born 11 Oct 1864 in Thornton, Boone Co., IN; died 28 Feb 1942.

1213. Esther[7] **Bovee** (David[6], Elisha[5], Cornelius[4], Rykert[3], Nicholas[2], Mathieu[1]), born 1844 in Boone Co., IN. She married in Sep 1885 Thomas Bass.

Children of Esther Bovee and Thomas Bass were as follows:

| 2227 | i | Bertha[8] **Bass**. |

1214. John Sylvester[7] **Bovee** (David[6], Elisha[5], Cornelius[4], Rykert[3], Nicholas[2], Mathieu[1]), born Jul 1849 in Boone Co., IN. He married (1) on 1 Jan 1871 in Richland Center, Richland Co., WI Hattie Woodman, born abt 1854; died 3 Jan 1874 in Dayton Twp, Richland Co., WI; (2) abt 1880 Ethel Z Dillon, born Sep 1861 in Basswood, Richland Co., WI.

Children of John Sylvester Bovee and Hattie Woodman were as follows:

| 2228 | i | Edward M[8] **Bovee**, born Aug 1872 in WI. He married on 31 Jul 1899 in Spokane, Spokane Co.,WA **Mary Meyer**, born 1881 in Germany, daughter of Henry Meyer and Sophia Koster. |
| 2229 | ii | David[8] **Bovee**, born 4 Nov 1873; died 4 Dec 1873 in Richland Center, Richland Co., WI. |

Children of John Sylvester Bovee and Ethel Z Dillon were as follows:

| 2230 | i | John Wesley[8] **Bovee**, born Jan 1881 in WI. He married **Myrtle (---)**, born abt 1894 in OR; died 1 Aug 1952 in Sunnyside, Yakima Co., WA. |
| 2231 | ii | Jay Ora[8] **Bovee**, born 14 Dec 1883 in Basswood, Richland Co., WI; died 29 Feb 1956 in Yolo Co., CA. |

1215. Jacob Newton[7] **Bovee** (David[6], Elisha[5], Cornelius[4], Rykert[3], Nicholas[2], Mathieu[1]), born 2 Feb 1854 in Richland Co., WI; died 2 Dec 1916 in Shevlin, Clearwater Co., MN. He married on 21 Sep 1878 in Richland Center, Richland Co., WI Martha A Davis, born Mar 1857 in IN; died 9 Oct 1906 in Shevlin, Clearwater Co., MN.

Children of Jacob Newton Bovee and Martha A Davis were as follows:

	2232	i	Lola B[8] **Bovee**, born Aug 1883 in MN. She married **Avery Hoffman**.
+	2233	ii	Walter Richard[8] **Bovee**, born 22 Jan 1885 in MN; died 12 Sep 1929 in Bain, MN. He married **Lena McFarland**.
+	2234	iii	Roderick[8] **Bovee**, born 13 Jul 1887 in Grey Eagle, Todd Co., MN; died Oct 1963. He married **Alice Sveve**.
	2235	iv	Bessie Blanche[8] **Bovee**, born Nov 1890 in MN. She married **Burt Rounds**.
	2236	v	Ivan B[8] **Bovee**, born Aug 1893 in MN; died 26 Feb 1931 in Hennepin Co., MN. He married **Lily (---)**.
	2237	vi	Flora[8] **Bovee**. She married **Vernon Farr**.

1216. Cornelius[7] **Bovee** (Jonas Nicholas[6], Nicholas[5], Cornelius[4], Rykert[3], Nicholas[2], Mathieu[1]), born 1840 in Pinckney, Lewis Co., NY; died 17 Dec 1899 in Fairchild, Eau Claire Co., WI. He married (1) on 30 Aug 1859 Mary Hindman, died 3 Jan 1860 in Alma, Jackson Co., WI; (2) on 22 Feb 1863 in Hixton, Jackson Co., WI Hannah M Pettis, born 4 Nov 1844 in Smyrna, Chenago Co., NY; died 5 Jan 1927 in Fairchild, Eau Claire Co., WI, daughter of Hiram N Pettis and Melinda Taylor.

Children of Cornelius Bovee and Hannah M Pettis were as follows:

	2238	i	Leonard Alpheus[8] **Bovee**, born 28 Mar 1869 in Garden Valley, Jackson Co., WI; died 30 Jul 1940 in Ozaukee Co.,WI. He married **Nettie Vander Berg**.
+	2239	ii	George F[8] **Bovee**, born 1 Jun 1873 in Clayton, Polk Co., WI. He married **Lillian Adelia Brown**.
	2240	iii	Charles Homer[8] **Bovee**, born 9 Aug 1876 in Clayton, Polk Co.,WI. He married in Feb 1902 in Eau Claire, Eau Claire Co., WI **Melinda Benitt**.
	2241	iv	Nellie J[8] **Bovee**, born 6 Jul 1879 in Clayton, Polk Co., WI.
+	2242	v	Hiram Nelson[8] **Bovee**, born 15 Sep 1882 in WI; died 21 Nov 1946 in Lebanon, Linn Co., OR.. He married **Ruby Grace Chatterson**.
	2243	vi	Truman M[8] **Bovee**, born 10 Jan 1886 in WI.

1217. Julia[7] **Bovee** (Jonas Nicholas[6], Nicholas[5], Cornelius[4], Rykert[3], Nicholas[2], Mathieu[1]), born abt 1842 in Pinckney, Lewis Co., NY. She married on 6 Jun 1856 in Jackson Co., WI Truman A Hoisington.

Children of Julia Bovee and Truman A Hoisington were as follows:

2244	i	William[8] **Hoisington**.
2245	ii	Fred[8] **Hoisington**.

1218. Truman Andrew[7] **Bovee** (Jonas Nicholas[6], Nicholas[5], Cornelius[4], Rykert[3], Nicholas[2], Mathieu[1]), born abt 1845 in Pinckney, Lewis Co., NY; died 9 Oct 1897 in Clayton, Polk Co., WI. He married (1) on 27 Jul 1862 in Hautonburg, WI, divorced Eliza Hamlin, daughter of Orin Hamlin and Roxana (---); (2) on 12 Sep 1871 in Menomonie, Dunn Co., WI Eliza Jane Hamlin, daughter of Orin Hamlin and Roxana (---); (3) Julia Pettis Peysen, born abt 1842.

Children of Truman Andrew Bovee and Julia Pettis Peysen were as follows:

+ 2246 i William Alfred^8 **Bovee**, born 31 Oct 1870 in MN; died 22 Feb 1933 in Minneapolis, Hennepin Co., MN. He married (1) **Jennie E Anderson**; (2) **Mary A Wells**.

1220. Celestia^7 **Bovee** (Jonas Nicholas^6, Nicholas^5, Cornelius^4, Rykert^3, Nicholas^2, Mathieu^1), born 26 Apr 1852 in NY. She married on 21 Nov 1880 in Jackson Co., WI Calvin W Letson.

Children of Celestia Bovee and Calvin W Letson were as follows:

2247 i Carl^8 **Letson**, born abt 1882.
2248 ii Florence Lillieth^8 **Letson**, born abt 1885.

1222. Silas N^7 **Bovee** (Jonas Nicholas^6, Nicholas^5, Cornelius^4, Rykert^3, Nicholas^2, Mathieu^1), born Oct 1855 in NY; died 12 Jan 1933 in Eau Claire Co., WI. He married on 7 Oct 1877 in Jackson Co., WI Caroline W Bovee (see 1235), born 1862 in WI, daughter of Zebulon Bovee and Waity Brundige.

Children of Silas N Bovee and Caroline W Bovee were as follows:

2249 i Edward^8 **Bovee**, born Feb 1881 in WI.
2250 ii Alfred^8 **Bovee**, born Feb 1886 in WI.
2251 iii Minnie^8 **Bovee**, born Jun 1890 in WI.

1223. Annie Malvina^7 **Bovee** (Silas Lewis^6, Nicholas^5, Cornelius^4, Rykert^3, Nicholas^2, Mathieu^1), born abt 1843 in Lewis Co., NY. She married on 19 Feb 1861 in Hixton, Jackson Co., WI Joseph Olver, born in Batavia, WI, son of John Olver and Elizabeth Castle.

Children of Annie Malvina Bovee and Joseph Olver were as follows:

2252 i Sarah Elizabeth^8 **Olver**.
2253 ii John^8 **Olver**.
2254 iii Frank^8 **Olver**.

1224. Sarah Jane^7 **Bovee** (Silas Lewis^6, Nicholas^5, Cornelius^4, Rykert^3, Nicholas^2, Mathieu^1), born 23 Jan 1845 in Pinckney, Lewis Co., NY; died 11 Feb 1921 in Long Beach, Los Angeles Co., CA. She married on 1 Jan 1861 in Hixton, Jackson Co., WI Isaac Shoemaker Hallenbeck, born 10 Nov 1836 in Chemung Co., NY; died 2 Aug 1921.

Children of Sarah Jane Bovee and Isaac Shoemaker Hallenbeck were as

follows:

| 2255 | i | William Henry[8] **Hallenbeck**, born 20 Dec 1861; died 28 Mar 1956. |

- 2255 i William Henry[8] **Hallenbeck**, born 20 Dec 1861; died 28 Mar 1956.
- 2256 ii James Lewis[8] **Hallenbeck**, born 5 Jan 1863; died 24 Aug 1934.
- 2257 iii Sarah Ann (Sadie)[8] **Hallenbeck**, born 13 Feb 1866; died 18 Mar 1934.
- 2258 iv Eleanor Jane[8] **Hallenbeck**, born 1868; died 1868.
- 2259 v Child[8] **Hallenbeck**, born abt 1870; died abt 1870.
- 2260 vi Isaac Shoemaker[8] **Hallenbeck** Jr., born 15 Jul 1874; died 11 Jan 1956.
- 2261 vii Nina Elizabeth[8] **Hallenbeck**, born 4 Oct 1886.

1226. Mary Josephine[7] **Bovee** (Silas Lewis[6], Nicholas[5], Cornelius[4], Rykert[3], Nicholas[2], Mathieu[1]), born 25 Feb 1850 in Pinckney, Lewis Co., NY; died 15 Jan 1925 in Minneapolis, Hennepin Co., MN. She married on 9 Mar 1865 in Jackson Co., WI Henry Olver.

Children of Mary Josephine Bovee and Henry Olver were as follows:

- 2262 i Florence[8] **Olver**.
- 2263 ii Otto[8] **Olver**.
- 2264 iii Roy[8] **Olver**.

1227. Electa[7] **Bovee** (Silas Lewis[6], Nicholas[5], Cornelius[4], Rykert[3], Nicholas[2], Mathieu[1]), born 1852. She married on 28 Aug 1869 Alexander Meek, son of Andrew Meek and Margaret (---).

Children of Electa Bovee and Alexander Meek were as follows:

- 2265 i Silas[8] **Meek**.
- 2266 ii Ella[8] **Meek**.
- 2267 iii Mark[8] **Meek**, born 25 Dec 1880 in Alma Center, Jackson Co., WI; died 21 Dec 1968 in Black River Falls, Jackson Co., WI.

1230. Gilbert Humphrey[7] **Bovee** (Silas Lewis[6], Nicholas[5], Cornelius[4], Rykert[3], Nicholas[2], Mathieu[1]), born Apr 1862 in WI. He married on 9 Jul 1893 in Moroe Co., WI Jessie L Warren, born Nov 1872 in WI, daughter of James Morris Warren.

Children of Gilbert Humphrey Bovee and Jessie L Warren were as follows:

- 2268 i Birding J[8] **Bovee**, born Apr 1894 in SD.
- 2269 ii Lloyd L[8] **Bovee**, born 6 Dec 1896 in SD; died Jul 1974 in SD. He married **Marie Lawrence**, born 1 Mar 1904; died 1974.

2270	iii	Dorothy A[8] **Bovee**, born May 1899 in SD. She married (---) **Babcock**.
2271	iv	Margaret Irene[8] **Bovee**, born abt 1903 in SD. She married (---) **Hankins**.
2272	v	Winnefred E[8] **Bovee**, born abt 1905 in SD. She married (---) **Walner**, son of James Warren Walner.
2273	vi	Ruth W[8] **Bovee**, born abt 1909 in SD. She married **Greble (---)**.
2274	vii	Gwendalyn Jean[8] **Bovee**, born 12 Mar 1916 in SD; died 27 Nov 1981 in San Joaquin, Fresno Co., CA.

1231. Silas Lewis[7] Bovee Jr (Silas Lewis[6], Nicholas[5], Cornelius[4], Rykert[3], Nicholas[2], Mathieu[1]), born Sep 1864 in WI. He married on 24 Mar 1887 in Jackson Co., WI Della A Warren, born Jan 1871 in WI.

Children of Silas Lewis Bovee Jr and Della A Warren were as follows:

2275	i	Grace[8] **Bovee**, born Nov 1887 in WI.
2276	ii	Warren A[8] **Bovee**, born 29 Apr 1889 in WI; died Oct 1970.
+ 2277	iii	Claire Lewis[8] **Bovee**, born 31 Dec 1891 in WI; died May 1977 in IA. He married **Ida Gilles**.
2278	iv	Vivian G[8] **Bovee**, born 1 Nov 1893 in WI.
2279	v	Marjorie M[8] **Bovee**, born 26 Mar 1899 in WI.
2280	vi	Kathleen[8] **Bovee**, born 6 Oct 1901 in Jackson Co., WI.

1232. Joseph Milford[7] Bovee (Zebulon[6], Nicholas[5], Cornelius[4], Rykert[3], Nicholas[2], Mathieu[1]), born 18 Jun 1855 in Alma, Buffalo Co., WI. He married on 18 Dec 1877 in Alma, Jackson Co., WI Mary Christensen, born 20 Sep 1861 in Waupun, Fond du Lac Co., WI; died 27 Sep 1947 in Merrillan, Jackson Co., WI.

Children of Joseph Milford Bovee and Mary Christensen were as follows:

| + 2281 | i | James Joseph[8] **Bovee**, born 11 Jan 1879 in Alma Center, Jackson Co., WI; died 1946 in Regina, Saskatchewan, Canada. He married **Mary Gertrude Nelson**. |

1233. Charlotte Melissa[7] Bovee (Zebulon[6], Nicholas[5], Cornelius[4], Rykert[3], Nicholas[2], Mathieu[1]), born abt 1858 in Jackson Co., WI. She married on 4 Jul 1873 in Jackson Co., WI Andrew J Stafford.

Children of Charlotte Melissa Bovee and Andrew J Stafford were as follows:

| 2282 | i | Alex[8] **Stafford**, born 15 Sep 1881 in Greenwood, Clark Co., WI. |
| 2283 | ii | Elmer James[8] **Stafford**, born 16 May 1885 in Greenwood, Clark Co., WI. |

1236. Lucretia M[7] **Bovee** (Zebulon[6], Nicholas[5], Cornelius[4], Rykert[3], Nicholas[2], Mathieu[1]), born 1863 in WI. She married on 25 Jul 1886 in Jackson Co., WI Charles Edward Burnett.

Children of Lucretia M Bovee and Charles Edward Burnett were as follows:

2284   i   Orin Cyrus[8] **Burnett**, born 18 Jul 1895 in Jackson Co., WI.

1246. Harriet[7] **Bovee** (James R[6], Cornelius[5], Cornelius[4], Rykert[3], Nicholas[2], Mathieu[1]), born abt 1856. She married George A Graves, born abt 1854.

Children of Harriet Bovee and George A Graves were as follows:

2285   i   William[8] **Graves**. He married in 1910 **Nancy B (---)**.

1247. Edmund L[7] **Bovee** (James R[6], Cornelius[5], Cornelius[4], Rykert[3], Nicholas[2], Mathieu[1]), born abt 1860 in Elk Creek, Erie Co., PA. He married Ada E Campbell, born Jul 1859 in PA, daughter of Alexander Campbell and Jennett (---).

Children of Edmund L Bovee and Ada E Campbell were as follows:

+   2286   i   Lee Elmer[8] **Bovee**, born 2 Jun 1883; died Feb 1971 in Pittsburgh, Allegheny Co., PA. He married **Edna (---)**.

    2287   ii   Russell L[8] **Bovee**, born 29 Jun 1887 in PA; died 11 Aug 1959.

1248. Alice[7] **Bovee** (James R[6], Cornelius[5], Cornelius[4], Rykert[3], Nicholas[2], Mathieu[1]), born 14 Feb 1863. She married Henry Billet.

Children of Alice Bovee and Henry Billet were as follows:

2288   i   Harriet[8] **Billet**.

1249. James Elmer[7] **Bovee** (James R[6], Cornelius[5], Cornelius[4], Rykert[3], Nicholas[2], Mathieu[1]), born abt 1864. He married on 12 Dec 1883 in Defiance, Defiance Co., OH Susan Beard.

Children of James Elmer Bovee and Susan Beard were as follows:

2289   i   Harvey[8] **Bovee**, born abt 1886 in Pageville, PA; died 5 May 1962 in Pageville, PA.

2290   ii   Charles[8] **Bovee**, born 28 Jul 1896 in Lake City, Erie Co., PA; died Sep 1968. He married **Eleanor (---)**, born abt 1900.

1258. George Frederick[7] **Bovie** (Frederick Morgan[6], Frederick[5], Cornelius[4], Rykert[3], Nicholas[2], Mathieu[1]), born 21 Dec 1872 in Gallia Co., OH; died 25 Sep

1943. He married (1) on 2 Jun 1897 in Gallipolis, Gallia Co., OH Nellie
Gatewood, died 25 Aug 1907 in Gallipolis, Gallia Co., OH; (2) in 1910 in
Saginaw, Saginaw Co., MI Gladys Carpenter, born 1884 in Minneapolis,
Hennepin Co., MN.

Children of George Frederick Bovie and Nellie Gatewood were as follows:
+ 2291 i Lucy Virginia ^{8} **Bovie**, born 1899 in Gallipolis, Gallia Co.,
OH. She married **Ray Long**.

Children of George Frederick Bovie and Gladys Carpenter were as follows:
2292 i George Frederick ^{8} **Bovie**, born 1910; died 1990. He
married **Marguerite Worthen**.
2293 ii JaneAnn ^{8} **Bovie**, born 13 Jun 1914 in Gallipolis, Gallia
Co., OH; died 27 Jun 1957.
+ 2294 iii Smith Palmer ^{8} **Bovie**, born 24 Dec 1917 in Gallipolis,
Gallia Co., OH. He married **Maria Feiler**.

1259. Joseph Harley Clark ^{7} **Bovie** (Frederick Morgan ^{6}, Frederick ^{5}, Cornelius ^{4},
Rykert ^{3}, Nicholas ^{2}, Mathieu ^{1}), born 9 Nov 1874 in Gallipolis, Gallia Co., OH; died
1959. He married in 1899 Emma G Geissler, born 6 Nov 1878 in OH; buried in
Mound Hill Cem, Gallipolis, Gallia Co., OH, daughter of Earnest Geissler and
Anna Steigert.

Children of Joseph Harley Clark Bovie and Emma G Geissler were as
follows:
+ 2295 i Frederick Ernest ^{8} **Bovie**, born 2 Feb 1901 in Gallipolis,
Gallia Co., OH; died 19 Apr 1980 in Jackson, Jackson Co.,
OH. He married **Jeanetta Jones**.
+ 2296 ii Katherine Elizabeth ^{8} **Bovie**, born 1 Sep 1905 in Gallipolis,
Gallia Co., OH. She married **John Kircher**.

1260. Vernon Morgan ^{7} **Bovie** (Frederick Morgan ^{6}, Frederick ^{5}, Cornelius ^{4},
Rykert ^{3}, Nicholas ^{2}, Mathieu ^{1}), born 10 Mar 1878 in Gallipolis, Gallia Co., OH;
died 9 Mar 1926 in San Francisco, San Francisco Co., CA. He married on 26
Nov 1902 in New York, New York Co., NY Mary Roland Tinker, born abt 1873 in
PA, daughter of Henry Griswald Tinker.

Children of Vernon Morgan Bovie and Mary Roland Tinker were as follows:
+ 2297 i Henry Tinker ^{8} **Bovie**, born abt 1902 in NJ; died 10 Jul
1941 in Paraguay, South America. He married **Mary
Rowlad Tucker**.

1261. Elizabeth ^{7} **Bovie** (Frederick Morgan ^{6}, Frederick ^{5}, Cornelius ^{4}, Rykert ^{3},
Nicholas ^{2}, Mathieu ^{1}), born 8 Mar 1879 in Gallia Co., OH; died 1951. She married
on 11 Oct 1905 Everette Humphrey Morgan, born 11 Aug 1876; died 11 Feb
1957, son of David J Morgan and Mary Davis.

Children of Elizabeth Bovie and Everette Humphrey Morgan were as follows:

2298   i   Everett B[8] **Morgan**, born 27 Aug 1906 in Eagle, Harrison Co.,WV; died 16 Dec 1971 in Athens, Athens Co., OH.

2299   ii   David J[8] **Morgan**, born 8 Jun 1908 in Eagle, Harrison Co.,WV; died 1937.

2300   iii   Elizabeth Bovee[8] **Morgan**, born 25 Oct 1910 in Eagle, Harrison Co.,WV.

2301   iv   Roger G B[8] **Morgan**, born 1918.

1262. Marilla[7] **Bovie** (Frederick Morgan[6], Frederick[5], Cornelius[4], Rykert[3], Nicholas[2], Mathieu[1]), born Jul 1882 in Gallia Co., OH; died 1960. She married Dr. Ira J Kail.

Children of Marilla Bovie and Dr. Ira J Kail were as follows:

2302   i   Samuel[8] **Kail**, born 7 Jan 1915.

2303   ii   Joseph[8] **Kail**.

2304   iii   Mary Marilla[8] **Kail**, born 18 Sep 1924.

1264. Frank Merton[7] **Bovee** (Emory John[6], Peter[5], Cornelius[4], Rykert[3], Nicholas[2], Mathieu[1]), born 29 Mar 1868 in Kingsville Twp, Ashtabula Co., OH; died 29 Nov 1950 in Kingsville Twp, Ashtabula Co., OH. He married on 7 Sep 1892 Eleanor Camham, born May 1868.

Children of Frank Merton Bovee and Eleanor Camham were as follows:

2305   i   Cecil E[8] **Bovee**, born 25 Feb 1893; died May 1972 in Struthers, Mahoning Co., OH.

2306   ii   Hardy R[8] **Bovee**, born 18 Aug 1895; died Dec 1981 in Kingsville, Ashtabula Co.,OH.

2307   iii   Albert W[8] **Bovee**, born 4 Dec 1897.

+   2308   iv   Perry[8] **Bovee**, born 10 May 1900. He married **Ruth Alice Avery**.

2309   v   Walter G[8] **Bovee**, born 4 Oct 1903 in Kingsville, Ashtabula Co.,OH; died Nov 1960 in Ashtabula Co.,OH. He married **Irene Ferguson**, born 29 Oct 1907; died 8 Feb 1991.

2310   vi   Eleanor[8] **Bovee**, born 22 Mar 1907; died 14 Mar 1909.

1287. Archibald Melrose[7] **Bovee** (John[6], John[5], Nicholas M[4], Matthew[3], Nicholas[2], Mathieu[1]), born 25 Jul 1838 in Wayne Co., IL; died 25 Dec 1900 in Blair, Washington Co., NE. He married on 27 Oct 1864 in Heyworth, McClean Co., IL Evaline C Gossard, born 10 Oct 1847 in Harrison Co, OH; died 10 Feb 1927 in Craig, Burt Co, NE, daughter of John Garrison Gossard and Elizabeth (---).

Children of Archibald Melrose Bovee and Evaline C Gossard were as follows:

+ 2311 i William Harlan[8] **Bovee**, born 4 Oct 1865 in McClean Co., IL; died 8 Feb 1916 in Yuma, Yuma Co., AZ. He married **Elizabeth C Spencer**.

2312 ii Minnie E[8] **Bovee**, born 23 Dec 1868 in IL; died 7 Jan 1883.

+ 2313 iii Luella M[8] **Bovee**, born 5 Jun 1870 in McClean Co., IL; died 19 Jul 1904. She married **William George Fowler**.

2314 iv Ida Bell[8] **Bovee**, born 3 Jun 1873; died 20 Sep 1875.

+ 2315 v Robert Raymond[8] **Bovee**, born 27 Apr 1875 in Vacoma, Washington Co., NE; died 1956. He married **Ester Johnson**.

2316 vi Oliver B[8] **Bovee**, born 3 Oct 1877; died 4 Jan 1879.

2317 vii Gertrude L[8] **Bovee**, born 7 Mar 1878; died 22 Mar 1883.

+ 2318 viii Orlie M[8] **Bovee**, born 1 Jul 1879 in Vacoma, Washington Co., NE; died 21 Jul 1901. He married **Grace Lavina Oberst**.

+ 2319 ix Archibald Theodore[8] **Bovee**, born 9 Jan 1884 in Vacoma, Washington Co., NE; died 5 Aug 1979 in Swiftcurrent, Saskatchewan, Canada. He married **Winnifred Davis**.

+ 2320 x Harry F[8] **Bovee**, born 10 Aug 1887 in Vacoma, Washington Co., NB; died 1970 in British Columbia, Canada. He married **Mattie Gleen Dulaney**.

+ 2321 xi Opal M[8] **Bovee**, born 6 Apr 1890 in Vacoma, Washington Co., NE; died 1983. She married **William Brunton**.

2322 xii Bertie[8] **Bovee**.

1288. Nicholas Aaron[7] **Bovee** (John[6], John[5], Nicholas M[4], Matthew[3], Nicholas[2], Mathieu[1]), born 17 Jan 1841 in Fairfield, Wayne Co., IL; died 20 Mar 1916 in IA. He married on 24 Aug 1865 in DeWitt Co., IL Anna Maria Betzer, born 14 Jul 1847 in OH; died 3 Apr 1905.

Children of Nicholas Aaron Bovee and Anna Maria Betzer were as follows:

2323 i Elfie[8] **Bovee**, born abt 1867 in IL.

2324 ii Myrtle Frances[8] **Bovee**, born 24 Jan 1875 in IA. She married on 26 Feb 1896 **John Loftis**, born 21 Mar 1874; died 1956, son of Caleb Loftus and Mary Elizabeth Bovee.

2325 iii Edith Bessie[8] **Bovee**, born 12 Apr 1877 in IA. She married on 2 Mar 1899 **Leigh Richman Fletcher**.

+ 2326 iv Raymond H[8] **Bovee**, born 10 Aug 1879 in IA; died 2 Dec 1945. He married **Minnie Pearl Gillman**.

2327 v William G[8] **Bovee**, born 26 Sep 1881; died 6 Dec 1920.

1289. John Wesley[7] **Bovee** (John[6], John[5], Nicholas M[4], Matthew[3], Nicholas[2], Mathieu[1]), born 16 Aug 1843 in Wayne Co., IL; died 15 Jan 1914 in Salem, Marion Co., OR. He married on 1 Jan 1867 in McClean Co, IL Margaret Critchfield, born 24 Nov 1847 in Coshocton Co., OH; died 20 Apr 1919 in

Helmville, Powel Co., MT, daughter of Samuel Critchfield and Lydia Ann Duncan.

Children of John Wesley Bovee and Margaret Critchfield were as follows:

2328 i   Adda Jane[8] **Bovee**, born 17 Oct 1867; died 10 Apr 1959 in Fulton, Callaway Co., MO. She married on 22 Aug 1894 **Ellis Bradford**.

+ 2329 ii   Henry Hopkins[8] **Bovee**, born 5 Oct 1869 in De Kalb, Buchanan Co., MO; died 5 Nov 1950. He married **Florence Eleanor Putzker**.

2330 iii   Lizzie Evoline[8] **Bovee**, born 21 Dec 1871; died Dec 1872.

+ 2331 iv   William James[8] **Bovee**, born 20 Jan 1874 in Hamilton, Caldwell Co., MO; died 20 Nov 1944 in Los Angeles, Los Angeles Co., CA. He married **Anita Putzker**.

2332 v   Mamie[8] **Bovee**, born 15 Nov 1878 in Lindley, Grundy Co., MO; died 9 May 1888.

2333 vi   Anna Bell[8] **Bovee**, born 5 Apr 1882 in MO; died 18 Dec 1962. She married on 27 Dec 1904 in Norfolk, Madison Co., NE **Louis Rautenberg**.

+ 2334 vii   Arthur Roy[8] **Bovee**, born 12 May 1885 in St Paul, Howard Co., NE; died 2 Jun 1953 in Pierce, Pierce Co., NE. He married **Otelia Magdalena Machmueller**.

+ 2335 viii Carl Howard[8] **Bovee**, born 8 May 1888 in Norfolk, Madison Co., NE; died May 1961. He married **Emma Potras**.

1290. Jacob Nelson[7] **Bovee** (John[6], John[5], Nicholas M[4], Matthew[3], Nicholas[2], Mathieu[1]), born 5 Sep 1845 in Wayne Co., IL; died 10 Jun 1904 in Vashon Island, King Co., WA. He married on 9 Apr 1875 in Coalport Church, Lockridge, Jefferson Co., IA Mary Jennie Heron, born 1838 in PA; died 15 Nov 1915 in Seattle, King Co., WA, daughter of David Heron and Janet Garrett.

Children of Jacob Nelson Bovee and Mary Jennie Heron were as follows:

+ 2336 i   Carrie Agnes[8] **Bovee**, born 26 Apr 1876 in Walker, Linn Co., IA; died Sep 1947 in Santa Ana, Orange Co., CA. She married **Andrew Eli Griswold**.

2337 ii   Justin O[8] **Bovee**, born 14 Jun 1879 in Bremer Co., IA. He married **Diane (---)**.

1300. Nelson LeGrande[7] **Bovee** (Aaron Milton[6], John[5], Nicholas M[4], Matthew[3], Nicholas[2], Mathieu[1]), born 5 Aug 1846 in IL. He married on 18 Jan 1872 in Iowa Co., WI Martha Jane Kuison, born 4 Feb 1848 in WI; died aft 1920 in Beloit, Rock Co., WI.

Children of Nelson LeGrande Bovee and Martha Jane Kuison were as follows:

2338 i   Serina[8] **Bovee**, born abt 1873 in WI.

2339 ii   Francis J[8] **Bovee**, born 1875 in WI. He married on 13 Jun

1896 in Fennimore, Grant Co., WI **Julia Kirkpatrick**.

+ 2340 iii Albert[8] **Bovee**, born abt 1877 in WI. He married **Annie (---)**.

1303. Charles Franklin Leroy[7] **Bovee** (Aaron Milton[6], John[5], Nicholas M[4], Matthew[3], Nicholas[2], Mathieu[1]), born 24 Feb 1853 in WI; died 6 Apr 1905. He married on 26 Dec 1882 in Grant Co., WI Josephine Amidon, born Jul 1856; died 30 Sep 1906.

Children of Charles Franklin Leroy Bovee and Josephine Amidon were as follows:

2341 i William[8] **Bovee**, born Mar 1884 in IA.
2342 ii Frank[8] **Bovee**, born Apr 1887 in IA.
2343 iii Adeline[8] **Bovee**, born Feb 1890 in IA.
2344 iv Minnie[8] **Bovee**, born Dec 1892 in IA.
2345 v Grace[8] **Bovee**, born Mar 1894 in IA.

1304. Ida Ann[7] **Bovee** (Aaron Milton[6], John[5], Nicholas M[4], Matthew[3], Nicholas[2], Mathieu[1]), born 29 Mar 1855; died 27 Jan 1942. She married on 22 Dec 1875 in Monfort, Grant Co., WI David Jackson DeVoe, born 21 Dec 1845 in Greene Co., OH; died 29 Dec 1918, son of Robert Jackson DeVoe and Lydia E Kendrick.

Children of Ida Ann Bovee and David Jackson DeVoe were as follows:

2346 i Homer[8] **DeVoe**, born 29 Sep 1876; died 26 Nov 1959 in Monfort, Grant Co., WI.
2347 ii Louisa L[8] **DeVoe**, born aft 1876.

1305. William Levant[7] **Bovee** (Aaron Milton[6], John[5], Nicholas M[4], Matthew[3], Nicholas[2], Mathieu[1]), born 4 Aug 1857 in WI; died 1936. He married on 29 Sep 1886 Pauline M Minerta, born 26 Mar 1866 in IA; died 1952.

Children of William Levant Bovee and Pauline M Minerta were as follows:

+ 2348 i Lillian[8] **Bovee**, born abt 1882; died 1962. She married **Charles Fathers**.

1310. John McClellan[7] **Bovee** (Wesley[6], John[5], Nicholas M[4], Matthew[3], Nicholas[2], Mathieu[1]), born 6 Jun 1863 in IL; died 1 Jul 1932 in Los Angeles, Los Angeles Co., CA. He married on 12 Jun 1889 in Quincy, Adams Co., IL Laura May Mosely, born May 1867 in Frankford, Pike Co., MO, daughter of Lewis Henry Mosely and Bathilda (---).

Children of John McClellan Bovee and Laura May Mosely were as follows:

+ 2349 i William Vivian[8] **Bovee**, born 21 Nov 1890 in Winchester, Scott Co., IL; died 28 Mar 1969 in Pleasant Hill, Pike Co., IL. He married **Alice Marie Gant**.

2350 ii   Morina B[8] **Bovee**, born 15 Mar 1893 in IL; died Feb 1918. She married on 20 Sep 1915 **Arthur Schleper**.

2351 iii   John Merlin[8] **Bovee**, born Sep 1894 in Bellvue, Calhoun Co., IL; died aft 1900.

+ 2352 iv   Faith M[8] **Bovee**, born 15 Oct 1896 in Bellvue, Calhoun Co., IL; died 4 Apr 1988 in MT. She married **Fred R Uhde**.

2353 v   Hallie May[8] **Bovee**, born 31 Aug 1898 in Bellvue, Calhoun Co., IL; died Aug 1984.

2354 vi   Mary Florine[8] **Bovee**, born 27 Jan 1901 in IL. She married **R K Roberts**.

2355 vii   Evelyn Beatrice[8] **Bovee**, born 12 Mar 1903 in IL; died Mar 1903.

2356 viii   Emma Louise[8] **Bovee**, born 9 Nov 1908.

+ 2357 ix   Eugene Burdette[8] **Bovee**, born 27 Sep 1911 in Calhoun Co., IL; died 17 Feb 1989. He married **Marjorie Irene Johnson**.

1315. Nancy Jane[7] **Bovee** (Nelson John[6], John[5], Nicholas M[4], Matthew[3], Nicholas[2], Mathieu[1]), born 9 Jul 1849 in Wayne Co., IL; died 25 Nov 1909 in Randolph, Cedar Co., NE. She married on 15 Jun 1874 in Blair, Washington Co., NE Thomas Jefferson Howarth, born 28 Jan 1844 in Andover, Essex Co., MA; died 2 Jan 1929 in Pittsburgh, Allegheny Co., PA, son of Thomas Howarth and Hannah Pearl Marston.

Children of Nancy Jane Bovee and Thomas Jefferson Howarth were as follows:

2358 i   William[8] **Howarth**, born 25 Apr 1875 in Washington Co., NE; died 26 Sep 1881.

2359 ii   Mary Elizabeth[8] **Howarth**, born 17 Dec 1877 in Washington Co., NE; died 31 Jul 1985.

2360 iii   Nelson[8] **Howarth**, born 19 Jul 1879 in Washington Co., NE; died 25 Dec 1949.

2361 iv   Victor[8] **Howarth**, born 11 Jul 1881 in Vacoma, Washington Co., NE; died 23 Oct 1960 in Rupert, Minidoka Co., ID.

2362 v   Hermon[8] **Howarth**, born 29 Jan 1883 in Washington Co., NE; died 14 Apr 1890.

2363 vi   Harrison[8] **Howarth**, born 8 Aug 1884 in Washington Co., NE; died 20 Feb 1969.

2364 vii   Clara Pearl[8] **Howarth**, born 1 Apr 1886 in Washington Co., NE; died 6 Jan 1918.

2365 viii   Cora Merton[8] **Howarth**, born 15 Nov 1887 in Washington Co., NE; died 10 Jul 1972.

2366 ix   Frank[8] **Howarth**, born 5 May 1889 in Washington Co., NE; died 2 Feb 1978.

2367 x   Jessie May[8] **Howarth**, born 8 Apr 1891 in Carroll, Wayne

Co., NE; died 31 Mar 1985.

2368 xi Thomas Walton[8] **Howarth**, born 13 Aug 1894 in Carroll, Wayne Co., NE; died 29 Jun 1962.

1316. Mary Elizabeth[7] **Bovee** (Nelson John[6], John[5], Nicholas M[4], Matthew[3], Nicholas[2], Mathieu[1]), born 11 Dec 1850 in IL; died 5 Apr 1901. She married on 16 Mar 1871 in Wayne Co., IL Caleb Loftus, born 2 Dec 1847; died 30 Nov 1934.

Children of Mary Elizabeth Bovee and Caleb Loftus were as follows:

2369 i George[8] **Loftis**, born 25 Dec 1871; died 2 Feb 1940 in Blair, Washington Co., NE.

2370 ii John[8] **Loftis**, born 21 Mar 1874; died 1956. He married on 26 Feb 1896 **Myrtle Frances Bovee**, born 24 Jan 1875 in IA, daughter of Nicholas Aaron Bovee and Anna Maria Betzer.

2371 iii Lizzie[8] **Loftis**, born 13 Mar 1876; died 15 Oct 1883.

2372 iv Nancy Emma[8] **Loftis**, born 21 Apr 1878.

2373 v Frank[8] **Loftis**, born 18 Jan 1881; died 29 Jan 1941.

2374 vi Charlie[8] **Loftis**, born 18 Mar 1883; died 10 Jul 1890.

2375 vii Bert Nelson[8] **Loftis**, born 9 May 1885; died 17 Dec 1952. He married **E Grace**, born 4 Dec 1881; died 30 Oct 1947.

2376 viii Minnie[8] **Loftis**, born 1 May 1887.

2377 ix Mary Olive[8] **Loftis**, born 25 Oct 1889.

2378 x Ora Edith[8] **Loftis**, born 2 Oct 1891; died 10 Oct 1949.

2379 xi Ray Warden[8] **Loftis**, born 21 Aug 1893; died 18 Feb 1899.

1318. John Milton[7] **Bovee** (Nelson John[6], John[5], Nicholas M[4], Matthew[3], Nicholas[2], Mathieu[1]), born 25 Oct 1853 in IL; died 2 Apr 1940. He married Clara Dulceina Hancock, born Jan 1861 in PA.

Children of John Milton Bovee and Clara Dulceina Hancock were as follows:

+ 2380 i Elmer N[8] **Bovee**, born Oct 1882 in Nebo, Pike Co., IL. He married **Myrtle M (---)**.

+ 2381 ii Lee M[8] **Bovee**, born Jul 1884 in NE; died 19 Mar 1963 in Los Angeles, Los Angeles Co., CA. He married **Olive Emily Mennell**.

+ 2382 iii Walter[8] **Bovee**, born Feb 1888 in NE. He married **Alice W (---)**.

2383 iv Ada M[8] **Bovee**, born 22 Oct 1890 in NE; died Jan 1982 in Craig, Burt Co., NE.

1319. Sarah Catherine[7] **Bovee** (Nelson John[6], John[5], Nicholas M[4], Matthew[3], Nicholas[2], Mathieu[1]), born 20 Jan 1855 in Wayne Co., IL; died 2 Apr 1881 in

Tekama, Burt Co., NB. She married on 13 Mar 1879 in NE George Calvin Geary.

Children of Sarah Catherine Bovee and George Calvin Geary were as follows:

2384   i   Jessie Catherine[8] **Geary**.

1321. James Massey[7] **Bovee** (Nelson John[6], John[5], Nicholas M[4], Matthew[3], Nicholas[2], Mathieu[1]), born 3 Mar 1860 in Fairfield, Wayne Co., IL; died 10 Apr 1938 in Laramie, Albany Co., WY. He married on 6 Mar 1887 in NE Sarah Ann Flanagan, born 22 Jun 1861 in Barnsville, Belmont Co., OH; died 27 Apr 1934 in Wheatland, Platte Co., WY, daughter of Peter Flanagan and Maria Miller.

Children of James Massey Bovee and Sarah Ann Flanagan were as follows:

+   2385   i   Glenn Peter[8] **Bovee**, born 13 Apr 1888 in Glenrock, Converse Co., WY; died 31 Dec 1956 in Shawnee, Pottawatomie Co., OK. He married **Vina Irene Sauter**.

      2386   ii   Gladys Gertrude[8] **Bovee**, born 14 Nov 1890 in Omaha, Douglas Co., NE; died 11 Jan 1935 in Basi, Big Horn Co., WY.

+   2387   iii   Gail Margaret[8] **Bovee**, born 7 Apr 1895 in Fletcher, Washington Co., NE; died 8 Apr 1986 in Laramie, Albany Co., WY. She married **John Wesley Johnson**.

      2388   iv   Gretchen[8] **Bovee**, born 4 Aug 1898 in Blair, Washington Co., WY; died 28 Aug 1981 in CA. She married on 4 Jun 1933 in Los Angeles, Los Angeles Co., CA **Thomas Charles Gallagher**, son of Bart James Gallagher and Ada Marie Rogers.

1322. Emma Louise[7] **Bovee** (Nelson John[6], John[5], Nicholas M[4], Matthew[3], Nicholas[2], Mathieu[1]), born 10 Feb 1862 in Wayne Co., IL; died 17 Nov 1948. She married on 6 May 1884 in Blair, Washington Co., NE Jefferson H Gossard, born 7 Jan 1840 in Ross Co., OH; died 1 May 1889 in Washington Co., NE.

Children of Emma Louise Bovee and Jefferson H Gossard were as follows:

2389   i   Bessie Edith[8] **Gossard**.
2390   ii   Jefferson Wilbur[8] **Gossard**.

1323. Margaret Olive[7] **Bovee** (Nelson John[6], John[5], Nicholas M[4], Matthew[3], Nicholas[2], Mathieu[1]), born 17 Apr 1864 in Wayne Co., IL; died 20 Nov 1955 in Wayne, Wayne Co., NE. She married on 1 Jan 1884 in Blair, Washington Co., NE Amzi Phillip Gossard, born 29 Apr 1862 in McClean Co., IL; died 7 Nov 1941 in Wayne, Wayne Co., NE, son of Philip J Gossard and Mary E Leper.

Children of Margaret Olive Bovee and Amzi Phillip Gossard were as follows:

2391   i   Bert Jackson[8] **Gossard**.

2392   ii   Leonard Nelson[8] **Gossard**.

2393   iii   Earl Amzi[8] **Gossard**.

2394   iv   Richard Kelly[8] **Gossard**.

2395   v   Mabel Olive **Gossard**.

2396   vi   Wayne Theodore[8] **Gossard**.

1346. Jasper Lincoln[7] **Bovee** (Joseph Smith[6], Mathew[5], Nicholas M[4], Matthew[3], Nicholas[2], Mathieu[1]), born 21 May 1866 in Denver Denver Co., CO; died 25 Jun 1941 in Wheatland, Platte Co., WY. He married on 20 May 1884 in Cheyenne, Laramie Co., WY Rosa Quincy Shanks, born 6 Feb 1867 in Springfield, Sangamon Co., IL; died 16 Mar 1944 in Wheatland, Platte Co., WY, daughter of Samuel Shanks.

Children of Jasper Lincoln Bovee and Rosa Quincy Shanks were as follows:

2397   i   Clara Belle[8] **Bovee**, born 27 Sep 1892 in Cheyenne, Laramie Co., WY; died 14 Jul 1966. She married on 8 Jun 1911 **William Selby**.

2398   ii   Floyd Norman[8] **Bovee**, born 3 Mar 1893 in Cheyenne, Laramie Co., WY; died Nov 1894 in Cheyenne, Laramie Co., WY.

+ 2399   iii   Nettie Elizabeth[8] **Bovee**, born 9 Aug 1893 in Cheyenne, Laramie Co., WY; died 4 Nov 1980 in Wheatland, Platte Co., WY. She married **Horace Cleveland Wilson**.

2400   iv   Florence M[8] **Bovee**, born 3 May 1896; died Died young.

2401   v   Clyde G[8] **Bovee**, born 21 Jul 1900 in Wheatland, Platte Co., WY; died 5 Oct 1986 in Twisp, Okanogan Co., WA.

2402   vi   Halbert L[8] **Bovee**, born 18 Jan 1902 in Wheatland, Platte Co., WY; died Mar 1987 in Twisp, Okanogan Co., WA.

2403   vii   Donald Ray[8] **Bovee**, born 2 Dec 1910 in Wheatland, Platte Co., WY; died 8 Feb 1981. He married **Edith Adams**, born 1922; died 1997.

1350. Lester La Grand[7] **Bovee** (Joseph Smith[6], Mathew[5], Nicholas M[4], Matthew[3], Nicholas[2], Mathieu[1]), born 22 Feb 1878. He married on 25 Apr 1907 in Cheyanne, Laramie Co., WY Nellie Bollin, born 13 Apr 1888; died 9 Apr 1970.

Children of Lester La Grand Bovee and Nellie Bollin were as follows:

+ 2404   i   Raymond A[8] **Bovee**, born 8 Jan 1908 in Cheyenne, Laramie Co., WY; died 9 Mar 1991 in Cheyenne, Laramie Co., WY. He married **Marie Dykeman**.

+ 2405   ii   Joseph Earl[8] **Bovee**, born 28 Mar 1910 in Cheyenne, Laramie Co., WY. He married (1) **Frances Berry**; (2) **Evelyn (---)**.

1360. Marvin W[7] **Bovee** (Benedict Arnold[6], Mathias Jacob[5], Jacob Mathias[4],

Matthew[3], Nicholas[2], Mathieu[1]), born 31 Jan 1859 in Eagle, Waukesha Co., WI; died 25 Nov 1947 in Eagle, Waukesha Co., WI. He married on 30 Aug 1888 in Chicago, Cook Co., IL Mararet Robinson, born 27 Jul 1858 in Forest Glenn, IL; died 16 Dec 1943 in Eagle, Waukesha Co., WI, daughter of James Robinson and Anna Harrington.

Children of Marvin W Bovee and Mararet Robinson were as follows:

+ 2406 i Benedict Arthur[8] **Bovee**, born 6 Jun 1889 in Eagle, Waukesha Co., WI; died 14 Apr 1985 in Fort Lauderdale, Broward Co., FL. He married **Myrtle L Manwaring**.

  2407 ii Leslie H[8] **Bovee**, born 18 Sep 1891 in Eagle, Waukesha Co., WI; died 11 Sep 1894.

+ 2408 iii James Francis[8] **Bovee**, born 3 Dec 1895 in Eagle, Waukesha Co., WI; died 9 Jan 1992. He married **Fern A Marty**.

  2409 iv Katherine A[8] **Bovee**, born 31 Oct 1897 in Eagle, Waukesha Co., WI; died 9 Jun 2000 in Waukesha, Waukesha Co., WI. She married in 1935 **Allen M Howard**, died 25 May 1963.

  2410 v Francis M[8] **Bovee**, born 22 Mar 1900; died 20 Jan 1919 in Eagle, Waukesha Co., WI.

1361. Manley W[7] **Bovee** (William Reid[6], Mathias Jacob[5], Jacob Mathias[4], Matthew[3], Nicholas[2], Mathieu[1]), born 25 Feb 1849 in Eagle, Waukesha Co., WI; died 7 Feb 1919 in Bartlesville, Washington Co., OK. He married Elizabeth Ford McCool, born Apr 1851.

Children of Manley W Bovee and Elizabeth Ford McCool were as follows:

+ 2411 i William David[8] **Bovee**, born 26 Dec 1872 in PA. He married **Mary Elizabeth Shutt**.

+ 2412 ii Jesse D[8] **Bovee**, born 13 Feb 1874 in PA; died 30 Jan 1959. He married (1) **Hattie Powell**; (2) **Della Baker**; (3) **Minnie Fescus**.

  2413 iii John Snover[8] **Bovee**, born 17 Sep 1879 in PA; died 21 Jun 1921 in Bartlesville, Washington Co., OK. He married on 10 Jul 1901 **Myrtle McCool**.

  2414 iv George Lester[8] **Bovee**, born 20 Dec 1884 in Salem, Clarion Co., PA. He married (1) on 22 Jun 1904 **Ada Fogel**; (2) on 6 May 1919 **Carrie B Ward**; (3) in 1928 **Maude McMillen**.

1364. Maude[7] **Bovee** (Marvin Henry[6], Mathias Jacob[5], Jacob Mathias[4], Matthew[3], Nicholas[2], Mathieu[1]). She married Halbert L Halverson.

Children of Maude Bovee and Halbert L Halverson were as follows:

  2415 i Keneth B[8] **Halverson**.

1375. Dewitt Clinton[7] **Bovee** (Edward Livingston[6], Mathias Jacob[5], Jacob Mathias[4], Matthew[3], Nicholas[2], Mathieu[1]), born 21 Jan 1861 in WI; died 17 Sep 1908 in Chicago, Cook Co., IL. He married Nettie (---).

Children of Dewitt Clinton Bovee and Nettie (---) were as follows:

2416   i   Ralph[8] **Bovee**, born 31 Aug 1885; died 31 Jan 1886 in Chicago, Cook Co., IL.

1376. Herbert Stephen[7] **Bovee** (Edward Livingston[6], Mathias Jacob[5], Jacob Mathias[4], Matthew[3], Nicholas[2], Mathieu[1]), born 17 Sep 1863 in WI. He married on 4 Nov 1885 in East Troy, Walworth Co., WI Edith F Burgit, born 23 Jul 1865 in Joliet, Will Co., IL; died 9 Dec 1899 in East Troy, Walworth Co., WI, daughter of William J Burgit and Maria J Burleigh.

Children of Herbert Stephen Bovee and Edith F Burgit were as follows:

2417   i   Roy E[8] **Bovee**, born 7 Jan 1887 in Eagle, Waukesha Co., WI; died Jan 1967 in Jenkintown,Montgomery Co., PA. He married (1) on 13 Sep 1912 in Wilmington,New Castle Co., DE **Elizabeth A Schwartz**; (2) aft 1912 **Mae (---)**.

2418   ii   William Clayton[8] **Bovee**, born 4 Aug 1888 in Elkhorn, Walworth Co., WI; died 1976 in PA. He married on 14 Jul 1915 **Emilie Barstow Dixon**.

2419   iii   Harold Burgit[8] **Bovee**, born 8 Oct 1892 in East Troy, Walworth Co., WI; died Jul 1986 in Philadelphia, Philidelphia Co., PA. He married on 26 Dec 1925 in Philadelphia, Philidelphia Co., PA **Sara Maysee Closs**.

2420   iv   Ruth Estelle[8] **Bovee**, born 31 Jul 1895 in East Troy, Walworth Co., WI; died 23 Jun 1902 in Elkhorn, Walworth Co., WI.

2421   v   Hubert I[8] **Bovee**, born 31 Jul 1895 in Elkhorn, Walworth Co., WI; died Jun 1902.

+ 2422   vi   Marvin Burleigh[8] **Bovee**, born 30 Mar 1897 in East Troy, Walworth Co., WI; died 10 Oct 1961 in WI. He married (1) **Nina Verginia Wilkinson**; (2) **Doris Anna Bedard**.

2423   vii   Helen Emily[8] **Bovee**, born 13 May 1898 in Ridgeway, Iowa Co., WI; died 22 Mar 1903.

2424   viii   Allen Dwight[8] **Bovee**, born 18 Oct 1899 in Lakeside, IL; died 28 Jan 1900 in East Troy, Walworth Co., WI.

1378. Marvin W[7] **Bovee** (Edward Livingston[6], Mathias Jacob[5], Jacob Mathias[4], Matthew[3], Nicholas[2], Mathieu[1]), born 27 Jan 1868 in WI. He married abt 1890 Mabel Gilman, born Jun 1868.

Children of Marvin W Bovee and Mabel Gilman were as follows:

2425   i   Kenneth[8] **Bovee**, born 24 Aug 1894 in Walworth Co., WI.

1379. Emily L[7] **Bovee** (Edward Livingston[6], Mathias Jacob[5], Jacob Mathias[4], Matthew[3], Nicholas[2], Mathieu[1]), born 17 Oct 1869 in WI; died 15 May 1958. She married on 23 Apr 1891 in Eagle, Waukesha Co., WI Jonathan Malin Jones, born 4 May 1866; died 5 Jul 1926.

Children of Emily L Bovee and Jonathan Malin Jones were as follows:

2426	i	Dorothy Bovee[8] **Jones**.
2427	ii	Edward[8] **Jones**.
2428	iii	Edna[8] **Jones**.

1390. John Walker[7] **Bovee** (Thomas Pittman[6], Philip Vedder[5], Jacob Mathias[4], Matthew[3], Nicholas[2], Mathieu[1]), born May 1865; died 1933 in Plainfield, Waushara Co., WI. He married Mary A Margeson, born Jul 1872 in WI; died 1947 in Plainfield, Waushara Co., WI.

Children of John Walker Bovee and Mary A Margeson were as follows:

+ 2429   i   Lloyd Horace[8] **Bovee**, born 19 Oct 1894 in WI; died 30 Jun 1981 in Plainfield, Waushara Co., WI. He married **Bernice Reed**.
+ 2430   ii   Bessie Lillian[8] **Bovee**, born 6 Oct 1897 in WI. She married **James Doolittle**.
   2431   iii   George M[8] **Bovee**, born 8 Mar 1903.
+ 2432   iv   Harold Vincent[8] **Bovee**, born 19 Aug 1914. He married unknown.

1396. Wilbert Lemuel[7] **Bovee** (Lemuel Jacob[6], Philip Vedder[5], Jacob Mathias[4], Matthew[3], Nicholas[2], Mathieu[1]), born abt 1869 in WI; died 24 Jun 1938. He married abt 1895 Anna Betts, born abt 1875.

Children of Wilbert Lemuel Bovee and Anna Betts were as follows:

2433	i	Dora[8] **Bovee**, born 1896.
2434	ii	Lena[8] **Bovee**.
2435	iii	Philip Lemuel[8] **Bovee**, born abt 1902 in TX; died Dec 1964 in El Paso, El Paso Co., TX..

1397. Jonathan Betts[7] **Bovee** (Lemuel Jacob[6], Philip Vedder[5], Jacob Mathias[4], Matthew[3], Nicholas[2], Mathieu[1]), born 26 Feb 1871 in WI. He married Addie Belle Lamphere, born 21 Dec 1877; died 3 May 1944 in Los Angeles, Los Angeles Co., CA.

Children of Jonathan Betts Bovee and Addie Belle Lamphere were as follows:

+ 2436   i   John Lemuel Franklin[8] **Bovee**, born 1897; died 1964. He married **Margaret Kepler Fowler**.

2437　ii　　　Catherine Leona[8] **Bovee**, born 1899; died 1981.

2438　iii　　Minnie May[8] **Bovee**, born 10 Jul 1903; died 12 May 1951 in Los Angeles Co., CA. She married **(---) Mack**.

2439　iv　　Esma Elizabeth[8] **Bovee**, born 1906; died 1970.

1399. Minnie Susan[7] **Bovee** (Lemuel Jacob[6], Philip Vedder[5], Jacob Mathias[4], Matthew[3], Nicholas[2], Mathieu[1]), born 11 Dec 1874 in WI; died 30 Aug 1894. She married Charles Tuttle.

Children of Minnie Susan Bovee and Charles Tuttle were as follows:

2440　i　　　Harry[8] **Tuttle**, born Aug 1894; died 13 Sep 1894.

1400. Elmer Ford[7] **Bovee** (Lemuel Jacob[6], Philip Vedder[5], Jacob Mathias[4], Matthew[3], Nicholas[2], Mathieu[1]), born 22 Feb 1882. He married on 18 May 1910 Helen Ione Harland.

Children of Elmer Ford Bovee and Helen Ione Harland were as follows:

2441　i　　　Harland Ford[8] **Bovee**, born 12 Mar 1911 in CO; died 29 Sep 1991 in COntra Costa Co., CA.

1402. Charles Eugene[7] **Bovee** (Lemuel Jacob[6], Philip Vedder[5], Jacob Mathias[4], Matthew[3], Nicholas[2], Mathieu[1]), born 15 Aug 1892. He married on 23 Dec 1912 Pansy Van Clive.

Children of Charles Eugene Bovee and Pansy Van Clive were as follows:

+　2442　i　　　Elurde Charles[8] **Bovee**, born 12 Mar 1914 in Oconto Co., WI. He married **Ethel (---)**.

+　2443　ii　　Elmer C[8] **Bovee**, born 12 Mar 1914 in Oconto Co., WI; died Jul 1986 in Yuma, Yuma Co., AZ. He married unknown.

2444　iii　　Mildred[8] **Bovee**, born abt 1897; died abt 1915.

2445　iv　　Ruth[8] **Bovee**.

1409. Grace M[7] **Bovee** (John Isaac[6], Philip Vedder[5], Jacob Mathias[4], Matthew[3], Nicholas[2], Mathieu[1]), born 4 Feb 1879; died Aug 1916. She married Dr. Frank Markey.

Children of Grace M Bovee and Dr. Frank Markey were as follows:

2446　i　　　John[8] **Markey**.

1410. Philip LaRue[7] **Bovee** (Eugene Charles[6], Philip Vedder[5], Jacob Mathias[4], Matthew[3], Nicholas[2], Mathieu[1]), born 14 Jul 1875 in Denver, Denver Co., CO; died 1924. He married Ava Graves, born 5 Nov 1877; died Mar 1974 in Newhall,

Los Angeles Co., CA.

Children of Philip LaRue Bovee and Ava Graves were as follows:

2447   i   Eloise[8] **Bovee**, born Jan 1900 in CO.

2448   ii   Lillian[8] **Bovee**, born 1901 in CO.

2449   iii   Beverly Martha[8] **Bovee**, born 1903 in CO. She married **(--) Barnard**.

+   2450   iv   Eugene Philip[8] **Bovee**, born 27 Nov 1904. He married **Zadie Elizabeth Currie**.

+   2451   v   John Larue[8] **Bovee**, born 24 Mar 1907 in CO; died Dec 1972 in CO. He married **Barbara Bendell**.

2452   vi   Helen[8] **Bovee**, born abt 1916. She married **(---) Venegas**.

1422. George Willard[7] Bovee (William Henry[6], John Grant[5], John[4], Matthew[3], Nicholas[2], Mathieu[1]), born 4 Jun 1853 in Clayton, Jefferson Co., NY; died 11 Dec 1944. He married (1) on 1 Jan 1878 Jessie W Harris, born abt 1862; died 4 Dec 1899 in Chaumont, Jefferson Co., NY; (2) Mattie McIvor, born in French Cnada; (3) Eleanor Carpenter.

Children of George Willard Bovee and Jessie W Harris were as follows:

2453   i   Ward L[8] **Bovee**, born Jul 1881 in Jefferson Co., NY; died bef 1944.

2454   ii   Edith E[8] **Bovee**, born Jul 1883 in Jefferson Co., NY. She married **Gilmore (---)**.

2455   iii   Carrie E[8] **Bovee**, born Mar 1896 in Jefferson Co., NY. She married **Charles Campbell**.

Children of George Willard Bovee and Mattie McIvor were as follows:

2456   i   Lillian[8] **Bovee**, born abt 1904 in Chaumont, Jefferson Co., NY. She married **Paul Cummings**.

2457   ii   Helen[8] **Bovee**, born abt 1906 in Chaumont, Jefferson Co., NY. She married **Ralph Viau**.

1424. Frederick Charles[7] Bovee (William Henry[6], John Grant[5], John[4], Matthew[3], Nicholas[2], Mathieu[1]), born 20 Aug 1859 in Jefferson Co., NY; died 15 Jun 1929 in Watertown, Jefferson Co., NY. He married (1) Elizabeth McKeever, born Feb 1861 in Canada; died 30 Apr 1903 in Chaumont, Jefferson Co., NY; (2) on 8 Nov 1905 Ida May Juby.

Children of Frederick Charles Bovee and Elizabeth McKeever were as follows:

+   2458   i   Frederick Charles[8] **Bovee** Jr, born Jan 1884 in Three Mile Bay, Jefferson Co., NY; died 5 Jul 1961. He married **Harriet Steele**.

+   2459   ii   Edward J[8] **Bovee**, born Jun 1895 in NY. He married **Anna Emerson**.

2460   iii   Margaret E[8] **Bovee**, born Jan 1899. She married **Earnest**

Giblow.

Children of Frederick Charles Bovee and Ida May Juby were as follows:

 2461 i Mary Bovee, born abt 1906. She married **(---) Roberts**.

+ 2462 ii Stella Bovee, born 24 Sep 1911. She married (1) **James E Denslow**; (2) **Paul DuFrene**.

+ 2463 iii Eunice Bovee, born 14 Oct 1914. She married **Norman Westcott**.

 2464 iv Laura Bovee, born abt 1915.

 2465 v Minny Bovee, born Aug 1916; died 3 Nov 1917.

 2466 vi Alice Bovee, born abt 1917.

+ 2467 vii George Bovee, born 27 Nov 1917 in Watertown, Jefferson Co., NY; died 24 Nov 1978 in Watertown, Jefferson Co., NY. He married **Mary Murphy**.

+ 2468 viii Ralph Perl Bovee, born 22 Dec 1920 in Watertown, Jefferson Co., NY; died 11 Apr 1996 in Watertown, Jefferson Co., NY. He married **Betty J Desormeau**.

1427. Hiram David^7 Bovee (William Henry^6, John Grant^5, John^4, Matthew^3, Nicholas^2, Mathieu^1), born abt 1866; died 1944 in Clayton, Jefferson Co., NY. He married on 28 Jan 1906 Lana M Jondrew.

Children of Hiram David Bovee and Lana M Jondrew were as follows:

+ 2469 i Fanny Bovee, born 4 Mar 1907; died 24 Nov 1930. She married **John Russell**.

+ 2470 ii Florence M Bovee, born 4 Oct 1908. She married **Stanley E Farr**.

+ 2471 iii Harold L Bovee, born 14 Dec 1912 in Depauville, Clayton Twp., Jefferson Co., NY; died 3 Feb 1975 in St Petersburg, Pinellas Co., FL. He married **Evelyn Gertrude Constance**.

+ 2472 iv Gladys Leota Bovee, born 30 Sep 1913 in Clayton, Jefferson Co., NY; died 20 Dec 1985. She married **Perry W Shely**.

 2473 v Ada K Bovee, born 24 Nov 1914. She married abt 1930 **Lowell Kiethley**.

1430. Bruce^7 Bovee (William Henry^6, John Grant^5, John^4, Matthew^3, Nicholas^2, Mathieu^1), born Oct 1873 in NY; died bef 1927. He married Martha I Wakefield, born 1881 in Canada.

Children of Bruce Bovee and Martha I Wakefield were as follows:

 2474 i Mary K Bovee, born abt 1903 in Clayton., Jefferson Co., NY.

 2475 ii Max L Bovee, born abt 1905 in Clayton., Jefferson Co., NY; died 10 Sep 1924 in Depauville, Clayton Twp.,

1431. Burton G[7] **Bovee** (William Henry[6], John Grant[5], John[4], Matthew[3], Nicholas[2], Mathieu[1]), born abt 1874; died 7 Jan 1912 in Depauville, Clayton Twp., Jefferson Co., NY. He married (1) Grace M Walrath, born abt 1874 in Depauville, Clayton Twp., Jefferson Co., NY; died 9 Aug 1903 in Clayton Jefferson Co., NY; (2) L Maude De Rosia, born May 1883.

Children of Burton G Bovee and Grace M Walrath were as follows:

2476	i	Nina S[8] **Bovee**, born abt 1893; died 11 Mar 1963. She married (1) **Francis Plummer**; (2) **(---) Redden**.
2477	ii	Agnes S[8] **Bovee**, born abt 1896.
2478	iii	Emma B[8] **Bovee**, born abt 1902.
2479	iv	John[8] **Bovee**, born 15 Aug 1902 in Clayton Jefferson Co., NY; died 16 Aug 1902 in Clayton Jefferson Co., NY.

Children of Burton G Bovee and L Maude De Rosia were as follows:

	2480	i	Child[8] **Bovee**.
	2481	ii	Elbridge B[8] **Bovee**, born 13 Sep 1906 in Clayton Jefferson Co., NY.
+	2482	iii	Walter Everette[8] **(Bovee)** De ROSIA, born 1 Jun 1909 in Clayton Jefferson Co., NY; died 21 Nov 1971 in Carthage, Jefferson Co., NY. He married (1) unknown; (2) **(---) Soluri**.

1444. Franklin E[7] **Bovee** (John Wesley[6], John Grant[5], John[4], Matthew[3], Nicholas[2], Mathieu[1]), born 26 Aug 1865 in Springfield, Sangamon Co., IL; buried in Forest Cem, Camden, Oneida Co., NY. He married on 13 Jan 1887 in Redfield, Oswego Co., NY Helen L Flagg, born Dec 1865 in NY, daughter of James E Flagg and Eunice Babcock.

Children of Franklin E Bovee and Helen L Flagg were as follows:

| + | 2483 | i | Anna Irene[8] **Bovee**, born 18 Jun 1892 in Redfield, Oswego Co., NY. She married **Lloyd E Watkins**. |
| + | 2484 | ii | Edward Milton[8] **Bovee**, born 11 Apr 1894 in Redfield, Oswego Co., NY; died 27 Dec 1968 in St. Cloud, Osceola Co., FL. He married **Bertha P Spellicy**. |

1445. Milton H[7] **Bovee** (John Wesley[6], John Grant[5], John[4], Matthew[3], Nicholas[2], Mathieu[1]), born Jun 1871 in Redfield, Oswego Co., NY. He married Minnie Redman, born 1874; buried in Forest Lawn Cem, Camden, Oneida Co., NY.

Children of Milton H Bovee and Minnie Redman were as follows:

| 2485 | i | Irene Pearl[8] **Bovee**, born Jun 1898 in Redfield, Oswego Co., NY. She married **John Baker**. |
| 2486 | ii | Mary Alice[8] **Bovee**. She married **Thomas Sherman**. |

2487   iii   Jane[8] **Bovee**. She married **John Webb**.

1466. Jennie[7] **Bovee** (Levi[6], John Henry[5], John Henry[4], Matthew[3], Nicholas[2], Mathieu[1]), born abt 1867. She married James E Marvin.

Children of Jennie Bovee and James E Marvin were as follows:

2488   i   William Claude[8] **Marvin**, born 9 Jun 1886 in Dover Twp., Lenawee Co., MI..

1468. Grosvenor A[7] **Bovee** (Levi[6], John Henry[5], John Henry[4], Matthew[3], Nicholas[2], Mathieu[1]), born 4 Apr 1871 in Lake Co., MI. He married Viola E Boren, born Nov 1868 in IN.

Children of Grosvenor A Bovee and Viola E Boren were as follows:

2489   i   Lillian Leone[8] **Bovee**, born 27 Mar 1895 in IN. She married on 28 Dec 1916 in Fort Wayne, Allen Co., IN **Floyde Paul Brown**.

1469. Woodbury H[7] **Bovee** (Hiram[6], John Henry[5], John Henry[4], Matthew[3], Nicholas[2], Mathieu[1]), born 15 Oct 1859 in North Star Twp., Gratiot Co., MI; died 12 Jul 1917. He married on 6 Feb 1887 in Gratiot Co., MI Jeanette Vedder, born 6 Feb 1868 in Lewanee Co., MI; died abt 1940, daughter of Clark Vedder and Sarah Ann Deline.

Children of Woodbury H Bovee and Jeanette Vedder were as follows:

2490   i   Agnes[8] **Bovee**, born 3 Dec 1888 in Gratiot Co., MI; died abt 1888 in Gratiot Co., MI.

2491   ii   Florence A[8] **Bovee**, born 14 Sep 1890 in North Star Twp., Gratiot Co., MI.

2492   iii   Lois L[8] **Bovee**, born Jan 1893 in North Star Twp., Gratiot Co., MI. She married **(---) Maxwell**.

+ 2493   iv   Cecil W[8] **Bovee**, born 29 Jan 1896 in North Star Twp., Gratiot Co., MI; died Jun 1973. He married **Dora L Zimmerman**.

+ 2494   v   Glen Howard[8] **Bovee**, born 18 Jul 1898 in North Star Twp., Gratiot Co., MI; died 22 Feb 1971 in Plymouth, Wayne Co., MI. He married **Charlotte T Teachman**.

+ 2495   vi   Hiram C (Harry)[8] **Bovee**, born 7 Nov 1901 in North Star Twp., Gratiot Co., MI; died 1960. He married **Rosamond I Parling**.

2496   vii   Royal O[8] **Bovee**, born 19 Nov 1905 in North Star Twp., Gratiot Co., MI; died Sep 1974 in FL.

1470. Clara A[7] **Bovee** (Hiram[6], John Henry[5], John Henry[4], Matthew[3], Nicholas[2], Mathieu[1]), born 25 Jan 1864 in North Star Twp., Gratiot Co., MI; died 1 Dec 1910 in St Johns, Clinton Co., MI. She married on 18 Jun 1879 Calvin A Crandell, born 8 May 1859; died 8 Jan 1929.

Children of Clara A Bovee and Calvin A Crandell were as follows:

2497	i	W Fletcher^8 **Crandell**, born 7 Mar 1880; died 14 Oct 1886.
2498	ii	Leon H^8 **Crandell**, born 5 Oct 1884; died 19 Apr 1885.
2499	iii	Evaline F^8 **Crandell**, born 7 Oct 1886.
2500	iv	Chauncey L^8 **Crandell**, born 20 Mar 1890.
2501	v	Inez Fern^8 **Crandell**, born 21 Mar 1893.
2502	vi	N B^8 **Crandell**, born 17 Sep 1895; died abt 1895.
2503	vii	Child^8 **Crandell**, born 9 Jul 1901; died abt 1901.

1477. Ida A^7 **Bovee** (Andrew J^6, Mathew^5, John Henry^4, Matthew^3, Nicholas^2, Mathieu^1), born Apr 1863; died 22 Mar 1924 in Minneapolis, Hennepin Co., MN.. She married abt 1887 Myron Stearns, born Sep 1865 in OH.

Children of Ida A Bovee and Myron Stearns were as follows:

2504	i	Mamie C^8 **Stearns**, born Apr 1888 in MI.
2505	ii	Vanessa^8 **Stearns**.

1478. Edward Hill^7 **Bovee** (Andrew J^6, Mathew^5, John Henry^4, Matthew^3, Nicholas^2, Mathieu^1), born 18 Sep 1864 in Flint, Genesee Co., MI; died 18 Jun 1960 in Girard, Erie Co. PA. He married on 25 Dec 1897 Adelia Ann Schutte, born 26 Aug 1878 in PA; died 20 May 1949, daughter of August Schutte and Sarah Williams.

Children of Edward Hill Bovee and Adelia Ann Schutte were as follows:

	2506	i	Viola May^8 **Bovee**, born 18 Oct 1898 in PA.
+	2507	ii	Archie Edward^8 **Bovee**, born 30 Jan 1900 in PA; died Dec 1980 in Bay View, Erie Co., OH. He married **Nellie I Beck**.
	2508	iii	Ethel Margaret^8 **Bovee**, born 28 Feb 1903; died Apr 1981 in PA.
	2509	iv	George Watson^8 **Bovee**, born 16 Apr 1904; died 1956 in Ripley, Chautauqua Co., NY.
	2510	v	Clyde August^8 **Bovee**, born 2 Sep 1908 in PA.
+	2511	vi	Raymond Arthur^8 **Bovee**, born 28 Jan 1910 in MN; died 22 Nov 1985 in Erie, Erie Co., PA. He married **Florence Edna Olmstead**.
	2512	vii	Myron Fred^8 **Bovee**, born 24 Jan 1912 in MN; died in Elizabeth, Allegheny Co., PA.
	2513	viii	Charles Andrew^8 **Bovee**, born abt 1914 in OH; died bef 1960.

1479. Selden Martin[7] **Bovee** (Andrew J[6], Mathew[5], John Henry[4], Matthew[3], Nicholas[2], Mathieu[1]), born 19 Sep 1872 in Hudson, Lenawee Co., MI; died 28 Apr 1950 in Sonoma, Sonoma Co., CA. He married (1) in OH Ethel Bates, born 13 Oct 1876; died 12 Feb 1940 in Los Angeles Co., CA; (2) Elizabeth (---), born 1881; died 1960.

Children of Selden Martin Bovee and Ethel Bates were as follows:

2514	i	Ruth Augusta[8] **Bovee**, born 1 Oct 1897 in OH; died 22 May 1988 in Los Angeles Co., CA. She married **(---) Savage**.
2515	ii	Marian Adele[8] **Bovee**, born 31 Oct 1901 in OH; died 5 Apr 1991 in Los Angeles Co., CA. She married **(---) Moore**.

1480. Daisy Mae[7] **Bovee** (Andrew J[6], Mathew[5], John Henry[4], Matthew[3], Nicholas[2], Mathieu[1]), born 30 Jan 1876 in Hudson, Lenawee Co., MI. She married (1) abt 1900 William T Dalton; (2) on 2 Aug 1930 in Bergland, Ontonagon Co.,MI. Richard W Schoonmaker, born in Rock Rapids, Lyon Co., IA..

Children of Daisy Mae Bovee and William T Dalton were as follows:

2516	i	Eugene Wesley[8] **Dalton**, born Oct 1901.
2517	ii	Thelma Mae[8] **Dalton**.

1481. Calvin O[7] **Bovee** (Grosvenor D[6], Mathew[5], John Henry[4], Matthew[3], Nicholas[2], Mathieu[1]), born Sep 1867 in Woodstock Twp., Lenawee Co., MI; died 27 Oct 1929. He married on 14 Nov 1894 in Tecumseh, Lenawee Co, MI Olcea Owen, born Aug 1876 in MI.

Children of Calvin O Bovee and Olcea Owen were as follows:

+	2518	i	Harland[8] **Bovee**, born 22 Dec 1896 in Hudson, Lenawee Co., MI; died 6 Jun 1963. He married **Beulah Laura Deline**.
	2519	ii	McDonald[8] **Bovee**, born 3 Dec 1898; died Sep 1964.
	2520	iii	Carl[8] **Bovee**, born 4 Feb 1904; died Oct 1970 in Grant, Newago Co., MI.
	2521	iv	Alice[8] **Bovee**, born abt 1906. She married **(---) Hoff**.

1486. Marion Lysander[7] **Bovee** (Elijah[6], Jacob[5], John Henry[4], Matthew[3], Nicholas[2], Mathieu[1]), born 14 Mar 1855 in MI; died 1 Dec 1913. He married on 7 Oct 1877 Lucy M Chalker, born 29 May 1858; died 28 Feb 1941.

Children of Marion Lysander Bovee and Lucy M Chalker were as follows:

	2522	i	Philena May[8] **Bovee**, born 4 May 1879 in MI; died 12 Feb 1889.
+	2523	ii	Paul R[8] **Bovee**, born 25 Apr 1881 in MI; died 1935. He married **Alice M Scully**.

+ 2524   iii   Mary Lucy[8] **Bovee**, born 25 Jan 1883 in MI; died Feb 1947. She married **Joseph Miller**.

+ 2525   iv   Marion Elijah[8] **Bovee**, born 22 Sep 1888 in MI; died Aug 1970 in Lexington, Salinac Co., MI. He married (1) **Anna Moorhouse**; (2) **Maude Loveless**.

+ 2526   v   John Wesley[8] **Bovee**, born 31 Dec 1890 in MI; died 30 Jan 1972 in Royal Oak, Oakland Co., MI. He married **Verley Madeline Stevens**.

1489. Elmore Mary[7] **Bovee** (Ezra[6], Jacob[5], John Henry[4], Matthew[3], Nicholas[2], Mathieu[1]), born 24 Dec 1867; died 8 Jun 1910. She married on 20 Nov 1883 in Clayton, Lenawee Co., MI George N Smith.

Children of Elmore Mary Bovee and George N Smith were as follows:

2527   i   Ray E[8] **Smith**, born Jul 1890.

2528   ii   Lisle[8] **Smith**, born Aug 1895.

1492. Lillian[7] **Bovee** (Albert[6], Jacob[5], John Henry[4], Matthew[3], Nicholas[2], Mathieu[1]), born 25 Jul 1855 in MI; died 1 Mar 1937. She married on 12 Sep 1875 Francis Leroy Cook, born Sep 1851 in NY; died 12 May 1931.

Children of Lillian Bovee and Francis Leroy Cook were as follows:

2529   i   Albert Earl[8] **Cook**, born 28 Feb 1877; died 1965.

2530   ii   Daisy Pearl[8] **Cook**, born 8 Oct 1878; died 11 Jun 1963.

2531   iii   Vernon Orlo[8] **Cook**, born 15 Apr 1881 in OH; died 27 Apr 1956.

2532   iv   Leon Herbert[8] **Cook**, born 7 May 1888 in MI; died 16 Apr 1957.

2533   v   Mildred Eliza[8] **Cook**, born 3 Feb 1890; died 2 Feb 1895.

1493. Fremont[7] **Bovee** (Albert[6], Jacob[5], John Henry[4], Matthew[3], Nicholas[2], Mathieu[1]), born 9 Dec 1856 in MI; died 8 Nov 1933. He married on 9 Dec 1877 in VA Martha Older, born 8 Aug 1857 in OH; died 30 May 1934.

Children of Fremont Bovee and Martha Older were as follows:

+ 2534   i   Erma[8] **Bovee**, born 17 Aug 1880 in Gratiot Co., MI; died Jan 1967. He married **Minerva Carpenter**.

2535   ii   Florence K[8] **Bovee**, born 27 Jul 1889 in MI; died 12 May 1945. She married **Harry Hazelton**.

1494. Virgil Albert[7] **Bovee** (Albert[6], Jacob[5], John Henry[4], Matthew[3], Nicholas[2], Mathieu[1]), born 27 Sep 1861 in MI; died 1 Aug 1943 in San Diego Co., CA. He married on 27 Mar 1887 in Spencer. Tioga Co., NY Bertha Jane Cook, born 21 Jun 1861 in PA; died 18 Aug 1951.

Children of Virgil Albert Bovee and Bertha Jane Cook were as follows:

+ 2536   i   Beulah Belle^8 **Bovee**, born 20 Sep 1889 in Montcalm Co., MI. She married (1) **Merle A Russell**; (2) **Herman Randolph**.

+ 2537   ii   Elizabeth^8 **Bovee**, born 18 Aug 1894 in Montcalm Co., MI. She married **Thomas Stanford Clayton**.

1496. Herbert Warren^7 **Bovee** (Milo^6, Jacob^5, John Henry^4, Matthew^3, Nicholas^2, Mathieu^1), born 27 Jul 1867 in Dover, Lenawee Co., MI; died 22 Nov 1936. He married on 1 Sep 1897 Mary McFetridge, born 14 Feb 1872 in MI; died 1956.

Children of Herbert Warren Bovee and Mary McFetridge were as follows:

+ 2538   i   Marshall Claude^8 **Bovee**, born 22 Apr 1901; died 10 Mar 1989 in Wayne Co., MI. He married **Laura Blanche Rose**.

+ 2539   ii   Wayne Hunter^8 **Bovee**, born 21 Apr 1905 in MI; died 27 Aug 1982 in TX. He married **Alice Louise Murphy**.

+ 2540   iii   Julia^8 **Bovee**, born 9 Dec 1907. She married **Floyd V Schultze**.

1497. Dora Arvilla^7 **Bovee** (Milo^6, Jacob^5, John Henry^4, Matthew^3, Nicholas^2, Mathieu^1), born 10 Nov 1868 in Dover, Lenawee Co., MI; died 1944. She married on 21 Dec 1891 Frank Bryant.

Children of Dora Arvilla Bovee and Frank Bryant were as follows:

2541   i   Sumner^8 **Bryant**.

2542   ii   Gertrude^8 **Bryant**.

1498. Cornelius Anson^7 **Bovee** (Milo^6, Jacob^5, John Henry^4, Matthew^3, Nicholas^2, Mathieu^1), born 15 Apr 1872 in Dover, Lenawee Co., MI; died 25 Sep 1961. He married on 15 Sep 1897 Gertrude Seton Chapelle.

Children of Cornelius Anson Bovee and Gertrude Seton Chapelle were as follows:

2543   i   Muriel^8 **Bovee**, born 30 Dec 1902 in Adrian, Lenawee Co., MI; died 6 Jun 1990.

+ 2544   ii   Seton Chapelle^8 **Bovee**, born 18 Apr 1907 in Adrian, Lenawee Co., MI; died 13 Feb 1977 in Coldwater, Branch Co., MI. He married **Clara W McKarghan**.

1499. Emma^7 **Bovee** (Arthur^6, Jacob^5, John Henry^4, Matthew^3, Nicholas^2, Mathieu^1), born 13 Jul 1863 in Dover, Lenawee Co., MI; died 24 Jul 1942. She married on 27 May 1889 William Shepherd, died 26 May 1925.

Children of Emma Bovee and William Shepherd were as follows:

2545   i   William M^{8} **Shepherd**.

2546   ii   Esther R^{8} **Shepherd**.

1500. Ella L^{7} **Bovee** (Arthur^{6}, Jacob^{5}, John Henry^{4}, Matthew^{3}, Nicholas^{2}, Mathieu^{1}), born 15 Nov 1865 in Dover, Lenawee Co., MI. She married George H Deline, born 15 Sep 1861; died 16 May 1898.

Children of Ella L Bovee and George H Deline were as follows:

2547   i   Lynn^{8} **Deline**, born 6 Jun 1892 in Dover, Lenawee Co., MI; died 10 Jul 1892.

1506. Aurilla^{7} **Bovee** (Hamilton^{6}, Jacob^{5}, John Henry^{4}, Matthew^{3}, Nicholas^{2}, Mathieu^{1}), born 3 Dec 1876; died 16 Dec 1954. She married on 26 Oct 1902, divorced Willis Tracey.

Children of Aurilla Bovee and Willis Tracey were as follows:

2548   i   Marie Agnes^{8} **Tracey**, born 6 May 1903.

1509. Archie Dell^{7} **Bovee** (Hamilton^{6}, Jacob^{5}, John Henry^{4}, Matthew^{3}, Nicholas^{2}, Mathieu^{1}), born 8 Apr 1884 in Gratiot Co., MI; died Jan 1969 in Ithaca, Gratiot Co., MI. He married on 29 Oct 1909 Hazel Ellen Greenlee.

Children of Archie Dell Bovee and Hazel Ellen Greenlee were as follows:

2549   i   Kenneth LaVern^{8} **Bovee**, born 2 Nov 1910; died 23 Jun 1952.

1510. Carl Aaron^{7} **Bovee** (Hamilton^{6}, Jacob^{5}, John Henry^{4}, Matthew^{3}, Nicholas^{2}, Mathieu^{1}), born 7 Feb 1888 in Gratiot Co., MI; died 22 Feb 1956. He married on 25 Dec 1909 Zora Palmer.

Children of Carl Aaron Bovee and Zora Palmer were as follows:

2550   i   Leo Dale^{8} **Bovee**, born 23 Oct 1911; died 2 Aug 1991. He married on 1 Aug 1936 **Dorothy Smith**, born abt 1916.

1514. Earl Eugene^{7} **Bovee** (Myron^{6}, Jacob^{5}, John Henry^{4}, Matthew^{3}, Nicholas^{2}, Mathieu^{1}), born 19 Jun 1872 in Clinton Co., MI; died 4 Feb 1951 in San Luis Obispo, San Luis Obispo Co., CA. He married (1) on 10 Aug 1904 in Richmond, Jefferson Co., OH Martha Nora Johnson, born 27 Jun 1882 in Steubenville, Jefferson Co., OH; died 3 Feb 1935 in Sioux City, Woodbury Co., IA, daughter of Rezin Beall Johnson and Anne Dance; (2) on 6 Mar 1937 Maude Fair, born 17 Sep 1887 in Pierson, Woodbury Co.,IA; died 25 Apr 1940 in Sioux City, Woodbury Co., IA.

Children of Earl Eugene Bovee and Martha Nora Johnson were as follows:

+ 2551 i David Victor[8] **Bovee**, born 10 Nov 1911 in Sioux City, Woodbury Co., IA; died 23 Jan 1983 in Springfield, Greene Co., MO. He married **Lois Margery Munderloh**.

+ 2552 ii Eugene Cleveland[8] **Bovee**, born 1 Apr 1915 in Sioux City, Woodbury Co., IA. He married (1) **Maezene Belle Wamsley**; (2) **Elizabeth Alice, Moss**.

+ 2553 iii Esther Anne[8] **Bovee**, born 5 Jun 1916 in Sioux City, Woodbury Co., IA. She married **Don Frost Crippin**.

1515. Cora May[7] **Bovee** (Myron[6], Jacob[5], John Henry[4], Matthew[3], Nicholas[2], Mathieu[1]), born 29 Oct 1874 in Clayton, Lenawee Co., MI; died Feb 1956. She married on 13 Apr 1901 in Perrington, Gratiot Co., MI Franklin Delmore Powell, born 13 Aug 1865 in Benton Ridge, Hancock Co., OH; died 21 Nov 1938 in Lansing, Ingham Co., MI, son of Rev. Peter Powell and Frances Margaret (---).

Children of Cora May Bovee and Franklin Delmore Powell were as follows:

2554 i Olive May[8] **Powell**, born 29 Jun 1902 in Fulton Center, Gratiot Co., MI.

2555 ii Ethel Treva[8] **Powell**, born 18 Feb 1904 in Fulton Center, Gratiot Co., MI.

2556 iii Crayton Arthur[8] **Powell**, born 30 Aug 1905 in Fulton Center, Gratiot Co., MI; died 10 Jul 1966.

2557 iv Mildred Imis[8] **Powell**, born 22 Mar 1907 in Fulton Center, Gratiot Co., MI.

2558 v Howard Wilson[8] **Powell**, born 26 Mar 1913 in Crystal Twp., Montcalm Co., MI; died 9 Nov 1969 in Dunedin, Pinellas Co., FL.

1516. Orlin Henry[7] **Bovee** (Myron[6], Jacob[5], John Henry[4], Matthew[3], Nicholas[2], Mathieu[1]), born 1 Aug 1876 in Lenawee Co., MI; died 25 Nov 1973. He married (1) on 23 Dec 1900 in Bowling Green, Wood Co., OH Elnora Stearns, born 3 May 1880; died 1959, daughter of Benton Stearns; (2) on 6 Jun 1961 Mazell Stearns, daughter of Benton Stearns.

Children of Orlin Henry Bovee and Elnora Stearns were as follows:

2559 i Child[8] **Bovee**, born 1902; died 1902.

+ 2560 ii Leo Myron[8] **Bovee**, born 22 Nov 1904 in Bowling Green, Wood Co., OH; died 15 May 1989. He married (1) **Eva Laurette Linton**; (2) **Frances Knight**.

+ 2561 iii Murlin Orlin[8] **Bovee**, born 16 Jan 1906 in Arcadia, Hancock Co., OH; died 18 May 1993. He married **Eva Karn**.

2562 iv Rena Lucille[8] **Bovee**, born 29 Nov 1908 in Arcadia, Hancock Co., OH; died 4 Apr 1961.

2563 v Avis Christina[8] **Bovee**, born 9 Feb 1910 in Arcadia, Hancock Co., OH. She married on 23 Dec 1948 **Robert**

Francis Ingham.

+ 2564 vi Dessie Elnora^8 **Bovee**, born 24 May 1918 in Arcadia, Hancock Co., OH; buried in Arcadia Cem, Arcadia, Hancock Co., OH. She married **Kenneth Vernell Anderson**.

1518. Arthur Jewett^7 **Bovee** (Myron^6, Jacob^5, John Henry^4, Matthew^3, Nicholas^2, Mathieu^1), born 30 Jun 1880; died 17 Aug 1953. He married on 31 Mar 1910 in St Paul, Ramsey Co., MN Marian Christina McInnis, born 2 Aug 1881 in Toledo, Lucas Co., OH; died 18 Dec 1945, daughter of Charles McInnis and Annie (---).

Children of Arthur Jewett Bovee and Marian Christina McInnis were as follows:

+ 2565 i Bonnie Mulla^8 **Bovee**, born 25 Feb 1911. She married **John C Alt Jr**.
+ 2566 ii Arthur Jewett^8 **Bovee** Jr, born 22 Mar 1912. He married **Frances Warne**.
+ 2567 iii Frances Roberta^8 **Bovee**, born 2 Jun 1913. She married **Lyle D Smith**.
+ 2568 iv Jennie Christie^8 **Bovee**, born 15 Jun 1916. She married **Leonard James Nesseth**.
+ 2569 v Rachael Ellen^8 **Bovee**, born 6 Sep 1919. She married **Raleigh A Lawson**.

1519. Addie Elizabeth^7 **Bovee** (Myron^6, Jacob^5, John Henry^4, Matthew^3, Nicholas^2, Mathieu^1), born 27 Oct 1882 in Gratiot Co., MI; died 24 Feb 1965 in Gratiot Co., MI. She married on 19 Dec 1903 in Perrington, Gratiot Co., MI Charles Misenhelder, born 2 Jul 1881 in Newark Twp., Gratiot Co., MI; died 29 Dec 1967 in Gratiot Co., MI, son of Christian Misenhelder and Katherine (---).

Children of Addie Elizabeth Bovee and Charles Misenhelder were as follows:

2570 i Rhea Elizabeth^8 **Misenhelder**, born 19 Jul 1904.
2571 ii Othel Christian^8 **Misenhelder**, born 18 Nov 1909.
2572 iii Katherine Irene^8 **Misenhelder**, born 3 Jul 1911.
2573 iv Carol Onalee^8 **Misenhelder**, born 12 Dec 1919.
2574 v Charles Dale^8 **Misenhelder**, born 22 Jul 1921.

1520. Harlow^7 **Bovee** (Myron^6, Jacob^5, John Henry^4, Matthew^3, Nicholas^2, Mathieu^1), born 30 Nov 1885 in North Star Twp., Gratiot Co., MI; died 27 Sep 1951. He married (1) on 31 Dec 1904 in Perrington, Gratiot Co., MI Cora Edna Munson, born 3 Mar 1888; died 11 Jul 1927 in Pompeii, Gratiot Co., MI; (2) on 30 Apr 1928 Jessie Murray Sarich, born 21 Jul 1890; died 6 Nov 1948.

Children of Harlow Bovee and Cora Edna Munson were as follows:

+ 2575 i Ardee Lewis^8 **Bovee**, born 31 Jan 1906; died 5 Mar 1969 in Clinton Co., MI. He married **Eileen Morley**.

+	2576	ii	Lola May[8] **Bovee**, born 9 Aug 1908. She married **Covert Walter**.
+	2577	iii	Beulah Faye[8] **Bovee**, born 15 Oct 1914; died 29 Sep 1964. She married **Joseph Skaryd**.
+	2578	iv	Olan Ford[8] **Bovee**, born 17 Mar 1917 in Gratiot Co., MI; died 2 Jun 1968. He married (1) **Helen Campbell**; (2) **Frances Robinson Bond**.
	2579	v	Oma Lee[8] **Bovee**, born 1 Oct 1925; died 1 Jul 1934.

Children of Harlow Bovee and Jessie Murray Sarich were as follows:

+	2580	i	Wanda Harriet[8] **Bovee**. She married (1) **Raymond Newlove**; (2) **Dean Frederick**; (3) **Robert D Beamer**.

1521. Ethel Alta[7] **Bovee** (Myron[6], Jacob[5], John Henry[4], Matthew[3], Nicholas[2], Mathieu[1]), born 21 Nov 1889 in Fulton Center, Gratiot Co., MI; died 5 Nov 1984. She married on 1 Jan 1915 in Carson City, Montcalm Co., MI Earnest Sorrell, born 2 Mar 1893; died 4 Jun 1948, son of John Sorrell and Ida (---).

Children of Ethel Alta Bovee and Earnest Sorrell were as follows:

2581	i	Hattie May[8] **Sorrell**, born 6 Jun 1916.
2582	ii	Donal Earnest[8] **Sorrell**, born 3 Dec 1917.
2583	iii	Anna Elizabeth[8] **Sorrell**, born 16 Sep 1918.
2584	iv	Robert Eugene[8] **Sorrell**, born 2 Jan 1921.
2585	v	RalphEverett[8] **Sorrell**, born 1 May 1922 in MIddleton, Gratiot Co., MI.
2586	vi	Gordo B[8] **Sorrell**, born 7 Feb 1925.
2587	vii	Shirley Ruth[8] **Sorrell**, born 29 Dec 1926.
2588	viii	Melvin James[8] **Sorrell**, born 5 Dec 1928.
2589	ix	Irvin Lee[8] **Sorrell**.
2590	x	Lyle John[8] **Sorrell**.

1522. Vena Imis[7] **Bovee** (Myron[6], Jacob[5], John Henry[4], Matthew[3], Nicholas[2], Mathieu[1]), born 16 Dec 1893 in Fulton Center, Gratiot Co., MI; died 13 May 1986. She married on 19 Feb 1919 in Sioux City, Woodbury Co., IA John Wesley Ritz, born 17 Apr 1894; died 26 Nov 1964, son of Philip E Ritz.

Children of Vena Imis Bovee and John Wesley Ritz were as follows:

2591	i	Lawrence Henry[8] **Ritz**, born 29 Mar 1920.
2592	ii	Phyllis Marie[8] **Ritz**, born 15 Mar 1921.
2593	iii	Evelyn Jane[8] **Ritz**, born 31 Jul 1924; died Nov 1964.
2594	iv	Willis Myron[8] **Ritz**, born 25 Nov 1926; died 28 Nov 1926.

1548. Echo H[7] **Bovee** (Alda[6], Jacob[5], John Henry[4], Matthew[3], Nicholas[2], Mathieu[1]), born 15 Apr 1892 in Dover, Lenawee Co., MI; died 29 Oct 1954 in Mt

Carmel Hosp, Detroit, Wayne Co., MI. He married Florence Shattuck, born 18 Mar 1895 in MI; died 1 Oct 1972 in Big Rapids, Mecosta Co., MI, daughter of Tom Shattuck and Jane Lusty.

Children of Echo H Bovee and Florence Shattuck were as follows:

2595	i	Eleanor[8] **Bovee**, born 6 Aug 1918.
2596	ii	Irene[8] **Bovee**, born 15 Apr 1921.
2597	iii	Gladys[8] **Bovee**, born 29 Apr 1922.

1549. Harold L[7] **Bovee** (Alda[6], Jacob[5], John Henry[4], Matthew[3], Nicholas[2], Mathieu[1]), born 17 Jan 1900 in Dover Twp., Lenawee Co., MI; died 24 Sep 1953 in Adrian, Lenawee Co., MI. He married on 15 Aug 1929 Ruth Barnes, born 15 Mar 1908.

Children of Harold L Bovee and Ruth Barnes were as follows:

| 2598 | i | Timothy[8] **Bovee**, born abt 1930. |

1551. Fred Mayfield[7] **Bovee** (Devillow[6], Jacob[5], John Henry[4], Matthew[3], Nicholas[2], Mathieu[1]), born 18 Nov 1895 in Cambria, San Luis Obispo Co., CA; died 4 Jan 1981. He married on 21 Nov 1917 Lydia Maxine Dominguez, born 23 May 1902 in Santa Maria, Santa Barbara Co., CA; died 1 Sep 1959 in IOOF Cem, San Luis Obispo, San Luis Obispo Co., CA.

Children of Fred Mayfield Bovee and Lydia Maxine Dominguez were as follows:

+	2599	i	Eleanor Maxine[8] **Bovee**, born 5 Jul 1918. She married **James Merrill McGrath**.
+	2600	ii	Florence[8] **Bovee**, born 1 Mar 1921. She married **Kenneth W Jones**.
+	2601	iii	Marilyn Enid[8] **Bovee**, born 12 Feb 1925 in San Luis Obispo, San Luis Obispo Co., CA. She married **David Henry Hildebran**.
+	2602	iv	Edmond James[8] **Bovee**, born 6 Apr 1926 in San Luis Obispo, San Luis Obispo Co., CA. He married **Addie Evelyn Johnson**.
	2603	v	Fred Mayfield[8] **Bovee**, born Jan 1927; died Jun 1927.
	2604	vi	Frances Marie[8] **Bovee**, born 13 Jan 1929. She married on 10 Jan 1947 in San Louis Obispo Co., CA. **Harold John Broerman**, born 3 Feb 1923 in IA.
	2605	vii	Donald Colbert[8] **Bovee**.
	2606	viii	Mary Ethel[8] **Bovee**.
	2607	ix	David[8] **Bovee**.

1555. James Byron[7] **Bovee** (James H[6], Peter[5], John Henry[4], Matthew[3], Nicholas[2], Mathieu[1]), born 1879 in Steuben Co., IN; died 1954. He married

Myrtle Mae Collins, born Aug 1879; died 1925.

Children of James Byron Bovee and Myrtle Mae Collins were as follows:

+ 2608   i   Russell E[8] **Bovee**, born 19 Oct 1903; died 10 Jul 1965 in IN. He married **Dorcas Bell**.

+ 2609   ii   Ruth[8] **Bovee**, born 1908. She married **Jess Shields**.

+ 2610   iii   Harold[8] **Bovee**, born 4 Dec 1910; died Jul 1986 in Wolcottville, La Grange Co., IN. He married **Retha Cook**.

+ 2611   iv   Wava[8] **Bovee**, born 29 Apr 1913 in Hudson, Steuben Co., IN; died Apr 1988. She married **Robert McKee**.

1558. Edward E[7] **Bovie** (Chester A[6], John E[5], Jacob[4], Abraham[3], Nicholas[2], Mathieu[1]), born 1844 in MI; died 15 Sep 1879. He married on 30 May 1867 in Allegan Co., MI Marcie E Richards.

Children of Edward E Bovie and Marcie E Richards were as follows:

2612   i   Hattie O[8] **Bovie**, born 5 Sep 1869 in Allegan Co., MI.

1559. Clare Byron[7] **Bovie** (Chester A[6], John E[5], Jacob[4], Abraham[3], Nicholas[2], Mathieu[1]), born abt 1857 in Kalamazoo, Kalamazoo Co., MI; died 5 Sep 1921 in Milford, Iroquois Co., IL. He married on 16 Dec 1885 in Milford, Iroquois Co., IL Jessie Rebecca Merriam, born 28 May 1860 in Sandwich, De Kalb Co., IL; died 21 May 1914 in Milford, Iroquois Co., IL.

Children of Clare Byron Bovie and Jessie Rebecca Merriam were as follows:

2613   i   Walter Harvey[8] **Bovie**, born 24 Feb 1888 in Jamestown, Stutsman Co., ND; died 5 Jun 1905 in Jamestown, Stutsman Co., ND.

2614   ii   Carrie J[8] **Bovie**, born abt 1890 in Jamestown, Stutsman Co., ND. She married on 3 Jul 1910 **Joseph R Peska**, born abt 1886 in Grand Junction, Van Buren Co., MI, son of Joseph Peska and Kate Rosenska.

1562. William T[7] **Bovie** (William T[6], John E[5], Jacob[4], Abraham[3], Nicholas[2], Mathieu[1]), born 11 Sep 1882 in Augusta, Kalamazoo Co., MI; died 1 Jan 1958 in Fairfield, Somerset Co., ME. He married on 15 Sep 1909 Martha Adams, daughter of Fealden A Adams.

Children of William T Bovie and Martha Adams were as follows:

2615   i   William Adams[8] **Bovie**, born 5 May 1914; died 1994 in Oakland, Kennebec Co., ME.

1568. Isaac Warren[7] **Bovee** II (Isaac Warren I[6], Isaac[5], Jacob[4], Abraham[3], Nicholas[2], Mathieu[1]), born 26 Jun 1855. He married Cora Slade, died 26 Mar 1922, daughter of Philip Slade and Angeline (---).

Children of Isaac Warren Bovee II and Cora Slade were as follows:

+ 2616   i   Isaac Warren^8 **Bovee** III, born 7 Aug 1881. He married **Helen Thayer Webster**.

+ 2617   ii   Sara Angeline^8 **Bovee**, born abt 1885 in Rensselaer Co., NY. She married **George Savery**.

+ 2618   iii   George White^8 **Bovee**, born 27 Nov 1888 in Hoosick, Rensselaer Co., NY; died 1965 in Hoosick, Rensselaer Co., NY. He married **Charlotte B Cook**.

1573. Alfred^7 **Bovee** II (Alfred^6, Jacob^5, Jacob^4, Abraham^3, Nicholas^2, Mathieu^1), born in Hoosick, Rensselaer Co., NY. He married unknown.

Children of Alfred Bovee II were as follows:

2619   i   Alfred^8 **Bovee** III.

1582. John Jacob^7 **Bovie** (Jacob F W^6, William G^5, Jacob^4, Abraham^3, Nicholas^2, Mathieu^1), born 28 Apr 1878 in Pittstown, Rensselaer Co, NY; died 12 Nov 1941 in Spokane, Spokane Co., WA. He married on 18 Nov 1911 in Spokane, Spokane Co., WA Gertrude Jones, born 23 Dec 1887 in Iowa City, Johnson Co., IA; died 22 May 1977 in Spokane, Spokane Co., WA, daughter of Oliver Charles Jones and Ella Graff (---).

Children of John Jacob Bovie and Gertrude Jones were as follows:

+ 2620   i   Walter James^8 **Bovee**, born 24 Jul 1913 in Spokane, Spokane Co., WA; died 9 Jun 1988. He married **Doris Maxine Kavachevich**.

2621   ii   Robert John^8 **Bovee**, born 7 Nov 1915 in Spokane, Spokane Co., WA. He married on 9 Mar 1940 **Mabel Arlene Vandevanter**, born 6 Aug 1914 in Idaho; died 22 Dec 1991 in San Diego, San Diego Co., CA.

1597. Grace Gertrude^7 **Bovee** (John Oscar^6, Peter^5, Matthew^4, Abraham^3, Nicholas^2, Mathieu^1), born 14 Mar 1868 in PA; died 7 Oct 1909. She married John Lawrence Herman, born 30 Nov 1863 in McHenry Twp., PA.

Children of Grace Gertrude Bovee and John Lawrence Herman were as follows:

2622   i   Rae Lorene^8 **Herman**, born 7 Jul 1886 in Newberry, Lycoming Co., PA.

2623   ii   Katherine Fredericka^8 **Herman**, born 11 Mar 1888 in Newberry, Lycoming Co., PA.

2624   iii   Mary Gertrude^8 **Herman**, born 15 Nov 1889 in Newberry, Lycoming Co., PA.

2625   iv   Hester Roberta^8 **Herman**, born 16 Feb 1892.

2626   v   Grace^8 **Herman**, born 2 Aug 1893 in Newberry, Lycoming

Co., PA.

| 2627 | vi | Vin Hope[8] **Herman**, born 17 Dec 1897 in Newberry, Lycoming Co., PA. |
| 2628 | vii | John Henry[8] **Herman**, born 11 Jan 1900 in Newberry, Lycoming Co., PA. |

1598. David Bussler[7] **Bovee** (John Oscar[6], Peter[5], Matthew[4], Abraham[3], Nicholas[2], Mathieu[1]), born 5 Oct 1876 in Newberry, Lycoming Co., PA; died 1940 in Bolivar,Allegany Co., NY. He married (1) in 1902 May Sloan; (2) on 17 Jun 1913 in Olean, Cattaraugus Co., NY Burdette Fish.

Children of David Bussler Bovee and Burdette Fish were as follows:

| 2629 | i | Catherine B[8] **Bovee**, born 5 Jan 1921 in Buffalo, Erie Co., NY; died 10 Mar 1988 in Wellsville,Alegany Co., NY. She married **Edgar D Holliday**. |
| + 2630 | ii | Luray[8] **Bovee**. She married **Clifford O Mills**. |

1599. Pearl Lorena[7] **Bovee** (John Oscar[6], Peter[5], Matthew[4], Abraham[3], Nicholas[2], Mathieu[1]), born 8 Jun 1883 in Olean, Cattaraugus Co., NY; died in Berwyn, Cook Co., IL. She married on 25 Dec 1903 Raymond Uriah Meyers, born 18 Mar 1879 in Turbotville, Northumberland Co., PA.

Children of Pearl Lorena Bovee and Raymond Uriah Meyers were as follows:

2631	i	Marguerite Bovee[8] **Meyers**, born 28 Oct 1904 in Newberry, Lycoming Co., PA.
2632	ii	Raymond John[8] **Meyers**, born 9 Aug 1914 in Chicago, Cook Co., IL.
2633	iii	Charles[8] **Meyers**.

1600. Charles Oscar[7] **Bovee** Sr (John Oscar[6], Peter[5], Matthew[4], Abraham[3], Nicholas[2], Mathieu[1]), born 7 Mar 1891 in Newberry, Lycoming Co., PA; died 3 Feb 1964 in Houston, Harris Co., TX. He married on 9 May 1924 Lucy Elizabeth Yxera, born 3 Oct 1894 in Minneapolis, Hennepin Co., MN; died 16 Aug 1992 in Friendswood, Galveston Co., TX.

Children of Charles Oscar Bovee Sr and Lucy Elizabeth Yxera were as follows:

| + 2634 | i | Charles Oscar[8] **Bovee** Jr, born 1 Mar 1925 in Houston, Harris Co., TX. He married **Lena Faye Duggan**. |
| 2635 | ii | Thomas Yxera[8] **Bovee**, born 18 Jul 1928. He married **Sherri (---)**. |

1601. Alice Estella[7] **Bovee** (George Burton[6], Peter[5], Matthew[4], Abraham[3], Nicholas[2], Mathieu[1]), born 31 Mar 1867 in Hepburnville, Lycoming Co., PA. She married on 15 May 1890 David Augustus Edler, born 7 Oct 1867 in Cogan Station, Lycoming Co., PA.

Children of Alice Estella Bovee and David Augustus Edler were as follows:

2636   i   Hazel Ruth **Edler**[8], born 15 Feb 1893 in Hepburnville, Lycoming Co., PA.

1602. Samuel Ball[7] **Bovee** (George Burton[6], Peter[5], Matthew[4], Abraham[3], Nicholas[2], Mathieu[1]), born 29 Jul 1869 in Hepburnville, Lycoming Co., PA; died 2 Jan 1916. He married on 14 Jun 1888 Sarah Catherine Blair, born 19 Oct 1871 in Balls Mills, Lycoming Co., PA; died 1921.

Children of Samuel Ball Bovee and Sarah Catherine Blair were as follows:

+   2637   i   Chester Emerson[8] **Bovee**, born 15 Jan 1889 in Hepburnville, Lycoming Co., PA. He married **Lucy Ann Mason**.
+   2638   ii   Bertha Ellen[8] **Bovee**, born 20 Mar 1891 in Hepburnville, Lycoming Co., PA. She married **Charles August Raub**.
    2639   iii   Verus Carl[8] **Bovee**, born 9 May 1893 in Hepburnville, Lycoming Co., PA; died 3 Aug 1914 in Hepburnville, Lycoming Co., PA.
+   2640   iv   Meredith Roger Leon[8] **Bovee**, born 15 Sep 1896 in Hepburnville, Lycoming Co., PA. He married **Charlotte Marguerite Frost**.
+   2641   v   Mary Elizabeth[8] **Bovee**, born 24 Dec 1898 in Hepburnville, Lycoming Co., PA; died 1978. She married **Robert Samuel Pindar**.
    2642   vi   Samuel Arthur[8] **Bovee**, born 1901 in Hepburnville, Lycoming Co., PA; died 1918.
    2643   vii   Arthur[8] **Bovee**.
+   2644   viii   Clyde LaRue[8] **Bovee**, born 12 Jan 1908; died 19 Jul 1971 in Oneida, Madison Co., NY. He married **Martha s Stebbins**.

1603. Burton Raymond[7] **Bovee** (George Burton[6], Peter[5], Matthew[4], Abraham[3], Nicholas[2], Mathieu[1]), born 28 Jun 1872 in Hepburnville, Lycoming Co., PA. He married Katherine Jane Snyder, born 2 Dec 1873 in Balls Mills, Lycoming Co., PA.

Children of Burton Raymond Bovee and Katherine Jane Snyder were as follows:

2645   i   Clara Elizabeth[8] **Bovee**, born 25 Jan 1898 in Balls Mills, Lycoming Co., PA. She married **C V Perron**.
2646   ii   Daniel Snyder[8] **Bovee**, born 13 Aug 1900 in Newberry, Lycoming Co., PA; died 23 Jul 1983 in Orange Co., CA.

1604. Ervin Emerson Edward[7] **Bovee** (George Burton[6], Peter[5], Matthew[4], Abraham[3], Nicholas[2], Mathieu[1]), born 20 Jun 1878 in PA; died 17 Aug 1945 in San Bernardino, San Bernardino Co., CA. He married Edna E Litz, born 28 Mar 1862; died 11 Jul 1952 in San Bernardino, San Bernardino Co., CA.

Children of Ervin Emerson Edward Bovee and Edna E Litz were as follows:

2647   i   George E[8] **Bovee**, born 3 Jul 1902 in PA; died 18 Nov 1984 in San Bernardino, San Bernardino Co., CA. He married **Ruth (---)**, born 5 Nov 1900 in CA; died 14 Oct 1975 in San Bernardino, San Bernardino Co., CA.

1605. Lemon Peter[7] **Bovee** (Perry Henry[6], Peter[5], Matthew[4], Abraham[3], Nicholas[2], Mathieu[1]), born 28 Oct 1871 in Newberry, Lycoming Co., PA; died 1928. He married (1) Mildred Kyler, buried in Mound Cem, Williamsport, Lycoming Co., PA; (2) Catherine Louise Owens.

Children of Lemon Peter Bovee and Mildred Kyler were as follows:

2648   i   Ada Ruth[8] **Bovee**, born 17 Apr 1900 in Newberry, Lycoming Co., PA.

2649   ii   Lewis Paul[8] **Bovee**, born 20 Jan 1902 in Newberry, Lycoming Co., PA.

+ 2650   iii   Helen[8] **Bovee**, born 5 Mar 1904 in Newberry, Lycoming Co., PA. She married **(---) Brown**.

Children of Lemon Peter Bovee and Catherine Louise Owens were as follows:

+ 2651   i   Robert Owen[8] **Bovee**, born 26 Dec 1910 in Newberry, Lycoming Co., PA; died 19 Feb 1964. He married **Frances McDermott**.

2652   ii   Thomas Peter[8] **Bovee**, born 24 Dec 1912 in Newberry, Lycoming Co., PA.

1607. George Gregg[7] **Bovee** (Perry Henry[6], Peter[5], Matthew[4], Abraham[3], Nicholas[2], Mathieu[1]), born 16 Jun 1875 in Newberry, Lycoming Co., PA. He married on 16 Apr 1901 Maud Delilah Love, born 8 Dec 1881 in Lavelle, Schuylkill Co., PA.

Children of George Gregg Bovee and Maud Delilah Love were as follows:

2653   i   Dorothy Love[8] **Bovee**, born 23 Feb 1902 in Newberry, Lycoming Co., PA.

2654   ii   Donald Gregg[8] **Bovee**, born 3 May 1904 in Newberry, Lycoming Co., PA.

2655   iii   Grace Gertrude[8] **Bovee**, born 13 Dec 1905 in Newberry, Lycoming Co., PA; died 20 Nov 1948 in Los Angeles, Los Angeles Co., CA. She married **(---) Saxton**.

1608. Gertrude Grace[7] **Bovee** (Perry Henry[6], Peter[5], Matthew[4], Abraham[3], Nicholas[2], Mathieu[1]), born 27 Sep 1877 in Newberry, Lycoming Co., PA. She married on 25 May 1898 Charles Eugene Alden.

Children of Gertrude Grace Bovee and Charles Eugene Alden were as follows:

2656   i   John[8] **Alden**, born 25 Feb 1899 in Newberry, Lycoming Co., PA.

1609. Blanche[7] **Bovee** (Perry Henry[6], Peter[5], Matthew[4], Abraham[3], Nicholas[2], Mathieu[1]), born 2 Jan 1880 in PA. She married on 15 Nov 1904 Archibald Miller Hoagland, born 30 Jun 1876 in Williamsport, Lycoming Co., PA.

Children of Blanche Bovee and Archibald Miller Hoagland were as follows:

2657   i   John Pleasant[8] **Hoagland**, born 11 Dec 1905 in Williamsport, Lycoming Co., PA.

2658   ii   Archibald Miller[8] **Hoagland**, born 5 Jul 1909 in Newberry, Lycoming Co., PA.

2659   iii   Robert Bovee[8] **Hoagland**, born 3 Oct 1912 in Williamsport, Lycoming Co., PA; died 1 Feb 1914.

2660   iv   Miriam[8] **Hoagland**, born 18 Feb 1915 in Williamsport, Lycoming Co., PA.

1611. Luther Martin[7] **Bovee** (Perry Henry[6], Peter[5], Matthew[4], Abraham[3], Nicholas[2], Mathieu[1]), born 18 Oct 1883 in Newberry, Lycoming Co., PA. He married Elsie May Grimsley, born 10 Dec 1888 in Braddock, Allegheny Co., PA.

Children of Luther Martin Bovee and Elsie May Grimsley were as follows:

2661   i   Jack[8] **Bovee**, born 26 Nov 1913; died 26 Nov 1913.

2662   ii   Luther Martin[8] **Bovee** Jr, born 27 Aug 1914.

2663   iii   Thelma Jean[8] **Bovee**, born 24 Feb 1921 in PA; died 7 Oct 1996 in Los Angeles, Los Angeles Co., CA. She married **(---) Horton**.

1613. Perry Graham[7] **Bovee** (Perry Henry[6], Peter[5], Matthew[4], Abraham[3], Nicholas[2], Mathieu[1]), born 29 Apr 1889 in Newberry, Lycoming Co., PA; died 25 Jul 1917. He married (1) Mabel (---), born abt 1895; (2) Grace (---).

Children of Perry Graham Bovee and Mabel (---) were as follows:

2664   i   Richard H[8] **Bovee**.

2665   ii   Lillian M[8] **Bovee**.

2666   iii   Perry J[8] **Bovee** Jr.

2667   iv   Earl C[8] **Bovee**.

Children of Perry Graham Bovee and Grace (---) were as follows:

| 2668 | i | Laucetta B[8] **Bovee**. |
| 2669 | ii | Enid H[8] **Bovee**. |

1615. Lottie May[7] **Bovee** (Walter Haywood[6], Peter[5], Matthew[4], Abraham[3], Nicholas[2], Mathieu[1]), born 31 Aug 1879 in Sundbury, Northumberland Co., PA. She married on 31 Aug 1898 Harry James Lincoln, born 13 Apr 1878 in Shamokin, Northumberland Co., PA.

Children of Lottie May Bovee and Harry James Lincoln were as follows:

| 2670 | i | Margaret Emily[8] **Lincoln**, born 28 Mar 1904 in Williamsport, Lycoming Co., PA. |

1616. Eva Lee[7] **Bovee** (Walter Haywood[6], Peter[5], Matthew[4], Abraham[3], Nicholas[2], Mathieu[1]), born 2 Apr 1881 in Sundbury, Northumberland Co., PA. She married Lionelle Hornberger.

Children of Eva Lee Bovee and Lionelle Hornberger were as follows:

| 2671 | i | Lionelle[8] **Hornberger**, born Dec 1905. |

1617. Alva Davis[7] **Bovee** (Walter Haywood[6], Peter[5], Matthew[4], Abraham[3], Nicholas[2], Mathieu[1]), born 21 Jun 1886 in Newberry, Lycoming Co., PA. He married on 23 Feb 1908 Florence Wheeler, born abt 1888.

Children of Alva Davis Bovee and Florence Wheeler were as follows:

| 2672 | i | Walter[8] **Bovee**, born 1 Nov 1909 in Williamsport, Lycoming Co., PA; died Sep 1969. |
| 2673 | ii | Perry[8] **Bovee**, born Sep 1912 in Hagerstown, Washington Co., MD. |

1618. Lulu Hartman[7] **Bovee** (Walter Haywood[6], Peter[5], Matthew[4], Abraham[3], Nicholas[2], Mathieu[1]), born 25 Nov 1889 in Newberry, Lycoming Co., PA. She married William Edward Young, born 13 Aug 1886 in Philadelphia, Philadelphia Co., PA.

Children of Lulu Hartman Bovee and William Edward Young were as follows:

| 2674 | i | Thurman Thomas[8] **Young**, born 8 Jan 1908 in Pedricktown, Salem Co., NJ. |

1620. LeRoy George[7] **Bovee** (Walter Haywood[6], Peter[5], Matthew[4], Abraham[3], Nicholas[2], Mathieu[1]), born 1 Dec 1895; died in Phoenix, Maricopa Co., AZ. He married (1) Rita E Smith; (2) Oleta Alberta Kern, born 23 Jun 1901 in Albany, Delaware Co., IN; died 20 Jul 1989 in Phoenix, Maricopa Co., AZ.

Children of LeRoy George Bovee and Oleta Alberta Kern were as follows:

	2675	i	Margaret[8] **Bovee**.

2675   i   Margaret[8] **Bovee**.

2676   ii   Lorraine Alberta[8] **Bovee**.

2677   iii   Raymond Albert[8] **Bovee**.

+ 2678   iv   Robert Russell[8] **Bovee**, born 1924. He married **Glenetta Mae Lemons**.

1627. Donald Wright[7] **Bovee** (Wright Ingraham[6], Orrin Primmer[5], John[4], Abraham[3], Nicholas[2], Mathieu[1]), born Mar 1900 in Calhoun Co., MI. He married (---) Wortinger, born in Kalamazoo Co., MI.

Children of Donald Wright Bovee and (---) Wortinger were as follows:

+ 2679   i   June Odette[8] **Bovee**, born 8 Oct 1921 in CA; died 25 Jan 1997 in Lassen Co., CA. She married **Leon Ellena (---)**.

+ 2680   ii   Cherie Ann[8] **Bovee**, born abt 1923. She married **Robert Hendrickson**.

+ 2681   iii   Phyllis Elaine[8] **Bovee**, born abt 1930. She married **(---) Holiday**.

+ 2682   iv   Donald[8] **Bovee**. He married unknown.

1644. John W[7] **Bovee** (John W[6], Cornelius[5], Abraham[4], Abraham[3], Nicholas[2], Mathieu[1]), born 16 Dec 1861 in Groveland, Livingston Co., NY; died 1943 in NY. He married in 1891 in Groveland, Livingston Co., NY Martha Fleck, born Jan 1873 in Antrim, Ireland; died bef 1910, daughter of William Fleck and Sarah McCauley.

Children of John W Bovee and Martha Fleck were as follows:

2683   i   William J[8] **Bovee**, born 29 Jan 1890 in Groveland, Livingston Co., NY; died 2 Mar 1897 in Groveland, Livingston Co., NY.

+ 2684   ii   Victor David[8] **Bovee**, born 4 Apr 1891 in Groveland, Livingston Co., NY; died 14 May 1961 in Groveland, Livingston Co., NY. He married **Mary A Mastin**.

2685   iii   Isabella[8] **Bovee**, born 23 Dec 1893 in Groveland, Livingston Co., NY. She married on 27 Jun 1918 **Oswald Brenning**.

2686   iv   Elizabeth Martha[8] **Bovee**, born 14 Feb 1895 in Groveland, Livingston Co., NY; died 7 Feb 1920. She married **John W Stewart**.

+ 2687   v   Edith Mae[8] **Bovee**, born 7 Mar 1897 in Groveland, Livingston Co., NY; died 25 Jan 1977. She married **Meryle Dermyre Toland**.

+ 2688   vi   Sarah[8] **Bovee**, born 25 Sep 1899 in Groveland, Livingston Co., NY; died 4 Dec 1975 in Dansville, Livingston Co., NY. She married **James Noble**.

2689   vii   Josephine[8] **Bovee**, born abt 1902 in Groveland, Livingston Co., NY. She married **Harold Rorke**.

1646. Frederick[7] **Bovee** (John W[6], Cornelius[5], Abraham[4], Abraham[3], Nicholas[2], Mathieu[1]), born Apr 1867 in NY; died 1934 in NY. He married on 24 Mar 1890 in Mt Morris, Livingston Co., NY Jennie Van Valkenberg, born Jul 1869; died 1944, daughter of Daniel Van Valkenberg and Mary A.

Children of Frederick Bovee and Jennie Van Valkenberg were as follows:

+ 2690   i   Laverne[8] **Bovee**, born 14 Jan 1891 in Groveland, Livingston Co., NY; died 27 Oct 1967 in Steuben Co., NY. He married **Elizabeth Lowdin**.

+ 2691   ii   Mary[8] **Bovee**, born 26 Dec 1892 in Mt. Morris, Livingston Co., NY. She married **Emory Drew**.

+ 2692   iii   Edward[8] **Bovee**, born 21 Jan 1894 in Groveland, Livingston Co., NY; died 1977 in Dansville, Livingston Co., NY. He married **Ion Burns**.

+ 2693   iv   Frederick[8] **Bovee**, born 23 Jul 1897 in Groveland, Livingston Co., NY; died 17 Jul 1968 in Rochester, Monroe Co., NY. He married **Catherine (---)**.

   2694   v   John Merville[8] **Bovee**, born 7 Jan 1899 in Sparta, Livingston Co., NY; died in Rochester, Monroe Co., NY.

   2695   vi   Jennie[8] **Bovee**, born 1901 in Livingston Co., NY.

1663. Clara Leone[7] **Bovee** (Henry M[6], Cornelius[5], Abraham[4], Abraham[3], Nicholas[2], Mathieu[1]), born 31 Jan 1874 in Rathbone, Steuben Co., NY; christened 27 Apr 1895 in St Peter's Episcopal Ch, Dansville, Steuben Co., NY. She married on 27 Apr 1895 in S Dansville, Steuben Co., NY William James Jackson.

Children of Clara Leone Bovee and William James Jackson were as follows:

   2696   i   Clifford[8] **Jackson**.

   2697   ii   Paul[8] **Jackson**.

   2698   iii   William Raymond[8] **Jackson**.

   2699   iv   Laura[8] **Jackson**.

   2700   v   Arlita[8] **Jackson**.

   2701   vi   William[8] **Jackson** Jr.

1667. Jesse Clayton[7] **Bovee** (Henry M[6], Cornelius[5], Abraham[4], Abraham[3], Nicholas[2], Mathieu[1]), born 29 Nov 1882 in Portville, Cattaraugus Co., NY; christened 27 Apr 1895 in St Peter's Episcopal Ch, Dansville, Steuben Co., NY; died 3 Aug 1962 in Hornell, Steuben Co., NY. He married on 24 Aug 1903 in Groveland, Livingston Co., NY Dora Elva Welch, born 1886; died 19 Oct 1918 in Galeton, Potter Co., PA, daughter of William M Welch and Mary Harrington.

Children of Jesse Clayton Bovee and Dora Elva Welch were as follows:

+ 2702   i   Regis Renee[8] **Bovee**, born 21 Jun 1905 in Rathbone,

Steuben Co., NY; died in Canisteo,Steuben Co., NY. She married (1) **Harold Corbin**; (2) **Glen Ripley**.

2703   ii   Twila Joyce[8] **Bovee**, born 21 Apr 1907 in Rathbone, Steuben Co., NY; died 2 May 1928 in Canisteo, Steuben Co., NY.

+   2704   iii   Vera Doris[8] **Bovee**, born 4 Jul 1910 in Rathbone, Steuben Co., NY. She married **Harry Van Scoter Lemen**.

2705   iv   Leah Elaine[8] **Bovee**, born 12 Jan 1913 in Rathbone, Steuben Co., NY; died in Wellsville, Allegany Co., NY. She married in E Cobleskill, Schoharie Co., NY **Robert Feller**.

2706   v   Daisy Leone[8] **Bovee**, born 13 Mar 1914 in Galeton, Potter Co., PA. She married on 13 Apr 1934 in Canisteo, Steuben Co., NY **Rev John Frederick G Harrison**.

+   2707   vi   Margaret Helene[8] **Bovee**, born 11 Sep 1917 in Galeton, Potter Co., PA. She married **Clair William Norton**.

1668. Mabel Melvina[7] **Bovee** (Henry M[6], Cornelius[5], Abraham[4], Abraham[3], Nicholas[2], Mathieu[1]), born 17 Jul 1888 in Rathbone, Steuben Co., NY; christened 27 Apr 1895 in St Peter's Episcopal Ch, Dansville, Steuben Co., NY; died 1962 in Hornell, Steuben Co., NY. She married (1) aft 1930 Bert Angel, born in NY; (2) in Steuben Co., NY Samuel L Bickford, born 1881; died 1956 in Hornell, Steuben Co., NY.

Children of Mabel Melvina Bovee and Bert Angel were as follows:

2708   i   Delores[8] **Angel**.

1669. Laura Bonabel[7] **Bovee** (Henry M[6], Cornelius[5], Abraham[4], Abraham[3], Nicholas[2], Mathieu[1]), born 7 Jan 1890 in Groveland, Livingston Co., NY; christened 27 Apr 1895 in St Peter's Episcopal Ch, Dansville, Steuben Co., NY. She married in Steuben Co., NY Dorr Lieb.

Children of Laura Bonabel Bovee and Dorr Lieb were as follows:

2709   i   Alexander[8] **Lieb**.

1671. Edith Mildred[7] **Bovee** (Henry M[6], Cornelius[5], Abraham[4], Abraham[3], Nicholas[2], Mathieu[1]), born 29 Dec 1894 in Dansville, Steuben Co., NY; christened 27 Apr 1895 in St Peter's Episcopal Ch, Dansville, Steuben Co., NY; died 1948 in Portville, Cattaraugus Co., NY. She married abt 1909 in Town Line, Erie Co., NY Clyde G Bridenbaker, born 8 Jul 1887 in Town Line, Erie Co., NY; died 10 Jun 1978 in Brockport, Monroe Co., NY, son of Gilbert Bridenbaker.

Children of Edith Mildred Bovee and Clyde G Bridenbaker were as follows:

2710   i   Lyle[8] **Bridenbaker**, born abt 1912 in NY.

2711   ii   Glen[8] **Bridenbaker**, born 7 Apr 1913 in NY; died Jun 1971 in NY.

2712	iii	Neil [8] **Bridenbaker**, born abt 1914 in NY.
2713	iv	Henry [8] **Bridenbaker**, born 9 Apr 1917 in NY; died 1 Feb 1993.
2714	v	Bonnibel Margaret [8] **Bridenbaker**, born in NY; died in NY.

1672. Earl Erwin [7] **Bovee** (Henry M [6], Cornelius [5], Abraham [4], Abraham [3], Nicholas [2], Mathieu [1]), born 22 Nov 1898 in Short Tract, Allegany Co., NY; died in Hornell, Steuben Co., NY. He married on 9 Dec 1920 in Hornell, Steuben Co., NY Minnie Smith, born in Altoona, Blair Co., PA; died in Hornell, Steuben Co., NY, daughter of Harry E Smith and Lydia A.

Children of Earl Erwin Bovee and Minnie Smith were as follows:

+	2715	i	Carl Norman [8] **Bovee**, born abt 1920 in Canisteo, Steuben Co, NY; died 19 Aug 1999. He married **Ruth (---)**.
+	2716	ii	Earl Erwin [8] **Bovee** Jr, born 1922. He married **Geraldine Predmore**.
	2717	iii	Gordon L [8] **Bovee**, born abt 1924.
	2718	iv	Mabel [8] **Bovee**. She married in Dansville, Livingston Co., NY **(---) Rider**, born abt 1926.

1674. George William [7] **Bovee** (William R [6], Abraham [5], Abraham [4], Abraham [3], Nicholas [2], Mathieu [1]), born 17 Feb 1868 in Oshkosh, Winnebago Co., WI; died 6 Dec 1934 in Manawa, Waupaca Co., WI. He married on 16 Mar 1889 in Manawa, Waupaca Co., WI Olive M Bozile, born 17 Apr 1873 in Little Wolf Twp, Manawa, Waupaca Co., WI; died 6 May 1898 in Manawa, Waupaca Co., WI, daughter of Joseph Bozile and Harriet R Marshall.

Children of George William Bovee and Olive M Bozile were as follows:

	2719	i	Mary [8] **Bovee**, born 13 Apr 1890 in Little Wolf Twp., Waupaca Co., WI; died 19 Apr 1890.
	2720	ii	Ella C [8] **Bovee**, born 27 Nov 1892; died 10 Feb 1919 in Manawa, Waupaca Co., WI.
+	2721	iii	Viola F [8] **Bovee**, born 24 Jan 1895 in WI; died 27 Aug 1926. She married **William Thomas Vaughan**.
	2722	iv	George M [8] **Bovee**, born 1 May 1898.

1675. Arthur Vernon [7] **Bovee** (William R [6], Abraham [5], Abraham [4], Abraham [3], Nicholas [2], Mathieu [1]), born 13 Feb 1871 in Oshkosh, Winnebago Co., WI; died 13 Apr 1939 in Manawa, Waupaca Co., WI. He married on 26 Aug 1894 in Symco, Waupaca Co., WI Augusta Ernestina Ferg, born 25 Aug 1876 in Bloomfield, Waushara Co., WI; died 11 Apr 1974 in Manawa, Waupaca Co., WI, daughter of August Ferg and Amelia Koepp.

Children of Arthur Vernon Bovee and Augusta Ernestina Ferg were as follows:

+	2723	i	Vernon Harold [8] **Bovee**, born 22 Mar 1895 in Little Wolf

Twp., Waupaca Co., WI; died 1 Jan 1972 in Waushara Co., WI. He married **Minnie Michalski**.

+ 2724 ii Arthur Vernon[8] **Bovee** Jr, born 10 May 1897 in Manawa, Waupaca Co., WI; died Aug 1967 in Brea, Orange Co., CA. He married **Henrietta (---)**.

2725 iii Dorothy[8] **Bovee**, born 11 May 1898 in Little Wolf Twp., Waupaca Co., WI. She married **Emil Kitzman**.

+ 2726 iv Charlotte[8] **Bovee**, born abt 1899. She married **Henry Pauzig**.

+ 2727 v Carl Clifford[8] **Bovee**, born 28 Apr 1900 in Manawa, Waupaca Co., WI; died 24 Feb 1987 in Big Falls, Waupaca Co., WI. He married **Lilliam Emma Pauline Ruppenthal**.

+ 2728 vi Leland M[8] **Bovee**, born 27 Aug 1901 in Waupaca Co., WI; died 30 May 1985 in Antigo, Langlade Co., WI. He married **Ellen Giese**.

+ 2729 vii Gordon Lester[8] **Bovee**, born 26 Oct 1905 in Manawa, Waupaca Co., WI; died 27 Jul 1979 in Antigo, Langlade Co., WI. He married **Minnie Amelia Hansen**.

+ 2730 viii Everette Vivian[8] **Bovee**, born 9 Dec 1906 in Little Wolf Twp., Waupaca Co., WI; died 4 Nov 1984 in New London, Waupaca Co., WI. He married **Evelyn Hope Myers**.

2731 ix Sherida[8] **Bovee**, born 1909.

2732 x Irene L[8] **Bovee**, born 2 Nov 1915 in Manawa, Waupaca Co., WI; died 22 Jan 1937 in Manawa, Waupaca Co., WI.

1678. Maude[7] **Bovee** (William R[6], Abraham[5], Abraham[4], Abraham[3], Nicholas[2], Mathieu[1]), born 7 Jun 1881 in Manawa, Waupaca Co., WI. She married Avery J Baldwin.

Children of Maude Bovee and Avery J Baldwin were as follows:

2733 i Evan V[8] **Baldwin**, born abt 1903 in WI.

2734 ii Reginald W[8] **Baldwin**, born abt 1906 in WI.

2735 iii Lyle J[8] **Baldwin**, born abt 1908 in WI.

2736 iv Emma M[8] **Baldwin**, born abt 1910 in WI.

2737 v George W[8] **Baldwin**, born abt 1915 in WI.

2738 vi Gerald J[8] **Baldwin**, born abt 1916 in WI.

2739 vii Robert W[8] **Baldwin**, born abt 1918 in WI.

1698. George Lewis[7] **Bovee** (Minard[6], Abraham[5], Abraham[4], Abraham[3], Nicholas[2], Mathieu[1]), born 9 May 1879 in Stockbridge, Calumet Co., WI; died Jul 1963. He married on 16 Dec 1901 in Oshkosh, Winnebago Co., WI Mabel A Mallory, born abt 1883, daughter of West Mallory and Mary Casey.

Children of George Lewis Bovee and Mabel A Mallory were as follows:

2740 i Clair[8] **Bovee**, born 1903 in Manawa, Waupaca Co., WI.

2741	ii	Leona[8] **Bovee**, born abt 1907 in WI. She married **(---) Christenson**.
2742	iii	Merle[8] **Bovee**, born abt 1909.
2743	iv	Carol[8] **Bovee**, born abt 1913 in WI.
+ 2744	v	Ned Allen[8] **Bovee**, born 4 Jul 1916 in Presque Isle, Vilas Co., WI; died 5 Feb 1994 in Laurim, Houghton Co., MI. He married **Mildred Louise Hanson**.
2745	vi	Patricia[8] **Bovee**, born in WI. She married **(---) Aldridge**.

1705. Howard Norman[7] **Bovee** (Minard[6], Abraham[5], Abraham[4], Abraham[3], Nicholas[2], Mathieu[1]), born 7 Jan 1898 in Manawa, Waupaca Co., WI; died 1974 in Clintonville, Waupaca Co., WI. He married in 1919 Linda Henrietta Helms, born abt 1900.

Children of Howard Norman Bovee and Linda Henrietta Helms were as follows:

2746	i	Geraldine[8] **Bovee**, born aft 1919. She married **Fred Augustin**.
2747	ii	Howard W[8] **Bovee**, born aft 1919.

1707. Ella Rose[7] **Bovee** (Abraham[6], Abraham[5], Abraham[4], Abraham[3], Nicholas[2], Mathieu[1]), born 26 Aug 1881 in New London, Waupaca Co., WI; died 18 Mar 1965. She married on 29 Apr 1899 in Langlade Co., WI Martin Elliot.

Children of Ella Rose Bovee and Martin Elliot were as follows:

2748	i	Gladys[8] **Elliot**.
2749	ii	George[8] **Elliot**.
2750	iii	Beatrice[8] **Elliot**.
2751	iv	Donna[8] **Elliot**.

1708. Michael James[7] **Bovee** (Abraham[6], Abraham[5], Abraham[4], Abraham[3], Nicholas[2], Mathieu[1]), born 27 Apr 1883; died 23 Mar 1976 in Antigo, Langlade Co., WI. He married on 22 Oct 1912 in Antigo, Langlade Co., WI Frances Marciniak, born 17 Aug 1892 in Antigo, Langlade Co., WI; died 23 Oct 1963 in Antigo, Langlade Co., WI, daughter of Albert Marciniak and Josephine Bonczyk.

Children of Michael James Bovee and Frances Marciniak were as follows:

2752	i	Viginia Mary[8] **Bovee**, born 24 Jul 1913 in Antigo, Langlade Co., WI. She married on 13 Oct 1936 in Antigo, Langlade Co., WI **Edward R Yarie**.
2753	ii	Albert[8] **Bovee**, born 9 Nov 1914 in Antigo, Langlade Co., WI.
2754	iii	Madelime R[8] **Bovee**, born 4 Jul 1916 in Antigo, Langlade Co., WI; died 26 Jan 1983 in Antigo, Langlade Co., WI.
2755	iv	Gertrude Frances[8] **Bovee**, born 14 Jul 1918 in Antigo,

2756 v Francis Victor[8] **Bovee**, born 1 Dec 1926 in Antigo, Langlade Co., WI; died 12 Feb 1938 in Antigo, Langlade Co., WI.

1709. John Byron[7] **Bovee** (Abraham[6], Abraham[5], Abraham[4], Abraham[3], Nicholas[2], Mathieu[1]), born 18 Feb 1885 in Langlade Co., WI; died 3 Oct 1960 in Antigo, Langlade Co., WI. He married Mabel J Gould, born 13 Aug 1884 in Ashfield, Franklin Co., MA; died 1 Jan 1945 in Langlade Co., WI.

Children of John Byron Bovee and Mabel J Gould were as follows:

2757 i Child[8] **Bovee**, born 9 Jun 1918 in Antigo, Langlade Co., WI.

1712. Marie Pearl[7] **Bovee** (Abraham[6], Abraham[5], Abraham[4], Abraham[3], Nicholas[2], Mathieu[1]), born 27 Apr 1897 in Antigo, Langlade Co., WI; died 31 Jul 1983. She married on 5 Jun 1917 in Antigo, Langlade Co., WI Thomas J McGoff, born abt 1894 in Canada, son of Michael McGoff.

Children of Marie Pearl Bovee and Thomas J McGoff were as follows:

2758 i Marjorie M[8] **McGoff**, born 1918 in Antigo, Langlade Co., WI.
2759 ii Donald[8] **McGoff**, born 26 Apr 1924.
2760 iii Betty[8] **McGoff**, born in Wausau, Marathon Co., WI.

1713. William H[7] **Bovee** (Erastus[6], Abraham[5], Abraham[4], Abraham[3], Nicholas[2], Mathieu[1]), born May 1880 in WI; died abt 1908. He married Emma (---), born abt 1883.

Children of William H Bovee and Emma (---) were as follows:

2761 i Elaine[8] **Bovee**, born abt 1908 in WI.

1715. Clarence Abraham[7] **Bovee** (Erastus[6], Abraham[5], Abraham[4], Abraham[3], Nicholas[2], Mathieu[1]), born 28 Sep 1883 in WI; died 5 Jul 1960. He married Odela Luckow, born 28 May 1891; died Jun 1973.

Children of Clarence Abraham Bovee and Odela Luckow were as follows:

+ 2762 i Earl Clarence[8] **Bovee**, born 5 May 1908 in WI; died 11 Jul 1969 in OH. He married **Helen Wells**.
+ 2763 ii Merrill Frederick[8] **Bovee**, born 11 Jan 1915 in WI; died Jan 1975. He married **Dorothy Grebe**.
2764 iii Alice Mabel[8] **Bovee**, born 10 Aug 1916. She married **Courtland Huerion**.

1716. Edward C[7] **Bovee** (Erastus[6], Abraham[5], Abraham[4], Abraham[3], Nicholas[2], Mathieu[1]), born 25 Dec 1890 in Antigo, Langlade Co., WI; died 28 Aug 1961. He married on 24 Sep 1912 Hazel Thisdale, born 8 May 1897; died 9 Feb 1985 in Niagara, Marinette Co., WI.

Children of Edward C Bovee and Hazel Thisdale were as follows:

+ 2765 i Edward Harold[8] **Bovee**, born 6 Apr 1913; died 18 May 1991. He married **Florence F Peron**.

 2766 ii Gladys[8] **Bovee**, born abt 1914 in WI.

 2767 iii Thelma[8] **Bovee**, born abt 1920 in WI.

1724. Bertha Antionete[7] **Bovee** (William Edgar[6], Frederick Brown[5], Abraham[4], Abraham[3], Nicholas[2], Mathieu[1]), born 22 Dec 1872 in Stockbridge, Calumet Co., WI; died 22 Sep 1971 in Stockbridge, Calumet Co., WI. She married on 26 Jul 1891 in Stockbridge, Calumet Co., WI Warren Bruce Millar, born 15 Dec 1864 in Lamartine, Fond du Lac Co., WI, son of Daniel J Millar and Luca A (---).

Children of Bertha Antionete Bovee and Warren Bruce Millar were as follows:

 2768 i George Harvey[8] **Millar**, born 6 Jul 1892.

 2769 ii Olive Catherine[8] **Millar**, born Nov 1893.

 2770 iii Mildred Lucille[8] **Millar**, born 15 Mar 1897.

 2771 iv Ruth Muriel[8] **Millar**, born 18 Jun 1902; died 21 May 1994 in Racine, Racine Co., WI.

1726. Lotta May[7] **Bovee** (William Edgar[6], Frederick Brown[5], Abraham[4], Abraham[3], Nicholas[2], Mathieu[1]), born 25 Jun 1876 in Stockbridge, Calumet Co., WI; died abt 1962. She married on 26 Jul 1895 Arthur Floyd Dutcher, died abt 1930, son of Edgar Dutcher and Glowina Elizabeth (---).

Children of Lotta May Bovee and Arthur Floyd Dutcher were as follows:

 2772 i Child 1[8] **Dutcher**, born abt 1896; died abt 1906 in Milwaukee, Milwaukee Co., WI.

 2773 ii William F[8] **Dutcher**, born abt 1898.

1730. Albert[7] **Bovee** (Ervin[6], Frederick Brown[5], Abraham[4], Abraham[3], Nicholas[2], Mathieu[1]), born 4 Dec 1892 in MO; died May 1971 in Concord, Merrimac Co., NH. He married Elizabeth Heberlein, born 1897 in Germany.

Children of Albert Bovee and Elizabeth Heberlein were as follows:

 2774 i Edith[8] **Bovee**, born 27 Apr 1916 in Calumet Co., WI. She married **(---) Pitting**.

 2775 ii Frederick H[8] **Bovee**, born 24 Feb 1918 in Calumet Co., WI; died 8 Apr 1988 in Chino, San Bernardino Co.,CA.

+ 2776 iii Irving[8] **Bovee**, born 24 Dec 1919 in WI. He married

Shirley Giermoth.
+ 2777 iv John William[8] **Bovee**, born 23 Oct 1921 in Oakfield, Fond du Lac Co., WI; died 14 Jan 1991. He married **Ruth Angeline Grubish**.
+ 2778 v Alfred[8] **Bovee** Sr, born 8 Sep 1923; died 13 Nov 1993 in Loveland, Larimer Co., CO. He married **Mildred S (---)**.

1733. Andrew Jackson[7] **Bovee** Jr (Andrew Jackson[6], Henry[5], Abraham[4], Abraham[3], Nicholas[2], Mathieu[1]), born 23 Jul 1887 in Antigo, Langlade Co., WI; died 5 Nov 1918 in St Paul, Ramsey Co., MN. He married on 16 Sep 1908 Edith Tenney, born 11 May 1886 in Langlade Co., WI; died 15 Mar 1914.

Children of Andrew Jackson Bovee Jr and Edith Tenney were as follows:
+ 2779 i Lester M[8] **Bovee**, born 8 Oct 1909 in Bellingham, Whatcom Co., WA; died 24 Jan 2001 in Bellingham, Whatcom Co., WA. He married **Deloris Ehle**.
  2780 ii Norma[8] **Bovee**, born 11 Jun 1911 in Bellingham, Whatcom Co., WA; died 9 Aug 1922.

1734. Jesse Arthur[7] **Bovee** (Andrew Jackson[6], Henry[5], Abraham[4], Abraham[3], Nicholas[2], Mathieu[1]), born 9 Oct 1889 in Antigo, Langlade Co., WI; died 18 Sep 1946 in St Paul, Ramsey Co., MN. He married (1) on 24 Sep 1912 in St Paul, Ramsey Co., MN Attie Anne Victoria Nelson, born 25 Apr 1888 in Antigo, Langlade Co., WI; died 3 May 1929, daughter of Charles Nelson and Ida Christine Johnson; (2) on 28 Jun 1932 Gertrude Caroline Fitzpatrick.

Children of Jesse Arthur Bovee and Attie Anne Victoria Nelson were as follows:
  2781 i Muriel Marjorie[8] **Bovee**, born 13 Oct 1913; died Jan 1914.
+ 2782 ii Arlene Marion[8] **Bovee**, born abt 1914. She married **Fremont Marins Nelson**.
  2783 iii Vernon Eugene[8] **Bovee**, born 11 Apr 1915 in St Paul, Ramsey Co., MN; died 25 Oct 1930 in Washington Co., MN.
  2784 iv Wayne Aaron[8] **Bovee**, born 11 Oct 1918. He married **Dorothy Whitehead**.
+ 2785 v Carley May[8] **Bovee**, born 8 May 1924. She married **Raymond R Fronek**.
  2786 vi Child[8] **Bovee**.
  2787 vii Lois June[8] **Bovee**.

Children of Jesse Arthur Bovee and Gertrude Caroline Fitzpatrick were as follows:
  2788 i Gene Arthur[8] **Bovee**, born in St Paul, Ramsey Co., MN. He married **Nancy S**.

1735. Nellie Elizabeth[7] **Bovee** (Andrew Jackson[6], Henry[5], Abraham[4], Abraham[3], Nicholas[2], Mathieu[1]), born 9 Oct 1892 in Antigo, Langlade Co., WI; died 13 Jun 1965. She married (1) on 14 Jun 1920 in Lake Co., IN Clarence J Leen; (2) abt 1910 unknown.

Children of Nellie Elizabeth Bovee were as follows:

2789　i　　　　Ione[8] **(---)**, born 1911 in MI.

1737. Isabel Louise[7] **Bovee** (Andrew Jackson[6], Henry[5], Abraham[4], Abraham[3], Nicholas[2], Mathieu[1]), born 3 Jun 1897 in Antigo, Langlade Co., WI; died 1 Jul 1986 in Olympia, Thurston Co., WA. She married (1) on 25 Dec 1912 Jesse P Gooding, born 1879; died 2 Mar 1920 in Bellingham, Whatcom Co., WA; (2) on 26 Oct 1920 in Helena, Lewis & Clark Co., MT Frank George Starring, son of Frank Benjamin Starring.

Children of Isabel Louise Bovee and Jesse P Gooding were as follows:

2790　i　　　　Jessie Isabel[8] **Gooding**, born 29 Mar 1916 in Bellingham, Whatcom Co., WA.

Children of Isabel Louise Bovee and Frank George Starring were as follows:

2791　i　　　　Cheri Mai[8] **Starring**, born 29 Aug 1928 in Helena, Lewis & Clark Co., MT.

1741. Grace Evelyn[7] **Bovee** (Warren Henry[6], Henry[5], Abraham[4], Abraham[3], Nicholas[2], Mathieu[1]), born 24 Jun 1879 in Chilton, Calumet Co., WI; died in Appleton, Outagamie Co., WI. She married on 26 May 1897 in Chilton, Calumet Co., WI Clifford Bishop.

Children of Grace Evelyn Bovee and Clifford Bishop were as follows:

2792　i　　　　James[8] **Bishop**.
2793　ii　　　Doris[8] **Bishop**.
2794　iii　　Gladys[8] **Bishop**.
2795　iv　　　Riley[8] **Bishop**.
2796　v　　　Evelyn[8] **Bishop**.
2797　vi　　　Edward[8] **Bishop**.

1742. Robert Clare[7] **Bovee** (Warren Henry[6], Henry[5], Abraham[4], Abraham[3], Nicholas[2], Mathieu[1]), born 30 Mar 1881 in Calumet Co., WI; died bef 1963 in Fairfax,VA. He married Catherine (---), died aft 1963 in Fairfax,VA.

Children of Robert Clare Bovee and Catherine (---) were as follows:

2798　i　　　　Child[8] **Bovee**.
2799　ii　　　Child[8] **Bovee**.
2800　iii　　Child[8] **Bovee**.
2801　iv　　　Child[8] **Bovee**.

1744. John Henry[7] Bovee (Warren Henry[6], Henry[5], Abraham[4], Abraham[3], Nicholas[2], Mathieu[1]), born 19 Jul 1887; died 21 Aug 1944 in Calumet Co., WI. He married on 22 Nov 1910 Rose Winkle, died 1956.

Children of John Henry Bovee and Rose Winkle were as follows:

	2802	i	Iola Anne[8] **Bovee**, born 16 Jun 1913. She married (1) on 22 Nov 1945 **Matthew Zahringer**; (2) on 11 May 1963 **Wallace Stumpenhorst**.
	2803	ii	Cyril[8] **Bovee**, born 6 Jan 1915; died 6 Jan 1915.
+	2804	iii	Madeline Margaret[8] **Bovee**, born 12 Aug 1923; died in Stockbridge, Calumet Co., WI. She married **Sylvester Jacob Penning**.

1745. Lyman George[7] Bovee (Franklin Gibson[6], Aaron[5], Henry[4], Abraham[3], Nicholas[2], Mathieu[1]), born Apr 1878 in Danby, Thomkins Co., NY. He married Evaleen Elizabeth Thomas, born 26 Feb 1880 in New York, New York Co., NY, daughter of William Henry Thomas and Martha Moore.

Children of Lyman George Bovee and Evaleen Elizabeth Thomas were as follows:

+	2805	i	Lawrence Erwin[8] **Bovee**, born 11 Oct 1901; died 23 Dec 1927. He married **Hilda M Harris**.
	2806	ii	Richard Franklin[8] **Bovee**, born 19 Feb 1903. He married on 15 Nov 1926 in Binghamton, Broome Co., NY **Gladys Cook**.
	2807	iii	Frances Mildred[8] **Bovee**, born 10 Nov 1905. She married on 15 Nov 1926 **Mark Duane Simpson**.
	2808	iv	Lillian Hosley[8] **Bovee**, born 15 Nov 1906; died 20 Oct 1918.
+	2809	v	Burton George[8] **Bovee**, born 17 May 1912. He married **Alice Mae Lane**.
	2810	vi	Dorcas Louise[8] **Bovee**, born 30 Jun 1915. She married **Joseph Lewis**.

1746. Charles W[7] Bovee (Franklin Gibson[6], Aaron[5], Henry[4], Abraham[3], Nicholas[2], Mathieu[1]), born Sep 1879 in Tomkins Co., NY. He married on 2 Feb 1901 Louise Davis, born abt 1883 in PA.

Children of Charles W Bovee and Louise Davis were as follows:

	2811	i	Eugene[8] **Bovee**, born 12 Nov 1903; died Oct 1973. He married **Dorothy R (---)**, born 31 Jul 1904; died Feb 1975 in Binghamton, Broome Co., NY.

1750. Lucille Monica[7] Bovee (John Ira[6], John[5], Henry[4], Abraham[3], Nicholas[2],

Mathieu[1]), born 1910. She married Oswald Ronald Gravelle.

Children of Lucille Monica Bovee and Oswald Ronald Gravelle were as follows:

2812	i	Stephen[8] **Gravelle**, born in Ramsey Co., MN.
2813	ii	Davon[8] **Gravelle**, born in Ramsey Co., MN.
2814	iii	Elizabeth[8] **Gravelle**, born in Hennepin Co., MN.

1751. Gerald P[7] **Bovee** (John Ira[6], John[5], Henry[4], Abraham[3], Nicholas[2], Mathieu[1]), born 10 Jun 1915; died 20 Jan 1990 in St. Paul, Ramsey Co., MN. He married Florence M Neitje, born 13 Jul 1905; died 7 Oct 1993 in St. Paul, Ramsey Co., MN.

Children of Gerald P Bovee and Florence M Neitje were as follows:

2815	i	Marie Ann[8] **Bovee**.
2816	ii	Jeanne Lou[8] **Bovee**, born 22 Oct 1947; died 27 Oct 1947.

1752. Mary Helen[7] **Bovee** (John Ira[6], John[5], Henry[4], Abraham[3], Nicholas[2], Mathieu[1]), died 6 Dec 2000 in Saint Paul, Ramsey Co., MN. She married on 9 Sep 1935 William Anthony Cassen.

Children of Mary Helen Bovee and William Anthony Cassen were as follows:

2817	i	Joanne[8] **Cassen**, born in Ramsey Co., MN.
2818	ii	William Anthony[8] **Cassen**.
2819	iii	Kathleen[8] **Cassen**, born in Hennepin Co., MN.

1755. Rachel Eliza[7] **Bovee** (Charles J[6], John[5], Henry[4], Abraham[3], Nicholas[2], Mathieu[1]), born 18 Oct 1915 in Plaza, Mountrail Co., ND; died 27 Jun 1992 in Portland, Multnoma Co., OR. She married on 5 Apr 1935 Lloyd Jacob Walters, born 5 Apr 1905 in LeRoy, Mower Co., MN; died 14 Apr 1981 in Ocean Park, Pacific Co., WA, son of John Carpenter Walters and Edith Jenks.

Children of Rachel Eliza Bovee and Lloyd Jacob Walters were as follows:

2820	i	Charles Lloyd[8] **Walters**, born in Jamestown, Stutsman Co., ND.
2821	ii	Fay addison[8] **Walters**, born in Jamestown, Stutsman Co., ND.
2822	iii	John Harry[8] **Walters**, born in Jamestown, Stutsman Co., ND.

1756. Charles Avery[7] **Bovee** (Charles J[6], John[5], Henry[4], Abraham[3], Nicholas[2], Mathieu[1]), born in Jamestown, Stutsman Co., ND. He married on 8 Feb 1950 in Jamestown, Stutsman Co., ND Mary Jane Parkhouse, born in Arthur, Cass Co., ND.

Children of Charles Avery Bovee and Mary Jane Parkhouse were as follows:

+ 2823 i   Susan Ina[8] **Bovee**, born in Jamestown, Stutsman Co., ND. She married (1) **Steven Swanson**; (2) **Ron Staiger**.
+ 2824 ii   Charles James[8] **Bovee**, born in Minot, Ward Co., ND. He married **Jennie (---)**.
+ 2825 iii Steven Craig[8] **Bovee**, born in Minot, Ward Co., ND. He married **Susan Parizek**.
+ 2826 iv   Laurie Ann[8] **Bovee**, born in Minot, Ward Co., ND. She married **Jeffrey Wood**.

1757. Florence Marie[7] **Bovee** (Myron Edgar[6], Cornelius[5], Peter[4], Abraham[3], Nicholas[2], Mathieu[1]), born 1 Apr 1898 in Mendon. Clayton Co., IA; died 16 Aug 1979 in St Petersburg, Pinellas Co., FL. She married Charles Sawvell, born 21 Aug 1871; died 28 Mar 1968.

Children of Florence Marie Bovee and Charles Sawvell were as follows:

2827 i   Violet[8] **Sawvell**.
2828 ii   Tillie[8] **Sawvell**.
2829 iii Arnold[8] **Sawvell**.
2830 iv   Elmer[8] **Sawvell**.
2831 v   Evelyn[8] **Sawvell**.
2832 vi   Edward[8] **Sawvell**.

1759. Edward Wheeler[7] **Bovee** (Myron Edgar[6], Cornelius[5], Peter[4], Abraham[3], Nicholas[2], Mathieu[1]), born 12 Dec 1900 in Mendon. Clayton Co., IA; died Jul 1987 in Cottonwood, Yavapai Co., AZ. He married Amy Bass, born 28 Sep 1903; died May 1976 in Cottonwood, Yavapai Co., AZ, daughter of George Bass.

Children of Edward Wheeler Bovee and Amy Bass were as follows:

2833 i   John[8] **Bovee**, born abt 1930.
2834 ii   Ralph[8] **Bovee**, born abt 1930.

1760. Roy Alvin[7] **Bovee** (Myron Edgar[6], Cornelius[5], Peter[4], Abraham[3], Nicholas[2], Mathieu[1]), born 5 Aug 1902 in Mendon. Clayton Co., IA; died 20 Feb 1983 in S Beloit, Winnebego Co., IL. He married on 6 Aug 1937 Ellen A Taylor, born 16 Sep 1907; died 4 May 1972.

Children of Roy Alvin Bovee and Ellen A Taylor were as follows:

2835 i   Robert[8] **Bovee**.

1761. Arthur Cornelius[7] **Bovee** (Myron Edgar[6], Cornelius[5], Peter[4], Abraham[3], Nicholas[2], Mathieu[1]), born 24 Mar 1904 in Mendon. Clayton Co., IA; died Oct 1970 in McGregor, Clayton Co., IA. He married Emma Schultz, born 29 Jun

1907; died 2 Apr 1994 in McGregor, Clayton Co., IA.

Children of Arthur Cornelius Bovee and Emma Schultz were as follows:

+ 2836   i   Joyce Darlene[8] **Bovee**. She married **Dwain Alvin Nading**.

2837   ii   Glenn Arthur[8] **Bovee**, born 10 Feb 1940; died 1989. He married **Juliene Kay Lansing**.

1764. Marie Ellen[7] **Bovee** (Myron Edgar[6], Cornelius[5], Peter[4], Abraham[3], Nicholas[2], Mathieu[1]), born 8 Feb 1911 in Mendon. Clayton Co., IA; died 11 Jun 1977 in McGregor, Clayton Co., IA. She married Mark Daniel Wilson, born 1 Sep 1899 in IA, son of William Wilson and Mary Pierce.

Children of Marie Ellen Bovee and Mark Daniel Wilson were as follows:

2838   i   John R[8] **Wilson**, died in WW II.

1765. Raymond Ralph[7] **Bovee** (Myron Edgar[6], Cornelius[5], Peter[4], Abraham[3], Nicholas[2], Mathieu[1]), born 14 Jan 1916; died 17 Nov 1984 in McGregor, Clayton Co., IA. He married Arlene Kruse.

Children of Raymond Ralph Bovee and Arlene Kruse were as follows:

2839   i   Lori Lee[8] **Bovee**.

2840   ii   Gene Raymond[8] **Bovee**.

1766. Ethel May[7] **Bovee** (Myron Edgar[6], Cornelius[5], Peter[4], Abraham[3], Nicholas[2], Mathieu[1]), born 21 Mar 1918. She married (1) on 9 Dec 1936 Charley phalen; (2) in Nov 1949 Erwin Mann.

Children of Ethel May Bovee and Charley phalen were as follows:

2841   i   Doris Darlene[8] **phalen**.

2842   ii   Patricia Dorothy[8] **phalen**.

1770. Delila Sarah[7] **Bovee** (Jacob[6], Philip[5], Jacob Philip[4], Philip[3], Nicholas[2], Mathieu[1]), born 7 Nov 1853 in Cherry Valley, Ashtabula Co., OH; died 20 Feb 1926 in Los Angeles, Los Angeles Co., CA. She married on 12 Apr 1870 in Jefferson, Ashtabula Co., OH Henry D Miner, born 10 May 1835 in Lyndon, Cattaraugus Co., NY; died 22 Oct 1921 in Los Angeles, Los Angeles Co., CA.

Children of Delila Sarah Bovee and Henry D Miner were as follows:

2843   i   Clyde Dennison[8] **Miner**, born 22 Dec 1871 in Colebrook, Ashtabula Co., OH; died 27 Oct 1959 in Los Angeles, Los Angeles Co., CA.

2844   ii   Fred Jacob[8] **Miner**, born 6 Jun 1876 in Colebrook, Ashtabula Co., OH; died 23 Feb 1952 in Los Angeles, Los Angeles Co., CA.

| 2845 | iii | Rollin H (Ralph Henry)[8] **Miner**, born 25 Jun 1883 in Colebrook, Ashtabula Co., OH; died 11 Nov 1885 in Colebrook, Ashtabula Co., OH. |
| 2846 | iv | Mary Isabelle[8] **Miner**, born 23 Aug 1891 in Colebrook, Ashtabula Co., OH; died 22 Dec 1973 in Los Angeles, Los Angeles Co., CA. |

1781. Julia Jane[7] **Bovee** (Philip[6], Philip[5], Jacob Philip[4], Philip[3], Nicholas[2], Mathieu[1]), born Jun 1850 in Ashtabula Co., OH. She married George Washington Frost, born abt 1844 in NY.

Children of Julia Jane Bovee and George Washington Frost were as follows:

2847	i	Mary[8] **Frost**, born abt 1867 in MI.
2848	ii	Frank L[8] **Frost**, born abt 1869 in IA.
2849	iii	James[8] **Frost**, born abt 1870 in IA.
2850	iv	William Henry[8] **Frost**, born Oct 1874 in IA.
2851	v	Cora[8] **Frost**, born abt 1877.
2852	vi	Ida[8] **Frost**, born 1881.
2853	vii	Nettie Belle[8] **Frost**, born Sep 1885 in Jackson Co., IA.
2854	viii	Clara L[8] **Frost**, born Oct 1889 in IL.
2855	ix	George W[8] **Frost**, born Mar 1894 in IL.

1784. Hannah[7] **Bovee** (Philip[6], Philip[5], Jacob Philip[4], Philip[3], Nicholas[2], Mathieu[1]), born 19 Oct 1856 in Grand Rapids, Kent Co., MI; died 2 Dec 1923. She married on 5 Jul 1875 in Central City, Merrick Co., NE Henry Roswell Reed, born 11 Sep 1852 in CT; died 24 Mar 1901 in Scottsbluff, Scotts Bluff Co., NE, son of Harlow Reed and Fidellia Griffin.

Children of Hannah Bovee and Henry Roswell Reed were as follows:

2856	i	Cora F[8] **Reed**, born 28 Aug 1876 in Merrick Co., NE; died 2 Jan 1914.
2857	ii	Mary O[8] **Reed**, born 7 Jun 1878 in Merrick Co., NE; died 6 Apr 1936 in CA.
2858	iii	Ruth Ellen[8] **Reed**, born 30 Mar 1880; died 28 Aug 1880.
2859	iv	Frank Howard[8] **Reed**, born 2 Jun 1881; died 16 Feb 1927.
2860	v	Lottie E[8] **Reed**, born 5 Jul 1883; died 24 Nov 1924.
2861	vi	Henry Roswell[8] **Reed** Jr, born 30 Jun 1885.
2862	vii	Robert Eugene[8] **Reed**, born 3 Dec 1887 in Dawes Co., NE.
2863	viii	Viena Amelia[8] **Reed**, born 28 Dec 1889 in Dawes Co., NE.
2864	ix	Harlow Augustus[8] **Reed**, born 28 Mar 1892 in Crawford, Dawes Co., NE; died 22 Sep 1969 in Myrtle Point, Coos Co., OR. He married **Emily Alice LaFlame**.
2865	x	Nettie Jane[8] **Reed**, born 21 May 1894; died 24 Nov 1980.

2866   xi   Effie Pearl[8] **Reed**, born 31 Jul 1896 in Dawes Co., NE.

2867   xii   Maggie May[8] **Reed**, born 18 Aug 1898 in Dawes Co., NE.

2868   xiii   Edith Julien[8] **Reed**, born 24 Oct 1900; died 11 Feb 1906.

1785. Emily Melvina[7] **Bovee** (Philip[6], Philip[5], Jacob Philip[4], Philip[3], Nicholas[2], Mathieu[1]), born 19 Jan 1859 in Dorr, Allegan Co., MI; died 3 May 1930 in Central City, Merrick Co., NE. She married on 3 Oct 1875 in Marrick Co,. NE William Moss Clark, born abt 1848 in PA, son of Benjamin Clark and Maria Baxter.

Children of Emily Melvina Bovee and William Moss Clark were as follows:

2869   i   Minnie Otilla[8] **Clark**, born 13 May 1876 in Central City, Merrick Co., NE; died 22 Jul 1958 in Green Co., WI. She married on 13 Feb 1901 **George Morris Frye**, died 1 Apr 1967.

2870   ii   Josephine[8] **Clark**, born 1 Apr 1879 in Central City, Merrick Co., NE; died 16 Feb 1967 in Anaheim, Orange Co., CA. She married on 28 Feb 1904 in Central City, Merrick Co., NE **John Adelbert Dillon**.

2871   iii   Oscar R[8] **Clark**, born 9 Dec 1881 in Central City, Merrick Co., NE; died 15 Feb 1969 in Central City, Merrick Co., NE.

2872   iv   Florence[8] **Clark**, born 20 Oct 1884 in Central City, Merrick Co., NE; died 14 May 1898 in Central City, Merrick Co., NE.

2873   v   Lela Alice[8] **Clark**, born 30 Nov 1887 in Central City, Merrick Co., NE; died 15 Aug 1960 in Central City, Merrick Co., NE.

2874   vi   Estella E[8] **Clark**, born 12 Mar 1893 in Central City, Merrick Co., NE; died 6 May 1943 in Central City, Merrick Co., NE.

1787. Byron J[7] **Bovee** (Philip[6], Philip[5], Jacob Philip[4], Philip[3], Nicholas[2], Mathieu[1]), born 26 Jan 1868 in Allegan Co., MI. He married (1) abt 1994 Florence (---), born abt 1864 in IA; (2) in 1930 Laura (---), born abt 1863 in WA.

Children of Byron J Bovee and Florence (---) were as follows:

2875   i   John A[8] **Bovee**, born 24 Jan 1895 in Spkane, Spokane Co., WA; died 9 Jul 1971 in Niland, Imperial Co., CA.

+ 2876   ii   Ernest Fred[8] **Bovee**, born 17 Mar 1899 in WA; died Jun 1968. He married **Jessie Victoria Hinman**.

1788. Arthur E[7] **Bovee** (Philip[6], Philip[5], Jacob Philip[4], Philip[3], Nicholas[2], Mathieu[1]), born 10 Aug 1873 in NE. He married Melinda (---), born abt 1895 in KY.

Children of Arthur E Bovee and Melinda (---) were as follows:

2877   i   Molly S[8] **Bovee**, born abt 1912 in KY.

1790. Manfred[7] **Bovee** (George[6], Philip[5], Jacob Philip[4], Philip[3], Nicholas[2], Mathieu[1]), born Aug 1858 in Jefferson Co., IA. He married Martha Parker, born 1872 in OR.

Children of Manfred Bovee and Martha Parker were as follows:

2878	i	Walter[8] **Bovee**, born 20 Sep 1892 in OR; died Feb 1968.
2879	ii	Olive[8] **Bovee**, born May 1896 in Canada.

1791. Orbie O[7] **Bovee** (George[6], Philip[5], Jacob Philip[4], Philip[3], Nicholas[2], Mathieu[1]), born 23 Jan 1862 in Jefferson Co., IA; died 3 Jun 1930 in Wenatchee. Chelan Co., WA. He married on 30 May 1888 in Pendleton,Umatilla Co., OR May Florence Parker, born 19 Nov 1869 in Portland, Multnoma Co., OR; died 22 May 1945.

Children of Orbie O Bovee and May Florence Parker were as follows:

	2880	i	Eloise Mabel[8] **Bovee**, born 9 Mar 1889 in OR.
	2881	ii	Harriet Angeline[8] **Bovee**, born 14 Jun 1891 in OR; died 1895 in Vernon, British Columbia, Canada.
	2882	iii	Child[8] **Bovee**, born 19 Oct 1893 in Athena, Umatilla Co., OR; died Oct 1893.
	2883	iv	Arthur Franklin[8] **Bovee**, born 28 Feb 1896 in Vernon, British Columbia, Canada; died Dec 1981 in E Wenatche, Wenatche Co., WA. He married **Alma (---)**.
+	2884	v	Louis Grant[8] **Bovee**, born 7 Jun 1897 in Vernon, British Columbia, Canada. He married (1) **Irene G Alspach**; (2) **Hilma Kimes**.
	2885	vi	Hazel May[8] **Bovee**, born 6 Oct 1899 in Vernon, British Columbia, Canada.
	2886	vii	Elsie Ellen[8] **Bovee**, born 29 Jan 1902 in Vernon, British Columbia, Canada; died 1905.
	2887	viii	Florence Hallie[8] **Bovee**, born 15 Jan 1907 in Vernon, British Columbia, Canada; died in Wenatchee, Chelan Co., WA.
	2888	ix	Orbe Claude[8] **Bovee**, born 18 Dec 1907 in Vernon, British Columbia, Canada; died 19 Dec 1933.

1798. Vida A[7] **Bovee** (Byron E[6], Philip[5], Jacob Philip[4], Philip[3], Nicholas[2], Mathieu[1]), born Oct 1884; died 3 Oct 1964 in Adrian, Lewanee Co., MI. She married Ray Fachman.

Children of Vida A Bovee and Ray Fachman were as follows:

2889	i	Doris Marie[8] **Fachman**, died 1929.

1810. Charles H^7 **Bovee** (Job Hedden^6, John^5, Jacob Philip^4, Philip^3, Nicholas^2, Mathieu^1), born Apr 1878. He married Elizabeth Morrison, born abt 1884; died 11 Mar 1952 in Monroe Co., NY.

Children of Charles H Bovee and Elizabeth Morrison were as follows:

2890   i   Morrison C^8 **Bovee**, born 8 Jan 1902; died 23 Oct 1967 in Ticonderoga, Essex Co., NY. He married **(---) Laureen**.

1812. Frederick Germond^7 **Bovee** (Nicholas^6, John^5, Jacob Philip^4, Philip^3, Nicholas^2, Mathieu^1), born abt 1855 in Rawsonville, Wayne Co., MI; died 25 Apr 1935 in Plymouth, Wayne Co., MI. He married on 13 Dec 1883 Elsie L Bridger, born 22 Dec 1857 in Sumpter Twp., Wayne Co., MI; died 1 Nov 1946 in Wayne Co., MI, daughter of William Bridger and Caroline Eddy.

Children of Frederick Germond Bovee and Elsie L Bridger were as follows:

2891   i   Minnie^8 **Bovee**, born 28 Apr 1885; died 16 Jan 1906.

+ 2892   ii   Charles Henry^8 **Bovee**, born 4 Jun 1887 in Rawsonville, Wayne Co., MI; died 16 Dec 1951 in Novi, Oakland Co., MI. He married (1) **Tena Louise Packard**; (2) **Ina (---)**; (3) **Nina May Weber**.

2893   iii   Earl Lee^8 **Bovee**, born 23 Dec 1895; died 23 Oct 1952. He married (1) on 20 Oct 1920 **Mabel Lewis**; (2) on 3 Aug 1935 **Marie Higgens**; (3) on 21 Jul 1945 **Gertrude Longhurst**.

1813. Alfretta^7 **Bovee** (Nicholas^6, John^5, Jacob Philip^4, Philip^3, Nicholas^2, Mathieu^1), born 12 Aug 1861 in Ypsilanti, Washtenaw Co., MI; died 21 Mar 1943 in Wayne Co., MI. She married on 18 Jun 1879 Frederick Forsythe.

Children of Alfretta Bovee and Frederick Forsythe were as follows:

2894   i   Ernest^8 **Forsythe**.

1815. John Edwin^7 **Bovee** (Edwin Henry^6, John^5, Jacob Philip^4, Philip^3, Nicholas^2, Mathieu^1), born 16 Jul 1866 in Johnson Co., IA; died 11 Jun 1955. He married on 12 Jun 1890 Bessie A Babcock, born 31 Dec 1868 in Washington Co., IA; died 10 Jan 1907, daughter of Nathan L Babcock and Ophelia Smith.

Children of John Edwin Bovee and Bessie A Babcock were as follows:

2895   i   Viola Charlotta^8 **Bovee**, born 1891; died abt 1891.

2896   ii   Edith^8 **Bovee**, born May 1892 in IA. She married **Glenn S Zaring**.

+ 2897   iii   Nathan H^8 **Bovee**, born 6 Nov 1894 in IA; died 22 Mar 1964 in Tucson, Pima Co., AZ. He married **Vera Lucille Crosby**.

2898   iv   Henry^8 **Bovee**, born abt 1896.

2899   v   Bessie B^8 **Bovee**, born 19 Jun 1897 in IA. She married on

1818. Beatrice Ann[7] **Bovee** (Joseph W[6], John[5], Jacob Philip[4], Philip[3], Nicholas[2], Mathieu[1]), born 10 Apr 1874 in Morenci, Lewanee Co., MI. She married Byron Silvernail, born abt 1874 in Hudson, Lenawee Co., MI.

Children of Beatrice Ann Bovee and Byron Silvernail were as follows:

2900	i	Inez M[8] **Silvernail**, born 1898.
2901	ii	Jason W[8] **Silvernail**, born abt 1902.
2902	iii	Levi Byron[8] **Silvernail**, born 20 Mar 1903 in Lawton, Van Buren Co., MI; died 13 Nov 1960 in San Bernardino, San Bernardino Co., CA.
2903	iv	Elgie L[8] **Silvernail**, born 18 Apr 1904 in MI; died 31 Oct 1963 in Chico, Butte Co., CA.
2904	v	Irene B[8] **Silvernail**, born abt 1907.
2905	vi	Lyle A[8] **Silvernail**, born abt 1910.

1824. Frank J[7] **Bovee** (Francis M[6], John[5], Jacob Philip[4], Philip[3], Nicholas[2], Mathieu[1]), born Jan 1868 in MI. He married Clara Bartholomew.

Children of Frank J Bovee and Clara Bartholomew were as follows:

| 2906 | i | Pearl D[8] **Bovee**, born 8 Jul 1898; died 24 Jun 1984. She married (1) unknown; (2) **Emil O Bluhm**, born 14 Oct 1897; died 24 Jul 1972. |

1828. Freeman[7] **Bovee** (Charles P[6], Nicholas[5], Jacob Philip[4], Philip[3], Nicholas[2], Mathieu[1]), born Jul 1864 in MI. He married Abbie Terry, born Dec 1865 in OH.

Children of Freeman Bovee and Abbie Terry were as follows:

+	2907	i	Charles[8] **Bovee**, born 17 May 1886 in MI; died Jul 1966 in Cleveland, Cuyahoga Co., OH. He married **Mertie Esther Booker**.
+	2908	ii	Forest F[8] **Bovee**, born 14 May 1892 in Seneca Twp., Lenawee Co., MI; died 17 Jan 1948 in Seneca Twp., Lenawee Co., MI. He married **Helena Lemke**.
	2909	iii	Nora[8] **Bovee**, born 2 Jun 1893.
+	2910	iv	Uvah[8] **Bovee**, died 1954. She married **Leo Driscoll**.

1830. Seymour Nelson[7] **Bovee** (Nelson H[6], Nicholas[5], Jacob Philip[4], Philip[3], Nicholas[2], Mathieu[1]), born 25 Jun 1868 in Lenawee Co., MI; died 28 Dec 1953 in Detroit, Wayne Co., MI. He married on 17 Sep 1894 in Adrian, Lewanee Co., MI Bertha H Votzka, born Oct 1874 in Germany; died 1945, daughter of John Votzka and Fredricka Sholtz.

Children of Seymour Nelson Bovee and Bertha H Votzka were as follows:

+ 2911 i Fern[8] **Bovee**, born May 1896. She married **Ray D Post**.
+ 2912 ii Faye[8] **Bovee**, born Jan 1898 in MI. She married **Paul H Glaumer**.
    2913 iii Beula L[8] **Bovee**, born 1899; died Jan 1940.
    2914 iv Hazel W[8] **Bovee**, born 1904; died 3 Jan 1940. She married **Clare Tuttle**, born 1898; died 1950.
+ 2915 v Max Nelson[8] **Bovee**, born 1906 in MI; died 1963. He married **Irena Elsie Benfield**.

1832. Cora Bell[7] **Bovee** (Nelson H[6], Nicholas[5], Jacob Philip[4], Philip[3], Nicholas[2], Mathieu[1]), born 11 Oct 1876 in Seneca, Lenawee Co., MI; died 1960. She married Clyde L Onweller, born Sep 1876 in OH; died 1964.

Children of Cora Bell Bovee and Clyde L Onweller were as follows:
    2916 i Burton L[8] **Onweller**, born 2 Jan 1912 in OH.

1835. Floyd B[7] **Bovee** (Nelson H[6], Nicholas[5], Jacob Philip[4], Philip[3], Nicholas[2], Mathieu[1]), born Apr 1884 in MI; died 1948. He married (1) Mable Darling, born abt 1893 in OH; (2) Effie Humble.

Children of Floyd B Bovee and Mable Darling were as follows:
    2917 i Merritt[8] **Bovee**, born 18 Oct 1911 in OH; died Dec 1982 in Sylvania, Lucas Co., OH.
    2918 ii Mack[8] **Bovee**, born 19 Aug 1913; died 6 Oct 1913.
+ 2919 iii Miner[8] **Bovee**, born abt 1914. He married **Myrtle Clingingpeel**.
    2920 iv Donald[8] **Bovee**, born 1917; died 22 Apr 1931.
    2921 v Dale[8] **Bovee**, born 1918.
    2922 vi Mildred[8] **Bovee**, born 1919; died 1988. She married **Donald Dennis**, born 1909; died 1970.
    2923 vii Clarence C[8] **Bovee**, born Oct 1920; died 6 Jan 1921.

Children of Floyd B Bovee and Effie Humble were as follows:
    2924 i Vonnie[8] **Bovee**.
    2925 ii William O'Neal[8] **Bovee**.

1836. Charles Henry[7] **Bovee** (Nelson H[6], Nicholas[5], Jacob Philip[4], Philip[3], Nicholas[2], Mathieu[1]), born May 1885 in MI; died 1 Oct 1940. He married (1) abt 1910 Verlie Seevey, born 7 May 1884; died 1939; (2) abt 1914 Effie Roop, born 14 Oct 1887; died 14 Apr 1969 in Risingsun, Wood Co., OH.

Children of Charles Henry Bovee and Verlie Seevey were as follows:
    2926 i Ossie John[8] **Bovee**, born 16 Feb 1911; died Dec 1978 in

Children of Charles Henry Bovee and Effie Roop were as follows:

2927   i   Ira Dell^8 **Bovee**, born 24 Mar 1915; died Jun 1972 in Swanton, Fulton Co., OH. He married **Leta (---)**.

+ 2928   ii   Sidney Richard^8 **Bovee**, born 26 Sep 1915 in Whitehouse, Lucas Co., OH; died 27 Feb 1985 in Walbridge, Wood Co., OH. He married **Beatrice Irene Harmon**.

+ 2929   iii   Raymond Lewis^8 **Bovee**, born 17 Apr 1919; died Jul 1985 in Toledo, Lucas Co., OH. He married (1) **Genevieve (---)**; (2) **Helen (---)**.

+ 2930   iv   Eskell Charles^8 **Bovee**, born 13 Feb 1921 in OH; died Feb 1967. He married unknown.

1842. Jeremiah W^7 **Bovee** (William R^6, Daniel R^5, Nicholas P^4, Philip^3, Nicholas^2, Mathieu^1), born 22 Apr 1839 in NY. He married Maria Hungerford, born abt 1848 in NY, daughter of Henry Hungerford and Nancy (---).

Children of Jeremiah W Bovee and Maria Hungerford were as follows:

+ 2931   i   Charles D^8 **Bovee**, born abt 1867 in PA. He married **Frances J Twichell**.

1843. Daniel Reynolds^7 **Bovee** (William R^6, Daniel R^5, Nicholas P^4, Philip^3, Nicholas^2, Mathieu^1), born 10 Feb 1840 in Gainesville, Wyoming Co., NY; died 21 Jun 1926 in Lowville, Erie Co., PA. He married on 3 Jul 1864 in Corry, Erie Co., PA Lucina Raymond, born 8 Mar 1845 in Greenfield, Erie Co., PA; died 12 May 1931 in Wattsburg, Erie Co., PA, daughter of Silas Raymond and Sarah Smith.

Children of Daniel Reynolds Bovee and Lucina Raymond were as follows:

+ 2932   i   Ada C^8 **Bovee**, born 23 Jul 1866 in Erie Co., PA; died Apr 1957 in Washington, DC. She married (1) **Fred E Allen**; (2) **Prof Victor C Zebley**.

+ 2933   ii   June Raymond^8 **Bovee**, born 11 Jul 1870 in Greenfield, Erie Co., PA; died 20 Jun 1952 in Elizabethtown, Lancaster Co., PA. He married **Mabel Maria Cook**.

+ 2934   iii   Irl C^8 **Bovee**, born 23 Oct 1882 in Erie Co., PA. He married **Sarah Chess**.

1846. Charles Dexter^7 **Bovee** (William R^6, Daniel R^5, Nicholas P^4, Philip^3, Nicholas^2, Mathieu^1), born 12 Oct 1846 in Springville, Erie Co., NY; died 6 Dec 1923 in Erie, Erie Co., PA. He married on 21 Apr 1872 in N Springville, Erie Co., PA Almira E Smith, born 30 Aug 1845 in N Springville, Erie Co., PA; died 6 Nov 1920 in Swanville, Erie Co., PA, daughter of Lyman Smith and Hannah Brown.

Children of Charles Dexter Bovee and Almira E Smith were as follows:

+	2935	i	Glenn Dexter^8 **Bovee**, born 1 Mar 1873 in N Springfield, Erie Co., PA; died 8 Dec 1959 in Swanville, Erie Co., PA. He married **Jesse Tuttle**.
+	2936	ii	Harriet M^8 **Bovee**, born 29 Jul 1874 in N Springfield, Erie Co., PA; died 3 May 1964 in E Springfield, Erie Co., PA. She married (1) **Jonas Spencer Parker**; (2) **Charles Pickney**.
	2937	iii	Nellie G^8 **Bovee**, born 6 May 1877 in N Springfield, Erie Co., PA; died 8 Feb 1938 in Ionia, Ionia Co., MI. She married **Lyman Simmons**.
	2938	iv	Lyman S^8 **Bovee**, born 22 Dec 1879 in N Springfield, Erie Co., PA; died Aug 1973 in FL. He married **Eleanor Rollins**, died 1955.
+	2939	v	Frederick Charles^8 **Bovee**, born 24 Dec 1881 in N Springfield, Erie Co., PA; died 9 May 1957 in Erie, Erie Co., PA. He married **Mayme Esther Parker**.
	2940	vi	Aris R^8 **Bovee**, born 14 Sep 1884 in N Springfield, Erie Co., PA; died 2 Oct 1960 in E Springfield, Erie Co., PA. She married **Fred Egan**.
+	2941	vii	Ida E^8 **Bovee**, born 28 Apr 1887 in N Springfield, Erie Co., PA; died 1957. She married **Jacob Seib**.

1848. Mary Jane^7 **Bovee** (Nicholas^6, Jacob^5, Nicholas P^4, Philip^3, Nicholas^2, Mathieu^1), born 9 Sep 1830 in Chautauqua Co., NY; died 28 Sep 1861. She married on 8 Jul 1847 Amos Benton, born abt 1820, son of Herman Benton and Charlotte Morse.

Children of Mary Jane Bovee and Amos Benton were as follows:

	2942	i	Pauline^8 **Benton**, born 3 Jun 1848.
	2943	ii	Emma^8 **Benton**, born 3 Jun 1852.
	2944	iii	Helen W^8 **Benton**, born 23 Apr 1855 in IL; died 27 Jul 1871 in Clinton Co., MI.
	2945	iv	Edwin W^8 **Benton**, born 19 Nov 1858.

1849. Harper W^7 **Bovee** (Nicholas^6, Jacob^5, Nicholas P^4, Philip^3, Nicholas^2, Mathieu^1), born 21 Feb 1832 in Chautauqua Co., NY; died 30 Nov 1916. He married on 21 Feb 1853 Susan Benton, born 1833 in OH.

Children of Harper W Bovee and Susan Benton were as follows:

	2946	i	Clara^8 **Bovee**, born 30 Oct 1866 in OH.
+	2947	ii	Edward C^8 **Bovee**, born 2 Jul 1869. He married **Jennie M (---)**.
+	2948	iii	George A^8 **Bovee**, born 2 Nov 1873 in OH. He married **Ruth (---)**.
	2949	iv	Curtis Mathew^8 **Bovee**, born 12 Jun 1875 in OH; died 8 Oct 1948 in Los Angeles, Los Angeles Co., CA. He

married **Ida M**.

1850. Lorenzo Dow[7] **Bovee** (Nicholas[6], Jacob[5], Nicholas P[4], Philip[3], Nicholas[2], Mathieu[1]), born 17 Jan 1834 in Edmeston, Otsego Co., NY; died 25 Apr 1911 in Miami, Dade Co., FL. He married on 23 Sep 1863 in Bloomington, McLean Co., IL Ellen G Goodrich, born 20 Apr 1843 in Edmeston, Ostego Co., NY; died 15 Aug 1933 in Monte Vista, Rio Grande Co., CO, daughter of David F Goodrich.

Children of Lorenzo Dow Bovee and Ellen G Goodrich were as follows:

+ 2950   i   Floyd D[8] **Bovee**, born 8 Jun 1864 in Grundy Co.,IL; died 2 Sep 1914 in Durando, La Plata Co., CO. He married **Fanny D Kirby**.

   2951   ii   Fred Nicholas[8] **Bovee**, born 26 Dec 1869 in Chetopa, Labette Co., KS; died 28 Sep 1949 in Denison, Grayson Co., TX.

+ 2952   iii   Nella B[8] **Bovee**, born 12 Dec 1871 in Chetopa, Labette Co., KS; died 18 Nov 1938 in Antonito, Conejos Co., CO. She married **Alfred LaMar Strawn**.

   2953   iv   Vida[8] **Bovee**, born 7 Aug 1874 in Chetopa, Labette Co., KS; died 1933 in Pagos Springs, Archuleta Co., KS.

   2954   v   Zone N[8] **Bovee**, born 10 Dec 1876 in Chetopa, Labette Co., KS; died 1918 in Durando, La Plata Co., CO. He married abt 1900 **Cora Greene**, born abt 1880.

1851. Eunice S[7] **Bovee** (Nicholas[6], Jacob[5], Nicholas P[4], Philip[3], Nicholas[2], Mathieu[1]), born 10 Dec 1835 in Ashtabula Co., OH; died 18 Sep 1883. She married on 23 Nov 1854 Alex Loucks.

Children of Eunice S Bovee and Alex Loucks were as follows:

   2955   i   Ida[8] **Loucks**, born 15 Oct 1855.

   2956   ii   Della[8] **Loucks**, born 4 Oct 1856.

   2957   iii   Alton[8] **Loucks**, born 12 Feb 1858; died 21 Jan 1940.

   2958   iv   Nora[8] **Loucks**, born 12 Feb 1860.

   2959   v   Charles[8] **Loucks**, born 25 Aug 1863 in Jackson Twp., Will Co., IL; died 21 Dec 1927.

   2960   vi   Milton Scott[8] **Loucks**, born 25 Jun 1865 in Elwood, Will Co., IL; died 19 Jan 1946.

   2961   vii   Hattie[8] **Loucks**, born 22 Jun 1872 in Jackson Twp., Will Co., IL.

1852. Hannah Marie[7] **Bovee** (Nicholas[6], Jacob[5], Nicholas P[4], Philip[3], Nicholas[2], Mathieu[1]), born 23 Sep 1837 in Ashtabula Co., OH; died 12 Jan 1918. She married Benjamin Cahoon.

Children of Hannah Marie Bovee and Benjamin Cahoon were as follows:

2962	i	Franklin Henry[8] **Cahoon**, born 20 Nov 1859.
2963	ii	Ella Louise[8] **Cahoon**, born 11 Nov 1861 in Elwood, Will Co., IL.
2964	iii	Ulysses Grant[8] **Cahoon**, born 6 Aug 1864 in Elwood, Will Co., IL.
2965	iv	Florence[8] **Cahoon**, born 9 Jun 1868 in Elwood, Will Co., IL.
2966	v	Elmer S[8] **Cahoon**, born 14 Dec 1874 in Elwood, Will Co., IL.

1853. Emily E[7] **Bovee** (Nicholas[6], Jacob[5], Nicholas P[4], Philip[3], Nicholas[2], Mathieu[1]), born 11 Jun 1840 in Ashtabula Co., OH; died 3 Feb 1923. She married (1) on 4 Nov 1857 Antone Lahmar; (2) on 11 Oct 1863 Abner Loucks; (3) Charles Wilkins; (4) on 2 May 1893 John Kanagy.

Children of Emily E Bovee and Antone Lahmar were as follows:

2967	i	Adelbert[8] **Lahmar**, born 8 Sep 1858; died 26 Apr 1906.

Children of Emily E Bovee and Abner Loucks were as follows:

2968	i	Anna[8] **Loucks**, born 9 Aug 1865; died Jul 1937.
2969	ii	George[8] **Loucks**, born 21 Dec 1867; died 22 Feb 1925.
2970	iii	Julia[8] **Loucks**, born 13 Sep 1874.

Children of Emily E Bovee and Charles Wilkins were as follows:

2971	i	Clarence[8] **Wilkins**.
2972	ii	George[8] **Wilkins**.

1854. Harriet Augusta[7] **Bovee** (Nicholas[6], Jacob[5], Nicholas P[4], Philip[3], Nicholas[2], Mathieu[1]), born 24 Jun 1845 in Ashtabula Co., OH; died 3 Apr 1925 in Morris, Grundy Co., IL. She married on 30 Oct 1863 George Wickes.

Children of Harriet Augusta Bovee and George Wickes were as follows:

2973	i	Carrie E[8] **Wickes**, born 8 Jun 1868.
2974	ii	Minnie Mae[8] **Wickes**, born 4 Jun 1871.
2975	iii	Fred Clinton[8] **Wickes**, born 19 Dec 1875.
2976	iv	George C[8] **Wickes**, born 21 Sep 1876; died 12 Jun 1878.
2977	v	Athuur Frank[8] **Wickes**, born 17 Jul 1880.
2978	vi	Grace G[8] **Wickes**, born 27 Aug 1884.

1855. Harmon E[7] **Bovee** (Nicholas[6], Jacob[5], Nicholas P[4], Philip[3], Nicholas[2], Mathieu[1]), born 8 Oct 1847 in Kingsville, Ashtabula Co., OH; died 15 May 1910. He married on 8 Jan 1871 Marietta Wickes, born 28 Oct 1852.

Children of Harmon E Bovee and Marietta Wickes were as follows:

2979	i	Edwin F[8] **Bovee**, born 8 Jun 1872 in Jackson, Will Co., IL; died 7 Jan 1916.

2979   i   Edwin F[8] **Bovee**, born 8 Jun 1872 in Jackson, Will Co., IL; died 7 Jan 1916.

+   2980   ii   Charles H[8] **Bovee**, born 21 May 1874 in Jackson, Will Co., IL; died 7 Dec 1949. He married **Una Agnes Blair**.

+   2981   iii   Guy Clinton[8] **Bovee**, born 24 Apr 1877; died 26 Feb 1934 in Jackson, Will Co., IL. He married **Emiline C Lorenz**.

    2982   iv   Earl[8] **Bovee**, born 16 Mar 1879; died 15 Jul 1922. He married (1) on 12 Nov 1902 **Jessie M McIntyre**; (2) on 14 Feb 1920 **Alice Fairchild**.

    2983   v   Florence E[8] **Bovee**, born 17 Jan 1881; died 9 Nov 1881.

+   2984   vi   Irving[8] **Bovee**, born 28 Aug 1882; died 21 Jul 1951 in McAllen, Hidalgo Co., TX. He married (1) **Sylvia Hartman**; (2) **Hazel (---)**.

    2985   vii   Jessie[8] **Bovee**, born 12 Sep 1884. She married **Elmer S Colton**.

    2986   viii   Chester A[8] **Bovee**, born 17 Sep 1886. He married on 4 Oct 1911 **Alma Grace Caswell**.

    2987   ix   Harry L[8] **Bovee**, born 4 Nov 1888 in Jackson, Will Co., IL; died Jun 1969 in Elmwood, Peoria Co., IL. He married on 20 Nov 1912 **Ruth Selena Casewell**.

    2988   x   Lulu[8] **Bovee**, born 25 Oct 1890. She married **(---) Harbin**.

    2989   xi   Gladys[8] **Bovee**, born 20 Oct 1895; died 1 Jul 1929.

    2990   xii   Child[8] **Bovee**.

1863. Viola[7] **Bovee** (Harper R[6], Jacob[5], Nicholas P[4], Philip[3], Nicholas[2], Mathieu[1]), born 1854 in MI; died Mar 1929. She married on 11 Sep 1876 in Mecosta Co., MI Paris Banfield.

Children of Viola Bovee and Paris Banfield were as follows:

    2991   i   Harry M[8] **Banfield**, born 7 Aug 1877 in MI; died 14 Oct 1941 in Los Angeles, Los Angeles Co., CA.

1864. Eva Rachel[7] **Bovee** (Harper R[6], Jacob[5], Nicholas P[4], Philip[3], Nicholas[2], Mathieu[1]), born 6 Jun 1858 in Wayne Co., MI; died 1931. She married on 11 Jan 1882 in Mecosta Co., MI George Willard Trowbridge, born 6 Jan 1845 in Troy, Oakland Co., MI; died 19 Oct 1904 in Big Rapids, Mecosta Co., MI, son of A C Trowbridge and Rhoda Postal.

Children of Eva Rachel Bovee and George Willard Trowbridge were as follows:

    2992   i   Willard Fay[8] **Trowbridge**, born 1882; died 1918.

    2993   ii   Nellie[8] **Trowbridge**.

    2994   iii   George[8] **Trowbridge**.

1871. Frank[7] **Bovee** (John C[6], Jacob[5], Nicholas P[4], Philip[3], Nicholas[2], Mathieu[1]), born 11 Mar 1857 in Howard Co., IA. He married on 28 Jul 1886 in Oakland Co., MI Mary E Strator, born Dec 1865 in MI.

Children of Frank Bovee and Mary E Strator were as follows:

2995	i	Bertha Mae^8 **Bovee**, born Jul 1887.
2996	ii	Charles A^8 **Bovee**, born Nov 1889.

1872. Frank E^7 **Bovee** (Daniel^6, Jacob^5, Nicholas P^4, Philip^3, Nicholas^2, Mathieu^1), born 2 Nov 1847 in WI; died 9 Jun 1917 in Rochester, Monroe Co., NY. He married Flora Cole, born Mar 1847 in Canada, daughter of (---) Cole and Cornelia (---).

Children of Frank E Bovee and Flora Cole were as follows:

+	2997	i	Hattie^8 **Bovee**, born Sep 1869 in Canada. She married **Raymond Harris**.

1878. Norman^7 **Bovee** Jr (Norman^6, Harper^5, Nicholas P^4, Philip^3, Nicholas^2, Mathieu^1), born abt 1845 in NY; died abt 1899. He married on 19 Feb 1866 in Will Co., IL Addie S Green, born abt 1843 in PA.

Children of Norman Bovee Jr and Addie S Green were as follows:

2998	i	Emma^8 **Bovee**, born abt 1867 in IL. She married on 15 Oct 1885 in Lake Co., IN **Edwim M Stockwell**.
2999	ii	Addie Bell^8 **Bovee**, born abt 1870 in IL. She married on 7 Feb 1893 in Will Co., IL **Ward Hunt**.
3000	iii	Fred V^8 **Bovee**, born abt 1874 in IL; died 10 Jun 1940 in East Chicago, Lake Co., IN. He married (1) in 1900 in Wright Co., IA **(---) Moles**; (2) on 27 Jun 1911 in La Porte Co., IN **Catherine W Lahey**.

1879. Alson L^7 **Bovee** (Norman^6, Harper^5, Nicholas P^4, Philip^3, Nicholas^2, Mathieu^1), born 1847 in NY. He married on 19 Nov 1867 in Willmington, Will Co., IL Sarah Jane Stebbins, born May 1844 in MN.

Children of Alson L Bovee and Sarah Jane Stebbins were as follows:

3001	i	Agnes Permelia^8 **Bovee**, born abt 1868 in Dakota Territory.
3002	ii	Jennie Amorette^8 **Bovee**, born 1870 in Dakota Territory.
3003	iii	Alson Norman^8 **Bovee**, born abt 1874 in Dakota Territory.
3004	iv	Sadie Ellen^8 **Bovee**, born Feb 1878 in SD.
3005	v	Mary^8 **Bovee**, born abt 1882; died 1893.
3006	vi	Lelia M^8 **Bovee**, born Apr 1885.
3007	vii	June A^8 **Bovee**, born Jun 1888.

1880. Charles Elliott[7] **Bovee** (Harmon[6], Harper[5], Nicholas P[4], Philip[3], Nicholas[2], Mathieu[1]), born 23 Apr 1851 in Pennline, Crawford Co., PA. He married Clara (---), born 1851 in VT.

Children of Charles Elliott Bovee and Clara (---) were as follows:

+ 3008   i   Arthur C[8] **Bovee**, born abt 1872 in WI. He married **Florence Weakens**.

1881. Lydia Jane[7] **Bovee** (Harmon[6], Harper[5], Nicholas P[4], Philip[3], Nicholas[2], Mathieu[1]), born 7 Aug 1854 in Pennline, Crawford Co., PA. She married (1) (---) Winslow, born Mar 1862 in Canada; (2) bef 1900 Hugh McMillan, born Mar 1862 in Canada.

Children of Lydia Jane Bovee and (---) Winslow were as follows:

3009   i   Frederick Bertie[8] **Winslow**, born 10 Mar 1871 in WI; died 24 Feb 1942 in Los Angeles, Los Angeles Co., CA.

1882. George Edmond[7] **Bovee** (Harmon[6], Harper[5], Nicholas P[4], Philip[3], Nicholas[2], Mathieu[1]), born 21 Apr 1857 in Rockville, Kankakee Co., IL. He married Verna M (---), born Jul 1858 in WV.

Children of George Edmond Bovee and Verna M (---) were as follows:

3010   i   Jennie E[8] **Bovee**, born Nov 1892 in MN.

1883. William Harmon[7] **Bovee** (Harmon[6], Harper[5], Nicholas P[4], Philip[3], Nicholas[2], Mathieu[1]), born 16 Apr 1863 in Hammond, St Croix Co., WI. He married Nellie B (---), born Jul 1866 in Canada.

Children of William Harmon Bovee and Nellie B (---) were as follows:

3011   i   Nallie G[8] **Bovee**, born 1891 in MN.

1893. Catherine[7] **Bovee** (Eliad E[6], Jacob Nicholas[5], Nicholas Jacob[4], Jacob[3], Nicholas[2], Mathieu[1]), born abt 1837 in Saratoga Co., NY. She married on 7 Mar 1865 in Washtenaw Co., MI Edward Pelton.

Children of Catherine Bovee and Edward Pelton were as follows:

3012   i   William[8] **Pelton**, born 27 Nov 1865.
3013   ii   Hattie[8] **Pelton**, born 4 Jul 1866.

1895. John N[7] **Bovee** (Eliad E[6], Jacob Nicholas[5], Nicholas Jacob[4], Jacob[3], Nicholas[2], Mathieu[1]), born abt 1843 in Charlton, Saratoga Co., NY; died bef 1915. He married Ann Elizabeth Shivley, born in PA.

Children of John N Bovee and Ann Elizabeth Shivley were as follows:

3014　i　　Frank Gervias^8 **Bovee**, born 1869; died 1896.

+　3015　ii　　Arthur Gibbon^8 **Bovee**, born 17 Feb 1882 in Washington, DC; died 6 May 1961 in Aiken, Aiken Co., SC. He married (1) **Martha L (---)**; (2) **Julia Lyons**.

1897. Eliad A^7 **Bovee** (Eliad E^6, Jacob Nicholas^5, Nicholas Jacob^4, Jacob^3, Nicholas^2, Mathieu^1), born 3 Jul 1848 in Glenville Twp., Schenectady Co., NY; died 23 Jan 1917 in Ypsilanti, Washtenaw Co., MI. He married on 2 Jan 1867 in Northville, Wayne Co., MI Jennie L Cady, born 23 Jan 1851 in MI; died 23 Sep 1913 in Ypsilanti, Washtenaw Co., MI, daughter of Daniel Cady and Lucinda Williams Knapp.

Children of Eliad A Bovee and Jennie L Cady were as follows:

+　3016　i　　Frank M^8 **Bovee**, born Jan 1868 in Northville Wayne Co., MI. He married **Mary S (---)**.

3017　ii　　Helen N^8 **Bovee**, born 2 Feb 1879 in Northville Wayne Co., MI.

1905. Howard L^7 **Bovee** (Eliad E^6, Jacob Nicholas^5, Nicholas Jacob^4, Jacob^3, Nicholas^2, Mathieu^1), born Jul 1869 in MI. He married Nettie Blanch Farwell, born 28 Mar 1870; died 17 Jan 1955, daughter of Ruben Farwell and Ann E Knickerbocker.

Children of Howard L Bovee and Nettie Blanch Farwell were as follows:

3018　i　　Bonabell^8 **Bovee**. She married **(---) Fazzha**.

3019　ii　　Harold B^8 **Bovee**, born 24 Sep 1902 in MI; died 20 Oct 1994 in New Hudson, Oakland Co., MI. He married **Ruth L Wright**.

1907. Stillman^7 **Bovee** (Mathew J^6, Jacob Nicholas^5, Nicholas Jacob^4, Jacob^3, Nicholas^2, Mathieu^1), born Mar 1850 in Saratoga Co., NY. He married Josephine (---), born Jul 1851 in WI.

Children of Stillman Bovee and Josephine (---) were as follows:

3020　i　　Frederick G^8 **Bovee**, born Aug 1876 in IL.

3021　ii　　Frank J^8 **Bovee**, born 1879 in IL; died 7 Jan 1893 in Chicago, Cook Co., IL.

+　3022　iii　　James Henry^8 **Bovee**, born 16 Jul 1881 in IL; died Feb 1968 in Dunellen, Middlesex Co., NJ. He married **Martha (---)**.

3023　iv　　Katherine M^8 **Bovee**, born Jun 1883 in IL; died 27 Sep 1900 in Chicago, Cook Co., IL.

+　3024　v　　William A^8 **Bovee**, born 13 Jan 1890 in Chicago, Cook Co., IL; died Feb 1965. He married **Georgia Rose**.

3025　vi　　Stillman V^8 **Bovee**, born 25 May 1893 in Chicago, Cook Co., IL; died 22 Dec 1908 in Chicago, Cook Co., IL.

1910. John M^7 **Bovee** (Isaac^6, Jacob Nicholas^5, Nicholas Jacob^4, Jacob^3, Nicholas^2, Mathieu^1), born Apr 1850 in Charlton, Saratoga Co., NY. He married abt 1875 Ida M Houghton, born Jul 1858 in MI.

Children of John M Bovee and Ida M Houghton were as follows:

+ 3026 i Guy A^8 **Bovee**, born Oct 1875 in Woodland, Barry Co., MI; died 30 Mar 1916. He married **Minnie E Gilson**.
  3027 ii Jay^8 **Bovee**, born Jun 1876 in Woodland, Barry Co., MI.
  3028 iii Child^8 **Bovee**.

1913. Jacob^7 **Bovee** (Isaac^6, Jacob Nicholas^5, Nicholas Jacob^4, Jacob^3, Nicholas^2, Mathieu^1), born 1858 in Plynouth, Wayne co., MI; died abt 1886. He married Cora A Hotchkiss, born Nov 1862 in MI.

Children of Jacob Bovee and Cora A Hotchkiss were as follows:

+ 3029 i Lyle J^8 **Bovee**, born 21 Mar 1887 in MI; died Sep 1968 in Lowell, Kent Co., MI. He married **Mabel Keyser**.

1927. Christian^7 **Bovee** (Peter^6, Peter^5, Jacob^4, Jacob^3, Nicholas^2, Mathieu^1), born 18 Aug 1843 in Kingston, Ulster Co., NY; died 18 Mar 1908 in Dayton, Montgomery Co., OH. He married abt 1867 in Woodstock, Ulster Co., NY Jane Jay, born 1851 in NY; died 19 Feb 1897 in Roland, Pike Co., PA.

Children of Christian Bovee and Jane Jay were as follows:

+ 3030 i Clara^8 **Bovee**, born 24 Jul 1868 in NY. She married **Sidney Garrison**.
  3031 ii Arthur^8 **Bovee**, born 1871 in PA.
+ 3032 iii John Addison^8 **Bovee**, born 5 Apr 1873 in PA; died Apr 1942. He married (1) **Peets Sarah Baker**; (2) **Jennie M Brown**.
  3033 iv Alfred^8 **Bovee**, born 5 Apr 1875 in PA.
  3034 v Jennie^8 **Bovee**, born 29 Sep 1878 in PA.
  3035 vi Lida^8 **Bovee**, born 28 Jun 1882.
  3036 vii Alvina^8 **Bovee**, born 30 May 1885.
  3037 viii Charles^8 **Bovee**, born 1 May 1888.
  3038 ix William B^8 **Bovee**, born 6 Jun 1894; died Feb 1979 in Bath, Steuben Co., NY.

1931. Lorenzo^7 **Bovee** (Peter^6, Peter^5, Jacob^4, Jacob^3, Nicholas^2, Mathieu^1), born Oct 1854. He married in Oct 1889 Jennie Wood, born Apr 1869.

Children of Lorenzo Bovee and Jennie Wood were as follows:

+ 3039 i Ethel E^8 **Bovee**, born 31 Mar 1891 in Bethel, Sullivan Co.,

NY; died 10 Aug 1972. She married **Aldon M McCrabie**.

+ 3040 ii Chauncy William[8] **Bovee**, born 7 Sep 1892 in Long Eddy, Sullivan Co., NY; died Jan 1978 in Waltron, Delaware Co., NY. He married **Mildred Roberta King MacRabie**.

+ 3041 iii Edith M[8] **Bovee**, born Jun 1895. She married **Paul Krause**.

3042 iv Mabel Eliza[8] **Bovee**, born 24 Nov 1897; died 19 Sep 1898.

3043 v Ira McKinley[8] **Bovee**, born 27 Oct 1899 in NY; died 5 Mar 1917.

+ 3044 vi Harold Mark[8] **Bovee**, born abt 1903; died 1924 in Orange Co., NY. He married **Emma Caskey**.

1932. Samuel[7] **Bovee** (Peter[6], Peter[5], Jacob[4], Jacob[3], Nicholas[2], Mathieu[1]), born Mar 1857. He married in 1882 Nina J (---), born Apr 1867 in PA.

Children of Samuel Bovee and Nina J (---) were as follows:

3045 i Louis C[8] **Bovee**, born Jun 1883 in PA.

3046 ii Florence[8] **Bovee**, born Dec 1887 in Long Island, New York Co., NY.

3047 iii LeRoy[8] **Bovee**, born 1890; died 1892.

3048 iv Inez[8] **Bovee**, born Sep 1893 in NY.

3049 v Myrtle[8] **Bovee**, born 8 Dec 1898 in NY.

3050 vi Lester[8] **Bovee**, born 27 Feb 1902; died Oct 1975.

1933. George A[7] **Bovee** (Jacob Clayton[6], Peter[5], Jacob[4], Jacob[3], Nicholas[2], Mathieu[1]), born 15 Apr 1837 in Greene Co., NY. He married Mary Geddes.

Children of George A Bovee and Mary Geddes were as follows:

3051 i Richard C[8] **Bovee**. He married abt 1890 **Ida P Merritt**.

+ 3052 ii Lewis B[8] **Bovee**, born Jun 1868; died 1948. He married **Anna C Rightmeyer**.

3053 iii Etta[8] **Bovee**.

+ 3054 iv Ernest Winchel[8] **Bovee**, born 25 Nov 1872; died 23 Sep 1958. He married **Lucretia M Buckbee**.

3055 v Irving[8] **Bovee**, born 19 Apr 1878 in CT; died Feb 1966 in St Petersburg, Pinellas Co., FL.

3056 vi Sarah[8] **Bovee**.

3057 vii William[8] **Bovee**.

3058 viii Julia[8] **Bovee**.

3059 ix Mary[8] **Bovee**.

1934. Pliny L[7] **Bovee** (Jacob Clayton[6], Peter[5], Jacob[4], Jacob[3], Nicholas[2], Mathieu[1]), born 2 Apr 1841 in Ulster Co., NY. He married on 2 Apr 1864 Melissa Longendyke, born 2 Jul 1845 in NY, daughter of James Longendyke and Sara

Burhans.

Children of Pliny L Bovee and Melissa Longendyke were as follows:

+   3060   i   Franklin[8] **Bovee**, born 20 Dec 1864 in West Saugerties, Ulster Co., NY. He married **Grace DeWitt**.

     3061   ii   Frederick[8] **Bovee**, born 18 Jun 1868 in West Saugerties, Ulster Co., NY; died 19 Apr 1880.

+   3062   iii   Nelson[8] **Bovee**, born 4 Dec 1879 in West Saugerties, Ulster Co., NY. He married **Bertha Ostrander**.

1935. Jacob Henry[7] **Bovee** (Jacob Clayton[6], Peter[5], Jacob[4], Jacob[3], Nicholas[2], Mathieu[1]), born 1843 in Ulster Co., NY; died 22 Jun 1919 in Saugerties, Ulster Co., NY.. He married Sarah Brink, born abt 1848; died 14 Jun 1911.

Children of Jacob Henry Bovee and Sarah Brink were as follows:

     3063   i   Emma[8] **Bovee**, born abt 1871.

     3064   ii   Julia[8] **Bovee**, born abt 1875. She married **Burton Morse Spring**.

     3065   iii   Clarence[8] **Bovee**, born abt 1879; died 7 Jun 1925 in Saugerties, Ulster Co., NY..

     3066   iv   Theodore[8] **Bovee**, born 13 May 1886.

+   3067   v   Ward[8] **Bovee**, born 1 May 1887; died Oct 1967 in Haines Falls, Greene Co., NY. He married **Lulu E Schoonmaker**.

1936. Elijah[7] **Bovee** (Jacob Clayton[6], Peter[5], Jacob[4], Jacob[3], Nicholas[2], Mathieu[1]), born May 1846. He married Anna Dederick, born Mar 1851.

Children of Elijah Bovee and Anna Dederick were as follows:

     3068   i   Jennie[8] **Bovee**, born Sep 1874.

     3069   ii   Jessie[8] **Bovee**, born 1877.

     3070   iii   Daisy[8] **Bovee**, born Jul 1878.

     3071   iv   Mary[8] **Bovee**, born Nov 1880.

+   3072   v   Grover[8] **Bovee**, born Apr 1883. He married **Anna Carl**.

1937. Edgar[7] **Bovee** (Jacob Clayton[6], Peter[5], Jacob[4], Jacob[3], Nicholas[2], Mathieu[1]), born 1849 in Saugerties, Ulster Co., NY; died 9 Oct 1896 in Kingston, Ulster Co., NY. He married Alice Russel, born abt 1852; died 22 Sep 1928 in Poughkeepsie, Dutchess Co., NY.

Children of Edgar Bovee and Alice Russel were as follows:

+   3073   i   Charles[8] **Bovee**, born abt 1873 in NY. He married unknown.

     3074   ii   William[8] **Bovee**, born aft 1876.

3075   iii   Elmer[8] **Bovee**, born abt 1880; died 4 Oct 1902 in Saugerties, Ulster Co., NY.

1938. Hiram[7] **Bovee** (Jacob Clayton[6], Peter[5], Jacob[4], Jacob[3], Nicholas[2], Mathieu[1]), born abt 1851; died 1 Nov 1919 in Woodstock, Ulster Co., NY.. He married Martha Kierstede, born Nov 1850; died 1 Mar 1932 in Woodstock, Ulster Co., NY..

Children of Hiram Bovee and Martha Kierstede were as follows:

3076   i   Hattie[8] **Bovee**, born Jun 1882.

3077   ii   Florence[8] **Bovee**, born Oct 1884.

1939. Aldo Harris[7] **Bovee** (Isaac[6], Isaac[5], Jacob[4], Jacob[3], Nicholas[2], Mathieu[1]), born 22 Jan 1845 in OH. He married on 7 Oct 1869 Harriet Lucetta Mugg, born 19 Jan 1841 in Sandusky Co., OH; died 1914 in Elkhart, Elkhart Co., IN, daughter of Rev. Marcus Mugg.

Children of Aldo Harris Bovee and Harriet Lucetta Mugg were as follows:

3078   i   Mabel[8] **Bovee**, born 26 Dec 1879; died 27 Jan 1880.

+ 3079   ii   Mary Philena[8] **Bovee**, born 15 Apr 1883. She married **Frederick Charles Victor Graff**.

1944. William Irvin[7] **Bovee** (Isaac[6], Isaac[5], Jacob[4], Jacob[3], Nicholas[2], Mathieu[1]), born 28 Mar 1854 in Cayahoga Co., OH; died 4 Apr 1928 in Los Angeles, Los Angeles Co., CA. He married on 20 Jun 1881 Mary Etta Young, born 11 Feb 1859 in Centerville, Ontario, Canada, daughter of John Young and Harriet (---).

Children of William Irvin Bovee and Mary Etta Young were as follows:

+ 3080   i   James Ashley[8] **Bovee**, born 23 Mar 1882 in Edwardsburg,Cass Co., MI; died Nov 1983 in Phoenix, Maricopa Co., AZ. He married (1) **Myrtle Eleanor Conrad**; (2) **Mildred Ferguson**.

3081   ii   Etta May[8] **Bovee**, born 20 Oct 1883; died May 1943.

+ 3082   iii   Ransom Young[8] **Bovee**, born 9 Aug 1885 in Edwardsburg,Cass Co., MI; died Aug 1964. He married **Bessie Willeford**.

+ 3083   iv   Harriett Victoria[8] **Bovee**, born 5 Sep 1888 in Albion Boone Co., NE. She married **Sam Hansen**.

3084   v   Royal[8] **Bovee**, born 1890; died abt 1892.

3085   vi   Lillian[8] **Bovee**, born 1892; died abt 1892.

+ 3086   vii   Lacute Ruth[8] **Bovee**, born 12 Feb 1896 in Longmont, Boulder Co., CO; died Oct 1956. She married **Ray Ahbrook Tull**.

+ 3087   viii   Florence Helen[8] **Bovee**, born 25 Aug 1898 in Longmont, Boulder Co., CO. She married **Dr Paul Jon Bostick**.

1946. Edwin Orville[7] **Bovee** (Benjamin[6], Philip[5], Jacob[4], Jacob[3], Nicholas[2], Mathieu[1]), born Jan 1847 in NY. He married on 21 Sep 1867 in Albion Twp., Butler Co., IA Almira R Eggleston, born abt 1845 in NY, daughter of Ambrose Eggleston and M Abby.

Children of Edwin Orville Bovee and Almira R Eggleston were as follows:

+ 3088   i   Delia Minerva[8] **Bovee**, born 8 Sep 1868 in Parkersburg, Butler Co., IA. She married **Frank Huron Loomis**.

1949. Ezra[7] **Bovee** (Jacob[6], Philip[5], Jacob[4], Jacob[3], Nicholas[2], Mathieu[1]), born 20 Oct 1865 in Kane, Kane Co., IL; died 18 Nov 1956 in Sturgis, Meade Co., SD. He married on 18 Jan 1892 in Deadwood, Lawrence Co., SD Lois Lomeda Baker, born 7 Feb 1870 in IA; died 9 Jun 1962, daughter of (---) Baker and Marianne Bolton.

Children of Ezra Bovee and Lois Lomeda Baker were as follows:

+ 3089   i   Myrtle Helen[8] **Bovee**, born 7 Aug 1893 in SD; died 29 Jul 1979. She married **George Vodden**.
+ 3090   ii   Earl Richard[8] **Bovee**, born 1 Feb 1895 in SD; died 16 Feb 1992 in SD. He married **Julia E Sutter**.
   3091   iii   Ester Ruth[8] **Bovee**, born 24 Mar 1897 in Meade Co., SD. She married on 5 Aug 1917 **Gilbert Waterhouse**.
+ 3092   iv   Gladys Elizabeth[8] **Bovee**, born 17 Oct 1899 in Sturgis, Meade Co., SD. She married **Hollis C Dever**.
   3093   v   Hazel Emma[8] **Bovee**, born 16 Sep 1902 in Sturgis, Meade Co., SD; died 2 Jan 1997 in Laramie, Albany Co., WY. She married on 26 Jul 1958 **Isaac Selvig**.
+ 3094   vi   Amos Philip[8] **Bovee**, born 26 Jan 1905 in Sturgis, Meade Co., SD; died 4 Feb 1995. He married **Ethelyn Hershey**.
   3095   vii   Harold Samuel[8] **Bovee**, born 15 Jan 1907 in Sturgis, Meade Co., SD; died 6 Apr 1999 in Sturgis, Meade Co., SD. He married on 15 Sep 1934 **Maxine Seeley**.
   3096   viii   Herbert Ezra[8] **Bovee**, born 8 Aug 1909 in Sturgis, Meade Co., SD; died 6 Apr 1910.
+ 3097   ix   Sumner Eugene[8] **Bovee**, born 15 Jul 1910 in Sturgis, Meade Co., SD; died 12 Mar 1959 in Sturgis, Meade Co., SD. He married **Ester Fruth**.

1972. James V[7] **Bovee** (Abel W[6], Henry[5], Jacob[4], Jacob[3], Nicholas[2], Mathieu[1]), born Feb 1861 in NY. He married (1) Ella Bentley; (2) Marian (---).

Children of James V Bovee and Ella Bentley were as follows:

+ 3098   i   Mary[8] **Bovee**, born abt 1881. She married **Edwin Gardinier**.

1983. Manley S[7] **Bovee** (Marquis[6], Jacob I[5], Isaac[4], Jacob[3], Nicholas[2],
Mathieu[1]), born Oct 1869 in WI. He married (1) Mary W (---), born 1872 in WI;
(2) Martha (---), born Jul 1869; died 21 Jul 1902 in Chicago, Cook Co., IL.

  Children of Manley S Bovee and Martha (---) were as follows:
  3099 i   Robert M[8] **Bovee**, born 2 Mar 1899 in IL; died Jun 1970 in
               Portland, Multmoma Co., OR. He married **Gertrude L (---**
).

1984. Charles A[7] **Bovee** (Marquis[6], Jacob I[5], Isaac[4], Jacob[3], Nicholas[2],
Mathieu[1]), born Nov 1872 in WI. He married Amanda (---), born Jan 1876.

  Children of Charles A Bovee and Amanda (---) were as follows:
  3100 i   Child[8] **Bovee**, born Nov 1899.

1988. Selena Viola[7] **Bovee** (Myndert[6], Daniel[5], Matthew[4], Jacob[3], Nicholas[2],
Mathieu[1]), born 1842 in Lenawee Co., MI. She married (1) on 29 Feb 1860 in
Ionia Co., MI Nathan E Stoughton, born 6 Sep 1836 in MI; died 26 Feb 1872, son
of Samuel Elmer Stoughton and Emily H Park; (2) on 4 Mar 1873 John C
Stoughton, born 13 Jul 1844 in Ionia Co., MI, son of Samuel Elmer Stoughton
and Emily H Park.

  Children of Selena Viola Bovee and Nathan E Stoughton were as follows:
  3101 i   Lila[8] **Stoughton**, born abt 1860 in MI.
  3102 ii   Georgina[8] **Stoughton**, born abt 1864.
  3103 iii   George[8] **Stoughton**, born abt 1865 in MI.
  3104 iv   Grace[8] **Stoughton**, born abt 1865 in MI.

  Children of Selena Viola Bovee and John C Stoughton were as follows:
  3105 i   Elmer B[8] **Stoughton**, born 14 Apr 1879 in Greenville,
               Montcalm Co., MI.

1990. Selinda H[7] **Bovee** (Myndert[6], Daniel[5], Matthew[4], Jacob[3], Nicholas[2],
Mathieu[1]), born 1847. She married in Dec 1865 in Grand Rapids, Kent Co., MI
James J Norris, born abt 1834 in NY.

  Children of Selinda H Bovee and James J Norris were as follows:
  3106 i   Frank Leslie[8] **Norris**, born abt 1865.
  3107 ii   Grace[8] **Norris**, born abt 1869.
  3108 iii   Ethel Agatha[8] **Norris**, born 17 Oct 1871 in MI; died 21 Sep
               1956 in Los Angeles, Los Angeles Co., CA. She married
               (---) Squiers.

1999. John Livingston[7] **Bovee** (Cornelius[6], Daniel[5], Matthew[4], Jacob[3], Nicholas[2],

Mathieu[1]), born 3 Jul 1846 in NY; died 2 Apr 1917 in Seward, Seward Co., NB. He married on 9 Oct 1866 in Henderson Co., IL Elizabeth Bell Andrews, born 29 Jan 1849 in IN; died 13 Feb 1927 in Havelock, Lancaster Co., NE, daughter of John C Andrews and Chirena (---).

Children of John Livingston Bovee and Elizabeth Bell Andrews were as follows:

+   3109   i   Daniel Walter[8] **Bovee**, born 17 Jun 1868 in IL; died Feb 1923. He married **Sarah Amanda Boyd**.

     3110   ii   Edward F[8] **Bovee**, born 17 Jul 1870 in IL; died 15 Sep 1958.

+   3111   iii   Harry Carl[8] **Bovee**, born 9 Jan 1875 in Shenandoah, Page Co., IA; died 16 Dec 1943 in NE. He married **Myrtle Grace Siddens**.

+   3112   iv   Maude[8] **Bovee**, born abt 1877. She married **(---) Marvell**.

2001. Jacob C[7] **Bovee** (Cornelius[6], Daniel[5], Matthew[4], Jacob[3], Nicholas[2], Mathieu[1]), born Feb 1850 in MI. He married on 12 Nov 1873 in Oquawka, Henderson Co., IL Jenevieve Fox, born Aug 1854 in IL.

Children of Jacob C Bovee and Jenevieve Fox were as follows:

     3113   i   Hattie[8] **Bovee**, born Nov 1874 in IL.

     3114   ii   Cora M[8] **Bovee**, born Aug 1876 in IL.

+   3115   iii   Franklin Cornelius[8] **Bovee**, born 11 Feb 1879 in Oquawka, Henderson Co., IL. He married **Daisy M (---)**.

     3116   iv   William J[8] **Bovee**, born Mar 1881 in IA.

     3117   v   Robert H[8] **Bovee**, born May 1883 in IA. He married **Bessie Donahue**, born abt 1895 in IA.

     3118   vi   Fred[8] **Bovee**, born Feb 1885 in IA.

     3119   vii   Mable M[8] **Bovee**, born Jan 1889 in IA.

     3120   viii   Blanche[8] **Bovee**, born Nov 1897 in IA.

2003. Sarah E[7] **Bovee** (Daniel D[6], Daniel[5], Matthew[4], Jacob[3], Nicholas[2], Mathieu[1]), born 1859 in IL. She married Wesley McEwen.

Children of Sarah E Bovee and Wesley McEwen were as follows:

     3121   i   Carl Clint[8] **McEwen**, born 6 Jan 1886 in KS; died 12 Feb 1955 in Los Angeles, Los Angeles Co., CA.

2009. Jacob Lorenzo[7] **Bovee** (Abraham[6], Jacob[5], Matthew[4], Jacob[3], Nicholas[2], Mathieu[1]), born 9 May 1845 in NY; died 18 Oct 1921 in Richford, Tioga Co., NY. He married (1) abt 1860 Malona A (---), born 1845 in NY; died 20 Aug 1888 in Bergen, Genesee Co., NY; (2) abt 1890 Catherine (---), born 16 Sep 1850 in England; died 10 Jun 1904 in Richford, Tioga Co., NY; (3) on 9 May 1905 Frances H Belden, born abt 1863; died 29 Nov 1925 in Berkshire, Tioga Co., NY, daughter of (---) Belden and Meranda (---).

Children of Jacob Lorenzo Bovee and Malona A (---) were as follows:

3122   i   Delevan E[8] **Bovee**, born Sep 1863 in Riga, Monroe Co., NY; died 1938. He married **Jennie M Brodie**, daughter of Peter Brodie and Christine Campbell.

3123   ii   Clatie J[8] **Bovee**, born 13 Dec 1866; died 30 Nov 1867.

3124   iii   Lottie May[8] **Bovee**, born May 1871 in Monroe Co., NY; died 14 Feb 1920 in Monroe Co., NY. She married on 19 Apr 1890 in Bergen, Genesee Co., NY **William Ludington Bovee** (see 2042), born Apr 1867 in Genesee Co., NY; died 20 Dec 1926 in Riga, Monroe Co., NY, son of Cornelius Elihu Bovee and Harriet M Ludington.

2024. Wayland Henry[7] **Bovee** (Henry Jacob[6], Jacob[5], Matthew[4], Jacob[3], Nicholas[2], Mathieu[1]), born 24 Oct 1860 in Riga, Monroe Co., NY; christened 10 May 1862 in Congregational Ch, Riga, Monroe Co., NY; died 9 Jun 1919 in Oakland, Alameda Co., CA. He married (1) abt 1890, divorced Ida May Bartlett Shibley, born 13 Jun 1865 in Ontario, Canada; died 10 Aug 1899 in Vancouver, British Columbia, Canada; (2) on 18 Aug 1897 in Kansas City, Jackson Co., MO, divorced Pauline Morton Houk, born Jul 1870 in MO; died 7 Dec 1955 in MO; (3) aft 1901 Florence L Houk, born abt 1869; died 8 Jun 1918 in Woodland, Yolo Co., CA.

Children of Wayland Henry Bovee and Ida May Bartlett Shibley were as follows:

+   3125   i   Evelyn[8] **Bovee**, born 24 May 1891 in Ravenna, Los Angeles Co., CA; died 30 Jan 1978 in Portland, Multnomah Co., OR. She married **Guy Russell Gorton**.

Children of Wayland Henry Bovee and Pauline Morton Houk were as follows:

+   3126   i   Meda Emogene[8] **Bovee**, born 14 Sep 1899 in Speed, MO; died 13 May 1981 in Kansas City, Jackson Co., MO. She married (1) **Luther W Dugger**; (2) **William H Sigman**; (3) **James H Moss**; (4) **Earl F Swain**.

+   3127   ii   Lorene Houk[8] **Bovee**, born 11 Oct 1901 in Kansas City, Jackson Co., MO; died 26 Apr 1991 in Kansas City, Jackson Co., MO. She married **Carl Gilbert Lamb**.

2042. William Ludington[7] **Bovee** (Cornelius Elihu[6], Cornelius Schermerhorn[5], Matthew[4], Jacob[3], Nicholas[2], Mathieu[1]), born Apr 1867 in Genesee Co., NY; died 20 Dec 1926 in Riga, Monroe Co., NY. He married on 19 Apr 1890 in Bergen, Genesee Co., NY Lottie May Bovee (see 3124), born May 1871 in Monroe Co., NY; died 14 Feb 1920 in Monroe Co., NY, daughter of Jacob Lorenzo Bovee and Malona A (---).

Children of William Ludington Bovee and Lottie May Bovee were as follows:

3128   i   Beulah[8] **Bovee**, born Nov 1894. She married unknown.

+ 3129 ii Kenneth Jacob^8 **Bovee**, born 24 Sep 1897; died 3 Mar 1954. He married (1) **Irene Hofer**; (2) **Florence (---)**.

3130 iii Olive^8 **Bovee**, born 20 Feb 1899; died 24 Apr 1967. She married unknown.

3131 iv Floyd G^8 **Bovee**, born 27 May 1902; died 25 Jan 1974.

3132 v Everett^8 **Bovee**, born 20 Jan 1906; died 9 Sep 1970.

3133 vi Ruby Wilhelmina^8 **Bovee**, born 21 Feb 1908 in Chili, Monroe Co., NY. She married unknown.

3134 vii Dorothy M^8 **Bovee**, born 27 Jun 1911 in Chili, Monroe Co., NY; died Dec 1990.

2043. George W^7 **Bovee** (Cornelius Elihu^6, Cornelius Schermerhorn^5, Matthew^4, Jacob^3, Nicholas^2, Mathieu^1), born Nov 1868 in Genesee Co., NY; died 30 Jan 1925 in Stone Church, Genesee Co., NY. He married abt 1895 in Genesee Co., NY Matilda (---), born Sep 1879 in NY; died 1921.

Children of George W Bovee and Matilda (---) were as follows:

3135 i Leon I^8 **Bovee**, born 25 Apr 1895 in LeRoy, Genesee Co., NY; died 22 Aug 1898 in LeRoy, Genesee Co., NY.

3136 ii child^8 **Bovee**, born bef 1898 in Genesee Co., NY.

3137 iii Leola^8 **Bovee**, born Sep 1898. She married **Earl Wood**.

+ 3138 iv Lawrence Nelson^8 **Bovee**, born 24 Jul 1901 in Stone Church, Genesee Co., NY; died Jul 1991 in LeRoy, Genesee Co., NY. He married **Doris Sturble**.

3139 v Charles G^8 **Bovee**, born 13 Nov 1903 in Stone Church, Genesee Co., NY; died 3 May 1985 in West Palm Beach, Palm Beach Co., FL. He married in Palm Beach, Palm Beach Co., FL **Esther (---)**, born 17 Dec 1905; died 18 Feb 1987 in Palm Beach, Palm Beach Co., FL.

3140 vi Eugene M^8 **Bovee**, born 27 Nov 1905 in Bergen, Genesee Co., NY; died Jul 1983 in Rochester, Monroe Co., NY.

3141 vii Helen B^8 **Bovee**, born 22 Jul 1908 in Bergen, Genesee Co., NY.

3142 viii Child^8 **Bovee**, born 27 Sep 1910; died bef 1915.

3143 ix Emily Ann^8 **Bovee**, born aft 1910.

2053. George^7 **Bovee** (Luther^6, Jacob^5, Anthony^4, Gerrit^3, Anthony^2, Mathieu^1), born 13 Jun 1853 in Saratoga Co., NY; died 29 Sep 1924 in Utica Oneida Co., NY. He married (1) on 8 Dec 1880 Endora Austin; (2) on 28 Oct 1886 Frances Lindsey, born 8 Aug 1857 in NY; died 7 May 1934.

Children of George Bovee and Frances Lindsey were as follows:

3144 i Edward Lewis^8 **Bovee**, born 2 Apr 1888 in Gloversville, Fulton Co., NY; died 15 Oct 1985 in Gloversville, Fulton Co., NY. He married (1) **Florence Butler**, born 1887; died 1943; (2) on 22 Nov 1945 in Moravia, Cayuga Co., NY

Nina Isabell Sloan, born 28 Sep 1907; died Nov 1977, daughter of Charles N Sloan and Olive E Burldorf.

3145   ii   Harry Raymond^8 **Bovee**, born 27 May 1892 in Gloversville, Fulton Co., NY; died 20 May 1969. He married (1) **Bertha Goevick**; (2) **Florence Beman**.

2054. Hiram^7 **Bovee** (Luther^6, Jacob^5, Anthony^4, Gerrit^3, Anthony^2, Mathieu^1), born 10 Sep 1855 in Saratoga Co., NY; died bef 1900. He married Emile Daniels, born 1861 in NY.

Children of Hiram Bovee and Emile Daniels were as follows:

+   3146   i   Albert A^8 **Bovee**, born 1878. He married (1) **Allice Kelly**; (2) **Helen E Hogan**.

     3147   ii   Gertrude^8 **Bovee**, born Aug 1882.

2056. Henry L^7 **Bovee** (Luther^6, Jacob^5, Anthony^4, Gerrit^3, Anthony^2, Mathieu^1), born 14 Aug 1859 in Saratoga Co., NY; died 1928 in Glens Falls, Warren Co., NY. He married on 4 Sep 1885 Mary Noonan, born Jan 1855 in Ireland; died 20 Jan 1904 in Moreau Twp., Saratoga Co., NY.

Children of Henry L Bovee and Mary Noonan were as follows:

+   3148   i   Lewis F^8 **Bovee**, born Dec 1886 in NY. He married **Louisa Cody**.

     3149   ii   Amanda E^8 **Bovee**, born 2 Aug 1888; died 1981 in NY. She married **Edmund F Bombard**, born 1880; died 1959.

+   3150   iii   Walter W^8 **Bovee**, born Mar 1890. He married **Olive Mesink**.

     3151   iv   Dudley A^8 **Bovee**, born 17 Dec 1891; died Jan 1981.

+   3152   v   Beecher A^8 **Bovee**, born 12 Dec 1893 in Saratoga Co., NY; died Nov 1982 in Hudson Falls, Washington Co., NY. He married **Ella T White**.

     3153   vi   Edward M^8 **Bovee**, born 3 Sep 1895; died 1990. He married **Agnes O'Dell**.

     3154   vii   Harriet J^8 **Bovee**, born 3 Jun 1897; died 25 Dec 1921. She married **Frank Suthard**.

+   3155   viii   Marcus Sherman^8 **Bovee**, born 26 Apr 1899 in Hartford, Washington Co., NY; died 27 Feb 1977. He married **Kathryn Nichols**.

     3156   ix   Harold^8 **Bovee**, born 25 Jun 1901; died 23 Nov 1983 in Glens Falls, Warren Co., NY. He married **Frances M Parrow**, born 28 Apr 1905; died 1 Jun 1969.

2058. Orra Martin^7 **Bovee** (Luther^6, Jacob^5, Anthony^4, Gerrit^3, Anthony^2, Mathieu^1), born 27 Feb 1864 in Saratoga Co., NY; died 10 Jul 1936 in Lake Luzerne, Warren Co., NY. He married on 28 Nov 1896 in Hadley, Saratoga Co., NY Agnes Mary Reed, born 1 Jan 1879; died Apr 1924.

Children of Orra Martin Bovee and Agnes Mary Reed were as follows:

3157   i   Philip William[8] **Bovee**, born 27 Sep 1910 in Lake Luzerne, Warren Co., NY. He married (1) on 27 Nov 1931 **Mary Jalet**, born 1 Jul 1911; (2) **Sophia Jabieski**, born 22 Jun 1914.

2060. Fred[7] **Bovee** (Luther[6], Jacob[5], Anthony[4], Gerrit[3], Anthony[2], Mathieu[1]), born 26 Jun 1867 in Saratoga Co., NY; died 19 Nov 1934 in Conklinville, Saratoga Co., NY. He married Lydia Ann Ovitt, born 16 Jul 1870; died 17 Apr 1932.

Children of Fred Bovee and Lydia Ann Ovitt were as follows:

3158   i   Emmet[8] **Bovee**, born 13 Jul 1892; died 26 Oct 1963 in Conklinville, Broome Co., NY.

+   3159   ii   George Melvin[8] **Bovee**, born 3 Apr 1895; died 18 Nov 1960 in Day, Saratoga Co., NY. He married **Ethel Jenkins**.

3160   iii   Melvin[8] **Bovee**, born Sep 1899.

3161   iv   Florence M[8] **Bovee**, born 21 Jun 1902. She married **Joseph Harold LeBarron**.

3162   v   Clinton[8] **Bovee**, born 24 Sep 1908; died Nov 1971.

2070. Henry Harrison[7] **Bovee** (Orra[6], Jacob[5], Anthony[4], Gerrit[3], Anthony[2], Mathieu[1]), born 18 Apr 1888 in Saranac, Clinton Co., NY. He married in 1911 Mary A (---), born abt 1888 in Canada.

Children of Henry Harrison Bovee and Mary A (---) were as follows:

3163   i   Kenneth[8] **Bovee**, born 23 Oct 1912 in NY; died Jun 1974 in Philadelphia, Philadelphia Co., PA. He married **Louise Keyser**.

3164   ii   Gerald[8] **Bovee**, born 13 Jul 1915 in NY; died 23 Nov 1989.

2073. Frank[7] **Bovee** (Norman[6], Jacob[5], Anthony[4], Gerrit[3], Anthony[2], Mathieu[1]), born Sep 1863; died 1940. He married Alice May Bovee (see 2068), born Jul 1870 in NY; died 1920, daughter of Orra Bovee and Louise Daniels.

Children of Frank Bovee and Alice May Bovee were as follows:

3165   i   Child[8] **Bovee**, born abt 1886; died 17 May 1886.

+   3166   ii   Albert H[8] **Bovee**, born Jan 1888 in NY; died 1959. He married **Effie Marcellus**.

3167   iii   Louise[8] **Bovee**, born Apr 1889.

+   3168   iv   Warren[8] **Bovee**, born 2 Jun 1892 in Day, Saratoga Co., NY; died 28 Feb 1957. He married **Eva Belle White**.

3169   v   Zelpha J[8] **Bovee**, born 9 Jul 1893; died 13 Dec 1925. She married **Charles S White**, born 1899.

3170	vi	Emma Hazel[8] **Bovee**. She married **Franklin B Jenkins**.
3171	vii	Nellie[8] **Bovee**, born 18 Oct 1900.

2075. Charles[7] **Bovee** (Norman[6], Jacob[5], Anthony[4], Gerrit[3], Anthony[2], Mathieu[1]). He married Ada Carel, born 1879; died 1943.

Children of Charles Bovee and Ada Carel were as follows:

+	3172	i	Harold[8] **Bovee**, born 20 Jul 1903; died 6 Oct 1976. He married **Charlotte Thompson**.
	3173	ii	Floyd[8] **Bovee**, born 12 Jun 1904; died Jul 1966. He married on 21 Aug 1948 **Mary Arminos**, born 24 Jul 1924 in Mayfield, Fulton Co., NY.
	3174	iii	Ethyl[8] **Bovee**, born abt 1906. She married (1) **(---) Masaitie**; (2) **(---) Sanborn**.
	3175	iv	Eva[8] **Bovee**, born abt 1908.
	3176	v	Leo[8] **Bovee**, born 1913.
+	3177	vi	Clinton[8] **Bovee**, born 17 Feb 1915; died 16 Oct 1992. He married **Nancy M (---)**.
+	3178	vii	Carl Harvey[8] **Bovee**, born 10 Apr 1920. He married **Jane O'Donnell**.

2076. Cora L[7] **Bovee** (Norman[6], Jacob[5], Anthony[4], Gerrit[3], Anthony[2], Mathieu[1]), born 24 Mar 1857; died 5 Jan 1915. She married on 12 Apr 1891 Charles L Frasier.

Children of Cora L Bovee and Charles L Frasier were as follows:

3179	i	Charles Willet[8] **Frasier**.
3180	ii	Orange H[8] **Frasier**, born 10 Nov 1904.
3181	iii	Ashley[8] **Frasier**.

2077. Rosalie[7] **Bovee** (Norman[6], Jacob[5], Anthony[4], Gerrit[3], Anthony[2], Mathieu[1]), born 1872. She married in Apr 1890 Ulysses Grant Frasier, born 1865.

Children of Rosalie Bovee and Ulysses Grant Frasier were as follows:

3182	i	Bessie E[8] **Frasier**.
3183	ii	Sheridan[8] **Frasier**.
3184	iii	Sherman[8] **Frasier**, born 1897.
3185	iv	Walter S[8] **Frasier**, born 1899.
3186	v	Berton M[8] **Frasier**, born 1902.
3187	vi	Clifford A[8] **Frasier**, born 1905.
3188	vii	Violet E[8] **Frasier**, born 1908.
3189	viii	Grace I[8] **Frasier**, born 1910.

2079. Mary Ardell[7] **Bovee** (Norman[6], Jacob[5], Anthony[4], Gerrit[3], Anthony[2], Mathieu[1]), born 28 Jul 1875; died 1959. She married Truman E Frasier, born 1869; died 1939.

Children of Mary Ardell Bovee and Truman E Frasier were as follows:

3190	i	William E[8] **Frasier**, born 1893.
3191	ii	Jennie E[8] **Frasier**, born 1895.
3192	iii	Celeste E[8] **Frasier**, born 1898.
3193	iv	Cora E[8] **Frasier**, born 1900.
3194	v	Bertha E[8] **Frasier**, born 1901.

2081. Orange[7] **Bovee** (Norman[6], Jacob[5], Anthony[4], Gerrit[3], Anthony[2], Mathieu[1]), born 22 Dec 1878; died Jan 1968. He married Emma Wells Orton.

Children of Orange Bovee and Emma Wells Orton were as follows:

3195	i	Sheldon Leonard[8] **Bovee**.

2082. Lester[7] **Bovee** (Norman[6], Jacob[5], Anthony[4], Gerrit[3], Anthony[2], Mathieu[1]), born Mar 1881. He married Carrie Carleton.

Children of Lester Bovee and Carrie Carleton were as follows:

	3196	i	Kenneth[8] **Bovee**, born 25 Nov 1908; died 1952.
+	3197	ii	Leon[8] **Bovee**, born 5 Apr 1910 in Day, Saratoga Co., NY; died 19 Jun 1992 in Glens Falls, Warren Co., NY. He married **Ernestine Ellithorpe Ovitt**.
+	3198	iii	Owen L[8] **Bovee**, born 18 Mar 1912; died 9 Oct 1992 in Day, Saratoga Co., NY. He married **Iva Ovitt**.
+	3199	iv	Carl L[8] **Bovee**, born 11 May 1915 in Day, Saratoga Co., NY; died 26 Jul 2000. He married **Gladys I Ralph**.
+	3200	v	Eleanor[8] **Bovee**, born abt 1914; died 1957. She married unknown.
+	3201	vi	Beatrice[8] **Bovee**, born 17 May 1917; died Jun 1976 in Conklinville, Saratoga co., NY. She married **Scott Houghton**.
+	3202	vii	Gerald[8] **Bovee**, born 21 Jun 1918; died Aug 1986. He married **Shirley M Ralph**.
+	3203	viii	Nancy F[8] **Bovee**, born 7 Aug 1922; died 10 Oct 1989 in Day, Saratoga Co., NY. She married **(---) Bovee**.
+	3204	ix	Willard L[8] **Bovee**, born 14 Dec 1924 in Day, Saratoga Co., NY; died 26 Jan 2000. He married **Marie Scoville**.
	3205	x	Margaret[8] **Bovee**, born 1927; died 1940.
+	3206	xi	Cora[8] **Bovee**, born 29 Jul 1929 in Day, Saratoga Co., NY; died 9 Nov 1997 in Amsterdam, Montgomery Co., NY. She married **Aloysius E Zawilomski**.

2083. Anna Lorra[7] **Bovee** (Norman[6], Jacob[5], Anthony[4], Gerrit[3], Anthony[2], Mathieu[1]), born 30 Jul 1882; died 1962 in Gloversville, Fulton Co., NY. She married Roscoe White, born 1884; died 1945.

Children of Anna Lorra Bovee and Roscoe White were as follows:

3207	i	Lela[8] **White**.
3208	ii	Kenneth[8] **White**, born 1 Jan 1908.
3209	iii	Leona[8] **White**, born 1909.
3210	iv	Laura[8] **White**, born 28 Apr 1913 in Day, Saratoga Co., NY.
3211	v	Isla[8] **White**, born 22 Feb 1915.
3212	vi	Cecil[8] **White**.
3213	vii	Josephine[8] **White**, born 21 Oct 1918.
3214	viii	Clyde[8] **White**.
3215	ix	Milton[8] **White**, born 30 Jan 1923.
3216	x	Walton[8] **White**, born 23 Sep 1924.

2086. Luther E[7] **Bovee** (Wallace[6], Jacob[5], Anthony[4], Gerrit[3], Anthony[2], Mathieu[1]), born Apr 1865 in NY; died 4 May 1939. He married (1) Mary Jane Swart, born Feb 1860 in Herkimer Co., NY; died 16 Aug 1905, daughter of Daniel Swart and Sarah (---); (2) on 14 Apr 1907 Mayme J Morris.

Children of Luther E Bovee and Mary Jane Swart were as follows:

| 3217 | i | Anna[8] **Bovee**, born Jul 1887 in Hagaman, Montgomery Co., NY. |

2087. Jacob H[7] **Bovee** (Wallace[6], Jacob[5], Anthony[4], Gerrit[3], Anthony[2], Mathieu[1]), born Jan 1868 in NY; died 1945. He married Ida May Stewart, born Jan 1876 in NY; died 1952.

Children of Jacob H Bovee and Ida May Stewart were as follows:

| 3218 | i | Carleton[8] **Bovee**, born 20 Jun 1895; died Mar 1976 in Hagaman, Montgomery Co., NY. He married **Bessie Connelly**. |
| 3219 | ii | Harley[8] **Bovee**, born Aug 1896; died 1932. |

2090. David Duff[7] **Bovee** (Wallace[6], Jacob[5], Anthony[4], Gerrit[3], Anthony[2], Mathieu[1]), born Mar 1877. He married Sarah M Davidson, born Oct 1884, daughter of James M Davidson.

Children of David Duff Bovee and Sarah M Davidson were as follows:

| 3220 | i | Gladys Lorette[8] **Bovee**. |

2092. Marshall[7] **Bovee** (Wallace[6], Jacob[5], Anthony[4], Gerrit[3], Anthony[2],

Mathieu[1]), born Feb 1881 in NY. He married on 23 Jun 1900 Mable Tissue.

Children of Marshall Bovee and Mable Tissue were as follows:

3221   i   Cecelia Mary[8] **Bovee**, born 1 Feb 1908. She married **Charles Ballou**, born 7 Apr 1907; died Oct 1981.

3222   ii   Margaret[8] **Bovee**, born 1 Aug 1910; died 1912.

2098. Mac Henry[7] **Bovee** (Henry Joseph[6], Joseph[5], Anthony[4], Gerrit[3], Anthony[2], Mathieu[1]), born 8 Oct 1903 in Cozad, Dawson Co., NE; died 20 Aug 1951. He married E Blandena Johnson, born 12 Feb 1905; died 9 Dec 1992.

Children of Mac Henry Bovee and E Blandena Johnson were as follows:

+   3223   i   Mary Jane[8] **Bovee**, born in Cozad, Dawson Co., NE. She married **William Vasey**.

     3224   ii   Phyllis Ellen[8] **Bovee**, born in Cozad, Dawson Co., NE.

2102. Guy Harrison[7] **Bovee** (Eugene M[6], Joseph[5], Anthony[4], Gerrit[3], Anthony[2], Mathieu[1]), born 1 Jan 1889 in Burr Oak, Winneshiek Co., IA; died May 1964 in CA. He married Mary Isabel Fillipe, born 24 May 1900; died 25 Apr 1988 in Castro Valley, Alemeda Co., CA.

Children of Guy Harrison Bovee and Mary Isabel Fillipe were as follows:

     3225   i   Charles[8] **Bovee**, born 11 Nov 1921; died 1922.

     3226   ii   Carlos Robert[8] **Bovee**, born 11 Nov 1921; died 1988 in Yreka, Siskiyou Co., CA.

     3227   iii   Doris B[8] **Bovee**, born 1923; died 1971. She married (1) **Albert Holmes**; (2) **George Jump**; (3) **Buck Powers**.

+   3228   iv   Edward LeRoy[8] **Bovee**, born 24 Oct 1925. He married **Katherine Bouden**.

     3229   v   Keith[8] **Bovee**, born 1927; died dy.

     3230   vi   Kevin[8] **Bovee**, born 1927; died dy.

     3231   vii   Keitha[8] **Bovee**, born 1927; died dy.

2103. Claude Alva[7] **Bovee** (Eugene M[6], Joseph[5], Anthony[4], Gerrit[3], Anthony[2], Mathieu[1]), born 5 Feb 1898 in MT; died Jun 1969 in Reedpoint, Stillwater Co. MT. He married (1) in 1920 in Stillwater Co., MT Mamie (---), born abt 1899 in MO; (2) Catherine Lannen, born 6 Apr 1905; died 4 Feb 1995 in MT, daughter of John Francis Lannen and Mildred Davis.

Children of Claude Alva Bovee and Mamie (---) were as follows:

+   3232   i   Gayle[8] **Bovee**, born 21 Feb 1921; died 20 Nov 1995 in Danville, VA. He married (1) **Jesse (---)**; (2) **Margaret (---)**.

     3233   ii   Elaine[8] **Bovee**, born abt 1923. She married **George Sprout**.

Children of Claude Alva Bovee and Catherine Lannen were as follows:

3234   i   Claude Alvin[8] **Bovee**, born 1924; died Jul 1944 in Saipan.
+ 3235   ii   Rex Everett[8] **Bovee**, born 23 Jan 1926. He married (1) **Dolly Rickman**; (2) **Bertha Gwin Heaps**.

2109. U N[7] **Bovee** (Peter B[6], Gerrit[5], Peter[4], Gerrit[3], Anthony[2], Mathieu[1]). He married Melissa (---), born abt 1869.

Children of U N Bovee and Melissa (---) were as follows:
+ 3236   i   Earl H[8] **Bovee**, born abt 1895. He married **Florence (---)**.

2121. Charles Howard[7] **Bovee** (David[6], Jonathan[5], Peter[4], Gerrit[3], Anthony[2], Mathieu[1]), born 14 Jul 1861 in Coldwater, Branch Co., MI; died 2 May 1906 in Reno, Washo Co., NV. He married on 21 Jun 1890 Bessie Grosvenor, born 12 Aug 1870 in IL; died 11 Sep 1959.

Children of Charles Howard Bovee and Bessie Grosvenor were as follows:
+ 3237   i   David Grosvenor[8] **Bovee**, born 16 Jul 1895 in Coldwater, Branch Co., MI; died May 1975 in Seattle, King Co., WA. He married **Grace Donnelly**.

2123. Edwin Anson[7] **Bovee** (Eli William[6], Jonathan[5], Peter[4], Gerrit[3], Anthony[2], Mathieu[1]), born 30 Sep 1851 in Litchfield, Hillsdale Co., MI; died 16 Dec 1910 in Grand Rapids, Kent Co., MI. He married (1) on 24 Dec 1868 in Reading, Hillsdale Co., MI Jullia A Session, born 28 Feb 1849; died 19 Sep 1871; (2) on 15 Oct 1874 in 1st Congregational Ch, Royalton Twp., Berrien Co., MI Adeline Elizabeth Stevens, born 15 Oct 1854 in Chatfield, Crawford Co., OH; died 24 Sep 1930 in Traverse City, Grand Traverse Co., MI, daughter of William Stevens and Leah Dill.

Children of Edwin Anson Bovee and Jullia A Session were as follows:
3238   i   Nellie[8] **Bovee**, born 30 Aug 1871 in Hillsdale Co., MI; died 21 Aug 1872 in Hillsdale Co., MI.

Children of Edwin Anson Bovee and Adeline Elizabeth Stevens were as follows:
+ 3239   i   Carrie Leah[8] **Bovee**, born 1 Nov 1875 in MI; died 15 Jan 1899 in Benton Harbor, Berrien Co., MI. She married **Bert Seeley**.
+ 3240   ii   William Arthur[8] **Bovee**, born 26 Jan 1878 in St Joseph, Berrien Co., MI; died 29 Aug 1954 in Traverse City, Grand Traverse Co., MI. He married (1) **Letitia Bixler**; (2) **Mildred P Champlin**.
3241   iii   Myrtle Jennie[8] **Bovee**, born 21 Aug 1879 in St Joseph, Berrien Co., MI; died 23 Oct 1923 in Grand Rapids, Kent Co., MI. She married on 5 Apr 1905 in Grand Rapids,

Kent Co., MI **William P Praetorius**, born 1871; died 1962 in Elks National Home.

+ 3242 iv David Lloyd[8] **Bovee**, born 29 Jun 1882 in Holland, Ottawa Co.,MI; died 21 Nov 1953 in Grand Rapids, Kent Co., MI. He married **Maude Jeanette Wright**.

+ 3243 v Nellie Andrea[8] **Bovee**, born 13 Sep 1885 in St Joseph, Berrien Co., MI; christened in Congregational Ch, Grand Rapids, Kent Co., MI; died 22 Nov 1969 in Irving, Dallas Co., TX. She married **Harry Peter Willwerth**.

+ 3244 vi Ruth Winnifred[8] **Bovee**, born 22 Jan 1890 in St Joseph, Berrien Co., MI; christened 22 Apr 1973 in Immanuel Presb Ch, Grand Rapids, Kent Co., MI; died 3 Dec 1975 in Grand Rapids, Kent Co., MI. She married **Clarence W Strouse**.

2124. Ella Jane[7] **Bovee** (Eli William[6], Jonathan[5], Peter[4], Gerrit[3], Anthony[2], Mathieu[1]), born 29 Jan 1854 in Coldwater, Branch Co., MI; died Nov 1936 in Benton Harbor, Berrien Co., MI. She married on 18 Dec 1873 Henry W Kent, born 30 Sep 1843 in Bronson, Branch Co., MI.

Children of Ella Jane Bovee and Henry W Kent were as follows:

+ 3245 i Maxine[8] **Kent**, born 2 Apr 1892 in Benton Harbor, Berrien Co., MI; died 22 Dec 1937 in Benton Harbor, Berrien Co., MI. She married **(---) Butler**.

3246 ii Jim[8] **Kent**.

2126. Carolyn Amelia[7] **Bovee** (Eli William[6], Jonathan[5], Peter[4], Gerrit[3], Anthony[2], Mathieu[1]), born 29 Jan 1858 in Coldwater, Branch Co., MI; died 11 Jun 1936 in St Joseph, Berrien Co., MI. She married on 21 Aug 1875 in St.Joseph, Berrien Co., MI Henry Joseph Lewis.

Children of Carolyn Amelia Bovee and Henry Joseph Lewis were as follows:

3247 i Jennie Georgiana[8] **Lewis**, born abt 1877; died 1950.

2131. Jonathan Orly[7] **Bovee** (Clark[6], Jonathan[5], Peter[4], Gerrit[3], Anthony[2], Mathieu[1]), born 4 Jul 1858 in Algansee Twp., Branch Co., MI; died 9 Dec 1925. He married (1) on 26 Nov 1883 in Branch Co., MI Ida M Camp, born 8 Mar 1857 in Algansee, Branch Co., MI; died 20 Feb 1886, daughter of Isaac Fuller Camp and Frances Arvilla Vermilya; (2) Ada W Pruce, born 22 Aug 1858 in OH; died 11 Dec 1944.

Children of Jonathan Orly Bovee and Ida M Camp were as follows:

+ 3248 i William Eli[8] **Bovee**, born 18 Jun 1884 in MI; died 21 Oct 1917. He married **Hazel Purmanter**.

Children of Jonathan Orly Bovee and Ada W Pruce were as follows:

+ 3249 i Grace May[8] **Bovee**, born 1 Jun 1890 in Algansee, Branch

Co., MI. She married **Walter Charles Camfield**.

2132. Elmer Ellsworth[7] **Bovee** (Clark[6], Jonathan[5], Peter[4], Gerrit[3], Anthony[2], Mathieu[1]), born 30 Aug 1859 in Algansee Twp., Branch Co.,MI; died 11 Jul 1938 in Algansee Twp., Branch Co., MI. He married on 26 Nov 1890 Nettie Follette, born 10 Nov 1866 in OH.

Children of Elmer Ellsworth Bovee and Nettie Follette were as follows:

+ 3250   i   Paul Elmer[8] **Bovee**, born 29 May 1902 in Chicago, Cook Co., IL; died Oct 1973. He married **Florence (---)**.
+ 3251   ii   Carl Folette[8] **Bovee**, born 15 Aug 1905 in Chicago, Cook Co., IL; died 13 Oct 1979 in Kissimmee, Osceola Co., FL. He married **Mildred Beatrice Novotney**.

2133. Lucy Lovina[7] **Bovee** (Clark[6], Jonathan[5], Peter[4], Gerrit[3], Anthony[2], Mathieu[1]), born 30 Aug 1862 in Algansee, Branch Co.,MI. She married on 14 Apr 1878 in Branch Co., MI Walter Frank.

Children of Lucy Lovina Bovee and Walter Frank were as follows:

3252   i   Maude Dora[8] **Frank**, born 1 Aug 1881. She married on 3 Oct 1896 **Charles Bruce Woodward**.
3253   ii   Harvey Edward[8] **Frank**, born 7 Aug 1883.
3254   iii   Alta[8] **Frank**, born Jan 1885. She married on 19 Oct 1904 **Ernest Brown**.
3255   iv   Linie[8] **Frank**, born 27 May 1888. She married **Ray From**.
3256   v   Abraham Clark[8] **Frank**, born 11 May 1890; died 20 Aug 1890.

2135. Henry Orgo[7] **Bovee** (Clark[6], Jonathan[5], Peter[4], Gerrit[3], Anthony[2], Mathieu[1]), born 14 Sep 1867 in Algansee Twp., Branch Co., MI; died 4 Apr 1938 in Coldwater, Branch Co., MI. He married on 6 Oct 1892 Dora Quimby, born 24 Jun 1870 in MI; died 22 Jan 1962.

Children of Henry Orgo Bovee and Dora Quimby were as follows:

+ 3257   i   Upton Randall[8] **Bovee**, born 16 Dec 1895 in MI; died 12 Sep 1963. He married (1) **Mildred Filled**; (2) **Bernice Sorter**; (3) **Arda Bartholomy Hallock**.
+ 3258   ii   Kenneth Clark[8] **Bovee**, born 1 Sep 1902 in WI; died 13 Jul 1948. He married (1) **Adelma Lillian Dickey**; (2) **Alice W (---)**.

2137. Edward Clark[7] **Bovee** (Clark[6], Jonathan[5], Peter[4], Gerrit[3], Anthony[2], Mathieu[1]), born 16 Jul 1872 in Algansee, Branch Co.,MI; died aft 1938. He married Inez Mae Brainard.

Children of Edward Clark Bovee and Inez Mae Brainard were as follows:

3259   i   Corlan Drury^8 **Bovee**, born 30 Jun 1915; died 6 Jan 1977 in Livonia, Wayne Co., MI.

2138. Charles A^7 **Bovee** (Abraham^6, William W^5, Peter^4, Gerrit^3, Anthony^2, Mathieu^1), born abt 1873 in NY. He married Clara K Jones, born abt 1868 in NY; died 26 Jul 1922 in Syracuse, Onondaga Co., NY.

Children of Charles A Bovee and Clara K Jones were as follows:

3260   i   Roy J^8 **Bovee**, born abt 1904 in NY.

2147. Frank^7 **Bovee** (Moses S^6, Peter^5, Jacob^4, Gerrit^3, Anthony^2, Mathieu^1), born 9 Apr 1865 in VT; died 17 Dec 1904. He married on 5 Sep 1885 Elsie Freeman, born 1871 in VT; died 17 Dec 1939.

Children of Frank Bovee and Elsie Freeman were as follows:

3261   i   Grace **Bovee**.
3262   ii   Ernest Otis^8 **Bovee**.
3263   iii   Alice A^8 **Bovee**.
3264   iv   Eric Ashley^8 **Bovee**.

2149. William Francis^7 **Bovee** (William W^6, Moses R^5, Jacob^4, Gerrit^3, Anthony^2, Mathieu^1), born abt 1869 in Australia; died 16 Sep 1931 in Santa Barbara Co., CA. He married in 1884 in IA Minnie May Isenhart, born 20 Nov 1865 in IL; died 8 Mar 1955 in Santa Barbara Co., CA, daughter of John Isenhart.

Children of William Francis Bovee and Minnie May Isenhart were as follows:

+   3265   i   John William^8 **Bovee**, born 1 Mar 1887 in Green Mountain, Mareshal Co., IA; died 23 Mar 1924 in Visalia, Tulare Co., CA. He married **Jeannette Perry Conable**.
  3266   ii   Elizabeth^8 **Bovee**. She married **Howard A Irwin**.
+   3267   iii   Paul Worden^8 **Bovee**, born 24 Oct 1893; died 29 Apr 1974 in Sant Barbara, Santa Barbara Co., CA. He married **Meda Logan**.
  3268   iv   Hazel^8 **Bovee**.
  3269   v   Gertrude^8 **Bovee**, died abt 1940. She married in 1922 **Harold Raugh**.

2151. Henry M^7 **Bovee** (William W^6, Moses R^5, Jacob^4, Gerrit^3, Anthony^2, Mathieu^1), born 10 Jan 1862 in Australia; died 29 Jul 1942 in Monrovia, Los Angeles Co., CA. He married Georgia V Cooper, born 6 Nov 1875 in NB; died Nov 1973 in Baldwin Park, Los Angeles Co., CA.

Children of Henry M Bovee and Georgia V Cooper were as follows:

3270   i   George C^8 **Bovee**, born 2 Dec 1895 in CA; died Jul 1962 in CA.

2154. Ernest A^7 **Bovee** (William W^6, Moses R^5, Jacob^4, Gerrit^3, Anthony^2, Mathieu^1), born 5 Oct 1871 in Marshall Co., IA; died 17 Dec 1945 in Los Angeles, Los Angeles Co., CA. He married WinnieA Valentine, born 27 Feb 1878 in OH; died 9 Feb 1981 in Monrovia, Los Angeles Co., CA.

Children of Ernest A Bovee and WinnieA Valentine were as follows:

3271   i   Muriel^8 **Bovee**, born 2 Nov 1904; died 10 Oct 1991 in Ventura, Ventura Co., CA.

+   3272   ii   Hartson^8 **Bovee**, born 1 Mar 1908; died 17 May 1997 in Ventura Co., CA. He married **Ruth Horn**.

2157. Frank Luther^7 **Bovee** (Moses C^6, Moses R^5, Jacob^4, Gerrit^3, Anthony^2, Mathieu^1), born 4 Jul 1865 in Marshall Co., IA; died 30 Dec 1949. He married Jessie Elizabeth Isenhart, born Oct 1867 in IL, daughter of John Isenhart.

Children of Frank Luther Bovee and Jessie Elizabeth Isenhart were as follows:

3273   i   Blanche F^8 **Bovee**, born 21 Dec 1890 in IA; died 1959 in Marshall Co., IA. She married **Elmer Connor**.

+   3274   ii   Benjamin Samuel^8 **Bovee**, born 6 May 1892 in Green Mountain, Marshall Co., IA; died 23 Dec 1981 in Brandenton, Manatee Co., FL. He married **Eleanor Ceser**.

+   3275   iii   Lloyd D^8 **Bovee**, born 10 Apr 1894 in IA; died Feb 1967 in Greenville, Hunt Co., TX. He married **Cora (---)**.

3276   iv   Harold L^8 **Bovee**, born 8 Oct 1896 in IA; died 15 Nov 1948.

3277   v   Margaret^8 **Bovee**, born 1903 in IA. She married **Henry Harding**.

2162. Charles Edward^7 **Bovee** (Moses C^6, Moses R^5, Jacob^4, Gerrit^3, Anthony^2, Mathieu^1), born 13 May 1878 in Marshall Co., IA; died 17 Oct 1963 in Marshall Co., IA. He married on 21 Jan 1914 in Marshalltown, Marshall Co., IA Bertha Harriet Lampman, born 22 Dec 1890; died 13 Sep 1943 in Marshall Co., IA.

Children of Charles Edward Bovee and Bertha Harriet Lampman were as follows:

3278   i   Ada Helen^8 **Bovee**, born 29 Sep 1915. She married **Jack Wikle**.

+   3279   ii   Homer Charles^8 **Bovee**, born 18 Nov 1917; died 18 May 2004 in Green Mountain, Marshall Co., IA. He married **Vera Thurston**.

3280   iii   Grace Edna^8 **Bovee**, born 20 Sep 1919. She married **Ray**

Ireland.

3281	iv	Fred Burt[8] **Bovee**, born 27 Sep 1921.
3282	v	Ethel Mary[8] **Bovee**, born 3 Aug 1923. She married **Lowel Stiles**.
3283	vi	Betty Jane[8] **Bovee**, born 10 Oct 1925. She married **Richard Miller**.
3284	vii	Ruth Ann[8] **Bovee**, born 5 Mar 1928. She married on 27 Jul 1947 **Rex Beach**.
3285	viii	Cora Marie[8] **Bovee**. She married **Lawrence Halter**.

2164. Clyde Charles[7] **Bovee** (James B[6], Moses R[5], Jacob[4], Gerrit[3], Anthony[2], Mathieu[1]), born 18 Nov 1864 in Marshall Co., IA; died 1956. He married on 15 Mar 1889 Alice C Shearer, born 29 Oct 1862 in Barnet, Caledonia Co., VT, daughter of Thomas James Shearer and Caroline C Somers.

Children of Clyde Charles Bovee and Alice C Shearer were as follows:

+	3286	i	Homer Thomas[8] **Bovee**, born 27 Dec 1889 in Laurens,Pocahontas Co., IA; died 4 Jul 1965 in WA. He married **Lois H T Roller**.
+	3287	ii	Earle Clyde[8] **Bovee**, born 24 Jul 1891 in IA; died Feb 1984. He married **Muriel Sanderson**.
	3288	iii	Joyce Elizabeth[8] **Bovee**, born 13 Mar 1893 in Havelock, Pocahontas Co., IA; died 1933.
	3289	iv	Margaret Alice[8] **Bovee**, born 14 Jan 1899 in Ware, Pocahontas Co., IA. She married **Herbert Lofquist**.

2168. George M[7] **Bovee** (Mark[6], Moses R[5], Jacob[4], Gerrit[3], Anthony[2], Mathieu[1]), born 10 Nov 1862; died 13 Aug 1893 in Laurens, Pocahontas Co., IA. He married Minnie M Kahley, born 2 May 1864 in Davenport, Scott Co., IA.

Children of George M Bovee and Minnie M Kahley were as follows:

+	3290	i	Mark C[8] **Bovee**, born 6 Sep 1886 in IA; died 17 Dec 1971. He married **Ruth Ilene Pennington**.
	3291	ii	Louis M[8] **Bovee**, born 8 Apr 1890 in IA; died 26 Feb 1990. He married **Mildred Grace Copp**.
+	3292	iii	George[8] **Bovee**, born 25 Feb 1892 in IA. He married **Myrtle Ethel Churning**.

2169. Phineas Arno[7] **Bovee** (Mark[6], Moses R[5], Jacob[4], Gerrit[3], Anthony[2], Mathieu[1]), born 27 Jul 1864 in Peacham, Caledonia Co., VT; died 17 Jan 1917 in Marshal Co., IA. He married on 1 Jan 1889 Lucinda Owen.

Children of Phineas Arno Bovee and Lucinda Owen were as follows:

	3293	i	Clara[8] **Bovee**, born 19 Jul 1897 in Green Mountain, Marshall Co., IA; died 5 Mar 1949 in Waterloo, Black Hawk Co., IA.

3294	ii	Flora[8] **Bovee**.
3295	iii	Jennie[8] **Bovee**.
3296	iv	(---)[8] **Bovee**.

2172. Thaddeus Fairbanks[7] **Bovee** (Mark[6], Moses R[5], Jacob[4], Gerrit[3], Anthony[2], Mathieu[1]), born 9 Jun 1873 in Marshall Co., IA; died 3 Mar 1952. He married (1) abt 1903 Elizabeth Wilson, born 25 Sep 1875 in KS; died 1909; (2) abt 1911 Mabel C Hayes, born 1881 in IL; died 23 Feb 1958 in Los Angeles, Los Angeles Co., CA.

Children of Thaddeus Fairbanks Bovee and Elizabeth Wilson were as follows:

	3297	i	Helen Mary Wilson[8] **Bovee**, born 23 Jul 1904 in CAnada; died 21 Feb 1996. She married **Norman Tobias Carl**.
+	3298	ii	Glenn Thaddeus[8] **Bovee**, born 12 Aug 1906 in Saskatchewan, Canada; died Oct 1984 in San Diego, San Diego Co., CA. He married (1) **Helen Hurst**; (2) **Marion Olson**.
	3299	iii	Vincent[8] **Bovee**, born 1907 in Craik, Saskatchewan, Canada; died 1907.

2178. Harry W[7] **Bovee** (Otis M[6], Courtland[5], Jacob[4], Gerrit[3], Anthony[2], Mathieu[1]), born 12 Feb 1884 in IA; died 1959. He married Ruth Mercedes Findlay.

Children of Harry W Bovee and Ruth Mercedes Findlay were as follows:

	3300	i	Alan Findlay[8] **Bovee**, born 8 Sep 1915 in CAnada. He married on 25 Oct 1940 **Margaret Mosier**.
+	3301	ii	John Colin[8] **Bovee**, born 15 Dec 1918 in Maryfield, Saskatchewan, Canada; died 1959. He married **Barbara Winston**.
	3302	iii	Mary Marcel[8] **Bovee**, born 1920 in Maryfield, Saskatchewan, Canada; died 19 Feb 1992. She married **Robert Matthew**.

2179. William Courtland[7] **Bovee** (Otis M[6], Courtland[5], Jacob[4], Gerrit[3], Anthony[2], Mathieu[1]), born 25 Jul 1885 in IA; died 10 Jul 1966 in Red Bluff, Tehama Co., CA. He married on 25 Feb 1915 in Des Moines, Polk Co., IA Pearl Lorraine Van Hoesen, born 18 May 1875; died Oct 1976 in Red Bluff, Tehama Co., CA.

Children of William Courtland Bovee and Pearl Lorraine Van Hoesen were as follows:

+	3303	i	Courtney Van[8] **Bovee**, born 27 Jun 1919 in Maryfield, Saskatchewan, Canada. He married **Shirley Patricia Shepherd**.

Generation 8

2182. Bert[8] **Bovee** (Edward H[7], Stephen[6], Philip[5], Mathew[4], Philip[3], Mathieu[2], Mathieu[1]), born 24 Mar 1883 in NY; died Sep 1962 in NY. He married Lila (---), born abt 1893 in NY.

Children of Bert Bovee and Lila (---) were as follows:

3304   i   Arlene L[9] **Bovee**, born abt 1924.

3305   ii   Leonard L[9] **Bovee**, born abt 1930.

2194. Richard Curtis[8] **Bovie** (Richard Heman[7], Richard H[6], Henry[5], John[4], Rykert[3], Nicholas[2], Mathieu[1]), born 30 Apr 1896 in Cambridge, Washington Co., NY; died 18 May 1976 in Bennington, Bennington Co., VT. He married on 7 Feb 1931 Orpha Anna Cain, born 9 Dec 1894 in Sand Lake, Rensselaer Co., NY; died 8 Sep 1982 in Cambridge, Washington Co., NY.

Children of Richard Curtis Bovie and Orpha Anna Cain were as follows:

+   3306   i   Frederick Richard[9] **Bovie**, born in Rennselaer Co., NY. He married **Carole Eva Monroe**.

2195. Sanford Harold[8] **Bovie** (Charles S[7], Sanford S[6], Henry[5], John[4], Rykert[3], Nicholas[2], Mathieu[1]), born 13 Oct 1892; died 2 Jul 1969 in Hoosick, Rensselaer Co., NY. He married on 29 May 1918 in Hoosick, Rensselaer Co., NY Sarah Albertine Turner, born 15 Aug 1890 in Hoosick Falls, Rensselear Co., NY; died 13 May 1977 in Bennington, Bennington Co., VT, daughter of Albert Turner and Ida May Stone.

Children of Sanford Harold Bovie and Sarah Albertine Turner were as follows:

3307   i   Ruth Elizabeth[9] **Bovie**, born 28 Nov 1922 in Bennington, Bennington Co., VT. She married on 20 Jul 1946 **Lyman Arnstrong Rudd**, son of Lyman Rudd and Sarah Armstrong.

2198. George P[8] **Bovie** (William H[7], Parker R.[6], John[5], John[4], Rykert[3], Nicholas[2], Mathieu[1]), born May 1862 in NY; died abt 1920 in Chicago, Cook Co., IL. He married abt 1890 Elizabeth (---), born Sep 1872.

Children of George P Bovie and Elizabeth (---) were as follows:

3308   i   Elwood[9] **Bovie**, born Mar 1891; died 24 Aug 1908 in Chicago, Cook Co., IL.

3309   ii   William[9] **Bovie**, born 28 Sep 1893 in Chicago, Cook Co., IL; died May 1969 in Chicago, Cook Co., IL. He married **Ella (---)**.

+   3310   iii   George P[9] **Bovie**, born Jun 1895 in Chicago, Cook Co., IL. He married **Bettie (---)**.

3311   iv   John[9] **Bovie**, born Jan 1897 in Chicago, Cook Co., IL.

3312	v	Elizabeth[9] **Bovie**, born Jun 1898 in Chicago, Cook Co., IL.
3313	vi	Joseph[9] **Bovie**, born May 1900 in Chicago, Cook Co., IL.
3314	vii	Robert O[9] **Bovie**, born abt 1903 in Chicago, Cook Co., IL.

2202. Richard Harrison[8] **Bovee** (John Nelson[7], Richard[6], Elisha[5], Cornelius[4], Rykert[3], Nicholas[2], Mathieu[1]), born 24 May 1875 in Pilla Twp., Ford Co., IL; died 28 Apr 1957. He married on 19 Jan 1902 Jennie O Towne, born abt 1879 in IA.

Children of Richard Harrison Bovee and Jennie O Towne were as follows:

	3315	i	Althea Marie[9] **Bovee**, born abt 1904. She married **(---) Bruinn**.
	3316	ii	Lois E[9] **Bovee**, born abt 1908 in CA. She married **(---) Nightingale**.
	3317	iii	Jennie E[9] **Bovee**, born abt 1910 in CA. She married **Nightingale (---)**.
+	3318	iv	Frances H[9] **Bovee**, born abt 1911. She married (1) **Glen Hess**; (2) **Gaylord Huddleston**.
+	3319	v	John R[9] **Bovee**, born abt 1913 in CA. He married **Margaret (---)**.
+	3320	vi	Bert J[9] **Bovee**, born abt 1918 in CA. He married **Dolores (---)**.

2204. John Earl LeRoy[8] **Bovee** (John Nelson[7], Richard[6], Elisha[5], Cornelius[4], Rykert[3], Nicholas[2], Mathieu[1]), born 22 Jun 1879 in WI; died 2 Nov 1967 in Anaheim, Orange Co., CA. He married Daisy L McFie, born 22 Jan 1884; died Jan 1987 in LaHabra, Orange Co., CA.

Children of John Earl LeRoy Bovee and Daisy L McFie were as follows:

3321	i	Aloise M[9] **Bovee**, born abt 1907 in CO.
3322	ii	John Leroy[9] **Bovee** Jr, born abt 1909 in CO.
3323	iii	Grace M[9] **Bovee**, born abt 1912 in CO.

2206. Manley Glenn[8] **Bovee** (John Nelson[7], Richard[6], Elisha[5], Cornelius[4], Rykert[3], Nicholas[2], Mathieu[1]), born 31 Dec 1884 in Richland Center, Richland Co., WI; died 20 Dec 1953 in San Diego, San Diego Co., CA. He married on 17 Apr 1910 in Imperial Co., CA Anna Frances Taylor, born 23 Sep 1890 in Roby, Texas Co., MO; died 26 Jun 1939 in Imperial Co., CA.

Children of Manley Glenn Bovee and Anna Frances Taylor were as follows:

| + | 3324 | i | Glenn Nelson[9] **Bovee**, born 30 Jan 1911 in Heber Ranch, Imperial, Imperial Co., CA; died 23 Feb 1972 in CA. He married (1) **Helen Margaret Gates**; (2) **Doris Jane Jackson Arvine**. |
| + | 3325 | ii | Lillburn Robert[9] **Bovee**, born 3 Aug 1912 in Heber Ranch, Imperial Co., CA. He married **Ruth Phyllis McGregor**. |

3326   iii   Althea Lelia[9] **Bovee**, born 7 Jan 1914 in Heber Ranch, Imperial, Imperial Co., CA. She married (1) in Jul 1943, divorced **Bud Wilder**; (2) on 30 Jan 1959 in Imperial, Imperial Co., CA **Philip E Nelson**, born 4 Dec 1911 in KS; died 26 Mar 1986.

+   3327   iv   Allan Douglas[9] **Bovee**, born 12 Dec 1916 in Heber Ranch, Imperial, Imperial Co., CA; died 20 Feb 2000 in Hemet, Riverside Co., CA. He married **Elizabeth Pearl Hobbs**.

+   3328   v   Alice Elizabeth[9] **Bovee**, born 22 Oct 1918 in Imperial, Imperial Co., CA; died 10 Apr 1964. She married **William Flores**.

+   3329   vi   Leslie Gerald[9] **Bovee**, born 7 Nov 1920 in Holtville, Imperial Co., CA. He married **Irene R Jackman**.

+   3330   vii   Ester Esmond[9] **Bovee**, born 26 Aug 1922 in Holtville, Imperial Co., CA. She married **Floyd Vernon Piper**.

3331   viii   Ernest Franklin[9] **Bovee**, born 7 Sep 1924 in Santa Barbara, Santa Barbara Co., CA. He married on 1 Jan 1953 in Yuma, Yuma Co., AZ **Carvella Mills**, born 17 Nov 1923 in Norman, Cleveland Co., OK, daughter of Jesse Walker Mills and Fannie Mae Yandell.

+   3332   ix   Paul Leroy[9] **Bovee**, born 12 Oct 1926 in Holtville, Imperial Co., CA; died 11 May 1977 in Denver, Denver Co., CO.. He married (1) **Dorothy Elinor Baxter Morris**; (2) **Roberta Alexander**.

3333   x   George Kenneth[9] **Bovee**, born 1 Feb 1928 in Holtville, Imperial Co., CA; died 24 Jan 1931 in Holtville, Imperial Co., CA.

+   3334   xi   Billy Ray[9] **Bovee**, born in Holtville, Imperial Co., CA. He married **Florence Linnea Anderson**.

+   3335   xii   Lena Ann[9] **Bovee**, born in Holtville, Imperial Co., CA. She married **Norman C Wingerd**.

2207. Ira Burt[8] **Bovee** (John Nelson[7], Richard[6], Elisha[5], Cornelius[4], Rykert[3], Nicholas[2], Mathieu[1]), born 15 Jan 1891 in Otero Co., CO; died 6 Jun 1948 in Lawson, Clay Co., MO. He married on 20 May 1914 in Pueblo, Pueblo Co., CO Blanche Christine Atterbury, born 24 Aug 1891 in Lawson, Clay Co., MO; died Sep 1983 in Lakewood, Denver Co., CO.

Children of Ira Burt Bovee and Blanche Christine Atterbury were as follows:

3336   i   Thelma Lois[9] **Bovee**, born 20 Sep 1917 in CO. She married on 17 Aug 1940 **Robert Allen Austin**.

3337   ii   Virginia Dorothy[9] **Bovee**, born 25 Jan 1919 in CO. She married on 10 May 1941 **William Strawn**.

+   3338   iii   Burt Richard[9] **Bovee**, born 31 Aug 1922. He married **Peggy Prey**.

+   3339   iv   Erma Jean[9] **Bovee**, born 12 Jun 1927. She married **Richard G Himes**.

2209. Jesse Morris[8] **Bovee** (John Nelson[7], Richard[6], Elisha[5], Cornelius[4], Rykert[3], Nicholas[2], Mathieu[1]), born 3 Oct 1897 in La Junta, Otero Co., CO; died 22 Jun 1956 in Santa Clara, Santa Clara Co., CA. He married on 24 Jul 1918 Mary Jane Spearman, born abt 1900 in CO.

Children of Jesse Morris Bovee and Mary Jane Spearman were as follows:

3340   i   Donald[9] **Bovee**, born abt 1920 in CO.

2220. Lulu Victoria[8] **Bovee** (David William[7], Durfee[6], Elisha[5], Cornelius[4], Rykert[3], Nicholas[2], Mathieu[1]), born Mar 1879 in WI. She married on 29 Dec 1903 in Black Hawk Co., IA Bert Lincoln Morrow, born 1876 in IA; died 1969, son of Isaac Morrow and Lucy (---).

Children of Lulu Victoria Bovee and Bert Lincoln Morrow were as follows:

3341   i   Evelyn[9] **Morrow**, born 1904 in IA; died 1911.
3342   ii   William[9] **Morrow**, born 1905 in IA.
3343   iii   Russell[9] **Morrow**, born 1907 in IA.
3344   iv   Marion[9] **Morrow**, born 1910 in IA.
3345   v   Robert[9] **Morrow**, born 1913 in IA; died 1973.

2221. Helen A[8] **Bovee** (David William[7], Durfee[6], Elisha[5], Cornelius[4], Rykert[3], Nicholas[2], Mathieu[1]), born 6 Jul 1897 in IA; died Oct 1987. She married aft 1920 Rillmond W Schear, son of Augustus A Schear and Alta Benner.

Children of Helen A Bovee and Rillmond W Schear were as follows:

3346   i   Dwight[9] **Schear**, born 17 Aug 1922 in Waterloo, Black Hawk Co., IA.
3347   ii   Nancy[9] **Schear**, born 12 Jun 1926 in Waterloo, Black Hawk Co., IA.
3348   iii   Sally[9] **Schear**, born in Seattle, King Co., WA.
3349   iv   Barbara[9] **Schear**, born in Seattle, King Co., WA.
3350   v   Marcy[9] **Schear**, born in Seattle, King Co., WA.
3351   vi   Rillmond[9] **Schear**, born in Seattle, King Co., WA.

2233. Walter Richard[8] **Bovee** (Jacob Newton[7], David[6], Elisha[5], Cornelius[4], Rykert[3], Nicholas[2], Mathieu[1]), born 22 Jan 1885 in MN; died 12 Sep 1929 in Bain, MN. He married Lena McFarland, born 22 Feb 1889 in Gladstone, Henderson Co., IL; died 15 Aug 1970 in Duluth, St Louis Co., MN, daughter of James McFarland and Nettie Welch.

Children of Walter Richard Bovee and Lena McFarland were as follows:

+   3352   i   Kermit R[9] **Bovee**, born 1 Oct 1908 in Lengby, Polk Co., MN; died 19 Aug 1982 in Solon Springs, Douglas Co., WI. He married **Helen Priem**.

	3353	ii	Walter D^9 **Bovee**, born 1910; died 10 May 1985 in Duluth, St Louis Co., MN.
+	3354	iii	Vartone D^9 **Bovee**, born 8 Mar 1913 in Climax, Polk Co., MN. He married **Ethel Hartzberg**.
+	3355	iv	Maxine M^9 **Bovee**, born 9 Mar 1916 in Comstock Clay Co., MN. She married **Edward Borgolte**.
+	3356	v	Forrest W^9 **Bovee**, born 22 Nov 1926 in Bain, MN. He married **Marian Joyce Smith**.
+	3357	vi	Gloria L^9 **Bovee**, born 18 Aug 1929 in Bain, MN. She married **Dorence Thorson**.

2234. Roderick^8 **Bovee** (Jacob Newton^7, David^6, Elisha^5, Cornelius^4, Rykert^3, Nicholas^2, Mathieu^1), born 13 Jul 1887 in Grey Eagle, Todd Co., MN; died Oct 1963. He married Alice Sveve, born 14 Nov 1894 in Norman Co., MN.

Children of Roderick Bovee and Alice Sveve were as follows:

+	3358	i	Caryl Roger^9 **Bovee**, born 3 Dec 1913; died 3 Sep 1970 in Fosston, Polk Co., MN. He married **Doris Jorgenson**.
+	3359	ii	Iva Lee^9 **Bovee**. She married **John William Graupman**.
+	3360	iii	Alice May^9 **Bovee**. She married **Eugene Hegland**.
+	3361	iv	John Richard^9 **Bovee**, born 29 Jul 1929 in Fosston, Polk Co., MN. He married (1) **Grace Ellen Hanson**; (2) **Terry jaakkola**.

2238. Leonard Alpheus^8 **Bovee** (Cornelius^7, Jonas Nicholas^6, Nicholas^5, Cornelius^4, Rykert^3, Nicholas^2, Mathieu^1), born 28 Mar 1869 in Garden Valley, Jackson Co., WI; died 30 Jul 1940 in Ozaukee Co.,WI. He married on 11 Oct 1891 in Garden Valley, Jackson Co., WI Nettie Vander Berg, born Apr 1872 in Garden Valley, Jackson Co., WI; died 22 Jun 1935, daughter of William Vander Berg and Mary (---).

Children of Leonard Alpheus Bovee and Nettie Vander Berg were as follows:

	3362	i	Cornelius Frank^9 **Bovee**, born 6 Oct 1892 in WI; died May 1967 in Eau Claire, Eau Claire Co., WI.
	3363	ii	William^9 **Bovee**, born Aug 1899.
	3364	iii	Edward^9 **Bovee**.
	3365	iv	Myryle M^9 **Bovee**, born abt 1901.
	3366	v	Marie^9 **Bovee**.
	3367	vi	Sherman Lee^9 **Bovee**, born 17 Jul 1902 in Fairchild, Eau Claire Co., WI.
	3368	vii	Elgie N^9 **Bovee**, born abt 1904.

2239. George F^8 **Bovee** (Cornelius^7, Jonas Nicholas^6, Nicholas^5, Cornelius^4, Rykert^3, Nicholas^2, Mathieu^1), born 1 Jun 1873 in Clayton, Polk Co., WI. He married on 21 Aug 1901 in Fairchild, Eau Claire Co., WI Lillian Adelia Brown.

Children of George F Bovee and Lillian Adelia Brown were as follows:

+ 3369   i   Myron[9] **Bovee**, born 30 Aug 1902 in WI; died Aug 1974 in Kent King Co., WA. He married **Hazel Reed**.

   3370   ii   Helen[9] **Bovee**. She married (1) **George Fleck**; (2) **Edward Leschak**.

   3371   iii   Elsie[9] **Bovee**. She married **Emil Peterson**.

+ 3372   iv   Alton E[9] **Bovee**, born 30 Jul 1914; died 7 Feb 2001 in Park Rapids, Hubbard Co., MN. He married **Phyllis Coon**.

+ 3373   v   Harold[9] **Bovee**, born 28 Jul 1917 in WI; died 27 Aug 1985 in Ft Lauderdale, Broward Co., FL. He married **Beryl (---)**.

   3374   vi   Warren Everett[9] **Bovee**, born 29 Apr 1921 in Bridge Cr Twp., Eau Claire Co., WI; died Apr 1971 in Los Angeles Co., CA.

+ 3375   vii   Janice Lurine[9] **Bovee**, born abt 1924. She married (1) **Lenard Guy Revels**; (2) **Bernard Lawton**.

2242. Hiram Nelson[8] **Bovee** (Cornelius[7], Jonas Nicholas[6], Nicholas[5], Cornelius[4], Rykert[3], Nicholas[2], Mathieu[1]), born 15 Sep 1882 in WI; died 21 Nov 1946 in Lebanon, Linn Co., OR.. He married on 17 Jun 1906 in Eau Claire, Eau Claire Co., WI Ruby Grace Chatterson, born 20 Jul 1880 in Fairchild, Eau Claire Co., WI; died 17 Mar 1984 in Albany, Linn Co., OR, daughter of Washington Chatterson and Laura Ann Winn.

Children of Hiram Nelson Bovee and Ruby Grace Chatterson were as follows:

   3376   i   Cleve Winn[9] **Bovee**, born 26 Sep 1906 in Fairchild, Eau Claire Co., WI; died Dec 1992 in Mesa, Maricopa Co., AZ. He married on 8 Jun 1923 in International Falls, Koochiching Co., MN **Susan Elsa Cerosky**.

+ 3377   ii   Ruth Viola[9] **Bovee**, born 1 Nov 1907 in Eau Claire Co., WI; died 1907 in Eau Claire Co., WI. She married **Edward Anthony**.

+ 3378   iii   Belva Marie[9] **Bovee**, born 14 May 1917 in WI. She married **Kenneth Taylor Hughes**.

+ 3379   iv   Erma Mildred[9] **Bovee**, born 18 Apr 1918 in WI. She married **Joseph Anthony**.

   3380   v   Eleanor Beatrice[9] **Bovee**, born abt 1919 in WI. She married **Walter Keisling**.

+ 3381   vi   Duane Lorenzo[9] **Bovee**, born in International Falls, Koochiching Co., MN. He married **Della Caston**.

+ 3382   vii   Wayne Andrew[9] **Bovee**, born in International Falls, Koochiching Co., MN. He married **Mary Katheryn Campbell**.

2246. William Alfred[8] **Bovee** (Truman Andrew[7], Jonas Nicholas[6], Nicholas[5], Cornelius[4], Rykert[3], Nicholas[2], Mathieu[1]), born 31 Oct 1870 in MN; died 22 Feb 1933 in Minneapolis, Hennepin Co., MN. He married (1) on 24 Dec 1891 in Polk Co., WI Jennie E Anderson, born Dec 1877 in Sweden; (2) on 14 Feb 1917 in Miles City, Custer Co., MT Mary A Wells, born abt 1888 in PA.

Children of William Alfred Bovee and Jennie E Anderson were as follows:

+ 3383 i Truman Alphie[9] **Bovee**, born 15 Mar 1893 in Richardson Polk Co., MN; died 24 Sep 1990 in Miles City, Custer Co., MT. He married **Rose Lewis**.

+ 3384 ii Robert Alvin[9] **Bovee**, born 23 Mar 1895 in WI; died abt 1918. He married **Helma (---)**.

+ 3385 iii Lloyd Laverne[9] **Bovee**, born 23 Aug 1897 in WI; died 15 Apr 1957 in Minot, Ward Co., ND. He married **Rueh L Rued**.

3386 iv Mytrle Julia[9] **Bovee**, born 7 Jun 1899 in WI.

Children of William Alfred Bovee and Mary A Wells were as follows:

3387 i William[9] **Bovee**, born 17 Nov 1920. He married **Eileen (---)**.

3388 ii Ellen[9] **Bovee**, born 1923.

3389 iii John[9] **Bovee**, born 1925.

3390 iv June[9] **Bovee**, born 1927.

2277. Claire Lewis[8] **Bovee** (Silas Lewis[7], Silas Lewis[6], Nicholas[5], Cornelius[4], Rykert[3], Nicholas[2], Mathieu[1]), born 31 Dec 1891 in WI; died May 1977 in IA. He married Ida Gilles.

Children of Claire Lewis Bovee and Ida Gilles were as follows:

+ 3391 i Warren[9] **Gilles**, born 2 Jan 1922; died 7 Jul 2003 in Milwaukee, Milwaukee Co., WI. He married **Gladys Helen Rose**.

2281. James Joseph[8] **Bovee** (Joseph Milford[7], Zebulon[6], Nicholas[5], Cornelius[4], Rykert[3], Nicholas[2], Mathieu[1]), born 11 Jan 1879 in Alma Center, Jackson Co., WI; died 1946 in Regina, Saskatchewan, Canada. He married in 1907 in Regina, Saskatchewan, Canada Mary Gertrude Nelson, born 9 Aug 1884 in Mount Forest, Ontario, Canada; died 16 Mar 1967 in Avonlea, Saskatchewan, Canada, daughter of Charles Nelson and Mary Jane Nixon.

Children of James Joseph Bovee and Mary Gertrude Nelson were as follows:

3392 i Charles Joseph[9] **Bovee**, born 24 Jan 1908 in Rouleau, Saskatchewan, Canada. He married on 3 May 1941 **Edith Mary Chapman**.

3393 ii Edna Mary[9] **Bovee**, born 13 Sep 1909 in New Warren, Saskatchewan, Canada. She married in 1960 in Avonlea,

Saskatchewan, Canada **Leslie Mayne Babcock**.

3394 iii Frederick Edward^9 **Bovee**, born 1911 in Avonlea, Saskatchewan, Canada; died 1925 in Avonlea, Saskatchewan, Canada.

3395 iv Ethel Maybel^9 **Bovee**, born 1913 in Avonlea, Saskatchewan, Canada; died 1916.

3396 v Roy Nelson^9 **Bovee**, born 15 Jun 1915 in Avonlea, Saskatchewan, Canada; died 29 Apr 1997 in Edmonton Alberta, Canada. He married on 14 May 1941 in Regina, Saskatchewan, Canada **Jeanetta Mae Speed**, died 31 Oct 1995 in Edmonton Alberta, Canada.

3397 vi Ada G^9 **Bovee**, born 21 Dec 1917 in Avonlea, Saskatchewan, Canada. She married on 27 Dec 1946 in Regina, Saskatchewan, Canada **Dick Bird**.

2286. Lee Elmer^8 **Bovee** (Edmund L^7, James R^6, Cornelius^5, Cornelius^4, Rykert^3, Nicholas^2, Mathieu^1), born 2 Jun 1883; died Feb 1971 in Pittsburgh, Allegheny Co., PA. He married Edna (---), born 21 Jun 1892; died Apr 1992 in Pittsburgh, Allegheny Co., PA.

Children of Lee Elmer Bovee and Edna (---) were as follows:

3398 i Dorothy^9 **Bovee**, born abt 1915.

2291. Lucy Virginia^8 **Bovie** (George Frederick^7, Frederick Morgan^6, Frederick^5, Cornelius^4, Rykert^3, Nicholas^2, Mathieu^1), born 1899 in Gallipolis, Gallia Co., OH. She married abt 1920 Ray Long.

Children of Lucy Virginia Bovie and Ray Long were as follows:

3399 i Ray^9 **Long**, born abt 1921.

2294. Smith Palmer^8 **Bovie** (George Frederick^7, Frederick Morgan^6, Frederick^5, Cornelius^4, Rykert^3, Nicholas^2, Mathieu^1), born 24 Dec 1917 in Gallipolis, Gallia Co., OH. He married Maria Feiler.

Children of Smith Palmer Bovie and Maria Feiler were as follows:

3400 i Claudia^9 **Bovie**.

3401 ii Sharon Carpenter^9 **Bovie**.

3402 iii Eric Carpenter^9 **Bovie**.

2295. Frederick Ernest^8 **Bovie** (Joseph Harley Clark^7, Frederick Morgan^6, Frederick^5, Cornelius^4, Rykert^3, Nicholas^2, Mathieu^1), born 2 Feb 1901 in Gallipolis, Gallia Co., OH; died 19 Apr 1980 in Jackson, Jackson Co., OH. He married Jeanetta Jones, born 19 Jun 1910, daughter of Reese O Jones and Lola McCoy.

Children of Frederick Ernest Bovie and Jeanetta Jones were as follows:

+   3403   i   Robert Jones^9 **Bovie**. He married **Margaret W Evans**.
+   3404   ii   David Frederick^9 **Bovie**. He married **Marian L Evans**.
+   3405   iii   James Edward^9 **Bovie**, born 10 Sep 1933; died 19 Nov 1990. He married **Gretchen Henderson**.
+   3406   iv   Stephen Clark^9 **Bovie**. He married **Delee Jennings**.

2296. Katherine Elizabeth^8 **Bovie** (Joseph Harley Clark^7, Frederick Morgan^6, Frederick^5, Cornelius^4, Rykert^3, Nicholas^2, Mathieu^1), born 1 Sep 1905 in Gallipolis, Gallia Co., OH. She married John Kircher.

Children of Katherine Elizabeth Bovie and John Kircher were as follows:

3407   i   John Frederick^9 **Kircher**, born 31 Jan 1929.
3408   ii   Katherine Joan^9 **Kircher**. She married **John Hughes Bonnell**.

2297. Henry Tinker^8 **Bovie** (Vernon Morgan^7, Frederick Morgan^6, Frederick^5, Cornelius^4, Rykert^3, Nicholas^2, Mathieu^1), born abt 1902 in NJ; died 10 Jul 1941 in Paraguay, South America. He married abt 1925 in New York, New York Co., NY Mary Rowlad Tucker.

Children of Henry Tinker Bovie and Mary Rowlad Tucker were as follows:

3409   i   Vernon H^9 **Bovie**, born abt 1923.
3410   ii   Mary Ellen^9 **Bovie**.

2308. Perry^8 **Bovee** (Frank Merton^7, Emory John^6, Peter^5, Cornelius^4, Rykert^3, Nicholas^2, Mathieu^1), born 10 May 1900. He married on 4 May 1929 in Detroit, Wayne Co., MI Ruth Alice Avery.

Children of Perry Bovee and Ruth Alice Avery were as follows:

3411   i   Robert Paul^9 **Bovee**, born in Albuquerque, Bernalillo Co., NM.
3412   ii   Dorthy Alice^9 **Bovee**, born in Tuba City, Coconino Co., AZ.

2311. William Harlan^8 **Bovee** (Archibald Melrose^7, John^6, John^5, Nicholas M^4, Matthew^3, Nicholas^2, Mathieu^1), born 4 Oct 1865 in McClean Co., IL; died 8 Feb 1916 in Yuma, Yuma Co., AZ. He married on 4 Jul 1886 in Blair, Washington Co., NE Elizabeth C Spencer, born 18 Jan 1866 in PA; died 5 Apr 1900 in Everett, Snohomish Co., WA.

Children of William Harlan Bovee and Elizabeth C Spencer were as follows:

+   3413   i   Claude Harley^9 **Bovee**, born 21 Jun 1887 in Stockton, San Joaquin Co., CA; died 12 Apr 1971 in Everett, Snohomish Co., WA. He married **Irma B Adams**.

+ 3414 ii Ethol^9 **Bovee**, born Aug 1889 in Arlington, Snohomish Co., WA; died 1930 in Arlington, Snohomish Co., WA. She married **David Spotten**.

3415 iii Robert Bell^9 **Bovee**, born 15 Mar 1891 in Everett, Snohomish Co., WA; died 29 Aug 1947 in Everett, Snohomish Co., WA. He married in Everett, Snohomish Co., WA **Blanche Leo**.

2313. Luella M^8 **Bovee** (Archibald Melrose^7, John^6, John^5, Nicholas M^4, Matthew^3, Nicholas^2, Mathieu^1), born 5 Jun 1870 in McClean Co., IL; died 19 Jul 1904. She married on 24 Dec 1889 William George Fowler, son of Joshua Fowler and Elizabeth Wes.

Children of Luella M Bovee and William George Fowler were as follows:

3416 i Joy^9 **Fowler**.
3417 ii Ruth^9 **Fowler**, born 10 Oct 1893; died 19 Dec 1983.
3418 iii Ray^9 **Fowler**.

2315. Robert Raymond^8 **Bovee** (Archibald Melrose^7, John^6, John^5, Nicholas M^4, Matthew^3, Nicholas^2, Mathieu^1), born 27 Apr 1875 in Vacoma, Washington Co., NE; died 1956. He married abt 1900 Ester Johnson, born abt 1884.

Children of Robert Raymond Bovee and Ester Johnson were as follows:

3419 i Harold Leslie^9 **Bovee**, born abt 1910.
3420 ii Delores^9 **Bovee**, born abt 1912.
3421 iii Opal^9 **Bovee**, born 1913.
3422 iv Ray^9 **Bovee**, born abt 1914.
3423 v Fay^9 **Bovee**, born 1915.

2318. Orlie M^8 **Bovee** (Archibald Melrose^7, John^6, John^5, Nicholas M^4, Matthew^3, Nicholas^2, Mathieu^1), born 1 Jul 1879 in Vacoma, Washington Co., NE; died 21 Jul 1901. He married on 27 Sep 1897 Grace Lavina Oberst, born Aug 1879.

Children of Orlie M Bovee and Grace Lavina Oberst were as follows:

3424 i Thelma^9 **Bovee**, born abt 1898.
3425 ii Eunice^9 **Bovee**, born abt 1900.

2319. Archibald Theodore^8 **Bovee** (Archibald Melrose^7, John^6, John^5, Nicholas M^4, Matthew^3, Nicholas^2, Mathieu^1), born 9 Jan 1884 in Vacoma, Washington Co., NE; died 5 Aug 1979 in Swiftcurrent, Saskatchewan, Canada. He married Winnifred Davis, born 6 Feb 1884 in Herman, Washington Co., NE.

Children of Archibald Theodore Bovee and Winnifred Davis were as follows:

3426 i Lloyd^9 **Bovee**, born 27 Nov 1909 in Lake Stevens,

Snohomish Co., WA.

+ 3427 ii Hugh Archibald[9] **Bovee**, born 16 Dec 1912. He married **Edna Lelia Hunter**.

3428 iii Rex[9] **Bovee**, born abt 1920. He married **Alice Louise Minor**.

2320. Harry F[8] **Bovee** (Archibald Melrose[7], John[6], John[5], Nicholas M[4], Matthew[3], Nicholas[2], Mathieu[1]), born 10 Aug 1887 in Vacoma, Washington Co., NB; died 1970 in British Columbia, Canada. He married on 11 Jan 1912 in Barlett, Washington Co., NE Mattie Gleen Dulaney, born abt 1888, daughter of John Dulaney and Vilena Belle Wild.

Children of Harry F Bovee and Mattie Gleen Dulaney were as follows:

3429 i Lyle[9] **Bovee**, born abt 1914.

3430 ii Harriet[9] **Bovee**.

3431 iii Phil[9] **Bovee**, born abt 1918.

2321. Opal M[8] **Bovee** (Archibald Melrose[7], John[6], John[5], Nicholas M[4], Matthew[3], Nicholas[2], Mathieu[1]), born 6 Apr 1890 in Vacoma, Washington Co., NE; died 1983. She married in 1909 William Brunton, died 1950.

Children of Opal M Bovee and William Brunton were as follows:

3432 i Orland[9] **Brunton**, born abt 1910 in Burt Co., NE.

3433 ii Earl[9] **Brunton**, born aft 1910 in Burt Co., NE.

3434 iii Keith[9] **Brunton**, born 1914 in Burt Co., NE.

3435 iv William B[9] **Brunton**, born in Burt Co., NE.

3436 v Evelyn[9] **Brunton**, born 1922 in Burt Co., NE.

2326. Raymond H[8] **Bovee** (Nicholas Aaron[7], John[6], John[5], Nicholas M[4], Matthew[3], Nicholas[2], Mathieu[1]), born 10 Aug 1879 in IA; died 2 Dec 1945. He married on 21 Mar 1906 Minnie Pearl Gillman, born 3 Jan 1882 in NE; died 20 May 1955.

Children of Raymond H Bovee and Minnie Pearl Gillman were as follows:

3437 i Helen I[9] **Bovee**, born abt 1908 in NE.

3438 ii Ethel M[9] **Bovee**, born abt 1910 in NE.

2329. Henry Hopkins[8] **Bovee** (John Wesley[7], John[6], John[5], Nicholas M[4], Matthew[3], Nicholas[2], Mathieu[1]), born 5 Oct 1869 in De Kalb, Buchanan Co., MO; died 5 Nov 1950. He married on 7 Jun 1910 Florence Eleanor Putzker, born 25 Jul 1887 in CA; died Jul 1982.

Children of Henry Hopkins Bovee and Florence Eleanor Putzker were as follows:

3439	i	Caroline Marjorie^9 **Bovee**, born 1 Apr 1911 in Oxnard, Ventura Co., CA; died 24 Sep 1992 in Landers, Yucca Valley Co., CA.. She married **John Lewis Smith**.
+ 3440	ii	Henry Hopkins^9 **Bovee** Jr, born 16 Jan 1915 in Oxnard, Ventura Co., CA; died 23 Apr 1994 in Los Angeles, Los Angeles Co., CA. He married **Ruth Conklin**.
3441	iii	Janet Helen^9 **Bovee**, born abt 1917 in Oxnard, Ventura Co., CA. She married **Glen Williams**.
3442	iv	John Wesley^9 **Bovee**, born 2 Mar 1923 in Owensmouth, CA; died 23 Nov 1989 in Prescott, Yavapai Co., AZ. He married **Mary America Lee**.
3443	v	Donald Dale^9 **Bovee**, born 22 Feb 1925 in Ontario, San Bernardino Co., CA. He married **Alverda L Hall**.

2331. William James^8 **Bovee** (John Wesley^7, John^6, John^5, Nicholas M^4, Matthew^3, Nicholas^2, Mathieu^1), born 20 Jan 1874 in Hamilton, Caldwell Co., MO; died 20 Nov 1944 in Los Angeles, Los Angeles Co., CA. He married aft 1900 Anita Putzker, born abt 1864; died 3 Apr 1934 in Los Angeles, Los Angeles Co., CA, daughter of Albin Putzker and Caroline Reimer.

Children of William James Bovee and Anita Putzker were as follows:

+ 3444	i	Clifton Willard^9 **Bovee**, born 23 Sep 1913 in Santa Anna, Orange Co., CA.. He married (1) **Sharlie Evelyn Carpenter**; (2) **Jonita Ruth Benham**.
3445	ii	Dorothy^9 **Bovee**. She married **(---) Carpenter**.

2334. Arthur Roy^8 **Bovee** (John Wesley^7, John^6, John^5, Nicholas M^4, Matthew^3, Nicholas^2, Mathieu^1), born 12 May 1885 in St Paul, Howard Co., NE; died 2 Jun 1953 in Pierce, Pierce Co., NE. He married on 3 Nov 1910 in Norfolk, Madison Co., NE Otelia Magdalena Machmueller, born 8 Jan 1886 in Norfolk, Madison Co., NE; died 29 Dec 1961 in Pierce, Pierce Co., NE, daughter of J Martin Machmueller and Louise Buettow.

Children of Arthur Roy Bovee and Otelia Magdalena Machmueller were as follows:

3446	i	Dorothy Edna^9 **Bovee**, born 10 Apr 1912 in Pierce Co., NE; died Oct 1980 in Norfolk, Madisoon Co., NE. She married on 8 Aug 1948 in Zion Lutheran Ch, Pierce, Pierce Co., NE **Lester Gallagher**.
+ 3447	ii	Harley Ray^9 **Bovee**, born 1 Jun 1913 in Pierce Co., NE. He married **Henrietta Clara Elfrieda Faudel**.

2335. Carl Howard^8 **Bovee** (John Wesley^7, John^6, John^5, Nicholas M^4, Matthew^3, Nicholas^2, Mathieu^1), born 8 May 1888 in Norfolk, Madison Co., NE; died May 1961. He married on 30 Jan 1911 Emma Potras.

Children of Carl Howard Bovee and Emma Potras were as follows:

3448   i   Harold^9 **Bovee**, born 1 Mar 1914; died 11 Dec 1949 in San Bernardino, San Bernardino Co., CA.

3449   ii   Mildred^9 **Bovee**, born bef 1917. She married **Harold Long**.

+   3450   iii   Howard Francis^9 **Bovee**, born 27 Aug 1917; died Jun 1978. He married **Maxine Babcock**.

2336. Carrie Agnes^8 **Bovee** (Jacob Nelson^7, John^6, John^5, Nicholas M^4, Matthew^3, Nicholas^2, Mathieu^1), born 26 Apr 1876 in Walker, Linn Co., IA; died Sep 1947 in Santa Ana, Orange Co., CA. She married in 1901 in Seattle, King Co., WA Andrew Eli Griswold, born 9 Nov 1875 in La Crosse, La Crosse Co., WI; died 14 Jul 1961 in Redlands, San Bernardino Co., CA.

Children of Carrie Agnes Bovee and Andrew Eli Griswold were as follows:

3451   i   Harlan Benham^9 **Griswold**, born 3 Mar 1903 in Seattle, King Co., WA; died 24 Oct 1997 in Fallbrook, San Diego Co., CA.

3452   ii   Melba W^9 **Griswold**, born 8 Jan 1905 in Seattle, King Co., WA; died 9 Jan 1968.

2340. Albert^8 **Bovee** (Nelson LeGrande^7, Aaron Milton^6, John^5, Nicholas M^4, Matthew^3, Nicholas^2, Mathieu^1), born abt 1877 in WI. He married Annie (---), born abt 1875.

Children of Albert Bovee and Annie (---) were as follows:

3453   i   Ralph^9 **Bovee**, born 24 Aug 1901 in WI; died Jun 1970 in St Petersburg, Pinellas Co., FL.

3454   ii   Wilhemina^9 **Bovee**, born 17 Jan 1905 in WI.

3455   iii   Edwin^9 **Bovee**, born 8 May 1906 in WI; died 2 Aug 1991.

3456   iv   Lenora^9 **Bovee**, born abt 1909 in WI.

3457   v   Roland Ritchie^9 **Bovee**, born 16 Nov 1912 in IL; died 10 Aug 1989 in Orlando, Orange Co., FL.

2348. Lillian^8 **Bovee** (William Levant^7, Aaron Milton^6, John^5, Nicholas M^4, Matthew^3, Nicholas^2, Mathieu^1), born abt 1882; died 1962. She married Charles Fathers.

Children of Lillian Bovee and Charles Fathers were as follows:

3458   i   Lloyd^9 **Fathers**, born 1903; died abt 1989 in Seattle, King Co., WA.

3459   ii   Russell Charles^9 **Fathers**, born abt 1907; died 1982 in Seattle, King Co., WA.

2349. William Vivian^8 **Bovee** (John McClellan^7, Wesley^6, John^5, Nicholas M^4, Matthew^3, Nicholas^2, Mathieu^1), born 21 Nov 1890 in Winchester, Scott Co., IL; died 28 Mar 1969 in Pleasant Hill, Pike Co., IL. He married on 9 Dec 1919 in Nebo, Pike Co., IL Alice Marie Gant, daughter of Robert Green Gant and Anna Flora.

Children of William Vivian Bovee and Alice Marie Gant were as follows:

3460	i	William Vivian^9 **Bovee** Jr, born 21 Jan 1921 in Pleasant Hill, Pike Co., IL.
+ 3461	ii	Robert Wesley^9 **Bovee**, born 1 Dec 1923 in Pleasant Hill, Pike Co., IL. He married **Ruth Ann Silvus**.
3462	iii	Albert Merlin^9 **Bovee**, born 2 Nov 1925 in Compton, Los Angeles Co., CA.
3463	iv	Eugene Orland^9 **Bovee**, born 5 Aug 1929 in Compton, Los Angeles Co., CA.

2352. Faith M^8 **Bovee** (John McClellan^7, Wesley^6, John^5, Nicholas M^4, Matthew^3, Nicholas^2, Mathieu^1), born 15 Oct 1896 in Bellvue, Calhoun Co., IL; died 4 Apr 1988 in MT. She married on 8 Jun 1920 in Rawlings, Carbon Co., WY Fred R Uhde, born 31 Jan 1901 in Storm Lake, Beuna Vista Co., IA; died 15 Jul 1972 in Rollins, Lake Co., MT.

Children of Faith M Bovee and Fred R Uhde were as follows:

3464	i	Mary^9 **Uhde**, born 7 Apr 1921.
3465	ii	Richard^9 **Uhde**, born 15 Oct 1922.
3466	iii	James^9 **Uhde**, born 24 Jan 1924 in Blanchard, Skagit Co., WA.
3467	iv	Paul^9 **Uhde**, born 20 Sep 1927; died 1 Apr 1930.
3468	v	Caroline^9 **Uhde**, born 26 May 1929.

2357. Eugene Burdette^8 **Bovee** (John McClellan^7, Wesley^6, John^5, Nicholas M^4, Matthew^3, Nicholas^2, Mathieu^1), born 27 Sep 1911 in Calhoun Co., IL; died 17 Feb 1989. He married on 4 Feb 1936 in Yuma, Yuma Co., AZ Marjorie Irene Johnson, born 3 Aug 1912; died 11 Jun 1989.

Children of Eugene Burdette Bovee and Marjorie Irene Johnson were as follows:

+ 3469	i	Beverly J^9 **Bovee**, born 2 Jan 1939 in Compton, Los Angeles Co., CA; died 12 Sep 2001 in Helena, Lewis & Clarck Co., MT. She married **(---) Shilder**.
+ 3470	ii	Stanley^9 **Bovee**, born in Compton, Los Angeles Co., CA. He married **Bambi (---)**.
+ 3471	iii	Nancy^9 **Bovee**, born in Compton, Los Angeles Co., CA. She married **Joel (---)**.

2380. Elmer N^8 **Bovee** (John Milton^7, Nelson John^6, John^5, Nicholas M^4, Matthew^3, Nicholas^2, Mathieu^1), born Oct 1882 in Nebo, Pike Co., IL. He married Myrtle M (---), born abt 1888 in NE.

Children of Elmer N Bovee and Myrtle M (---) were as follows:

3472	i	Mildred A^9 **Bovee**, born 1909 in NE.
3473	ii	Helen M^9 **Bovee**, born 1911 in NE.
3474	iii	Leone M^9 **Bovee**, born 1913 in NE.
3475	iv	Dorothy L^9 **Bovee**, born 1920 in NE.
3476	v	Laverne^9 **Bovee**, born 4 Jun 1922 in NE; died 20 Nov 1993 in Orange Co., CA.

2381. Lee M^8 **Bovee** (John Milton^7, Nelson John^6, John^5, Nicholas M^4, Matthew^3, Nicholas^2, Mathieu^1), born Jul 1884 in NE; died 19 Mar 1963 in Los Angeles, Los Angeles Co., CA. He married Olive Emily Mennell, born 24 Aug 1888 in NE; died 3 Feb 1945 in Los Angeles, Los Angeles Co., CA.

Children of Lee M Bovee and Olive Emily Mennell were as follows:

3477	i	Milton E^9 **Bovee**, born 24 Jun 1917 in CA; died 1 Oct 1969 in Los Angeles Co., CA. He married **Alice Ruth (---) Pike**.

2382. Walter^8 **Bovee** (John Milton^7, Nelson John^6, John^5, Nicholas M^4, Matthew^3, Nicholas^2, Mathieu^1), born Feb 1888 in NE. He married Alice W (---), born 12 Jan 1889 in NE; died Jul 1984 in Tekamah, Burt Co., NE.

Children of Walter Bovee and Alice W (---) were as follows:

3478	i	Adelaide^9 **Bovee**, born abt 1926 in NE.

2385. Glenn Peter^8 **Bovee** (James Massey^7, Nelson John^6, John^5, Nicholas M^4, Matthew^3, Nicholas^2, Mathieu^1), born 13 Apr 1888 in Glenrock, Converse Co., WY; died 31 Dec 1956 in Shawnee, Pottawatomie Co., OK. He married on 16 Nov 1912 in Shawnee, Pottawatomie Co., OK Vina Irene Sauter, born 15 Aug 1890 in Newell, Buena Vista Co., IA; died 11 Nov 1973 in Shawnee, Pottawatomie Co., OK, daughter of Frederick Lewis Sauter and Jennie Grace Robinson.

Children of Glenn Peter Bovee and Vina Irene Sauter were as follows:

	3479	i	Glenn Harold^9 **Bovee**, born 7 Nov 1918 in Shawnee, Pottawatomie Co., OK; died 10 Jul 1919 in Cheyenne, Laramie Co., WY.
+	3480	ii	Kenneth Eugene^9 **Bovee**, born 19 Aug 1920 in Shawnee, Pottawatomie Co., OK. He married **Ora Lee Laster**.
+	3481	iii	Keith Alan^9 **Bovee**, born 16 Dec 1921 in Shawnee, Pottawatomie Co., OK. He married **Pauline Elizabeth Dunbar**.

+ 3482 iv Reta Eunice^9 **Bovee**, born in Shawnee, Pottawatomie Co., OK. She married (1) **Kenneth Darrell Miller**; (2) **William Thomas Henderson**.

2387. Gail Margaret^8 **Bovee** (James Massey^7, Nelson John^6, John^5, Nicholas M^4, Matthew^3, Nicholas^2, Mathieu^1), born 7 Apr 1895 in Fletcher, Washington Co., NE; died 8 Apr 1986 in Laramie, Albany Co., WY. She married on 12 Nov 1919 in Cheyenne, Laramie Co., WY John Wesley Johnson, born 7 Oct 1892 in Albany Co., WY; died 24 Sep 1973 in Albany Co., WY, son of Jacob Elge Johnson and Sofia S Kampe.

Children of Gail Margaret Bovee and John Wesley Johnson were as follows:

3483 i Everette Elge^9 **Johnson**, born 5 Jul 1921 in Cheyenne, Laramie Co., WY.

3484 ii Carol Ann^9 **Johnson**, born in Laramie, Albany Co., WY.

2399. Nettie Elizabeth^8 **Bovee** (Jasper Lincoln^7, Joseph Smith^6, Mathew^5, Nicholas M^4, Matthew^3, Nicholas^2, Mathieu^1), born 9 Aug 1893 in Cheyenne, Laramie Co., WY; died 4 Nov 1980 in Wheatland, Platte Co., WY. She married on 4 May 1916 in Wheatland, Platte Co., WY Horace Cleveland Wilson, born 10 Jun 1889 in Burke Co., NC; died 19 Oct 1965 in Wheatland, Platte Co., WY.

Children of Nettie Elizabeth Bovee and Horace Cleveland Wilson were as follows:

3485 i Harold^9 **Wilson**.

3486 ii Donald Lee^9 **Wilson**, born 20 Jun 1921 in Wheatland, Platte Co., WY.

2404. Raymond A^8 **Bovee** (Lester La Grand^7, Joseph Smith^6, Mathew^5, Nicholas M^4, Matthew^3, Nicholas^2, Mathieu^1), born 8 Jan 1908 in Cheyenne, Laramie Co., WY; died 9 Mar 1991 in Cheyenne, Laramie Co., WY. He married Marie Dykeman.

Children of Raymond A Bovee and Marie Dykeman were as follows:

3487 i Virginia^9 **Bovee**.

3488 ii Vivian^9 **Bovee**.

3489 iii Wayne^9 **Bovee**.

2405. Joseph Earl^8 **Bovee** (Lester La Grand^7, Joseph Smith^6, Mathew^5, Nicholas M^4, Matthew^3, Nicholas^2, Mathieu^1), born 28 Mar 1910 in Cheyenne, Laramie Co., WY. He married (1) Frances Berry; (2) abt 1947 Evelyn (---).

Children of Joseph Earl Bovee and Frances Berry were as follows:

3490 i Joan^9 **Bovee**.

3491 ii David^9 **Bovee**.

3492   iii   Barbara[9] **Bovee**.

Children of Joseph Earl Bovee and Evelyn (---) were as follows:

3493   i   Pamela[9] **Bovee**.

2406. Benedict Arthur[8] **Bovee** (Marvin W[7], Benedict Arnold[6], Mathias Jacob[5], Jacob Mathias[4], Matthew[3], Nicholas[2], Mathieu[1]), born 6 Jun 1889 in Eagle, Waukesha Co., WI; died 14 Apr 1985 in Fort Lauderdale, Broward Co., FL. He married on 10 Sep 1913 Myrtle L Manwaring.

Children of Benedict Arthur Bovee and Myrtle L Manwaring were as follows:

3494   i   Kenneth M[9] **Bovee**, born 25 Jul 1914; died 6 Nov 1992. He married **Marjorie Wheeler**.

3495   ii   Mildred E[9] **Bovee**, born 30 Oct 1918. She married **Robert A McKoun**.

3496   iii   Frances E[9] **Bovee**, born 5 Feb 1920. She married **Philip S Bechtel**.

3497   iv   Joyce M[9] **Bovee**, born 17 Feb 1926. She married **Harry C Blatcheley**.

3498   v   Jack B[9] **Bovee**, born 17 Feb 1926. He married **Joan Wise**.

2408. James Francis[8] **Bovee** (Marvin W[7], Benedict Arnold[6], Mathias Jacob[5], Jacob Mathias[4], Matthew[3], Nicholas[2], Mathieu[1]), born 3 Dec 1895 in Eagle, Waukesha Co., WI; died 9 Jan 1992. He married on 6 Jul 1922 Fern A Marty, born 17 Dec 1895 in Dayton, Greene Co., WI; died 7 May 1990.

Children of James Francis Bovee and Fern A Marty were as follows:

3499   i   Dorothy[9] **Bovee**, born 21 Mar 1925 in Eagle, Waukesha Co.,WI. She married on 4 Sep 1954 **William F Clark**.

+   3500   ii   James Marty[9] **Bovee**, born in Eagle, Waukesha Co.,WI. He married **Marlene Jahnke**.

2411. William David[8] **Bovee** (Manley W[7], William Reid[6], Mathias Jacob[5], Jacob Mathias[4], Matthew[3], Nicholas[2], Mathieu[1]), born 26 Dec 1872 in PA. He married in Grand Valley, Warren Co., PA Mary Elizabeth Shutt, born 30 Sep 1875 in Fagundus, Warren Co.,PA; died 9 Jan 1957, daughter of Wallace Shutt and Ruby Eliza.

Children of William David Bovee and Mary Elizabeth Shutt were as follows:

+   3501   i   Wallace M[9] **Bovee**, born 21 Oct 1897; died 8 Sep 1961 in Jamestown, Chautauqua Vo., NY. He married **Dorothy M Fink**.

+   3502   ii   Harold Ezra[9] **Bovee**, born 2 Jul 1900 in PA. He married **Ruth Madge Powell**.

+   3503   iii   Rhea B[9] **Bovee**, born 24 Feb 1908 in Grand Valley,

Warren Co., PA. She married **Percy James Lanning**.

2412. Jesse D^8 **Bovee** (Manley W^7, William Reid^6, Mathias Jacob^5, Jacob Mathias^4, Matthew^3, Nicholas^2, Mathieu^1), born 13 Feb 1874 in PA; died 30 Jan 1959. He married (1) on 13 Feb 1894 Hattie Powell; (2) on 12 Sep 1927 Della Baker; (3) in 1933 Minnie Fescus.

Children of Jesse D Bovee and Hattie Powell were as follows:

3504   i   William^9 **Bovee**, born 1904 in PA.

2422. Marvin Burleigh^8 **Bovee** (Herbert Stephen^7, Edward Livingston^6, Mathias Jacob^5, Jacob Mathias^4, Matthew^3, Nicholas^2, Mathieu^1), born 30 Mar 1897 in East Troy, Walworth Co., WI; died 10 Oct 1961 in WI. He married (1) on 21 Aug 1918 in Spartanburg, Spartanburg Co., SC Nina Verginia Wilkinson, born 5 Mar 1899 in Minneapolis, Hennepin Co., MN; died 4 Nov 1947 in Minneapolis, Hennepin Co., MN, daughter of James Patton Wilkinson and Emma R Fornhof; (2) Doris Anna Bedard, born 10 Jan 1910, daughter of Earnest William Bedard and Laura Mary Archambould.

Children of Marvin Burleigh Bovee and Nina Verginia Wilkinson were as follows:

3505   i   Jean Beatrice^9 **Bovee**.
+ 3506   ii   Virginia Ora^9 **Bovee**. She married **Donald Emmet Carlson**.

Children of Marvin Burleigh Bovee and Doris Anna Bedard were as follows:

3507   i   Marianne Doris^9 **Bovee**.
+ 3508   ii   Mark Bedard^9 **Bovee**, born in Superior, Douglas Co., WI. He married **Janice Holisky**.

2429. Lloyd Horace^8 **Bovee** (John Walker^7, Thomas Pittman^6, Philip Vedder^5, Jacob Mathias^4, Matthew^3, Nicholas^2, Mathieu^1), born 19 Oct 1894 in WI; died 30 Jun 1981 in Plainfield, Waushara Co., WI. He married in Mar 1922 Bernice Reed, born 1900.

Children of Lloyd Horace Bovee and Bernice Reed were as follows:

3509   i   Raymond H^9 **Bovee**, born 10 Aug 1923; died 1923.
3510   ii   Paul^9 **Bovee**, born 31 Oct 1925.

2430. Bessie Lillian^8 **Bovee** (John Walker^7, Thomas Pittman^6, Philip Vedder^5, Jacob Mathias^4, Matthew^3, Nicholas^2, Mathieu^1), born 6 Oct 1897 in WI. She married on 25 May 1918 James Doolittle.

Children of Bessie Lillian Bovee and James Doolittle were as follows:

3511   i   Wayne J^9 **Doolittle**, born 18 Sep 1919.

3512　　ii　　　　Jean[9] **Doolittle**, born 20 Jun 1923.

2432. Harold Vincent[8] **Bovee** (John Walker[7], Thomas Pittman[6], Philip Vedder[5], Jacob Mathias[4], Matthew[3], Nicholas[2], Mathieu[1]), born 19 Aug 1914. He married unknown.

Children of Harold Vincent Bovee were as follows:

3513　　i　　　　Mary Lou[9] **Bovee**. She married **David Renner**.
3514　　ii　　　Roger William[9] **Bovee**, born in WI.

2436. John Lemuel Franklin[8] **Bovee** (Jonathan Betts[7], Lemuel Jacob[6], Philip Vedder[5], Jacob Mathias[4], Matthew[3], Nicholas[2], Mathieu[1]), born 1897; died 1964. He married in Jun 1938 in Fairfield, Fairfield Co., CT Margaret Kepler Fowler, born 1899; died 24 Nov 1958 in Los Angeles Co., CA, daughter of John Francis Fowler.

Children of John Lemuel Franklin Bovee and Margaret Kepler Fowler were as follows:

3515　　i　　　　John Francis[9] **Bovee**.
3516　　ii　　　Michael Christopher[9] **Bovee**.

2442. Elurde Charles[8] **Bovee** (Charles Eugene[7], Lemuel Jacob[6], Philip Vedder[5], Jacob Mathias[4], Matthew[3], Nicholas[2], Mathieu[1]), born 12 Mar 1914 in Oconto Co., WI. He married Ethel (---).

Children of Elurde Charles Bovee and Ethel (---) were as follows:

3517　　i　　　　Janice[9] **Bovee**, born bef 1993; died bef 1993.
3518　　ii　　　Donald[9] **Bovee**.
3519　　iii　　Gary[9] **Bovee**.

2443. Elmer C[8] **Bovee** (Charles Eugene[7], Lemuel Jacob[6], Philip Vedder[5], Jacob Mathias[4], Matthew[3], Nicholas[2], Mathieu[1]), born 12 Mar 1914 in Oconto Co., WI; died Jul 1986 in Yuma, Yuma Co., AZ. He married unknown.

Children of Elmer C Bovee were as follows:

+　　3520　　i　　　　Lawrence[9] **Bovee**. He married unknown.
+　　3521　　ii　　　Leslie Charles[9] **Bovee**. He married unknown.

2450. Eugene Philip[8] **Bovee** (Philip LaRue[7], Eugene Charles[6], Philip Vedder[5], Jacob Mathias[4], Matthew[3], Nicholas[2], Mathieu[1]), born 27 Nov 1904. He married Zadie Elizabeth Currie, born 14 Sep 1906.

Children of Eugene Philip Bovee and Zadie Elizabeth Currie were as follows:

	3522	i	Robert Eugene[9] **Bovee**, born 11 Mar 1928; died 14 Jul 1999 in Littleton, Arapahoe Co., CO. He married **Mary Alice Russell**.
	3523	ii	Velda Lorraine[9] **Bovee**, born 1 Jun 1929.
+	3524	iii	Mary Louise[9] **Bovee**. She married **Bruce E Hanson**.
	3525	iv	Paul Eugene[9] **Bovee**. He married **Mary Lou Kaufman**.
	3526	v	Jane Ellen[9] **Bovee**. She married **(---) McMullen**.

2451. John Larue[8] **Bovee** (Philip LaRue[7], Eugene Charles[6], Philip Vedder[5], Jacob Mathias[4], Matthew[3], Nicholas[2], Mathieu[1]), born 24 Mar 1907 in CO; died Dec 1972 in CO. He married Barbara Bendell.

Children of John Larue Bovee and Barbara Bendell were as follows:

+	3527	i	John Ronald[9] **Bovee**, born in CO. He married **Judith Lou Russell**.

2458. Frederick Charles[8] **Bovee** Jr (Frederick Charles[7], William Henry[6], John Grant[5], John[4], Matthew[3], Nicholas[2], Mathieu[1]), born Jan 1884 in Three Mile Bay, Jefferson Co., NY; died 5 Jul 1961. He married Harriet Steele, died 28 Apr 1957.

Children of Frederick Charles Bovee Jr and Harriet Steele were as follows:

+	3528	i	Lena[9] **Bovee**, born 13 Jan 1910; died Oct 1987 in Carthage, Jefferson Co., NY. She married **Myron Oliver**.
	3529	ii	Edith[9] **Bovee**, born 27 Jun 1911. She married **(---) Schultz**.
+	3530	iii	Richard[9] **Bovee**, born 1 May 1915 in Dexter, Jefferson Co., NY. He married **Ruth White**.
+	3531	iv	Eva[9] **Bovee**, born 4 Sep 1916 in Canada; died 23 May 1997 in Contra Costa Co., CA. She married **James F McMillan**.
	3532	v	Charles[9] **Bovee**, born abt 1921; died 25 Oct 1944 in At Sea, Battle of Leyte, USS Swanee.

2459. Edward J[8] **Bovee** (Frederick Charles[7], William Henry[6], John Grant[5], John[4], Matthew[3], Nicholas[2], Mathieu[1]), born Jun 1895 in NY. He married Anna Emerson, born 16 Jul 1894; died Dec 1971 in Watertown, Jefferson Co., NY.

Children of Edward J Bovee and Anna Emerson were as follows:

	3533	i	Stanley E[9] **Bovee**, born abt 1917; died abt 1961. He married **Gladys Paquette**.
+	3534	ii	Glenn S[9] **Bovee**, born 1919; died 18 Mar 1996. He married **Totsuyu Tumatu**.
	3535	iii	Pauline[9] **Bovee**, born abt 1920. She married **(---) Jones**.
	3536	iv	Frank[9] **Bovee**, born abt 1922.

2462. Stella[8] **Bovee** (Frederick Charles[7], William Henry[6], John Grant[5], John[4], Matthew[3], Nicholas[2], Mathieu[1]), born 24 Sep 1911. She married (1) on 26 Nov 1938 James E Denslow; (2) abt 1944 Paul DuFrene.

Children of Stella Bovee and James E Denslow were as follows:

3537 i Barbara J[9] **Denslow**.
3538 ii Nancy C[9] **Denslow**.

Children of Stella Bovee and Paul DuFrene were as follows:

3539 i Norma[9] **DuFrene**.

2463. Eunice[8] **Bovee** (Frederick Charles[7], William Henry[6], John Grant[5], John[4], Matthew[3], Nicholas[2], Mathieu[1]), born 14 Oct 1914. She married on 24 Nov 1932 Norman Westcott.

Children of Eunice Bovee and Norman Westcott were as follows:

3540 i Robert[9] **Westcott**.
3541 ii Arlene[9] **Westcott**.
3542 iii Paul[9] **Westcott**.
3543 iv Ronald[9] **Westcott**.

2467. George[8] **Bovee** (Frederick Charles[7], William Henry[6], John Grant[5], John[4], Matthew[3], Nicholas[2], Mathieu[1]), born 27 Nov 1917 in Watertown, Jefferson Co., NY; died 24 Nov 1978 in Watertown, Jefferson Co., NY. He married in Feb 1942 Mary Murphy, born abt 1922.

Children of George Bovee and Mary Murphy were as follows:

3544 i George[9] **Bovee** Jr.

2468. Ralph Perl[8] **Bovee** (Frederick Charles[7], William Henry[6], John Grant[5], John[4], Matthew[3], Nicholas[2], Mathieu[1]), born 22 Dec 1920 in Watertown, Jefferson Co., NY; died 11 Apr 1996 in Watertown, Jefferson Co., NY. He married on 18 Jul 1942 in Watertown, Jefferson Co., NY Betty J Desormeau, born 3 Apr 1922 in Watertown, Jefferson Co., NY, daughter of Henry Desormeau and Bessie Cummings.

Children of Ralph Perl Bovee and Betty J Desormeau were as follows:

3545 i Ralph Perl[9] **Bovee** Jr, born in Watertown, Jefferson Co., NY. He married on 18 Feb 1967 in Dallas/ Dallas Co., TX **Marie P**.
+ 3546 ii Larry A[9] **Bovee**, born in Watertown, Jefferson Co., NY. He married **Constance M Mallow**.
3547 iii Linda A[9] **Bovee**, born in Watertown, Jefferson Co., NY. She married **Gary Smith**.

+ 3548 iv James W^9 **Bovee**, born 30 Jun 1948; died 8 Nov 1989. He married **Frances (---)**.

2469. Fanny^8 **Bovee** (Hiram David^7, William Henry^6, John Grant^5, John^4, Matthew^3, Nicholas^2, Mathieu^1), born 4 Mar 1907; died 24 Nov 1930. She married on 29 May 1926 John Russell.

Children of Fanny Bovee and John Russell were as follows:
3549 i Josephine^9 **Russell**, born 30 Mar 1927.
3550 ii Hiram^9 **Russell**, born 2 Feb 1929.

2470. Florence M^8 **Bovee** (Hiram David^7, William Henry^6, John Grant^5, John^4, Matthew^3, Nicholas^2, Mathieu^1), born 4 Oct 1908. She married on 13 Nov 1923 Stanley E Farr.

Children of Florence M Bovee and Stanley E Farr were as follows:
3551 i Willard Clarkson^9 **Farr**, born 28 Mar 1924.
3552 ii Stanley^9 **Farr** Jr.
3553 iii Richard James^9 **Farr**.

2471. Harold L^8 **Bovee** (Hiram David^7, William Henry^6, John Grant^5, John^4, Matthew^3, Nicholas^2, Mathieu^1), born 14 Dec 1912 in Depauville, Clayton Twp., Jefferson Co., NY; died 3 Feb 1975 in St Petersburg, Pinellas Co., FL. He married on 28 Oct 1934 Evelyn Gertrude Constance, daughter of Charles Constance and Elizabeth White.

Children of Harold L Bovee and Evelyn Gertrude Constance were as follows:
+ 3554 i Mary Elizabeth^9 **Bovee**. She married **William H Dasno**.
+ 3555 ii Marilyn Mae^9 **Bovee**, born in Watertown, Jefferson Co., NY. She married **Robert Edward Dailey**.
+ 3556 iii Nancy Ann^9 **Bovee**, born in Jefferson Co., NY. She married **Donald W Rhodes**.
3557 iv Valerie Frances^9 **Bovee**, born in Jefferson Co., NY. She married on 13 Jun 1970 in LaFargeville, Jefferson Co., NY **James Michael Ramakka**.

2472. Gladys Leota^8 **Bovee** (Hiram David^7, William Henry^6, John Grant^5, John^4, Matthew^3, Nicholas^2, Mathieu^1), born 30 Sep 1913 in Clayton, Jefferson Co., NY; died 20 Dec 1985. She married on 9 Mar 1932 in Clayton., Jefferson Co., NY Perry W Shely.

Children of Gladys Leota Bovee and Perry W Shely were as follows:
3558 i Donald F^9 **Shely**, born in Clayton, Jefferson Co., NY.
3559 ii Sharon Louise^9 **Shely**, born 9 Mar 1942; died 7 May 1960

2482. Walter Everette[8] **(Bovee)** De ROSIA (Burton G[7], William Henry[6], John Grant[5], John[4], Matthew[3], Nicholas[2], Mathieu[1]), born 1 Jun 1909 in Clayton Jefferson Co., NY; died 21 Nov 1971 in Carthage, Jefferson Co., NY. He married (1) unknown; (2) (---) Soluri.

Children of Walter Everette (Bovee) De ROSIA were as follows:

3560   i   Buddy[9] **(Bovee)**.

2483. Anna Irene[8] **Bovee** (Franklin E[7], John Wesley[6], John Grant[5], John[4], Matthew[3], Nicholas[2], Mathieu[1]), born 18 Jun 1892 in Redfield, Oswego Co., NY. She married on 17 Jun 1914 Lloyd E Watkins.

Children of Anna Irene Bovee and Lloyd E Watkins were as follows:

3561   i   Keith Elihu[9] **Watkins**, born 30 Jan 1917.
3562   ii   Helen Harriett[9] **Watkins**, born 24 Oct 1918.

2484. Edward Milton[8] **Bovee** (Franklin E[7], John Wesley[6], John Grant[5], John[4], Matthew[3], Nicholas[2], Mathieu[1]), born 11 Apr 1894 in Redfield, Oswego Co., NY; died 27 Dec 1968 in St. Cloud, Osceola Co., FL. He married on 2 Sep 1914 in Camden, Oneida Co., NY Bertha P Spellicy, born 27 Aug 1894 in Florence, Oneida Co., NY; died May 1972 in Camden, Oneida Co., NY, daughter of Andrew Spellicy and Mary Waith.

Children of Edward Milton Bovee and Bertha P Spellicy were as follows:

+   3563   i   Edward Ellsworth[9] **Bovee**, born 22 Dec 1915; died Jan 1984. He married (1) **Hazel Zeaman**; (2) **Helen Boucher**.
+   3564   ii   Pauline Elizabeth[9] **Bovee**, born 8 Sep 1916 in Camden, Oneida Co., NY. She married **Clyde Frederick Relyea**.
     3565   iii Eunice Ethel[9] **Bovee**, born 20 Feb 1919 in Camden, Oneida Co., NY; died Nov 2002 in Royal Palm Beach, Palm Beach Co., FL. She married (1) **Joseph L Hevern**; (2) **Joseph Brosius**.
+   3566   iv   Anna Margaret[9] **Bovee**, born 31 Jan 1921 in Camden, Oneida Co., NY. She married (1) **Victor Seabrook**; (2) **Lawrence Desmond**; (3) **Donald Brosius**.
+   3567   v   Harold Lloyd[9] **Bovee**, born 11 Jun 1922 in NY; died 19 Jun 1999. He married **Lucile Grace Paddock**.
+   3568   vi   Ruth Eva[9] **Bovee**, born 16 Jun 1923 in Camden, Oneida Co., NY; died 26 Dec 2002 in Syracuse, Onondaga Co., NY. She married **Charles Kirch**.

2493. Cecil W[8] **Bovee** (Woodbury H[7], Hiram[6], John Henry[5], John Henry[4], Matthew[3], Nicholas[2], Mathieu[1]), born 29 Jan 1896 in North Star Twp., Gratiot

Co., MI; died Jun 1973. He married abt 1920 Dora L Zimmerman, born 1905; died 1997.

Children of Cecil W Bovee and Dora L Zimmerman were as follows:

3569	i	Evelyn M[9] **Bovee**. She married **Frederick Hicks**.
+ 3570	ii	Cecil Dale[9] **Bovee**, born abt 1927. He married **Margaret Hall**.
3571	iii	Ramon Woodberry[9] **Bovee**.

2494. Glen Howard[8] **Bovee** (Woodbury H[7], Hiram[6], John Henry[5], John Henry[4], Matthew[3], Nicholas[2], Mathieu[1]), born 18 Jul 1898 in North Star Twp., Gratiot Co., MI; died 22 Feb 1971 in Plymouth, Wayne Co., MI. He married on 30 Jun 1925 Charlotte T Teachman, born 30 Apr 1900; died Jul 1972 in Livonia, Wayne Co., MI.

Children of Glen Howard Bovee and Charlotte T Teachman were as follows:

+ 3572	i	Charlotte Jean[9] **Bovee**, born Nov 1925. She married **Robert R Rutila**.

2495. Hiram C (Harry)[8] **Bovee** (Woodbury H[7], Hiram[6], John Henry[5], John Henry[4], Matthew[3], Nicholas[2], Mathieu[1]), born 7 Nov 1901 in North Star Twp., Gratiot Co., MI; died 1960. He married Rosamond I Parling, born 1907; died 1986.

Children of Hiram C (Harry) Bovee and Rosamond I Parling were as follows:

+ 3573	i	Hiram C (Harry)[9] **Bovee** Jr, born 1924; died 1997. He married **Lois M Stone**.
3574	ii	Virginia Irene[9] **Bovee**, born aft 1924. She married **Earnest R Williams**.
+ 3575	iii	Richard Lee[9] **Bovee**, born aft 1924. He married unknown.
3576	iv	Jeannette Harriet[9] **Bovee**.
3577	v	Doris Kay[9] **Bovee**.
+ 3578	vi	Roger Lee[9] **Bovee**. He married **Sharon (---)**.

2507. Archie Edward[8] **Bovee** (Edward Hill[7], Andrew J[6], Mathew[5], John Henry[4], Matthew[3], Nicholas[2], Mathieu[1]), born 30 Jan 1900 in PA; died Dec 1980 in Bay View, Erie Co., OH. He married on 6 Feb 1924 in North Girard, PA Nellie I Beck, died 27 Dec 1968 in San Diego, San Diego Co., CA, daughter of William Beck and Lizzie McClean.

Children of Archie Edward Bovee and Nellie I Beck were as follows:

+ 3579	i	Howard Edward[9] **Bovee**, born 13 Dec 1924. He married **Elizabeth Jane McBride**.

2511. Raymond Arthur[8] **Bovee** (Edward Hill[7], Andrew J[6], Mathew[5], John Henry[4],

Matthew[3], Nicholas[2], Mathieu[1]), born 28 Jan 1910 in MN; died 22 Nov 1985 in Erie, Erie Co., PA. He married Florence Edna Olmstead, born 11 Feb 1911 in Conneaut, Ashtabula Co., OH; died 26 Jul 1975 in Millsboro, Sussex Co., DE.

Children of Raymond Arthur Bovee and Florence Edna Olmstead were as follows:

	3580	i	Orville Fred[9] **Bovee**.
+	3581	ii	Raymond Arthur[9] **Bovee** Jr, born in Girard, Erie Co., PA. He married **Doris May English**.
	3582	iii	Joanne Gertrude[9] **Bovee**.
	3583	iv	Mary Jane[9] **Bovee**.
	3584	v	Beverly Arlene[9] **Bovee**.
	3585	vi	Evelyn May[9] **Bovee**.

2518. Harland[8] **Bovee** (Calvin O[7], Grosvenor D[6], Mathew[5], John Henry[4], Matthew[3], Nicholas[2], Mathieu[1]), born 22 Dec 1896 in Hudson, Lenawee Co., MI; died 6 Jun 1963. He married Beulah Laura Deline, born 19 Sep 1899 in Lenawee Co., MI; died 12 Feb 1984 in Lansing, Ingham Co., MI, daughter of Edgar Alvi Deline and Hattie M Walworth.

Children of Harland Bovee and Beulah Laura Deline were as follows:

	3586	i	Mildred Louise[9] **Bovee**, born 1919; died 25 Jul 1995 in Lansing, Ingham Co., MI. She married on 17 Jun 1938 **Kenneth C Boroff**.
	3587	ii	Grace L[9] **Bovee**.
	3588	iii	George[9] **Bovee**.
	3589	iv	W[9] **Bovee**.
	3590	v	Sharon[9] **Bovee**.
	3591	vi	L[9] **Bovee**.
+	3592	vii	Roy L[9] **Bovee**. He married **Doris M (---)**.

2523. Paul R[8] **Bovee** (Marion Lysander[7], Elijah[6], Jacob[5], John Henry[4], Matthew[3], Nicholas[2], Mathieu[1]), born 25 Apr 1881 in MI; died 1935. He married on 30 Jun 1903 Alice M Scully, born abt 1883.

Children of Paul R Bovee and Alice M Scully were as follows:

3593	i	Lucy J[9] **Bovee**, born 4 Feb 1904. She married **Glen Daley**.
3594	ii	Paul R[9] **Bovee** Jr, born 10 Nov 1906; died 9 Apr 1914.
3595	iii	Mattie Elaine[9] **Bovee**, born 18 Jun 1910. She married on 29 Jun 1929 **Carl Schroeder**.

2524. Mary Lucy[8] **Bovee** (Marion Lysander[7], Elijah[6], Jacob[5], John Henry[4], Matthew[3], Nicholas[2], Mathieu[1]), born 25 Jan 1883 in MI; died Feb 1947. She married Joseph Miller.

Children of Mary Lucy Bovee and Joseph Miller were as follows:

3596   i   Joseph[9] **Miller**.

2525. Marion Elijah[8] **Bovee** (Marion Lysander[7], Elijah[6], Jacob[5], John Henry[4], Matthew[3], Nicholas[2], Mathieu[1]), born 22 Sep 1888 in MI; died Aug 1970 in Lexington, Salinac Co., MI. He married (1) on 5 Jun 1912 Anna Moorhouse, died 26 Jun 1920; (2) on 22 Feb 1922 Maude Loveless.

Children of Marion Elijah Bovee and Anna Moorhouse were as follows:

3597   i   Geraldine[9] **Bovee**, born 13 May 1915.

Children of Marion Elijah Bovee and Maude Loveless were as follows:

+ 3598   i   Noreen Loveless[9] **Bovee**, born 8 Apr 1923. She married **Wesley Zebley**.
   3599   ii   Wayne Marion[9] **Bovee**, born 18 Nov 1926. He married **Margaret Cromwell**.
   3600   iii   Leo Thomas[9] **Bovee**, born 9 Feb 1929. He married **Eileen Bentley**.

2526. John Wesley[8] **Bovee** (Marion Lysander[7], Elijah[6], Jacob[5], John Henry[4], Matthew[3], Nicholas[2], Mathieu[1]), born 31 Dec 1890 in MI; died 30 Jan 1972 in Royal Oak, Oakland Co., MI. He married on 3 May 1912 Verley Madeline Stevens, died 24 Jun 1958 in Wayne Co., MI, daughter of Edward J Stevens and Alice Ede.

Children of John Wesley Bovee and Verley Madeline Stevens were as follows:

3601   i   Glen Wesley[9] **Bovee**, born 3 Dec 1912; died 3 Dec 1912.
3602   ii   Melvin John[9] **Bovee**, born 3 Sep 1914; died 24 Jan 1993 in Royal Oak, Oakland Co., MI.
3603   iii   Marvin Paul[9] **Bovee**, born 9 May 1916; died 7 Sep 1916.
3604   iv   Marion Edward[9] **Bovee**, born 9 May 1916; died 8 Sep 1916.
3605   v   Hazel Virginia[9] **Bovee**, born 25 Feb 1919.
3606   vi   Donald Clayton[9] **Bovee**, born 11 Jul 1921.

2534. Erma[8] **Bovee** (Fremont[7], Albert[6], Jacob[5], John Henry[4], Matthew[3], Nicholas[2], Mathieu[1]), born 17 Aug 1880 in Gratiot Co., MI; died Jan 1967. He married Minerva Carpenter, born abt 1879.

Children of Erma Bovee and Minerva Carpenter were as follows:

3607   i   Veva Fern[9] **Bovee**.
3608   ii   Kylie[9] **Bovee**, born 13 May 1900; died Dec 1966 in Ithaca,

Gratiot Co., MI. He married **Pauline Ennis**.

3609   iii   Marjorie[9] **Bovee**, born 29 Jul 1904.

2536. Beulah Belle[8] **Bovee** (Virgil Albert[7], Albert[6], Jacob[5], John Henry[4], Matthew[3], Nicholas[2], Mathieu[1]), born 20 Sep 1889 in Montcalm Co., MI. She married (1) on 19 Aug 1914 Merle A Russell, born Oct 1889; (2) on 13 Jun 1936 Herman Randolph.

Children of Beulah Belle Bovee and Merle A Russell were as follows:

3610   i   Martha Joyce[9] **Russell**, born 16 Sep 1917.

3611   ii   Ruth Eleanor[9] **Russell**, born 18 Feb 1922.

2537. Elizabeth[8] **Bovee** (Virgil Albert[7], Albert[6], Jacob[5], John Henry[4], Matthew[3], Nicholas[2], Mathieu[1]), born 18 Aug 1894 in Montcalm Co., MI. She married on 19 Jul 1917 Thomas Stanford Clayton, born 25 Aug 1894.

Children of Elizabeth Bovee and Thomas Stanford Clayton were as follows:

3612   i   Thomas Stanford[9] **Clayton** Jr, born 2 May 1922.

3613   ii   Robert[9] **Clayton**, born 1 Jul 1927.

2538. Marshall Claude[8] **Bovee** (Herbert Warren[7], Milo[6], Jacob[5], John Henry[4], Matthew[3], Nicholas[2], Mathieu[1]), born 22 Apr 1901; died 10 Mar 1989 in Wayne Co., MI. He married on 1 Jan 1923 Laura Blanche Rose, born 31 May 1902.

Children of Marshall Claude Bovee and Laura Blanche Rose were as follows:

3614   i   Oliver Herbert[9] **Bovee**, born 1923; died Sep 2003.

+   3615   ii   Marshall Gaylord[9] **Bovee**, born 1928 in Monroe Co., MI. He married **Carmen (---)**.

+   3616   iii   Janice Laurene[9] **Bovee**, born 22 Aug 1930 in Petersburg, Monroe Co., MI; died 14 Dec 2001 in Manitou Beach, Lenawee Co., MI. She married **Caroll (John) Hassenzahl**.

3617   iv   Susan Rose[9] **Bovee**.

2539. Wayne Hunter[8] **Bovee** (Herbert Warren[7], Milo[6], Jacob[5], John Henry[4], Matthew[3], Nicholas[2], Mathieu[1]), born 21 Apr 1905 in MI; died 27 Aug 1982 in TX. He married on 12 Jun 1927 Alice Louise Murphy, born 1 May 1905.

Children of Wayne Hunter Bovee and Alice Louise Murphy were as follows:

3618   i   Richard Warren[9] **Bovee**.

2540. Julia[8] **Bovee** (Herbert Warren[7], Milo[6], Jacob[5], John Henry[4], Matthew[3],

Nicholas^2, Mathieu^1), born 9 Dec 1907. She married on 25 Jun 1932 Floyd V Schultze, born 7 Nov 1910.

Children of Julia Bovee and Floyd V Schultze were as follows:

3619   i   Karl Herbert^9 **Schultze.**

2544. Seton Chapelle^8 **Bovee** (Cornelius Anson^7, Milo^6, Jacob^5, John Henry^4, Matthew^3, Nicholas^2, Mathieu^1), born 18 Apr 1907 in Adrian, Lenawee Co., MI; died 13 Feb 1977 in Coldwater, Branch Co., MI. He married on 10 Aug 1930 Clara W McKarghan, born 6 Apr 1908; died 12 Dec 1988 in Coldwater, Branch Co., MI.

Children of Seton Chapelle Bovee and Clara W McKarghan were as follows:

+   3620   i   Seton Chapelle^9 **Bovee** Jr. He married **Barbara L (---).**
    3621   ii   Natalie Morgan^9 **Bovee.** She married **(---) Hutson.**

2551. David Victor^8 **Bovee** (Earl Eugene^7, Myron^6, Jacob^5, John Henry^4, Matthew^3, Nicholas^2, Mathieu^1), born 10 Nov 1911 in Sioux City, Woodbury Co., IA; died 23 Jan 1983 in Springfield, Greene Co., MO. He married on 12 Sep 1937 in Beemer, Cuming Co., NE Lois Margery Munderloh, born Oct 1914.

Children of David Victor Bovee and Lois Margery Munderloh were as follows:

+   3622   i   Barbara Jane^9 **Bovee.** She married **Leon Polk.**
    3623   ii   David Victor^9 **Bovee** Jr. He married (1) on 26 Jan 1967 in Saratoga Springs, Saratoga Co., NY, divorced **Elizabeth Ann McCleod**; (2) on 10 Feb 1983, divorced **Mary Alice Douglas**; (3) on 10 Sep 1994 in Ann Arbor, Washtenaw Co., MI **Marjorie Slabi**.
    3624   iii   Susan Bly^9 **Bovee**, born in Springfield, Green Co., MO.

2552. Eugene Cleveland^8 **Bovee** (Earl Eugene^7, Myron^6, Jacob^5, John Henry^4, Matthew^3, Nicholas^2, Mathieu^1), born 1 Apr 1915 in Sioux City, Woodbury Co., IA. He married (1) on 18 May 1942 in Kahoka, Clark Co., MO Maezene Belle Wamsley, born 4 May 1924 in Clarksville, Butler Co., IA; (2) on 9 May 1968 in Santa Monica, Los Angeles Co., CA Elizabeth Alice, Moss, born 5 Aug 1931 in Los Angeles, Los Angeles Co., CA; died 18 Dec 1996 in Lawrence, Douglas Co., KS.

Children of Eugene Cleveland Bovee and Maezene Belle Wamsley were as follows:

    3625   i   Frances Ann^9 **Bovee**, born in Waverly, Bremer Co., IA. She married on 3 Nov 1968 in Topanga, Los Angeles Co., CA **Roger Adams Young**.
+   3626   ii   Gregory Joe^9 **Bovee**, born in Cedar Falls, Black Hawk Co., IA. He married (1) **Carolyn Scrogum**; (2) **Martha**

Lois Haegler.

+ 3627 iii Matthew Wamsley[9] **Bovee**, born in Gainesville, Alachua Co., FL. He married (1) **Kellie Ann White**; (2) **Alison Ibbotson**.

2553. Esther Anne[8] **Bovee** (Earl Eugene[7], Myron[6], Jacob[5], John Henry[4], Matthew[3], Nicholas[2], Mathieu[1]), born 5 Jun 1916 in Sioux City, Woodbury Co., IA. She married on 28 May 1937 in Sioux City, Woodbury Co., IA Don Frost Crippin, born 18 Feb 1913 in Sioux City, Woodbury Co., IA; died 27 Aug 1994 in Sierra Vista, Cochise Co., AZ.

Children of Esther Anne Bovee and Don Frost Crippin were as follows:

3628 i Dennis Bovee[9] **Crippin**, born in Sioux City, Woodbury Co., IA.

3629 ii Robert Bruce[9] **Crippin**, born in San Diego, San Diego Co., CA.

2560. Leo Myron[8] **Bovee** (Orlin Henry[7], Myron[6], Jacob[5], John Henry[4], Matthew[3], Nicholas[2], Mathieu[1]), born 22 Nov 1904 in Bowling Green, Wood Co., OH; died 15 May 1989. He married (1) on 12 Aug 1925, divorced Eva Laurette Linton; (2) on 27 Nov 1947 Frances Knight, born 26 Jul 1906 in OH; died 3 Aug 1988 in AZ.

Children of Leo Myron Bovee and Eva Laurette Linton were as follows:

+ 3630 i Barbara Eleanor[9] **Bovee**, born 22 Mar 1926. She married **Charles West**.

2561. Murlin Orlin[8] **Bovee** (Orlin Henry[7], Myron[6], Jacob[5], John Henry[4], Matthew[3], Nicholas[2], Mathieu[1]), born 16 Jan 1906 in Arcadia, Hancock Co., OH; died 18 May 1993. He married on 6 May 1925 Eva Karn, born 23 Feb 1906; died 16 Apr 1988 in OH.

Children of Murlin Orlin Bovee and Eva Karn were as follows:

+ 3631 i Dessie Louise[9] **Bovee**, born 29 Sep 1925. She married **William Robert Shireman**.

+ 3632 ii Murl Gene[9] **Bovee**, born 12 Feb 1927. He married **Wilma Irene Farthing**.

+ 3633 iii Parley Eldon[9] **Bovee**, born 23 Oct 1929. He married **Jacquelyn Leibecker**.

2564. Dessie Elnora[8] **Bovee** (Orlin Henry[7], Myron[6], Jacob[5], John Henry[4], Matthew[3], Nicholas[2], Mathieu[1]), born 24 May 1918 in Arcadia, Hancock Co., OH; buried in Arcadia Cem, Arcadia, Hancock Co., OH. She married on 5 Sep 1937 Kenneth Vernell Anderson, born 2 Jul 1917 in Findlay, Hancock Co., OH.

Children of Dessie Elnora Bovee and Kenneth Vernell Anderson were as

follows:

3634   i   Janis Elnora^9 **Anderson**, born in Findlay, Hancock Co., OH.

3635   ii   Nancy Louise^9 **Anderson**.

3636   iii   Lee Vernell^9 **Anderson**.

3637   iv   Joyce Annette^9 **Anderson**.

2565. Bonnie Mulla^8 **Bovee** (Arthur Jewett^7, Myron^6, Jacob^5, John Henry^4, Matthew^3, Nicholas^2, Mathieu^1), born 25 Feb 1911. She married on 20 Oct 1946 John C Alt Jr, born 28 Mar 1913.

Children of Bonnie Mulla Bovee and John C Alt Jr were as follows:

3638   i   Arthur John^9 **Alt**.

2566. Arthur Jewett^8 **Bovee** Jr (Arthur Jewett^7, Myron^6, Jacob^5, John Henry^4, Matthew^3, Nicholas^2, Mathieu^1), born 22 Mar 1912. He married in 1933 Frances Warne, born 14 Feb 1913; died 27 Jan 1992 in Del Mar, San Diego Co., CA.

Children of Arthur Jewett Bovee Jr and Frances Warne were as follows:

3639   i   Martha Lois^9 **Bovee**.

+ 3640   ii   Arthur David^9 **Bovee**. He married **Barbara Louise Miller**.

2567. Frances Roberta^8 **Bovee** (Arthur Jewett^7, Myron^6, Jacob^5, John Henry^4, Matthew^3, Nicholas^2, Mathieu^1), born 2 Jun 1913. She married on 26 Aug 1940 Lyle D Smith, born 1908; died 7 Aug 1944.

Children of Frances Roberta Bovee and Lyle D Smith were as follows:

3641   i   Lyle Arthur^9 **Smith**.

2568. Jennie Christie^8 **Bovee** (Arthur Jewett^7, Myron^6, Jacob^5, John Henry^4, Matthew^3, Nicholas^2, Mathieu^1), born 15 Jun 1916. She married on 9 Jun 1945 Leonard James Nesseth, born 28 Mar 1915.

Children of Jennie Christie Bovee and Leonard James Nesseth were as follows:

3642   i   Christie Ann^9 **Nesseth**.

3643   ii   Laura Jean^9 **Nesseth**.

2569. Rachael Ellen^8 **Bovee** (Arthur Jewett^7, Myron^6, Jacob^5, John Henry^4, Matthew^3, Nicholas^2, Mathieu^1), born 6 Sep 1919. She married on 16 Aug 1947 Raleigh A Lawson.

Children of Rachael Ellen Bovee and Raleigh A Lawson were as follows:

3644	i	Donald Raleigh^9 **Lawson**.
3645	ii	Mark James^9 **Lawson**.
3646	iii	Julie Marie^9 **Lawson**.

2575. Ardee Lewis^8 **Bovee** (Harlow^7, Myron^6, Jacob^5, John Henry^4, Matthew^3, Nicholas^2, Mathieu^1), born 31 Jan 1906; died 5 Mar 1969 in Clinton Co., MI. He married on 31 Oct 1925 Eileen Morley, born 14 Mar 1909; died 29 Dec 1982 in Lansing, Ingham Co., MI.

Children of Ardee Lewis Bovee and Eileen Morley were as follows:

+ 3647 i Miron Lewis^9 **Bovee**, born 3 Jun 1926; died 28 Oct 1988 in Sarasota, Sarasota Co., FL. He married **Jean DeClercy**.

3648 ii Joyce Kathleen^9 **Bovee**, born 11 Jan 1928. She married (1) in 1947 **Alfred Barker**; (2) **Hal Conklyn**.

3649 iii Kenneth Ardee^9 **Bovee**, born 3 Jul 1929; died 3 Jul 1929.

3650 iv Marjorie^9 **Bovee**, born abt 1930; died abt 1930.

3651 v Phyllis May^9 **Bovee**.

3652 vi Larry May^9 **Bovee**.

2576. Lola May^8 **Bovee** (Harlow^7, Myron^6, Jacob^5, John Henry^4, Matthew^3, Nicholas^2, Mathieu^1), born 9 Aug 1908. She married on 8 Apr 1928 Covert Walter, born 1 Dec 1909; died 25 Oct 1985.

Children of Lola May Bovee and Covert Walter were as follows:

3653 i William Lee^9 **Walter**, died 29 Feb 1948.

3654 ii Marilyn Jean^9 **Walter**.

3655 iii Helen Ann^9 **Walter**.

3656 iv Janet Elizabeth^9 **Walter**.

2577. Beulah Faye^8 **Bovee** (Harlow^7, Myron^6, Jacob^5, John Henry^4, Matthew^3, Nicholas^2, Mathieu^1), born 15 Oct 1914; died 29 Sep 1964. She married on 22 Oct 1930 Joseph Skaryd, born 12 Aug 1907.

Children of Beulah Faye Bovee and Joseph Skaryd were as follows:

3657 i Lillian Beulah^9 **Skaryd**.

3658 ii Shirley Ann^9 **Skaryd**.

3659 iii Douglas Joseph^9 **Skaryd**.

3660 iv James^9 **Skaryd**.

2578. Olan Ford^8 **Bovee** (Harlow^7, Myron^6, Jacob^5, John Henry^4, Matthew^3, Nicholas^2, Mathieu^1), born 17 Mar 1917 in Gratiot Co., MI; died 2 Jun 1968. He married (1) on 7 Sep 1935 Helen Campbell, born 29 May 1916; died 7 Sep 1944; (2) in 1945 Frances Robinson Bond.

Children of Olan Ford Bovee and Helen Campbell were as follows:

+ 3661 i Edna Mae^9 **Bovee**. She married **Lonnie Prososki**.
+ 3662 ii Billie Jean^9 **Bovee**. She married **Norval Wiseman**.
  3663 iii Gordon Olan^9 **Bovee**.

Children of Olan Ford Bovee and Frances Robinson Bond were as follows:

  3664 i James Lee^9 **Bovee**.
  3665 ii Richard^9 **Bovee**.
  3666 iii Michael Allen^9 **Bovee**.

2580. Wanda Harriet^8 **Bovee** (Harlow^7, Myron^6, Jacob^5, John Henry^4, Matthew^3, Nicholas^2, Mathieu^1). She married (1) on 22 Jun 1947, divorced Raymond Newlove, born 5 Dec 1925; (2) on 12 Feb 1956 Dean Frederick, died 8 Mar 1965; (3) aft 1956 Robert D Beamer.

Children of Wanda Harriet Bovee and Raymond Newlove were as follows:

  3667 i David Harlow^9 **Newlove**.
  3668 ii Donald^9 **Newlove**.

Children of Wanda Harriet Bovee and Dean Frederick were as follows:

  3669 i Deanna^9 **Frederick**.
  3670 ii Wendy^9 **Frederick**.
  3671 iii Michael^9 **Frederick**.

Children of Wanda Harriet Bovee and Robert D Beamer were as follows:

  3672 i Robyn^9 **Beamer**.

2599. Eleanor Maxine^8 **Bovee** (Fred Mayfield^7, Devillow^6, Jacob^5, John Henry^4, Matthew^3, Nicholas^2, Mathieu^1), born 5 Jul 1918. She married in 1940 James Merrill McGrath, born 22 Dec 1914, son of Clayton McGrath and Gretchen (---).

Children of Eleanor Maxine Bovee and James Merrill McGrath were as follows:

  3673 i Nenai Lee^9 **McGrath**. She married on 17 Jun 1962 **Rodger Edwin Vierre**.
  3674 ii Michael James^9 **McGrath**. He married on 23 Mar 1968 **Marie Louise Jensen**.
  3675 iii Margaret Ann^9 **McGrath**. She married on 22 Jun 1974 in Morro Bay, San Luis Obispo Co., CA **James Edward McLaughlin**.
  3676 iv Kelly Maureen^9 **McGrath**.

2600. Florence^8 **Bovee** (Fred Mayfield^7, Devillow^6, Jacob^5, John Henry^4,

Matthew[3], Nicholas[2], Mathieu[1]), born 1 Mar 1921. She married Kenneth W Jones, born 29 May 1917.

Children of Florence Bovee and Kenneth W Jones were as follows:

3677   i   Herbert Charles[9] **Jones**.

2601. Marilyn Enid[8] **Bovee** (Fred Mayfield[7], Devillow[6], Jacob[5], John Henry[4], Matthew[3], Nicholas[2], Mathieu[1]), born 12 Feb 1925 in San Luis Obispo, San Luis Obispo Co., CA. She married on 30 May 1952 in San Luis Obispo, San Luis Obispo Co., CA David Henry Hildebran, born 2 Jul 1925.

Children of Marilyn Enid Bovee and David Henry Hildebran were as follows:

3678   i   Steven James[9] **Hildebran**, born in San Luis Obispo, CA. He married on 29 Dec 1977 **Marlene Briaske**.

3679   ii   David Thomas[9] **Hildebran**, born in San Luis Obispo, CA. He married on 6 May 1977 **Holly Eileen Leake**.

3680   iii   Susan Jane[9] **Hildebran**, born in San Luis Obispo, CA. She married on 21 Sep 1978 **Eugene McCrary**.

3681   iv   Mary Jo[9] **Hildebran**, born in San Luis Obispo, CA. She married on 18 Jun 1983 **Scott William Berg**.

2602. Edmond James[8] **Bovee** (Fred Mayfield[7], Devillow[6], Jacob[5], John Henry[4], Matthew[3], Nicholas[2], Mathieu[1]), born 6 Apr 1926 in San Luis Obispo, San Luis Obispo Co., CA. He married on 25 Jun 1948 in San Luis Obispo, San Luis Obispo Co., CA Addie Evelyn Johnson.

Children of Edmond James Bovee and Addie Evelyn Johnson were as follows:

+   3682   i   Diana Sue[9] **Bovee**. She married (1) **Daniel Lee McCrory**; (2) **Edward Francis Lakjer**.

+   3683   ii   Rodney James[9] **Bovee**, born in San Luis Obispo, San Luis Obispo Co., CA. He married **Kelly Ann Dennis**.

2608. Russell E[8] **Bovee** (James Byron[7], James H[6], Peter[5], John Henry[4], Matthew[3], Nicholas[2], Mathieu[1]), born 19 Oct 1903; died 10 Jul 1965 in IN. He married Dorcas Bell.

Children of Russell E Bovee and Dorcas Bell were as follows:

+   3684   i   James Eugene[9] **Bovee**. He married unknown.

2609. Ruth[8] **Bovee** (James Byron[7], James H[6], Peter[5], John Henry[4], Matthew[3], Nicholas[2], Mathieu[1]), born 1908. She married Jess Shields.

Children of Ruth Bovee and Jess Shields were as follows:

3685   i   Jerome[9] **Shields**.

2610. Harold[8] **Bovee** (James Byron[7], James H[6], Peter[5], John Henry[4], Matthew[3], Nicholas[2], Mathieu[1]), born 4 Dec 1910; died Jul 1986 in Wolcottville, La Grange Co., IN. He married Retha Cook, born 22 Nov 1909; died 17 Mar 1979 in Wolcottville, La Grange Co., IN, daughter of Irvin Cook and Vera (---).

Children of Harold Bovee and Retha Cook were as follows:

+ 3686   i   Beverly[9] **Bovee**. She married **Blaine Alan Gilliland**.
+ 3687   ii   Nancy Jane[9] **Bovee**, born in Kendallville, Noble Co., IN. She married **Ned H Stump**.
+ 3688   iii   Harold[9] **Bovee**, born in Kendallville, Noble Co., IN. He married **Linda Dorsett**.
   3689   iv   Norman Allen[9] **Bovee**, born in Kendallville, Noble Co., IN. He married on 28 Dec 1967 **Joan Guildenbecker**.

2611. Wava[8] **Bovee** (James Byron[7], James H[6], Peter[5], John Henry[4], Matthew[3], Nicholas[2], Mathieu[1]), born 29 Apr 1913 in Hudson, Steuben Co., IN; died Apr 1988. She married Robert McKee.

Children of Wava Bovee and Robert McKee were as follows:

   3690   i   Donald[9] **McKee**.
   3691   ii   William[9] **McKee**.

2616. Isaac Warren[8] **Bovee** III (Isaac Warren[7], Isaac Warren I[6], Isaac[5], Jacob[4], Abraham[3], Nicholas[2], Mathieu[1]), born 7 Aug 1881. He married Helen Thayer Webster, born 17 Aug 1884, daughter of Dyer R Webster.

Children of Isaac Warren Bovee III and Helen Thayer Webster were as follows:

   3692   i   Isaac Warren[9] **Bovee** IV, born abt 1910.

2617. Sara Angeline[8] **Bovee** (Isaac Warren[7], Isaac Warren I[6], Isaac[5], Jacob[4], Abraham[3], Nicholas[2], Mathieu[1]), born abt 1885 in Rensselaer Co., NY. She married in Elmhurst, Du Page Co., IL George Savery.

Children of Sara Angeline Bovee and George Savery were as follows:

   3693   i   Harold[9] **Savery**.
   3694   ii   Helen[9] **Savery**.

2618. George White[8] **Bovee** (Isaac Warren[7], Isaac Warren I[6], Isaac[5], Jacob[4], Abraham[3], Nicholas[2], Mathieu[1]), born 27 Nov 1888 in Hoosick, Rensselaer Co., NY; died 1965 in Hoosick, Rensselaer Co., NY. He married on 1 Apr 1918 in Hoosick, Rensselaer Co., NY Charlotte B Cook, born 1896 in Boytonville, NY?.

Children of George White Bovee and Charlotte B Cook were as follows:

3695   i   Robert^9 **Bovee**, born abt 1920.

2620. Walter James^8 **Bovee** (John Jacob^7, Jacob F W^6, William G^5, Jacob^4, Abraham^3, Nicholas^2, Mathieu^1), born 24 Jul 1913 in Spokane, Spokane Co., WA; died 9 Jun 1988. He married on 29 Sep 1946 in Santa Cruz, San Fransanciso Co., CA Doris Maxine Kavachevich, born 5 Sep 1922 in Provo, Utah Co., UT; christened 16 Jan 1923 in Salt Lake City, Salt Lake Co., UT, daughter of William Kavachevich and Helga Bunting.

Children of Walter James Bovee and Doris Maxine Kavachevich were as follows:

3696   i   Jo Ann^9 **Bovee**, born in Ross, Marin Co.,CA. She married on 15 Aug 1970 **Frank William Bauman**.

3697   ii   John William^9 **Bovee**, born in Escondido, San Diego Co., CA. He married on 25 Nov 1978 **Maureen Gray Mello**.

3698   iii   Nancy Jean^9 **Bovee**, born in Castro Valley, Alameda Co., CA. She married on 15 Feb 1975 **Steven Neal McEachern**.

2630. Luray^8 **Bovee** (David Bussler^7, John Oscar^6, Peter^5, Matthew^4, Abraham^3, Nicholas^2, Mathieu^1). She married on 20 Apr 1932 in Wellsville, Allegany Co., NY Clifford O Mills, born 23 Jan 1910 in Hume, Allegany Co., NY; died 19 Dec 1990 in Wellsville, Allegany Co., NY, son of Chester Mills and Mabel Dennis.

Children of Luray Bovee and Clifford O Mills were as follows:

3699   i   David Chester^9 **Mills**.

3700   ii   Robert Joseph^9 **Mills**.

3701   iii   Maureen Lee^9 **Mills**.

2634. Charles Oscar^8 **Bovee** Jr (Charles Oscar^7, John Oscar^6, Peter^5, Matthew^4, Abraham^3, Nicholas^2, Mathieu^1), born 1 Mar 1925 in Houston, Harris Co., TX. He married Lena Faye Duggan.

Children of Charles Oscar Bovee Jr and Lena Faye Duggan were as follows:

3702   i   Susanne^9 **Bovee**, born in Houston, Harris Co., TX. She married on 24 Aug 1974 in Friendswood, Galviston Co., TX **Ronny James Newberry**.

3703   ii   Sally Lynn^9 **Bovee**. She married on 24 Nov 1984 in Friendswood, Galviston Co., TX **John Bryant Fox**.

2637. Chester Emerson^8 **Bovee** (Samuel Ball^7, George Burton^6, Peter^5, Matthew^4, Abraham^3, Nicholas^2, Mathieu^1), born 15 Jan 1889 in Hepburnville, Lycoming Co., PA. He married on 10 May 1913 Lucy Ann Mason, born 9 Apr

1897 in Gordon, Schuykill Co., PA; died 20 Aug 1981 in Healdton, Carter Co., OK, daughter of John Mason and Regina (---).

Children of Chester Emerson Bovee and Lucy Ann Mason were as follows:

3704   i   Florence Elizabeth^{9} **Bovee**, born 17 Mar 1915 in Perrysville, Allegheny Co., PA; died Aug 1982 in Halton City, Tarrant Co., TX. She married **(---) Yost**.

3705   ii   Sarah Catherine^{9} **Bovee**, born 21 Dec 1920 in Williamsport, Lycoming Co., PA; died 5 Oct 2000 in Fort Worth Tarrant Co., TX.

\+   3706   iii   Meredith Roger Leon^{9} **Bovee**, born 20 Jul 1923 in Sullivan, Madison Co., NY; died 27 Dec 2001 in Fort Worth Tarrant Co., TX. He married (1) **Lillian May Rolfe**; (2) **Carol Lynne Crowell**; (3) **Nancy Joan Davis**.

2638. Bertha Ellen^{8} **Bovee** (Samuel Ball^{7}, George Burton^{6}, Peter^{5}, Matthew^{4}, Abraham^{3}, Nicholas^{2}, Mathieu^{1}), born 20 Mar 1891 in Hepburnville, Lycoming Co., PA. She married on 20 Mar 1911 Charles August Raub.

Children of Bertha Ellen Bovee and Charles August Raub were as follows:

3707   i   Charles Samuel^{9} **Raub**, born 26 Sep 1911 in Lopez, Sullivan Co., PA.

3708   ii   Kenneth^{9} **Raub**.

3709   iii   Arthur Leon^{9} **Raub**.

3710   iv   Child^{9} **Raub**.

2640. Meredith Roger Leon^{8} **Bovee** (Samuel Ball^{7}, George Burton^{6}, Peter^{5}, Matthew^{4}, Abraham^{3}, Nicholas^{2}, Mathieu^{1}), born 15 Sep 1896 in Hepburnville, Lycoming Co., PA. He married on 8 Dec 1916 Charlotte Marguerite Frost.

Children of Meredith Roger Leon Bovee and Charlotte Marguerite Frost were as follows:

3711   i   Dorothy^{9} **Bovee**, born abt 1916 in Syracuse, Onandaga Co., NY.

3712   ii   Charlotte^{9} **Bovee**, born abt 1919 in Syracuse, Onandaga Co., NY.

3713   iii   Lois^{9} **Bovee**, born May 1926 in Syracuse, Onandaga Co., NY.

2641. Mary Elizabeth^{8} **Bovee** (Samuel Ball^{7}, George Burton^{6}, Peter^{5}, Matthew^{4}, Abraham^{3}, Nicholas^{2}, Mathieu^{1}), born 24 Dec 1898 in Hepburnville, Lycoming Co., PA; died 1978. She married Robert Samuel Pindar, born 1891; died 1972.

Children of Mary Elizabeth Bovee and Robert Samuel Pindar were as follows:

3714   i   Robert Samuel^{9} **Pindar** Jr, born 1 Oct 1918 in Munnsville,

2644. Clyde LaRue[8] **Bovee** (Samuel Ball[7], George Burton[6], Peter[5], Matthew[4], Abraham[3], Nicholas[2], Mathieu[1]), born 12 Jan 1908; died 19 Jul 1971 in Oneida, Madison Co., NY. He married on 20 Sep 1930 Martha s Stebbins, born 4 Oct 1906 in Oneida Co., NY, daughter of Bertrand H Stebbins and Blanche (---).

    Children of Clyde LaRue Bovee and Martha s Stebbins were as follows:

    3715   i   Arthur Blair[9] **Bovee**, born 21 Dec 1934 in Syracuse, Onondaga Co., NY; died 16 Sep 1941 in Oneida Co., NY.

    3716   ii   Catherine[9] **Bovee**, born in Syracuse, Onondaga Co., NY. She married (1) **(---) Keeler**; (2) on 17 Oct 1978 in Syracuse, Onondaga Co., NY **H M Jerome**.

    3717   iii   Barbara[9] **Bovee**.

2650. Helen[8] **Bovee** (Lemon Peter[7], Perry Henry[6], Peter[5], Matthew[4], Abraham[3], Nicholas[2], Mathieu[1]), born 5 Mar 1904 in Newberry, Lycoming Co., PA. She married (---) Brown.

    Children of Helen Bovee and (---) Brown were as follows:

    3718   i   Linda[9] **Brown**.

2651. Robert Owen[8] **Bovee** (Lemon Peter[7], Perry Henry[6], Peter[5], Matthew[4], Abraham[3], Nicholas[2], Mathieu[1]), born 26 Dec 1910 in Newberry, Lycoming Co., PA; died 19 Feb 1964. He married Frances McDermott, born abt 1914.

    Children of Robert Owen Bovee and Frances McDermott were as follows:

+   3719   i   Deborah J[9] **Bovee**. She married **Leo Damaska**.

+   3720   ii   Roberta O[9] **Bovee**. She married **William Webster**.

+   3721   iii   Gail L[9] **Bovee**. She married **Paul Sober**.

2678. Robert Russell[8] **Bovee** (LeRoy George[7], Walter Haywood[6], Peter[5], Matthew[4], Abraham[3], Nicholas[2], Mathieu[1]), born 1924. He married Glenetta Mae Lemons.

    Children of Robert Russell Bovee and Glenetta Mae Lemons were as follows:

+   3722   i   Jenne Ann[9] **Bovee**. She married **Gerald Stephen Collins**.

    3723   ii   Russell Glen[9] **Bovee**. He married **Bernadette Ingalllina**.

    3724   iii   Robert[9] **Bovee**.

2679. June Odette[8] **Bovee** (Donald Wright[7], Wright Ingraham[6], Orrin Primmer[5],

John[4], Abraham[3], Nicholas[2], Mathieu[1]), born 8 Oct 1921 in CA; died 25 Jan 1997 in Lassen Co., CA. She married Leon Ellena (---), born abt 1919.

Children of June Odette Bovee and Leon Ellena (---) were as follows:

3725   i   Jeffrey[9] **Ellena**.

3726   ii   Michael[9] **Ellena**.

2680. Cherie Ann[8] **Bovee** (Donald Wright[7], Wright Ingraham[6], Orrin Primmer[5], John[4], Abraham[3], Nicholas[2], Mathieu[1]), born abt 1923. She married Robert Hendrickson.

Children of Cherie Ann Bovee and Robert Hendrickson were as follows:

3727   i   Barbara Ann[9] **Hendrickson**.

3728   ii   Cherie Louise[9] **Hendrickson**, born 22 Feb 1946 in Lasen Co., CA; died 22 Feb 1946.

3729   iii   James[9] **Hendrickson**.

3730   iv   Steven[9] **Hendrickson**.

2681. Phyllis Elaine[8] **Bovee** (Donald Wright[7], Wright Ingraham[6], Orrin Primmer[5], John[4], Abraham[3], Nicholas[2], Mathieu[1]), born abt 1930. She married (---) Holiday.

Children of Phyllis Elaine Bovee and (---) Holiday were as follows:

3731   i   Pattie Elaine[9] **Holiday**.

2682. Donald[8] **Bovee** (Donald Wright[7], Wright Ingraham[6], Orrin Primmer[5], John[4], Abraham[3], Nicholas[2], Mathieu[1]). He married unknown.

Children of Donald Bovee were as follows:

3732   i   Donald[9] **(---)**.

3733   ii   Thomas[9] **Bovee**.

3734   iii   David W[9] **Bovee**, born 14 Dec 1968; died 16 Dec 1968 in Lassen Co., CA.

2684. Victor David[8] **Bovee** (John W[7], John W[6], Cornelius[5], Abraham[4], Abraham[3], Nicholas[2], Mathieu[1]), born 4 Apr 1891 in Groveland, Livingston Co., NY; died 14 May 1961 in Groveland, Livingston Co., NY. He married on 2 Jan 1915 Mary A Mastin, born 29 Apr 1891; died Oct 1973 in Groveland, Livingston Co., NY.

Children of Victor David Bovee and Mary A Mastin were as follows:

3735   i   Dorothy G[9] **Bovee**, born 1915 in Livingston Co., NY.

3736   ii   Marion V[9] **Bovee**, born 1918 in Livingston Co., NY.

3737   iii   Marjorie S[9] **Bovee**, born 1923 in Groveland, Livingston Co., NY.

3738   iv   Alice[9] **Bovee**, born 1924 in Groveland, Livingston Co., NY.

2687. Edith Mae[8] **Bovee** (John W[7], John W[6], Cornelius[5], Abraham[4], Abraham[3], Nicholas[2], Mathieu[1]), born 7 Mar 1897 in Groveland, Livingston Co., NY; died 25 Jan 1977. She married on 8 Sep 1915 Meryle Dermyre Toland.

Children of Edith Mae Bovee and Meryle Dermyre Toland were as follows:

3739	i	Mary[9] **Toland**, born abt 1916. She married **Howard Schery**.
3740	ii	Isabel[9] **Toland**.
3741	iii	Sara[9] **Toland**.
3742	iv	Roxy[9] **Toland**.
3743	v	Robert[9] **Toland**, born abt 1925.
3744	vi	Marie[9] **Toland**, born abt 1927.
3745	vii	Alex[9] **Toland**, born abt 1929.
3746	viii	Russell[9] **Toland**.

2688. Sarah[8] **Bovee** (John W[7], John W[6], Cornelius[5], Abraham[4], Abraham[3], Nicholas[2], Mathieu[1]), born 25 Sep 1899 in Groveland, Livingston Co., NY; died 4 Dec 1975 in Dansville, Livingston Co., NY. She married on 20 Nov 1920 in Geneseo, Livingston Co., NY James Noble, born 1895 in NY; died 1979 in NY.

Children of Sarah Bovee and James Noble were as follows:

3747	i	Donald J[9] **Noble**, born 18 Sep 1921 in NY; died 3 Apr 1981 in Dansville, Livingston Co., NY.
3748	ii	Sarah Jean[9] **Noble**, born 18 Jun 1926.
3749	iii	John Murray[9] **Noble**, born 21 Oct 1928.
3750	iv	James Morton[9] **Noble**, born 24 Aug 1934 in NY; died 1943 in NY.

2690. Laverne[8] **Bovee** (Frederick[7], John W[6], Cornelius[5], Abraham[4], Abraham[3], Nicholas[2], Mathieu[1]), born 14 Jan 1891 in Groveland, Livingston Co., NY; died 27 Oct 1967 in Steuben Co., NY. He married in Groveland, Livingston Co., NY Elizabeth Lowdin, born 4 Oct 1904; died 23 May 1980 in Groveland, Livingston Co., NY, daughter of James Lowdin and Mary Ann McKown.

Children of Laverne Bovee and Elizabeth Lowdin were as follows:

+	3751	i	Glenn S[9] **Bovee**, born 10 Feb 1924 in Groveland, Livingston Co., NY. He married **Lena Mustrella**.
+	3752	ii	Robert J[9] **Bovee**, born abt 1930 in Groveland, Livingston Co., NY. He married **Jean Hellier**.
+	3753	iii	Harold E[9] **Bovee**, born aft 1930 in Groveland, Livingston Co., NY. He married **Thelma Appeline**.
+	3754	iv	Shirley Hugh[9] **Bovee**, born 27 May 1932 in Groveland,

Livingston Co., NY; died 23 Aug 1955 in Groveland, Livingston Co., NY. He married **Lillian M Gilbert**.

2691. Mary[8] **Bovee** (Frederick[7], John W[6], Cornelius[5], Abraham[4], Abraham[3], Nicholas[2], Mathieu[1]), born 26 Dec 1892 in Mt. Morris, Livingston Co., NY. She married on 30 Sep 1907 in Mt Morris, Livingston Co., NY Emory Drew, son of Homer Drew.

Children of Mary Bovee and Emory Drew were as follows:

3755	i	Child[9] **Drew**, born abt 1908 in NY; died abt 1909 in NY.
3756	ii	Lena[9] **Drew**, born Feb 1909 in NY.

2692. Edward[8] **Bovee** (Frederick[7], John W[6], Cornelius[5], Abraham[4], Abraham[3], Nicholas[2], Mathieu[1]), born 21 Jan 1894 in Groveland, Livingston Co., NY; died 1977 in Dansville, Livingston Co., NY. He married Ion Burns, born 1899; died 1964 in Dansville, Steuben Co., NY.

Children of Edward Bovee and Ion Burns were as follows:

+	3757	i	Margaret[9] **Bovee**, born 1918 in Groveland,Livingston Co., NY. She married **(---) Bus**.
	3758	ii	Olive S[9] **Bovee**, born 1923 in Groveland, Livingston Co., NY. She married **(---) Gardner**.
+	3759	iii	Laura[9] **Bovee**. She married **Frank Schirmer**.

2693. Frederick[8] **Bovee** (Frederick[7], John W[6], Cornelius[5], Abraham[4], Abraham[3], Nicholas[2], Mathieu[1]), born 23 Jul 1897 in Groveland, Livingston Co., NY; died 17 Jul 1968 in Rochester, Monroe Co., NY. He married Catherine (---), born abt 1903.

Children of Frederick Bovee and Catherine (---) were as follows:

3760	i	Alice[9] **Bovee**.

2702. Regis Renee[8] **Bovee** (Jesse Clayton[7], Henry M[6], Cornelius[5], Abraham[4], Abraham[3], Nicholas[2], Mathieu[1]), born 21 Jun 1905 in Rathbone, Steuben Co., NY; died in Canisteo,Steuben Co., NY. She married (1) on 19 Mar 1925 in Canisteo,Steuben Co., NY Harold Corbin, born in Bennettsville, Chenango Co., NY; died 5 Aug 1972 in Wellsville, Allegany Co., NY; (2) on 11 Oct 1975 in Canisteo,Steuben Co., NY Glen Ripley, born in NY.

Children of Regis Renee Bovee and Harold Corbin were as follows:

3761	i	Eileen Neva[9] **Corbin**, born 9 Oct 1927 in Canisteo,Steuben Co., NY.
3762	ii	Carol Louise[9] **Corbin**, born 26 Jul 1929 in Canisteo,Steuben Co., NY.
3763	iii	Dorr Orrin[9] **Corbin**, born in Canisteo,Steuben Co., NY.

2704. Vera Doris[8] **Bovee** (Jesse Clayton[7], Henry M[6], Cornelius[5], Abraham[4], Abraham[3], Nicholas[2], Mathieu[1]), born 4 Jul 1910 in Rathbone, Steuben Co., NY. She married on 29 Dec 1933 in Canisteo,Steuben Co., NY Harry Van Scoter Lemen, son of Charles T Lemen.

Children of Vera Doris Bovee and Harry Van Scoter Lemen were as follows:

3764   i   David Robert[9] **Lemen**, born in Hornell, Steuben Co., NY.

3765   ii   Linda Lou[9] **Lemen**, born in Hornell, Steuben Co., NY.

2707. Margaret Helene[8] **Bovee** (Jesse Clayton[7], Henry M[6], Cornelius[5], Abraham[4], Abraham[3], Nicholas[2], Mathieu[1]), born 11 Sep 1917 in Galeton, Potter Co., PA. She married on 14 Jul 1934 in Canestio, Steuben Co., NY, divorced Clair William Norton.

Children of Margaret Helene Bovee and Clair William Norton were as follows:

3766   i   Barbara Jean[9] **Norton**, born in Canisteo,Steuben Co., NY.

3767   ii   Jacquelyn Sue[9] **Norton**, born in Hornell, Steuben Co., NY.

3768   iii   Sandra Lee[9] **Norton**, born in Hornell, Steuben Co., NY.

3769   iv   Richard Clair[9] **Norton**, born in Hornell, Steuben Co., NY.

3770   v   Gary William[9] **Norton**, born in Hornell, Steuben Co., NY.

2715. Carl Norman[8] **Bovee** (Earl Erwin[7], Henry M[6], Cornelius[5], Abraham[4], Abraham[3], Nicholas[2], Mathieu[1]), born abt 1920 in Canisteo, Steuben Co, NY; died 19 Aug 1999. He married Ruth (---), born abt 1928.

Children of Carl Norman Bovee and Ruth (---) were as follows:

3771   i   Carl Norman[9] **Bovee** Jr, born 1949 in Hornell, Steuben Co., NY; died 1949 in Hornell, Steuben Co., NY.

2716. Earl Erwin[8] **Bovee** Jr (Earl Erwin[7], Henry M[6], Cornelius[5], Abraham[4], Abraham[3], Nicholas[2], Mathieu[1]), born 1922. He married in Steuben Co, NY Geraldine Predmore, daughter of (---) Predmore and Gladys (---).

Children of Earl Erwin Bovee Jr and Geraldine Predmore were as follows:

+   3772   i   Sherry May[9] **Bovee**. She married (1) **Robert Matacle**; (2) **Michael Henry**.

2721. Viola F[8] **Bovee** (George William[7], William R[6], Abraham[5], Abraham[4], Abraham[3], Nicholas[2], Mathieu[1]), born 24 Jan 1895 in WI; died 27 Aug 1926. She married on 27 Nov 1913 in Manawa, Waupaca Co., WI William Thomas Vaughan, born 3 May 1893 in Little Wolf Twp., Waupaca Co., WI; died 28 Feb

1954 in Appleton, Outagamie Co., WI, son of Walter G Vaughan and Anna Behnke.

Children of Viola F Bovee and William Thomas Vaughan were as follows:

3773   i   Wilbur Francis^9 **Vaughan**, born 5 Jan 1915 in Little Wolf Twp., Waupaca Co., WI.

3774   ii   Earl Thomas^9 **Vaughan**, born 24 Jan 1916 in Little Wolf Twp., Waupaca Co., WI; died 15 Jul 1987.

3775   iii   Lester William^9 **Vaughan**, born 3 Aug 1918 in Little Wolf Twp., Waupaca Co., WI; died 17 Sep 1975 in Marshfield, Wood Co., WI.

3776   iv   Roger George^9 **Vaughan**, born 21 May 1921 in Little Wolf Twp., Waupaca Co., WI.

2723. Vernon Harold^8 **Bovee** (Arthur Vernon^7, William R^6, Abraham^5, Abraham^4, Abraham^3, Nicholas^2, Mathieu^1), born 22 Mar 1895 in Little Wolf Twp., Waupaca Co., WI; died 1 Jan 1972 in Waushara Co., WI. He married on 22 Jun 1918 Minnie Michalski.

Children of Vernon Harold Bovee and Minnie Michalski were as follows:

+ 3777   i   Lyle William^9 **Bovee**, born 8 Jun 1918 in Farmington Twp., Waupaca Co., WI. He married **Laverna M Marburger**.

+ 3778   ii   Florence Cecilia^9 **Bovee**, born 17 Dec 1919 in Farmington Twp., Waupaca Co., WI. She married **Claude William Byrion Sr**.

+ 3779   iii   Vivian May^9 **Bovee**, born 31 Jul 1921 in Farmington Twp., Waupaca Co., WI. She married **Vernon Byrion**.

3780   iv   Harold Vernon^9 **Bovee**, born 6 Feb 1924 in Farmington Twp., Waupaca Co., WI.

+ 3781   v   Isabell Agnes^9 **Bovee**, born 9 May 1929 in Farmington Twp., Waupaca Co., WI. She married **Lyle Jolin Sr**.

+ 3782   vi   Augusta Tresa^9 **Bovee**, born in Farmington Twp., Waupaca Co., WI. She married **Hugh A Stewart**.

2724. Arthur Vernon^8 **Bovee** Jr (Arthur Vernon^7, William R^6, Abraham^5, Abraham^4, Abraham^3, Nicholas^2, Mathieu^1), born 10 May 1897 in Manawa, Waupaca Co., WI; died Aug 1967 in Brea, Orange Co., CA. He married Henrietta (---).

Children of Arthur Vernon Bovee Jr and Henrietta (---) were as follows:

+ 3783   i   Arthur William^9 **Bovee**, died in La Mirada, Los Angeles Co., CA. He married **Henrietta Bessie Meyer**.

2726. Charlotte^8 **Bovee** (Arthur Vernon^7, William R^6, Abraham^5, Abraham^4, Abraham^3, Nicholas^2, Mathieu^1), born abt 1899. She married Henry Pauzig.

Children of Charlotte Bovee and Henry Pauzig were as follows:

3784   i   Kenneth^9 **Pauzig**.

3785   ii   Dolores^9 **Pauzig**.

3786   iii   Henry^9 **Pauzig** Jr..

2727. Carl Clifford^8 **Bovee** (Arthur Vernon^7, William R^6, Abraham^5, Abraham^4, Abraham^3, Nicholas^2, Mathieu^1), born 28 Apr 1900 in Manawa, Waupaca Co., WI; died 24 Feb 1987 in Big Falls, Waupaca Co., WI. He married on 4 Nov 1925 in Big Falls, Waupaca Co., WI. Lilliam Emma Pauline Ruppenthal, born 28 Apr 1903; died 1975.

Children of Carl Clifford Bovee and Lilliam Emma Pauline Ruppenthal were as follows:

+   3787   i   Carol Mae^9 **Bovee**, born 7 Aug 1926 in Big Falls, Waupaca Co., WI.. She married **John Phiip Kernan**.

+   3788   ii   Douglas Arthur^9 **Bovee**, born in Big Falls, Waupaca Co., WI.. He married **Betty Carol Blaydes**.

    3789   iii   Yvonne Rae^9 **Bovee**, born 23 Jul 1935; died 10 Jan 1937.

    3790   iv   Donald Carl^9 **Bovee**, born 23 Jul 1935; died 23 Jul 1935.

    3791   v   Donna Rae^9 **Bovee**, born in Big Falls, Waupaca Co., WI.. She married on 29 Jun 1957 in Waulegan, Lake Co., IL. **James Forest Rustad**.

2728. Leland M^8 **Bovee** (Arthur Vernon^7, William R^6, Abraham^5, Abraham^4, Abraham^3, Nicholas^2, Mathieu^1), born 27 Aug 1901 in Waupaca Co., WI; died 30 May 1985 in Antigo, Langlade Co., WI. He married Ellen Giese, born 19 Nov 1906; died 12 Jun 1981 in Antigo, Langlade Co., WI.

Children of Leland M Bovee and Ellen Giese were as follows:

    3792   i   Roland E^9 **Bovee**, born abt 1924.

    3793   ii   Leland M^9 **Bovee** Jr, born 14 Jun 1928; died 17 Jul 1928.

+   3794   iii   Roger^9 **Bovee**, born abt 1929. He married **Elode Gast**.

    3795   iv   Jeanette^9 **Bovee**. She married (1) **Herbert Malliest**; (2) **Conrad Biersdorf**.

    3796   v   Mary Lee^9 **Bovee**.

2729. Gordon Lester^8 **Bovee** (Arthur Vernon^7, William R^6, Abraham^5, Abraham^4, Abraham^3, Nicholas^2, Mathieu^1), born 26 Oct 1905 in Manawa, Waupaca Co., WI; died 27 Jul 1979 in Antigo, Langlade Co., WI. He married on 6 May 1925 in Big Falls, Waupaca Co., WI Minnie Amelia Hansen, born 27 Jun 1909 in WI; died 17 Jun 1988 in Antigo, Langlade Co., WI.

Children of Gordon Lester Bovee and Minnie Amelia Hansen were as follows:

+   3797   i   Elaine^9 **Bovee**, born 3 Jan 1926 in Tigerton, Shawano

Co., WI. She married **Laddie Schwartz Jr**.

+ 3798   ii   Gordon W^{9} **Bovee**, born 31 Mar 1928 in Antigo, Langlade Co., WI. He married **Rita Wachal**.

+ 3799   iii   Shirley M^{9} **Bovee**, born in Antigo, Langlade Co., WI. She married **Richard F Kestley**.

+ 3800   iv   Helen Jane^{9} **Bovee**, born in Antigo, Langlade Co., WI. She married **Thomas Fermanich**.

+ 3801   v   Irene L^{9} **Bovee**, born in Antigo, Langlade Co., WI. She married **Howard L Wagner**.

2730. Everette Vivian^{8} **Bovee** (Arthur Vernon^{7}, William R^{6}, Abraham^{5}, Abraham^{4}, Abraham^{3}, Nicholas^{2}, Mathieu^{1}), born 9 Dec 1906 in Little Wolf Twp., Waupaca Co., WI; died 4 Nov 1984 in New London, Waupaca Co., WI. He married on 20 Mar 1929 in Big Falls, Waupaca Co., WI Evelyn Hope Myers, born 3 Jan 1910 in Hancock,Waushara Co., WI.; died 21 Oct 1999 in New London, Waushara Co., WI., daughter of Del Myers and Lana Emmot.

Children of Everette Vivian Bovee and Evelyn Hope Myers were as follows:

+ 3802   i   Robert Eugene^{9} **Bovee**, born 22 Jun 1929 in Wyoming, Waupaca Co., WI.. He married **Betty Ann Surorise**.

+ 3803   ii   Everette Vivian^{9} **Bovee** Jr, born in Big Falls, Waupaca Co., WI.. He married **Phyllis Mahn**.

+ 3804   iii   Donald Lee^{9} **Bovee**, born in Wyoming Twp., Waupac Co., WI. He married (1) **Patty Jo Prinson**; (2) **Elizabeth (---)**.

+ 3805   iv   Tony Lee^{9} **Bovee**, born in Seoul, Korea. He married **Denise Marie Kubinski**.

3806   v   Judy Lynn^{9} **Bovee**, born in Seoul, Korea.

2744. Ned Allen^{8} **Bovee** (George Lewis^{7}, Minard^{6}, Abraham^{5}, Abraham^{4}, Abraham^{3}, Nicholas^{2}, Mathieu^{1}), born 4 Jul 1916 in Presque Isle, Vilas Co., WI; died 5 Feb 1994 in Laurim, Houghton Co., MI. He married on 17 Feb 1940 in Eagle River, Vilas Co., WI Mildred Louise Hanson.

Children of Ned Allen Bovee and Mildred Louise Hanson were as follows:

+ 3807   i   Melissa Gail^{9} **Bovee**. She married **Paul Goulette**.

3808   ii   Brian Bradley^{9} **Bovee**. He married (1) in 1969 **Constance Stuart**; (2) **Barbara (---)**.

+ 3809   iii   Mary Helen^{9} **Bovee**. She married **Jerry Bybee**.

+ 3810   iv   Melanie Ann^{9} **Bovee**. She married (1) **Michael Thomas Steen**; (2) **Kenneth Despain**.

2762. Earl Clarence^{8} **Bovee** (Clarence Abraham^{7}, Erastus^{6}, Abraham^{5}, Abraham^{4}, Abraham^{3}, Nicholas^{2}, Mathieu^{1}), born 5 May 1908 in WI; died 11 Jul 1969 in OH. He married Helen Wells, born 2 Mar 1911.

Children of Earl Clarence Bovee and Helen Wells were as follows:

3811 i   Mary Lee[9] **Bovee**. She married **James E Racine**.

2763. Merrill Frederick[8] **Bovee** (Clarence Abraham[7], Erastus[6], Abraham[5], Abraham[4], Abraham[3], Nicholas[2], Mathieu[1]), born 11 Jan 1915 in WI; died Jan 1975. He married Dorothy Grebe, born 14 Feb 1921.

Children of Merrill Frederick Bovee and Dorothy Grebe were as follows:

+ 3812 i   Sue Ann[9] **Bovee**. She married **Maurice Wayne Poe**.

 3813 ii   Cathy Lou[9] **Bovee**.

2765. Edward Harold[8] **Bovee** (Edward C[7], Erastus[6], Abraham[5], Abraham[4], Abraham[3], Nicholas[2], Mathieu[1]), born 6 Apr 1913; died 18 May 1991. He married Florence F Peron, born 17 Apr 1910.

Children of Edward Harold Bovee and Florence F Peron were as follows:

+ 3814 i   Jan Merrill[9] **Bovee**, born in Niagara, Marinette Co., WI. He married **Anita Louise (---)**.

+ 3815 ii   Gary Edward[9] **Bovee**, born 1943 in Norway, Dickinson Co., MI; died abt 1997. He married **Patricia A Tohulka**.

 3816 iii   Carolyn[9] **Bovee**.

 3817 iv   Marlene[9] **Bovee**. She married **(---) Chartier**.

2776. Irving[8] **Bovee** (Albert[7], Ervin[6], Frederick Brown[5], Abraham[4], Abraham[3], Nicholas[2], Mathieu[1]), born 24 Dec 1919 in WI. He married Shirley Giermoth.

Children of Irving Bovee and Shirley Giermoth were as follows:

3818 i   Jim[9] **Bovee**. He married **Pat (---)**.

3819 ii   Margaret[9] **Bovee**.

3820 iii   Joseph[9] **Bovee**.

2777. John William[8] **Bovee** (Albert[7], Ervin[6], Frederick Brown[5], Abraham[4], Abraham[3], Nicholas[2], Mathieu[1]), born 23 Oct 1921 in Oakfield, Fond du Lac Co., WI; died 14 Jan 1991. He married Ruth Angeline Grubish, born 28 Mar 1924.

Children of John William Bovee and Ruth Angeline Grubish were as follows:

3821 i   John Martin[9] **Bovee**, born in Steele Co., MN. He married on 6 Oct 1962 in Trinity Evangelical United Brethern Church, Lomira, Dodge Co., WI. **Jacquelyn Joy Jordan**, daughter of Arden W Jordan and Hazel H Gusse.

3822 ii   Judith[9] **Bovee**.

3823 iii   Gary William[9] **Bovee**, born in Steele Co., MN.

3824 iv   Richard Sylvester[9] **Bovee**, born in Steele Co., MN.

2778. Alfred[8] **Bovee** Sr (Albert[7], Ervin[6], Frederick Brown[5], Abraham[4], Abraham[3], Nicholas[2], Mathieu[1]), born 8 Sep 1923; died 13 Nov 1993 in Loveland, Larimer Co., CO. He married Mildred S (---).

Children of Alfred Bovee Sr and Mildred S (---) were as follows:

3825	i	Alfred[9] **Bovee** Jr.
3826	ii	Robert[9] **Bovee**.
3827	iii	Alan[9] **Bovee**.
3828	iv	Carra[9] **Bovee**.

2779. Lester M[8] **Bovee** (Andrew Jackson[7], Andrew Jackson[6], Henry[5], Abraham[4], Abraham[3], Nicholas[2], Mathieu[1]), born 8 Oct 1909 in Bellingham, Whatcom Co., WA; died 24 Jan 2001 in Bellingham, Whatcom Co., WA. He married on 26 Jun 1932 in Bellingham, Whatcom Co., WA Deloris Ehle.

Children of Lester M Bovee and Deloris Ehle were as follows:

| + | 3829 | i | Aloha[9] **Bovee**. She married **Clyde Wells**. |
| + | 3830 | ii | Edith[9] **Bovee**. She married **Philip Hansen**. |

2782. Arlene Marion[8] **Bovee** (Jesse Arthur[7], Andrew Jackson[6], Henry[5], Abraham[4], Abraham[3], Nicholas[2], Mathieu[1]), born abt 1914. She married Fremont Marins Nelson.

Children of Arlene Marion Bovee and Fremont Marins Nelson were as follows:

| 3831 | i | Fremont Ronald[9] **Nelson**, born in Ramsey Co., MN. |
| 3832 | ii | David Michael[9] **Nelson**, born in Ramsey Co., MN. |

2785. Carley May[8] **Bovee** (Jesse Arthur[7], Andrew Jackson[6], Henry[5], Abraham[4], Abraham[3], Nicholas[2], Mathieu[1]), born 8 May 1924. She married on 19 Jul 1945 Raymond R Fronek.

Children of Carley May Bovee and Raymond R Fronek were as follows:

3833	i	Tim[9] **Fronek**.
3834	ii	Richard[9] **Fronek**.
3835	iii	Martin[9] **Fronek**.
3836	iv	Vernon[9] **Fronek**.

2804. Madeline Margaret[8] **Bovee** (John Henry[7], Warren Henry[6], Henry[5], Abraham[4], Abraham[3], Nicholas[2], Mathieu[1]), born 12 Aug 1923; died in Stockbridge, Calumet Co., WI. She married on 16 Jun 1942 Sylvester Jacob

Penning.

Children of Madeline Margaret Bovee and Sylvester Jacob Penning were as follows:

3837	i	Sandra Lee[9] **Penning**.
3838	ii	Bonita Lee[9] **Penning**.
3839	iii	Sharon Rose[9] **Penning**.
3840	iv	Lynn Mary[9] **Penning**.

2805. Lawrence Erwin[8] **Bovee** (Lyman George[7], Franklin Gibson[6], Aaron[5], Henry[4], Abraham[3], Nicholas[2], Mathieu[1]), born 11 Oct 1901; died 23 Dec 1927. He married on 27 Sep 1919 in Binghampton, Broome Co., NY Hilda M Harris, born abt 1903.

Children of Lawrence Erwin Bovee and Hilda M Harris were as follows:

+	3841	i	Robert Lawrence[9] **Bovee**, born 13 Oct 1922. He married **Julienne Marie (---)**.
	3842	ii	Barbara[9] **Bovee**. She married **(---) Tripp**.
	3843	iii	Betty[9] **Bovee**. She married **(---) Orzel**.

2809. Burton George[8] **Bovee** (Lyman George[7], Franklin Gibson[6], Aaron[5], Henry[4], Abraham[3], Nicholas[2], Mathieu[1]), born 17 May 1912. He married on 6 Jun 1930 Alice Mae Lane.

Children of Burton George Bovee and Alice Mae Lane were as follows:

3844	i	Jean[9] **Bovee**.
3845	ii	Jane[9] **Bovee**.
3846	iii	Joan[9] **Bovee**.
3847	iv	Gary L[9] **Bovee**.

2823. Susan Ina[8] **Bovee** (Charles Avery[7], Charles J[6], John[5], Henry[4], Abraham[3], Nicholas[2], Mathieu[1]), born in Jamestown, Stutsman Co., ND. She married (1) on 26 Dec 1970 in Minot, Ward Co., ND Steven Swanson; (2) in May 1978 in Minot, Ward Co., ND Ron Staiger.

Children of Susan Ina Bovee and Steven Swanson were as follows:

3848	i	Jaseon Paul[9] **Swanson**, born in Bismark, Burleigh Co., ND.

Children of Susan Ina Bovee and Ron Staiger were as follows:

3849	i	Cassie Faye[9] **Staiger**, born in Minot, Ward Co., ND.
3850	ii	Andrew Ray[9] **Staiger**, born in Bismark, Burleigh Co., ND.

2824. Charles James[8] **Bovee** (Charles Avery[7], Charles J[6], John[5], Henry[4],

Abraham^3, Nicholas^2, Mathieu^1), born in Minot, Ward Co., ND. He married on 28 Apr 1990 Jennie (---).

Children of Charles James Bovee and Jennie (---) were as follows:

3851   i   Allison Marie^9 **Bovee**, born in Antioch, Lake Co., IL.

2825. Steven Craig^8 **Bovee** (Charles Avery^7, Charles J^6, John^5, Henry^4, Abraham^3, Nicholas^2, Mathieu^1), born in Minot, Ward Co., ND. He married on 11 Jul 1981 Susan Parizek.

Children of Steven Craig Bovee and Susan Parizek were as follows:

3852   i   Kami Jane^9 **Bovee**, born in Minot, Ward Co., ND.

3853   ii   Stephen Craig^9 **Bovee** Jr, born in Minot, Ward Co., ND.

2826. Laurie Ann^8 **Bovee** (Charles Avery^7, Charles J^6, John^5, Henry^4, Abraham^3, Nicholas^2, Mathieu^1), born in Minot, Ward Co., ND. She married on 1 Dec 1978 in Minot, Ward Co., ND Jeffrey Wood.

Children of Laurie Ann Bovee and Jeffrey Wood were as follows:

3854   i   Justin Gene^9 **Wood**, born in Minot, Ward Co., ND.

2836. Joyce Darlene^8 **Bovee** (Arthur Cornelius^7, Myron Edgar^6, Cornelius^5, Peter^4, Abraham^3, Nicholas^2, Mathieu^1). She married Dwain Alvin Nading.

Children of Joyce Darlene Bovee and Dwain Alvin Nading were as follows:

3855   i   Kim^9 **Nading**.

3856   ii   Brian Lee^9 **Nading**.

2876. Ernest Fred^8 **Bovee** (Byron J^7, Philip^6, Philip^5, Jacob Philip^4, Philip^3, Nicholas^2, Mathieu^1), born 17 Mar 1899 in WA; died Jun 1968. He married on 20 Mar 1924 in Stevens Co., WA Jessie Victoria Hinman.

Children of Ernest Fred Bovee and Jessie Victoria Hinman were as follows:

3857   i   Ester S^9 **Bovee**.

2884. Louis Grant^8 **Bovee** (Orbie O^7, George^6, Philip^5, Jacob Philip^4, Philip^3, Nicholas^2, Mathieu^1), born 7 Jun 1897 in Vernon, British Columbia, Canada. He married (1) on 30 Jun 1923 Irene G Alspach, died 5 Jul 1964; (2) on 26 Feb 1966 in Palm Springs, Riverside Co., CA Hilma Kimes.

Children of Louis Grant Bovee and Irene G Alspach were as follows:

+   3858   i   Lois Lucille^9 **Bovee**, born 30 Jul 1925. She married **William Currie**.

+ 3859 ii Elizabeth Mae[9] **Bovee**, born 8 Nov 1928. She married **Raymond Roy pierce.**

+ 3860 iii Clifford Dan[9] **Bovee**. He married (1) **Mary Lou Livermore**; (2) **Debbie (---).**

2892. Charles Henry[8] **Bovee** (Frederick Germond[7], Nicholas[6], John[5], Jacob Philip[4], Philip[3], Nicholas[2], Mathieu[1]), born 4 Jun 1887 in Rawsonville, Wayne Co., MI; died 16 Dec 1951 in Novi, Oakland Co., MI. He married (1) on 21 Jun 1905 Tena Louise Packard, born abt 1881 in MI; died 1926 in Plymouth, Wayne Co., MI; (2) Ina (---); (3) aft 1927 Nina May Weber, born 26 May 1896 in MI; died 8 Nov 1984 in Wayne, Wayne Co., MI, daughter of Albert Weber and Elizabeth (---).

Children of Charles Henry Bovee and Tena Louise Packard were as follows:

+ 3861 i Donald F[9] **Bovee**, born 23 Jul 1906 in Rawsonville, Wayne Co., MI; died 25 May 1979 in Pacific Grove, Monterey Co., CA. He married **Katherine Louise Hammer.**

+ 3862 ii Muriel Ferne[9] **Bovee**, born 5 Aug 1908; died 1991 in FL. She married (1) **Frank Brown**; (2) **Elbert Martin.**

3863 iii Ralph[9] **Bovee**, born 29 Jan 1911; died 2 Jan 1932 in Shattuck, TX.

+ 3864 iv Norvall Charles[9] **Bovee**, born 17 Mar 1917 in Salem, Washtenaw Co., MI; died 11 Dec 1970 in Mt Pleasant, Isabella Co., MI. He married **Evelyn Mary Gagnon.**

Children of Charles Henry Bovee and Ina (---) were as follows:

3865 i Beverly[9] **Bovee**, born 1927. She married **Bruce McAllister.**

2897. Nathan H[8] **Bovee** (John Edwin[7], Edwin Henry[6], John[5], Jacob Philip[4], Philip[3], Nicholas[2], Mathieu[1]), born 6 Nov 1894 in IA; died 22 Mar 1964 in Tucson, Pima Co., AZ. He married on 15 Jun 1922 Vera Lucille Crosby, born 3 Oct 1900 in AZ; died 13 Oct 1990.

Children of Nathan H Bovee and Vera Lucille Crosby were as follows:

+ 3866 i John Edwin[9] **Bovee**, born 1922. He married **Elizabeth (---).**

3867 ii Robert[9] **Bovee**, born 24 May 1924.

+ 3868 iii Henry Russell[9] **Bovee**, born 18 Nov 1926. He married **Nancy Williams.**

3869 iv Mary Jean[9] **Bovee**. She married **Don Hardy.**

2907. Charles[8] **Bovee** (Freeman[7], Charles P[6], Nicholas[5], Jacob Philip[4], Philip[3], Nicholas[2], Mathieu[1]), born 17 May 1886 in MI; died Jul 1966 in Cleveland, Cuyahoga Co., OH. He married Mertie Esther Booker, born 11 Nov 1889; died

20 Feb 1966.

Children of Charles Bovee and Mertie Esther Booker were as follows:

3870   i   Dolores[9] **Bovee**, born abt 1907. She married **Lyle Easton**.

2908. Forest F[8] **Bovee** (Freeman[7], Charles P[6], Nicholas[5], Jacob Philip[4], Philip[3], Nicholas[2], Mathieu[1]), born 14 May 1892 in Seneca Twp., Lenawee Co., MI; died 17 Jan 1948 in Seneca Twp., Lenawee Co., MI. He married Helena Lemke, born 1898; died 1988.

Children of Forest F Bovee and Helena Lemke were as follows:

+ 3871 i   Burton[9] **Bovee**, born 15 Feb 1919 in MI; died 5 Apr 1980 in Morenci, Lenawee Co., MI. He married (1) **Madelyn Lucille Johnson**; (2) **Vivian Harger**.

+ 3872 ii   Keith N[9] **Bovee**, born 11 May 1923; died 22 Aug 1982 in Adrian, Lenawee Co., MI. He married **Helen Rathbun**.

    3873 iii   Marlene[9] **Bovee.** She married **Glenn Kelly**.

+ 3874 iv   Forrest Burdette[9] **Bovee**. He married **Rosetta Diane Nichols**.

2910. Uvah[8] **Bovee** (Freeman[7], Charles P[6], Nicholas[5], Jacob Philip[4], Philip[3], Nicholas[2], Mathieu[1]), died 1954. She married Leo Driscoll, born 1890; died 1964.

Children of Uvah Bovee and Leo Driscoll were as follows:

3875   i   Dorothy Ellen[9] **Driscoll**, born 2 Aug 1920; died 2 Mar 1997 in Orange Co., CA. She married **(---) Russell**.

2911. Fern[8] **Bovee** (Seymour Nelson[7], Nelson H[6], Nicholas[5], Jacob Philip[4], Philip[3], Nicholas[2], Mathieu[1]), born May 1896. She married Ray D Post.

Children of Fern Bovee and Ray D Post were as follows:

3876   i   Donna[9] **Post**.

2912. Faye[8] **Bovee** (Seymour Nelson[7], Nelson H[6], Nicholas[5], Jacob Philip[4], Philip[3], Nicholas[2], Mathieu[1]), born Jan 1898 in MI. She married Paul H Glaumer.

Children of Faye Bovee and Paul H Glaumer were as follows:

3877   i   Dwight[9] **Glaumer**.

3878   ii   Keith[9] **Glaumer**.

2915. Max Nelson[8] **Bovee** (Seymour Nelson[7], Nelson H[6], Nicholas[5], Jacob

Philip[4], Philip[3], Nicholas[2], Mathieu[1]), born 1906 in MI; died 1963. He married on 18 Apr 1928 Irena Elsie Benfield, born 1910; died 19 Dec 1955, daughter of William Holmes.

Children of Max Nelson Bovee and Irena Elsie Benfield were as follows:

+ 3879   i   Norval Seymour[9] **Bovee**. He married **Jocelyn Gurnee Larrabee**.

+ 3880   ii   Mavis Irena[9] **Bovee**. She married **Richard Dirlam**.

2919. Miner[8] **Bovee** (Floyd B[7], Nelson H[6], Nicholas[5], Jacob Philip[4], Philip[3], Nicholas[2], Mathieu[1]), born abt 1914. He married Myrtle Clingingpeel, born 13 Mar 1916.

Children of Miner Bovee and Myrtle Clingingpeel were as follows:

3881   i   Patsey Louise[9] **Bovee**, born 17 Mar 1937; died 20 Mar 1937.

3882   ii   Floyd[9] **Bovee**.

3883   iii   Cindy[9] **Bovee**.

+ 3884   iv   Dale Allen[9] **Bovee**. He married (1) **Barbara O'Hare**; (2) **Fay Maness**.

3885   v   Jimmy[9] **Bovee**.

2928. Sidney Richard[8] **Bovee** (Charles Henry[7], Nelson H[6], Nicholas[5], Jacob Philip[4], Philip[3], Nicholas[2], Mathieu[1]), born 26 Sep 1915 in Whitehouse, Lucas Co., OH; died 27 Feb 1985 in Walbridge, Wood Co., OH. He married on 13 Nov 1938 Beatrice Irene Harmon, born 28 Aug 1922.

Children of Sidney Richard Bovee and Beatrice Irene Harmon were as follows:

3886   i   Sandra Anne[9] **Bovee**, born in Bowling Green, Wood Co., OH. She married **(---) True**.

+ 3887   ii   Richard Eugene[9] **Bovee**. He married **Brenda Harrison Fallon**.

+ 3888   iii   Roger Lee[9] **Bovee**. He married **Sandra Meys**.

3889   iv   Regina Rae[9] **Bovee**, born in Toledo, Lucas Co., OH.

2929. Raymond Lewis[8] **Bovee** (Charles Henry[7], Nelson H[6], Nicholas[5], Jacob Philip[4], Philip[3], Nicholas[2], Mathieu[1]), born 17 Apr 1919; died Jul 1985 in Toledo, Lucas Co., OH. He married (1) Genevieve (---); (2) Helen (---).

Children of Raymond Lewis Bovee and Genevieve (---) were as follows:

3890   i   Raymond[9] **Bovee** Jr.

3891   ii   Shirley[9] **Bovee**.

3892   iii   Sharon[9] **Bovee**.

Children of Raymond Lewis Bovee and Helen (---) were as follows:

3893   i   Raymond^9 **Bovee** Jr.

3894   ii   Leslie^9 **Bovee**.

3895   iii   Child^9 **Bovee**.

2930. Eskell Charles^8 **Bovee** (Charles Henry^7, Nelson H^6, Nicholas^5, Jacob Philip^4, Philip^3, Nicholas^2, Mathieu^1), born 13 Feb 1921 in OH; died Feb 1967. He married in Hawaii unknown.

Children of Eskell Charles Bovee were as follows:

3896   i   Diane^9 **Bovee**.

2931. Charles D^8 **Bovee** (Jeremiah W^7, William R^6, Daniel R^5, Nicholas P^4, Philip^3, Nicholas^2, Mathieu^1), born abt 1867 in PA. He married on 2 Sep 1890 Frances J Twichell.

Children of Charles D Bovee and Frances J Twichell were as follows:

3897   i   Ada^9 **Bovee**, born abt 1892.

+ 3898   ii   George Earl^9 **Bovee**, born 15 Jun 1895 in Edinboro, Erie Co., PA; christened 26 May 1929 in Pensacola, Escambia Co., FL; died 2 Jun 1972 in Pensacola, Escambia Co., FL. He married **Daisy L Long**.

3899   iii   Charles^9 **Bovee**, born abt 1901.

3900   iv   Bertha^9 **Bovee**, born abt 1906.

3901   v   Mabel^9 **Bovee**, born 1909.

2932. Ada C^8 **Bovee** (Daniel Reynolds^7, William R^6, Daniel R^5, Nicholas P^4, Philip^3, Nicholas^2, Mathieu^1), born 23 Jul 1866 in Erie Co., PA; died Apr 1957 in Washington, DC. She married (1) on 27 May 1886 in Erie Co., PA Fred E Allen; (2) Prof Victor C Zebley.

Children of Ada C Bovee and Prof Victor C Zebley were as follows:

3902   i   June^9 **Zebley**.

2933. June Raymond^8 **Bovee** (Daniel Reynolds^7, William R^6, Daniel R^5, Nicholas P^4, Philip^3, Nicholas^2, Mathieu^1), born 11 Jul 1870 in Greenfield, Erie Co., PA; died 20 Jun 1952 in Elizabethtown, Lancaster Co., PA. He married Mabel Maria Cook, born 12 Jun 1872 in Venango, Wattsburg Co., PA; died 23 Dec 1949 in Elizabethtown, Lancaster Co., PA, daughter of Grinsitte Hood Cook and Martha Skinner.

Children of June Raymond Bovee and Mabel Maria Cook were as follows:

+ 3903   i   Lynn Albert^9 **Bovee**, born 18 Oct 1889 in Venango, Crawford Co., PA; died 24 Jul 1963 in Orange, Orange

Co., CA. He married **Lena Anderson**.

+ 3904 ii Frank Grencett[9] **Bovee**, born 16 Oct 1891 in Erie Co., PA; died 13 Dec 1916. He married **Mary Louise Berger**.

2934. Irl C[8][1] **Bovee** (Daniel Reynolds[7], William R[6], Daniel R[5], Nicholas P[4], Philip[3], Nicholas[2], Mathieu[1]), born 23 Oct 1882 in Erie Co., PA. He married Sarah Chess, born abt 1879; died 1956.

Children of Irl C Bovee and Sarah Chess were as follows:

3905 i Alberta[9] **Bovee**, born abt 1916. She married **George Hacodale**.

2935. Glenn Dexter[8] **Bovee** (Charles Dexter[7], William R[6], Daniel R[5], Nicholas P[4], Philip[3], Nicholas[2], Mathieu[1]), born 1 Mar 1873 in N Springfield, Erie Co., PA; died 8 Dec 1959 in Swanville, Erie Co., PA. He married Jesse Tuttle.

Children of Glenn Dexter Bovee and Jesse Tuttle were as follows:

+ 3906 i Aris[9] **Bovee**, born 5 Nov 1901 in Swanville, Erie Co., PA; died in Erie, Erie Co., PA. She married **Ross Reed**.

2936. Harriet M[8] **Bovee** (Charles Dexter[7], William R[6], Daniel R[5], Nicholas P[4], Philip[3], Nicholas[2], Mathieu[1]), born 29 Jul 1874 in N Springfield, Erie Co., PA; died 3 May 1964 in E Springfield, Erie Co., PA. She married (1) abt 1928 Jonas Spencer Parker, born 11 Jun 1845 in Millcreek Twp., Erie Co., PA; died 30 Aug 1929 in Erie, Erie Co., PA, son of Dean Parker and Mary Ann Shattuck; (2) Charles Pickney.

Children of Harriet M Bovee and Charles Pickney were as follows:

3907 i Vernon[9] **Pickney**.

2939. Frederick Charles[8] **Bovee** (Charles Dexter[7], William R[6], Daniel R[5], Nicholas P[4], Philip[3], Nicholas[2], Mathieu[1]), born 24 Dec 1881 in N Springfield, Erie Co., PA; died 9 May 1957 in Erie, Erie Co., PA. He married on 28 Aug 1913 in Dunkirk, Chautauqua Co., NY Mayme Esther Parker, born 13 Nov 1889 in Summit Twp., Erie Co., PA; died 16 Jan 1986 in Erie, Erie Co., PA, daughter of Jonas Spencer Parker and Mary Emeline Pinney.

Children of Frederick Charles Bovee and Mayme Esther Parker were as follows:

+ 3908 i Ruth Adella[9] **Bovee**, born 22 Sep 1918 in Erie, Erie Co., PA. She married (1) **Merton Smith Bartels**; (2) **Howard Westley**; (3) **John L Beecher**.

3909 ii Howard Parker[9] **Bovee**, born 12 Aug 1920. He married on 15 Apr 1942 **Rose Smitti**.

+ 3910 iii Frederick Lyman[9] **Bovee**, born 27 Feb 1923. He married

Jeanette Nardo.

+ 3911 iv Harry Spencer[9] **Bovee**, born 10 Dec 1924. He married **Dorothy Brakeman**.

2941. Ida E[8] **Bovee** (Charles Dexter[7], William R[6], Daniel R[5], Nicholas P[4], Philip[3], Nicholas[2], Mathieu[1]), born 28 Apr 1887 in N Springfield, Erie Co., PA; died 1957. She married on 3 Apr 1913 in Swanville, Erie Co., PA Jacob Seib, born 1883; died 1953.

Children of Ida E Bovee and Jacob Seib were as follows:

3912 i Almira[9] **Seib**, born 28 Apr 1914.

3913 ii Charles[9] **Seib**, born 11 Aug 1919.

3914 iii Harold[9] **Seib**, born 25 Oct 1926.

3915 iv Leatrice[9] **Seib**.

2947. Edward C[8] **Bovee** (Harper W[7], Nicholas[6], Jacob[5], Nicholas P[4], Philip[3], Nicholas[2], Mathieu[1]), born 2 Jul 1869. He married Jennie M (---), born abt 1875.

Children of Edward C Bovee and Jennie M (---) were as follows:

3916 i Lurlynn[9] **Bovee**, born Nov 1893. She married **James William Neff**.

2948. George A[8] **Bovee** (Harper W[7], Nicholas[6], Jacob[5], Nicholas P[4], Philip[3], Nicholas[2], Mathieu[1]), born 2 Nov 1873 in OH. He married Ruth (---), born abt 1877.

Children of George A Bovee and Ruth (---) were as follows:

3917 i Ruth[9] **Bovee**, born 5 Nov 1900; died Oct 1975 in San Bernardino Co., CA.

3918 ii Marion[9] **Bovee**, born abt 1901 in OH.

3919 iii Charles[9] **Bovee**, born 20 Jan 1906; died Jul 1981 in Paramount, Los Angeles Co., CA.

3920 iv Edith[9] **Bovee**, born abt 1911 in CA.

2950. Floyd D[8] **Bovee** (Lorenzo Dow[7], Nicholas[6], Jacob[5], Nicholas P[4], Philip[3], Nicholas[2], Mathieu[1]), born 8 Jun 1864 in Grundy Co.,IL; died 2 Sep 1914 in Durando, La Plata Co., CO. He married on 23 Sep 1891 in Oswego, Labette Co., KS Fanny D Kirby, born 7 Jul 1868 in Coffee Co., TN, daughter of John Andrew Kirby and Elizabeth A Pearson.

Children of Floyd D Bovee and Fanny D Kirby were as follows:

3921 i Byron Merle[9] **Bovee**, born 26 Feb 1893 in Oswego, Labette Co., KS; died 12 Oct 1937 in Denver, Denver Co., CO. He married on 26 Dec 1916 **Bessie L Downing**.

+ 3922 ii Thelma[9] **Bovee**, born 30 Jan 1895 in Oswego, Labette Co., KS; died 20 Apr 1939 in Golden, Jefferson Co., CO. She married **Horace R Davies**.

+ 3923 iii Alta[9] **Bovee**, born 19 Nov 1899 in Durango, La Plata Co., CO. She married **Walter James Kemper**.

3924 iv Alla[9] **Bovee**, born 19 Nov 1899 in Durango, La Plata Co., CO. She married on 4 Nov 1923 in Denver, Denver Co., CO **Leonard U Carlson**.

2952. Nella B[8] **Bovee** (Lorenzo Dow[7], Nicholas[6], Jacob[5], Nicholas P[4], Philip[3], Nicholas[2], Mathieu[1]), born 12 Dec 1871 in Chetopa, Labette Co., KS; died 18 Nov 1938 in Antonito, Conejos Co., CO. She married on 24 Aug 1893 in Monte Vista, Rio Grande Co., CO Alfred LaMar Strawn, born 1 Mar 1867 in Strawn, Coffey Co., KS; died 4 Nov 1940 in Antonito, Conejos Co., CO, son of James Carson Strawn and Fedelia Grinnell.

Children of Nella B Bovee and Alfred LaMar Strawn were as follows:

3925 i Paul LeMar[9] **Strawn**, born 5 Jul 1894 in Durango, La Plata Co., CO; died 24 May 1958 in Antonito, Conejos Co., CO.

3926 ii James Ivan[9] **Strawn**, born 7 Jun 1897 in Chetopa, Labette Co., KS; died 26 Mar 1946 in Albuquerque, Bernalillo Co., NM.

3927 iii Edmund LeRoy[9] **Strawn**, born 31 Aug 1900 in Durango, La Plata Co., CO; died 26 Mar 1919 in Sunny Side Mine, CO.

3928 iv Floyd Lamont[9] **Strawn**, born 24 Mar 1904 in Pagosa Springs, Archuleta Co., CO; died 8 Sep 1967 in Torrance, Los Angeles Co., CA.

3929 v Frederick Harold[9] **Strawn**, born 6 Apr 1906 in Pagosa Springs, Archuleta Co., CO; died 5 Jul 1973 in Los Angeles, Los Angeles Co., CA.

3930 vi Helen[9] **Strawn**, born 13 Nov 1909 in Monte Vista, Rio Grande Co., CO; died 29 Jul 1934 in Avalon, Los Angeles Co., CA.

2980. Charles H[8] **Bovee** (Harmon E[7], Nicholas[6], Jacob[5], Nicholas P[4], Philip[3], Nicholas[2], Mathieu[1]), born 21 May 1874 in Jackson, Will Co., IL; died 7 Dec 1949. He married Una Agnes Blair, born Mar 1875; died 8 Apr 1928 in Mower Co., MN, daughter of (---) Blair and Mary (---).

Children of Charles H Bovee and Una Agnes Blair were as follows:

3931 i Mary[9] **Bovee**, born Feb 1898.

3932 ii Ruth[9] **Bovee**, born abt 1903.

2981. Guy Clinton[8] **Bovee** (Harmon E[7], Nicholas[6], Jacob[5], Nicholas P[4], Philip[3], Nicholas[2], Mathieu[1]), born 24 Apr 1877; died 26 Feb 1934 in Jackson, Will Co.,

IL. He married on 14 Apr 1904 Emiline C Lorenz, born abt 1884; died 6 Aug 1940.

Children of Guy Clinton Bovee and Emiline C Lorenz were as follows:

+ 3933   i   Esther^{9} **Bovee**, born 28 May 1906. She married **Chester L Christianson**.

+ 3934   ii   George Henry^{9} **Bovee**, born 9 Mar 1908; died Jun 1975. He married **Helen Dessie Gornason**.

    3935   iii   Lawrence Harmon^{9} **Bovee**, born abt 1912; died 6 May 1927 in Jackson Twp., Will Co., IL.

2984. Irving^{8} **Bovee** (Harmon E^{7}, Nicholas^{6}, Jacob^{5}, Nicholas P^{4}, Philip^{3}, Nicholas^{2}, Mathieu^{1}), born 28 Aug 1882; died 21 Jul 1951 in McAllen, Hidalgo Co., TX. He married (1) Sylvia Hartman, died 9 Jan 1940; (2) Hazel (---), born 29 Dec 1896; died Sep 1979 in Port Isabel Isl, Cameron Co., TX.

Children of Irving Bovee and Sylvia Hartman were as follows:

+ 3936   i   Donald C^{9} **Bovee**, born 31 Oct 1925; died 22 Jan 1995 in Willmington, Will Co., IL. He married **Ruth L (---)**.

Children of Irving Bovee and Hazel (---) were as follows:

    3937   i   Beatrice B^{9} **Bovee**. She married **(---) Connor**.

2997. Hattie^{8} **Bovee** (Frank E^{7}, Daniel^{6}, Jacob^{5}, Nicholas P^{4}, Philip^{3}, Nicholas^{2}, Mathieu^{1}), born Sep 1869 in Canada. She married Raymond Harris, born Apr 1872 in NY.

Children of Hattie Bovee and Raymond Harris were as follows:

    3938   i   Dianna^{9} **Harris**, born Apr 1896 in MI.

3008. Arthur C^{8} **Bovee** (Charles Elliott^{7}, Harmon^{6}, Harper^{5}, Nicholas P^{4}, Philip^{3}, Nicholas^{2}, Mathieu^{1}), born abt 1872 in WI. He married Florence Weakens, born Oct 1873 in IL, daughter of (---) Weakens and Sarah A.

Children of Arthur C Bovee and Florence Weakens were as follows:

    3939   i   Ralph Bouty^{9} **Bovee**, born 18 Jul 1894 in MN; died Jan 1969 in San Bernardino, San Bernardino Co., CA. He married **Cassie (---)**, born 20 Dec 1893; died Jan 1986.

3015. Arthur Gibbon^{8} **Bovee** (John N^{7}, Eliad E^{6}, Jacob Nicholas^{5}, Nicholas Jacob^{4}, Jacob^{3}, Nicholas^{2}, Mathieu^{1}), born 17 Feb 1882 in Washington, DC; died 6 May 1961 in Aiken, Aiken Co., SC. He married (1) abt 1909 Martha L (---), born 15 Apr 1889 in France; died 19 Jul 1973 in Los Angeles, Los Angeles Co., CA; (2) on 12 Feb 1937 Julia Lyons, born 27 Feb 1907; died 12 Jan 1990.

Children of Arthur Gibbon Bovee and Martha L (---) were as follows:

3940 i Martha Gibbon[9] **Bovee**, born abt 1910 in IL.

3941 ii Arthur Bishop[9] **Bovee**.

Children of Arthur Gibbon Bovee and Julia Lyons were as follows:

3942 i Bonnie[9] **Bovee**.

3016. Frank M[8] **Bovee** (Eliad A[7], Eliad E[6], Jacob Nicholas[5], Nicholas Jacob[4], Jacob[3], Nicholas[2], Mathieu[1]), born Jan 1868 in Northville Wayne Co., MI. He married Mary S (---), born abt 1880 in NH.

Children of Frank M Bovee and Mary S (---) were as follows:

3943 i E Arthur[9] **Bovee**, born 17 Sep 1902 in OH; died Aug 1969 in Battle Creek, Calhoun Co., MI.

3944 ii Edward S[9] **Bovee**, born 23 May 1905 in MI; died Apr 1983 in Battle Creek, Calhoun Co., MI.

3945 iii Frank W[9] **Bovee**, born abt 1914 in MI.

3022. James Henry[8] **Bovee** (Stillman[7], Mathew J[6], Jacob Nicholas[5], Nicholas Jacob[4], Jacob[3], Nicholas[2], Mathieu[1]), born 16 Jul 1881 in IL; died Feb 1968 in Dunellen, Middlesex Co., NJ. He married Martha (---), born abt 1886.

Children of James Henry Bovee and Martha (---) were as follows:

3946 i Helen Evelyn[9] **Bovee**, born 7 Jun 1904.

3947 ii Ruth Josephine[9] **Bovee**, born 14 Sep 1906; died 23 Jun 1952.

3024. William A[8] **Bovee** (Stillman[7], Mathew J[6], Jacob Nicholas[5], Nicholas Jacob[4], Jacob[3], Nicholas[2], Mathieu[1]), born 13 Jan 1890 in Chicago, Cook Co., IL; died Feb 1965. He married Georgia Rose, born abt 1892 in IA, daughter of (---) Rose and Hannah (---).

Children of William A Bovee and Georgia Rose were as follows:

3948 i William[9] **Bovee**, born 9 Feb 1916 in IL; died 17 Oct 1988 in Tinley Park, Cook Co., IL.

3949 ii Robert[9] **Bovee**, born 17 Apr 1918; died 5 Nov 1989 in Glendale, Maricopa Co., AZ.

3026. Guy A[8] **Bovee** (John M[7], Isaac[6], Jacob Nicholas[5], Nicholas Jacob[4], Jacob[3], Nicholas[2], Mathieu[1]), born Oct 1875 in Woodland, Barry Co., MI; died 30 Mar 1916. He married on 7 Jan 1897 in Lake Odessa, Ionia Co., MI Minnie E Gilson, born Mar 1876 in Sunfield, Eaton Co., MI.

Children of Guy A Bovee and Minnie E Gilson were as follows:

3950   i   Leo J[9] **Bovee**, born 15 Dec 1897; died Dec 1968 in Brooklyn, Jackson Co., MI. He married **Gladys (---)**.

3951   ii   Cleo C[9] **Bovee**, born abt 1903; died 30 Mar 1920.

3952   iii   Kathe[9] **Bovee**, born abt 1909.

3029. Lyle J[8] **Bovee** (Jacob[7], Isaac[6], Jacob Nicholas[5], Nicholas Jacob[4], Jacob[3], Nicholas[2], Mathieu[1]), born 21 Mar 1887 in MI; died Sep 1968 in Lowell, Kent Co., MI. He married in 1908 Mabel Keyser, born 23 Aug 1887 in Lowell, Kent Co., MI; died May 1981 in Lowell, Kent Co., MI.

Children of Lyle J Bovee and Mabel Keyser were as follows:

3953   i   Child[9] **Bovee**, born bef 1917.

3954   ii   Vercel Lyle[9] **Bovee**. He married **Marilyn Green**.

+ 3955   iii   Glendon Charles[9] **Bovee**, born 8 Jul 1917 in Smith, Ionia Co., MI. He married **Janet A Haselweidt**.

3030. Clara[8] **Bovee** (Christian[7], Peter[6], Peter[5], Jacob[4], Jacob[3], Nicholas[2], Mathieu[1]), born 24 Jul 1868 in NY. She married abt 1887 Sidney Garrison, born Sep 1859.

Children of Clara Bovee and Sidney Garrison were as follows:

3956   i   Louisa A[9] **Garrison**, born Jun 1889.

3957   ii   Wilfred C[9] **Garrison**, born May 1891.

3958   iii   Ina M[9] **Garrison**, born Aug 1893.

3959   iv   Olive E[9] **Garrison**, born Aug 1895.

3960   v   Bernice P[9] **Garrison**, born Mar 1898.

3032. John Addison[8] **Bovee** (Christian[7], Peter[6], Peter[5], Jacob[4], Jacob[3], Nicholas[2], Mathieu[1]), born 5 Apr 1873 in PA; died Apr 1942. He married (1) on 5 Jul 1905 Peets Sarah Baker; (2) on 12 Aug 1922 Jennie M Brown.

Children of John Addison Bovee and Peets Sarah Baker were as follows:

+ 3961   i   Frank Walter[9] **Bovee**, born 22 May 1907 in East Branch, Delaware Co., NY; died 22 Aug 1976 in Syracuse, Onondaga Co., NY. He married **Gertrude Louise MacFarlane**.

3962   ii   Lena[9] **Bovee**, born 6 Feb 1909; died 24 Dec 1913.

3963   iii   Freda May[9] **Bovee**, born 25 Jul 1911.

3039. Ethel E[8] **Bovee** (Lorenzo[7], Peter[6], Peter[5], Jacob[4], Jacob[3], Nicholas[2], Mathieu[1]), born 31 Mar 1891 in Bethel, Sullivan Co., NY; died 10 Aug 1972. She married on 11 Oct 1911 Aldon M McCrabie.

Children of Ethel E Bovee and Aldon M McCrabie were as follows:

3964　i　　　Vernone^9 **McCrabie**.

3965　ii　　Robert^9 **McCrabie**.

3966　iii　　Pearl^9 **McCrabie**.

3967　iv　　Hilda^9 **McCrabie**.

3968　v　　　Ethel^9 **McCrabie**.

3969　vi　　Helena^9 **McCrabie**.

3970　vii　　Hope^9 **McCrabie**.

3040. Chauncy William^8 **Bovee** (Lorenzo^7, Peter^6, Peter^5, Jacob^4, Jacob^3, Nicholas^2, Mathieu^1), born 7 Sep 1892 in Long Eddy, Sullivan Co., NY; died Jan 1978 in Waltron, Delaware Co., NY. He married on 25 Dec 1912 Mildred Roberta King MacRabie, born 17 Oct 1892; died 24 Jun 1986 in Walton, Delaware Co., NY.

Children of Chauncy William Bovee and Mildred Roberta King MacRabie were as follows:

3971　i　　　Madelyn^9 **Bovee**, born 17 Sep 1915; died 15 Jun 1997.

3972　ii　　Martin C^9 **Bovee**, born 10 May 1925; died 1999 in Walton, Delaware Co., NY.

3041. Edith M^8 **Bovee** (Lorenzo^7, Peter^6, Peter^5, Jacob^4, Jacob^3, Nicholas^2, Mathieu^1), born Jun 1895. She married on 19 Mar 1914 Paul Krause.

Children of Edith M Bovee and Paul Krause were as follows:

3973　i　　　Oliver^9 **Krause**.

3974　ii　　Jim C^9 **Krause**.

3044. Harold Mark^8 **Bovee** (Lorenzo^7, Peter^6, Peter^5, Jacob^4, Jacob^3, Nicholas^2, Mathieu^1), born abt 1903; died 1924 in Orange Co., NY. He married abt 1922 Emma Caskey, born abt 1905, daughter of Charles Caskey and Hester Jenning.

Children of Harold Mark Bovee and Emma Caskey were as follows:

+　3975　i　　　Raymond Harold^9 **Bovee**, born 23 Feb 1923 in Middletown, Orange Co., NY; died 7 Oct 1969 in San Diego, San Diego Co., CA. He married **Louise May, Harper**.

3052. Lewis B^8 **Bovee** (George A^7, Jacob Clayton^6, Peter^5, Jacob^4, Jacob^3, Nicholas^2, Mathieu^1), born Jun 1868; died 1948. He married Anna C Rightmeyer, born Feb 1870.

Children of Lewis B Bovee and Anna C Rightmeyer were as follows:

+　3976　i　　　Lewis Laverne^9 **Bovee**, born 30 Oct 1889 in NY; died

1963. He married **Lilah Layman**.

3054. Ernest Winchel[8] **Bovee** (George A[7], Jacob Clayton[6], Peter[5], Jacob[4], Jacob[3], Nicholas[2], Mathieu[1]), born 25 Nov 1872; died 23 Sep 1958. He married Lucretia M Buckbee, born 24 Aug 1880; died 30 Oct 1918.

Children of Ernest Winchel Bovee and Lucretia M Buckbee were as follows:

+   3977   i   Barton[9] **Bovee**, born 1 Jun 1900 in CT; died Jan 1982 in CT. He married **E Georgetta (---)**.

3060. Franklin[8] **Bovee** (Pliny L[7], Jacob Clayton[6], Peter[5], Jacob[4], Jacob[3], Nicholas[2], Mathieu[1]), born 20 Dec 1864 in West Saugerties, Ulster Co., NY. He married Grace DeWitt, born Dec 1874.

Children of Franklin Bovee and Grace DeWitt were as follows:

     3978   i   Edith[9] **Bovee**, born abt 1900.

3062. Nelson[8] **Bovee** (Pliny L[7], Jacob Clayton[6], Peter[5], Jacob[4], Jacob[3], Nicholas[2], Mathieu[1]), born 4 Dec 1879 in West Saugerties, Ulster Co., NY. He married on 8 Mar 1905 in Woodstock, Ulster Co., NY Bertha Ostrander, daughter of Maurice Ostrander.

Children of Nelson Bovee and Bertha Ostrander were as follows:

     3979   i   Ethel M[9] **Bovee**, born 24 May 1905 in Hurley, Ulster Co., NY.

     3980   ii   William[9] **Bovee**, born 17 Mar 1907 in Hurley, Ulster Co., NY.

     3981   iii   Clayton S[9] **Bovee**, born 21 Mar 1909 in West Hurley, Ulster Co., NY; died Nov 1979 in New Paltz, Ulster Co., NY.

     3982   iv   Beatrice E[9] **Bovee**, born 18 Aug 1911 in Esopus, Ulster Co., NY. She married **(---) Asker**.

     3983   v   Kenneth N[9] **Bovee**, born 15 Oct 1915 in Esopus, Ulster Co., NY.

     3984   vi   Percy N[9] **Bovee**, born 27 Oct 1917 in Ulster Co., NY; died Jun 1986 in Port Ewen, Ulster Co., NY.

+   3985   vii   Lester Eugene[9] **Bovee**, born abt 1921 in Saugerties, Ulster Co., NY. He married **Bertha Ruth Sickler**.

3067. Ward[8] **Bovee** (Jacob Henry[7], Jacob Clayton[6], Peter[5], Jacob[4], Jacob[3], Nicholas[2], Mathieu[1]), born 1 May 1887; died Oct 1967 in Haines Falls, Greene Co., NY. He married Lulu E Schoonmaker.

Children of Ward Bovee and Lulu E Schoonmaker were as follows:

     3986   i   Leo L[9] **Bovee**, born abt 1917 in Saugerties, Ulster Co.,

3072. Grover[8] **Bovee** (Elijah[7], Jacob Clayton[6], Peter[5], Jacob[4], Jacob[3], Nicholas[2], Mathieu[1]), born Apr 1883. He married Anna Carl.

Children of Grover Bovee and Anna Carl were as follows:

3987	i	Jessie[9] **Bovee**. She married **(---) DelVecchio**.
3988	ii	Urias E[9] **Bovee**, born 15 Dec 1910; died 27 Sep 1984 in Broward Co., FL.
3989	iii	Georgiana[9] **Bovee**. She married **Hugo Haebler**.
+ 3990	iv	Ray D[9] **BoVee**, born 21 Jul 1914 in Younkers, Westchester Co., NY; died 8 Sep 1982 in Seber Shores, Sandy Creek, Oswego Co., NY. He married **Regina Reed**.
3991	v	Charles E[9] **Bovee**.

3073. Charles[8] **Bovee** (Edgar[7], Jacob Clayton[6], Peter[5], Jacob[4], Jacob[3], Nicholas[2], Mathieu[1]), born abt 1873 in NY. He married unknown.

Children of Charles Bovee were as follows:

| 3992 | i | Gertrude[9] **Bovee**. |

3079. Mary Philena[8] **Bovee** (Aldo Harris[7], Isaac[6], Isaac[5], Jacob[4], Jacob[3], Nicholas[2], Mathieu[1]), born 15 Apr 1883. She married on 18 Jan 1906 in College, New York Co., NY Frederick Charles Victor Graff, son of Joseph Graff and Elizabeth Knosf.

Children of Mary Philena Bovee and Frederick Charles Victor Graff were as follows:

3993	i	Charles Amiel[9] **Graff**, born 19 Oct 1906.
3994	ii	Louis Kenwood[9] **Graff**, born 2 Jun 1908; died 4 Oct 1971.
3995	iii	Worthie Lee[9] **Graff**, born 26 Mar 1911.
3996	iv	Elsie Josephine[9] **Graff**, born 25 Sep 1912.
3997	v	Frances Myrtle[9] **Graff**, born 23 Sep 1914.
3998	vi	Merl Willard[9] **Graff**, born 1 Aug 1916.
3999	vii	Gertrude Juanita[9] **Graff**, born 4 Apr 1919.

3080. James Ashley[8] **Bovee** (William Irvin[7], Isaac[6], Isaac[5], Jacob[4], Jacob[3], Nicholas[2], Mathieu[1]), born 23 Mar 1882 in Edwardsburg, Cass Co., MI; died Nov 1983 in Phoenix, Maricopa Co., AZ. He married (1) on 31 Mar 1909 Myrtle Eleanor Conrad, born 21 Oct 1888 in Breckenridge, Summit Co., CO, daughter of Ernest Conrad and Lucina Viana Albee; (2) on 6 Oct 1946 Mildred Ferguson, died abt 1990.

Children of James Ashley Bovee and Myrtle Eleanor Conrad were as follows:

4000   i   Vianna Dawn[9] **Bovee**, born 15 Apr 1910 in Denver, Denver Co., CO. She married on 7 Nov 1995 **Richard Carlson**.

4001   ii   Eleanor Constance[9] **Bovee**, born 9 Jul 1911 in Denver, Denver Co., CO. She married (1) **Charles L Driscoll**; (2) **(---) Pendergast**.

4002   iii   James Ashley[9] **Bovee** Jr, born 3 Nov 1913 in Denver, Denver Co., CO; died Dec 1976 in San Diego, San Diego Co., CA. He married **Audrey S Bovee**.

+   4003   iv   Ransom Irvin[9] **Bovee**, born 2 Jul 1917 in Denver, Denver Co., CO; died 29 Aug 1984 in HI. He married **Audrey Stoskopf**.

4004   v   Ernest Myron[9] **Bovee**, born 2 Jul 1917 in Denver, Denver Co., CO.

3082. Ransom Young[8] **Bovee** (William Irvin[7], Isaac[6], Isaac[5], Jacob[4], Jacob[3], Nicholas[2], Mathieu[1]), born 9 Aug 1885 in Edwardsburg,Cass Co., MI; died Aug 1964. He married in 1910 in Denver, Denver Co., CO Bessie Willeford, born 5 Jul 1892; died Aug 1964, daughter of George Willeford and Emma Pittington.

Children of Ransom Young Bovee and Bessie Willeford were as follows:

+   4005   i   Marguerite E[9] **Bovee**, born 15 Dec 1911 in Colorado; died 16 Mar 1995 in Los Angeles, Los Angeles Co., CA. She married (1) **Harry Lake**; (2) **Forrest Newcomb**.

+   4006   ii   Bonnie[9] **Bovee**, born 26 Dec 1913. She married (1) **Dale Warner**; (2) **Dale Stanley**.

4007   iii   Robert Young[9] **Bovee**, born 13 Dec 1917. He married in Nov 1958 **Nina Flores**.

3083. Harriett Victoria[8] **Bovee** (William Irvin[7], Isaac[6], Isaac[5], Jacob[4], Jacob[3], Nicholas[2], Mathieu[1]), born 5 Sep 1888 in Albion Boone Co., NE. She married in 1915 Sam Hansen.

Children of Harriett Victoria Bovee and Sam Hansen were as follows:

4008   i   James William[9] **Hansen**, born 18 Aug 1915 in San Diego, San Diego Co., CA.

3086. Lacute Ruth[8] **Bovee** (William Irvin[7], Isaac[6], Isaac[5], Jacob[4], Jacob[3], Nicholas[2], Mathieu[1]), born 12 Feb 1896 in Longmont, Boulder Co., CO; died Oct 1956. She married in 1921 Ray Ahbrook Tull, born 1 Apr 1896 in WIndsor, Shelby Co., IL, son of Jessie Tull and Minnie Ashbrook.

Children of Lacute Ruth Bovee and Ray Ahbrook Tull were as follows:

4009   i   Florence[9] **Tull**, born 19 Feb 1922 in Denver, Denver Co.,

4010   ii   Ray Ashbrook[9] **Tull** Jr, born 23 Apr 1926 in Denver, Denver Co., CO.

3087. Florence Helen[8] **Bovee** (William Irvin[7], Isaac[6], Isaac[5], Jacob[4], Jacob[3], Nicholas[2], Mathieu[1]), born 25 Aug 1898 in Longmont, Boulder Co., CO. She married on 15 Jun 1918 Dr Paul Jon Bostick, born 30 Jan 1897.

Children of Florence Helen Bovee and Dr Paul Jon Bostick were as follows:

4011   i   Paul Jon[9] **Bostick**.

3088. Delia Minerva[8] **Bovee** (Edwin Orville[7], Benjamin[6], Philip[5], Jacob[4], Jacob[3], Nicholas[2], Mathieu[1]), born 8 Sep 1868 in Parkersburg, Butler Co., IA. She married Frank Huron Loomis, born 12 Dec 1861.

Children of Delia Minerva Bovee and Frank Huron Loomis were as follows:

4012   i   Ralph[9] **Loomis**, born Oct 1891 in SD.
4013   ii   George[9] **Loomis**, born Sep 1893 in SD.
4014   iii   Fay[9] **Loomis**, born Sep 1895 in IA.
4015   iv   Viola[9] **Loomis**, born Apr 1898 in WA.
4016   v   Gladys[9] **Loomis**.

3089. Myrtle Helen[8] **Bovee** (Ezra[7], Jacob[6], Philip[5], Jacob[4], Jacob[3], Nicholas[2], Mathieu[1]), born 7 Aug 1893 in SD; died 29 Jul 1979. She married George Vodden.

Children of Myrtle Helen Bovee and George Vodden were as follows:

4017   i   Juanita[9] **Vodden**, born 31 Dec 1913.
4018   ii   George[9] **Vodden** Jr, born 15 Mar 1915.
4019   iii   Donald[9] **Vodden**, born 17 Jul 1917.
4020   iv   Duane[9] **Vodden**, born 18 Mar 1920.
4021   v   Lucille[9] **Vodden**, born 8 Nov 1922.
4022   vi   Wallace[9] **Vodden**, born 1924.
4023   vii   Marian[9] **Vodden**, born 9 May 1927.

3090. Earl Richard[8] **Bovee** (Ezra[7], Jacob[6], Philip[5], Jacob[4], Jacob[3], Nicholas[2], Mathieu[1]), born 1 Feb 1895 in SD; died 16 Feb 1992 in SD. He married Julia E Sutter, born 5 Jan 1895; died 12 Dec 1950.

Children of Earl Richard Bovee and Julia E Sutter were as follows:

4024   i   Lesta Helen[9] **Bovee**, born 18 Oct 1920.
+ 4025   ii   Evelyn Mae[9] **Bovee**, born 6 Jun 1922. She married **(---) Downey**.

4026   iii   Earlene Elizabeth[9] **Bovee**, born 13 Dec 1931; died 30 Dec 1931.

3092. Gladys Elizabeth[8] **Bovee** (Ezra[7], Jacob[6], Philip[5], Jacob[4], Jacob[3], Nicholas[2], Mathieu[1]), born 17 Oct 1899 in Sturgis, Meade Co., SD. She married on 22 Feb 1920 Hollis C Dever.

Children of Gladys Elizabeth Bovee and Hollis C Dever were as follows:

4027   i   Janice[9] **Dever**.
4028   ii   Ann Joann[9] **Dever**.

3094. Amos Philip[8] **Bovee** (Ezra[7], Jacob[6], Philip[5], Jacob[4], Jacob[3], Nicholas[2], Mathieu[1]), born 26 Jan 1905 in Sturgis, Meade Co., SD; died 4 Feb 1995. He married on 10 Jun 1948 Ethelyn Hershey.

Children of Amos Philip Bovee and Ethelyn Hershey were as follows:

4029   i   Susan[9] **Bovee**.
4030   ii   Philip[9] **Bovee**.
4031   iii   Harold[9] **Bovee**.
4032   iv   Debra[9] **Bovee**.

3097. Sumner Eugene[8] **Bovee** (Ezra[7], Jacob[6], Philip[5], Jacob[4], Jacob[3], Nicholas[2], Mathieu[1]), born 15 Jul 1910 in Sturgis, Meade Co., SD; died 12 Mar 1959 in Sturgis, Meade Co., SD. He married on 2 Jan 1934 Ester Fruth.

Children of Sumner Eugene Bovee and Ester Fruth were as follows:

4033   i   Eugene[9] **Bovee**.
4034   ii   Barbara[9] **Bovee**.
4035   iii   Sherilee[9] **Bovee**.

3098. Mary[8] **Bovee** (James V[7], Abel W[6], Henry[5], Jacob[4], Jacob[3], Nicholas[2], Mathieu[1]), born abt 1881. She married on 23 Aug 1899 in Gloversville, Fulton Co., NY Edwin Gardinier.

Children of Mary Bovee and Edwin Gardinier were as follows:

4036   i   Franklin[9] **Gardinier**.

3109. Daniel Walter[8] **Bovee** (John Livingston[7], Cornelius[6], Daniel[5], Matthew[4], Jacob[3], Nicholas[2], Mathieu[1]), born 17 Jun 1868 in IL; died Feb 1923. He married Sarah Amanda Boyd, born 29 Aug 1872 in OH; died 11 Nov 1959.

Children of Daniel Walter Bovee and Sarah Amanda Boyd were as follows:

	4037	i	Hazel Virginia[9] **Bovee**, born Mar 1892 in NE. She married **(---) Stinchfield**.
+	4038	ii	Frank Leslie[9] **Bovee**, born 13 Dec 1893 in NE; died 5 Jul 1959 in Cascade Co., MT. He married **Effie Alvina Biesemier**.
+	4039	iii	LeRoy[9] **Bovee**, born 23 Apr 1896 in NE; died 13 Jan 1949. He married **Harriet (---)**.
	4040	iv	Ethel Mae[9] **Bovee**, born Oct 1899 in NE; died 1928. She married **(---) Hoops**.
	4041	v	Wilbur Boyd[9] **Bovee**, born 30 Nov 1902; died May 1971 in Cody, Park Co., WY.
+	4042	vi	Paul Henry[9] **Bovee**, born 31 May 1909; died Mar 1982 in Park, Park Co., WY. He married **Arlene Kells**.

3111. Harry Carl[8] **Bovee** (John Livingston[7], Cornelius[6], Daniel[5], Matthew[4], Jacob[3], Nicholas[2], Mathieu[1]), born 9 Jan 1875 in Shenandoah, Page Co., IA; died 16 Dec 1943 in NE. He married on 19 Feb 1900 in NE Myrtle Grace Siddens, born 5 Sep 1884 in Crounse, Lansaster Co., NE; died 30 Dec 1951 in NE, daughter of James A Siddens and Marada A.

Children of Harry Carl Bovee and Myrtle Grace Siddens were as follows:

	4043	i	Bessie Blanch[9] **Bovee**, born 2 Oct 1900 in Bee, Seward Co., NE. She married on 28 Feb 1918 **Roy Edward Miller**.
	4044	ii	Cecil Glenn[9] **Bovee**, born 14 Dec 1902 in Bee, Seward Co., NE; died 11 Sep 1903.
	4045	iii	Lillian Bell[9] **Bovee**, born 26 Jul 1904 in Bee, Seward Co., NE. She married on 14 Jun 1926 **Eelzie McGuire**.
	4046	iv	Harry Raymond[9] **Bovee**, born 18 Apr 1907 in Bee, Seward Co., NE.
	4047	v	Vesta Ruth[9] **Bovee**, born 11 Sep 1909 in Bee, Seward Co., NE.
	4048	vi	James Edward[9] **Bovee**, born 24 Jan 1912 in Bee, Seward Co., NE.
	4049	vii	Alva Vern[9] **Bovee**, born 18 Jun 1914 in Bee, Seward Co., NE; died 9 Feb 1975 in Independence, Jackson Co., MO.
+	4050	viii	LaVeta Grace[9] **Bovee**, born 6 Jan 1917 in Bee, Seward Co., NE. She married **Berry Thomas**.
	4051	ix	Ethel Rose[9] **Bovee**, born 31 May 1919 in Bee, Seward Co., NE.
+	4052	x	Ilene Marie[9] **Bovee**, born 11 Mar 1922 in Lincoln, Lancaster Co., NE. She married **Donald Bruce Watson**.
	4053	xi	Joan Marilyn[9] **Bovee**, born 1 Apr 1929 in Havelock, Lancaster Co., NE.
	4054	xii	Donald[9] **Bovee**, born 1931; died 1931.

3112. Maude[8] **Bovee** (John Livingston[7], Cornelius[6], Daniel[5], Matthew[4], Jacob[3], Nicholas[2], Mathieu[1]), born abt 1877. She married (---) Marvell.

Children of Maude Bovee and (---) Marvell were as follows:

4055   i   Mabel[9] **Marvell**, born 15 May 1897 in NE.

3115. Franklin Cornelius[8] **Bovee** (Jacob C[7], Cornelius[6], Daniel[5], Matthew[4], Jacob[3], Nicholas[2], Mathieu[1]), born 11 Feb 1879 in Oquawka, Henderson Co., IL. He married abt 1897 Daisy M (---), born Jan 1880.

Children of Franklin Cornelius Bovee and Daisy M (---) were as follows:

4056   i   Ethel F[9] **Bovee**, born May 1898 in IA.

3125. Evelyn[8] **Bovee** (Wayland Henry[7], Henry Jacob[6], Jacob[5], Matthew[4], Jacob[3], Nicholas[2], Mathieu[1]), born 24 May 1891 in Ravenna, Los Angeles Co., CA; died 30 Jan 1978 in Portland, Multnomah Co., OR. She married on 19 Jun 1919 in San Francisco, San Francisco Co., CA Guy Russell Gorton.

Children of Evelyn Bovee and Guy Russell Gorton were as follows:

4057   i   Robert Lewis[9] **Gorton**.

3126. Meda Emogene[8] **Bovee** (Wayland Henry[7], Henry Jacob[6], Jacob[5], Matthew[4], Jacob[3], Nicholas[2], Mathieu[1]), born 14 Sep 1899 in Speed, MO; died 13 May 1981 in Kansas City, Jackson Co., MO. She married (1) in 1921 Luther W Dugger; (2), divorced William H Sigman; (3) on 8 Dec 1934 in Kansas City, Jackson Co., MO, divorced James H Moss; (4) on 16 May 1939 in Platte City, Platte Co., MO Earl F Swain.

Children of Meda Emogene Bovee and Earl F Swain were as follows:

4058   i   Wendell Earl[9] **Swain**.

3127. Lorene Houk[8] **Bovee** (Wayland Henry[7], Henry Jacob[6], Jacob[5], Matthew[4], Jacob[3], Nicholas[2], Mathieu[1]), born 11 Oct 1901 in Kansas City, Jackson Co., MO; died 26 Apr 1991 in Kansas City, Jackson Co., MO. She married on 19 Apr 1930 in Parkville, Platte Co., MO Carl Gilbert Lamb, born 10 Apr 1904 in Peculiar, Cass Co., MO; died 19 Jan 1991 in Kansas City, Jackson Co., MO, son of William Lamb and Mary Etta Reeder.

Children of Lorene Houk Bovee and Carl Gilbert Lamb were as follows:

4059   i   Jay Gilbert[9] **Lamb**, born in Kansas City, Jackson Co., MO.
4060   ii   Judy Kay[9] **Lamb**, born in Kansas City, Jackson Co., MO.

3129. Kenneth Jacob[8] **Bovee** (William Ludington[7], Cornelius Elihu[6], Cornelius Schermerhorn[5], Matthew[4], Jacob[3], Nicholas[2], Mathieu[1]), born 24 Sep 1897; died

3 Mar 1954. He married (1) Irene Hofer, born 1899; died 24 Apr 1951; (2) Florence (---).

Children of Kenneth Jacob Bovee and Irene Hofer were as follows:

+ 4061   i   Kenneth Frederick^9 **Bovee**, born 20 Jan 1921 in Monroe Co., NY; died 29 Mar 1990. He married **Ann Nixon**.

   4062   ii   Virginia^9 **Bovee**, born in Monroe Co,. NY. She married **Russell Harris**.

   4063   iii   Leona^9 **Bovee**, born in Monroe Co,. NY. She married **Donald Pimm**.

   4064   iv   Alta^9 **Bovee**, born in Monroe Co,. NY. She married **Jack Brew**.

   4065   v   Betty^9 **Bovee**, born in Monroe Co,. NY; died 9 Sep 1980. She married **Richard Wilkes**.

   4066   vi   Shirley^9 **Bovee**, born in Monroe Co,. NY. She married (1) **Robert Wilkes**; (2) **Marvin Kadrie**.

   4067   vii   William L^9 **Bovee**, born 25 Nov 1933 in Monroe Co,. NY; died 5 Oct 1980. He married **Melba Kiskie**.

3138. Lawrence Nelson^8 Bovee (George W^7, Cornelius Elihu^6, Cornelius Schermerhorn^5, Matthew^4, Jacob^3, Nicholas^2, Mathieu^1), born 24 Jul 1901 in Stone Church, Genesee Co., NY; died Jul 1991 in LeRoy, Genesee Co., NY. He married abt 1934 Doris Sturble, born 29 Sep 1914 in NY; died Dec 1982 in LeRoy, Genesee Co., NY.

Children of Lawrence Nelson Bovee and Doris Sturble were as follows:

   4068   i   Child^9 **Bovee**.

   4069   ii   Joan^9 **Bovee**.

   4070   iii   George^9 **Bovee**.

   4071   iv   Carl^9 **Bovee**.

3146. Albert A^8 Bovee (Hiram^7, Luther^6, Jacob^5, Anthony^4, Gerrit^3, Anthony^2, Mathieu^1), born 1878. He married (1) Allice Kelly; (2) on 2 Jul 1922 Helen E Hogan.

Children of Albert A Bovee and Allice Kelly were as follows:

+ 4072   i   Roswell^9 **Bovee**, born 19 Jul 1907; died 1980. He married **Susana Kesier**.

   4073   ii   Mildred^9 **Bovee**, born abt 1908; died abt 1950. She married **Gerold Goodnoe**.

+ 4074   iii   Claude Henry^9 **Bovee**, born 16 Nov 1909 in Fenimore, NY; died 11 May 1996 in Glens Falls, Warren Co., NY. He married **Julia Sarah Gilbert**.

   4075   iv   Gertrude^9 **Bovee**.

   4076   v   Lena^9 **Bovee**.

   4077   vi   Mary^9 **Bovee**.

Children of Albert A Bovee and Helen E Hogan were as follows:

4078   i   Mary^9 **Bovee**, born abt 1923. She married on 6 Jun 1946 **John J Bethel**.

3148. Lewis F^8 **Bovee** (Henry L^7, Luther^6, Jacob^5, Anthony^4, Gerrit^3, Anthony^2, Mathieu^1), born Dec 1886 in NY. He married Louisa Cody.

Children of Lewis F Bovee and Louisa Cody were as follows:

4079   i   Edward^9 **Bovee**.

3150. Walter W^8 **Bovee** (Henry L^7, Luther^6, Jacob^5, Anthony^4, Gerrit^3, Anthony^2, Mathieu^1), born Mar 1890. He married Olive Mesink, born 1894.

Children of Walter W Bovee and Olive Mesink were as follows:

+   4080   i   Donald Marcus^9 **Bovee**, born 1915. He married (1) **Rouette C Bush**; (2) **Eva Pashley**.

3152. Beecher A^8 **Bovee** (Henry L^7, Luther^6, Jacob^5, Anthony^4, Gerrit^3, Anthony^2, Mathieu^1), born 12 Dec 1893 in Saratoga Co., NY; died Nov 1982 in Hudson Falls, Washington Co., NY. He married on 6 Oct 1915 Ella T White, born 20 Feb 1896; died Feb 1981 in Hudson Falls, Washington Co., NY, daughter of Alfred White and Susie Thompson.

Children of Beecher A Bovee and Ella T White were as follows:

+   4081   i   Gerald Arthur^9 **Bovee**, born 30 Jul 1928 in NY. He married **Jean Brown**.

     4082   ii   Wilda McKnight^9 **Bovee**.

3155. Marcus Sherman^8 **Bovee** (Henry L^7, Luther^6, Jacob^5, Anthony^4, Gerrit^3, Anthony^2, Mathieu^1), born 26 Apr 1899 in Hartford, Washington Co., NY; died 27 Feb 1977. He married on 3 Aug 1927 Kathryn Nichols, born 21 Jun 1897 in Hartford, Washington Co., NY; died 23 Mar 1992.

Children of Marcus Sherman Bovee and Kathryn Nichols were as follows:

+   4083   i   Marcus Trevor^9 **Bovee**. He married (1) **Beverly Mae LaRich**; (2) **Ingeborg Meyer**.

3159. George Melvin^8 **Bovee** (Fred^7, Luther^6, Jacob^5, Anthony^4, Gerrit^3, Anthony^2, Mathieu^1), born 3 Apr 1895; died 18 Nov 1960 in Day, Saratoga Co., NY. He married on 28 Jul 1917 Ethel Jenkins, born 23 Jun 1899; died 18 Apr 1981 in Day, Saratoga Co., NY, daughter of John Jenkins and Adah Manning.

Children of George Melvin Bovee and Ethel Jenkins were as follows:

	4084	i	Adah Charity[9] **Bovee**, born abt 1917; died 1957 in Day, Saratoga Co., NY.
	4085	ii	George Melvin[9] **Bovee** Jr, born 6 Nov 1919 in Day, Saratoga Co., NY; died 12 Nov 1919 in Day, Saratoga Co., NY.
	4086	iii	Lene Alzoa[9] **Bovee**, born abt 1921. She married **Anthony Vidulich**.
	4087	iv	Virginia Alberta[9] **Bovee**, born abt 1924; died 1966 in Day, Saratoga Co., NY. She married **Porter Brownell**.
+	4088	v	Daniel John[9] **Bovee**, born abt 1930. He married **Dawn Arsenault**.
	4089	vi	Julia Marie[9] **Bovee**. She married **Charles Wadsworth**.
	4090	vii	Betty Jean[9] **Bovee**. She married **John Olson**.

3166. Albert H[8] **Bovee** (Frank[7], Norman[6], Jacob[5], Anthony[4], Gerrit[3], Anthony[2], Mathieu[1]), born Jan 1888 in NY; died 1959. He married abt 1912 Effie Marcellus.

Children of Albert H Bovee and Effie Marcellus were as follows:

| | 4091 | i | Ernest G[9] **Bovee**, died 28 Jul 1945. He married **Helen (---)**. |
| | 4092 | ii | Beatrice L[9] **Bovee**, born 28 Jul 1917; died 7 Apr 1993. She married in 1943 **Charles White**. |

3168. Warren[8] **Bovee** (Frank[7], Norman[6], Jacob[5], Anthony[4], Gerrit[3], Anthony[2], Mathieu[1]), born 2 Jun 1892 in Day, Saratoga Co., NY; died 28 Feb 1957. He married in Jun 1914 Eva Belle White, born 22 Jan 1898 in Conklinville, Saratoga Co., NY; died 6 Feb 1975 in Greenwich, Washington Co., NY.

Children of Warren Bovee and Eva Belle White were as follows:

	4093	i	Milton[9] **Bovee**, born abt 1916.
	4094	ii	Warren Franklin[9] **Bovee**.
	4095	iii	Alice[9] **Bovee**, born 2 Jul 1918 in Day Center, Saratoga Co., NY. She married on 5 Oct 1935 **Sydney S Squires**.
	4096	iv	Kieth Lincoln[9] **Bovee**, born 23 Dec 1921 in Day Center, Saratoga Co., NY; died 17 Jan 1956 in Ft Miller, Washington Co., NY. He married on 24 Oct 1947 **Madeline Brockway**.
+	4097	v	Maurice T[9] **Bovee**, born 28 Jan 1923; died 20 Feb 1968. He married **Delores Grieve Beagle**.

3172. Harold[8] **Bovee** (Charles[7], Norman[6], Jacob[5], Anthony[4], Gerrit[3], Anthony[2], Mathieu[1]), born 20 Jul 1903; died 6 Oct 1976. He married on 10 Feb 1929 Charlotte Thompson, born 19 Oct 1908; died 9 Feb 1991, daughter of Clarence Thompson and Gertrude Warner.

Children of Harold Bovee and Charlotte Thompson were as follows:

+ 4098   i   Francis Clarence[9] **Bovee**, born 1930; died 10 Feb 1994. He married **Margaret Long**.
+ 4099   ii   Robert Charles[9] **Bovee**. He married **Pamela Wilcox**.
   4100   iii   Carmeta[9] **Bovee**.

3177. Clinton[8] **Bovee** (Charles[7], Norman[6], Jacob[5], Anthony[4], Gerrit[3], Anthony[2], Mathieu[1]), born 17 Feb 1915; died 16 Oct 1992. He married Nancy M (---), born abt 1920.

Children of Clinton Bovee and Nancy M (---) were as follows:

   4101   i   Laverne[9] **Bovee**.
   4102   ii   Dana[9] **Bovee**.

3178. Carl Harvey[8] **Bovee** (Charles[7], Norman[6], Jacob[5], Anthony[4], Gerrit[3], Anthony[2], Mathieu[1]), born 10 Apr 1920. He married in 1937 Jane O'Donnell, born 12 May 1921; died 26 Jan 2004 in NY.

Children of Carl Harvey Bovee and Jane O'Donnell were as follows:

   4103   i   Harvey Carl[9] **Bovee**.
   4104   ii   Janet Theresa[9] **Bovee**. She married **Julius Blackwood**.
   4105   iii   Floyd Charles[9] **Bovee**, born 5 Dec 1941; died 1979 in HI.
+ 4106   iv   Dannie Harold[9] **Bovee**. He married (1) **Kaye Louise Bryngelson**; (2) **Sheryl (---)**.
   4107   v   Thomas[9] **Bovee**. He married **Sharyn (---)**.
   4108   vi   Carol[9] **Bovee**.
   4109   vii   Noel[9] **Bovee**.
   4110   viii   Lorraine[9] **Bovee**. She married **John Chun**.

3197. Leon[8] **Bovee** (Lester[7], Norman[6], Jacob[5], Anthony[4], Gerrit[3], Anthony[2], Mathieu[1]), born 5 Apr 1910 in Day, Saratoga Co., NY; died 19 Jun 1992 in Glens Falls, Warren Co., NY. He married Ernestine Ellithorpe Ovitt, born 20 Oct 1909.

Children of Leon Bovee and Ernestine Ellithorpe Ovitt were as follows:

   4111   i   David[9] **Bovee**.

3198. Owen L[8] **Bovee** (Lester[7], Norman[6], Jacob[5], Anthony[4], Gerrit[3], Anthony[2], Mathieu[1]), born 18 Mar 1912; died 9 Oct 1992 in Day, Saratoga Co., NY. He married abt 1943 Iva Ovitt, died 21 Aug 1958.

Children of Owen L Bovee and Iva Ovitt were as follows:

   4112   i   Owen L[9] **Bovee** Jr. He married **Betty (---)**.
   4113   ii   Ralph[9] **Bovee**.

4114	iii	Carl^9 **Bovee**.
4115	iv	Carrie Jean^9 **Bovee**. She married **George Howe**.
4116	v	Kenneth^9 **Bovee**.
4117	vi	Leon^9 **Bovee**.
4118	vii	Crystal^9 **Bovee**. She married **Eli Bombard**.
4119	viii	Nicholas^9 **Bovee**.

3199. Carl L^8 **Bovee** (Lester^7, Norman^6, Jacob^5, Anthony^4, Gerrit^3, Anthony^2, Mathieu^1), born 11 May 1915 in Day, Saratoga Co., NY; died 26 Jul 2000. He married Gladys I Ralph.

Children of Carl L Bovee and Gladys I Ralph were as follows:

| 4120 | i | Charles F^9 **Bovee**. |

3200. Eleanor^8 **Bovee** (Lester^7, Norman^6, Jacob^5, Anthony^4, Gerrit^3, Anthony^2, Mathieu^1), born abt 1914; died 1957. She married unknown.

Children of Eleanor Bovee were as follows:

| 4121 | i | Donald^9 **Francis**. |
| 4122 | ii | Margaret^9 **(---)**. She married **Ralph Harold Jr.**. |

3201. Beatrice^8 **Bovee** (Lester^7, Norman^6, Jacob^5, Anthony^4, Gerrit^3, Anthony^2, Mathieu^1), born 17 May 1917; died Jun 1976 in Conklinville, Saratoga co., NY. She married Scott Houghton, born 1903; died 19 Sep 1996.

Children of Beatrice Bovee and Scott Houghton were as follows:

| 4123 | i | Ellen^9 **Houghton**. |
| 4124 | ii | Jeanne May^9 **Houghton**. |

3202. Gerald^8 **Bovee** (Lester^7, Norman^6, Jacob^5, Anthony^4, Gerrit^3, Anthony^2, Mathieu^1), born 21 Jun 1918; died Aug 1986. He married Shirley M Ralph, born abt 1930.

Children of Gerald Bovee and Shirley M Ralph were as follows:

4125	i	Gerald L^9 **Bovee**, born 30 Jan 1951 in Corinth, Saratoga Co., NY; died 3 Feb 1998.
4126	ii	Kristine^9 **Bovee**. She married **John,Dingman (---)**.
4127	iii	Michael^9 **Bovee**. He married **Shawn (---)**.
4128	iv	Norman^9 **Bovee**. He married **Cindy Eggleston**.
4129	v	Brandy^9 **Bovee**. She married **Kenneth Potter**.

3203. Nancy F^8 **Bovee** (Lester^7, Norman^6, Jacob^5, Anthony^4, Gerrit^3, Anthony^2,

Mathieu[1]), born 7 Aug 1922; died 10 Oct 1989 in Day, Saratoga Co., NY. She married (---) Bovee.

Children of Nancy F Bovee and (---) Bovee were as follows:

4130	i	Gerald[9] **Bovee**.
4131	ii	Lewis[9] **Bovee**.
4132	iii	Carol[9] **Bovee**.

3204. Willard L[8] **Bovee** (Lester[7], Norman[6], Jacob[5], Anthony[4], Gerrit[3], Anthony[2], Mathieu[1]), born 14 Dec 1924 in Day, Saratoga Co., NY; died 26 Jan 2000. He married in Sep 1947 in Corinth, Saratoga Co., NY Marie Scoville, born 30 Dec 1928.

Children of Willard L Bovee and Marie Scoville were as follows:

+ 4133　i　Willard L[9] **Bovee**. He married (1) **Barbara Grimes**; (2) **Betty Stedman**.

+ 4134　ii　James Kenneth[9] **Bovee**. He married **Sharon Allenon**.

　4135　iii　Robert Edward[9] **Bovee**.

　4136　iv　John Richard[9] **Bovee**, born 7 Dec 1951; died 29 May 1970.

+ 4137　v　Henry Frederick[9] **Bovee**. He married (1) **Deborah,Stert (---)**; (2) **Melanie (---)**.

　4138　vi　Rose Marie[9] **Bovee**.

3206. Cora[8] **Bovee** (Lester[7], Norman[6], Jacob[5], Anthony[4], Gerrit[3], Anthony[2], Mathieu[1]), born 29 Jul 1929 in Day, Saratoga Co., NY; died 9 Nov 1997 in Amsterdam, Montgomery Co., NY. She married on 21 Jul 1952 Aloysius E Zawilomski, born 4 May 1925; died 15 Jan 1973 in Amsterdam, Montgomery Co., NY.

Children of Cora Bovee and Aloysius E Zawilomski were as follows:

　4139　i　Terry A[9] **Zawilomski**. He married **Ester Garner**.

　4140　ii　Donald J[9] **Zawilomski**, born in Amsterdam, Montgomery Co., NY.

3223. Mary Jane[8] **Bovee** (Mac Henry[7], Henry Joseph[6], Joseph[5], Anthony[4], Gerrit[3], Anthony[2], Mathieu[1]), born in Cozad, Dawson Co., NE. She married William Vasey.

Children of Mary Jane Bovee and William Vasey were as follows:

4141	i	Douglas Kent[9] **Vasey**.
4142	ii	Susan[9] **Vasey**.
4143	iii	Nancy[9] **Vasey**.

3228. Edward LeRoy[8] **Bovee** (Guy Harrison[7], Eugene M[6], Joseph[5], Anthony[4], Gerrit[3], Anthony[2], Mathieu[1]), born 24 Oct 1925. He married Katherine Bouden.

Children of Edward LeRoy Bovee and Katherine Bouden were as follows:

+   4144   i   Michael Lynn[9] **Bovee**. He married (1) **Denise Dilley**; (2) **Joanne Benninghoven**.
     4145   ii   Michelle Louise[9] **Bovee**. She married **Clyde Simpson**.
     4146   iii   Guy LaMont[9] **Bovee**.
     4147   iv   Mark LeRoy[9] **Bovee**.

3232. Gayle[8] **Bovee** (Claude Alva[7], Eugene M[6], Joseph[5], Anthony[4], Gerrit[3], Anthony[2], Mathieu[1]), born 21 Feb 1921; died 20 Nov 1995 in Danville, VA. He married (1) Jesse (---); (2) Margaret (---).

Children of Gayle Bovee and Jesse (---) were as follows:

     4148   i   Jenny[9] **Bovee**.
     4149   ii   Lee[9] **Bovee**.

Children of Gayle Bovee and Margaret (---) were as follows:

     4150   i   Gayle[9] **Bovee** Jr. He married **Becky (---)**.
     4151   ii   Thomas[9] **Bovee**.

3235. Rex Everett[8] **Bovee** (Claude Alva[7], Eugene M[6], Joseph[5], Anthony[4], Gerrit[3], Anthony[2], Mathieu[1]), born 23 Jan 1926. He married (1) Dolly Rickman; (2) Bertha Gwin Heaps.

Children of Rex Everett Bovee and Dolly Rickman were as follows:

     4152   i   Danny[9] **Bovee**.
+   4153   ii   Rex[9] **Bovee** Jr. He married **Vickie Haykin**.
     4154   iii   David[9] **Bovee**. He married **Valencia (---)**.

3236. Earl H[8] **Bovee** (U N[7], Peter B[6], Gerrit[5], Peter[4], Gerrit[3], Anthony[2], Mathieu[1]), born abt 1895. He married Florence (---), born abt 1901.

Children of Earl H Bovee and Florence (---) were as follows:

     4155   i   Barent[9] **Bovee**, born abt 1927.

3237. David Grosvenor[8] **Bovee** (Charles Howard[7], David[6], Jonathan[5], Peter[4], Gerrit[3], Anthony[2], Mathieu[1]), born 16 Jul 1895 in Coldwater, Branch Co., MI; died May 1975 in Seattle, King Co., WA. He married Grace Donnelly, born 6 Mar 1900 in Galveston, Galveston Co., TX; died 31 Aug 1989 in Seattle King Co., WA.

Children of David Grosvenor Bovee and Grace Donnelly were as follows:

4156   i   Elizabeth B[9] **Bovee**. She married **(---) Patterson**.

+ 4157   ii   Grace B[9] **Bovee**. She married **Doug Devin**.

3239. Carrie Leah[8] **Bovee** (Edwin Anson[7], Eli William[6], Jonathan[5], Peter[4], Gerrit[3], Anthony[2], Mathieu[1]), born 1 Nov 1875 in MI; died 15 Jan 1899 in Benton Harbor, Berrien Co., MI. She married on 14 Feb 1895 in Benton Harbor, Berrien Co., MI Bert Seeley, born 23 Feb 1876 in Augusta, Kalamzoo Co., MI; died abt 14 Nov 1942 in Benton Harbor, Berrien Co., MI, son of Nathan Seeley.

Children of Carrie Leah Bovee and Bert Seeley were as follows:

4158   i   Edith Marie[9] **Seeley**, born 14 Mar 1896 in Benton Harbor, Berrien Co., MI; died 14 Aug 1981 in Okemos, Ingham Co., MI. She married on 12 Feb 1916 in Holland, Ottawa Co., MI **Arthur Hilding**, born 6 Dec 1891 in South Bend, St Joseph Co., MI.

3240. William Arthur[8] **Bovee** (Edwin Anson[7], Eli William[6], Jonathan[5], Peter[4], Gerrit[3], Anthony[2], Mathieu[1]), born 26 Jan 1878 in St Joseph, Berrien Co., MI; died 29 Aug 1954 in Traverse City, Grand Traverse Co., MI. He married (1) in Jul 1898 in Benton Harbor, Berrien Co., MI Letitia Bixler, born Aug 1878 in PA; died 8 Jul 1905 in Williamsport, Lycoming Co., PA; (2) on 2 May 1908 in Grand Rapids, Kent Co., MI Mildred P Champlin, born 18 Jan 1886 in Grand Rapids, Kent Co., MI; died 15 Oct 1975 in Traverse City, Grand Traverse Co., MI, daughter of John Jacob Champlin and Sara Adelade Waring.

Children of William Arthur Bovee and Mildred P Champlin were as follows:

4159   i   Maxine LaVerne[9] **Bovee**, born 18 Apr 1911 in Grand Rapids, Kent Co., MI; died 14 Mar 1989 in Tucson, Pima Co., AZ.

+ 4160   ii   William Richard[9] **Bovee**, born 3 Jan 1918 in Traverse City, Grand Traverse Co., MI; christened in Traverse City, Grand Traverse Co., MI; died 4 Apr 1994 in Bay City, Bay Co., MI. He married (1) **Elizabeth J Kistler**; (2) **Marian (---)**.

+ 4161   iii Thomas R[9] **Bovee**, born 31 Jan 1920 in Traverse City, Grand Traverse Co., MI. He married **Elizabeth Jane Williams**.

+ 4162   iv Lloyd Champlin[9] **Bovee**, born 21 Oct 1923 in Traverse City, Grand Traverse Co., MI; died 16 May 1992 in Wapakoneta, Auglaize Co., OH. He married **Inez Ford Neiswonger**.

+ 4163   v   Elizabeth Lorrain[9] **Bovee**, born 16 Feb 1926 in Traverse City, Grand Traverse Co., MI; christened 24 Mar 1940 in Traverse City, Grand Traverse Co., MI; died 1 Aug 1997 in Tucson, Pima Co., AZ. She married **Otto J Olsson**.

3242. David Lloyd[8] **Bovee** (Edwin Anson[7], Eli William[6], Jonathan[5], Peter[4], Gerrit[3], Anthony[2], Mathieu[1]), born 29 Jun 1882 in Holland, Ottawa Co.,MI; died 21 Nov 1953 in Grand Rapids, Kent Co., MI. He married on 29 Jun 1904 in Grand Rapids, Kent Co., MI Maude Jeanette Wright, born 13 Aug 1884 in Grand Haven, Ottawa Co., MI; died 14 Nov 1961 in Athens, Calhoun Co., MI, daughter of Harry Wright and Lillian Anderson.

Children of David Lloyd Bovee and Maude Jeanette Wright were as follows:

	4164	i	Winnifred Loraine[9] **Bovee**, born 16 Jun 1905 in Grand Rapids, Kent Co., MI; died 25 Oct 1906 in Grand Rapids, Kent Co., MI.
+	4165	ii	Dorothy Irene[9] **Bovee**, born 14 Aug 1908 in Grand Rapids, Kent Co., MI; died 23 Jul 1982 in Hastings, Barry Co., MI. She married **Rev William Edgeworth Potts**.
+	4166	iii	Margaret Eileen[9] **Bovee**, born 22 Apr 1910 in Grand Rapids, Kent Co., MI; died Jan 2001. She married **Earl Paul Wagner**.
+	4167	iv	Lillian Mae[9] **Bovee**, born 20 Nov 1913 in Grand Rapids, Kent Co., MI; died 11 Mar 2000 in Grand Rapids, Kent Co., MI. She married **Arthur Oscar Holmberg**.
+	4168	v	Edwin Wright[9] **Bovee**, born 21 Mar 1917 in Grand Rapids, Kent Co., MI; died 31 Dec 1986 in Grand Rapids, Kent Co., MI. He married **Doris Elaine Bergers**.

3243. Nellie Andrea[8] **Bovee** (Edwin Anson[7], Eli William[6], Jonathan[5], Peter[4], Gerrit[3], Anthony[2], Mathieu[1]), born 13 Sep 1885 in St Joseph, Berrien Co., MI; christened in Congregational Ch, Grand Rapids, Kent Co., MI; died 22 Nov 1969 in Irving, Dallas Co., TX. She married on 30 Jun 1910 in Bates St. home, Grand Rapids, Kent Co., MI Harry Peter Willwerth, born 1 Mar 1884 in Grand Rapids, Kent Co., MI; christened in Congregational Ch, Grand Rapids, Kent Co., MI; died 4 Feb 1972 in Irving, Dallas Co., TX, son of Lorenzo Willwerth and Elizabeth Smith.

Children of Nellie Andrea Bovee and Harry Peter Willwerth were as follows:

4169	i	Robert Edwin[9] **Willwerth**, born 6 May 1911 in Grand Rapids, Kent Co., MI; died 14 Dec 1996 in San Jose, Santa Clara Co., CA. He married (1) on 6 Jun 1932 in South Bend, St Joseph Co., MI **Margaret Evelyn Kent**, born 1911; died Aug 1971 in San Jose, Santa Clara Co., CA; (2) on 22 Nov 1971 in Palo Alto, Santa Clara Co., CA **Sigrid Manuela Hagens**, born 6 Jul 1926 in Bremen, Germany.
4170	ii	Richard[9] **Willwerth**, born 1913 in Grand Rapids, Kent Co., MI; died 1913.
4171	iii	Harry Victor[9] **Willwerth**, born 18 Jan 1915 in Grand Rapids, Kent Co., MI; died 10 Feb 1995 in Los Angeles, Los Angeles Co., CA. He married on 8 Jun 1946 in Grand Rapids, Kent Co., MI **Margaret Bain Veenboer**, born 5 Jul 1915 in Grand Rapids, Kent Co., MI, daughter of Dr

William H Veenboer and Mary Bain.

4172   iv   Donald Wayne^9 **Willwerth**, born 29 Dec 1916 in Grand Rapids, Kent Co., MI; died 1998 in Irving, Dallas Co., TX. He married on 10 Jun 1939 in Grand Rapids, Kent Co., MI **Bertha Ruth Boschma**, born 11 Apr 1918 in Detroit, Wayne Co., MI; died 21 Dec 2001 in Irving, Dallas Co., TX, daughter of Arend Bernardus Boschma and Grace Prins.

4173   v   Thomas Roland^9 **Willwerth**, born 10 Jan 1919 in Grand Rapids, Kent Co., MI. He married on 3 Jul 1942 in Lowell, Kent Co., MI **Rita Jacqueline Day**, born 23 Apr 1921 in Lowell, Kent Co., MI.

4174   vi   Max Gerald^9 **Willwerth**, born 26 Sep 1923 in Grand Rapids, Kent Co., MI. He married on 20 Oct 1945 in Grand Rapids, Kent Co., MI **Carol Hedrick**, born 3 Aug 1923 in Adrian, Lenawee Co., MI.

3244. Ruth Winnifred^8 **Bovee** (Edwin Anson^7, Eli William^6, Jonathan^5, Peter^4, Gerrit^3, Anthony^2, Mathieu^1), born 22 Jan 1890 in St Joseph, Berrien Co., MI; christened 22 Apr 1973 in Immanuel Presb Ch, Grand Rapids, Kent Co., MI; died 3 Dec 1975 in Grand Rapids, Kent Co., MI. She married on 14 Mar 1912 in Grand Rapids, Kent Co., MI Clarence W Strouse, born 25 Mar 1890 in Auburn, De Kalb Co., IN; christened 22 Apr 1973 in Immanuel Presb Ch, Grand Rapids, Kent Co., MI; died 8 Aug 1975 in Grand Rapids, Kent Co., MI.

Children of Ruth Winnifred Bovee and Clarence W Strouse were as follows:

4175   i   Jack W^9 **Strouse**, born 29 Nov 1917 in Grand Rapids, Kent Co., MI; died 8 Mar 1976 in Pasadena, Los Angeles Co., CA. He married on 15 Aug 1964 in Las Vegas, Clark Co., NV **Lilian De Vries**, born in Leidsendam, Zuid, Netherlands.

4176   ii   William Robert^9 **Strouse**, born 18 Jul 1925 in Grand Rapids, Kent Co., MI. He married on 7 Jun 1947 in Grand Rapids, Kent Co., MI **Shirley Arline Millett**, born 22 Apr 1924 in Gardner, Worcester Co., MA; died 22 Jan 1986 in Waterloo, Black Hawk Co., IA.

3245. Maxine^8 **Kent** (Ella Jane^7 Bovee, Eli William^6, Jonathan^5, Peter^4, Gerrit^3, Anthony^2, Mathieu^1), born 2 Apr 1892 in Benton Harbor, Berrien Co., MI; died 22 Dec 1937 in Benton Harbor, Berrien Co., MI. She married (---) Butler.

Children of Maxine Kent and (---) Butler were as follows:

4177   i   Barbara^9 **Butler**, born Oct 1927; died 12 Dec 1937.

3248. William Eli^8 **Bovee** (Jonathan Orly^7, Clark^6, Jonathan^5, Peter^4, Gerrit^3, Anthony^2, Mathieu^1), born 18 Jun 1884 in MI; died 21 Oct 1917. He married on 19 Apr 1908 Hazel Purmanter, born abt 1888.

Children of William Eli Bovee and Hazel Purmanter were as follows:

4178   i   Arthur M^9 Bovee, born 10 Jan 1910; died 6 Sep 1939.

4179   ii   Wayne E^9 Bovee, born Mar 1914. He married on 9 Mar 1937 **Margery R Grange.**

4180   iii   Sylvan^9 Bovee, born 15 Feb 1916; died 21 Oct 1959.

3249. Grace May^8 Bovee (Jonathan Orly^7, Clark^6, Jonathan^5, Peter^4, Gerrit^3, Anthony^2, Mathieu^1), born 1 Jun 1890 in Algansee, Branch Co., MI. She married on 28 Oct 1911 Walter Charles Camfield.

Children of Grace May Bovee and Walter Charles Camfield were as follows:

4181   i   Alton^9 **Camfield.** He married **Beatrice Hassinger.**

4182   ii   Marie^9 **Camfield.**

4183   iii   Louise^9 **Camfield.**

3250. Paul Elmer^8 Bovee (Elmer Ellsworth^7, Clark^6, Jonathan^5, Peter^4, Gerrit^3, Anthony^2, Mathieu^1), born 29 May 1902 in Chicago, Cook Co., IL; died Oct 1973. He married Florence (---).

Children of Paul Elmer Bovee and Florence (---) were as follows:

4184   i   Robert^9 Bovee, born 1920; died 1930.

3251. Carl Folette^8 Bovee (Elmer Ellsworth^7, Clark^6, Jonathan^5, Peter^4, Gerrit^3, Anthony^2, Mathieu^1), born 15 Aug 1905 in Chicago, Cook Co., IL; died 13 Oct 1979 in Kissimmee, Osceola Co., FL. He married on 18 Sep 1931 Mildred Beatrice Novotney, born 1909; died aft 1988 in Leesburg, Lake Co., FL.

Children of Carl Folette Bovee and Mildred Beatrice Novotney were as follows:

+   4185   i   Kenneth Carl^9 Bovee, born in Chicago, Cook Co., IL. He married **Terry Lee Turner.**

    4186   ii   Curtis Carl^9 Bovee.

3257. Upton Randall^8 Bovee (Henry Orgo^7, Clark^6, Jonathan^5, Peter^4, Gerrit^3, Anthony^2, Mathieu^1), born 16 Dec 1895 in MI; died 12 Sep 1963. He married (1) Mildred Filled; (2) on 2 Jun 1917, divorced Bernice Sorter; (3) in 1957 Arda Bartholomy Hallock, born 22 May 1906 in Bad Axe, Huron Co., MI; died 18 Apr 1999 in Lenawee Medical Facility, Lenawee Co., MI, daughter of Frederick S Hallock and Minnie Weiland.

Children of Upton Randall Bovee and Bernice Sorter were as follows:

4187   i   John^9 Bovee, born abt 1920.

Children of Upton Randall Bovee and Arda Bartholomy Hallock were as

follows:

4188   i   John[9] **Bovee**.

3258. Kenneth Clark[8] **Bovee** (Henry Orgo[7], Clark[6], Jonathan[5], Peter[4], Gerrit[3], Anthony[2], Mathieu[1]), born 1 Sep 1902 in WI; died 13 Jul 1948. He married (1) on 15 Jun 1932 Adelma Lillian Dickey, born 23 Apr 1905; (2) Alice W (---), born abt 1889 in NE.

Children of Kenneth Clark Bovee and Adelma Lillian Dickey were as follows:

+   4189   i   Helen Jean[9] **Bovee**. She married **Jerry Groner**.

4190   ii   Carol Anne[9] **Bovee**.

3265. John William[8] **Bovee** (William Francis[7], William W[6], Moses R[5], Jacob[4], Gerrit[3], Anthony[2], Mathieu[1]), born 1 Mar 1887 in Green Mountain, Mareshal Co., IA; died 23 Mar 1924 in Visalia, Tulare Co., CA. He married on 4 Oct 1910 in Monrovia, Los Angeles Co., CA Jeannette Perry Conable.

Children of John William Bovee and Jeannette Perry Conable were as follows:

4191   i   Jeannette Conable[9] **Bovee**, born 3 Jul 1911. She married (1) on 23 Jun 1937 **John Edward Ettner**, born 4 Nov 1911 in Elgin, Kane Co., IL; (2) on 7 Mar 1967 in Tulare Co., CA **Bowen Daniel Jenkins**, born 7 Feb 1908; died 14 Dec 1992 in Tulare, Tulare Co., CA.

4192   ii   Hazel Ileen[9] **Bovee**, born 28 Feb 1913 in San Francisco, San Francisco Co., CA. She married **Edwin Gower Blaney**.

4193   iii   Mary Adelaide[9] **Bovee**, born 3 Mar 1914. She married **George Harper McCord**, born 21 Oct 1915 in San Francisco, San Francisco Co., CA.

3267. Paul Worden[8] **Bovee** (William Francis[7], William W[6], Moses R[5], Jacob[4], Gerrit[3], Anthony[2], Mathieu[1]), born 24 Oct 1893; died 29 Apr 1974 in Sant Barbara, Santa Barbara Co., CA. He married Meda Logan, born 4 Feb 1903 in KS; died 28 Oct 1997 in Sant Barbara, Santa Barbara Co., CA.

Children of Paul Worden Bovee and Meda Logan were as follows:

4194   i   William Logan[9] **Bovee**, died Age 5 Yrs..

4195   ii   Harold Worden[9] **Bovee**, born 23 Jan 1923; died 20 Mar 1943 in World War II.

3272. Hartson[8] **Bovee** (Ernest A[7], William W[6], Moses R[5], Jacob[4], Gerrit[3], Anthony[2], Mathieu[1]), born 1 Mar 1908; died 17 May 1997 in Ventura Co., CA. He married Ruth Horn, born 13 Apr 1909; died 1985.

Children of Hartson Bovee and Ruth Horn were as follows:

| 4196 | i | Barry^9 **Bovee**. He married **Nancy Smith**. |
| 4197 | ii | Sharon^9 **Bovee**, born 17 May 1942; died Jun 1975. She married **Samuel Hale**. |

3274. Benjamin Samuel^8 **Bovee** (Frank Luther^7, Moses C^6, Moses R^5, Jacob^4, Gerrit^3, Anthony^2, Mathieu^1), born 6 May 1892 in Green Mountain, Marshall Co., IA; died 23 Dec 1981 in Brandenton, Manatee Co., FL. He married Eleanor Ceser, born 1894 in MN; died 14 Aug 1954 in Elmhurst, Du Page Co., IL, daughter of John W Ceser and Ida Falk.

Children of Benjamin Samuel Bovee and Eleanor Ceser were as follows:

	4198	i	Arline Faith^9 **Bovee**, born 18 Oct 1920 in Racine, Racine Co., WI.
+	4199	ii	Cecil Lynn^9 **Bovee**, born 29 Sep 1922 in Minneapolis, Hennepin Co., MN. He married **Mildred Eddy**.
	4200	iii	Dale Eugene^9 **Bovee**, born 24 Jun 1924 in Chicago, Cook Co., IL; died 5 Sep 2004 in FL.

3275. Lloyd D^8 **Bovee** (Frank Luther^7, Moses C^6, Moses R^5, Jacob^4, Gerrit^3, Anthony^2, Mathieu^1), born 10 Apr 1894 in IA; died Feb 1967 in Greenville, Hunt Co., TX. He married Cora (---).

Children of Lloyd D Bovee and Cora (---) were as follows:

| 4201 | i | Bud^9 **Bovee**. |
| 4202 | ii | Gene W^9 **Bovee**, born in Carbondale, Jackson Co., IL. |

3279. Homer Charles^8 **Bovee** (Charles Edward^7, Moses C^6, Moses R^5, Jacob^4, Gerrit^3, Anthony^2, Mathieu^1), born 18 Nov 1917; died 18 May 2004 in Green Mountain, Marshall Co., IA. He married on 25 Oct 1942 Vera Thurston, born 17 May 1916.

Children of Homer Charles Bovee and Vera Thurston were as follows:

	4203	i	Loren Lee^9 **Bovee**. He married **(---) Kay**.
+	4204	ii	Ronald Craig^9 **Bovee**, born 18 Mar 1944; died 2001. He married **Kathleen Sandra Brown**.
	4205	iii	Deann Katherin^9 **Bovee**. She married on 22 Aug 1964 **Everette Raymond Pickerell**.
+	4206	iv	Dennis J^9 **Bovee**. He married **Darlene Ethel Drummer**.
	4207	v	Carol Ann^9 **Bovee**. She married on 22 Aug 1970 **Larry Luverne Perry**.

3286. Homer Thomas^8 **Bovee** (Clyde Charles^7, James B^6, Moses R^5, Jacob^4, Gerrit^3, Anthony^2, Mathieu^1), born 27 Dec 1889 in Laurens, Pocahontas Co., IA;

died 4 Jul 1965 in WA. He married on 19 Sep 1917 Lois H T Roller.

Children of Homer Thomas Bovee and Lois H T Roller were as follows:

4208 i Jane Aralia^9 **Bovee**, born 8 Jun 1918. She married **William S Brand**.

4209 ii Helen Alice^9 **Bovee**, born 2 Jan 1921. She married **Bruce D Finlayson**.

+ 4210 iii Charles Clyde^9 **Bovee**, born 11 Feb 1926. He married **Edyth Wessling**.

4211 iv Mary Lois^9 **Bovee**, born 11 Feb 1926. She married **Clifford John Taylor**.

3287. Earle Clyde^8 **Bovee** (Clyde Charles^7, James B^6, Moses R^5, Jacob^4, Gerrit^3, Anthony^2, Mathieu^1), born 24 Jul 1891 in IA; died Feb 1984. He married on 29 Sep 1915 Muriel Sanderson.

Children of Earle Clyde Bovee and Muriel Sanderson were as follows:

+ 4212 i Earl Clyde^9 **Bovee** Jr, born 20 Jun 1916 in Sumner, Pierce Co., WA. He married **Emily Mae Vicary**.

4213 ii Marbara Muriel^9 **Bovee**, born 8 May 1919; died 1978.

3290. Mark C^8 **Bovee** (George M^7, Mark^6, Moses R^5, Jacob^4, Gerrit^3, Anthony^2, Mathieu^1), born 6 Sep 1886 in IA; died 17 Dec 1971. He married Ruth Ilene Pennington, born 6 Jul 1891 in CO.

Children of Mark C Bovee and Ruth Ilene Pennington were as follows:

+ 4214 i Claude Lee^9 **Bovee**, born 26 May 1911; died Jan 1973 in CA. He married **Ethel Rose Austin**.

4215 ii Stella Jane^9 **Bovee**, born 8 Mar 1916 in NE. She married (1) **Marvin Brant**; (2) **Elroy Erickson**.

4216 iii Bess Evalyn^9 **Bovee**, born 22 Oct 1922. She married (1) **Doy LeRoy Francis**; (2) **Philip Joseph Rice**.

3292. George^8 **Bovee** (George M^7, Mark^6, Moses R^5, Jacob^4, Gerrit^3, Anthony^2, Mathieu^1), born 25 Feb 1892 in IA. He married on 5 Jan 1916 in Holyoke, Philips Co., CO Myrtle Ethel Churning, born 6 Jul 1895; died Nov 1973.

Children of George Bovee and Myrtle Ethel Churning were as follows:

4217 i Glennie^9 **Bovee**, born 27 Jan 1917; died Jul 1917.

4218 ii Marjorie Helen^9 **Bovee**, born 28 Jul 1918. She married **Billy H Conry**.

+ 4219 iii Leonard Burl^9 **Bovee**, born 13 Mar 1920. He married **Jeanette Reynolds**.

4220 iv Lester Marion^9 **Bovee**, born 9 Apr 1922. He married **Ruby Iva Norman**.

4221   v   Esther Mary[9] **Bovee**, born 9 Apr 1922. She married (1) **Edward Boone Basham**; (2) **Frank Roy Mayer**.

4222   vi   Ruth Lenore[9] **Bovee**, born 2 Aug 1925. She married (1) **Maurice M Frank**; (2) **Hugh A Banks**.

+ 4223   vii   George Raymond[9] **Bovee**. He married (1) **Nancy Rose Modisett**; (2) **Karen Nieda Sundt**.

3298. Glenn Thaddeus[8] **Bovee** (Thaddeus Fairbanks[7], Mark[6], Moses R[5], Jacob[4], Gerrit[3], Anthony[2], Mathieu[1]), born 12 Aug 1906 in Saskatchewan, Canada; died Oct 1984 in San Diego, San Diego Co., CA. He married (1) on 12 Jan 1929 Helen Hurst, born 17 Feb 1907 in IN; died 3 Feb 1988; (2) in Sep 1969 Marion Olson.

Children of Glenn Thaddeus Bovee and Helen Hurst were as follows:

4224   i   Joanne Patricia[9] **Bovee**. She married **Frank Joseph Hickey**.

4225   ii   Merolyn Lou[9] **Bovee**. She married **Douglas Emery Stephenson**.

4226   iii   Jerolyn Sue[9] **Bovee**. She married on 8 Jul 1967 **David Gordon Thompson**.

4227   iv   Ronald S[9] **Bovee**.

3301. John Colin[8] **Bovee** (Harry W[7], Otis M[6], Courtland[5], Jacob[4], Gerrit[3], Anthony[2], Mathieu[1]), born 15 Dec 1918 in Maryfield, Saskatchewan, Canada; died 1959. He married on 24 Nov 1944 Barbara Winston.

Children of John Colin Bovee and Barbara Winston were as follows:

4228   i   John Winston[9] **Bovee**, born in CA. He married **Patricia Bolek**.

+ 4229   ii   James Findlay[9] **Bovee**, born in CA. He married **Brenda Bond**.

4230   iii   Louise[9] **Bovee**, born in CA.

3303. Courtney Van[8] **Bovee** (William Courtland[7], Otis M[6], Courtland[5], Jacob[4], Gerrit[3], Anthony[2], Mathieu[1]), born 27 Jun 1919 in Maryfield, Saskatchewan, Canada. He married on 24 Aug 1940 in Carson City, Montcalm Co., MI Shirley Patricia Shepherd, born 16 Apr 1920 in CAnada.

Children of Courtney Van Bovee and Shirley Patricia Shepherd were as follows:

4231   i   Courtland Lowell[9] **Bovee**, born in Red Bluff, Tehama Co., CA.

4232   ii   Garland Courtney[9] **Bovee**, born in Red Bluff, Tehama Co., CA.

4233   iii   Lynell DeJon[9] **Bovee**. She married on 20 May 1978

Generation 9

3306. Frederick Richard^9 **Bovie** (Richard Curtis^8, Richard Heman^7, Richard H^6, Henry^5, John^4, Rykert^3, Nicholas^2, Mathieu^1), born in Rennselaer Co., NY. He married on 9 Jul 1956 in Greenwich, Washington Co., NY Carole Eva Monroe, daughter of John Thomas Monroe and Hazel Emma Lewis.

Children of Frederick Richard Bovie and Carole Eva Monroe were as follows:

4234	i	Douglas John^{10} **Bovie**.
4235	ii	Venetia Claire^{10} **Bovie**.
4236	iii	David Frederick^{10} **Bovie**.

3310. George P^9 **Bovie** (George P^8, William H^7, Parker R.^{6}, John^5, John^4, Rykert^3, Nicholas^2, Mathieu^1), born Jun 1895 in Chicago, Cook Co., IL. He married Bettie (---), born abt 1900.

Children of George P Bovie and Bettie (---) were as follows:

4237	i	Girard L^{10} **Bovie**, born 8 Feb 1922 in Chicago, Cook Co., IL; died Jul 1990.
4238	ii	Jean^{10} **Bovie**, born 1925; died abt 1928.

3318. Frances H^9 **Bovee** (Richard Harrison^8, John Nelson^7, Richard^6, Elisha^5, Cornelius^4, Rykert^3, Nicholas^2, Mathieu^1), born abt 1911. She married (1) Glen Hess; (2) Gaylord Huddleston.

Children of Frances H Bovee and Gaylord Huddleston were as follows:

4239	i	LeRoy^{10} **Huddleston**.
4240	ii	Ellen^{10} **Huddleston**.

3319. John R^9 **Bovee** (Richard Harrison^8, John Nelson^7, Richard^6, Elisha^5, Cornelius^4, Rykert^3, Nicholas^2, Mathieu^1), born abt 1913 in CA. He married Margaret (---).

Children of John R Bovee and Margaret (---) were as follows:

4241	i	Betty^{10} **Bovee**.
4242	ii	Robert^{10} **Bovee**.
4243	iii	Bernice^{10} **Bovee**.

3320. Bert J^9 **Bovee** (Richard Harrison^8, John Nelson^7, Richard^6, Elisha^5, Cornelius^4, Rykert^3, Nicholas^2, Mathieu^1), born abt 1918 in CA. He married Dolores (---).

Children of Bert J Bovee and Dolores (---) were as follows:

4244   i   Dorothy[10] **Bovee**. She married **Robert Hahn**.

3324. Glenn Nelson[9] **Bovee** (Manley Glenn[8], John Nelson[7], Richard[6], Elisha[5], Cornelius[4], Rykert[3], Nicholas[2], Mathieu[1]), born 30 Jan 1911 in Heber Ranch, Imperial, Imperial Co., CA; died 23 Feb 1972 in CA. He married (1) on 22 Mar 1933 in Holtville, Imperial Co., CA Helen Margaret Gates, born 10 Feb 1915 in Holtville, Imperial Co., CA; died 28 May 1999 in Glendale, Maricopa Co., AZ; (2) on 16 Nov 1947 in Los Angeles, Los Angeles Co., CA Doris Jane Jackson Arvine, born in Burlington, Des Moines Co., IA.

Children of Glenn Nelson Bovee and Helen Margaret Gates were as follows:

+   4245   i   Gerald Nelson[10] **Bovee**, born 11 Aug 1939 in San Diego, San Diego Co., CA; died Oct 2002 in Sun City, Maricopa Co., AZ. He married **Sharon Ann Morris**.

Children of Glenn Nelson Bovee and Doris Jane Jackson Arvine were as follows:

4246   i   Paul Nelson[10] **Bovee**, born in National City, San Diego Co., CA.

3325. Lillburn Robert[9] **Bovee** (Manley Glenn[8], John Nelson[7], Richard[6], Elisha[5], Cornelius[4], Rykert[3], Nicholas[2], Mathieu[1]), born 3 Aug 1912 in Heber Ranch, Imperial Co., CA. He married on 29 Aug 1942 in San Diego, San Diego Co., CA Ruth Phyllis McGregor, born 1 Sep 1920 in Erie, Whiteside Co., IL.

Children of Lillburn Robert Bovee and Ruth Phyllis McGregor were as follows:

+   4247   i   Roger Lee[10] **Bovee**, born in San Diego, San Diego Co., CA. He married **Constance Levac**.

+   4248   ii   Dennis Robert[10] **Bovee**, born in San Diego, San Diego Co., CA. He married **Robyn Renee Schmidt**.

+   4249   iii   Sharon Ann[10] **Bovee**, born in San Diego, San Diego Co., CA. She married **Michael Alan Marianno**.

3327. Allan Douglas[9] **Bovee** (Manley Glenn[8], John Nelson[7], Richard[6], Elisha[5], Cornelius[4], Rykert[3], Nicholas[2], Mathieu[1]), born 12 Dec 1916 in Heber Ranch, Imperial, Imperial Co., CA; died 20 Feb 2000 in Hemet, Riverside Co., CA. He married on 11 Oct 1940 in San Diego, San Diego Co., CA Elizabeth Pearl Hobbs, born 29 Apr 1919 in Norman, Cleveland Co., OK.

Children of Allan Douglas Bovee and Elizabeth Pearl Hobbs were as follows:

+   4250   i   Allan Wayne[10] **Bovee**, born in San Diego, San Diego Co., CA. He married **Judy Caroline Wilson**.

+   4251   ii   Steven Douglas[10] **Bovee**, born in Alhambra, Los Angeles Co., CA. He married **Shyrle Jeanne Darby**.

3328. Alice Elizabeth^9 **Bovee** (Manley Glenn^8, John Nelson^7, Richard^6, Elisha^5, Cornelius^4, Rykert^3, Nicholas^2, Mathieu^1), born 22 Oct 1918 in Imperial, Imperial Co., CA; died 10 Apr 1964. She married on 15 Aug 1936 in Imperial, Imperial Co., CA William Flores, born 29 May 1900; died 26 Sep 1968.

Children of Alice Elizabeth Bovee and William Flores were as follows:

4252	i	Marvin^{10} **Flores**.
4253	ii	Douglas^{10} **Flores**.
4254	iii	Diantha^{10} **Flores**, born 1 Apr 1944; died 27 Sep 1986.
4255	iv	Cynthia^{10} **Flores**.
4256	v	Donald^{10} **Flores**.
4257	vi	Allan^{10} **Flores**.
4258	vii	Mary Alice^{10} **Flores**.

3329. Leslie Gerald^9 **Bovee** (Manley Glenn^8, John Nelson^7, Richard^6, Elisha^5, Cornelius^4, Rykert^3, Nicholas^2, Mathieu^1), born 7 Nov 1920 in Holtville, Imperial Co., CA. He married on 10 Jul 1942 in LaMesa, San Diego Co., CA Irene R Jackman, born 23 Jul 1923.

Children of Leslie Gerald Bovee and Irene R Jackman were as follows:

+	4259	i	Karen Garnet^{10} **Bovee**, born in LaMesa, San Diego Co., CA. She married **James Talada**.
+	4260	ii	Colleen Rachel^{10} **Bovee**, born in San Diego, San Diego Co., CA. She married **James Morocco**.
+	4261	iii	Melody Layne^{10} **Bovee**, born in San Diego, San Diego Co., CA. She married **Gary Mills**.

3330. Ester Esmond^9 **Bovee** (Manley Glenn^8, John Nelson^7, Richard^6, Elisha^5, Cornelius^4, Rykert^3, Nicholas^2, Mathieu^1), born 26 Aug 1922 in Holtville, Imperial Co., CA. She married on 23 Jul 1944 in Key West, Monroe Co., FL Floyd Vernon Piper, son of John Piper and Pearl Smith.

Children of Ester Esmond Bovee and Floyd Vernon Piper were as follows:

| 4262 | i | Priscilla Ann^{10} **Piper**, born in Los Angeles, Los Angeles Co., CA. |
| 4263 | ii | Mark Vernon^{10} **Piper**, born in Ventura, Ventura Co., CA. |

3332. Paul Leroy^9 **Bovee** (Manley Glenn^8, John Nelson^7, Richard^6, Elisha^5, Cornelius^4, Rykert^3, Nicholas^2, Mathieu^1), born 12 Oct 1926 in Holtville, Imperial Co., CA; died 11 May 1977 in Denver, Denver Co., CO.. He married (1) on 2 Oct 1960 Dorothy Elinor Baxter Morris, born 28 Feb 1923; died 3 Oct 1998; (2) Roberta Alexander.

Children of Paul Leroy Bovee and Dorothy Elinor Baxter Morris were as follows:

4264	i	Audra[10] **Bovee**.
4265	ii	Nicole[10] **Bovee**.
4266	iii	Holly Elizabeth[10] **Bovee**.

Children of Paul Leroy Bovee and Roberta Alexander were as follows:

| 4267 | i | Paula[10] **Bovee**. |

3334. Billy Ray[9] **Bovee** (Manley Glenn[8], John Nelson[7], Richard[6], Elisha[5], Cornelius[4], Rykert[3], Nicholas[2], Mathieu[1]), born in Holtville, Imperial Co., CA. He married on 8 May 1954 in Turlock, Stanislaus Co., CA Florence Linnea Anderson, born in Newell, Butte Co., SD.

Children of Billy Ray Bovee and Florence Linnea Anderson were as follows:

| 4268 | i | Donna Ann[10] **Bovee**, born in Albuquerque, Bernalillo Co., NM. She married on 7 Apr 1989 in Los Gatos, Santa Clara Co., CA **Robert Witt**. |
| 4269 | ii | Daniel Ray[10] **Bovee**, born in Arcadia, Los Angeles Co., CA. He married on 20 Apr 1991 in Pismo Beach, San Luis Obispo Co., CA **Karen Schmidt**. |

3335. Lena Ann[9] **Bovee** (Manley Glenn[8], John Nelson[7], Richard[6], Elisha[5], Cornelius[4], Rykert[3], Nicholas[2], Mathieu[1]), born in Holtville, Imperial Co., CA. She married on 14 Dec 1953 in South San Gabriel, Rosemead Co., CA, divorced Norman C Wingerd, born in Hope, Dickinson Co., KS, son of Simon Cecil Wingerd and Catherine Aydelotte Smith.

Children of Lena Ann Bovee and Norman C Wingerd were as follows:

4270	i	Linda Louise[10] **Wingerd**, born in Alhambra, Los Angeles Co., CA.
4271	ii	Diane Elain[10] **Wingerd**, born in Alhambra, Los Angeles Co., CA.
4272	iii	Karen Eilene[10] **Wingerd**, born in Alhambra, Los Angeles Co., CA.

3338. Burt Richard[9] **Bovee** (Ira Burt[8], John Nelson[7], Richard[6], Elisha[5], Cornelius[4], Rykert[3], Nicholas[2], Mathieu[1]), born 31 Aug 1922. He married Peggy Prey.

Children of Burt Richard Bovee and Peggy Prey were as follows:

| + | 4273 | i | Keith R[10] **Bovee**. He married **Norma Jean (---)**. |

3339. Erma Jean[9] **Bovee** (Ira Burt[8], John Nelson[7], Richard[6], Elisha[5], Cornelius[4], Rykert[3], Nicholas[2], Mathieu[1]), born 12 Jun 1927. She married on 8 Jan 1943

Richard G Himes.

Children of Erma Jean Bovee and Richard G Himes were as follows:

4274   i   Richard[10] **Himes** Jr..

4275   ii   Child[10] **Himes**.

3352. Kermit R[9] **Bovee** (Walter Richard[8], Jacob Newton[7], David[6], Elisha[5], Cornelius[4], Rykert[3], Nicholas[2], Mathieu[1]), born 1 Oct 1908 in Lengby, Polk Co., MN; died 19 Aug 1982 in Solon Springs, Douglas Co., WI. He married Helen Priem, born 11 Apr 1910 in Douglas Co., WI.

Children of Kermit R Bovee and Helen Priem were as follows:

+ 4276   i   Kermit D[10] **Bovee** Jr, born 13 Mar 1928 in Remer, Cass Co., MN; died 22 May 1983 in Lewis & Clark Co., MT. He married **Beverly Bowman**.

+ 4277   ii   Bonnie Lee[10] **Bovee**. She married **Robert Lawrence Ferdelman**.

   4278   iii   Michael D[10] **Bovee**, born in Crosby, Crow Wing Co.,MN.

3354. Vartone D[9] **Bovee** (Walter Richard[8], Jacob Newton[7], David[6], Elisha[5], Cornelius[4], Rykert[3], Nicholas[2], Mathieu[1]), born 8 Mar 1913 in Climax, Polk Co., MN. He married abt 1940 Ethel Hartzberg, born 1920.

Children of Vartone D Bovee and Ethel Hartzberg were as follows:

4279   i   Warren[10] **Bovee**.

4280   ii   Nancy[10] **Bovee**.

3355. Maxine M[9] **Bovee** (Walter Richard[8], Jacob Newton[7], David[6], Elisha[5], Cornelius[4], Rykert[3], Nicholas[2], Mathieu[1]), born 9 Mar 1916 in Comstock Clay Co., MN. She married Edward Borgolte.

Children of Maxine M Bovee and Edward Borgolte were as follows:

4281   i   Edward[10] **Borgolte**.

3356. Forrest W[9] **Bovee** (Walter Richard[8], Jacob Newton[7], David[6], Elisha[5], Cornelius[4], Rykert[3], Nicholas[2], Mathieu[1]), born 22 Nov 1926 in Bain, MN. He married on 13 May 1950 Marian Joyce Smith, born 23 May 1933 in Palisade, Aitkin Co., MN; died 8 Mar 1998 in Hoyt Lakes, St Louis Co., MN, daughter of Arthur Smith and Alice Anderson.

Children of Forrest W Bovee and Marian Joyce Smith were as follows:

+ 4282   i   Lynda Karen[10] **Bovee**. She married **Darwin Michel Alar**.

+ 4283   ii   Wendy Ann[10] **Bovee**, born in Dallas, Dallas Co., TX. She married **Norik Assatourian**.

4284	iii	David Zane[10] **Bovee**, born in Superior, Douglas Co., WI.
4285	iv	William Howard[10] **Bovee**, born 12 Aug 1956; died 8 Aug 1975.
+ 4286	v	Cynthia Kay[10] **Bovee**, born in Hoyt Lakes, St Louis Co., MN. She married (1) **Kieth Norris Sigman**; (2) **Kieth Norris**.
+ 4287	vi	Becky Sue[10] **Bovee**, born in Wichita, Sedgwick Co., KS. She married **James Anthoy Reek**.

3357. Gloria L[9] **Bovee** (Walter Richard[8], Jacob Newton[7], David[6], Elisha[5], Cornelius[4], Rykert[3], Nicholas[2], Mathieu[1]), born 18 Aug 1929 in Bain, MN. She married Dorence Thorson.

Children of Gloria L Bovee and Dorence Thorson were as follows:

4288	i	Steven[10] **Thorson**.
4289	ii	Wanda[10] **Thorson**.
4290	iii	Debra[10] **Thorson**.

3358. Caryl Roger[9] **Bovee** (Roderick[8], Jacob Newton[7], David[6], Elisha[5], Cornelius[4], Rykert[3], Nicholas[2], Mathieu[1]), born 3 Dec 1913; died 3 Sep 1970 in Fosston, Polk Co., MN. He married on 24 Dec 1934 in McIntosh, Polk Co., MN Doris Jorgenson.

Children of Caryl Roger Bovee and Doris Jorgenson were as follows:

+ 4291	i	Peter Roger[10] **Bovee**. He married **Mary Nell Johnson**.
4292	ii	Susan Renee[10] **Bovee**.

3359. Iva Lee[9] **Bovee** (Roderick[8], Jacob Newton[7], David[6], Elisha[5], Cornelius[4], Rykert[3], Nicholas[2], Mathieu[1]). She married John William Graupman.

Children of Iva Lee Bovee and John William Graupman were as follows:

4293	i	Tim John[10] **Graupman**, born in Steele Co., MN.
4294	ii	Elizabeth Mae[10] **Graupman**, born in Yello Medicine Co., MN.
4295	iii	Mary Lee[10] **Graupman**, born in Yello Medicine Co., MN.
4296	iv	Jane Alice[10] **Graupman**, born in Beltrami Co., MN.
4297	v	John Louis[10] **Graupman**, born in Beltrami Co., MN.
4298	vi	Patrick Caryl[10] **Graupman**, born in Beltrami Co., MN.

3360. Alice May[9] **Bovee** (Roderick[8], Jacob Newton[7], David[6], Elisha[5], Cornelius[4], Rykert[3], Nicholas[2], Mathieu[1]). She married Eugene Hegland.

Children of Alice May Bovee and Eugene Hegland were as follows:

4299   i   Daniel[10] **Hegland**.

3361. John Richard[9] **Bovee** (Roderick[8], Jacob Newton[7], David[6], Elisha[5], Cornelius[4], Rykert[3], Nicholas[2], Mathieu[1]), born 29 Jul 1929 in Fosston, Polk Co., MN. He married (1) abt 1958 Grace Ellen Hanson; (2) on 9 May 1982 in Balon Co., MN Terry jaakkola.

Children of John Richard Bovee and Grace Ellen Hanson were as follows:

4300   i   Russell Jack[10] **Bovee**, born in Wilkin Co., MN. He married **Hye Kyong**.

4301   ii   Jean Ellen[10] **Bovee**, born in Crow Wing Co., MN. She married **James Gonzales**.

\+ 4302   iii   Roger Edward[10] **Bovee**. He married **Kelly Marie Aamodt**.

Children of John Richard Bovee and Terry jaakkola were as follows:

4303   i   Roderick Jock[10] **Bovee**.

4304   ii   Regon Joan[10] **Bovee**.

3369. Myron[9] **Bovee** (George F[8], Cornelius[7], Jonas Nicholas[6], Nicholas[5], Cornelius[4], Rykert[3], Nicholas[2], Mathieu[1]), born 30 Aug 1902 in WI; died Aug 1974 in Kent King Co., WA. He married Hazel Reed.

Children of Myron Bovee and Hazel Reed were as follows:

\+ 4305   i   William[10] **Bovee**. He married unknown.

\+ 4306   ii   Frank W[10] **Bovee**. He married (1) **Gladys (---)**; (2) **Myrtle (---)**.

4307   iii   Raymond[10] **Bovee**.

4308   iv   Robert[10] **Bovee**.

3372. Alton E[9] **Bovee** (George F[8], Cornelius[7], Jonas Nicholas[6], Nicholas[5], Cornelius[4], Rykert[3], Nicholas[2], Mathieu[1]), born 30 Jul 1914; died 7 Feb 2001 in Park Rapids, Hubbard Co., MN. He married Phyllis Coon.

Children of Alton E Bovee and Phyllis Coon were as follows:

4309   i   Fred[10] **Bovee**, born in Powell, Park Co., WY. He married **Constance Peterson**.

4310   ii   Linda[10] **Bovee**.

\+ 4311   iii   Richard[10] **Bovee**. He married **Karen (---)**.

4312   iv   Alton E[10] **Bovee** Jr.

4313   v   Duane[10] **Bovee**.

3373. Harold[9] **Bovee** (George F[8], Cornelius[7], Jonas Nicholas[6], Nicholas[5],

Cornelius[4], Rykert[3], Nicholas[2], Mathieu[1]), born 28 Jul 1917 in WI; died 27 Aug 1985 in Ft Lauderdale, Broward Co., FL. He married Beryl (---), born abt 1920.

Children of Harold Bovee and Beryl (---) were as follows:

4314   i   Glenn M[10] **Bovee**.

3375. Janice Lurine[9] **Bovee** (George F[8], Cornelius[7], Jonas Nicholas[6], Nicholas[5], Cornelius[4], Rykert[3], Nicholas[2], Mathieu[1]), born abt 1924. She married (1) Lenard Guy Revels; (2) Bernard Lawton.

Children of Janice Lurine Bovee and Lenard Guy Revels were as follows:

4315   i   Larry[10] **Revels**.
4316   ii   Nita Marie[10] **Revels**, born in St Louis Co., MN.
4317   iii   Rita May[10] **Revels**, born in St Louis Co., MN.

3377. Ruth Viola[9] **Bovee** (Hiram Nelson[8], Cornelius[7], Jonas Nicholas[6], Nicholas[5], Cornelius[4], Rykert[3], Nicholas[2], Mathieu[1]), born 1 Nov 1907 in Eau Claire Co., WI; died 1907 in Eau Claire Co., WI. She married Edward Anthony.

Children of Ruth Viola Bovee and Edward Anthony were as follows:

4318   i   Ray Allen[10] **Anthony**, born in Koochiching Co., MN.

3378. Belva Marie[9] **Bovee** (Hiram Nelson[8], Cornelius[7], Jonas Nicholas[6], Nicholas[5], Cornelius[4], Rykert[3], Nicholas[2], Mathieu[1]), born 14 May 1917 in WI. She married Kenneth Taylor Hughes.

Children of Belva Marie Bovee and Kenneth Taylor Hughes were as follows:

4319   i   Lucille Louise[10] **Hughes**, born in Koochiching Co., MN.

3379. Erma Mildred[9] **Bovee** (Hiram Nelson[8], Cornelius[7], Jonas Nicholas[6], Nicholas[5], Cornelius[4], Rykert[3], Nicholas[2], Mathieu[1]), born 18 Apr 1918 in WI. She married Joseph Anthony.

Children of Erma Mildred Bovee and Joseph Anthony were as follows:

4320   i   Jerry Andre[10] **Anthony**, born in Koochiching Co., MN.

3381. Duane Lorenzo[9] **Bovee** (Hiram Nelson[8], Cornelius[7], Jonas Nicholas[6], Nicholas[5], Cornelius[4], Rykert[3], Nicholas[2], Mathieu[1]), born in International Falls, Koochiching Co., MN. He married Della Caston.

Children of Duane Lorenzo Bovee and Della Caston were as follows:

+   4321   i   Robert[10] **Bovee**, born in Sacramento, Sacramento Co., CA. He married unknown.

+ 4322   ii   Diane Marie[10] **Bovee**, born in Lebanon, Linn Co., OR. She married (1) **Mark Hunter**; (2) **Glenn Shimp**.

3382. Wayne Andrew[9] **Bovee** (Hiram Nelson[8], Cornelius[7], Jonas Nicholas[6], Nicholas[5], Cornelius[4], Rykert[3], Nicholas[2], Mathieu[1]), born in International Falls, Koochiching Co., MN. He married on 26 Jan 1951 in Fairfield, Solano Co., CA Mary Katheryn Campbell, born in Wichita , Sedgwick Co., KS, daughter of Raymond Edward Campbell and Maxine Amanda Brewer.

Children of Wayne Andrew Bovee and Mary Katheryn Campbell were as follows:

+ 4323   i   Elaine Diane[10] **Bovee**, born in Fairfield, Solano Co., CA. She married **John James Keirnan**.
   4324   ii   Raymond Kent[10] **Bovee**.
   4325   iii   Grant Craig[10] **Bovee**.
   4326   iv   Reed Andrew[10] **Bovee**.

3383. Truman Alphie[9] **Bovee** (William Alfred[8], Truman Andrew[7], Jonas Nicholas[6], Nicholas[5], Cornelius[4], Rykert[3], Nicholas[2], Mathieu[1]), born 15 Mar 1893 in Richardson Polk Co., MN; died 24 Sep 1990 in Miles City, Custer Co., MT. He married on 22 Oct 1916 Rose Lewis, born 30 Mar 1898 in Hull Sioux Co., IA; died May 1988 in Miles City, Custer Co., MT, daughter of Charles Lewis and Lizzie Jane Holmes.

Children of Truman Alphie Bovee and Rose Lewis were as follows:

+ 4327   i   Truman Alphie[10] **Bovee** Jr, born 11 Jul 1918 in MT. He married **Mary Irene Williams**.
+ 4328   ii   Opal Jennie[10] **Bovee**, born 25 Nov 1919 in MT. She married **Lewis Bucholz**.
+ 4329   iii   Ruby Irene[10] **Bovee**, born 22 Aug 1921. She married **Samuel H Annalora**.
+ 4330   iv   Pearl Rose[10] **Bovee**, born 28 Jun 1923. She married (1) **Gary Martz**; (2) **Sylvestor St Peter**.
+ 4331   v   Robert William[10] **Bovee**, born 4 Jul 1925. He married **Dorothy Miller**.
   4332   vi   Boyd Bernard[10] **Bovee**, born 11 Apr 1927; died Apr 1932.

3384. Robert Alvin[9] **Bovee** (William Alfred[8], Truman Andrew[7], Jonas Nicholas[6], Nicholas[5], Cornelius[4], Rykert[3], Nicholas[2], Mathieu[1]), born 23 Mar 1895 in WI; died abt 1918. He married Helma (---), born 23 Oct 1906; died Jul 1972 in Montevideo,Chippewa Co., MN.

Children of Robert Alvin Bovee and Helma (---) were as follows:

+ 4333   i   Glenn M[10] **Bovee**, born abt 1917. He married **Marjorie (---)**.

3385. Lloyd Laverne[9] **Bovee** (William Alfred[8], Truman Andrew[7], Jonas Nicholas[6], Nicholas[5], Cornelius[4], Rykert[3], Nicholas[2], Mathieu[1]), born 23 Aug 1897 in WI; died 15 Apr 1957 in Minot, Ward Co., ND. He married on 29 Sep 1926 Rueh L Rued, born 5 May 1907 in Palmero, Mountrail Co., ND; died 22 Apr 1983 in Tacoma, Pierce Co., WA.

Children of Lloyd Laverne Bovee and Rueh L Rued were as follows:

+ 4334 i Lloyd Leroy[10] **Bovee**, born 21 Aug 1927 in Stanley, Mountrail Co., ND. He married **Phyliss E Swenke**.
  4335 ii Dianna Gay[10] **Bovee**, born in Minot, Ward Co., ND. She married **Craig Ramagoz**.
  4336 iii Dalen Curtis[10] **Bovee**, born 18 Oct 1939 in Deering, Mc Henry Co., ND; died 24 Dec 1939.

3391. Warren[9] **Gilles** (Claire Lewis[8], Silas Lewis[7], Silas Lewis[6], Nicholas[5], Cornelius[4], Rykert[3], Nicholas[2], Mathieu[1]), born 2 Jan 1922; died 7 Jul 2003 in Milwaukee, Milwaukee Co., WI. He married abt 1950 Gladys Helen Rose, born abt 1930.

Children of Warren Gilles and Gladys Helen Rose were as follows:

4337 i Christopher P[10] **Bovee**.
4338 ii Priscilla Denise[10] **Bovee**.
4339 iii David S[10] **Bovee**.
4340 iv Gregory Richard[10] **Bovee**, born 17 Jan 1955 in WI; died 1 Mar 1985 in Sioux City, Woodbury Co., IA.
4341 v John Goeffrey[10] **Bovee**.
4342 vi Paul Warren[10] **Bovee**.

3403. Robert Jones[9] **Bovie** (Frederick Ernest[8], Joseph Harley Clark[7], Frederick Morgan[6], Frederick[5], Cornelius[4], Rykert[3], Nicholas[2], Mathieu[1]). He married abt 1952 Margaret W Evans, daughter of David Brice Evans and Margaret Ethel Morgan.

Children of Robert Jones Bovie and Margaret W Evans were as follows:

+ 4343 i Robert Rhys[10] **Bovie**. He married unknown.
  4344 ii Mary Bryn[10] **Bovie**.
  4345 iii Stephen Richard[10] **Bovie**.
  4346 iv Jane Meagan[10] **Bovie**.
  4347 v Susan Bronwyn[10] **Bovie**.
  4348 vi David Penn[10] **Bovie**.

3404. David Frederick[9] **Bovie** (Frederick Ernest[8], Joseph Harley Clark[7], Frederick Morgan[6], Frederick[5], Cornelius[4], Rykert[3], Nicholas[2], Mathieu[1]). He

343

married Marian L Evans, daughter of David Brice Evans and Margaret Ethel Morgan.

Children of David Frederick Bovie and Marian L Evans were as follows:

- 4349   i   Barbara Sue[10] **Bovie**, born in Berea, Cuyahoga Co., OH.
- + 4350   ii   Sally Renee[10] **Bovie**, born in Pittsburg, Allegheny Co., PA. She married **Emmett Hume**.
- + 4351   iii   Rebecca Kim[10] **Bovie**, born in Plainfield, Union Co., NJ. She married **Peter Wright**.

3405. James Edward[9] **Bovie** (Frederick Ernest[8], Joseph Harley Clark[7], Frederick Morgan[6], Frederick[5], Cornelius[4], Rykert[3], Nicholas[2], Mathieu[1]), born 10 Sep 1933; died 19 Nov 1990. He married Gretchen Henderson, daughter of Verlin Henderson and Evelyn Vance.

Children of James Edward Bovie and Gretchen Henderson were as follows:

- 4352   i   Karen Lynn[10] **Bovie**.
- 4353   ii   Sandra Lee[10] **Bovie**.

3406. Stephen Clark[9] **Bovie** (Frederick Ernest[8], Joseph Harley Clark[7], Frederick Morgan[6], Frederick[5], Cornelius[4], Rykert[3], Nicholas[2], Mathieu[1]). He married Delee Jennings, daughter of Robert Jennings and Mary Louise Bash.

Children of Stephen Clark Bovie and Delee Jennings were as follows:

- 4354   i   Kyle Stephen[10] **Bovie**.
- 4355   ii   Aric Wade[10] **Bovie**.
- 4356   iii   Holley Leigh[10] **Bovie**.

3413. Claude Harley[9] **Bovee** (William Harlan[8], Archibald Melrose[7], John[6], John[5], Nicholas M[4], Matthew[3], Nicholas[2], Mathieu[1]), born 21 Jun 1887 in Stockton, San Joaquin Co., CA; died 12 Apr 1971 in Everett, Snohomish Co., WA. He married on 28 Jan 1918 in Everett, Snohomish Co., WA Irma B Adams, born 27 Jul 1898 in Arbela, Tuscola Co., MI; died 20 Jan 1977 in Arlington, Snohomish Co., WA.

Children of Claude Harley Bovee and Irma B Adams were as follows:

- + 4357   i   Harley Howard[10] **Bovee**, born 12 Dec 1918 in Edgecomb, Snohomish Co., WA. He married **Ila Beryl, Obert**.
- + 4358   ii   Robert Clare[10] **Bovee**, born 18 Mar 1921 in Arlington, Snohomish Co., WA. He married **Mary J Franck**.

3414. Ethol[9] **Bovee** (William Harlan[8], Archibald Melrose[7], John[6], John[5], Nicholas M[4], Matthew[3], Nicholas[2], Mathieu[1]), born Aug 1889 in Arlington, Snohomish Co., WA; died 1930 in Arlington, Snohomish Co., WA. She married David Spotten, born in MI.

Children of Ethol Bovee and David Spotten were as follows:

4359   i   Margaret^{10} **Spotten**, born 12 Mar 1909 in Ontonagon, Ontonagon Co., MI.

4360   ii   Glen^{10} **Spotten**, born in Aberdeen, Grays Harbor Co., WA; buried in Seattle, King Co., WA.

3427. Hugh Archibald^9 **Bovee** (Archibald Theodore^8, Archibald Melrose^7, John^6, John^5, Nicholas M^4, Matthew^3, Nicholas^2, Mathieu^1), born 16 Dec 1912. He married Edna Lelia Hunter, born 13 Jan 1919; died 1 Jan 1998 in Fort St. John, British Columbia, Canada.

Children of Hugh Archibald Bovee and Edna Lelia Hunter were as follows:

+   4361   i   Ivan Robert^{10} **Bovee**. He married **Leslie Maclachlin**.

+   4362   ii   Lynwood Wayne^{10} **Bovee**, born in Cabri, Saskatchewan, Canada. He married **Ellen Louise Groger**.

      4363   iii   Norma Dean^{10} **Bovee**. She married **Robert McRae**.

3440. Henry Hopkins^9 **Bovee** Jr (Henry Hopkins^8, John Wesley^7, John^6, John^5, Nicholas M^4, Matthew^3, Nicholas^2, Mathieu^1), born 16 Jan 1915 in Oxnard, Ventura Co., CA; died 23 Apr 1994 in Los Angeles, Los Angeles Co., CA. He married in Apr 1942 Ruth Conklin, born 9 Mar 1917 in Muskegan, Muskegan Co., MI.

Children of Henry Hopkins Bovee Jr and Ruth Conklin were as follows:

+   4364   i   William Roscoe^{10} **Bovee**, born 18 Jan 1938 in CA; died 16 Feb 1981 in Los Angeles, Los Angeles Co., CA. He married **Charlene Eleanor Bartlett**.

      4365   ii   Mariane^{10} **Bovee**. She married **Robert Lee Garrison**.

      4366   iii   Valerie Ruth^{10} **Bovee**. She married on 19 Mar 1967 **Robert Will Schempp**.

+   4367   iv   Jeffrey Alan^{10} **Bovee**. He married **Kathleen Dianne Ward**.

3444. Clifton Willard^9 **Bovee** (William James^8, John Wesley^7, John^6, John^5, Nicholas M^4, Matthew^3, Nicholas^2, Mathieu^1), born 23 Sep 1913 in Santa Anna, Orange Co., CA.. He married (1) Sharlie Evelyn Carpenter, born 10 Apr 1914; died 30 Nov 1988; (2) on 1 Sep 1951 Jonita Ruth Benham.

Children of Clifton Willard Bovee and Jonita Ruth Benham were as follows:

4368   i   Pamela Jean^{10} **Bovee**.

4369   ii   Anthony Andrea^{10} **Bovee**.

4370   iii   Gregory Rene^{10} **Bovee**.

4371   iv   Rene Andrea^{10} **Bovee**.

3447. Harley Ray[9] **Bovee** (Arthur Roy[8], John Wesley[7], John[6], John[5], Nicholas M[4], Matthew[3], Nicholas[2], Mathieu[1]), born 1 Jun 1913 in Pierce Co., NE. He married on 3 Sep 1939 in Pierce Co., NE Henrietta Clara Elfrieda Faudel, born 28 Jul 1915 in Pierce Co., NE, daughter of Charles Faudel and Augusta Alsie Groskursth.

Children of Harley Ray Bovee and Henrietta Clara Elfrieda Faudel were as follows:

+   4372   i   Ila Mae[10] **Bovee**, born in Pierce, Pierce Co., NE. She married **Frederick William Kraft**.

     4373   ii   LaDonna Kay[10] **Bovee**, born in Norfolk, Madison Co., NE. She married on 3 Sep 1966 in Pierce Co., NE **Gerald G Retzlaff**.

+   4374   iii   Rhonda Rae[10] **Bovee**, born in Norfolk, Madison Co., NE. She married **Charles Christopher Johnson**.

3450. Howard Francis[9] **Bovee** (Carl Howard[8], John Wesley[7], John[6], John[5], Nicholas M[4], Matthew[3], Nicholas[2], Mathieu[1]), born 27 Aug 1917; died Jun 1978. He married Maxine Babcock.

Children of Howard Francis Bovee and Maxine Babcock were as follows:

     4375   i   Stephen Francis[10] **Bovee**.

     4376   ii   Michael Scott[10] **Bovee**.

     4377   iii   Terese Ann[10] **Bovee**.

3461. Robert Wesley[9] **Bovee** (William Vivian[8], John McClellan[7], Wesley[6], John[5], Nicholas M[4], Matthew[3], Nicholas[2], Mathieu[1]), born 1 Dec 1923 in Pleasant Hill, Pike Co., IL. He married on 20 May 1950 in Compton, Los Angeles Co., CA Ruth Ann Silvus, daughter of Lawrence Newton Silvus and Stella Viola Schrecengost.

Children of Robert Wesley Bovee and Ruth Ann Silvus were as follows:

     4378   i   Alayne Maria[10] **Bovee**, born in Portsmouth, Independant City, VA.

+   4379   ii   John[10] **Bovee**, born in Bakersfield, Kern Co., CA. He married **Joanne Hussey**.

3469. Beverly J[9] **Bovee** (Eugene Burdette[8], John McClellan[7], Wesley[6], John[5], Nicholas M[4], Matthew[3], Nicholas[2], Mathieu[1]), born 2 Jan 1939 in Compton, Los Angeles Co., CA; died 12 Sep 2001 in Helena, Lewis & Clarck Co., MT. She married (---) Shilder.

Children of Beverly J Bovee and (---) Shilder were as follows:

     4380   i   Nicole[10] **Shilder**.

     4381   ii   Baron[10] **Shilder**.

3470. Stanley[9] **Bovee** (Eugene Burdette[8], John McClellan[7], Wesley[6], John[5], Nicholas M[4], Matthew[3], Nicholas[2], Mathieu[1]), born in Compton, Los Angeles Co., CA. He married on 17 Aug 1966 Bambi (---).

Children of Stanley Bovee and Bambi (---) were as follows:

4382   i   Eric[10] **Bovee**.

4383   ii   Isaac[10] **Bovee**.

3471. Nancy[9] **Bovee** (Eugene Burdette[8], John McClellan[7], Wesley[6], John[5], Nicholas M[4], Matthew[3], Nicholas[2], Mathieu[1]), born in Compton, Los Angeles Co., CA. She married on 14 Jul 1983 in San Francisco, San Francisco Co., CA Joel (---).

Children of Nancy Bovee and Joel (---) were as follows:

4384   i   Alexander[10] **(---)**.

4385   ii   Mathew[10] **(---)**.

3480. Kenneth Eugene[9] **Bovee** (Glenn Peter[8], James Massey[7], Nelson John[6], John[5], Nicholas M[4], Matthew[3], Nicholas[2], Mathieu[1]), born 19 Aug 1920 in Shawnee, Pottawatomie Co., OK. He married on 1 Sep 1940 in Seminole, Seminole Co., OK Ora Lee Laster, born 10 Aug 1922 in Asher, Pottawatomie Co., OK, daughter of Francis Terrell Laster and Lynn Deserah Glenn.

Children of Kenneth Eugene Bovee and Ora Lee Laster were as follows:

+   4386   i   Glenda Carol[10] **Bovee**, born in Shawnee, Pottawatommie Co., OK. She married **James Edward Vaughn**.

    4387   ii   Kenneth[10] **Bovee**, born in Shawnee, Pottawatomie Co., OK.

+   4388   iii   Janice Irene[10] **Bovee**, born in Shawnee, Pottawatomie Co., OK. She married **John Ray Harris**.

3481. Keith Alan[9] **Bovee** (Glenn Peter[8], James Massey[7], Nelson John[6], John[5], Nicholas M[4], Matthew[3], Nicholas[2], Mathieu[1]), born 16 Dec 1921 in Shawnee, Pottawatomie Co., OK. He married on 1 Sep 1942 in Washington, DC Pauline Elizabeth Dunbar, born 24 Nov 1919 in Tulsa Co., OK, daughter of Ralph Dunbar and Pauline Joyce Herron.

Children of Keith Alan Bovee and Pauline Elizabeth Dunbar were as follows:

+   4389   i   Timothy Keith[10] **Bovee**, born in Shawnee, Pottawatomie Co., OK. He married **Reiko Ogura**.

+   4390   ii   Douglas Alan[10] **Bovee**, born in Shawnee, Pottawatomie Co., OK. He married **Nancy Laura Burns**.

3482. Reta Eunice[9] **Bovee** (Glenn Peter[8], James Massey[7], Nelson John[6], John[5],

Nicholas M[4], Matthew[3], Nicholas[2], Mathieu[1]), born in Shawnee, Pottawatomie Co., OK. She married (1) on 17 Feb 1951 in Shawnee, Pottawatomie Co., OK, divorced Kenneth Darrell Miller; (2) on 22 Dec 1951 in Gainesville, Cook Co., TX William Thomas Henderson, born 29 Sep 1927 in Shawnee, Pottawatomie Co., OK, son of Oliver Wesley Henderson and Carolyn Frances Kellog.

Children of Reta Eunice Bovee and William Thomas Henderson were as follows:

4391	i	Thomas Ashley[10] **Henderson**, born in Shawnee, Pottawatomie Co., OK.
4392	ii	Alicia Renee[10] **Henderson**, born in Shawnee, Pottawatomie Co., OK.
4393	iii	Sarah Janell[10] **Henderson**, born in Shawnee, Pottawatomie Co., OK.
4394	iv	William Wesley[10] **Henderson**, born in Shawnee, Pottawatomie Co., OK.
4395	v	Laura Ellyn[10] **Henderson**, born in Aquana, Guam, Mariana Islands.

3500. James Marty[9] **Bovee** (James Francis[8], Marvin W[7], Benedict Arnold[6], Mathias Jacob[5], Jacob Mathias[4], Matthew[3], Nicholas[2], Mathieu[1]), born in Eagle, Waukesha Co.,WI. He married on 22 Aug 1953 Marlene Jahnke, born 11 Mar 1933; died 11 Sep 1982.

Children of James Marty Bovee and Marlene Jahnke were as follows:

4396	i	Scott Arthur[10] **Bovee**.
4397	ii	Steven James[10] **Bovee**.

3501. Wallace M[9] **Bovee** (William David[8], Manley W[7], William Reid[6], Mathias Jacob[5], Jacob Mathias[4], Matthew[3], Nicholas[2], Mathieu[1]), born 21 Oct 1897; died 8 Sep 1961 in Jamestown, Chautauqua Vo., NY. He married abt 1917 Dorothy M Fink, born 12 Aug 1897; died Jul 1970 in Jamestown, Chautauqua Vo., NY.

Children of Wallace M Bovee and Dorothy M Fink were as follows:

4398	i	George[10] **William**, born 1 Mar 1935; died 1 Mar 1935.
4399	ii	Mary Ellen[10] **Bovee**, born 30 Jul 1938; died 1 Aug 1938.

3502. Harold Ezra[9] **Bovee** (William David[8], Manley W[7], William Reid[6], Mathias Jacob[5], Jacob Mathias[4], Matthew[3], Nicholas[2], Mathieu[1]), born 2 Jul 1900 in PA. He married on 23 May 1923 Ruth Madge Powell, born 28 Jun 1900; died Feb 1985 in Greenville, Mercer Co., PA.

Children of Harold Ezra Bovee and Ruth Madge Powell were as follows:

4400	i	Dorothy Madge[10] **Bovee**, born 24 Nov 1924; died 20 Jan 1947. She married on 21 Jan 1941 **Earl Stallar**.
4401	ii	Joyce Ann[10] **Bovee**, born 23 Jul 1926; died 14 Oct 1930.

4402 iii Marjorie[10] **Bovee**.

3503. Rhea B[9] **Bovee** (William David[8], Manley W[7], William Reid[6], Mathias Jacob[5], Jacob Mathias[4], Matthew[3], Nicholas[2], Mathieu[1]), born 24 Feb 1908 in Grand Valley, Warren Co., PA. She married on 3 Jul 1931 Percy James Lanning.

Children of Rhea B Bovee and Percy James Lanning were as follows:
4403 i Mary Sue[10] **Lanning**.

3506. Virginia Ora[9] **Bovee** (Marvin Burleigh[8], Herbert Stephen[7], Edward Livingston[6], Mathias Jacob[5], Jacob Mathias[4], Matthew[3], Nicholas[2], Mathieu[1]). She married in 1947 Donald Emmet Carlson.

Children of Virginia Ora Bovee and Donald Emmet Carlson were as follows:
4404 i Peggy[10] **Carlson**, born in Hennepin Co., MN.
4405 ii Pamela[10] **Carlson**, born in Hennepin Co., MN.

3508. Mark Bedard[9] **Bovee** (Marvin Burleigh[8], Herbert Stephen[7], Edward Livingston[6], Mathias Jacob[5], Jacob Mathias[4], Matthew[3], Nicholas[2], Mathieu[1]), born in Superior, Douglas Co., WI. He married Janice Holisky, born in Two Harbors, Lake Co., MN.

Children of Mark Bedard Bovee and Janice Holisky were as follows:
4406 i Steven Mark[10] **Bovee**.
4407 ii Barbara Jo[10] **Bovee**, born in Salem, Marion Co., OR. She married **Mark Gossack**.
+ 4408 iii Michael Bren[10] **Bovee**, born in Salem, Marion Co., OR. He married **Trudy (---)**.

3520. Lawrence[9] **Bovee** (Elmer C[8], Charles Eugene[7], Lemuel Jacob[6], Philip Vedder[5], Jacob Mathias[4], Matthew[3], Nicholas[2], Mathieu[1]). He married unknown.

Children of Lawrence Bovee were as follows:
4409 i Deborah[10] **Bovee**.

3521. Leslie Charles[9] **Bovee** (Elmer C[8], Charles Eugene[7], Lemuel Jacob[6], Philip Vedder[5], Jacob Mathias[4], Matthew[3], Nicholas[2], Mathieu[1]). He married unknown.

Children of Leslie Charles Bovee were as follows:
4410 i Joseph William[10] **Bovee**.
4411 ii Angelia Lynn[10] **Bovee**.

3524. Mary Louise[9] **Bovee** (Eugene Philip[8], Philip LaRue[7], Eugene Charles[6], Philip Vedder[5], Jacob Mathias[4], Matthew[3], Nicholas[2], Mathieu[1]). She married Bruce E Hanson, born 21 Apr 1929.

Children of Mary Louise Bovee and Bruce E Hanson were as follows:

4412	i	Paul Kevin[10] **Hanson**.
4413	ii	Christine Ann[10] **Hanson**.
4414	iii	Brian Timothy[10] **Hanson**.
4415	iv	Philip[10] **Hanson**.

3527. John Ronald[9] **Bovee** (John Larue[8], Philip LaRue[7], Eugene Charles[6], Philip Vedder[5], Jacob Mathias[4], Matthew[3], Nicholas[2], Mathieu[1]), born in CO. He married on 9 May 1954 in Denver, Denver Co., CO Judith Lou Russell, born in Atchison, Atchison Co., KS, daughter of Loren Lee Russell and Gertrude Marie Estes.

Children of John Ronald Bovee and Judith Lou Russell were as follows:

4416	i	Robin LaRue[10] **Bovee**, born in Denver, Denver Co., CO.
4417	ii	Douglas Russell[10] **Bovee**, born in Denver, Denver Co., CO.

3528. Lena[9] **Bovee** (Frederick Charles[8], Frederick Charles[7], William Henry[6], John Grant[5], John[4], Matthew[3], Nicholas[2], Mathieu[1]), born 13 Jan 1910; died Oct 1987 in Carthage, Jefferson Co., NY. She married on 13 Oct 1930 in Watertown, Jefferson Co., NY Myron Oliver.

Children of Lena Bovee and Myron Oliver were as follows:

4418	i	Janet[10] **Oliver**.
4419	ii	Joan[10] **Oliver**.
4420	iii	Charles[10] **Oliver**.
4421	iv	Roger[10] **Oliver**.

3530. Richard[9] **Bovee** (Frederick Charles[8], Frederick Charles[7], William Henry[6], John Grant[5], John[4], Matthew[3], Nicholas[2], Mathieu[1]), born 1 May 1915 in Dexter, Jefferson Co., NY. He married Ruth White.

Children of Richard Bovee and Ruth White were as follows:

+	4422	i	Rev Martin W[10] **Bovee**. He married unknown.
	4423	ii	Melissa[10] **Bovee**. She married (---) **Drake**.
+	4424	iii	Mathew[10] **Bovee**. He married **Lois (---)**.
	4425	iv	Molly[10] **Bovee**. She married (---) **Stacy**.

3531. Eva^9 **Bovee** (Frederick Charles^8, Frederick Charles^7, William Henry^6, John Grant^5, John^4, Matthew^3, Nicholas^2, Mathieu^1), born 4 Sep 1916 in Canada; died 23 May 1997 in Contra Costa Co., CA. She married James F McMillan.

Children of Eva Bovee and James F McMillan were as follows:

4426	i	Richard^{10} **McMillan**.
4427	ii	Robert^{10} **McMillan**.
4428	iii	Ronald^{10} **McMillan**.

3534. Glenn S^9 **Bovee** (Edward J^8, Frederick Charles^7, William Henry^6, John Grant^5, John^4, Matthew^3, Nicholas^2, Mathieu^1), born 1919; died 18 Mar 1996. He married abt 1938 Totsuyu Tumatu.

Children of Glenn S Bovee and Totsuyu Tumatu were as follows:

| 4429 | i | John^{10} **Bovee**. |
| 4430 | ii | Linda^{10} **Bovee**. |

3546. Larry A^9 **Bovee** (Ralph Perl^8, Frederick Charles^7, William Henry^6, John Grant^5, John^4, Matthew^3, Nicholas^2, Mathieu^1), born in Watertown, Jefferson Co., NY. He married on 13 Nov 1964 in Watertown, Jefferson Co., NY Constance M Mallow, born in Watertown, Jefferson Co., NY, daughter of Edward P Mallow and Arlene Johnson.

Children of Larry A Bovee and Constance M Mallow were as follows:

| 4431 | i | Scott A^{10} **Bovee**. He married **Mary Cholla**. |
| 4432 | ii | Jeffrey L^{10} **Bovee**. |

3548. James W^9 **Bovee** (Ralph Perl^8, Frederick Charles^7, William Henry^6, John Grant^5, John^4, Matthew^3, Nicholas^2, Mathieu^1), born 30 Jun 1948; died 8 Nov 1989. He married Frances (---).

Children of James W Bovee and Frances (---) were as follows:

| 4433 | i | Stephanie^{10} **Bovee**. |
| 4434 | ii | Elizabeth^{10} **Bovee**. |

3554. Mary Elizabeth^9 **Bovee** (Harold L^8, Hiram David^7, William Henry^6, John Grant^5, John^4, Matthew^3, Nicholas^2, Mathieu^1). She married on 9 Jan 1960 in Clayton Jefferson Co., NY William H Dasno.

Children of Mary Elizabeth Bovee and William H Dasno were as follows:

| 4435 | i | Sandra Rae^{10} **Dasno**. |
| 4436 | ii | Susan K^{10} **Dasno**, born in Watertown, Jefferson Co., NY. |

3555. Marilyn Mae[9] **Bovee** (Harold L[8], Hiram David[7], William Henry[6], John Grant[5], John[4], Matthew[3], Nicholas[2], Mathieu[1]), born in Watertown, Jefferson Co., NY. She married on 19 Jun 1965 in Clayton Jefferson Co., NY Robert Edward Dailey, son of Donald Dailey and Frieda Quencer.

Children of Marilyn Mae Bovee and Robert Edward Dailey were as follows:

4437   i   Vincent Edward[10] **Dailey**, born in Batavia, Genesee Co., NY.

4438   ii   Donald Harold[10] **Dailey**, born in Batavia, Genesee Co., NY.

3556. Nancy Ann[9] **Bovee** (Harold L[8], Hiram David[7], William Henry[6], John Grant[5], John[4], Matthew[3], Nicholas[2], Mathieu[1]), born in Jefferson Co., NY. She married on 15 May 1965 in Clayton Jefferson Co., NY Donald W Rhodes.

Children of Nancy Ann Bovee and Donald W Rhodes were as follows:

4439   i   Christian[10] **Rhodes**.

3563. Edward Ellsworth[9] **Bovee** (Edward Milton[8], Franklin E[7], John Wesley[6], John Grant[5], John[4], Matthew[3], Nicholas[2], Mathieu[1]), born 22 Dec 1915; died Jan 1984. He married (1) Hazel Zeaman; (2) Helen Boucher.

Children of Edward Ellsworth Bovee and Hazel Zeaman were as follows:

+   4440   i   Edward[10] **Bovee**. He married **Carolyn Smith**.
+   4441   ii   Richard H[10] **Bovee**, born 12 Oct 1944; died 25 Feb 1993. He married **Nancy Plumley**.

Children of Edward Ellsworth Bovee and Helen Boucher were as follows:

4442   i   John Edward[10] **Bovee**, born 13 Oct 1962; died 22 Dec 1979.

4443   ii   Helen Jeanne[10] **Bovee**. She married on 12 Oct 1991 **John Tate**.

3564. Pauline Elizabeth[9] **Bovee** (Edward Milton[8], Franklin E[7], John Wesley[6], John Grant[5], John[4], Matthew[3], Nicholas[2], Mathieu[1]), born 8 Sep 1916 in Camden, Oneida Co., NY. She married on 29 Nov 1936 in Camden, Oneida Co., NY Clyde Frederick Relyea, born 9 Mar 1907 in Canastota, Madison Co., NY; died 15 May 1980 in Oneida, Madison Co., NY.

Children of Pauline Elizabeth Bovee and Clyde Frederick Relyea were as follows:

4444   i   Clyde Edward[10] **Relyea**, born in Camden, Oneida Co., NY. He married on 6 Jun 1960 **Nancy Lee Easter**.

4445   ii   Harold Clarence[10] **Relyea**, born in Camden, Oneida Co., NY. He married **Ruth Rhinesmith**.

3566. Anna Margaret[9] **Bovee** (Edward Milton[8], Franklin E[7], John Wesley[6], John Grant[5], John[4], Matthew[3], Nicholas[2], Mathieu[1]), born 31 Jan 1921 in Camden, Oneida Co., NY. She married (1) on 15 Mar 1941 Victor Seabrook; (2) Lawrence Desmond; (3) Donald Brosius.

Children of Anna Margaret Bovee and Victor Seabrook were as follows:

4446   i   Karen Ann[10] **Seabrook**.

Children of Anna Margaret Bovee and Lawrence Desmond were as follows:

4447   i   Lauranne[10] **Desmond**.

3567. Harold Lloyd[9] **Bovee** (Edward Milton[8], Franklin E[7], John Wesley[6], John Grant[5], John[4], Matthew[3], Nicholas[2], Mathieu[1]), born 11 Jun 1922 in NY; died 19 Jun 1999. He married on 1 Nov 1947 Lucile Grace Paddock, born 9 Nov 1924, daughter of Ross E Paddock and Mary Deeley.

Children of Harold Lloyd Bovee and Lucile Grace Paddock were as follows:

+   4448   i   Paul Ross[10] **Bovee**. He married **Chislaine LeBain**.
+   4449   ii   Mark Russell[10] **Bovee**. He married **Lisa Murphy**.
+   4450   iii   James Edward[10] **Bovee**. He married **Joanne Wilkinson**.

3568. Ruth Eva[9] **Bovee** (Edward Milton[8], Franklin E[7], John Wesley[6], John Grant[5], John[4], Matthew[3], Nicholas[2], Mathieu[1]), born 16 Jun 1923 in Camden, Oneida Co., NY; died 26 Dec 2002 in Syracuse, Onondaga Co., NY. She married on 1 Nov 1947 in Camden, NY Charles Kirch, born 11 Jun 1922.

Children of Ruth Eva Bovee and Charles Kirch were as follows:

4451   i   Ruth Lucille[10] **Kirch**.
4452   ii   Christine Anne[10] **Kirch**.
4453   iii   Karen A[10] **Kirch**.
4454   iv   Karol B[10] **Kirch**.
4455   v   Grace Harriet[10] **Kirch**.

3570. Cecil Dale[9] **Bovee** (Cecil W[8], Woodbury H[7], Hiram[6], John Henry[5], John Henry[4], Matthew[3], Nicholas[2], Mathieu[1]), born abt 1927. He married Margaret Hall, born abt 1927.

Children of Cecil Dale Bovee and Margaret Hall were as follows:

+   4456   i   David Ray[10] **Bovee**. He married unknown.
+   4457   ii   Thomas Dale[10] **Bovee**. He married **Debra Flowers**.
+   4458   iii   James Dean[10] **Bovee**. He married unknown.

3572. Charlotte Jean[9] **Bovee** (Glen Howard[8], Woodbury H[7], Hiram[6], John Henry[5], John Henry[4], Matthew[3], Nicholas[2], Mathieu[1]), born Nov 1925. She married on 20 Mar 1948 Robert R Rutila.

Children of Charlotte Jean Bovee and Robert R Rutila were as follows:

4459	i	Sherrilyn[10] **Rutila**.
4460	ii	Lori Ann[10] **Rutila**.
4461	iii	Kimberly[10] **Rutila**.
4462	iv	Janet[10] **Rutila**.

3573. Hiram C (Harry)[9] **Bovee** Jr (Hiram C (Harry)[8], Woodbury H[7], Hiram[6], John Henry[5], John Henry[4], Matthew[3], Nicholas[2], Mathieu[1]), born 1924; died 1997. He married Lois M Stone, born 1926.

Children of Hiram C (Harry) Bovee Jr and Lois M Stone were as follows:

	4463	i	Cheryl Jane[10] **Bovee**.
+	4464	ii	Gregory Lee[10] **Bovee**. He married (1) **Kathleen Evitis**; (2) **Paula F Tropp**.
	4465	iii	Pamela Sue[10] **Bovee**, born 22 Nov 1951; died 22 Nov 1951.
+	4466	iv	Michael Dee[10] **Bovee**. He married **Teresa (---)**.
+	4467	v	Daniel Joe[10] **Bovee**. He married **Deborah (---)**.

3575. Richard Lee[9] **Bovee** (Hiram C (Harry)[8], Woodbury H[7], Hiram[6], John Henry[5], John Henry[4], Matthew[3], Nicholas[2], Mathieu[1]), born aft 1924. He married unknown.

Children of Richard Lee Bovee were as follows:

4468	i	Terry Lee[10] **Bovee**.
4469	ii	Debbie Ann[10] **Bovee**.
4470	iii	Christopher Robin[10] **Bovee**.
4471	iv	Jane Ellen[10] **Bovee**.

3578. Roger Lee[9] **Bovee** (Hiram C (Harry)[8], Woodbury H[7], Hiram[6], John Henry[5], John Henry[4], Matthew[3], Nicholas[2], Mathieu[1]). He married Sharon (---).

Children of Roger Lee Bovee and Sharon (---) were as follows:

4472	i	Stephen R[10] **Bovee**.
4473	ii	Lori Lou[10] **Bovee**.
4474	iii	Shari[10] **Bovee**.

3579. Howard Edward[9] **Bovee** (Archie Edward[8], Edward Hill[7], Andrew J[6],

Mathew[5], John Henry[4], Matthew[3], Nicholas[2], Mathieu[1]), born 13 Dec 1924. He married Elizabeth Jane McBride.

Children of Howard Edward Bovee and Elizabeth Jane McBride were as follows:

4475	i	James Howard[10] **Bovee**.
+ 4476	ii	John R[10] **Bovee**. He married unknown.
4477	iii	Rosemary[10] **Bovee**. She married **(---) Kent**.
4478	iv	Linda Joan[10] **Bovee**.

3581. Raymond Arthur[9] **Bovee** Jr (Raymond Arthur[8], Edward Hill[7], Andrew J[6], Mathew[5], John Henry[4], Matthew[3], Nicholas[2], Mathieu[1]), born in Girard, Erie Co., PA. He married on 1 Nov 1952 in Conneaut, Ashtabula Co., OH Doris May English, born in Conneaut, Ashtabula Co., OH.

Children of Raymond Arthur Bovee Jr and Doris May English were as follows:

4479	i	Mathew Raymond[10] **Bovee**.
4480	ii	Daniel Joseph[10] **Bovee**.
4481	iii	Deborah Kay[10] **Bovee**.
4482	iv	James[10] **Bovee**.
+ 4483	v	Sandra Lynn[10] **Bovee**, born in Conneaut, Ashtabula Co., OH. She married **Theron Milo Huntley**.
4484	vi	Theresa Marie[10] **Bovee**.

3592. Roy L[9] **Bovee** (Harland[8], Calvin O[7], Grosvenor D[6], Mathew[5], John Henry[4], Matthew[3], Nicholas[2], Mathieu[1]). He married Doris M (---).

Children of Roy L Bovee and Doris M (---) were as follows:

4485	i	Douglas L[10] **Bovee**.
4486	ii	Gregory Scott[10] **Bovee**.
4487	iii	Michael R[10] **Bovee**.
4488	iv	Laura M[10] **Bovee**.

3598. Noreen Loveless[9] **Bovee** (Marion Elijah[8], Marion Lysander[7], Elijah[6], Jacob[5], John Henry[4], Matthew[3], Nicholas[2], Mathieu[1]), born 8 Apr 1923. She married in 1951 Wesley Zebley.

Children of Noreen Loveless Bovee and Wesley Zebley were as follows:

4489	i	Stephen[10] **Zebley**.

3615. Marshall Gaylord[9] **Bovee** (Marshall Claude[8], Herbert Warren[7], Milo[6], Jacob[5], John Henry[4], Matthew[3], Nicholas[2], Mathieu[1]), born 1928 in Monroe Co.,

MI. He married Carmen (---).

Children of Marshall Gaylord Bovee and Carmen (---) were as follows:
4490   i   Barbara[10] **Bovee**.
4491   ii   Janet[10] **Bovee**.
4492   iii   Marshall[10] **Bovee**.
4493   iv   Mitchael[10] **Bovee**.

3616. Janice Laurene[9] **Bovee** (Marshall Claude[8], Herbert Warren[7], Milo[6], Jacob[5], John Henry[4], Matthew[3], Nicholas[2], Mathieu[1]), born 22 Aug 1930 in Petersburg, Monroe Co., MI; died 14 Dec 2001 in Manitou Beach, Lenawee Co., MI. She married on 3 May 1947 in Angola, Steuben Co., IN Caroll (John) Hassenzahl, died 22 Mar 1977.

Children of Janice Laurene Bovee and Caroll (John) Hassenzahl were as follows:
4494   i   Carroll Jeff[10] **Hassenzahl**.
4495   ii   Doug[10] **Hassenzahl**.
4496   iii   Jack[10] **Hassenzahl**.
4497   iv   Dean[10] **Hassenzahl**.
4498   v   Joel[10] **Hassenzahl**.
4499   vi   Jennifer[10] **Hassenzahl**.

3620. Seton Chapelle[9] **Bovee** Jr (Seton Chapelle[8], Cornelius Anson[7], Milo[6], Jacob[5], John Henry[4], Matthew[3], Nicholas[2], Mathieu[1]). He married abt 1956 Barbara L (---).

Children of Seton Chapelle Bovee Jr and Barbara L (---) were as follows:
4500   i   Mark S[10] **Bovee**. He married **Karen (---)**.
4501   ii   Sarah[10] **Bovee**.
4502   iii   Rev Matthew D[10] **Bovee**.
4503   iv   William[10] **Bovee**.
4504   v   Susan[10] **Bovee**.

3622. Barbara Jane[9] **Bovee** (David Victor[8], Earl Eugene[7], Myron[6], Jacob[5], John Henry[4], Matthew[3], Nicholas[2], Mathieu[1]). She married on 29 Dec 1963 in Needham, Suffolk Co., MA, divorced Leon Polk, born in Lansing, Ingham Co., MI.

Children of Barbara Jane Bovee and Leon Polk were as follows:
4505   i   Kevin Scott[10] **Polk**, born in Ann Arbor, Washtenaw Co., MI.

3626. Gregory Joe[9] **Bovee** (Eugene Cleveland[8], Earl Eugene[7], Myron[6], Jacob[5], John Henry[4], Matthew[3], Nicholas[2], Mathieu[1]), born in Cedar Falls, Black Hawk Co., IA. He married (1) on 12 Sep 1972 in Lawrence, Douglas Co., KS, divorced Carolyn Scrogum; (2) on 14 Jun 1984, divorced Martha Lois Haegler, born in Tonganoxie, Leavenworth Co., KS.

Children of Gregory Joe Bovee and Carolyn Scrogum were as follows:

    4506   i   Alexander Eugene[10] **Bovee**, born in Lawrence, Douglas Co., KS.

3627. Matthew Wamsley[9] **Bovee** (Eugene Cleveland[8], Earl Eugene[7], Myron[6], Jacob[5], John Henry[4], Matthew[3], Nicholas[2], Mathieu[1]), born in Gainesville, Alachua Co., FL. He married (1) on 1 Aug 1981 in Portland, Cumberland Co., ME, divorced Kellie Ann White; (2) on 2 Aug 1991 in Grand Canyon, Conconino Co., AZ Alison Ibbotson, born in Farnborough, England.

Children of Matthew Wamsley Bovee and Alison Ibbotson were as follows:

    4507   i   Nicholas Joseph[10] **Bovee**, born in Farnborough, England.
    4508   ii   Jacob Rannoch[10] **Bovee**, born in Farnborough, England.
    4509   iii   Hannah June[10] **Bovee**, born in Overland Park, Johnson Co., KS.

3630. Barbara Eleanor[9] **Bovee** (Leo Myron[8], Orlin Henry[7], Myron[6], Jacob[5], John Henry[4], Matthew[3], Nicholas[2], Mathieu[1]), born 22 Mar 1926. She married on 11 Jul 1948 Charles West.

Children of Barbara Eleanor Bovee and Charles West were as follows:

    4510   i   Kathy Ann[10] **West**.
    4511   ii   Patricia Sue[10] **West**.
    4512   iii   Linda Diane[10] **West**.

3631. Dessie Louise[9] **Bovee** (Murlin Orlin[8], Orlin Henry[7], Myron[6], Jacob[5], John Henry[4], Matthew[3], Nicholas[2], Mathieu[1]), born 29 Sep 1925. She married on 11 Oct 1945 William Robert Shireman, born 3 Aug 1921.

Children of Dessie Louise Bovee and William Robert Shireman were as follows:

    4513   i   Nancy Kay[10] **Shireman**.
    4514   ii   Susan Jean[10] **Shireman**.

3632. Murl Gene[9] **Bovee** (Murlin Orlin[8], Orlin Henry[7], Myron[6], Jacob[5], John Henry[4], Matthew[3], Nicholas[2], Mathieu[1]), born 12 Feb 1927. He married on 4 Jun 1950 Wilma Irene Farthing, born 23 Oct 1929.

Children of Murl Gene Bovee and Wilma Irene Farthing were as follows:

+ 4515   i   Randall Jay^{10} **Bovee**. He married **Betty Jean Taylor**.
+ 4516   ii   Jeffrey Gene^{10} **Bovee**. He married **Pamela Alice Makres**.
+ 4517   iii   Mickey Orlin^{10} **Bovee**. He married **Barbara Elizabeth Krieger**.
   4518   iv   Karen Louise^{10} **Bovee**, born 24 Jan 1958; died 23 Nov 1976.
   4519   v   Annette Marie^{10} **Bovee**.

3633. Parley Eldon^9 **Bovee** (Murlin Orlin^8, Orlin Henry^7, Myron^6, Jacob^5, John Henry^4, Matthew^3, Nicholas^2, Mathieu^1), born 23 Oct 1929. He married on 23 Oct 1954 Jacquelyn Leibecker.

Children of Parley Eldon Bovee and Jacquelyn Leibecker were as follows:

   4520   i   Michael Lynn^{10} **Bovee**.
   4521   ii   Patrick Allen^{10} **Bovee**.

3640. Arthur David^9 **Bovee** (Arthur Jewett^8, Arthur Jewett^7, Myron^6, Jacob^5, John Henry^4, Matthew^3, Nicholas^2, Mathieu^1). He married in 1956 Barbara Louise Miller.

Children of Arthur David Bovee and Barbara Louise Miller were as follows:

   4522   i   Dana Louise^{10} **Bovee**.
   4523   ii   Lynne Elizabeth^{10} **Bovee**.

3647. Miron Lewis^9 **Bovee** (Ardee Lewis^8, Harlow^7, Myron^6, Jacob^5, John Henry^4, Matthew^3, Nicholas^2, Mathieu^1), born 3 Jun 1926; died 28 Oct 1988 in Sarasota, Sarasota Co., FL. He married on 15 Jul 1950 Jean DeClercy, born 28 Oct 1928.

Children of Miron Lewis Bovee and Jean DeClercy were as follows:

   4524   i   Thomas Michael^{10} **Bovee**.

3661. Edna Mae^9 **Bovee** (Olan Ford^8, Harlow^7, Myron^6, Jacob^5, John Henry^4, Matthew^3, Nicholas^2, Mathieu^1). She married Lonnie Prososki.

Children of Edna Mae Bovee and Lonnie Prososki were as follows:

   4525   i   Diana^{10} **Prososki**, born 20 Feb 1957; died 3 Dec 1977.

3662. Billie Jean^9 **Bovee** (Olan Ford^8, Harlow^7, Myron^6, Jacob^5, John Henry^4, Matthew^3, Nicholas^2, Mathieu^1). She married on 20 Jun 1957 Norval Wiseman.

Children of Billie Jean Bovee and Norval Wiseman were as follows:

4526	i	Rosemary J[10] **Wiseman**.
4527	ii	Infant[10] **Wiseman**, born 10 Jan 1959; died 10 Jan 1959.
4528	iii	Mark Edward[10] **Wiseman**, born 7 Feb 1960; died bef 1987.

3682. Diana Sue[9] **Bovee** (Edmond James[8], Fred Mayfield[7], Devillow[6], Jacob[5], John Henry[4], Matthew[3], Nicholas[2], Mathieu[1]). She married (1) on 14 Aug 1971 in San Luis Obispo, San Luis Obispo Co., CA Daniel Lee McCrory; (2) on 21 Aug 1982 in Atascodero, San Luis Obispo Co., CA Edward Francis Lakjer.

Children of Diana Sue Bovee and Daniel Lee McCrory were as follows:

| 4529 | i | Ryan Patrick[10] **McCrory**. |
| 4530 | ii | Andrew James[10] **McCrory**. |

Children of Diana Sue Bovee and Edward Francis Lakjer were as follows:

| 4531 | i | Kristan Elizabeth[10] **Lakjer**. |

3683. Rodney James[9] **Bovee** (Edmond James[8], Fred Mayfield[7], Devillow[6], Jacob[5], John Henry[4], Matthew[3], Nicholas[2], Mathieu[1]), born in San Luis Obispo, San Luis Obispo Co., CA. He married on 4 Sep 1976 Kelly Ann Dennis.

Children of Rodney James Bovee and Kelly Ann Dennis were as follows:

4532	i	Jennifer Ann[10] **Bovee**.
4533	ii	Natalie Maureen[10] **Bovee**.
4534	iii	Conner Mathew[10] **Bovee**, born in Stockton, San Joaquin Co., CA.

3684. James Eugene[9] **Bovee** (Russell E[8], James Byron[7], James H[6], Peter[5], John Henry[4], Matthew[3], Nicholas[2], Mathieu[1]). He married unknown.

Children of James Eugene Bovee were as follows:

4535	i	Bradley[10] **Bovee**.
4536	ii	Matt[10] **Bovee**.
4537	iii	Terry[10] **Bovee**.

3686. Beverly[9] **Bovee** (Harold[8], James Byron[7], James H[6], Peter[5], John Henry[4], Matthew[3], Nicholas[2], Mathieu[1]). She married on 22 Nov 1958 Blaine Alan Gilliland.

Children of Beverly Bovee and Blaine Alan Gilliland were as follows:

| 4538 | i | Brent Alan[10] **Gilliland**, born in LaGrange, LaGrange Co., IN. |
| 4539 | ii | Brian Arnold[10] **Gilliland**. |

4540	iii	Brenda Allene[10] **Gilliland**, died in LaGrange, LaGrange Co., IN.
4541	iv	Bradley Aaron[10] **Gilliland**, born in LaGrange, LaGrange Co., IN.
4542	v	Barbara Anne[10] **Gilliland**, born in LaGrange, LaGrange Co., IN.

3687. Nancy Jane[9] **Bovee** (Harold[8], James Byron[7], James H[6], Peter[5], John Henry[4], Matthew[3], Nicholas[2], Mathieu[1]), born in Kendallville, Noble Co., IN. She married on 23 May 1959 Ned H Stump.

Children of Nancy Jane Bovee and Ned H Stump were as follows:

4543	i	Crystal Amber[10] **Stump**.
4544	ii	Rebecca Sue[10] **Stump**.
4545	iii	Nathan Aaron[10] **Stump**.
4546	iv	Scott Alan[10] **Stump**.
4547	v	Kurt Irvin[10] **Stump**.

3688. Harold[9] **Bovee** (Harold[8], James Byron[7], James H[6], Peter[5], John Henry[4], Matthew[3], Nicholas[2], Mathieu[1]), born in Kendallville, Noble Co., IN. He married on 22 Nov 1962 Linda Dorsett, daughter of Louis Dorsett and Gladys Hendricks.

Children of Harold Bovee and Linda Dorsett were as follows:

4548	i	Michael[10] **Bovee**.
4549	ii	Jeffrey[10] **Bovee**.
4550	iii	Jonathan[10] **Bovee**.
4551	iv	Miranda[10] **Bovee**.

3706. Meredith Roger Leon[9] **Bovee** (Chester Emerson[8], Samuel Ball[7], George Burton[6], Peter[5], Matthew[4], Abraham[3], Nicholas[2], Mathieu[1]), born 20 Jul 1923 in Sullivan, Madison Co., NY; died 27 Dec 2001 in Fort Worth Tarrant Co., TX. He married (1) Lillian May Rolfe, born 18 Jul 1923 in Halifax, Nova Scotia, daughter of Ralph Rolfe and Gladys Allison; (2) on 25 Nov 1961 Carol Lynne Crowell, born in Brooklyn, Kings Co., NY, daughter of Thomas Crowell and Helen Walsh; (3) Nancy Joan Davis, born 23 Dec 1929 in Olney, Young Co., TX, daughter of Willia Davis and Mattie Bond.

Children of Meredith Roger Leon Bovee and Lillian May Rolfe were as follows:

4552	i	Meredeth Leon Roger[10] **Bovee**, born 1 Feb 1942 in New London, New London Co., CT; died 10 Apr 1988 in New London, New London Co., CT.

Children of Meredith Roger Leon Bovee and Carol Lynne Crowell were as follows:

4553	i	Lisa Marie [10] **Bovee**, born in Rockville Center, Nassau Co., NY. She married on 4 Oct 1999 **Christopher William Manville**, son of William Manville and Judith Columbia.
4554	ii	Denise Catherine [10] **Bovee**, born in New London, New London Co., CT. She married (1) **Kevin Bingle**; (2) **Steven Lazier**.
+ 4555	iii	Kurt Steven [10] **Bovee**, born in New London, New London Co., CT. He married **Caroline Godin**.

Children of Meredith Roger Leon Bovee and Nancy Joan Davis were as follows:

| + 4556 | i | Patrick Emerson Bovea [10] **Bovee**, born in Fort Worth Tarrant Co., TX. He married **Machelle (---)**. |

3719. Deborah J[9] Bovee (Robert Owen[8], Lemon Peter[7], Perry Henry[6], Peter[5], Matthew[4], Abraham[3], Nicholas[2], Mathieu[1]). She married Leo Damaska.

Children of Deborah J Bovee and Leo Damaska were as follows:

4557	i	Garth [10] **Damaska**.
4558	ii	James [10] **Damaska**.
4559	iii	Susan [10] **Damaska**.
4560	iv	Paula [10] **Damaska**.

3720. Roberta O[9] Bovee (Robert Owen[8], Lemon Peter[7], Perry Henry[6], Peter[5], Matthew[4], Abraham[3], Nicholas[2], Mathieu[1]). She married William Webster.

Children of Roberta O Bovee and William Webster were as follows:

| 4561 | i | William Robert [10] **Webster**. |
| 4562 | ii | Michelle Ann [10] **Webster**. |

3721. Gail L[9] Bovee (Robert Owen[8], Lemon Peter[7], Perry Henry[6], Peter[5], Matthew[4], Abraham[3], Nicholas[2], Mathieu[1]). She married abt 1957 Paul Sober.

Children of Gail L Bovee and Paul Sober were as follows:

| 4563 | i | Janet G [10] **Sober**. |
| 4564 | ii | Sharon E [10] **Sober**. |

3722. Jenne Ann[9] Bovee (Robert Russell[8], LeRoy George[7], Walter Haywood[6], Peter[5], Matthew[4], Abraham[3], Nicholas[2], Mathieu[1]). She married Gerald Stephen Collins.

Children of Jenne Ann Bovee and Gerald Stephen Collins were as follows:

| 4565 | i | Sonja Nichole [10] **Collins**. |

4566   ii   Anna Jenee[10] **Collins**.

3751. Glenn S[9] **Bovee** (Laverne[8], Frederick[7], John W[6], Cornelius[5], Abraham[4], Abraham[3], Nicholas[2], Mathieu[1]), born 10 Feb 1924 in Groveland, Livingston Co., NY. He married Lena Mustrella.

   Children of Glenn S Bovee and Lena Mustrella were as follows:

   4567   i   John[10] **Bovee**.
+ 4568   ii   Michael[10] **Bovee**. He married **Mona Wolfanger**.

3752. Robert J[9] **Bovee** (Laverne[8], Frederick[7], John W[6], Cornelius[5], Abraham[4], Abraham[3], Nicholas[2], Mathieu[1]), born abt 1930 in Groveland, Livingston Co., NY. He married Jean Hellier.

   Children of Robert J Bovee and Jean Hellier were as follows:

   4569   i   James[10] **Bovee**, born 30 Nov 1950; died 9 Oct 1957.
+ 4570   ii   Elizabeth[10] **Bovee**. She married **John Goho**.
+ 4571   iii   Robert J[10] **Bovee** Jr. He married **Christine Fournier**.

3753. Harold E[9] **Bovee** (Laverne[8], Frederick[7], John W[6], Cornelius[5], Abraham[4], Abraham[3], Nicholas[2], Mathieu[1]), born aft 1930 in Groveland, Livingston Co., NY. He married Thelma Appeline.

   Children of Harold E Bovee and Thelma Appeline were as follows:

+ 4572   i   Terry Edward[10] **Bovee**. He married **Penny Craft**.
+ 4573   ii   Gerald K[10] **Bovee**. He married **Hope (---)**.
+ 4574   iii   Dan[10] **Bovee**. He married unknown.

3754. Shirley Hugh[9] **Bovee** (Laverne[8], Frederick[7], John W[6], Cornelius[5], Abraham[4], Abraham[3], Nicholas[2], Mathieu[1]), born 27 May 1932 in Groveland, Livingston Co., NY; died 23 Aug 1955 in Groveland, Livingston Co., NY. He married Lillian M Gilbert, born 7 Feb 1929 in Dansville, Livingston Co., NY, daughter of Abner E Gilbert and Helen T Lang.

   Children of Shirley Hugh Bovee and Lillian M Gilbert were as follows:

+ 4575   i   Shirley Hugh[10] **Bovee**. She married **Richard C Seager**.

3757. Margaret[9] **Bovee** (Edward[8], Frederick[7], John W[6], Cornelius[5], Abraham[4], Abraham[3], Nicholas[2], Mathieu[1]), born 1918 in Groveland, Livingston Co., NY. She married (---) Bus.

   Children of Margaret Bovee and (---) Bus were as follows:

   4576   i   Roger[10] **Bus**.

4577 ii Edward[10] **Bus.**

3759. Laura[9] **Bovee** (Edward[8], Frederick[7], John W[6], Cornelius[5], Abraham[4], Abraham[3], Nicholas[2], Mathieu[1]). She married Frank Schirmer.

Children of Laura Bovee and Frank Schirmer were as follows:

4578 i Donald[10] **Schirmer.**
4579 ii Lawrence[10] **Schirmer.**
4580 iii Christine[10] **Schirmer.**

3772. Sherry May[9] **Bovee** (Earl Erwin[8], Earl Erwin[7], Henry M[6], Cornelius[5], Abraham[4], Abraham[3], Nicholas[2], Mathieu[1]). She married (1) on 27 May 1966 in Hornell, Steuben Co., NY Robert Matacle; (2) aft 1970 in NY Michael Henry, born in NY, son of (---) Henry and Agnes French.

Children of Sherry May Bovee and Robert Matacle were as follows:

4581 i Mary[10] **Matacle.**
4582 ii Steven[10] **Matacle.**
4583 iii David[10] **Matacle.**

3777. Lyle William[9] **Bovee** (Vernon Harold[8], Arthur Vernon[7], William R[6], Abraham[5], Abraham[4], Abraham[3], Nicholas[2], Mathieu[1]), born 8 Jun 1918 in Farmington Twp., Waupaca Co., WI. He married on 22 Sep 1944 in Greenville, Hunt Co., TX Laverna M Marburger, born 5 May 1920 in Hutchinson, Reno Co., KS.

Children of Lyle William Bovee and Laverna M Marburger were as follows:

4584 i Timothy J[10] **Bovee**, born in Bangor, Penobscot Co., ME.

3778. Florence Cecilia[9] **Bovee** (Vernon Harold[8], Arthur Vernon[7], William R[6], Abraham[5], Abraham[4], Abraham[3], Nicholas[2], Mathieu[1]), born 17 Dec 1919 in Farmington Twp., Waupaca Co., WI. She married on 27 Jun 1936 in Waupaca, Waupaca Co., WI Claude William Byrion Sr, born 21 Feb 1914 in Waupaca, Waupaca Co., WI, son of Joseph Byrion and Mabel Moore.

Children of Florence Cecilia Bovee and Claude William Byrion Sr were as follows:

4585 i Claude William[10] **Byrion.**
4586 ii Lorne[10] **Byrion.**
4587 iii Virgil Lee[10] **Byrion.**
4588 iv Patricia Ann[10] **Byrion.**
4589 v Michael Allen[10] **Byrion.**
4590 vi Kathleen Marie[10] **Byrion.**

4591   vii   Daniel Mark[10] **Byrion**.

4592   viii   Patricia Cecil[10] **Byrion**.

3779. Vivian May[9] **Bovee** (Vernon Harold[8], Arthur Vernon[7], William R[6], Abraham[5], Abraham[4], Abraham[3], Nicholas[2], Mathieu[1]), born 31 Jul 1921 in Farmington Twp., Waupaca Co., WI. She married Vernon Byrion, born 1921 in Waupaca, Waupaca Co., WI.

    Children of Vivian May Bovee and Vernon Byrion were as follows:

4593   i   Joane[10] **Byrion**.

3781. Isabell Agnes[9] **Bovee** (Vernon Harold[8], Arthur Vernon[7], William R[6], Abraham[5], Abraham[4], Abraham[3], Nicholas[2], Mathieu[1]), born 9 May 1929 in Farmington Twp., Waupaca Co., WI. She married in Jun 1946 Lyle Jolin Sr, born 1926 in Oskosh, Winnebago Co., WI.

    Children of Isabell Agnes Bovee and Lyle Jolin Sr were as follows:

4594   i   Lanette Isabel[10] **Jolin**, born in Oshkosh, Winnebago Co., WI.

4595   ii   Diona Mary[10] **Jolin**.

4596   iii   Lyle John[10] **Jolin**.

4597   iv   Roxanne Jane[10] **Jolin**.

4598   v   Gary Richard[10] **Jolin**.

4599   vi   Donald Lee[10] **Jolin**.

4600   vii   Deborah Kay[10] **Jolin**.

4601   viii   Darlene Carol[10] **Jolin**.

4602   ix   Lexene Grace[10] **Jolin**.

4603   x   Jeffrey James[10] **Jolin**.

4604   xi   Sheila Jean[10] **Jolin**.

3782. Augusta Tresa[9] **Bovee** (Vernon Harold[8], Arthur Vernon[7], William R[6], Abraham[5], Abraham[4], Abraham[3], Nicholas[2], Mathieu[1]), born in Farmington Twp., Waupaca Co., WI. She married on 9 Aug 1947 in Oskosh, Winnebago Co., WI Hugh A Stewart, born in Farmington Twp., Waupaca Co., WI.

    Children of Augusta Tresa Bovee and Hugh A Stewart were as follows:

4605   i   Richard Lee[10] **Stewart**.

4606   ii   Susan Marie[10] **Stewart**.

4607   iii   Marshall Allen[10] **Stewart**.

3783. Arthur William[9] **Bovee** (Arthur Vernon[8], Arthur Vernon[7], William R[6], Abraham[5], Abraham[4], Abraham[3], Nicholas[2], Mathieu[1]), died in La Mirada, Los Angeles Co., CA. He married Henrietta Bessie Meyer, born 13 Mar 1902 in

Oskosh, Winnebago Co., WI; died 13 Feb 1973 in Brea, Orange Co., CA.

Children of Arthur William Bovee and Henrietta Bessie Meyer were as follows:

4608 i Jean Delores[10] **Bovee**.

4609 ii Arlette Jane[10] **Bovee**.

4610 iii Arthur Wayne[10] **Bovee**, born in Big Falls, Waupaca Co., WI. He married (1) **Myrtle Bytell**; (2) in 1981 in Ontario, San Bernardino Co., CA **Sharon Weisman**.

4611 iv Joyce Sharon[10] **Bovee**, born in Milwaukee, Milwaukee Co., WI. She married (1) in 1959 in Milwaukee, Milwaukee Co., WI, divorced **Gail Hagel Barger**; (2) in 1981 in Las Vegas, Clark Co., NV **Gregory Rooinett**.

3787. Carol Mae[9] **Bovee** (Carl Clifford[8], Arthur Vernon[7], William R[6], Abraham[5], Abraham[4], Abraham[3], Nicholas[2], Mathieu[1]), born 7 Aug 1926 in Big Falls, Waupaca Co., WI.. She married on 7 Feb 1948 John Phiip Kernan, born 21 Mar 1924, son of John Philip Kernan and Margaret Kal.

Children of Carol Mae Bovee and John Phiip Kernan were as follows:

4612 i Candace Ann[10] **Kernan**.

4613 ii Michael John[10] **Kernan**.

4614 iii Mary Sue[10] **Kernan**.

3788. Douglas Arthur[9] **Bovee** (Carl Clifford[8], Arthur Vernon[7], William R[6], Abraham[5], Abraham[4], Abraham[3], Nicholas[2], Mathieu[1]), born in Big Falls, Waupaca Co., WI.. He married on 27 Jun 1959 in Barrington, Lake Co., IL Betty Carol Blaydes, born in Memphis, Shelby Co., TN., daughter of John W Blaydes and Margaret Cross.

Children of Douglas Arthur Bovee and Betty Carol Blaydes were as follows:

4615 i Lauren Elizabeth[10] **Bovee**, born in Inglewood, Los Angeles Co., CA.. She married on 26 Sep 1987 in Rancho Palos Verdes, Los Angeles Co., CA. **Chester Brach**.

4616 ii Paul Arthur[10] **Bovee**, born in Inglewood, Los Angeles Co., CA..

3794. Roger[9] **Bovee** (Leland M[8], Arthur Vernon[7], William R[6], Abraham[5], Abraham[4], Abraham[3], Nicholas[2], Mathieu[1]), born abt 1929. He married Elode Gast.

Children of Roger Bovee and Elode Gast were as follows:

4617 i Susan[10] **Bovee**, born in WI.

4618 ii Roger[10] **Bovee**, born in WI.

4619 iii Debbie[10] **Bovee**, born in WI.

4620 iv Mark^{10} **Bovee**, born in WI.

4621 v James^{10} **Bovee**, born in WI.

4622 vi Julie^{10} **Bovee**.

3797. Elaine^9 **Bovee** (Gordon Lester^8, Arthur Vernon^7, William R^6, Abraham^5, Abraham^4, Abraham^3, Nicholas^2, Mathieu^1), born 3 Jan 1926 in Tigerton, Shawano Co., WI. She married on 28 Oct 1945 in Antigo, Langlade Co., WI Laddie Schwartz Jr, born 26 Aug 1925 in Antigo, Langlade Co., WI.

Children of Elaine Bovee and Laddie Schwartz Jr were as follows:

4623 i Steven R^{10} **Schwartz**, born in Antigo, Langlade Co., WI. He married on 14 Jun 1969 in Antigo, Langlade Co., WI **Angela (---)**, born in Antigo, Langlade Co., WI.

4624 ii Craig E^{10} **Schwartz**.

3798. Gordon W^9 **Bovee** (Gordon Lester^8, Arthur Vernon^7, William R^6, Abraham^5, Abraham^4, Abraham^3, Nicholas^2, Mathieu^1), born 31 Mar 1928 in Antigo, Langlade Co., WI. He married on 2 Jul 1949 in Antigo, Langlade Co., WI Rita Wachal, born 30 Jul 1929 in Antigo, Langlade Co., WI.

Children of Gordon W Bovee and Rita Wachal were as follows:

4625 i Gordon J^{10} **Bovee**, born in Antigo, Langlade Co., WI.

4626 ii Cheryl A^{10} **Bovee**, born in Antigo, Langlade Co., WI.

4627 iii Charles^{10} **Bovee**, born in Pontiac, Oakland Co., MI.

4628 iv Thomas Allen^{10} **Bovee**, born in Pontiac, Oakland Co., MI.

3799. Shirley M^9 **Bovee** (Gordon Lester^8, Arthur Vernon^7, William R^6, Abraham^5, Abraham^4, Abraham^3, Nicholas^2, Mathieu^1), born in Antigo, Langlade Co., WI. She married on 13 May 1950 in Antigo, Langlade Co., WI Richard F Kestley, born 19 Aug 1928 in Shawano, Shawano Co., WI.

Children of Shirley M Bovee and Richard F Kestley were as follows:

4629 i John F^{10} **Kestley**.

3800. Helen Jane^9 **Bovee** (Gordon Lester^8, Arthur Vernon^7, William R^6, Abraham^5, Abraham^4, Abraham^3, Nicholas^2, Mathieu^1), born in Antigo, Langlade Co., WI. She married on 13 Jun 1953 in Antigo, Langlade Co., WI Thomas Fermanich, born 1 Dec 1927 in Matoon, Shawano Co., WI.

Children of Helen Jane Bovee and Thomas Fermanich were as follows:

4630 i Patrick B^{10} **Fermanich**.

4631 ii Michael G^{10} **Fermanich**.

4632 iii Timothy^{10} **Fermanich**.

4633　　iv　　　Jane Kay[10] **Fermanich**.

3801. Irene L[9] **Bovee** (Gordon Lester[8], Arthur Vernon[7], William R[6], Abraham[5], Abraham[4], Abraham[3], Nicholas[2], Mathieu[1]), born in Antigo, Langlade Co., WI. She married on 6 Aug 1956 in Antigo, Langlade Co., WI Howard L Wagner, born in Wittenberg, Shawano Co., WI.

Children of Irene L Bovee and Howard L Wagner were as follows:
4634　　i　　　David H[10] **Wagner**.
4635　　ii　　　John Paul[10] **Wagner**.

3802. Robert Eugene[9] **Bovee** (Everette Vivian[8], Arthur Vernon[7], William R[6], Abraham[5], Abraham[4], Abraham[3], Nicholas[2], Mathieu[1]), born 22 Jun 1929 in Wyoming, Waupaca Co., WI.. He married on 3 Sep 1951 in Bear Creek, Outagamie Co., WI. Betty Ann Surorise, born in Deer Creek, Outagamie Co., WI..

Children of Robert Eugene Bovee and Betty Ann Surorise were as follows:
+　4636　　i　　　David Robert[10] **Bovee**, born in New London, Waushara Co., WI.. He married **Rhonda Marie Slosarek**.
+　4637　　ii　　　Debra Ann[10] **Bovee**, born in New London, Waushara Co., WI.. She married **Donald James Flease**.

3803. Everette Vivian[9] **Bovee** Jr (Everette Vivian[8], Arthur Vernon[7], William R[6], Abraham[5], Abraham[4], Abraham[3], Nicholas[2], Mathieu[1]), born in Big Falls, Waupaca Co., WI.. He married on 20 Sep 1958 in Kaukauna, Outagami Co., WI. Phyllis Mahn, born in Kaukauna, Outagami Co., WI., daughter of Roy Francis Mahn and Phoebe Skenanders.

Children of Everette Vivian Bovee Jr and Phyllis Mahn were as follows:
4638　　i　　　Perry Roy[10] **Bovee**, born in Kaukauna, Outagami Co., WI.. He married on 2 Oct 1999 in Kimberly, Outagamie Co., WI. **Stephanie Ann Siske**.
+　4639　　ii　　　Peggy Sue[10] **Bovee**, born in Kaukauna, Outagami Co., WI.. She married **Timothy J Kasten**.
4640　　iii　　Bart Everette[10] **Bovee**, died 22 Nov 1986.

3804. Donald Lee[9] **Bovee** (Everette Vivian[8], Arthur Vernon[7], William R[6], Abraham[5], Abraham[4], Abraham[3], Nicholas[2], Mathieu[1]), born in Wyoming Twp., Waupac Co., WI. He married (1) on 3 Oct 1971 in Waukegan, Lake Co., IL Patty Jo Prinson, born in New London,Waupaca Co., WI; (2) Elizabeth (---).

Children of Donald Lee Bovee and Patty Jo Prinson were as follows:
+　4641　　i　　　Ronald Gordon[10] **Bovee**, born in New London,Waupaca Co., WI. He married (1) **Penny Marie Van Straten**; (2)

Cinnamon Lynn Chimelski.

+ 4642   ii   Jodi Lei[10] **Bovee**, born in New London, Waupaca Co., WI. She married **Mathew Young**.

3805. Tony Lee[9] **Bovee** (Everette Vivian[8], Arthur Vernon[7], William R[6], Abraham[5], Abraham[4], Abraham[3], Nicholas[2], Mathieu[1]), born in Seoul, Korea. He married on 3 Jul 1976 Denise Marie Kubinski.

Children of Tony Lee Bovee and Denise Marie Kubinski were as follows:

4643   i   Jason Charles[10] **Bovee**, born in New London, Waupaca Co., WI.

4644   ii   Nathan Lee[10] **Bovee**, born in New London, Waupaca Co., WI.

4645   iii   Zachary Daniel[10] **Bovee**, born in New London, Waupaca Co., WI.

3807. Melissa Gail[9] **Bovee** (Ned Allen[8], George Lewis[7], Minard[6], Abraham[5], Abraham[4], Abraham[3], Nicholas[2], Mathieu[1]). She married on 22 Apr 1961 in Sacred Heart Church, Calumet, Houghton Co., MI Paul Goulette, died 1994, son of Edwin Goulette and Marie (---).

Children of Melissa Gail Bovee and Paul Goulette were as follows:

4646   i   Jeffrey[10] **Goulette**.
4647   ii   Kristi Lee[10] **Goulette**.

3809. Mary Helen[9] **Bovee** (Ned Allen[8], George Lewis[7], Minard[6], Abraham[5], Abraham[4], Abraham[3], Nicholas[2], Mathieu[1]). She married in 1968 Jerry Bybee.

Children of Mary Helen Bovee and Jerry Bybee were as follows:

4648   i   Jason Vincent[10] **Bybee**.
4649   ii   Billi Jean[10] **Bybee**.
4650   iii   Danielle Marie[10] **Bybee**.

3810. Melanie Ann[9] **Bovee** (Ned Allen[8], George Lewis[7], Minard[6], Abraham[5], Abraham[4], Abraham[3], Nicholas[2], Mathieu[1]). She married (1) in 1969, divorced Michael Thomas Steen, born in Royal Oak, Oakland Co., MI; (2) in 1974 Kenneth Despain.

Children of Melanie Ann Bovee and Michael Thomas Steen were as follows:

4651   i   Brian Michael[10] **Steen**, born in Calumet, Houghton Co., MI.

Children of Melanie Ann Bovee and Kenneth Despain were as follows:

4652   i   Sara Louise[10] **Despain**.

3812. Sue Ann[9] Bovee (Merrill Frederick[8], Clarence Abraham[7], Erastus[6], Abraham[5], Abraham[4], Abraham[3], Nicholas[2], Mathieu[1]). She married Maurice Wayne Poe.

Children of Sue Ann Bovee and Maurice Wayne Poe were as follows:

4653	i	Kelly[10] **Poe.**
4654	ii	Cathy[10] **Poe.**

3814. Jan Merrill[9] Bovee (Edward Harold[8], Edward C[7], Erastus[6], Abraham[5], Abraham[4], Abraham[3], Nicholas[2], Mathieu[1]), born in Niagara, Marinette Co., WI. He married Anita Louise (---).

Children of Jan Merrill Bovee and Anita Louise (---) were as follows:

4655	i	Todd Anthony[10] **Bovee**, born 8 Apr 1962; died 16 Jun 1963.
4656	ii	Michael Joseph[10] **Bovee.**
4657	iii	Denyle Marie[10] **Bovee.**

3815. Gary Edward[9] Bovee (Edward Harold[8], Edward C[7], Erastus[6], Abraham[5], Abraham[4], Abraham[3], Nicholas[2], Mathieu[1]), born 1943 in Norway, Dickinson Co., MI; died abt 1997. He married Patricia A Tohulka.

Children of Gary Edward Bovee and Patricia A Tohulka were as follows:

4658	i	Eric[10] **Bovee.**
4659	ii	Edward[10] **Bovee.**
4660	iii	Brad Daniel[10] **Bovee.**
4661	iv	Bridget Eilene[10] **Bovee.**

3829. Aloha[9] Bovee (Lester M[8], Andrew Jackson[7], Andrew Jackson[6], Henry[5], Abraham[4], Abraham[3], Nicholas[2], Mathieu[1]). She married Clyde Wells.

Children of Aloha Bovee and Clyde Wells were as follows:

4662	i	Cindy[10] **Wells.**
4663	ii	Stanley[10] **Wells.**

3830. Edith[9] Bovee (Lester M[8], Andrew Jackson[7], Andrew Jackson[6], Henry[5], Abraham[4], Abraham[3], Nicholas[2], Mathieu[1]). She married in Bellinghan, Whatcom Co., WA Philip Hansen.

Children of Edith Bovee and Philip Hansen were as follows:

4664	i	Curtis[10] **Hansen.**

4665	ii	Timothy[10] **Hansen**.
4666	iii	Neil[10] **Hansen**.
4667	iv	Melanie[10] **Hansen**.

3841. Robert Lawrence[9] **Bovee** (Lawrence Erwin[8], Lyman George[7], Franklin Gibson[6], Aaron[5], Henry[4], Abraham[3], Nicholas[2], Mathieu[1]), born 13 Oct 1922. He married Julienne Marie (---), born 25 Jun 1922.

Children of Robert Lawrence Bovee and Julienne Marie (---) were as follows:

4668	i	Susanne Marie[10] **Bovee**.
4669	ii	Sally Anne[10] **Bovee**.

3858. Lois Lucille[9] **Bovee** (Louis Grant[8], Orbie O[7], George[6], Philip[5], Jacob Philip[4], Philip[3], Nicholas[2], Mathieu[1]), born 30 Jul 1925. She married on 13 Sep 1947 William Currie.

Children of Lois Lucille Bovee and William Currie were as follows:

4670	i	Laurel Irene[10] **Currie**.

3859. Elizabeth Mae[9] **Bovee** (Louis Grant[8], Orbie O[7], George[6], Philip[5], Jacob Philip[4], Philip[3], Nicholas[2], Mathieu[1]), born 8 Nov 1928. She married on 9 Jul 1949 Raymond Roy pierce.

Children of Elizabeth Mae Bovee and Raymond Roy pierce were as follows:

4671	i	Donald Grant[10] **Pierce**.

3860. Clifford Dan[9] **Bovee** (Louis Grant[8], Orbie O[7], George[6], Philip[5], Jacob Philip[4], Philip[3], Nicholas[2], Mathieu[1]). He married (1) Mary Lou Livermore; (2) Debbie (---).

Children of Clifford Dan Bovee and Mary Lou Livermore were as follows:

4672	i	Suzy[10] **Bovee**.
4673	ii	Brian[10] **Bovee**.

3861. Donald F[9] **Bovee** (Charles Henry[8], Frederick Germond[7], Nicholas[6], John[5], Jacob Philip[4], Philip[3], Nicholas[2], Mathieu[1]), born 23 Jul 1906 in Rawsonville, Wayne Co., MI; died 25 May 1979 in Pacific Grove, Monterey Co., CA. He married Katherine Louise Hammer, born 26 Jul 1905 in Detroit Wayne Co., MI; died 1 Nov 1968 in Livonia, Wayne Co., MI.

Children of Donald F Bovee and Katherine Louise Hammer were as follows:

+	4674	i	Robert Frederick[10] **Bovee**, born 12 Jun 1926 in Novi, Oakland Co., MI. He married **Fay Elaine Christensen**.

| | 4675 | ii | Joanne Carolyn^{10} **Bovee**, born in Detroit Wayne Co., MI. She married **William Zimmerman**. |
| + | | | |

+ 4675 ii Joanne Carolyn^{10} **Bovee**, born in Detroit Wayne Co., MI. She married **William Zimmerman**.

+ 4676 iii Keith Alvin^{10} **Bovee**. He married **Elnora Lanphierd**.

4677 iv Linda Ruth^{10} **Bovee**, born 1 Jul 1942 in Wayne Co., MI; died 2 Jul 1942 in Wayne Co., MI.

+ 4678 v Joyce Kay^{10} **Bovee**, born in Plymouth, Wayne Co., MI. She married **Ronald Moore**.

3862. Muriel Ferne^9 **Bovee** (Charles Henry^8, Frederick Germond^7, Nicholas^6, John^5, Jacob Philip^4, Philip^3, Nicholas^2, Mathieu^1), born 5 Aug 1908; died 1991 in FL. She married (1) in 1926 Frank Brown; (2) Elbert Martin.

Children of Muriel Ferne Bovee and Frank Brown were as follows:

4679 i James Douglas^{10} **Brown**, born 1927.

Children of Muriel Ferne Bovee and Elbert Martin were as follows:

4680 i Ralph^{10} **Martin**.

3864. Norvall Charles^9 **Bovee** (Charles Henry^8, Frederick Germond^7, Nicholas^6, John^5, Jacob Philip^4, Philip^3, Nicholas^2, Mathieu^1), born 17 Mar 1917 in Salem, Washtenaw Co., MI; died 11 Dec 1970 in Mt Pleasant, Isabella Co., MI. He married on 28 May 1941 in Nardin Park, MI Evelyn Mary Gagnon.

Children of Norvall Charles Bovee and Evelyn Mary Gagnon were as follows:

+ 4681 i Sue Evelyn^{10} **Bovee**. She married **Peter Woods**.

+ 4682 ii Kenneth Charles^{10} **Bovee**. He married **Stephanie (---)**.

3866. John Edwin^9 **Bovee** (Nathan H^8, John Edwin^7, Edwin Henry^6, John^5, Jacob Philip^4, Philip^3, Nicholas^2, Mathieu^1), born 1922. He married abt 1950 Elizabeth (---).

Children of John Edwin Bovee and Elizabeth (---) were as follows:

4683 i Mark^{10} **Bovee**, died abt 1950.

4684 ii Elizabeth^{10} **Bovee**.

4685 iii Kent^{10} **Bovee**.

4686 iv Kevin^{10} **Bovee**.

3868. Henry Russell^9 **Bovee** (Nathan H^8, John Edwin^7, Edwin Henry^6, John^5, Jacob Philip^4, Philip^3, Nicholas^2, Mathieu^1), born 18 Nov 1926. He married in 1950 Nancy Williams, born 20 Oct 1926.

Children of Henry Russell Bovee and Nancy Williams were as follows:

4687 i Nathan Robert^{10} **Bovee**.

4688 ii Wright Charles[10] **Bovee**.

3871. Burton[9] **Bovee** (Forest F[8], Freeman[7], Charles P[6], Nicholas[5], Jacob Philip[4], Philip[3], Nicholas[2], Mathieu[1]), born 15 Feb 1919 in MI; died 5 Apr 1980 in Morenci, Lenawee Co., MI. He married (1) Madelyn Lucille Johnson, born 12 Jun 1918 in Medina Twp., Lenawee Co., MI; died 7 Jul 1941 in Ann Arbor, Washtenaw Co., MI; (2) Vivian Harger.

Children of Burton Bovee and Vivian Harger were as follows:
4689 i Barbara[10] **Bovee**. She married **Doyle Southerland**.

3872. Keith N[9] **Bovee** (Forest F[8], Freeman[7], Charles P[6], Nicholas[5], Jacob Philip[4], Philip[3], Nicholas[2], Mathieu[1]), born 11 May 1923; died 22 Aug 1982 in Adrian, Lenawee Co., MI. He married abt 1950 Helen Rathbun.

Children of Keith N Bovee and Helen Rathbun were as follows:
4690 i Brian[10] **Bovee**. He married **Janet (---)**.
+ 4691 ii Forrest Fred[10] **Bovee**. He married unknown.
4692 iii Barry[10] **Bovee**. He married **Linda (---)**.
4693 iv Carol[10] **Bovee**.

3874. Forrest Burdette[9] **Bovee** (Forest F[8], Freeman[7], Charles P[6], Nicholas[5], Jacob Philip[4], Philip[3], Nicholas[2], Mathieu[1]). He married in 1961 Rosetta Diane Nichols.

Children of Forrest Burdette Bovee and Rosetta Diane Nichols were as follows:
+ 4694 i Megan Eileen[10] **Bovee**. She married **Christopher Cottle**.
+ 4695 ii Jenna Marlene[10] **Bovee**. She married **Robert Rainey**.
4696 iii Brigell Fay[10] **Bovee**. She married **Rex Vernier**.

3879. Norval Seymour[9] **Bovee** (Max Nelson[8], Seymour Nelson[7], Nelson H[6], Nicholas[5], Jacob Philip[4], Philip[3], Nicholas[2], Mathieu[1]). He married on 3 Aug 1951 Jocelyn Gurnee Larrabee.

Children of Norval Seymour Bovee and Jocelyn Gurnee Larrabee were as follows:
4697 i Scott N[10] **Bovee**.
4698 ii Shawn N[10] **Bovee**. He married **Denise Kathleen Hand**.

3880. Mavis Irena[9] **Bovee** (Max Nelson[8], Seymour Nelson[7], Nelson H[6], Nicholas[5], Jacob Philip[4], Philip[3], Nicholas[2], Mathieu[1]). She married Richard Dirlam.

Children of Mavis Irena Bovee and Richard Dirlam were as follows:

4699 i   Thomas[10] **Dirlam**.

4700 ii   Kyle R[10] **Dirlam**.

4701 iii   Melissa K[10] **Dirlam**.

3884. Dale Allen[9] **Bovee** (Miner[8], Floyd B[7], Nelson H[6], Nicholas[5], Jacob Philip[4], Philip[3], Nicholas[2], Mathieu[1]). He married (1) Barbara O'Hare; (2) Fay Maness.

Children of Dale Allen Bovee and Barbara O'Hare were as follows:

4702 i   Teresa Marie[10] **Bovee**. She married **Walter G Houston**.

4703 ii   Tammy Lynn[10] **Bovee**. She married **John Droullard**.

4704 iii   Darlene Ellen[10] **Bovee**.

4705 iv   Anette Lea[10] **Bovee**. She married **Darrin Ramsey**.

4706 v   Debra Ann[10] **Bovee**.

3887. Richard Eugene[9] **Bovee** (Sidney Richard[8], Charles Henry[7], Nelson H[6], Nicholas[5], Jacob Philip[4], Philip[3], Nicholas[2], Mathieu[1]). He married Brenda Harrison Fallon.

Children of Richard Eugene Bovee and Brenda Harrison Fallon were as follows:

4707 i   Richard E[10] **Bovee** Jr.

3888. Roger Lee[9] **Bovee** (Sidney Richard[8], Charles Henry[7], Nelson H[6], Nicholas[5], Jacob Philip[4], Philip[3], Nicholas[2], Mathieu[1]). He married Sandra Meys.

Children of Roger Lee Bovee and Sandra Meys were as follows:

4708 i   Michael[10] **Bovee**.

3898. George Earl[9] **Bovee** (Charles D[8], Jeremiah W[7], William R[6], Daniel R[5], Nicholas P[4], Philip[3], Nicholas[2], Mathieu[1]), born 15 Jun 1895 in Edinboro, Erie Co., PA; christened 26 May 1929 in Pensacola, Escambia Co., FL; died 2 Jun 1972 in Pensacola, Escambia Co., FL. He married Daisy L Long, born 16 Feb 1900 in Vancleave, Jackson Co., MS; christened 1 May 1910 in Theodore, Mobile Co., AL; died 27 Apr 1984 in Pensacola, Escambia Co., FL.

Children of George Earl Bovee and Daisy L Long were as follows:

+ 4709 i   Earl Wesley[10] **Bovee**, born 1 Mar 1918 in Pensacola, Escambia Co., FL; christened 21 Oct 1928 in Pensacola, Escambia Co., FL; died 5 Oct 1967 in Tampa, Hillsborough Co., FL. He married (1) **Lilly May Babb**; (2) **Mary L Ward**.

  4710 ii   Sybil Irene[10] **Bovee**, born 21 Aug 1921 in Pensacola,

Escambia Co., FL; christened 5 Feb 1923 in Pensacola, Escambia Co., FL; died 7 Aug 1993 in Pensacola, Escambia Co., FL. She married on 30 Apr 1937 **Harold Bruce Bradley**.

3903. Lynn Albert^{9} **Bovee** (June Raymond^{8}, Daniel Reynolds^{7}, William R^{6}, Daniel R^{5}, Nicholas P^{4}, Philip^{3}, Nicholas^{2}, Mathieu^{1}), born 18 Oct 1889 in Venango, Crawford Co., PA; died 24 Jul 1963 in Orange, Orange Co., CA. He married on 12 Sep 1912 in Westfield, Chautauqua Co., NY Lena Anderson, born 15 May 1882 in Westfield, Chautauqua Co., NY; died 16 Jun 1961 in Lawrence Park, Erie Co., PA, daughter of Mortimer Anderson and Alice J Hunt.

Children of Lynn Albert Bovee and Lena Anderson were as follows:

+ 4711   i   Neal Anderson^{10} **Bovee**, born 16 Dec 1914 in Westfield, Chautauqua Co., NY; died 29 Oct 1980 in Mc Alester, Pittsburg Co., OK. He married (1) **Ruth Marie Cousins**; (2) **Elaine Madeline Marie Tutiau**.

3904. Frank Grencett^{9} **Bovee** (June Raymond^{8}, Daniel Reynolds^{7}, William R^{6}, Daniel R^{5}, Nicholas P^{4}, Philip^{3}, Nicholas^{2}, Mathieu^{1}), born 16 Oct 1891 in Erie Co., PA; died 13 Dec 1916. He married Mary Louise Berger, born 22 Dec 1890; died 20 Mar 1967.

Children of Frank Grencett Bovee and Mary Louise Berger were as follows:

+ 4712   i   June^{10} **Bovee**, born 14 Apr 1915. She married **Arthur Shreve**.

3906. Aris^{9} **Bovee** (Glenn Dexter^{8}, Charles Dexter^{7}, William R^{6}, Daniel R^{5}, Nicholas P^{4}, Philip^{3}, Nicholas^{2}, Mathieu^{1}), born 5 Nov 1901 in Swanville, Erie Co., PA; died in Erie, Erie Co., PA. She married on 7 May 1928 Ross Reed.

Children of Aris Bovee and Ross Reed were as follows:

4713   i   Nancy^{10} **Reed**.

3908. Ruth Adella^{9} **Bovee** (Frederick Charles^{8}, Charles Dexter^{7}, William R^{6}, Daniel R^{5}, Nicholas P^{4}, Philip^{3}, Nicholas^{2}, Mathieu^{1}), born 22 Sep 1918 in Erie, Erie Co., PA. She married (1) on 23 Nov 1939 Merton Smith Bartels; (2) on 30 Jun 1960 Howard Westley; (3) on 13 Apr 1968 John L Beecher.

Children of Ruth Adella Bovee and Merton Smith Bartels were as follows:

4714   i   Eileen Rueh^{10} **Bartels**, born 17 Mar 1942; died 8 Jul 1958 in Wattsburg, Erie Co., PA.

4715   ii   Richard Charles^{10} **Bartels**.

4716   iii   Thomas Spencer^{10} **Bartels**.

3910. Frederick Lyman[9] **Bovee** (Frederick Charles[8], Charles Dexter[7], William R[6], Daniel R[5], Nicholas P[4], Philip[3], Nicholas[2], Mathieu[1]), born 27 Feb 1923. He married on 14 Sep 1946 Jeanette Nardo, daughter of Dominic Nardo and Angeline (---).

Children of Frederick Lyman Bovee and Jeanette Nardo were as follows:

+ 4717   i   Frederick Charles[10] **Bovee**. He married **Galia Straight**.
   4718   ii   William[10] **Bovee**.
   4719   iii   Tammy Ruth[10] **Bovee**. She married on 30 Sep 1989 **John Johnson**.

3911. Harry Spencer[9] **Bovee** (Frederick Charles[8], Charles Dexter[7], William R[6], Daniel R[5], Nicholas P[4], Philip[3], Nicholas[2], Mathieu[1]), born 10 Dec 1924. He married on 28 Feb 1947 Dorothy Brakeman.

Children of Harry Spencer Bovee and Dorothy Brakeman were as follows:

+ 4720   i   Sandra[10] **Bovee**. She married **James Mawhinney**.
+ 4721   ii   Harry S[10] **Bovee**. He married **Deborah Alberica**.

3922. Thelma[9] **Bovee** (Floyd D[8], Lorenzo Dow[7], Nicholas[6], Jacob[5], Nicholas P[4], Philip[3], Nicholas[2], Mathieu[1]), born 30 Jan 1895 in Oswego, Labette Co., KS; died 20 Apr 1939 in Golden, Jefferson Co., CO. She married on 22 Aug 1920 Horace R Davies.

Children of Thelma Bovee and Horace R Davies were as follows:

   4722   i   David Richard[10] **Davies**, born 30 Jul 1924 in Casper, Natrona Co., WY.
   4723   ii   Darlene Caryl[10] **Davies**, born 6 Apr 1929 in Denver, Denver Co., CO.

3923. Alta[9] **Bovee** (Floyd D[8], Lorenzo Dow[7], Nicholas[6], Jacob[5], Nicholas P[4], Philip[3], Nicholas[2], Mathieu[1]), born 19 Nov 1899 in Durango, La Plata Co., CO. She married on 28 Mar 1926 in Denver, Denver Co., CO Walter James Kemper.

Children of Alta Bovee and Walter James Kemper were as follows:

   4724   i   Evelyn Doris[10] **Kemper**, born 3 Feb 1927 in Denver, Denver Co., CO.

3933. Esther[9] **Bovee** (Guy Clinton[8], Harmon E[7], Nicholas[6], Jacob[5], Nicholas P[4], Philip[3], Nicholas[2], Mathieu[1]), born 28 May 1906. She married on 9 Apr 1936 Chester L Christianson.

Children of Esther Bovee and Chester L Christianson were as follows:

   4725   i   David L[10] **Christianson**.

4726　ii　　　Carol Louise [10] **Christianson**.

3934. George Henry [9] **Bovee** (Guy Clinton [8], Harmon E [7], Nicholas [6], Jacob [5], Nicholas P [4], Philip [3], Nicholas [2], Mathieu [1]), born 9 Mar 1908; died Jun 1975. He married on 9 Sep 1933 Helen Dessie Gornason.

Children of George Henry Bovee and Helen Dessie Gornason were as follows:

+　4727　i　　　Robert John [10] **Bovee**. He married **Patricia Werkle**.
　　4728　ii　　Nancy [10] **Bovee**.

3936. Donald C [9] **Bovee** (Irving [8], Harmon E [7], Nicholas [6], Jacob [5], Nicholas P [4], Philip [3], Nicholas [2], Mathieu [1]), born 31 Oct 1925; died 22 Jan 1995 in Willmington, Will Co., IL. He married Ruth L (---).

Children of Donald C Bovee and Ruth L (---) were as follows:

　　4729　i　　　Gayl R [10] **Bovee**.

3955. Glendon Charles [9] **Bovee** (Lyle J [8], Jacob [7], Isaac [6], Jacob Nicholas [5], Nicholas Jacob [4], Jacob [3], Nicholas [2], Mathieu [1]), born 8 Jul 1917 in Smith, Ionia Co., MI. He married Janet A Haselweidt.

Children of Glendon Charles Bovee and Janet A Haselweidt were as follows:

　　4730　i　　　Orla Lee [10] **Bovee**.
+　4731　ii　　Lewis Lyle [10] **Bovee**. He married unknown.

3961. Frank Walter [9] **Bovee** (John Addison [8], Christian [7], Peter [6], Peter [5], Jacob [4], Jacob [3], Nicholas [2], Mathieu [1]), born 22 May 1907 in East Branch, Delaware Co., NY; died 22 Aug 1976 in Syracuse, Onondaga Co., NY. He married on 21 Nov 1931 in Walton, Delaware Co., NY Gertrude Louise MacFarlane, born 4 Feb 1911 in Meridale, Delaware Co., NY; died 2 Sep 1975 in Delhi, Delaware Co., NY.

Children of Frank Walter Bovee and Gertrude Louise MacFarlane were as follows:

+　4732　i　　　John William [10] **Bovee**, born 17 Oct 1932 in Norwich, Chenango Co., NY; died 24 Oct 1994 in AZ. He married **June Irwin**.
+　4733　ii　　Frank Walter [10] **Bovee** Jr, born in Norwich, Chenango Co., NY. He married **Carol LaVonne Pipa**.
+　4734　iii　Donna Lee [10] **Bovee**, born in Norwich, Chenango Co., NY. She married (1) **Ronald J Hannon**; (2) **John Herrick**.
+　4735　iv　James Lewis [10] **Bovee**, born in Norwich, Chenango Co., NY. He married **Betty Ashcroft**.

+ 4736 v David Fred[10] **Bovee**, born 31 May 1944 in Norwich, Chenango Co., NY; died 5 Aug 1994. He married **Donna Mary Powers**.

4737 vi Susan Louise[10] **Bovee**, born in Norwich, Chenango Co., NY. She married (1), divorced **Brian Emple**; (2), divorced **Walter Miller**; (3), divorced **Robert Gray**.

3975. Raymond Harold[9] **Bovee** (Harold Mark[8], Lorenzo[7], Peter[6], Peter[5], Jacob[4], Jacob[3], Nicholas[2], Mathieu[1]), born 23 Feb 1923 in Middletown, Orange Co., NY; died 7 Oct 1969 in San Diego, San Diego Co., CA. He married in Sep 1943 in Dallas, Dallas Co., TX Louise May, Harper, born 14 Sep 1925 in Dallas, Dallas Co., TX, daughter of James J Harper and Louise Acker.

Children of Raymond Harold Bovee and Louise May, Harper were as follows:

4738 i Raymond Harold[10] **Bovee** Jr, born in Vallejo, Solano Co., CA. He married on 26 Nov 1966 in Seattle, King Co., WA **Barbara Maurine Gates**.

4739 ii Stephen Paul[10] **Bovee**, born in Dallas, Dallas Co., TX. He married (1) **Mary Jo (---)**; (2) **Sharon (---)**.

4740 iii Mary Ellen[10] **Bovee**, born in Dallas, Dallas Co., TX. She married **Roy Flahive**.

4741 iv Rita Ellen[10] **Bovee**, born in San Diego, San Diego Co., CA. She married **Mark Landis**.

4742 v Yvonne Elicia[10] **Bovee**, born in San Diego, San Diego Co., CA. She married **Steve Clark**.

4743 vi Theresa Irene[10] **Bovee**, born in San Diego, San Diego Co., CA. She married **Malcom Nicholson**.

4744 vii Louise Y[10] **Bovee**, born in Norfolk, VA. She married **Steve Stinchcomb**.

4745 viii Bridgette Louise[10] **Bovee**, born in Norfolk, VA.

4746 ix Yvette V[10] **Bovee**, born in San Diego, San Diego Co., CA. She married **William Barnett**.

3976. Lewis Laverne[9] **Bovee** (Lewis B[8], George A[7], Jacob Clayton[6], Peter[5], Jacob[4], Jacob[3], Nicholas[2], Mathieu[1]), born 30 Oct 1889 in NY; died 1963. He married Lilah Layman, born 13 Dec 1895.

Children of Lewis Laverne Bovee and Lilah Layman were as follows:

+ 4747 i Ehelyn[10] **Bovee**, born abt 1918. She married **Arnold Copping**.

4748 ii Marjorie[10] **Bovee**.

+ 4749 iii Jacqueline[10] **Bovee**, born abt 1928 in Saugerties, Ulster Co., NY.; died 24 Jan 2005 in Delmar, Albany Co., NY.. She married **David R Miller**.

3977. Barton[9] Bovee (Ernest Winchel[8], George A[7], Jacob Clayton[6], Peter[5], Jacob[4], Jacob[3], Nicholas[2], Mathieu[1]), born 1 Jun 1900 in CT; died Jan 1982 in CT. He married E Georgetta (---), born 15 Jan 1896.

    Children of Barton Bovee and E Georgetta (---) were as follows:

+   4750   i   Jean Patricia[10] **Bovee**. She married **Alan E Hanbury**.
+   4751   ii   Barton Winchel[10] **Bovee**. He married **Jean Lawton**.

3985. Lester Eugene[9] Bovee (Nelson[8], Pliny L[7], Jacob Clayton[6], Peter[5], Jacob[4], Jacob[3], Nicholas[2], Mathieu[1]), born abt 1921 in Saugerties, Ulster Co., NY. He married Bertha Ruth Sickler.

    Children of Lester Eugene Bovee and Bertha Ruth Sickler were as follows:

     4752   i   Lester Eugene[10] **Bovee** Jr. He married **Barbara Catherine Moffatt**.
     4753   ii   Leonard Arthur[10] **Bovee**. He married on 17 Jan 1965 **Eileen Mackerie**.

3990. Ray D[9] BoVee (Grover[8], Elijah[7], Jacob Clayton[6], Peter[5], Jacob[4], Jacob[3], Nicholas[2], Mathieu[1]), born 21 Jul 1914 in Younkers, Westchester Co., NY; died 8 Sep 1982 in Seber Shores, Sandy Creek, Oswego Co., NY. He married Regina Reed, born 8 May 1920; died Jan 1990.

    Children of Ray D BoVee and Regina Reed were as follows:

     4754   i   James[10] **Bovee**.
     4755   ii   Patricia[10] **Bovee**.
     4756   iii   Dorothy[10] **Bovee**.

4003. Ransom Irvin[9] Bovee (James Ashley[8], William Irvin[7], Isaac[6], Isaac[5], Jacob[4], Jacob[3], Nicholas[2], Mathieu[1]), born 2 Jul 1917 in Denver, Denver Co., CO; died 29 Aug 1984 in HI. He married abt 1949 Audrey Stoskopf, born 6 Jul 1917 in Seattle, Kings Co., WA, daughter of Frank Andrew Stoskopf and Minnie Wood.

    Children of Ransom Irvin Bovee and Audrey Stoskopf were as follows:

     4757   i   Lynn Ernest[10] **Bovee**, born in Seattle, King Co., WA.

4005. Marguerite E[9] Bovee (Ransom Young[8], William Irvin[7], Isaac[6], Isaac[5], Jacob[4], Jacob[3], Nicholas[2], Mathieu[1]), born 15 Dec 1911 in Colorado; died 16 Mar 1995 in Los Angeles, Los Angeles Co., CA. She married (1) in Oct 1929 Harry Lake; (2) in Dec 1938 Forrest Newcomb.

    Children of Marguerite E Bovee and Harry Lake were as follows:

     4758   i   JoAnn[10] **Lake**, born in Los Angeles, Los Angeles Co., CA.

4759　ii　　Nancy Lee[10] **Lake**, born in Los Angeles, Los Angeles Co., CA.

4006. Bonnie[9] **Bovee** (Ransom Young[8], William Irvin[7], Isaac[6], Isaac[5], Jacob[4], Jacob[3], Nicholas[2], Mathieu[1]), born 26 Dec 1913. She married (1) in Sep 1937 Dale Warner; (2) in Jan 1956 Dale Stanley.

Children of Bonnie Bovee and Dale Warner were as follows:

4760　i　　Diana[10] **Warner**, born in Oklahoma City, Oklahoma Co., OK.

4761　ii　　Ronald[10] **Warner**, born in Los Angeles, Los Angeles Co., CA.

4762　iii　　Yvonne Nina[10] **Warner**, born in Los Angeles, Los Angeles Co., CA.

4763　iv　　Camille Roberts[10] **Warner**, born in Los Angeles, Los Angeles Co., CA.

4025. Evelyn Mae[9] **Bovee** (Earl Richard[8], Ezra[7], Jacob[6], Philip[5], Jacob[4], Jacob[3], Nicholas[2], Mathieu[1]), born 6 Jun 1922. She married (---) Downey.

Children of Evelyn Mae Bovee and (---) Downey were as follows:

4764　i　　Lenor[10] **Downey**.

4765　ii　　Child[10] **Downey**.

4038. Frank Leslie[9] **Bovee** (Daniel Walter[8], John Livingston[7], Cornelius[6], Daniel[5], Matthew[4], Jacob[3], Nicholas[2], Mathieu[1]), born 13 Dec 1893 in NE; died 5 Jul 1959 in Cascade Co., MT. He married on 25 Dec 1917 Effie Alvina Biesemier, born 27 Feb 1892 in Sterling, Johnson Co., NE; died Aug 1980, daughter of Fred Biesemier and Leona (---).

Children of Frank Leslie Bovee and Effie Alvina Biesemier were as follows:

4766　i　　Charles Leslie[10] **Bovee**, born 2 Oct 1918. He married **Nora Elizabeth Wenzel**.

+　4767　ii　　Robert Dale[10] **Bovee**, born 4 Jul 1920. He married **Margaret (---)**.

4768　iii　　Melvin Merle[10] **Bovee**, born 24 Jan 1923; died 22 Jul 1924.

+　4769　iv　　Carroll Lee[10] **Bovee**, born 16 Dec 1924. He married **Bette (---)**.

4039. LeRoy[9] **Bovee** (Daniel Walter[8], John Livingston[7], Cornelius[6], Daniel[5], Matthew[4], Jacob[3], Nicholas[2], Mathieu[1]), born 23 Apr 1896 in NE; died 13 Jan 1949. He married Harriet (---), born in NE.

Children of LeRoy Bovee and Harriet (---) were as follows:

4770   i   Virginia^{10} **Bovee**, born in WY. She married **(---) Bishop**.

4042. Paul Henry^9 **Bovee** (Daniel Walter^8, John Livingston^7, Cornelius^6, Daniel^5, Matthew^4, Jacob^3, Nicholas^2, Mathieu^1), born 31 May 1909; died Mar 1982 in Park, Park Co., WY. He married Arlene Kells, born 19 Jul 1908; died Mar 1984 in Powell, Park Co., WY.

Children of Paul Henry Bovee and Arlene Kells were as follows:

4771   i   Delores Ethel^{10} **Bovee**. She married **George M Bleekman**.

+ 4772   ii   Janet Rae^{10} **Bovee**. She married **Robert E Burgess**.

4050. LaVeta Grace^9 **Bovee** (Harry Carl^8, John Livingston^7, Cornelius^6, Daniel^5, Matthew^4, Jacob^3, Nicholas^2, Mathieu^1), born 6 Jan 1917 in Bee, Seward Co., NE. She married Berry Thomas.

Children of LaVeta Grace Bovee and Berry Thomas were as follows:

4773   i   John^{10} **Thomas**.

4774   ii   Mary^{10} **Thomas**.

4775   iii   Janet^{10} **Thomas**.

4776   iv   Maureen^{10} **Thomas**.

4052. Ilene Marie^9 **Bovee** (Harry Carl^8, John Livingston^7, Cornelius^6, Daniel^5, Matthew^4, Jacob^3, Nicholas^2, Mathieu^1), born 11 Mar 1922 in Lincoln, Lancaster Co., NE. She married on 20 May 1944 in Oak Park, Cook Co., IL Donald Bruce Watson, born 28 Apr 1922 in Loami, Sangamon Co., IL, son of George Edric Watson and Ida Burghardt.

Children of Ilene Marie Bovee and Donald Bruce Watson were as follows:

4777   i   David Bruce^{10} **Watson**, born 28 Jun 1945 in Chicago, Cook Co., IL; died 26 Jan 1988 in St. Charles, Kane Co., IL.

4778   ii   Robert Bovee^{10} **Watson**, born in Elmhurst, Du Page Cp., IL.

4779   iii   Donald Edric^{10} **Watson**.

4780   iv   Deborah Jeanne^{10} **Watson**.

4061. Kenneth Frederick^9 **Bovee** (Kenneth Jacob^8, William Ludington^7, Cornelius Elihu^6, Cornelius Schermerhorn^5, Matthew^4, Jacob^3, Nicholas^2, Mathieu^1), born 20 Jan 1921 in Monroe Co., NY; died 29 Mar 1990. He married on 17 Apr 1943 Ann Nixon, born 21 Oct 1923 in Geneseo, Livingston Co., NY, daughter of Erwin Nixon and Helen Owens.

Children of Kenneth Frederick Bovee and Ann Nixon were as follows:

4781 i Gary Kenneth[10] **Bovee**, born in Batavia, Genesee Co., NY. He married on 31 Mar 1984 **June Burdick**.

+ 4782 ii Diane[10] **Bovee**, born in Batavia, Genesee Co., NY. She married **Dale Beardsley**.

4072. Roswell[9] **Bovee** (Albert A[8], Hiram[7], Luther[6], Jacob[5], Anthony[4], Gerrit[3], Anthony[2], Mathieu[1]), born 19 Jul 1907; died 1980. He married Susana Kesier.

Children of Roswell Bovee and Susana Kesier were as follows:

4783 i Mildred[10] **Bovee**.

4784 ii Gary John[10] **Bovee**, born 13 Nov 1935 in Lake Luzerne, Warren Co., NY; died 20 Aug 1993. He married **Ruth Elsie Austin**.

4785 iii Edward Philip[10] **Bovee**.

4786 iv Lawrence[10] **Bovee**.

4074. Claude Henry[9] **Bovee** (Albert A[8], Hiram[7], Luther[6], Jacob[5], Anthony[4], Gerrit[3], Anthony[2], Mathieu[1]), born 16 Nov 1909 in Fenimore, NY; died 11 May 1996 in Glens Falls, Warren Co., NY. He married on 10 Mar 1934 in Lake Luzern, Warren Co., NY Julia Sarah Gilbert, born 23 Nov 1916, daughter of Walter Edison Gilbert and Blanche Emma Taylor.

Children of Claude Henry Bovee and Julia Sarah Gilbert were as follows:

4787 i Patricia Ann[10] **Bovee**, born 19 Jun 1934; died 18 Apr 1995. She married (1) **Godfrey Waterman**; (2) **Thomas Murphy**.

4788 ii William[10] **Claude**.

+ 4789 iii Ronald[10] **Bovee**, born in Lake Luzerne, Warren Co., NY. He married **Janice Lois Stewart**.

4790 iv Sandra Lou[10] **Bovee**, born in Glens Falls, Warren Co., NY. She married (1) on 7 Nov 1981 **William Frederick Gorton**; (2) on 2 Mar 1987, divorced **Joseph David Gonyea**.

4791 v Terry Walter[10] **Bovee**, born in Corinth, Saratoga Co., NY. He married on 8 Aug 1964 **Roberta Barrett**.

4792 vi Judith Alice[10] **Bovee**, born in Glens Falls, Warren Co., NY. She married **Theodore Barrett**.

+ 4793 vii John Francis[10] **Bovee**, born in Glens Falls, Warren Co., NY. He married (1) **Mary Jane Ovitt**; (2) **Corine Stephens**.

+ 4794 viii James Wayne[10] **Bovee**, born in Glens Falls, Warren Co., NY. He married **Cathy Ann Mosher**.

4080. Donald Marcus[9] **Bovee** (Walter W[8], Henry L[7], Luther[6], Jacob[5], Anthony[4],

Gerrit³, Anthony², Mathieu¹), born 1915. He married (1) Rouette C Bush, born 17 Apr 1917; died Jul 1978; (2) Eva Pashley, born 1922; died 20 Nov 1992, daughter of Benjamine Pashley.

Children of Donald Marcus Bovee and Rouette C Bush were as follows:

4795	i	Donna¹⁰ **Bovee**. She married **(---) McGowan**.
4796	ii	Gail¹⁰ **Bovee**. She married **(---) Ridgeway**.
+ 4797	iii	Thomas W¹⁰ **Bovee**. He married **Carol (---)**.

4081. Gerald Arthur⁹ **Bovee** (Beecher A⁸, Henry L⁷, Luther⁶, Jacob⁵, Anthony⁴, Gerrit³, Anthony², Mathieu¹), born 30 Jul 1928 in NY. He married Jean Brown.

Children of Gerald Arthur Bovee and Jean Brown were as follows:

4798	i	David Gerald¹⁰ **Bovee**, born in NY.
4799	ii	Darrell Clayton¹⁰ **Bovee**, born in NY.
4800	iii	Kathryn Jean¹⁰ **Bovee**, born in NY.

4083. Marcus Trevor⁹ **Bovee** (Marcus Sherman⁸, Henry L⁷, Luther⁶, Jacob⁵, Anthony⁴, Gerrit³, Anthony², Mathieu¹). He married (1) on 10 May 1962 Beverly Mae LaRich; (2) on 8 Sep 1983 Ingeborg Meyer.

Children of Marcus Trevor Bovee and Beverly Mae LaRich were as follows:

4801	i	Marcus Trevor¹⁰ **Bovee** Jr.
4802	ii	Peter Trent¹⁰ **Bovee**.

4088. Daniel John⁹ **Bovee** (George Melvin⁸, Fred⁷, Luther⁶, Jacob⁵, Anthony⁴, Gerrit³, Anthony², Mathieu¹), born abt 1930. He married in 1955 Dawn Arsenault.

Children of Daniel John Bovee and Dawn Arsenault were as follows:

+ 4803	i	Kim Daniel¹⁰ **Bovee**. He married **Jane Blower**.
+ 4804	ii	Kelly Anthony¹⁰ **Bovee**. He married **Danita Brownell**.

4097. Maurice T⁹ **Bovee** (Warren⁸, Frank⁷, Norman⁶, Jacob⁵, Anthony⁴, Gerrit³, Anthony², Mathieu¹), born 28 Jan 1923; died 20 Feb 1968. He married abt 1950 Delores Grieve Beagle.

Children of Maurice T Bovee and Delores Grieve Beagle were as follows:

4805	i	Larry¹⁰ **Bovee**.
4806	ii	Keefe¹⁰ **Bovee**.
4807	iii	Jerry¹⁰ **Bovee**.

4098. Francis Clarence⁹ **Bovee** (Harold⁸, Charles⁷, Norman⁶, Jacob⁵, Anthony⁴,

Gerrit[3], Anthony[2], Mathieu[1]), born 1930; died 10 Feb 1994. He married Margaret Long.

Children of Francis Clarence Bovee and Margaret Long were as follows:

4808   i   Steven F[10] **Bovee**.

4809   ii   Carol[10] **Bovee**.

4810   iii   Jennette[10] **Bovee**.

4811   iv   Sherrie[10] **Bovee**. She married **(---) Richards**.

4099. Robert Charles[9] **Bovee** (Harold[8], Charles[7], Norman[6], Jacob[5], Anthony[4], Gerrit[3], Anthony[2], Mathieu[1]). He married Pamela Wilcox.

Children of Robert Charles Bovee and Pamela Wilcox were as follows:

4812   i   Wayne[10] **Bovee**.

4813   ii   Gary[10] **Bovee**.

4814   iii   Carmetta Gertrude[10] **Bovee**.

4106. Dannie Harold[9] **Bovee** (Carl Harvey[8], Charles[7], Norman[6], Jacob[5], Anthony[4], Gerrit[3], Anthony[2], Mathieu[1]). He married (1) on 15 Apr 1960 Kaye Louise Bryngelson; (2) Sheryl (---).

Children of Dannie Harold Bovee and Kaye Louise Bryngelson were as follows:

4815   i   Michael Lee[10] **Bovee**. He married **Teresa Marie German**.

4816   ii   Susan Louise[10] **Bovee**. She married **Lawrence Allan Donahue**.

4133. Willard L[9] **Bovee** (Willard L[8], Lester[7], Norman[6], Jacob[5], Anthony[4], Gerrit[3], Anthony[2], Mathieu[1]). He married (1) Barbara Grimes; (2) on 30 Nov 1996 Betty Stedman.

Children of Willard L Bovee and Barbara Grimes were as follows:

+   4817   i   Kevin John[10] **Bovee**. He married unknown.

+   4818   ii   Mathew Scott[10] **Bovee**. He married **Donna Sherwood**.

4134. James Kenneth[9] **Bovee** (Willard L[8], Lester[7], Norman[6], Jacob[5], Anthony[4], Gerrit[3], Anthony[2], Mathieu[1]). He married on 18 Feb 1969 Sharon Allenon.

Children of James Kenneth Bovee and Sharon Allenon were as follows:

4819   i   James K[10] **Bovee**. He married **Colleen Conroy**.

4820   ii   Jeffrey Scott[10] **Bovee**.

4821   iii   Tina Marie[10] **Bovee**. She married **Phillip Fuller**.

4137. Henry Frederick^9 **Bovee** (Willard L^8, Lester^7, Norman^6, Jacob^5, Anthony^4, Gerrit^3, Anthony^2, Mathieu^1). He married (1) Deborah,Stert (---); (2) Melanie (---).

Children of Henry Frederick Bovee and Melanie (---) were as follows:

4822   i   Brad^{10} **Bovee**.

4823   ii   Devin^{10} **Bovee**.

4824   iii   Aaron^{10} **Bovee**.

4144. Michael Lynn^9 **Bovee** (Edward LeRoy^8, Guy Harrison^7, Eugene M^6, Joseph^5, Anthony^4, Gerrit^3, Anthony^2, Mathieu^1). He married (1) Denise Dilley; (2) Joanne Benninghoven.

Children of Michael Lynn Bovee and Denise Dilley were as follows:

4825   i   Jason M^{10} **Bovee**.

4826   ii   Karrie A^{10} **Bovee**.

4827   iii   Shane M^{10} **Bovee**.

Children of Michael Lynn Bovee and Joanne Benninghoven were as follows:

4828   i   Breanne M^{10} **Bovee**.

4829   ii   Brett M^{10} **Bovee**.

4153. Rex^9 **Bovee** Jr (Rex Everett^8, Claude Alva^7, Eugene M^6, Joseph^5, Anthony^4, Gerrit^3, Anthony^2, Mathieu^1). He married Vickie Haykin.

Children of Rex Bovee Jr and Vickie Haykin were as follows:

4830   i   Beth^{10} **Bovee**.

4831   ii   Joanna^{10} **Bovee**.

4157. Grace B^9 **Bovee** (David Grosvenor^8, Charles Howard^7, David^6, Jonathan^5, Peter^4, Gerrit^3, Anthony^2, Mathieu^1). She married Doug Devin.

Children of Grace B Bovee and Doug Devin were as follows:

4832   i   Steve^{10} **Devin**.

4833   ii   Betsy^{10} **Devin**. She married **(---) Smith**.

4160. William Richard^9 **Bovee** (William Arthur^8, Edwin Anson^7, Eli William^6, Jonathan^5, Peter^4, Gerrit^3, Anthony^2, Mathieu^1), born 3 Jan 1918 in Traverse City, Grand Traverse Co., MI; christened in Traverse City, Grand Traverse Co., MI; died 4 Apr 1994 in Bay City, Bay Co., MI. He married (1) on 9 Mar 1946 in Central U M Ch, Traverse City, Grand Traverse Co., MI Elizabeth J Kistler, born 17 Apr 1922 in Traverse City, Grand Traverse Co., MI; christened in Bay City, Bay Co., MI; died 18 Apr 1982 in Bay City, Bay Co., MI, daughter of Hornisod

Kistler and Alma Meteen; (2) on 16 Feb 1991 in Bay City, Bay Co., MI Marian (---).

Children of William Richard Bovee and Elizabeth J Kistler were as follows:

4834   i   William Richard^{10} **Bovee** Jr, born in Traverse City, Grand Traverse Co., MI; christened in Bay City, Bay Co., MI. He married on 7 Dec 1968 in Bay City, Bay Co., MI **Janet Kirk**.

4835   ii   Barbara Jean^{10} **Bovee**, born in Saginaw, Saginaw Co., MI; christened in Bay City, Bay Co., MI.

4161. Thomas R^{9} **Bovee** (William Arthur^{8}, Edwin Anson^{7}, Eli William^{6}, Jonathan^{5}, Peter^{4}, Gerrit^{3}, Anthony^{2}, Mathieu^{1}), born 31 Jan 1920 in Traverse City, Grand Traverse Co., MI. He married on 22 Feb 1941 in Traverse City, Grand Traverse Co., MI Elizabeth Jane Williams, born 12 May 1922 in Traverse City, Grand Traverse Co., MI, daughter of Bert T Williams and Florence Skellett.

Children of Thomas R Bovee and Elizabeth Jane Williams were as follows:

4836   i   Sandra Lee^{10} **Bovee**, born in Traverse City, Grand Traverse Co., MI. She married **(---) Storrs**.

4837   ii   John Thomas^{10} **Bovee**, born in Traverse City, Grand Traverse Co., MI.

4162. Lloyd Champlin^{9} **Bovee** (William Arthur^{8}, Edwin Anson^{7}, Eli William^{6}, Jonathan^{5}, Peter^{4}, Gerrit^{3}, Anthony^{2}, Mathieu^{1}), born 21 Oct 1923 in Traverse City, Grand Traverse Co., MI; died 16 May 1992 in Wapakoneta, Auglaize Co., OH. He married on 12 Jun 1943 in Detroit, Wayne Co., MI Inez Ford Neiswonger, born 23 Sep 1923 in Cleveland, Cayahoga Co., OH, daughter of Kenneth George Neiswonger and Lena Oceola Ford.

Children of Lloyd Champlin Bovee and Inez Ford Neiswonger were as follows:

+   4838   i   Dianne Elizabeth^{10} **Bovee**, born in Traverse City, Grand Traverse Co., MI. She married **Karl Arthur Jenkins**.

4839   ii   Thomas Richard^{10} **Bovee**, born in Detroit, Wayne Co., MI.

4840   iii   Debra Lynn^{10} **Bovee**, born in Lima, Allen Co., OH. She married on 23 Sep 1990 in United Methodist Church, Wapakoneta, Auglaize Co., OH **Philip Kinstle**, born in Lima, Allen Co., OH, son of Herbert Kinstle and Marie Naylor.

4841   iv   Michael William^{10} **Bovee**, born in Lima, Allen Co., OH.

4163. Elizabeth Lorrain^{9} **Bovee** (William Arthur^{8}, Edwin Anson^{7}, Eli William^{6}, Jonathan^{5}, Peter^{4}, Gerrit^{3}, Anthony^{2}, Mathieu^{1}), born 16 Feb 1926 in Traverse City, Grand Traverse Co., MI; christened 24 Mar 1940 in Traverse City, Grand Traverse Co., MI; died 1 Aug 1997 in Tucson, Pima Co., AZ. She married on 18 Oct 1951 in Bellmore, Nassau Co., NY Otto J Olsson, born 30 Sep 1924 in

Bellmore, Nassau Co., NY, son of John Olof Olsson and Margit Elleretsen Morbekk.

Children of Elizabeth Lorrain Bovee and Otto J Olsson were as follows:

4842 i Dr John M[10] **Olsson**, born in Bay Shore, Suffolk Co., NY. He married on 24 Jun 1978 in Harrisburg, Dauphin Co., PA **Dr Miriam E Wildeman**.

4843 ii Karen L[10] **Olsson**, born in Suffolk Co., NY.

4844 iii David C[10] **Olsson**, born in West Islip, Suffolk Co., NY.

4845 iv Eric T[10] **Olsson**, born in West Islip, Suffolk Co., NY.

4165. Dorothy Irene[9] **Bovee** (David Lloyd[8], Edwin Anson[7], Eli William[6], Jonathan[5], Peter[4], Gerrit[3], Anthony[2], Mathieu[1]), born 14 Aug 1908 in Grand Rapids, Kent Co., MI; died 23 Jul 1982 in Hastings, Barry Co., MI. She married on 28 Aug 1935 in Grand Rapids, Kent Co., MI Rev William Edgeworth Potts, died 11 Feb 1961 in Ann Arbor, Washtenaw Co., MI.

Children of Dorothy Irene Bovee and Rev William Edgeworth Potts were as follows:

4846 i Mary Martha[10] **Potts**, born in Grand Rapids, Kent Co., MI. She married on 25 Jun 1966 in Athens, Calhoun Co., MI **Larry Melendy**.

4847 ii William Edgeworth[10] **Potts** Jr, born in Grand Rapids, Kent Co., MI. He married on 4 Oct 1969 **Noralee Carrier**.

4166. Margaret Eileen[9] **Bovee** (David Lloyd[8], Edwin Anson[7], Eli William[6], Jonathan[5], Peter[4], Gerrit[3], Anthony[2], Mathieu[1]), born 22 Apr 1910 in Grand Rapids, Kent Co., MI; died Jan 2001. She married on 15 Oct 1932 in Grand Rapids, Kent Co., MI Earl Paul Wagner, died 27 Feb 1976.

Children of Margaret Eileen Bovee and Earl Paul Wagner were as follows:

4848 i Joyce Eileen[10] **Wagner**, born in E Grand Rapids, Kent Co., MI. She married on 23 Jun 1951 **Donald Edward Brown**.

4167. Lillian Mae[9] **Bovee** (David Lloyd[8], Edwin Anson[7], Eli William[6], Jonathan[5], Peter[4], Gerrit[3], Anthony[2], Mathieu[1]), born 20 Nov 1913 in Grand Rapids, Kent Co., MI; died 11 Mar 2000 in Grand Rapids, Kent Co., MI. She married on 2 Jul 1937 in Grand Rapids, Kent Co., MI Arthur Oscar Holmberg, born 2 Feb 1901 in MI; died 8 Mar 1983 in Grand Rapids, Kent Co., MI.

Children of Lillian Mae Bovee and Arthur Oscar Holmberg were as follows:

4849 i David Carl[10] **Holmberg**, born in Grand Rapids, Kent Co., MI. He married on 29 Jul 1967 in Grand Rapids, Kent Co., MI **Yvonnne Marie Wisniewski**.

4850 ii Carol Jean[10] **Holmberg**, born in Grand Rapids, Kent Co.,

MI. She married on 12 Nov 1966 in Grand Rapids, Kent Co., MI **Richard James Vandenberg**, born 6 Mar 1941; died 17 Aug 1977 in Grand Rapids, Kent Co., MI.

4168. Edwin Wright[9] **Bovee** (David Lloyd[8], Edwin Anson[7], Eli William[6], Jonathan[5], Peter[4], Gerrit[3], Anthony[2], Mathieu[1]), born 21 Mar 1917 in Grand Rapids, Kent Co., MI; died 31 Dec 1986 in Grand Rapids, Kent Co., MI. He married on 22 Jun 1940 in Grand Rapids, Kent Co., MI Doris Elaine Bergers, born 18 Apr 1918; died 4 Jul 1992 in East Grand Rapids, Kent Co., MI.

Children of Edwin Wright Bovee and Doris Elaine Bergers were as follows:

+ 4851   i   Lloyd Martin[10] **Bovee**, born in Grand Rapids, Kent Co., MI. He married (1) **Madeline Judith Labree**; (2) **Gay Marie Chambers**.
+ 4852   ii   Byron Wright[10] **Bovee**, born in Grand Rapids, Kent Co., MI. He married (1) **Phyllis Ilene Haas**; (2) **Victoria Lee Vogel**; (3) **Priscilla Ann Hefferan**.
+ 4853   iii   Beverly Ann[10] **Bovee**, born in Grand Rapids, Kent Co., MI. She married **Kenneth Murray Stevens**.

4185. Kenneth Carl[9] **Bovee** (Carl Folette[8], Elmer Ellsworth[7], Clark[6], Jonathan[5], Peter[4], Gerrit[3], Anthony[2], Mathieu[1]), born in Chicago, Cook Co., IL. He married Terry Lee Turner, born in Malvern Chester Co., PA.

Children of Kenneth Carl Bovee and Terry Lee Turner were as follows:

4854   i   Benton[10] **Bovee**.
4855   ii   Child[10] **Bovee**.
4856   iii   Child[10] **Bovee**.

4189. Helen Jean[9] **Bovee** (Kenneth Clark[8], Henry Orgo[7], Clark[6], Jonathan[5], Peter[4], Gerrit[3], Anthony[2], Mathieu[1]). She married on 24 Jun 1957 Jerry Groner, born 9 Sep 1926.

Children of Helen Jean Bovee and Jerry Groner were as follows:

4857   i   Diane Lynn[10] **Groner**.

4199. Cecil Lynn[9] **Bovee** (Benjamin Samuel[8], Frank Luther[7], Moses C[6], Moses R[5], Jacob[4], Gerrit[3], Anthony[2], Mathieu[1]), born 29 Sep 1922 in Minneapolis, Hennepin Co., MN. He married Mildred Eddy.

Children of Cecil Lynn Bovee and Mildred Eddy were as follows:

4858   i   Jodeen[10] **Bovee**.
4859   ii   Kim[10] **Bovee**.
+ 4860   iii   Kevin[10] **Bovee**, born in Ypsilanti, Washtenaw Co., MI. He married unknown.

4204. Ronald Craig[9] **Bovee** (Homer Charles[8], Charles Edward[7], Moses C[6], Moses R[5], Jacob[4], Gerrit[3], Anthony[2], Mathieu[1]), born 18 Mar 1944; died 2001. He married on 17 Nov 1967 Kathleen Sandra Brown.

Children of Ronald Craig Bovee and Kathleen Sandra Brown were as follows:

| 4861 | i | Craig Richard[10] **Bovee**. He married **Erica Sue Roberts**. |
| 4862 | ii | Sherri Lynn[10] **Bovee**. |

4206. Dennis J[9] **Bovee** (Homer Charles[8], Charles Edward[7], Moses C[6], Moses R[5], Jacob[4], Gerrit[3], Anthony[2], Mathieu[1]). He married on 15 Jun 1968 Darlene Ethel Drummer.

Children of Dennis J Bovee and Darlene Ethel Drummer were as follows:

| 4863 | i | David John[10] **Bovee**. |
| 4864 | ii | Darla Jane[10] **Bovee**. |

4210. Charles Clyde[9] **Bovee** (Homer Thomas[8], Clyde Charles[7], James B[6], Moses R[5], Jacob[4], Gerrit[3], Anthony[2], Mathieu[1]), born 11 Feb 1926. He married Edyth Wessling, born 1924.

Children of Charles Clyde Bovee and Edyth Wessling were as follows:

4865	i	Michael Leigh[10] **Bovee**, born in Chattanooga, Hamilton Co., TN.
4866	ii	Michelle Kent[10] **Bovee**, born in Chattanooga, Hamilton Co., TN. She married (1) on 25 Aug 1979, divorced **Theodore Avery Wright**; (2) on 30 Jan 1995 **Joseph A Masters**.
+ 4867	iii	Kent Thomas[10] **Bovee**, born in Bristol, Sullivan Co., TN. He married **Dawn Georgia**.
+ 4868	iv	Mark Teroller[10] **Bovee**, born in Atlanta Fulton Co., GA. He married **Christianne Collette Rouland**.
4869	v	Geoffrey Spence[10] **Bovee**, born in Atlanta Fulton Co., GA.

4212. Earl Clyde[9] **Bovee** Jr (Earle Clyde[8], Clyde Charles[7], James B[6], Moses R[5], Jacob[4], Gerrit[3], Anthony[2], Mathieu[1]), born 20 Jun 1916 in Sumner, Pierce Co., WA. He married on 15 Jun 1940 Emily Mae Vicary, born 31 May 1916.

Children of Earl Clyde Bovee Jr and Emily Mae Vicary were as follows:

4870	i	Clyde Douglas[10] **Bovee**.
4871	ii	Janice Louise[10] **Bovee**. She married **Terry Hines**.
4872	iii	Walter Vicary[10] **Bovee**.

4214. Claude Lee^9 **Bovee** (Mark C^8, George M^7, Mark^6, Moses R^5, Jacob^4, Gerrit^3, Anthony^2, Mathieu^1), born 26 May 1911; died Jan 1973 in CA. He married Ethel Rose Austin.

Children of Claude Lee Bovee and Ethel Rose Austin were as follows:

+ 4873 i Claude Lee^{10} **Bovee** Jr. He married **Virginia Carol Jackson**.

4219. Leonard Burl^9 **Bovee** (George^8, George M^7, Mark^6, Moses R^5, Jacob^4, Gerrit^3, Anthony^2, Mathieu^1), born 13 Mar 1920. He married Jeanette Reynolds, born 7 May 1917; died 11 Jul 1988 in Van Nuys, Los Angeles Co., CA.

Children of Leonard Burl Bovee and Jeanette Reynolds were as follows:

+ 4874 i Leonard B^{10} **Bovee**, born in CA. He married (1) **Lynn Swanson**; (2) **Andrea Pepritsch**.
  4875 ii Linda Ann^{10} **Bovee**, born in CA. She married **Timothy Reed Ord**.

4223. George Raymond^9 **Bovee** (George^8, George M^7, Mark^6, Moses R^5, Jacob^4, Gerrit^3, Anthony^2, Mathieu^1). He married (1) Nancy Rose Modisett; (2) Karen Nieda Sundt.

Children of George Raymond Bovee and Nancy Rose Modisett were as follows:

+ 4876 i Raymond George^{10} **Bovee**, born in CA. He married **Debra Sue Bass**.
+ 4877 ii Scott Allyn^{10} **Bovee**, born in CA. He married **Lynn Eleanor McCartney**.
  4878 iii Shera Lynn^{10} **Bovee**, born 15 Jun 1957 in CA; died 4 Oct 1962.
+ 4879 iv Brett Lindsey^{10} **Bovee**, born in CA. He married **Kris Elise Kastney**.

4229. James Findlay^9 **Bovee** (John Colin^8, Harry W^7, Otis M^6, Courtland^5, Jacob^4, Gerrit^3, Anthony^2, Mathieu^1), born in CA. He married Brenda Bond.

Children of James Findlay Bovee and Brenda Bond were as follows:

  4880 i Daniel James^{10} **Bovee**, born in CA.
  4881 ii Brittany Jo^{10} **Bovee**, born in CA.

Generation 10

4245. Gerald Nelson^{10} **Bovee** (Glenn Nelson^9, Manley Glenn^8, John Nelson^7, Richard^6, Elisha^5, Cornelius^4, Rykert^3, Nicholas^2, Mathieu^1), born 11 Aug 1939 in

San Diego, San Diego Co., CA; died Oct 2002 in Sun City, Maricopa Co., AZ. He married on 31 Jan 1959 in Reno, Washoe Co., NV Sharon Ann Morris, born in Ashland, Jackson Co., OR.

Children of Gerald Nelson Bovee and Sharon Ann Morris were as follows:

4882	i	Kimberly Ann[11] **Bovee**, born in Klamath Falls, Klamath Co., OR.
+ 4883	ii	Leota Margaret[11] **Bovee**, born in Klamath Falls, Klamath Co., OR. She married **Kenneth Croft Gaddis**.
+ 4884	iii	David Nelson[11] **Bovee**, born in La Mesa, San Diego Co., CA. He married **Kris Ann Reed**.
+ 4885	iv	Gregory Preston[11] **Bovee**, born in La Mesa, San Diego Co., CA. He married (1) **Anne Marie Miller**; (2) **Lisa Christine Regalia**; (3) **Wendie Lynn Cartright**.

4247. Roger Lee[10] **Bovee** (Lillburn Robert[9], Manley Glenn[8], John Nelson[7], Richard[6], Elisha[5], Cornelius[4], Rykert[3], Nicholas[2], Mathieu[1]), born in San Diego, San Diego Co., CA. He married on 21 Jun 1980 in Acme, Whatcom Co., WA Constance Levac, born in Poughkeepsie, Dutchess Co., NY.

Children of Roger Lee Bovee and Constance Levac were as follows:

4886	i	Justin Roger[11] **Bovee**, born in Weber Co., UT.
4887	ii	Leighton Neil[11] **Bovee**, born in Weber Co., UT.

4248. Dennis Robert[10] **Bovee** (Lillburn Robert[9], Manley Glenn[8], John Nelson[7], Richard[6], Elisha[5], Cornelius[4], Rykert[3], Nicholas[2], Mathieu[1]), born in San Diego, San Diego Co., CA. He married on 15 Jan 1974 in San Diego, San Diego Co., CA Robyn Renee Schmidt, born in National City, San Diego Co., CA.

Children of Dennis Robert Bovee and Robyn Renee Schmidt were as follows:

4888	i	Jonathan Robert[11] **Bovee**, born in San Diego, San Diego Co., CA.

4249. Sharon Ann[10] **Bovee** (Lillburn Robert[9], Manley Glenn[8], John Nelson[7], Richard[6], Elisha[5], Cornelius[4], Rykert[3], Nicholas[2], Mathieu[1]), born in San Diego, San Diego Co., CA. She married on 18 Jul 1965 in Faifield, Solana Co., CA Michael Alan Marianno, born in Woodland, Yolo Co., CA, son of Frank A Marianno and Catherine Tierman.

Children of Sharon Ann Bovee and Michael Alan Marianno were as follows:

4889	i	Michael Alan[11] **Marianno** Jr., born in Fairfield, Solano Co., CA.
4890	ii	James Robert[11] **Marianno**, born in Fairfield, Solano Co., CA.

4250. Allan Wayne[10] **Bovee** (Allan Douglas[9], Manley Glenn[8], John Nelson[7], Richard[6], Elisha[5], Cornelius[4], Rykert[3], Nicholas[2], Mathieu[1]), born in San Diego, San Diego Co., CA. He married on 17 Jul 1971 in Oroville, Butte Co., CA Judy Caroline Wilson, born in Gridley, Butte Co., CA.

Children of Allan Wayne Bovee and Judy Caroline Wilson were as follows:

4891   i   Jill Nichole[11] **Bovee**, born in Modesto, Stanislaus Co., CA.

4892   ii   Steven Daniel[11] **Bovee**, born in Modesto, Stanislaus Co., CA.

4251. Steven Douglas[10] **Bovee** (Allan Douglas[9], Manley Glenn[8], John Nelson[7], Richard[6], Elisha[5], Cornelius[4], Rykert[3], Nicholas[2], Mathieu[1]), born in Alhambra, Los Angeles Co., CA. He married on 23 Jul 1967 in Covina, Los Angeles Co., CA Shyrle Jeanne Darby, born in Los Angeles, Los Angeles Co., CA.

Children of Steven Douglas Bovee and Shyrle Jeanne Darby were as follows:

4893   i   Brian Steven[11] **Bovee**, born in Bitborg, Germany.

4894   ii   Robine Diane[11] **Bovee**, born in Hemiet, Riverside Co., CA.

4259. Karen Garnet[10] **Bovee** (Leslie Gerald[9], Manley Glenn[8], John Nelson[7], Richard[6], Elisha[5], Cornelius[4], Rykert[3], Nicholas[2], Mathieu[1]), born in LaMesa, San Diego Co., CA. She married on 8 Jul 1966 in El Cajon, San Diego Co., CA James Talada.

Children of Karen Garnet Bovee and James Talada were as follows:

4895   i   Kevin Jay[11] **Talada**, born in San Diego, San Diego Co., CA.

4896   ii   Kandy Kim[11] **Talada**, born in San Diego, San Diego Co., CA.

4260. Colleen Rachel[10] **Bovee** (Leslie Gerald[9], Manley Glenn[8], John Nelson[7], Richard[6], Elisha[5], Cornelius[4], Rykert[3], Nicholas[2], Mathieu[1]), born in San Diego, San Diego Co., CA. She married on 7 Jun 1971 James Morocco.

Children of Colleen Rachel Bovee and James Morocco were as follows:

4897   i   Jamie Cayleen[11] **Morocco**.

4898   ii   Janelle Cara[11] **Morocco**.

4899   iii   Joshua Cary[11] **Morocco**.

4261. Melody Layne[10] **Bovee** (Leslie Gerald[9], Manley Glenn[8], John Nelson[7], Richard[6], Elisha[5], Cornelius[4], Rykert[3], Nicholas[2], Mathieu[1]), born in San Diego, San Diego Co., CA. She married on 21 Mar 1970 Gary Mills.

Children of Melody Layne Bovee and Gary Mills were as follows:

4900   i   Rachel Ann[11] **Mills**.

4901   ii   Tamera Michelle[11] **Mills**.

4273. Keith R[10] **Bovee** (Burt Richard[9], Ira Burt[8], John Nelson[7], Richard[6], Elisha[5], Cornelius[4], Rykert[3], Nicholas[2], Mathieu[1]). He married Norma Jean (---).

Children of Keith R Bovee and Norma Jean (---) were as follows:

4902   i   Weston[11] **Bovee**.

4903   ii   Grant[11] **Bovee**.

4276. Kermit D[10] **Bovee** Jr (Kermit R[9], Walter Richard[8], Jacob Newton[7], David[6], Elisha[5], Cornelius[4], Rykert[3], Nicholas[2], Mathieu[1]), born 13 Mar 1928 in Remer, Cass Co., MN; died 22 May 1983 in Lewis & Clark Co., MT. He married abt 1950 Beverly Bowman.

Children of Kermit D Bovee Jr and Beverly Bowman were as follows:

4904   i   Christine[11] **Bovee**.

4905   ii   Kevin[11] **Bovee**, born 27 Nov 1954; died Feb 1978 in Billings, Yellowstone Co., MT.

4906   iii   Brent[11] **Bovee**.

4277. Bonnie Lee[10] **Bovee** (Kermit R[9], Walter Richard[8], Jacob Newton[7], David[6], Elisha[5], Cornelius[4], Rykert[3], Nicholas[2], Mathieu[1]). She married Robert Lawrence Ferdelman.

Children of Bonnie Lee Bovee and Robert Lawrence Ferdelman were as follows:

4907   i   Mark Robert[11] **Ferdelman**, born in Hennepin Co., MN.

4908   ii   Jay Lawrence[11] **Ferdelman**, born in Hennepin Co., MN.

4909   iii   Scott Alan[11] **Ferdelman**, born in Hennepin Co., MN.

4910   iv   Tracy Lee[11] **Ferdelman**, born in Hennepin Co., MN.

4911   v   Bobbie Lee[11] **Ferdelman**, born in Hennepin Co., MN.

4282. Lynda Karen[10] **Bovee** (Forrest W[9], Walter Richard[8], Jacob Newton[7], David[6], Elisha[5], Cornelius[4], Rykert[3], Nicholas[2], Mathieu[1]). She married Darwin Michel Alar.

Children of Lynda Karen Bovee and Darwin Michel Alar were as follows:

4912   i   Rachel Lyn[11] **Alar**, born in St Louis Co., MN.

4913   ii   Christopher Michael[11] **Allar**, born in St Louis Co., MN.

4283. Wendy Ann^{10} **Bovee** (Forrest W^9, Walter Richard^8, Jacob Newton^7, David^6, Elisha^5, Cornelius^4, Rykert^3, Nicholas^2, Mathieu^1), born in Dallas, Dallas Co., TX. She married Norik Assatourian.

Children of Wendy Ann Bovee and Norik Assatourian were as follows:

4914   i   Lydia^{11} **Assatourian**.

4915   ii   Sevon^{11} **Assatourian**.

4286. Cynthia Kay^{10} **Bovee** (Forrest W^9, Walter Richard^8, Jacob Newton^7, David^6, Elisha^5, Cornelius^4, Rykert^3, Nicholas^2, Mathieu^1), born in Hoyt Lakes, St Louis Co., MN. She married (1) Kieth Norris Sigman; (2) Kieth Norris.

Children of Cynthia Kay Bovee and Kieth Norris Sigman were as follows:

4916   i   Michael Leroy^{11} **Sigman** Jr..

4917   ii   Damon Jeremy^{11} **Sigman**.

4287. Becky Sue^{10} **Bovee** (Forrest W^9, Walter Richard^8, Jacob Newton^7, David^6, Elisha^5, Cornelius^4, Rykert^3, Nicholas^2, Mathieu^1), born in Wichita, Sedgwick Co., KS. She married James Anthoy Reek.

Children of Becky Sue Bovee and James Anthoy Reek were as follows:

4918   i   Brandon James^{11} **Reek**, born in St Louis Co., MN.

4919   ii   Christopher Owen^{11} **Reek**, born in St Louis Co., MN.

4291. Peter Roger^{10} **Bovee** (Caryl Roger^9, Roderick^8, Jacob Newton^7, David^6, Elisha^5, Cornelius^4, Rykert^3, Nicholas^2, Mathieu^1). He married on 30 Aug 1958 Mary Nell Johnson.

Children of Peter Roger Bovee and Mary Nell Johnson were as follows:

+   4920   i   Chad Mathew^{11} **Bovee**, born in Bemidji, Beltrami Co., MN. He married **Mary Taylor**.

+   4921   ii   Joel Steven^{11} **Bovee**. He married **Naomi Helen Bjorg**.

     4922   iii   Patrick Roger^{11} **Bovee**.

4302. Roger Edward^{10} **Bovee** (John Richard^9, Roderick^8, Jacob Newton^7, David^6, Elisha^5, Cornelius^4, Rykert^3, Nicholas^2, Mathieu^1). He married Kelly Marie Aamodt.

Children of Roger Edward Bovee and Kelly Marie Aamodt were as follows:

4923   i   Cole Russell^{11} **Bovee**, born in Beltrami Co., MN.

4924   ii   Josie Rain^{11} **Bovee**, born in Wright Co., MN.

4305. William^{10} **Bovee** (Myron^9, George F^8, Cornelius^7, Jonas Nicholas^6, Nicholas^5, Cornelius^4, Rykert^3, Nicholas^2, Mathieu^1). He married unknown.

Children of William Bovee were as follows:

4925	i	William^{11} **Bovee** Jr.
4926	ii	Buddy^{11} **Bovee**.
4927	iii	Gail^{11} **Bovee**.

4306. Frank W^{10} **Bovee** (Myron^9, George F^8, Cornelius^7, Jonas Nicholas^6, Nicholas^5, Cornelius^4, Rykert^3, Nicholas^2, Mathieu^1). He married (1) Gladys (---); (2) Myrtle (---).

Children of Frank W Bovee and Gladys (---) were as follows:

| 4928 | i | Becky^{11} **Bovee**. |
| 4929 | ii | Myron^{11} **Bovee**. |

4311. Richard^{10} **Bovee** (Alton E^9, George F^8, Cornelius^7, Jonas Nicholas^6, Nicholas^5, Cornelius^4, Rykert^3, Nicholas^2, Mathieu^1). He married Karen (---).

Children of Richard Bovee and Karen (---) were as follows:

4930	i	Paul Richard^{11} **Bovee**.
4931	ii	Dustin Lynn^{11} **Bovee**.
+ 4932	iii	Aprille^{11} **Bovee**. She married **Norman Charles Wilson**.

4321. Robert^{10} **Bovee** (Duane Lorenzo^9, Hiram Nelson^8, Cornelius^7, Jonas Nicholas^6, Nicholas^5, Cornelius^4, Rykert^3, Nicholas^2, Mathieu^1), born in Sacramento, Sacramento Co., CA. He married unknown.

Children of Robert Bovee were as follows:

| 4933 | i | Child^{11} **Bovee**. |
| 4934 | ii | Robert (Robbie)^{11} **Bovee**. |

4322. Diane Marie^{10} **Bovee** (Duane Lorenzo^9, Hiram Nelson^8, Cornelius^7, Jonas Nicholas^6, Nicholas^5, Cornelius^4, Rykert^3, Nicholas^2, Mathieu^1), born in Lebanon, Linn Co., OR. She married (1) Mark Hunter; (2) Glenn Shimp.

Children of Diane Marie Bovee and Mark Hunter were as follows:

| 4935 | i | Elias^{11} **Hunter**. |

Children of Diane Marie Bovee and Glenn Shimp were as follows:

| 4936 | i | Justin^{11} **Shimp**. |

4323. Elaine Diane[10] **Bovee** (Wayne Andrew[9], Hiram Nelson[8], Cornelius[7], Jonas Nicholas[6], Nicholas[5], Cornelius[4], Rykert[3], Nicholas[2], Mathieu[1]), born in Fairfield, Solano Co., CA. She married on 6 Dec 1980 in Hammersmith, London, England John James Keirnan, born in Tramore, Waterford, Ireland.

Children of Elaine Diane Bovee and John James Keirnan were as follows:

4937	i	Katheryn Louise[11] **Keirnan**.
4938	ii	Mary Amanda[11] **Keirnan**, born in Renton, King Co., WA.
4939	iii	Rose Fiona[11] **Keirnan**, born in Burien, King Co., WA.
4940	iv	Claire Vevile[11] **Keirnan**, born in Anchorage, Southcentral, AK.

4327. Truman Alphie[10] **Bovee** Jr (Truman Alphie[9], William Alfred[8], Truman Andrew[7], Jonas Nicholas[6], Nicholas[5], Cornelius[4], Rykert[3], Nicholas[2], Mathieu[1]), born 11 Jul 1918 in MT. He married on 18 Apr 1942 Mary Irene Williams.

Children of Truman Alphie Bovee Jr and Mary Irene Williams were as follows:

4941	i	Sharine Roberta[11] **Bovee**, born in Miles City, Custer Co., MT.
4942	ii	Richard Alphie[11] **Bovee**, born in Miles City, Custer Co., MT. He married on 21 Dec 1969 **Madeline Crawford**.
4943	iii	Truman Alphie[11] **Bovee** III, born in Miles City, Custer Co., MT. He married on 20 Apr 1974 **Judy Richardson**.
4944	iv	William Alvin[11] **Bovee**, born in Miles City, Custer Co., MT.
4945	v	Mary Rose[11] **Bovee**, born in Miles City, Custer Co., MT.
4946	vi	Pamela Rose[11] **Bovee**, born in Miles City, Custer Co., MT.

4328. Opal Jennie[10] **Bovee** (Truman Alphie[9], William Alfred[8], Truman Andrew[7], Jonas Nicholas[6], Nicholas[5], Cornelius[4], Rykert[3], Nicholas[2], Mathieu[1]), born 25 Nov 1919 in MT. She married on 9 Sep 1945 Lewis Bucholz.

Children of Opal Jennie Bovee and Lewis Bucholz were as follows:

| 4947 | i | Barbara Jen[11] **Bucholz**, born in Portland, Multnomah Co., OR. |
| 4948 | ii | Ronald Lewis[11] **Bucholz**, born in Portland, Multnomah Co., OR. |

4329. Ruby Irene[10] **Bovee** (Truman Alphie[9], William Alfred[8], Truman Andrew[7], Jonas Nicholas[6], Nicholas[5], Cornelius[4], Rykert[3], Nicholas[2], Mathieu[1]), born 22 Aug 1921. She married on 24 Aug 1940 Samuel H Annalora.

Children of Ruby Irene Bovee and Samuel H Annalora were as follows:

| 4949 | i | Virginia Rose[11] **Annalora**, born in Miles City, Custer Co., MT. |

4950	ii	Julia Catherina [11] **Annalora**.
4951	iii	Jill Ann [11] **Annalora**.
4952	iv	Brian Joseph [11] **Annalora**.

4330. Pearl Rose [10] **Bovee** (Truman Alphie [9], William Alfred [8], Truman Andrew [7], Jonas Nicholas [6], Nicholas [5], Cornelius [4], Rykert [3], Nicholas [2], Mathieu [1]), born 28 Jun 1923. She married (1) on 21 Apr 1942 Gary Martz, died Jun 1945; (2) on 2 Jan 1947 Sylvestor St Peter, born 20 Jul 1920 in Miles City, Custer Co., MT.

Children of Pearl Rose Bovee and Sylvestor St Peter were as follows:

4953	i	Jeffrey Francis [11] **St Peter**, born in Phoenix, Maricopa Co., AZ.

4331. Robert William [10] **Bovee** (Truman Alphie [9], William Alfred [8], Truman Andrew [7], Jonas Nicholas [6], Nicholas [5], Cornelius [4], Rykert [3], Nicholas [2], Mathieu [1]), born 4 Jul 1925. He married on 25 May 1946 Dorothy Miller, born 24 Aug 1929 in Bridger, Carbon Co., MT, daughter of George Miller and Elise (---).

Children of Robert William Bovee and Dorothy Miller were as follows:

+	4954	i	David Lee [11] **Bovee**, born in Miles City, Custer Co., MT. He married **Terry Frazer**.
	4955	ii	Rodger Lee [11] **Bovee**, born in Miles City, Custer Co., MT. He married on 21 Oct 1971 **Rene Jane McBride**.
	4956	iii	Gregory Lee [11] **Bovee**, born in Helena, Lewis & Clark Co., MT.
	4957	iv	Judy Lynn [11] **Bovee**, born in Helena, Lewis & Clark Co., MT.

4333. Glenn M [10] **Bovee** (Robert Alvin [9], William Alfred [8], Truman Andrew [7], Jonas Nicholas [6], Nicholas [5], Cornelius [4], Rykert [3], Nicholas [2], Mathieu [1]), born abt 1917. He married abt 1940 Marjorie (---).

Children of Glenn M Bovee and Marjorie (---) were as follows:

	4958	i	Robert [11] **Bovee**.
	4959	ii	James A [11] **Bovee**.
	4960	iii	David [11] **Bovee**.
+	4961	iv	George Alden [11] **Bovee**. He married **Kimberlee Gay Kreft**.

4334. Lloyd Leroy [10] **Bovee** (Lloyd Laverne [9], William Alfred [8], Truman Andrew [7], Jonas Nicholas [6], Nicholas [5], Cornelius [4], Rykert [3], Nicholas [2], Mathieu [1]), born 21 Aug 1927 in Stanley, Mountrail Co., ND. He married on 5 Nov 1955 in Tacoma, Pierce Co., WA Phyliss E Swenke, daughter of Edward J Swenke and Mary M MacMillan.

Children of Lloyd Leroy Bovee and Phyliss E Swenke were as follows:

+ 4962 i Mary M[11] **Bovee**. She married **John Graves**.
+ 4963 ii Faith P[11] **Bovee**. She married **Warren J Holbrook**.
+ 4964 iii Hope[11] **Bovee**. She married (1) **Scott Eichman**; (2) **(---) Murray**.

4343. Robert Rhys[10] **Bovie** (Robert Jones[9], Frederick Ernest[8], Joseph Harley Clark[7], Frederick Morgan[6], Frederick[5], Cornelius[4], Rykert[3], Nicholas[2], Mathieu[1]). He married unknown.

Children of Robert Rhys Bovie were as follows:

4965 i Rhys Evan[11] **Bovie**.

4350. Sally Renee[10] **Bovie** (David Frederick[9], Frederick Ernest[8], Joseph Harley Clark[7], Frederick Morgan[6], Frederick[5], Cornelius[4], Rykert[3], Nicholas[2], Mathieu[1]), born in Pittsburg, Allegheny Co., PA. She married Emmett Hume.

Children of Sally Renee Bovie and Emmett Hume were as follows:

4966 i David Dylan[11] **Hume**.
4967 ii Cara Louise[11] **Hume**.

4351. Rebecca Kim[10] **Bovie** (David Frederick[9], Frederick Ernest[8], Joseph Harley Clark[7], Frederick Morgan[6], Frederick[5], Cornelius[4], Rykert[3], Nicholas[2], Mathieu[1]), born in Plainfield, Union Co., NJ. She married Peter Wright.

Children of Rebecca Kim Bovie and Peter Wright were as follows:

4968 i Daniel Irving[11] **Wright**.

4357. Harley Howard[10] **Bovee** (Claude Harley[9], William Harlan[8], Archibald Melrose[7], John[6], John[5], Nicholas M[4], Matthew[3], Nicholas[2], Mathieu[1]), born 12 Dec 1918 in Edgecomb, Snohomish Co., WA. He married on 14 Nov 1941 in Pasco, Franklin Co., WA Ila Beryl, Obert, born 11 Feb 1921 in Hamilton, Ravalli Co., MT, daughter of Leslie Ernest Obert and Beryl Patrick.

Children of Harley Howard Bovee and Ila Beryl, Obert were as follows:

+ 4969 i Peggy Lorene[11] **Bovee**, born in La Canada, Los Angeles Co., CA. She married **Nadar Friedman**.
  4970 ii Ila Kathryn[11] **Bovee**, born in Seattle, King Co., WA. She married in Jul 1966 in Seattle, King Co., WA **John Thomas**.
+ 4971 iii Betty Jane[11] **Bovee**, born in Oklahoma City, Oklahoma Co., OK. She married **John De Jurnatt**.
+ 4972 iv Donald Harley[11] **Bovee**, born in Seattle, King Co., WA.

He married **Nancy (---)**.

4358. Robert Clare[10] **Bovee** (Claude Harley[9], William Harlan[8], Archibald Melrose[7], John[6], John[5], Nicholas M[4], Matthew[3], Nicholas[2], Mathieu[1]), born 18 Mar 1921 in Arlington, Snohomish Co., WA. He married on 10 Jul 1942 in Seattle, King Co., WA Mary J Franck, born 25 Sep 1920 in Yakima, Yakima Co., WA.

Children of Robert Clare Bovee and Mary J Franck were as follows:

+ 4973   i   James Clair[11] **Bovee**, born in Seattle, King Co., WA. He married **Lynda Berry**.

   4974   ii   Joan Marie[11] **Bovee**, born in Seattle, King Co., WA. She married on 26 Oct 1966 in Seattle, King Co., WA **Frank Migliore**, son of Leonard Migliore and Rose Carbone.

+ 4975   iii   Robert Paul[11] **Bovee**, born in Seattle, King Co., WA. He married (1) **Vicki Corner**; (2) **Joan Johnson**.

   4976   iv   Therese Marie[11] **Bovee**, born in Seattle, King Co., WA. She married (1) on 31 May 1980 in Kenmore, King Co., WA **John Lewis Mladenovic**, son of Louis Mladenovic and Angie (---); (2) on 12 Aug 1989 in Bothel, King Co., WA **Craig McKelvey**.

4361. Ivan Robert[10] **Bovee** (Hugh Archibald[9], Archibald Theodore[8], Archibald Melrose[7], John[6], John[5], Nicholas M[4], Matthew[3], Nicholas[2], Mathieu[1]). He married Leslie Maclachlin.

Children of Ivan Robert Bovee and Leslie Maclachlin were as follows:

+ 4977   i   Jamie[11] **Bovee**. He married unknown.

   4978   ii   Terre[11] **Bovee**.

4362. Lynwood Wayne[10] **Bovee** (Hugh Archibald[9], Archibald Theodore[8], Archibald Melrose[7], John[6], John[5], Nicholas M[4], Matthew[3], Nicholas[2], Mathieu[1]), born in Cabri, Saskatchewan, Canada. He married Ellen Louise Groger, born in Fort St. John, British Columbia, Canada.

Children of Lynwood Wayne Bovee and Ellen Louise Groger were as follows:

   4979   i   Lisa Rae[11] **Bovee**, born in Fort St. John, British Columbia, Canada. She married **Tony Chisholm**.

+ 4980   ii   Derek Lynnwood[11] **Bovee**, born in Fort Staint John, British Columbia, Canada. He married **Michell (---)**.

   4981   iii   Kara Lorraine[11] **Bovee**, born in Fort St. John, British Columbia, Canada. She married in Fort St. John, British Columbia, Canada **Clem Corbeil**.

4364. William Roscoe[10] **Bovee** (Henry Hopkins[9], Henry Hopkins[8], John Wesley[7], John[6], John[5], Nicholas M[4], Matthew[3], Nicholas[2], Mathieu[1]), born 18 Jan 1938 in CA; died 16 Feb 1981 in Los Angeles, Los Angeles Co., CA. He married on 31 Jul 1964 Charlene Eleanor Bartlett.

Children of William Roscoe Bovee and Charlene Eleanor Bartlett were as follows:

4982   i   Amy Elizabeth[11] **Bovee**.

4367. Jeffrey Alan[10] **Bovee** (Henry Hopkins[9], Henry Hopkins[8], John Wesley[7], John[6], John[5], Nicholas M[4], Matthew[3], Nicholas[2], Mathieu[1]). He married on 20 Apr 1985 Kathleen Dianne Ward, born in Lafayette, Contra Costa Co., CA..

Children of Jeffrey Alan Bovee and Kathleen Dianne Ward were as follows:

4983   i   Jamison Alan[11] **Bovee**, born in Fallbrook, San Diego Co., CA..

4984   ii   Megan Alisya[11] **Bovee**, born in Fallbrook, San Diego Co., CA..

4372. Ila Mae[10] **Bovee** (Harley Ray[9], Arthur Roy[8], John Wesley[7], John[6], John[5], Nicholas M[4], Matthew[3], Nicholas[2], Mathieu[1]), born in Pierce, Pierce Co., NE. She married on 10 Jun 1961 in Valparaiso, Porter Co., IN Frederick William Kraft, born in Fort Wayne, Allen Co., IN, son of Frederick William Kraft and Edna Marie Ulmer.

Children of Ila Mae Bovee and Frederick William Kraft were as follows:

4985   i   Frederick William[11] **Kraft**, born in Chicago Heights, Cook Co., IL.

4986   ii   Elizabeth Lila[11] **Kraft**, born in Park Ridge, Cook Co,. IL.

4987   iii   Alison Marie[11] **Kraft**, born in Park Ridge, Cook Co,. IL.

4374. Rhonda Rae[10] **Bovee** (Harley Ray[9], Arthur Roy[8], John Wesley[7], John[6], John[5], Nicholas M[4], Matthew[3], Nicholas[2], Mathieu[1]), born in Norfolk, Madison Co., NE. She married on 29 Jun 1974 in Sioux Falls, Minnehaha Co., SD Charles Christopher Johnson.

Children of Rhonda Rae Bovee and Charles Christopher Johnson were as follows:

4988   i   Sarah Christine[11] **Johnson**, born in Grant Co, MN.

4989   ii   Emily Maria[11] **Johnson**, born in Pope Co., MN.

4379. John[10] **Bovee** (Robert Wesley[9], William Vivian[8], John McClellan[7], Wesley[6], John[5], Nicholas M[4], Matthew[3], Nicholas[2], Mathieu[1]), born in Bakersfield, Kern Co., CA. He married on 4 Jul 1990 Joanne Hussey.

Children of John Bovee and Joanne Hussey were as follows:

4990   i   Connor Douglas[11] **Bovee**, born in Sacramento, Sacramento Co., CA.

4991   ii   Griffin Wesley[11] **Bovee**, born in Sacramento, Sacramento Co., CA.

4992   iii   Parker[11] **Bovee**.

4386. Glenda Carol[10] **Bovee** (Kenneth Eugene[9], Glenn Peter[8], James Massey[7], Nelson John[6], John[5], Nicholas M[4], Matthew[3], Nicholas[2], Mathieu[1]), born in Shawnee, Pottawatommie Co., OK. She married on 4 Mar 1960 in Shawnee, Pottawatommie Co., OK James Edward Vaughn, born in Okema, Okfuskee Co., OK, son of Orbie Newton Vaughn and Edna Lou Baker.

Children of Glenda Carol Bovee and James Edward Vaughn were as follows:

4993   i   Kathryn Adonna[11] **Vaughn**, born in Shawnee, Pottawatomie Co., OK.

4994   ii   Kimberly Ann[11] **Vaughn**, born in Shawnee, Pottawatomie Co., OK.

4995   iii   Kelly Annette[11] **Vaughn**, born 26 Feb 1965 in Ardmore, Carter Co., OK; died 26 Feb 1965.

4388. Janice Irene[10] **Bovee** (Kenneth Eugene[9], Glenn Peter[8], James Massey[7], Nelson John[6], John[5], Nicholas M[4], Matthew[3], Nicholas[2], Mathieu[1]), born in Shawnee, Pottawatomie Co., OK. She married on 11 Feb 1975 in Little Rock, Pulaski Co., AR John Ray Harris, born in AR.

Children of Janice Irene Bovee and John Ray Harris were as follows:

4996   i   Kelly Lorene[11] **Harris**, born in Little Rock, Pulaski Co., AR.

4389. Timothy Keith[10] **Bovee** (Keith Alan[9], Glenn Peter[8], James Massey[7], Nelson John[6], John[5], Nicholas M[4], Matthew[3], Nicholas[2], Mathieu[1]), born in Shawnee, Pottawatomie Co., OK. He married on 22 Mar 1975 in Southern Japan Reiko Ogura, born in Japan, daughter of Kingo Ogura and Tsurue (---).

Children of Timothy Keith Bovee and Reiko Ogura were as follows:

4997   i   Hiroyuki Nicholas[11] **Bovee**, born in Tokyo, Japan.

4998   ii   Masayuki[11] **Bovee**, born 17 Oct 1976 in Tokyo, Japan; died 17 Oct 1976.

4390. Douglas Alan[10] **Bovee** (Keith Alan[9], Glenn Peter[8], James Massey[7], Nelson John[6], John[5], Nicholas M[4], Matthew[3], Nicholas[2], Mathieu[1]), born in Shawnee, Pottawatomie Co., OK. He married on 5 Jun 1970 in Wynnewood, Garvin Co., OK Nancy Laura Burns, daughter of Frank Bent Burns and Ester Westberg.

Children of Douglas Alan Bovee and Nancy Laura Burns were as follows:

4999	i	Kirsten Michelle[11] **Bovee**.
5000	ii	Katherine Elizabeth[11] **Bovee**.

4408. Michael Bren[10] **Bovee** (Mark Bedard[9], Marvin Burleigh[8], Herbert Stephen[7], Edward Livingston[6], Mathias Jacob[5], Jacob Mathias[4], Matthew[3], Nicholas[2], Mathieu[1]), born in Salem, Marion Co., OR. He married Trudy (---).

Children of Michael Bren Bovee and Trudy (---) were as follows:

5001	i	Bren Michael[11] **Bovee**, born in Salem, Marion Co., OR.

4422. Rev Martin W[10] **Bovee** (Richard[9], Frederick Charles[8], Frederick Charles[7], William Henry[6], John Grant[5], John[4], Matthew[3], Nicholas[2], Mathieu[1]). He married unknown.

Children of Rev Martin W Bovee were as follows:

5002	i	Child[11] **Bovee**.

4424. Mathew[10] **Bovee** (Richard[9], Frederick Charles[8], Frederick Charles[7], William Henry[6], John Grant[5], John[4], Matthew[3], Nicholas[2], Mathieu[1]). He married Lois (---).

Children of Mathew Bovee and Lois (---) were as follows:

5003	i	Child[11] **Bovee**.
5004	ii	Child[11] **Bovee**.

4440. Edward[10] **Bovee** (Edward Ellsworth[9], Edward Milton[8], Franklin E[7], John Wesley[6], John Grant[5], John[4], Matthew[3], Nicholas[2], Mathieu[1]). He married on 18 Apr 1970 Carolyn Smith.

Children of Edward Bovee and Carolyn Smith were as follows:

+	5005	i	Jodi Lynn[11] **Bovee**. She married **Scott Biezenbos**.

4441. Richard H[10] **Bovee** (Edward Ellsworth[9], Edward Milton[8], Franklin E[7], John Wesley[6], John Grant[5], John[4], Matthew[3], Nicholas[2], Mathieu[1]), born 12 Oct 1944; died 25 Feb 1993. He married on 5 Feb 1961 in Camden, Onieda Co., NY Nancy Plumley.

Children of Richard H Bovee and Nancy Plumley were as follows:

+	5006	i	Shari[11] **Bovee**. She married (1) **Jeffrey Smith**; (2) **Dale Wheeler**.
+	5007	ii	Nancy[11] **Bovee**. She married **William Burke**.
	5008	iii	Cindy[11] **Bovee**.

4448. Paul Ross[10] **Bovee** (Harold Lloyd[9], Edward Milton[8], Franklin E[7], John Wesley[6], John Grant[5], John[4], Matthew[3], Nicholas[2], Mathieu[1]). He married Chislaine LeBain, born in Belgium.

Children of Paul Ross Bovee and Chislaine LeBain were as follows:

5009   i   Daniel James[11] **Bovee**.
5010   ii   Vanessa Jynn[11] **Bovee**.

4449. Mark Russell[10] **Bovee** (Harold Lloyd[9], Edward Milton[8], Franklin E[7], John Wesley[6], John Grant[5], John[4], Matthew[3], Nicholas[2], Mathieu[1]). He married on 9 Feb 1991 Lisa Murphy.

Children of Mark Russell Bovee and Lisa Murphy were as follows:

5011   i   Korrie Lynn[11] **Bovee**.
5012   ii   Kristyn Lyneya[11] **Bovee**.
5013   iii   Conner Paul[11] **Bovee**.

4450. James Edward[10] **Bovee** (Harold Lloyd[9], Edward Milton[8], Franklin E[7], John Wesley[6], John Grant[5], John[4], Matthew[3], Nicholas[2], Mathieu[1]). He married on 25 Mar 1992 Joanne Wilkinson.

Children of James Edward Bovee and Joanne Wilkinson were as follows:

5014   i   Sarah Ashton[11] **Bovee**.
5015   ii   Jonathan Ross[11] **Bovee**.
5016   iii   Megan Elizabeth[11] **Bovee**.
5017   iv   Joshua Mack[11] **Bovee**.

4456. David Ray[10] **Bovee** (Cecil Dale[9], Cecil W[8], Woodbury H[7], Hiram[6], John Henry[5], John Henry[4], Matthew[3], Nicholas[2], Mathieu[1]). He married unknown.

Children of David Ray Bovee were as follows:

5018   i   Amy[11] **Bovee**.
5019   ii   Cara[11] **Bovee**.

4457. Thomas Dale[10] **Bovee** (Cecil Dale[9], Cecil W[8], Woodbury H[7], Hiram[6], John Henry[5], John Henry[4], Matthew[3], Nicholas[2], Mathieu[1]). He married abt 1980 Debra Flowers.

Children of Thomas Dale Bovee and Debra Flowers were as follows:

5020   i   Warren Thomas[11] **Bovee**.
5021   ii   Brett[11] **Bovee**.

4458. James Dean^{10} **Bovee** (Cecil Dale^9, Cecil W^8, Woodbury H^7, Hiram^6, John Henry^5, John Henry^4, Matthew^3, Nicholas^2, Mathieu^1). He married abt 1980 unknown.

Children of James Dean Bovee were as follows:

5022   i   Christie^{11} **Bovee**.
5023   ii   James^{11} **Bovee**.

4464. Gregory Lee^{10} **Bovee** (Hiram C (Harry)^9, Hiram C (Harry)^8, Woodbury H^7, Hiram^6, John Henry^5, John Henry^4, Matthew^3, Nicholas^2, Mathieu^1). He married (1) Kathleen Evitis; (2) Paula F Tropp.

Children of Gregory Lee Bovee and Kathleen Evitis were as follows:

5024   i   Justin Mathew^{11} **Bovee**.
5025   ii   Troy^{11} **Bovee**.
5026   iii   Wendy^{11} **Bovee**.
5027   iv   Chad^{11} **Bovee**.

4466. Michael Dee^{10} **Bovee** (Hiram C (Harry)^9, Hiram C (Harry)^8, Woodbury H^7, Hiram^6, John Henry^5, John Henry^4, Matthew^3, Nicholas^2, Mathieu^1). He married Teresa (---).

Children of Michael Dee Bovee and Teresa (---) were as follows:

5028   i   Michael Ryan^{11} **Bovee**.
5029   ii   Andrew Joseph^{11} **Bovee**.

4467. Daniel Joe^{10} **Bovee** (Hiram C (Harry)^9, Hiram C (Harry)^8, Woodbury H^7, Hiram^6, John Henry^5, John Henry^4, Matthew^3, Nicholas^2, Mathieu^1). He married Deborah (---).

Children of Daniel Joe Bovee and Deborah (---) were as follows:

5030   i   Preston^{11} **Bovee**.
5031   ii   Stephanie^{11} **Bovee**.

4476. John R^{10} **Bovee** (Howard Edward^9, Archie Edward^8, Edward Hill^7, Andrew J^6, Mathew^5, John Henry^4, Matthew^3, Nicholas^2, Mathieu^1). He married unknown.

Children of John R Bovee were as follows:

5032   i   Shawn M^{11} **Bovee**.
5033   ii   Kristie Annetta^{11} **Bovee**.

4483. Sandra Lynn^{10} **Bovee** (Raymond Arthur^9, Raymond Arthur^8, Edward Hill^7, Andrew J^6, Mathew^5, John Henry^4, Matthew^3, Nicholas^2, Mathieu^1), born in Conneaut, Ashtabula Co., OH. She married on 24 Feb 1978 in Pierpont, Ashtabula Co., OH Theron Milo Huntley, born in Pierpont, Ashtabila Co., OH.

Children of Sandra Lynn Bovee and Theron Milo Huntley were as follows:

5034	i	Ratmond Allen^{11} **Huntley**.
5035	ii	Stacey Lynn^{11} **Huntley**.
5036	iii	Scott Aron^{11} **Huntley**.
5037	iv	Katie Ann^{11} **Huntley**.

4515. Randall Jay^{10} **Bovee** (Murl Gene^9, Murlin Orlin^8, Orlin Henry^7, Myron^6, Jacob^5, John Henry^4, Matthew^3, Nicholas^2, Mathieu^1). He married on 31 Mar 1972 Betty Jean Taylor, born in Hancock Co., OH.

Children of Randall Jay Bovee and Betty Jean Taylor were as follows:

5038	i	Nancy Louise^{11} **Bovee**.
5039	ii	Child^{11} **Bovee**, born 23 Oct 1974; died 23 Oct 1974.
5040	iii	Dianna Marie^{11} **Bovee**.
5041	iv	Richard Gordon^{11} **Bovee**.

4516. Jeffrey Gene^{10} **Bovee** (Murl Gene^9, Murlin Orlin^8, Orlin Henry^7, Myron^6, Jacob^5, John Henry^4, Matthew^3, Nicholas^2, Mathieu^1). He married on 9 Apr 1977 Pamela Alice Makres.

Children of Jeffrey Gene Bovee and Pamela Alice Makres were as follows:

5042	i	Stephen Alexander^{11} **Bovee**.

4517. Mickey Orlin^{10} **Bovee** (Murl Gene^9, Murlin Orlin^8, Orlin Henry^7, Myron^6, Jacob^5, John Henry^4, Matthew^3, Nicholas^2, Mathieu^1). He married Barbara Elizabeth Krieger.

Children of Mickey Orlin Bovee and Barbara Elizabeth Krieger were as follows:

5043	i	Chad Dustin^{11} **Bovee**.

4555. Kurt Steven^{10} **Bovee** (Meredith Roger Leon^9, Chester Emerson^8, Samuel Ball^7, George Burton^6, Peter^5, Matthew^4, Abraham^3, Nicholas^2, Mathieu^1), born in New London, New London Co., CT. He married in MA Caroline Godin.

Children of Kurt Steven Bovee and Caroline Godin were as follows:

5044	i	Ryan S^{11} **Bovee**.

5045 ii Dylan S[11] **Bovee**.

4556. Patrick Emerson Bovea[10] **Bovee** (Meredith Roger Leon[9], Chester Emerson[8], Samuel Ball[7], George Burton[6], Peter[5], Matthew[4], Abraham[3], Nicholas[2], Mathieu[1]), born in Fort Worth Tarrant Co., TX. He married Machelle (---).

Children of Patrick Emerson Bovea Bovee and Machelle (---) were as follows:

5046 i Taylor Bovea[11] **Bovee**.
5047 ii Mattie Bovea[11] **Bovee**.

4568. Michael[10] **Bovee** (Glenn S[9], Laverne[8], Frederick[7], John W[6], Cornelius[5], Abraham[4], Abraham[3], Nicholas[2], Mathieu[1]). He married Mona Wolfanger.

Children of Michael Bovee and Mona Wolfanger were as follows:

5048 i Stephanie[11] **Bovee**.
5049 ii Heather[11] **Bovee**.
5050 iii Jena[11] **Bovee**.

4570. Elizabeth[10] **Bovee** (Robert J[9], Laverne[8], Frederick[7], John W[6], Cornelius[5], Abraham[4], Abraham[3], Nicholas[2], Mathieu[1]). She married John Goho.

Children of Elizabeth Bovee and John Goho were as follows:

5051 i Todd[11] **Goho**.
5052 ii Troy[11] **Goho**.

4571. Robert J[10] **Bovee** Jr (Robert J[9], Laverne[8], Frederick[7], John W[6], Cornelius[5], Abraham[4], Abraham[3], Nicholas[2], Mathieu[1]). He married Christine Fournier.

Children of Robert J Bovee Jr and Christine Fournier were as follows:

5053 i Jeramy[11] **Bovee**.
5054 ii Joshua[11] **Bovee**.
5055 iii Child[11] **Bovee**.
5056 iv Chold[11] **Bovee**.
5057 v Child[11] **Bovee**.

4572. Terry Edward[10] **Bovee** (Harold E[9], Laverne[8], Frederick[7], John W[6], Cornelius[5], Abraham[4], Abraham[3], Nicholas[2], Mathieu[1]). He married Penny Craft.

Children of Terry Edward Bovee and Penny Craft were as follows:

5058 i Amy[11] **Bovee**.

4573. Gerald K^{10} **Bovee** (Harold E^9, Laverne^8, Frederick^7, John W^6, Cornelius^5, Abraham^4, Abraham^3, Nicholas^2, Mathieu^1). He married Hope (---).

Children of Gerald K Bovee and Hope (---) were as follows:

5059   i   Michelle^{11} **Bovee**.

4574. Dan^{10} **Bovee** (Harold E^9, Laverne^8, Frederick^7, John W^6, Cornelius^5, Abraham^4, Abraham^3, Nicholas^2, Mathieu^1). He married unknown.

Children of Dan Bovee were as follows:

5060   i   Karl^{11} **Bovee**.
5061   ii   Kevin^{11} **Bovee**.
5062   iii   Christopher^{11} **Bovee**.

4575. Shirley Hugh l^{10} **Bovee** (Shirley Hugh^9, Laverne^8, Frederick^7, John W^6, Cornelius^5, Abraham^4, Abraham^3, Nicholas^2, Mathieu^1). She married on 16 May 1981 in Wheeler, Steuben Co., NY Richard C Seager, son of Richard F Seager and Marguerite Watson.

Children of Shirley Hugh Bovee and Richard C Seager were as follows:

5063   i   Matthew R^{11} **Seager**, born in Dansville, Livingston Co., NY.

4636. David Robert^{10} **Bovee** (Robert Eugene^9, Everette Vivian^8, Arthur Vernon^7, William R^6, Abraham^5, Abraham^4, Abraham^3, Nicholas^2, Mathieu^1), born in New London, Waushara Co., WI.. He married on 24 Jul 1976 in New London, Waushara Co., WI. Rhonda Marie Slosarek.

Children of David Robert Bovee and Rhonda Marie Slosarek were as follows:

5064   i   Sarah Marie^{11} **Bovee**.
5065   ii   Andrew Paul^{11} **Bovee**, born in New London, Waushara Co., WI..

4637. Debra Ann^{10} **Bovee** (Robert Eugene^9, Everette Vivian^8, Arthur Vernon^7, William R^6, Abraham^5, Abraham^4, Abraham^3, Nicholas^2, Mathieu^1), born in New London, Waushara Co., WI.. She married on 6 Jul 1973 in New London, Waushara Co., WI. Donald James Flease, born in New London, Waushara Co., WI..

Children of Debra Ann Bovee and Donald James Flease were as follows:

5066   i   Gina Kay^{11} **Flease**.

5067   ii   Jamie Ryan[11] **Flease**.

5068   iii   Jared Paul[11] **Flease**.

4639. Peggy Sue[10] **Bovee** (Everette Vivian[9], Everette Vivian[8], Arthur Vernon[7], William R[6], Abraham[5], Abraham[4], Abraham[3], Nicholas[2], Mathieu[1]), born in Kaukauna, Outagami Co., WI.. She married Timothy J Kasten, born in Sherwood, Calumet Co., WI..

Children of Peggy Sue Bovee and Timothy J Kasten were as follows:

5069   i   Timothy Everette[11] **Kasten**, born in Appleton, Outagamie Co., WI.

5070   ii   Erik Craig[11] **Kasten**, born in Appleton, Outagamie Co., WI.

5071   iii   Cody Bart[11] **Kasten**.

4641. Ronald Gordon[10] **Bovee** (Donald Lee[9], Everette Vivian[8], Arthur Vernon[7], William R[6], Abraham[5], Abraham[4], Abraham[3], Nicholas[2], Mathieu[1]), born in New London,Waupaca Co., WI. He married (1) Penny Marie Van Straten, born in New London,Waupaca Co., WI; (2) Cinnamon Lynn Chimelski, born in Fond du Lac, Fond du Lac Co., WI.

Children of Ronald Gordon Bovee and Penny Marie Van Straten were as follows:

5072   i   Britnay Christine[11] **Bovee**, born in Appleton, Outagami Co., WI.

5073   ii   Brandon Richard[11] **Bovee**, born in Appleton, Outagami Co., WI.

Children of Ronald Gordon Bovee and Cinnamon Lynn Chimelski were as follows:

5074   i   Bret[11] **Bovee**.

5075   ii   Daniel[11] **Bovee**, born in New London,Waupaca Co., WI.

5076   iii   David[11] **Bovee**, born in Green Bay, Brown Co., WI.

5077   iv   Jasmine[11] **Bovee**, born in New London,Waupaca Co., WI.

4642. Jodi Lei[10] **Bovee** (Donald Lee[9], Everette Vivian[8], Arthur Vernon[7], William R[6], Abraham[5], Abraham[4], Abraham[3], Nicholas[2], Mathieu[1]), born in New London,Waupaca Co., WI. She married on 1 Sep 1997 in WI Mathew Young.

Children of Jodi Lei Bovee and Mathew Young were as follows:

5078   i   Brady Wayne[11] **Young**, born in New London,Waupaca Co., WI.

5079   ii   Alleionna Hope[11] **Young**, born in New London,Waupaca Co., WI.

5080   iii   Ashlei[11] **Young**, born in New London,Waupaca Co., WI.

4674. Robert Frederick[10] **Bovee** (Donald F[9], Charles Henry[8], Frederick Germond[7], Nicholas[6], John[5], Jacob Philip[4], Philip[3], Nicholas[2], Mathieu[1]), born 12 Jun 1926 in Novi, Oakland Co., MI. He married on 20 Dec 1945 Fay Elaine Christensen, born 15 Sep 1924 in Grayling, Crawford Co., MI.

Children of Robert Frederick Bovee and Fay Elaine Christensen were as follows:

5081	i	Billie Fay[11] **Bovee**, born in Mt Pleasant, Isabelle Co., MI. She married on 25 Sep 1976 **Richard Anthony Smith**.
5082	ii	Dena Kay[11] **Bovee**, born in Grayling, Crawford Co., MI.

4675. Joanne Carolyn[10] **Bovee** (Donald F[9], Charles Henry[8], Frederick Germond[7], Nicholas[6], John[5], Jacob Philip[4], Philip[3], Nicholas[2], Mathieu[1]), born in Detroit Wayne Co., MI. She married on 12 Aug 1950 in MI William Zimmerman.

Children of Joanne Carolyn Bovee and William Zimmerman were as follows:

5083	i	Sharon[11] **Zimmerman**.
5084	ii	James[11] **Zimmerman**.

4676. Keith Alvin[10] **Bovee** (Donald F[9], Charles Henry[8], Frederick Germond[7], Nicholas[6], John[5], Jacob Philip[4], Philip[3], Nicholas[2], Mathieu[1]). He married on 2 Jun 1951 in MIdland, Midland Co., MI Elnora Lanphierd.

Children of Keith Alvin Bovee and Elnora Lanphierd were as follows:

5085	i	Samdra[11] **Bovee**.
5086	ii	Sally[11] **Bovee**.

4678. Joyce Kay[10] **Bovee** (Donald F[9], Charles Henry[8], Frederick Germond[7], Nicholas[6], John[5], Jacob Philip[4], Philip[3], Nicholas[2], Mathieu[1]), born in Plymouth, Wayne Co., MI. She married on 25 Jan 1964 in Livonia, Wayne Co., MI Ronald Moore.

Children of Joyce Kay Bovee and Ronald Moore were as follows:

5087	i	Belinda[11] **Moore**.
5088	ii	Christopher[11] **Moore**.
5089	iii	Katherine[11] **Moore**.

4681. Sue Evelyn[10] **Bovee** (Norvall Charles[9], Charles Henry[8], Frederick Germond[7], Nicholas[6], John[5], Jacob Philip[4], Philip[3], Nicholas[2], Mathieu[1]). She married Peter Woods.

Children of Sue Evelyn Bovee and Peter Woods were as follows:

5090	i	John Charles[11] **Woods**.

5091   ii   Melinda Sue[11] **Woods**.

4682. Kenneth Charles[10] **Bovee** (Norvall Charles[9], Charles Henry[8], Frederick Germond[7], Nicholas[6], John[5], Jacob Philip[4], Philip[3], Nicholas[2], Mathieu[1]). He married Stephanie (---).

   Children of Kenneth Charles Bovee and Stephanie (---) were as follows:
   5092   i   Daniel James[11] **Bovee**.
   5093   ii   Jessica[11] **Bovee**.

4691. Forrest Fred[10] **Bovee** (Keith N[9], Forest F[8], Freeman[7], Charles P[6], Nicholas[5], Jacob Philip[4], Philip[3], Nicholas[2], Mathieu[1]). He married abt 1970 unknown.

   Children of Forrest Fred Bovee were as follows:
   5094   i   Timothy[11] **Bovee**.

4694. Megan Eileen[10] **Bovee** (Forrest Burdette[9], Forest F[8], Freeman[7], Charles P[6], Nicholas[5], Jacob Philip[4], Philip[3], Nicholas[2], Mathieu[1]). She married Christopher Cottle.

   Children of Megan Eileen Bovee and Christopher Cottle were as follows:
   5095   i   Katherine[11] **Cottle**.
   5096   ii   Samuel[11] **Cottle**.

4695. Jenna Marlene[10] **Bovee** (Forrest Burdette[9], Forest F[8], Freeman[7], Charles P[6], Nicholas[5], Jacob Philip[4], Philip[3], Nicholas[2], Mathieu[1]). She married Robert Rainey.

   Children of Jenna Marlene Bovee and Robert Rainey were as follows:
   5097   i   Garritt[11] **Rainey**.
   5098   ii   Tess[11] **Rainey**.

4709. Earl Wesley[10] **Bovee** (George Earl[9], Charles D[8], Jeremiah W[7], William R[6], Daniel R[5], Nicholas P[4], Philip[3], Nicholas[2], Mathieu[1]), born 1 Mar 1918 in Pensacola, Escambia Co., FL; christened 21 Oct 1928 in Pensacola, Escambia Co., FL; died 5 Oct 1967 in Tampa, Hillsborough Co., FL. He married (1) in Pensacola, Escambia Co., FL Lilly May Babb, born Dec 1919; died 20 Apr 1996 in Pensacola, Escambia Co., FL; (2) on 2 Mar 1962 Mary L Ward, died 30 Aug 1987.

   Children of Earl Wesley Bovee and Lilly May Babb were as follows:
   5099   i   Wayne[11] **Bovee**.

5100	ii	Don[11] **Bovee**, born in Pensacola, Escambia Co., FL.

5100   ii   Don[11] **Bovee**, born in Pensacola, Escambia Co., FL.

5101   iii   Earlene[11] **Bovee**, born in Pensacola, Escambia Co., FL. She married **(---) Myers**.

5102   iv   Caroline[11] **Bovee**, born in Pensacola, Escambia Co., FL.

4711. Neal Anderson[10] **Bovee** (Lynn Albert[9], June Raymond[8], Daniel Reynolds[7], William R[6], Daniel R[5], Nicholas P[4], Philip[3], Nicholas[2], Mathieu[1]), born 16 Dec 1914 in Westfield, Chautauqua Co., NY; died 29 Oct 1980 in Mc Alester, Pittsburg Co., OK. He married (1) on 31 Oct 1936 in Erie, Erie Co., PA Ruth Marie Cousins, born 10 May 1918 in Erie, Erie Co., PA; died 11 Nov 1945 in Washington, DC, daughter of Russel Cousins and Elizabeth Taylor; (2) on 15 Apr 1948 in Paris, France Elaine Madeline Marie Tutiau, born 9 Oct 1920 in Cotes Dunord, Lanvalley, France, daughter of Alfred Marie Tutiau and Wilhemena Damann.

Children of Neal Anderson Bovee and Ruth Marie Cousins were as follows:

+   5103   i   Lynn Irl[11] **Bovee**, born in Erie, Erie Co., PA. He married **Dona Irene Nottier**.

+   5104   ii   Sandra Ruth[11] **Bovee**, born 9 Sep 1939 in Falls Church, VA; died 3 Apr 1977 in Perth Amboy, Middlesex Co., VA. She married (1) **William F Dickson**; (2) **(---) Taylor**.

+   5105   iii   David Brian[11] **Bovee**, born in Erie, Erie Co., PA. He married (1) **Carolyn Brassel**; (2) **Donna Lee Thompson**.

  5106   iv   Judith Lee[11] **Bovee**, born 25 Apr 1945 in Washington, DC; died 26 Oct 1957 in Anaheim, Orange Co., CA.

Children of Neal Anderson Bovee and Elaine Madeline Marie Tutiau were as follows:

+   5107   i   Carol Maria[11] **Bovee**, born in Seine, Neuilly, France; christened in Paris, France. She married **Antonio Luigi Arnoldi**.

+   5108   ii   Linda Marcella[11] **Bovee**, born in Seine, Neuilly, France. She married **Gregory Philip Spohr**.

4712. June[10] **Bovee** (Frank Grencett[9], June Raymond[8], Daniel Reynolds[7], William R[6], Daniel R[5], Nicholas P[4], Philip[3], Nicholas[2], Mathieu[1]), born 14 Apr 1915. She married on 14 Dec 1935 Arthur Shreve.

Children of June Bovee and Arthur Shreve were as follows:

  5109   i   June Kathleen[11] **Shreve**.

4717. Frederick Charles[10] **Bovee** (Frederick Lyman[9], Frederick Charles[8], Charles Dexter[7], William R[6], Daniel R[5], Nicholas P[4], Philip[3], Nicholas[2], Mathieu[1]). He married on 28 Feb 1970 Galia Straight.

Children of Frederick Charles Bovee and Galia Straight were as follows:

5110	i	Gregory[11] **Bovee**.
5111	ii	Stephanie Lynn[11] **Bovee**.

4720. Sandra[10] Bovee (Harry Spencer[9], Frederick Charles[8], Charles Dexter[7], William R[6], Daniel R[5], Nicholas P[4], Philip[3], Nicholas[2], Mathieu[1]). She married abt 1969 James Mawhinney.

Children of Sandra Bovee and James Mawhinney were as follows:

5112	i	James[11] **Mawhinney**.

4721. Harry S[10] Bovee (Harry Spencer[9], Frederick Charles[8], Charles Dexter[7], William R[6], Daniel R[5], Nicholas P[4], Philip[3], Nicholas[2], Mathieu[1]). He married on 27 Jun 1970 Deborah Alberica.

Children of Harry S Bovee and Deborah Alberica were as follows:

5113	i	Jean Marc[11] **Bovee**.
5114	ii	Nicholas[11] **Bovee**.

4727. Robert John[10] Bovee (George Henry[9], Guy Clinton[8], Harmon E[7], Nicholas[6], Jacob[5], Nicholas P[4], Philip[3], Nicholas[2], Mathieu[1]). He married Patricia Werkle.

Children of Robert John Bovee and Patricia Werkle were as follows:

	5115	i	Debbie Beverly[11] **Bovee**.
+	5116	ii	Robert Guy[11] **Bovee**. He married **Chandra Lee Paddock**.
	5117	iii	Glen David[11] **Bovee**.
	5118	iv	Tammi Ann[11] **Bovee**.
	5119	v	Kimberly[11] **Bovee**.
	5120	vi	Child[11] **Bovee**.

4731. Lewis Lyle[10] Bovee (Glendon Charles[9], Lyle J[8], Jacob[7], Isaac[6], Jacob Nicholas[5], Nicholas Jacob[4], Jacob[3], Nicholas[2], Mathieu[1]). He married unknown.

Children of Lewis Lyle Bovee were as follows:

5121	i	Christopher D[11] **Bovee**.
5122	ii	John Ross[11] **Bovee**.

4732. John William[10] Bovee (Frank Walter[9], John Addison[8], Christian[7], Peter[6], Peter[5], Jacob[4], Jacob[3], Nicholas[2], Mathieu[1]), born 17 Oct 1932 in Norwich, Chenango Co., NY; died 24 Oct 1994 in AZ. He married on 30 Jul 1955 in Worksop, England June Irwin, born in England.

Children of John William Bovee and June Irwin were as follows:

5123   i   Linda Denise[11] **Bovee**.

5124   ii   John William[11] **Bovee** Jr.

4733. Frank Walter[10] **Bovee** Jr (Frank Walter[9], John Addison[8], Christian[7], Peter[6], Peter[5], Jacob[4], Jacob[3], Nicholas[2], Mathieu[1]), born in Norwich, Chenango Co., NY. He married on 23 Sep 1962 in Delhi, Delaware Co., NY Carol LaVonne Pipa.

Children of Frank Walter Bovee Jr and Carol LaVonne Pipa were as follows:

5125   i   Brenda Jan[11] **Bovee**, born in Oneota, Ostego Co., NY. She married on 31 Jul 1993 **Dale Mertz**.

5126   ii   Pamela Joy[11] **Bovee**, born in Delhi, Delaware Co., NY. She married on 2 Aug 1997 **Christopher Carroll**.

4734. Donna Lee[10] **Bovee** (Frank Walter[9], John Addison[8], Christian[7], Peter[6], Peter[5], Jacob[4], Jacob[3], Nicholas[2], Mathieu[1]), born in Norwich, Chenango Co., NY. She married (1) on 11 Feb 1955, divorced Ronald J Hannon; (2) on 18 Oct 1974 in Norwich, Chenango Co., NY John Herrick.

Children of Donna Lee Bovee and Ronald J Hannon were as follows:

5127   i   Debbie Dawn[11] **Hannon**, born in Norwich, Chenango Co., NY.

5128   ii   Ronald J[11] **Hannon**, born in Norwich, Chenango Co., NY.

5129   iii   Alicia Jolene[11] **Hannon**, born in Norwich, Chenango Co., NY.

5130   iv   Lincoln Todd[11] **Hannon**.

4735. James Lewis[10] **Bovee** (Frank Walter[9], John Addison[8], Christian[7], Peter[6], Peter[5], Jacob[4], Jacob[3], Nicholas[2], Mathieu[1]), born in Norwich, Chenango Co., NY. He married on 9 Sep 1967 in Norwich, Chenango Co., NY Betty Ashcroft, born 1 Feb 1942 in Norwich, Chenango Co., NY; died 9 May 1994 in Norwich, Chenango Co., NY.

Children of James Lewis Bovee and Betty Ashcroft were as follows:

5131   i   Andrea L[11] **Bovee**, born in Norwich, Chenango Co., NY.

5132   ii   Angelique C[11] **Bovee**, born in Norwich, Chenango Co., NY.

5133   iii   Alaina[11] **Bovee**, born in Norwich, Chenango Co., NY.

4736. David Fred[10] **Bovee** (Frank Walter[9], John Addison[8], Christian[7], Peter[6], Peter[5], Jacob[4], Jacob[3], Nicholas[2], Mathieu[1]), born 31 May 1944 in Norwich, Chenango Co., NY; died 5 Aug 1994. He married in Jul 1965 in Holmsville, Chenango Co., NY Donna Mary Powers, born in New Berlin, Chenango Co., NY.

Children of David Fred Bovee and Donna Mary Powers were as follows:

5134 i   Wendy Lynn[11] **Bovee**, born in Norwich, Chenango Co., NY. She married on 29 Aug 1987 in South New Berlin, Chenango Co., NY **Monroe Edwin Wall**.

+ 5135 ii   David James[11] **Bovee**, born in Norwich, Chenango Co., NY. He married **Angela Benedict**.

5136 iii Kimberly Dawn[11] **Bovee**, born 6 Jan 1972 in Norwich, Chenango Co., NY; died 11 Apr 1987 in Norwich, Chenango Co., NY.

4747. Ehelyn[10] **Bovee** (Lewis Laverne[9], Lewis B[8], George A[7], Jacob Clayton[6], Peter[5], Jacob[4], Jacob[3], Nicholas[2], Mathieu[1]), born abt 1918. She married Arnold Copping, born abt 1909.

Children of Ehelyn Bovee and Arnold Copping were as follows:

5137 i   Robert[11] **Copping**.

4749. Jacqueline[10] **Bovee** (Lewis Laverne[9], Lewis B[8], George A[7], Jacob Clayton[6], Peter[5], Jacob[4], Jacob[3], Nicholas[2], Mathieu[1]), born abt 1928 in Saugerties, Ulster Co., NY.; died 24 Jan 2005 in Delmar, Albany Co., NY.. She married David R Miller.

Children of Jacqueline Bovee and David R Miller were as follows:

5138 i   David Stephen[11] **Miller**.

4750. Jean Patricia[10] **Bovee** (Barton[9], Ernest Winchel[8], George A[7], Jacob Clayton[6], Peter[5], Jacob[4], Jacob[3], Nicholas[2], Mathieu[1]). She married Alan E Hanbury.

Children of Jean Patricia Bovee and Alan E Hanbury were as follows:

5139 i   Robert Deane[11] **Hanbury**.

5140 ii   Alan Edgar[11] **Hanbury**.

5141 iii Richard Alan[11] **Hanbury**.

4751. Barton Winchel[10] **Bovee** (Barton[9], Ernest Winchel[8], George A[7], Jacob Clayton[6], Peter[5], Jacob[4], Jacob[3], Nicholas[2], Mathieu[1]). He married Jean Lawton.

Children of Barton Winchel Bovee and Jean Lawton were as follows:

5142 i   Barton Nicholas[11] **Bovee**.

5143 ii   Susan Dianne[11] **Bovee**.

5144 iii Linda Kathleen[11] **Bovee**.

5145 iv Margaret Elizabeth[11] **Bovee**.

4767. Robert Dale[10] **Bovee** (Frank Leslie[9], Daniel Walter[8], John Livingston[7], Cornelius[6], Daniel[5], Matthew[4], Jacob[3], Nicholas[2], Mathieu[1]), born 4 Jul 1920. He married abt 1945 Margaret (---).

Children of Robert Dale Bovee and Margaret (---) were as follows:

5146	i	Kenneth[11] **Bovee**.
5147	ii	Barbara[11] **Bovee**.
5148	iii	Beverly[11] **Bovee**.

4769. Carroll Lee[10] **Bovee** (Frank Leslie[9], Daniel Walter[8], John Livingston[7], Cornelius[6], Daniel[5], Matthew[4], Jacob[3], Nicholas[2], Mathieu[1]), born 16 Dec 1924. He married abt 1950 Bette (---), born abt 1930.

Children of Carroll Lee Bovee and Bette (---) were as follows:

5149	i	Danny[11] **Bovee**.
5150	ii	Debra[11] **Bovee**.
5151	iii	Beth[11] **Bovee**.
5152	iv	Lori[11] **Bovee**.

4772. Janet Rae[10] **Bovee** (Paul Henry[9], Daniel Walter[8], John Livingston[7], Cornelius[6], Daniel[5], Matthew[4], Jacob[3], Nicholas[2], Mathieu[1]). She married Robert E Burgess, born 12 Nov 1926.

Children of Janet Rae Bovee and Robert E Burgess were as follows:

| 5153 | i | Betsey[11] **Burgess**. |
| 5154 | ii | Nancy J[11] **Burgess**. |

4782. Diane[10] **Bovee** (Kenneth Frederick[9], Kenneth Jacob[8], William Ludington[7], Cornelius Elihu[6], Cornelius Schermerhorn[5], Matthew[4], Jacob[3], Nicholas[2], Mathieu[1]), born in Batavia, Genesee Co., NY. She married on 10 Mar 1966 in York, Livingston Co., NY Dale Beardsley.

Children of Diane Bovee and Dale Beardsley were as follows:

| 5155 | i | Lynn[11] **Beardsley**. |
| 5156 | ii | David[11] **Beardsley**. |

4789. Ronald[10] **Bovee** (Claude Henry[9], Albert A[8], Hiram[7], Luther[6], Jacob[5], Anthony[4], Gerrit[3], Anthony[2], Mathieu[1]), born in Lake Luzerne, Warren Co., NY. He married abt 1965 Janice Lois Stewart.

Children of Ronald Bovee and Janice Lois Stewart were as follows:

| + | 5157 | i | Ronald Albert[11] **Bovee**. He married **Lorie Pike**. |

5158	ii	Cynthia[11] **Bovee**, born in Glens Falls, Warren Co., NY. She married on 6 Jun 1992 **Steven Dearborn**.
+ 5159	iii	Michael Joseph[11] **Bovee**. He married **Darcy Dennison**.
+ 5160	iv	Gary Claude[11] **Bovee**, born in Glens Falls, Warren Co., NY. He married **Michelle Caldwell**.
+ 5161	v	Michelle[11] **Bovee**, born in Glens Falls, Warren Co., NY. She married **Tony Lucia**.
5162	vi	Todd[11] **Bovee**, born in Glens Falls, Warren Co., NY.
5163	vii	Jessica[11] **Bovee**, born in Glens Falls, Warren Co., NY.

4793. John Francis[10] **Bovee** (Claude Henry[9], Albert A[8], Hiram[7], Luther[6], Jacob[5], Anthony[4], Gerrit[3], Anthony[2], Mathieu[1]), born in Glens Falls, Warren Co., NY. He married (1) on 27 Jun 1970 Mary Jane Ovitt; (2) on 1 Sep 1989 Corine Stephens.

Children of John Francis Bovee and Mary Jane Ovitt were as follows:

5164	i	Janna May[11] **Bovee**, born in Glens Falls, Warren Co., NY.
5165	ii	Julia Jane[11] **Bovee**, born in Glens Falls, Warren Co., NY. She married on 31 Dec 1995 **Duane M Moulton**.
5166	iii	John Francis[11] **Bovee** Jr, born in Glens Falls, Warren Co., NY.

4794. James Wayne[10] **Bovee** (Claude Henry[9], Albert A[8], Hiram[7], Luther[6], Jacob[5], Anthony[4], Gerrit[3], Anthony[2], Mathieu[1]), born in Glens Falls, Warren Co., NY. He married on 5 Sep 1970 Cathy Ann Mosher.

Children of James Wayne Bovee and Cathy Ann Mosher were as follows:

+ 5167	i	James Terry[11] **Bovee**. He married (1) **Debby MacKentire**; (2) **Kimberly Mattrau**.
5168	ii	Paulete Cathlene[11] **Bovee**, born in Glens Falls, Warren Co., NY.

4797. Thomas W[10] **Bovee** (Donald Marcus[9], Walter W[8], Henry L[7], Luther[6], Jacob[5], Anthony[4], Gerrit[3], Anthony[2], Mathieu[1]). He married Carol (---).

Children of Thomas W Bovee and Carol (---) were as follows:

5169	i	Michael Walter[11] **Bovee**.
5170	ii	Joanna Lynn[11] **Bovee**.

4803. Kim Daniel[10] **Bovee** (Daniel John[9], George Melvin[8], Fred[7], Luther[6], Jacob[5], Anthony[4], Gerrit[3], Anthony[2], Mathieu[1]). He married on 22 Oct 1977 Jane Blower.

Children of Kim Daniel Bovee and Jane Blower were as follows:

5171	i	Joshua David[11] **Bovee**.

5172   ii   Charles Daniel[11] **Bovee.**

4804. Kelly Anthony[10] **Bovee** (Daniel John[9], George Melvin[8], Fred[7], Luther[6], Jacob[5], Anthony[4], Gerrit[3], Anthony[2], Mathieu[1]). He married on 7 Dec 1974 Danita Brownell.

Children of Kelly Anthony Bovee and Danita Brownell were as follows:

5173   i   Levi George[11] **Bovee.**
5174   ii   Lucas Emile[11] **Bovee.**
5175   iii   Catherine Ethel[11] **Bovee.**

4817. Kevin John[10] **Bovee** (Willard L[9], Willard L[8], Lester[7], Norman[6], Jacob[5], Anthony[4], Gerrit[3], Anthony[2], Mathieu[1]). He married unknown.

Children of Kevin John Bovee were as follows:

5176   i   Kamryn[11] **Bovee.**
5177   ii   Austin[11] **Bovee.**
5178   iii   Madison[11] **Bovee.**

4818. Mathew Scott[10] **Bovee** (Willard L[9], Willard L[8], Lester[7], Norman[6], Jacob[5], Anthony[4], Gerrit[3], Anthony[2], Mathieu[1]). He married on 8 Feb 1992 Donna Sherwood.

Children of Mathew Scott Bovee and Donna Sherwood were as follows:

5179   i   Brett M[11] **Bovee.**
5180   ii   Isaac[11] **Bovee.**
5181   iii   Dakota[11] **Bovee.**

4838. Dianne Elizabeth[10] **Bovee** (Lloyd Champlin[9], William Arthur[8], Edwin Anson[7], Eli William[6], Jonathan[5], Peter[4], Gerrit[3], Anthony[2], Mathieu[1]), born in Traverse City, Grand Traverse Co., MI. She married on 14 Jun 1969 in Wapakoneta, Auglaize Co., OH Karl Arthur Jenkins, born in Marion, Marion Co., OH, son of Omar Jenkins and Maxine (---).

Children of Dianne Elizabeth Bovee and Karl Arthur Jenkins were as follows:

5182   i   Christopher Allen[11] **Jenkins,** born in Lima, Allen Co., OH.
5183   ii   Jason Matthew[11] **Jenkins,** born in Lima, Allen Co., OH.
5184   iii   Jennifer Lynn[11] **Jenkins,** born in Lima, Allen Co., OH.

4851. Lloyd Martin[10] **Bovee** (Edwin Wright[9], David Lloyd[8], Edwin Anson[7], Eli William[6], Jonathan[5], Peter[4], Gerrit[3], Anthony[2], Mathieu[1]), born in Grand Rapids, Kent Co., MI. He married (1) on 6 Aug 1966, divorced Madeline Judith Labree;

(2) on 7 Jun 1980 Gay Marie Chambers.

Children of Lloyd Martin Bovee and Madeline Judith Labree were as follows:

5185 i Todd Michael[11] **Bovee**, born in Grand Rapids, Kent Co., MI.

5186 ii Melissa Anne[11] **Bovee**, born in Grand Rapids, Kent Co., MI; died 8 Dec 1994.

4852. Byron Wright[10] **Bovee** (Edwin Wright[9], David Lloyd[8], Edwin Anson[7], Eli William[6], Jonathan[5], Peter[4], Gerrit[3], Anthony[2], Mathieu[1]), born in Grand Rapids, Kent Co., MI. He married (1) on 2 Sep 1962 in KS, divorced Phyllis Ilene Haas; (2) on 9 Dec 1975 in Grand Rapids, Kent Co., MI, divorced Victoria Lee Vogel; (3) on 16 Oct 1981 in Grand Rapids, Kent Co., MI Priscilla Ann Hefferan.

Children of Byron Wright Bovee and Phyllis Ilene Haas were as follows:

5187 i Sherri Lynne[11] **Bovee**, born in Paris, France.

+ 5188 ii Kimberly[11] **Bovee**, born in Grand Rapids, Kent Co., MI. She married **Robert Slupe Jr**.

4853. Beverly Ann[10] **Bovee** (Edwin Wright[9], David Lloyd[8], Edwin Anson[7], Eli William[6], Jonathan[5], Peter[4], Gerrit[3], Anthony[2], Mathieu[1]), born in Grand Rapids, Kent Co., MI. She married on 2 Sep 1967 in Grand Rapids, Kent Co., MI Kenneth Murray Stevens.

Children of Beverly Ann Bovee and Kenneth Murray Stevens were as follows:

5189 i Karen Elain[11] **Stevens**, born in Grand Rapids, Kent Co., MI.

5190 ii Kenin Tyler[11] **Stevens**, born in Grand Rapids, Kent Co., MI.

4860. Kevin[10] **Bovee** (Cecil Lynn[9], Benjamin Samuel[8], Frank Luther[7], Moses C[6], Moses R[5], Jacob[4], Gerrit[3], Anthony[2], Mathieu[1]), born in Ypsilanti, Washtenaw Co., MI. He married unknown.

Children of Kevin Bovee were as follows:

5191 i Austin Dale[11] **Bovee**.

4867. Kent Thomas[10] **Bovee** (Charles Clyde[9], Homer Thomas[8], Clyde Charles[7], James B[6], Moses R[5], Jacob[4], Gerrit[3], Anthony[2], Mathieu[1]), born in Bristol, Sullivan Co., TN. He married Dawn Georgia.

Children of Kent Thomas Bovee and Dawn Georgia were as follows:

5192 i Julia Anna[11] **Bovee**.

5193 ii Marshall Ryan[11] **Bovee**.

5194   iii   Meridith Grace[11] **Bovee**.

4868. Mark Teroller[10] **Bovee** (Charles Clyde[9], Homer Thomas[8], Clyde Charles[7], James B[6], Moses R[5], Jacob[4], Gerrit[3], Anthony[2], Mathieu[1]), born in Atlanta Fulton Co., GA. He married Christianne Collette Rouland.

Children of Mark Teroller Bovee and Christianne Collette Rouland were as follows:

5195   i   Nicholas Rouland[11] **Bovee**.

4873. Claude Lee[10] **Bovee** Jr (Claude Lee[9], Mark C[8], George M[7], Mark[6], Moses R[5], Jacob[4], Gerrit[3], Anthony[2], Mathieu[1]). He married Virginia Carol Jackson, born in KS.

Children of Claude Lee Bovee Jr and Virginia Carol Jackson were as follows:

5196   i   Jeri Lea[11] **Bovee**, born in CO. She married **Gregg McAllister**.

+   5197   ii   Barry Loris[11] **Bovee**, born in CO. He married **Connie Sue Bean**.

5198   iii   Marci Rae[11] **Bovee**, born in CO. She married (1), divorced **Stuart Cerise**; (2) **Edward F Bilikiewicz**.

5199   iv   Chris Lyn[11] **Bovee**, died 2 Jul 1973.

4874. Leonard B[10] **Bovee** (Leonard Burl[9], George[8], George M[7], Mark[6], Moses R[5], Jacob[4], Gerrit[3], Anthony[2], Mathieu[1]), born in CA. He married (1) Lynn Swanson; (2) Andrea Pepritsch.

Children of Leonard B Bovee and Lynn Swanson were as follows:

5200   i   Brian Keith[11] **Bovee**, born in CA. He married **Natasha Hugo**.

5201   ii   Ronald Gregory[11] **Bovee**, born in CA.

Children of Leonard B Bovee and Andrea Pepritsch were as follows:

5202   i   Kasey Nivole[11] **Bovee**, born in CA.

5203   ii   Patrick[11] **Bovee**, born in CA.

4876. Raymond George[10] **Bovee** (George Raymond[9], George[8], George M[7], Mark[6], Moses R[5], Jacob[4], Gerrit[3], Anthony[2], Mathieu[1]), born in CA. He married Debra Sue Bass, born in UT.

Children of Raymond George Bovee and Debra Sue Bass were as follows:

5204   i   Shawn Raymond[11] **Bovee**, born in UT.

5205   ii   Wendy Sue[11] **Bovee**, born in UT.

| 5206 | iii | Katy Rose[11] **Bovee**, born in UT. |
| 5207 | iv | Nancy Marie[11] **Bovee**, born in UT. |

4877. Scott Allyn[10] **Bovee** (George Raymond[9], George[8], George M[7], Mark[6], Moses R[5], Jacob[4], Gerrit[3], Anthony[2], Mathieu[1]), born in CA. He married Lynn Eleanor McCartney.

Children of Scott Allyn Bovee and Lynn Eleanor McCartney were as follows:

| 5208 | i | Alex Sutton[11] **Bovee**, born in CA. |
| 5209 | ii | Derek Scott[11] **Bovee**, born in CA. |

4879. Brett Lindsey[10] **Bovee** (George Raymond[9], George[8], George M[7], Mark[6], Moses R[5], Jacob[4], Gerrit[3], Anthony[2], Mathieu[1]), born in CA. He married Kris Elise Kastney, born in SC.

Children of Brett Lindsey Bovee and Kris Elise Kastney were as follows:

| 5210 | i | Austin William[11] **Bovee**. |

Generation 11

4883. Leota Margaret[11] **Bovee** (Gerald Nelson[10], Glenn Nelson[9], Manley Glenn[8], John Nelson[7], Richard[6], Elisha[5], Cornelius[4], Rykert[3], Nicholas[2], Mathieu[1]), born in Klamath Falls, Klamath Co., OR. She married on 23 Jul 1983 in Las Vegas, Clark Co., NV Kenneth Croft Gaddis, born in Santa Cruz, Santa Cruz Co., CA, son of Robert Cassius Gaddis and Helen Louise Croft.

Children of Leota Margaret Bovee and Kenneth Croft Gaddis were as follows:

5211	i	Kenneth Croft[12] **Gaddis** Jr., born in Phoenix, Maricopa Co., AZ.
5212	ii	Andrew Nelson[12] **Gaddis**, born in Phoenix, Maricopa Co., AZ.
5213	iii	Michael Robert[12] **Gaddis**, born in Phoenix, Maricopa Co., AZ.

4884. David Nelson[11] **Bovee** (Gerald Nelson[10], Glenn Nelson[9], Manley Glenn[8], John Nelson[7], Richard[6], Elisha[5], Cornelius[4], Rykert[3], Nicholas[2], Mathieu[1]), born in La Mesa, San Diego Co., CA. He married on 9 Oct 1988 in Glendale, Maricopa Co., AZ Kris Ann Reed, daughter of Alvin Dwain Reed and Robin Lynn Davis.

Children of David Nelson Bovee and Kris Ann Reed were as follows:

| 5214 | i | Jeffrey David[12] **Bovee**, born in Glendale, Maricopa Co., AZ. |
| 5215 | ii | Jonathan Preston[12] **Bovee**, born in Phoenix, Maricopa Co., AZ. |

4885. Gregory Preston[11] **Bovee** (Gerald Nelson[10], Glenn Nelson[9], Manley Glenn[8], John Nelson[7], Richard[6], Elisha[5], Cornelius[4], Rykert[3], Nicholas[2], Mathieu[1]), born in La Mesa, San Diego Co., CA. He married (1) on 14 Feb 1988 in Glendale, Maricopa Co., AZ Anne Marie Miller, born in Mesa, Maricopa Co., AZ, daughter of Clyde William Miller and Kathryn Lee Randolph; (2) Lisa Christine Regalia; (3) on 21 Sep 1996 in Mesa, Maricopa Co., AZ Wendie Lynn Cartright.

Children of Gregory Preston Bovee and Anne Marie Miller were as follows:

5216　i　　Tracey Preston[12] **Bovee**, born in Phoenix, Maricopa Co., AZ.

Children of Gregory Preston Bovee and Lisa Christine Regalia were as follows:

5217　i　　Carlie Katherine[12] **Bovee**, born in Glendale, Maricopa Co., AZ.

4920. Chad Mathew[11] **Bovee** (Peter Roger[10], Caryl Roger[9], Roderick[8], Jacob Newton[7], David[6], Elisha[5], Cornelius[4], Rykert[3], Nicholas[2], Mathieu[1]), born in Bemidji,Beltrami Co., MN. He married on 8 Jun 1991 Mary Taylor, born in Rice Lake, Dodge Co., MN, daughter of Raymond Taylor and Cheri Anne Kritch.

Children of Chad Mathew Bovee and Mary Taylor were as follows:

5218　i　　Olivia Anne[12] **Bovee**.

4921. Joel Steven[11] **Bovee** (Peter Roger[10], Caryl Roger[9], Roderick[8], Jacob Newton[7], David[6], Elisha[5], Cornelius[4], Rykert[3], Nicholas[2], Mathieu[1]). He married Naomi Helen Bjorg.

Children of Joel Steven Bovee and Naomi Helen Bjorg were as follows:

5219　i　　Brooke[12] **Bovee**, born in Hennepin Co., MN.
5220　ii　　Maria Jo[12] **Bovee**, born in Hennepin Co., MN.

4932. Aprille[11] **Bovee** (Richard[10], Alton E[9], George F[8], Cornelius[7], Jonas Nicholas[6], Nicholas[5], Cornelius[4], Rykert[3], Nicholas[2], Mathieu[1]). She married Norman Charles Wilson.

Children of Aprille Bovee and Norman Charles Wilson were as follows:

5221　i　　Bracken Kim[12] **Wilson**, born in St Louis Co., MN.

4954. David Lee[11] **Bovee** (Robert William[10], Truman Alphie[9], William Alfred[8], Truman Andrew[7], Jonas Nicholas[6], Nicholas[5], Cornelius[4], Rykert[3], Nicholas[2], Mathieu[1]), born in Miles City, Custer Co., MT. He married on 28 May 1968 Terry

Frazer.

Children of David Lee Bovee and Terry Frazer were as follows:

5222   i   Blaine [12] **Bovee**.

5223   ii   Veronica [12] **Bovee**.

4961. George Alden [11] **Bovee** (Glenn M [10], Robert Alvin [9], William Alfred [8], Truman Andrew [7], Jonas Nicholas [6], Nicholas [5], Cornelius [4], Rykert [3], Nicholas [2], Mathieu [1]). He married Kimberlee Gay Kreft.

Children of George Alden Bovee and Kimberlee Gay Kreft were as follows:

5224   i   David Marlin [12] **Bovee**, born in Hennepin Co., MN.

5225   ii   Jonathan Miles [12] **Bovee**, born in Hennepin Co., MN.

5226   iii   Maryanne Margaret [12] **Bovee**, born in Ramsey Co., MN.

4962. Mary M [11] **Bovee** (Lloyd Leroy [10], Lloyd Laverne [9], William Alfred [8], Truman Andrew [7], Jonas Nicholas [6], Nicholas [5], Cornelius [4], Rykert [3], Nicholas [2], Mathieu [1]). She married on 27 Nov 1971 in Tacoma, Pierce Co., WA John Graves, born in Crookston, Polk Co., MN.

Children of Mary M Bovee and John Graves were as follows:

5227   i   Brian L [12] **Graves**, born in Honolulu, Honolulu Co., HI.

5228   ii   Nathan J [12] **Graves**, born in Honolulu, Honolulu, HI.

4963. Faith P [11] **Bovee** (Lloyd Leroy [10], Lloyd Laverne [9], William Alfred [8], Truman Andrew [7], Jonas Nicholas [6], Nicholas [5], Cornelius [4], Rykert [3], Nicholas [2], Mathieu [1]). She married on 15 Jun 1974 Warren J Holbrook, born in Auburn, Cayuga Co., NY, son of Albert W Holbrook and Ann E Sheified.

Children of Faith P Bovee and Warren J Holbrook were as follows:

5229   i   Trinity Estelle [12] **Holbrook**, born in Germany.

5230   ii   Mathew James [12] **Holbrook**, born in Tacoma, Pierce Co., WA.

4964. Hope [11] **Bovee** (Lloyd Leroy [10], Lloyd Laverne [9], William Alfred [8], Truman Andrew [7], Jonas Nicholas [6], Nicholas [5], Cornelius [4], Rykert [3], Nicholas [2], Mathieu [1]). She married (1) on 11 Aug 1979 Scott Eichman, born in Flushing, Queens Co., NY; (2) on 1 May 1989 (---) Murray.

Children of Hope Bovee and Scott Eichman were as follows:

5231   i   Rachael E [12] **Eichman**, born in Deer Park, Spokane Co., WA.

4969. Peggy Lorene^{11} **Bovee** (Harley Howard^{10}, Claude Harley^9, William Harlan^8, Archibald Melrose^7, John^6, John^5, Nicholas M^4, Matthew^3, Nicholas^2, Mathieu^1), born in La Canada, Los Angeles Co., CA. She married in Jul 1966 in Seattle, King Co., WA Nadar Friedman.

Children of Peggy Lorene Bovee and Nadar Friedman were as follows:

5232   i   Arnon A^{12} **Friedman**, born in Bellingham, Whatcom Co., WA.

5233   ii   Ron^{12} **Friedman**, born in Gurnee, Lake Co., IL.

4971. Betty Jane^{11} **Bovee** (Harley Howard^{10}, Claude Harley^9, William Harlan^8, Archibald Melrose^7, John^6, John^5, Nicholas M^4, Matthew^3, Nicholas^2, Mathieu^1), born in Oklahoma City, Oklahoma Co., OK. She married in Jul 1967 in Seattle, King Co., WA John De Jurnatt.

Children of Betty Jane Bovee and John De Jurnatt were as follows:

5234   i   Alexander^{12} **De Jurnatt**, born in Seattle, King Co., WA.

5235   ii   Maxmillian^{12} **De Jurnatt**, born in Seattle, King Co., WA.

4972. Donald Harley^{11} **Bovee** (Harley Howard^{10}, Claude Harley^9, William Harlan^8, Archibald Melrose^7, John^6, John^5, Nicholas M^4, Matthew^3, Nicholas^2, Mathieu^1), born in Seattle, King Co., WA. He married in 1977 in Carnation, King Co., WA Nancy (---).

Children of Donald Harley Bovee and Nancy (---) were as follows:

5236   i   Timothy^{12} **Bovee**, born in Seattle, King Co., WA.

4973. James Clair^{11} **Bovee** (Robert Clare^{10}, Claude Harley^9, William Harlan^8, Archibald Melrose^7, John^6, John^5, Nicholas M^4, Matthew^3, Nicholas^2, Mathieu^1), born in Seattle, King Co., WA. He married on 8 Aug 1964 in Dinuba, Tulare Co., CA Lynda Berry, born in Van Buren, Crawford Co., AR, daughter of Lee Berry and Letha Viola James.

Children of James Clair Bovee and Lynda Berry were as follows:

+   5237   i   James Clair^{12} **Bovee** Jr, born in Lamdore, CA. He married **Ann Elizabeth Hogsett**.

+   5238   ii   Stephanie Chelene^{12} **Bovee**, born in Seattle, King Co., WA. She married **Charles Dempsey Bronson IV**.

+   5239   iii   Laura Michelle^{12} **Bovee**, born in Seattle, King Co., WA. She married **Michael James Brundage**.

+   5240   iv   Michael Patrick^{12} **Bovee**, born in Seattle, King Co., WA. He married **Rachel Kerry Ruth Struckman Moritz**.

4975. Robert Paul^{11} **Bovee** (Robert Clare^{10}, Claude Harley^9, William Harlan^8,

Archibald Melrose^7, John^6, John^5, Nicholas M^4, Matthew^3, Nicholas^2, Mathieu^1), born in Seattle, King Co., WA. He married (1) abt 1975, divorced Vicki Corner; (2) in Apr 1979 in Reno, Washo Co., NV Joan Johnson, born in Waco, McLennan Co., TX, daughter of Kenneth Allen Johnson and Barbara Beth Christian.

Children of Robert Paul Bovee and Vicki Corner were as follows:

5241   i   Joshua^{12} **Bovee**.

Children of Robert Paul Bovee and Joan Johnson were as follows:

5242   i   Roxanne Carol^{12} **Bovee**, born in Bellevue, King Co., WA.
5243   ii   Aubry Marie^{12} **Bovee**, born in Bellevue, King Co., WA.

4977. Jamie^{11} **Bovee** (Ivan Robert^{10}, Hugh Archibald^9, Archibald Theodore^8, Archibald Melrose^7, John^6, John^5, Nicholas M^4, Matthew^3, Nicholas^2, Mathieu^1). He married unknown.

Children of Jamie Bovee were as follows:

5244   i   Jamie Robert^{12} **Bovee**.

4980. Derek Lynnwood^{11} **Bovee** (Lynwood Wayne^{10}, Hugh Archibald^9, Archibald Theodore^8, Archibald Melrose^7, John^6, John^5, Nicholas M^4, Matthew^3, Nicholas^2, Mathieu^1), born in Fort Staint John, British Columbia, Canada. He married Michell (---).

Children of Derek Lynnwood Bovee and Michell (---) were as follows:

5245   i   Justin James Lynwood^{12} **Bovee**.

5005. Jodi Lynn^{11} **Bovee** (Edward^{10}, Edward Ellsworth^9, Edward Milton^8, Franklin E^7, John Wesley^6, John Grant^5, John^4, Matthew^3, Nicholas^2, Mathieu^1). She married on 20 Apr 2002 in Savanah, Chatham Co., GA Scott Biezenbos.

Children of Jodi Lynn Bovee and Scott Biezenbos were as follows:

5246   i   Brenden^{12} **Biezenbos**.

5006. Shari^{11} **Bovee** (Richard H^{10}, Edward Ellsworth^9, Edward Milton^8, Franklin E^7, John Wesley^6, John Grant^5, John^4, Matthew^3, Nicholas^2, Mathieu^1). She married (1) on 17 May 1981 Jeffrey Smith; (2) on 5 Nov 1988 Dale Wheeler.

Children of Shari Bovee and Jeffrey Smith were as follows:

5247   i   Jeffrey^{12} **Smith**.
5248   ii   William^{12} **Smith**.

Children of Shari Bovee and Dale Wheeler were as follows:

5249   i   Emily^{12} **Wheeler**.

5007. Nancy^{11} **Bovee** (Richard H^{10}, Edward Ellsworth^{9}, Edward Milton^{8}, Franklin E^{7}, John Wesley^{6}, John Grant^{5}, John^{4}, Matthew^{3}, Nicholas^{2}, Mathieu^{1}). She married on 19 Dec 1980 William Burke.

Children of Nancy Bovee and William Burke were as follows:

5250   i   Tiffany^{12} **Burke**.

5251   ii   Ryan^{12} **Burke**.

5103. Lynn Irl^{11} **Bovee** (Neal Anderson^{10}, Lynn Albert^{9}, June Raymond^{8}, Daniel Reynolds^{7}, William R^{6}, Daniel R^{5}, Nicholas P^{4}, Philip^{3}, Nicholas^{2}, Mathieu^{1}), born in Erie, Erie Co., PA. He married on 23 Nov 1961 in Rubidoux, Riverside, Co., CA Dona Irene Nottier, born in Bellingham, Whatcom Co., WA.

Children of Lynn Irl Bovee and Dona Irene Nottier were as follows:

5252   i   Shelly Ann^{12} **Bovee**, born in Newport Beach, Orange Co., CA.

5253   ii   Daniel Neal^{12} **Bovee**, born in Newport Beach, Orange Co., CA.

5104. Sandra Ruth^{11} **Bovee** (Neal Anderson^{10}, Lynn Albert^{9}, June Raymond^{8}, Daniel Reynolds^{7}, William R^{6}, Daniel R^{5}, Nicholas P^{4}, Philip^{3}, Nicholas^{2}, Mathieu^{1}), born 9 Sep 1939 in Falls Church, VA; died 3 Apr 1977 in Perth Amboy, Middlesex Co., VA. She married (1) on 20 Jan 1968 in Las Vegas, Clark Co., NV William F Dickson, born 26 May 1929 in Newark, Essex Co., NJ; died 3 Apr 1977 in Perth Amboy, Middlesex Co., NJ; (2) (---) Taylor.

Children of Sandra Ruth Bovee and (---) Taylor were as follows:

5254   i   Lora Gail^{12} **Taylor**, born in Portland, Multnomah Co., OR.

5255   ii   Dwain Kertis^{12} **Taylor**, born in Elizabeth, Union Co., NJ.

5105. David Brian^{11} **Bovee** (Neal Anderson^{10}, Lynn Albert^{9}, June Raymond^{8}, Daniel Reynolds^{7}, William R^{6}, Daniel R^{5}, Nicholas P^{4}, Philip^{3}, Nicholas^{2}, Mathieu^{1}), born in Erie, Erie Co., PA. He married (1) on 12 Apr 1964, divorced Carolyn Brassel; (2) on 7 Nov 1984 in Katy, Harris Co., TX Donna Lee Thompson.

Children of David Brian Bovee and Carolyn Brassel were as follows:

5256   i   Vicky Lynn^{12} **Bovee**.

5257   ii   Cynthia Lee^{12} **Bovee**.

5107. Carol Maria^{11} **Bovee** (Neal Anderson^{10}, Lynn Albert^{9}, June Raymond^{8}, Daniel Reynolds^{7}, William R^{6}, Daniel R^{5}, Nicholas P^{4}, Philip^{3}, Nicholas^{2},

Mathieu^1), born in Seine, Neuilly, France; christened in Paris, France. She married on 20 May 1972 in Beirut, Lebanon Antonio Luigi Arnoldi, born in Brindisi, Italy; christened in Brindisi, Italy.

Children of Carol Maria Bovee and Antonio Luigi Arnoldi were as follows:

5258   i   Jennifer Lynn^{12} **Arnoldi**, born in Bairut, Lebanon.

5259   ii   Michael Anthony^{12} **Arnoldi**, born in San Jose, Santa Clara Co., CA.

5108. Linda Marcella^{11} **Bovee** (Neal Anderson^{10}, Lynn Albert^9, June Raymond^8, Daniel Reynolds^7, William R^6, Daniel R^5, Nicholas P^4, Philip^3, Nicholas^2, Mathieu^1), born in Seine, Neuilly, France. She married on 26 Jul 1980 in Lompoc, Santa Barbara Co., CA Gregory Philip Spohr, born in Paterson, Passiac Co., NJ, son of Joseph Conrad Spohr Jr. and Alice Rita Donohoue.

Children of Linda Marcella Bovee and Gregory Philip Spohr were as follows:

5260   i   Christopher Michael^{12} **Spohr**, born in Fontana, Riverside Co., CA.

5116. Robert Guy^{11} **Bovee** (Robert John^{10}, George Henry^9, Guy Clinton^8, Harmon E^7, Nicholas^6, Jacob^5, Nicholas P^4, Philip^3, Nicholas^2, Mathieu^1). He married on 18 Feb 1989 Chandra Lee Paddock.

Children of Robert Guy Bovee and Chandra Lee Paddock were as follows:

5261   i   Rhea Coutney^{12} **Bovee**.

5262   ii   Cailene Victoria^{12} **Bovee**.

5135. David James^{11} **Bovee** (David Fred^{10}, Frank Walter^9, John Addison^8, Christian^7, Peter^6, Peter^5, Jacob^4, Jacob^3, Nicholas^2, Mathieu^1), born in Norwich, Chenango Co., NY. He married Angela Benedict.

Children of David James Bovee and Angela Benedict were as follows:

5263   i   Gabrielle Audree^{12} **Bovee**, born in Norwich, Chenango Co., NY.

5157. Ronald Albert^{11} **Bovee** (Ronald^{10}, Claude Henry^9, Albert A^8, Hiram^7, Luther^6, Jacob^5, Anthony^4, Gerrit^3, Anthony^2, Mathieu^1). He married on 26 May 1990 Lorie Pike.

Children of Ronald Albert Bovee and Lorie Pike were as follows:

5264   i   Ronald^{12} **Bovee**.

5265   ii   Nicole^{12} **Bovee**.

5159. Michael Joseph[11] **Bovee** (Ronald[10], Claude Henry[9], Albert A[8], Hiram[7], Luther[6], Jacob[5], Anthony[4], Gerrit[3], Anthony[2], Mathieu[1]). He married Darcy Dennison.

Children of Michael Joseph Bovee and Darcy Dennison were as follows:

5266   i   Michael[12] **Bovee** Jr.

5267   ii   Kaitlyn[12] **Bovee.**

5268   iii   Tabitha[12] **Bovee.**

5160. Gary Claude[11] **Bovee** (Ronald[10], Claude Henry[9], Albert A[8], Hiram[7], Luther[6], Jacob[5], Anthony[4], Gerrit[3], Anthony[2], Mathieu[1]), born in Glens Falls, Warren Co., NY. He married Michelle Caldwell.

Children of Gary Claude Bovee and Michelle Caldwell were as follows:

5269   i   Gary[12] **Bovee** Jr.

5161. Michelle[11] **Bovee** (Ronald[10], Claude Henry[9], Albert A[8], Hiram[7], Luther[6], Jacob[5], Anthony[4], Gerrit[3], Anthony[2], Mathieu[1]), born in Glens Falls, Warren Co., NY. She married Tony Lucia.

Children of Michelle Bovee and Tony Lucia were as follows:

5270   i   Devon Michael[12] **Lucia.**

5271   ii   Austin William[12] **Lucia.**

5272   iii   Aubre Mae[12] **Lucia.**

5167. James Terry[11] **Bovee** (James Wayne[10], Claude Henry[9], Albert A[8], Hiram[7], Luther[6], Jacob[5], Anthony[4], Gerrit[3], Anthony[2], Mathieu[1]). He married (1) bef 1992 Debby MacKentire; (2) aft 1992 Kimberly Mattrau.

Children of James Terry Bovee and Debby MacKentire were as follows:

5273   i   Derrick James[12] **Bovee**, born in Glens Falls, Warren Co., NY.

Children of James Terry Bovee and Kimberly Mattrau were as follows:

5274   i   Timothy Wayne[12] **Bovee**, born in Glens Falls, Warren Co., NY.

5188. Kimberly[11] **Bovee** (Byron Wright[10], Edwin Wright[9], David Lloyd[8], Edwin Anson[7], Eli William[6], Jonathan[5], Peter[4], Gerrit[3], Anthony[2], Mathieu[1]), born in Grand Rapids, Kent Co., MI. She married on 18 May 1985 in Grand Rapids, Kent Co., MI Robert Slupe Jr.

Children of Kimberly Bovee and Robert Slupe Jr were as follows:

5275   i   Jennifer Rebecca[12] **Slupe**, born in Grand Rapids, Kent

Co., MI.

5276　ii　Stephanie Ranee[12] **Slupe**, born in Grand Rapids, Kent Co., MI.

5197. Barry Loris[11] **Bovee** (Claude Lee[10], Claude Lee[9], Mark C[8], George M[7], Mark[6], Moses R[5], Jacob[4], Gerrit[3], Anthony[2], Mathieu[1]), born in CO. He married Connie Sue Bean.

　　Children of Barry Loris Bovee and Connie Sue Bean were as follows:

5277　i　April Lynn[12] **Bovee**, born in OR.

5278　ii　Dustin Loris[12] **Bovee**, born in OR.

5279　iii　Ryan LeRoy[12] **Bovee**, born in CO.

Generation 12

5237. James Clair[12] **Bovee** Jr (James Clair[11], Robert Clare[10], Claude Harley[9], William Harlan[8], Archibald Melrose[7], John[6], John[5], Nicholas M[4], Matthew[3], Nicholas[2], Mathieu[1]), born in Lamdore, CA. He married on 29 Jul 1995 Ann Elizabeth Hogsett.

　　Children of James Clair Bovee Jr and Ann Elizabeth Hogsett were as follows:

5280　i　Jonathan Robert[13] **Bovee**.

5281　ii　Alec Christopher[13] **Bovee**.

5238. Stephanie Chelene[12] **Bovee** (James Clair[11], Robert Clare[10], Claude Harley[9], William Harlan[8], Archibald Melrose[7], John[6], John[5], Nicholas M[4], Matthew[3], Nicholas[2], Mathieu[1]), born in Seattle, King Co., WA. She married on 11 Jul 1993 Charles Dempsey Bronson IV.

　　Children of Stephanie Chelene Bovee and Charles Dempsey Bronson IV were as follows:

5282　i　Makisa Xiaoli[13] **Bronson**.

5283　ii　Cienne Guobao[13] **Bronson**.

5239. Laura Michelle[12] **Bovee** (James Clair[11], Robert Clare[10], Claude Harley[9], William Harlan[8], Archibald Melrose[7], John[6], John[5], Nicholas M[4], Matthew[3], Nicholas[2], Mathieu[1]), born in Seattle, King Co., WA. She married on 29 Oct 1994 Michael James Brundage.

　　Children of Laura Michelle Bovee and Michael James Brundage were as follows:

5284　i　Samanth LaRose Shoemaker[13] **Brundage**.

5285　ii　Beau James[13] **Brundage**.

5286 iii Sydney Mary[13] **Brundage**.

5240. Michael Patrick[12] **Bovee** (James Clair[11], Robert Clare[10], Claude Harley[9], William Harlan[8], Archibald Melrose[7], John[6], John[5], Nicholas M[4], Matthew[3], Nicholas[2], Mathieu[1]), born in Seattle, King Co., WA. He married on 23 Aug 2003 Rachel Kerry Ruth Struckman Moritz.

Children of Michael Patrick Bovee and Rachel Kerry Ruth Struckman Moritz were as follows:

5287 i Jessica Chelene[13] **Bovee**.
5288 ii Madison Riley[13] **Bovee**.

Index

1

3

4

5

7

9

Amanda (O'Brien)
(1829-1917), 23, 60
Amanda Catherine
(Robb) (1833-
1912), 46
Amanda E (1888-
1981), 240
Amanda Matilda
(1820-), 42
Amelia (Miller) (1838-
1887), 45, 103
Amelia (Thirley), 61
Amelia Jane (1826-),
42
Amelia Wraight
(Wager) (1846-
1929), 84, 160
Amity G (Lake) (1820-
1906), 33, 84
Amos (1837-), 77
Amos Philip (1905-
1995), 235, 316
Amy, 402, 405
Amy (1872-1872), 99
Amy (Bass) (1903-
1976), 128, 215
Amy Elizabeth, 399
Anatje (1790-1861),
27, 73
Andrea (Pepritsch),
389, 418
Andrea L, 412
Andrew (1770-), 5, 12
Andrew D (1837-
1864), 44
Andrew Elliott (1847-
1908), 37, 90
Andrew J (1837-), 47,
105
Andrew Jackson
(1848-1912), 60,
125
Andrew Jackson Jr
(1887-1918), 126,
211
Andrew Joseph, 403
Andrew Paul, 406
Anette Lea, 373
Angela (Benedict),
413, 425
Angelia Lynn, 349
Angelica (1849-), 59,
125

Angeline, 86
Angeline ((---)) (1835-
), 23, 62
Angeline L (Reynolds)
(-1928), 84, 160
Angelique C, 412
Angenette Lucinda
(Heath), 77
Anita (Putzker) (1864-
1934), 173, 264
Anita Louise ((---)),
297, 369
Ann (1802-), 12
Ann (1879-), 119
Ann (Nixon) (1923-),
319, 380
Ann Amelia (Cook)
(1827-1865), 80,
154
Ann E (1843-), 58
Ann Eliza (LeBaron)
(1830-1921), 23, 61
Ann Elizabeth (1827-
1869), 40, 94
Ann Elizabeth
(Hogsett), 422, 427
Ann Elizabeth
(Patterson) (1851-),
54, 116
Ann Elizabeth
(Shivley), 138, 229
Anna ((---)) (1763-
1815), 2, 8
Anna (1701-), 1
Anna (1727-), 2, 5
Anna (1775-), 23
Anna (1777-), 25, 68
Anna (1778-), 11
Anna (1805-1879), 20,
47
Anna (1857-), 150
Anna (1860-1951),
139
Anna (1887-), 244
Anna (Betts) (1875-),
99, 181
Anna (Carl), 233, 313
Anna (Cole), 2, 7, 9
Anna (Dederick)
(1851-), 140, 233
Anna (Emerson)
(1894-1971), 183,
272

Anna (Handy), 151
Anna (Lighthall)
(1790-), 25, 69
Anna (Moorhouse) (-
1920), 189, 278
Anna (Smith) (1868-
1952), 56, 117
Anna (Warner) (1776-
1824), 8, 18
Anna B (Duncan)
(1820-1911), 35, 86
Anna Bell (1882-
1962), 173
Anna C (Rightmeyer)
(1870-), 232, 311
Anna Caroline
(Palmer) (1856-
1936), 86, 163
Anna Elizabeth (1829-
1875), 41, 97
Anna Frances (Taylor)
(1890-1939), 162,
254
Anna Irene (1892-),
185, 275
Anna Julia (Smith)
(1863-1947), 85,
161
Anna Laura (1888-
1974), 123
Anna Lorra (1882-
1962), 151, 244
Anna M (1828-), 23
Anna M (Whitbeck)
(1844-1878), 85,
161
Anna Margaret (1921-
), 275, 353
Anna Maria (1822-),
33
Anna Maria (1852-),
113
Anna Maria (Betzer)
(1847-1905), 92,
172, 176
Annatie (1765-), 11
Annatie (1768-), 7
Annatje (1783-), 25
Annatje (1791-), 24
Annatje (1795-1795),
27
Annatje (1796-), 27,
72

Annatje (1797-), 26,
71
Anne (Bird) (1838-
1893), 71, 143
Anne Marie (Miller),
390, 420
Anneke (1743-), 4
Annette Marie, 358
Annie ((---)) (1875-),
174, 265
Annie (Allen) (1790-
1851), 20, 51, 84
Annie Malvina (1843-),
87, 166
Annis P (1822-), 64
Anthony (1696-), 1
Anthony (1707-), 1, 3,
4, 12
Anthony (1755-1822),
10, 28
Anthony (1767-), 11,
13, 30
Anthony (1784-), 11
Anthony (1816-1858),
77, 149
Anthony Andrea, 345
Antionette (Dailey)
(1851-1915), 59,
125
Antje (1735-), 4
Antje (1769-), 10
Antje (1794-), 27
April Lynn, 427
Aprille, 394, 420
Archibald Melrose
(1838-1900), 92,
171
Archibald Theodore
(1884-1979), 172,
262
Archie Dell (1884-
1969), 108, 191
Archie Edward (1900-
1980), 187, 276
Arda Bartholomy
(Hallock) (1906-
1999), 248, 329
Ardee Lewis (1906-
1969), 193, 283
Ariantje (1731-), 2, 5
Ariantje (1741-), 4
Ariantje (1772-), 10

Ariantje (Brouwer)
(1737-1818), 3, 4,
10
Aris (1901-), 305, 374
Aris R (1884-1960),
224
Arizona (Hoisington),
104
Arlene (Kells) (1908-
1984), 317, 380
Arlene (Kruse), 128,
216
Arlene L (1924-), 253
Arlene Marion (1914-),
211, 298
Arlette Jane, 365
Arline Faith (1920-),
331
Armanell E (1881-
1962), 148
Arthur, 199
Arthur (1838-1915),
48, 107
Arthur (1871-), 231
Arthur Bishop, 309
Arthur Blair (1934-
1941), 289
Arthur C (1872-), 229,
308
Arthur Cornelius
(1904-1970), 128,
215
Arthur David, 282, 358
Arthur E (1873-), 130,
218
Arthur Franklin (1896-
1981), 219
Arthur Gibbon (1882-
1961), 230, 308
Arthur Jewett (1880-
1953), 109, 193
Arthur Jewett Jr
(1912-), 193, 282
Arthur M (1910-1939),
329
Arthur Roy (1885-
1953), 173, 264
Arthur Vernon (1871-
1939), 121, 206
Arthur Vernon Jr
(1897-1967), 207,
294
Arthur Wayne, 365

Arthur William, 294,
364
Arvilla Jane (Bussler)
(1857-), 54, 115
Asa (1805-1872), 20,
52
Attie Anne Victoria
(Nelson) (1888-
1929), 126, 211
Aubry Marie, 423
Audra, 337
Audrey (Stoskopf)
(1917-), 314, 378
Audrey S, 314
Augusta (1855-), 139
Augusta E (1852-
1860), 104
Augusta Ernestina
(Ferg) (1876-1974),
121, 206
Augusta Tresa, 294,
364
Aurelia (1807-1854),
21, 55
Aurelia (Randall)
(1832-1911), 81,
155
Aurilla (1876-1954),
108, 191
Austin, 416
Austin Dale, 417
Austin William, 419
Ava (Graves) (1877-
1974), 101, 182
Avis Christina (1910-),
192
Azro (1844-1864), 82
Bambi ((---)), 266, 347
Barbara, 269, 289,
299, 316, 356, 372,
414
Barbara ((---)), 296
Barbara (Bendell),
183, 272
Barbara (Grimes),
324, 383
Barbara (O'Hare), 303,
373
Barbara (Winston),
252, 333
Barbara Catherine
(Moffatt), 378

Betty Carol (Blaydes),
295, 365
Betty J (Desormeau)
(1922-), 184, 273
Betty Jane, 397, 422
Betty Jane (1925-),
251
Betty Jean, 321
Betty Jean (Taylor),
358, 404
Beula L (1899-1940),
222
Beulah (1894-), 238
Beulah Belle (1889-),
190, 279
Beulah Faye (1914-
1964), 194, 283
Beulah Laura (Deline)
(1899-1984), 188,
277
Beverly, 286, 359, 414
Beverly (1927-), 301
Beverly (Bowman),
338, 392
Beverly Ann, 387, 417
Beverly Arlene, 277
Beverly J (1939-2001),
266, 346
Beverly Mae (LaRich),
320, 382
Beverly Martha (1903-
), 183
Billie Fay, 408
Billie Jean, 284, 358
Billy Ray, 255, 337
Birding J (1894-), 167
Blaine, 421
Blanche (1880-), 116,
201
Blanche (1881-), 121
Blanche (1897-), 237
Blanche (Leo), 262
Blanche Christine
(Atterbury) (1891-
1983), 162, 255
Blanche F (1890-
1959), 250
Bonabell, 230
Bonnie, 309
Bonnie (1913-), 314,
379
Bonnie Lee, 338, 392

Bonnie Mulla (1911-),
193, 282
Boyd Bernard (1927-
1932), 342
Brad, 384
Brad Daniel, 369
Bradley, 359
Brandon Richard, 407
Brandy, 323
Breanne M, 384
Bren Michael, 401
Brenda (Bond), 333,
389
Brenda Harrison
(Fallon), 303, 373
Brenda Jan, 412
Brent, 392
Bret, 407
Brett, 402
Brett Lindsey, 389,
419
Brett M, 384, 416
Brian, 370, 372
Brian Bradley, 296
Brian Keith, 418
Brian Steven, 391
Bridget Eilene, 369
Bridgette Louise, 377
Brigell Fay, 372
Britnay Christine, 407
Brittany Jo, 389
Brooke, 420
Bruce (1873-1927),
102, 184
Bud, 331
Buddy, 394
Burdette (Fish), 115,
198
Burt Richard (1922-),
255, 337
Burton (1919-1980),
302, 372
Burton G (1874-1912),
102, 185
Burton George (1912-
), 213, 299
Burton Raymond
(1872-), 116, 199
Byron E (1839-1911),
63, 131
Byron J (1868-), 130,
218
Byron Merle (1893-

1937), 306
Byron Wright, 387,
417
Cailene Victoria, 425
Caleb Drake (1829-
1854), 81, 155
Calvin O (1867-1929),
106, 188
Candace E (1836-), 85
Cara, 402
Carel (1744-), 4
Carl, 319, 323
Carl (1904-1970), 188
Carl Aaron (1888-
1956), 108, 191
Carl Clifford (1900-
1987), 207, 295
Carl Folette (1905-
1979), 248, 329
Carl G (1869-1892),
115
Carl Harvey (1920-),
242, 322
Carl Howard (1888-
1961), 173, 264
Carl L (1915-2000),
243, 323
Carl Norman (1920-
1999), 206, 293
Carl Norman Jr (1949-
1949), 293
Carleton (1895-1976),
244
Carley May (1924-),
211, 298
Carlie Katherine, 420
Carlos Robert (1921-
1988), 245
Carmen ((---)), 279,
356
Carmeta, 322
Carmetta Gertrude,
383
Carol, 322, 324, 372,
383
Carol ((---)), 382, 415
Carol (1913-), 208
Carol Ann, 331
Carol Anne, 330
Carol LaVonne (Pipa),
376, 412
Carol Lynne (Crowell),
288, 360

13

15

Chauncy William (1892-1978), 232, 311

Cherie Ann (1923-), 203, 290

Cheryl A, 366

Cheryl Jane, 354

Chester A (1886-), 227

Chester Emerson (1889-), 199, 287

Chester J (1892-1963), 124

Chester Peter (1891-1900), 117

Chester Willey Grant (1882-), 162

Child, 124, 185, 211, 212, 227, 231, 304, 319, 387, 394, 401, 405, 411

Child (1845-1845), 154

Child (1848-1865), 153

Child (1880-), 134

Child (1882-1882), 108

Child (1886-1886), 241

Child (1893-1893), 219

child (1898-), 239

Child (1899-), 236

Child (-1900), 118

Child (1900-), 128

Child (1902-1902), 192

Child (1910-1915), 239

Child (1917-), 310

Child (1918-), 209

Child (1974-1974), 404

Chislaine (LeBain), 353, 402

Chold, 405

Chris Lyn (-1973), 418

Christian (1843-1908), 140, 231

Christianne Collette (Rouland), 388, 418

Christie, 403

Christine, 392

Christine ((---)), 106

Christine (Fournier), 362, 405

Christopher, 406

Christopher D, 411

Christopher P, 343

Christopher Robin, 354

Cindy, 303, 401

Cindy (Eggleston), 323

Cinnamon Lynn (Chimelski), 368, 407

Claas (1728-), 2

Clair (1903-), 207

Claire Lewis (1891-1977), 168, 259

Clara ((---)) (1851-), 137, 229

Clara (1866-), 224

Clara (1868-), 231, 310

Clara (1897-1949), 251

Clara (Bartholomew), 133, 221

Clara A (1864-1910), 104, 186

Clara Belle (1892-1966), 178

Clara Dulceina (Hancock) (1861-), 94, 176

Clara Elizabeth (1898-), 199

Clara J ((---)) (1842-), 46, 105

Clara K (Jones) (1868-1922), 156, 249

Clara Leone (1874-), 120, 204

Clara M (1836-), 72, 143

Clara W (McKarghan) (1908-1988), 190, 280

Clarence (1867-), 137

Clarence (1879-1925), 233

Clarence Abraham

(1883-1960), 124, 209

Clarence C (1920-1921), 222

Clarence F (1859-1931), 143

Clarence J (1864-), 106

Clarissa (1819-1819), 62

Clarissa (Schermerhorn) (1794-), 27, 73

Clarissa Eliza (1844-), 76

Clarissa M (1841-1907), 134

Clark (1831-1908), 81, 155

Clark G (1840-1905), 83, 159

Clatie J (1866-1867), 238

Claude Alva (1898-1969), 152, 245

Claude Alvin (1924-1944), 246

Claude Harley (1887-1971), 261, 344

Claude Henry (1909-1996), 319, 381

Claude Lee (1911-1973), 332, 389

Claude Lee Jr, 389, 418

Clayton S (1909-1979), 312

Cleo C (1903-1920), 310

Cleve Winn (1906-1992), 258

Clifford Dan, 301, 370

Clifton Willard (1913-), 264, 345

Clinton (1908-1971), 241

Clinton (1915-1992), 242, 322

Clyde August (1908-), 187

Clyde Charles (1864-1956), 158, 251

Clyde Douglas, 388

Clyde G (1900-1986), 178
Clyde LaRue (1908-1971), 199, 289
Clyde M (1900-1976), 123
Cole Russell, 393
Colleen (Conroy), 383
Colleen Rachel, 336, 391
Conner Mathew, 359
Conner Paul, 402
Connie Sue (Bean), 418, 427
Connor Douglas, 400
Constance (Levac), 335, 390
Constance (Peterson), 340
Constance (Stuart), 296
Constance M (Mallow), 273, 351
Cora ((---)), 156, 250, 331
Cora (1868-), 139
Cora (1878-), 121
Cora (1881-), 163
Cora (1929-1997), 243, 324
Cora (Greene) (1880-), 225
Cora (Slade) (-1922), 113, 196
Cora A (Hotchkiss) (1862-), 139, 231
Cora Bell (1859-), 61
Cora Bell (1876-1960), 134, 222
Cora Edna (Munson) (1888-1927), 109, 193
Cora L (1857-1915), 150, 242
Cora M (1860-), 88
Cora M (1876-), 237
Cora Marie, 251
Cora May (1874-1956), 108, 192
Cora May (1874-1959), 94
Cordelia (Pool) (1828-1898), 72

Cordelia Annete (1825-1825), 79
Corina (Jergenson), 58, 124
Corine (Stephens), 381, 415
Corlan Drury (1915-1977), 249
Cornelia (1754-), 7, 14
Cornelia (1756-1786), 7, 16
Cornelia (1770-1805), 9
Cornelia (1779-), 8
Cornelia (1791-1874), 16, 39
Cornelia (1813-), 19
Cornelia (1878-), 118
Cornelia (Brouwer) (1691-), 1, 2
Cornelius (1765-1847), 7, 15
Cornelius (1800-), 22, 57
Cornelius (1824-1853), 74, 145
Cornelius (1832-1914), 23, 62
Cornelius (1839-), 37
Cornelius (1840-1899), 87, 165
Cornelius (1853-), 145
Cornelius Anson (1872-1961), 107, 190
Cornelius Elihu (1836-1911), 77, 148, 238
Cornelius Frank (1892-1967), 257
Cornelius Harvey (1857-), 62
Cornelius Jr (1799-1870), 15, 36
Cornelius Schermerhorn (1807-1839), 28, 76
Courtland (1800-1872), 30, 82
Courtland Lowell, 333
Courtney Van (1919-), 252, 333
Craig Richard, 388
Crystal, 323

Culver Nathaniel (1855-1913), 53, 114
Curtis Carl, 329
Curtis Mathew (1875-1948), 224
Cynthia, 415
Cynthia (Youmans) (1803-1860), 21, 54
Cynthia Ann (Eddy), 64, 133
Cynthia Ann (Goodman) (1821-1899), 80, 154
Cynthia Kay, 339, 393
Cynthia Lee, 424
Cyril (1915-1915), 213
Daisy (1835-), 81
Daisy (1878-), 233
Daisy L (Long) (1900-1984), 304, 373
Daisy L (McFie) (1884-1987), 162, 254
Daisy Leone (1914-), 205
Daisy M ((---)) (1880-), 237, 318
Daisy Mae (1876-), 105, 188
Dakota, 416
Dale (1918-), 222
Dale Allen, 303, 373
Dale Eugene (1924-2004), 331
Dalen Curtis (1939-1939), 343
Dan, 362, 406
Dana, 322
Dana Louise, 358
Daniel, 407
Daniel (1789-), 27
Daniel (1794-1860), 27, 73
Daniel (1818-), 65, 136
Daniel D (1833-1913), 74, 145
Daniel James, 389, 402, 409
Daniel Joe, 354, 403
Daniel John (1930-), 321, 382

Diana Sue, 285, 359
Diane, 304, 381, 414
Diane ((---)), 173
Diane Marie, 342, 394
Dianna Gay, 343
Dianna Marie, 404
Dianne Elizabeth, 385, 416
Dianne P (1838-), 83
Doan Elisha (1848-1867), 88
Dolly (1860-), 139
Dolly (Rickman), 246, 325
Dolly Ann (1838-1840), 54
Dolores ((---)), 254, 334
Dolores (1907-), 302
Don, 410
Dona Irene (Nottier), 410, 424
Donald, 203, 271, 290
Donald (1917-1931), 222
Donald (1920-), 256
Donald (1931-1931), 317
Donald C (1925-1995), 308, 376
Donald Carl (1935-1935), 295
Donald Clayton (1921-), 278
Donald Colbert, 195
Donald Dale (1925-), 264
Donald F (1906-1979), 301, 370
Donald Gregg (1904-), 200
Donald Harley, 397, 422
Donald Lee, 296, 367
Donald Marcus (1915-), 320, 381
Donald Ray (1910-1981), 178
Donald Wright (1900-), 118, 203
Donna, 382
Donna (Sherwood), 383, 416

Donna Ann, 337
Donna Lee, 376, 412
Donna Lee (Thompson), 410, 424
Donna Mary (Powers), 377, 412
Donna Rae, 295
Dora (1896-), 181
Dora (Quimby) (1870-1962), 156, 248
Dora Arvilla (1868-1944), 107, 190
Dora Elva (Welch) (1886-1918), 120, 204
Dora L (Zimmerman) (1905-1997), 186, 276
Dora May (1872-1948), 98
Dorcas (Bell), 196, 285
Dorcas Louise (1915-), 213
Doris (Jorgenson), 257, 339
Doris (Sturble) (1914-1982), 239, 319
Doris Anna (Bedard) (1910-), 180, 270
Doris B (1923-1971), 245
Doris Elaine (Bergers) (1918-1992), 327, 387
Doris Jane Jackson (Arvine), 254, 335
Doris Kay, 276
Doris M ((---)), 277, 355
Doris Maxine (Kavachevich) (1922-), 197, 287
Doris May (English), 277, 355
Dorothy, 264, 335, 378
Dorothy (1898-), 207
Dorothy (1915-), 260
Dorothy (1916-), 288
Dorothy (1925-), 269
Dorothy (Brakeman),

306, 375
Dorothy (Grebe) (1921-), 209, 297
Dorothy (Miller) (1929-), 342, 396
Dorothy (Smith) (1916-), 191
Dorothy (Whitehead), 211
Dorothy A (1899-), 168
Dorothy Edna (1912-1980), 264
Dorothy Elinor Baxter (Morris) (1923-1998), 255, 336
Dorothy G (1915-), 290
Dorothy Irene (1908-1982), 327, 386
Dorothy L (1920-), 267
Dorothy Love (1902-), 200
Dorothy M (1911-1990), 239
Dorothy M (1913-1981), 118
Dorothy M (Fink) (1897-1970), 269, 348
Dorothy Madge (1924-1947), 348
Dorothy R ((---)) (1904-1975), 213
Dorthy Alice, 261
Douglas Alan, 347, 400
Douglas Arthur, 295, 365
Douglas L, 355
Douglas Russell, 350
Dr John Wesley (1861-1927), 102
Duane, 340
Duane Lorenzo, 258, 341
Dudley A (1891-1981), 240
Durfee (1812-1887), 35, 86
Dustin Loris, 427
Dustin Lynn, 394
Dylan S, 405

20

Elizabeth (Van Olinda) (1789-1837), 12, 32

Elizabeth (Vedder) (1768-), 9, 26

Elizabeth (Whitaker) (1786-1854), 8, 21

Elizabeth (Wilson), 8, 21

Elizabeth (Wilson) (1875-1909), 159, 252

Elizabeth A (Schwartz), 180

Elizabeth Alice, (Moss) (1931-1996), 192, 280

Elizabeth Ann (McCleod), 280

Elizabeth B, 326

Elizabeth B (Hellier) (1840-1894), 42, 98

Elizabeth Bell (Andrews) (1849-1927), 145, 237

Elizabeth C (Spencer) (1866-1900), 172, 261

Elizabeth Ford (McCool) (1851-), 97, 179

Elizabeth J (Kistler) (1922-1982), 326, 384

Elizabeth Jane (McBride), 276, 355

Elizabeth Jane (Williams) (1922-), 326, 385

Elizabeth Lorrain (1926-1997), 326, 385

Elizabeth M (1865-1882), 157

Elizabeth Mae (1928-), 301, 370

Elizabeth Maria (1793-1884), 18, 26, 41

Elizabeth Martha (1895-1920), 203

Elizabeth Pearl (Hobbs) (1919-), 255, 335

Elizabeth R (1812-), 30, 83, 157

Elizabeth Redding (1829-), 82

Elizabeth Swan (Tasher) (1825-), 73, 144

Ella (1872-1875), 119

Ella (Bentley), 143, 235

Ella Ann (Frederick), 123

Ella C (1892-1919), 206

Ella E (1855-1857), 97

Ella Jane (1854-1936), 155, 247

Ella L (1858-), 131

Ella L (1865-), 107, 191

Ella Rose (1881-1965), 123, 208

Ella S (1861-), 133

Ella S (Robinson) (1853-), 83, 159

Ella T (White) (1896-1981), 240, 320

Ellen ((---)), 58

Ellen (1923-), 259

Ellen (Giese) (1906-1981), 207, 295

Ellen (Soper), 35, 87

Ellen A (Taylor) (1907-1972), 128, 215

Ellen D (1836-1841), 54

Ellen G (Goodrich) (1843-1933), 135, 225

Ellen Louise (Groger), 345, 398

Elma Jane (Bordine) (1844-1918), 46, 105

Elmer (1880-1902), 234

Elmer C (1914-1986), 182, 271

Elmer Ellsworth (1859-1938), 156, 248

Elmer Ford (1882-), 100, 182

Elmer N (1882-), 176, 267

Elmore Mary (1867-1910), 106, 189

Elnora (Lanphierd), 371, 408

Elnora (Stearns) (1880-1959), 109, 192

Elode (Gast), 295, 365

Eloise (1900-), 183

Eloise Mabel (1889-), 219

Elsie, 258

Elsie (1794-), 14

Elsie (1817-1897), 20, 50

Elsie (1851-1875), 48, 110

Elsie (Freeman) (1871-1939), 157, 249

Elsie Ellen (1902-1905), 219

Elsie L (Bridger) (1857-1946), 132, 220

Elsie May (Grimsley) (1888-), 116, 201

Elurde Charles (1914-), 182, 271

Elvira Priscilla (1809-1882), 30, 83

Emeline (Baird), 19, 45

Emile (Daniels) (1861-), 149, 240

Emilie Barstow (Dixon), 180

Emiline C (Lorenz) (1884-1940), 227, 308

Emily ((---)), 42

Emily (1830-), 45

Emily (1833-), 71

Emily (1835-), 63

Emily (1846-), 59

Emily (1849-1856), 129

Emily (Dun), 16

Emily (Harris) (1812-1870), 19, 44

Emily A (1811-1895), 21, 55

24

Frances J (Twichell), 223, 304
Frances L (1860-1938), 148
Frances L (Lumb) (-1871), 43, 101
Frances M (Parrow) (1905-1969), 240
Frances Maria (1838-1857), 77
Frances Maria (1838-1864), 79
Frances Marie (1929-), 195
Frances Mildred (1905-), 213
Frances Roberta (1913-), 193, 282
Frances Robinson (Bond), 194, 283
Francis Clarence (1930-1994), 322, 382
Francis H (1846-), 50
Francis J (1875-), 173
Francis M (1843-), 64, 133
Francis M (1900-1919), 179
Francis Victor (1926-1938), 209
Francois, 1, 4
Frank (1857-), 136, 227
Frank (1863-1940), 150, 241
Frank (1865-1904), 157, 249
Frank (1868-), 138
Frank (1887-), 174
Frank (1922-), 272
Frank A (1849-), 96
Frank Allen (1870-1893), 113
Frank C (1882-), 131
Frank E (1847-1917), 136, 228
Frank Gervias (1869-1896), 230
Frank Grencett (1891-1916), 305, 374
Frank H (1849-1853), 149

Frank H (1872-), 160
Frank J (1868-), 133, 221
Frank J (1879-1893), 230
Frank Leslie (1893-1959), 317, 379
Frank Luther (1865-1949), 158, 250
Frank M (1868-), 230, 309
Frank McClellan (1864-1927), 102
Frank Merton (1868-1950), 90, 171
Frank W, 340, 394
Frank W (1914-), 309
Frank Walter (1907-1976), 310, 376
Frank Walter Jr, 376, 412
Franklin (1864-), 233, 312
Franklin (1883-), 119
Franklin Cornelius (1879-), 237, 318
Franklin E (1865-), 103, 185
Franklin Gibson (1855-1918), 61, 127
Franklin O (1866-1924), 156
Fred, 340
Fred (1859-), 150
Fred (1867-1934), 149, 241
Fred (1885-), 237
Fred Burt (1921-), 251
Fred Mayfield (1895-1981), 111, 195
Fred Mayfield (1927-1927), 195
Fred Nicholas (1869-1949), 225
Fred V (1874-1940), 228
Freda May (1911-), 310
Frederick (1865-1934), 121
Frederick (1866-1943), 60

Frederick (1867-1934), 119, 204
Frederick (1868-1880), 233
Frederick (1897-1968), 204, 292
Frederick Brown (1812-1904), 22, 59
Frederick Charles, 375, 410
Frederick Charles (1859-1929), 102, 183
Frederick Charles (1881-1957), 224, 305
Frederick Charles Jr (1884-1961), 183, 272
Frederick D (1830-), 63
Frederick Edward (1911-1925), 260
Frederick G (1876-), 230
Frederick Germond (1855-1935), 132, 220
Frederick H (1918-1988), 210
Frederick L (1870-), 129
Frederick Lyman (1923-), 305, 375
Freeman (1864-), 133, 221
Fremont (1856-1933), 107, 189
Gabrielle Audree, 425
Gail, 382, 394
Gail L, 289, 361
Gail Margaret (1895-1986), 177, 268
Galia (Straight), 375, 410
Garland Courtney, 333
Gary, 271, 383
Gary Claude, 415, 426
Gary Edward (1943-1997), 297, 369
Gary John (1935-1993), 381
Gary Jr, 426

Gary Kenneth, 381
Gary L, 299
Gary William, 297
Gay Marie
  (Chambers), 387,
  417
Gayl R, 376
Gayle (1921-1995),
  245, 325
Gayle Jr, 325
Gene Arthur, 211
Gene Raymond, 216
Gene W, 331
Genevieve ((---)), 223,
  303
Geoffrey Spence, 388
George, 277, 319
George (1830-1862),
  63, 130
George (1851-), 140
George (1853-1924),
  149, 239
George (1854-), 132
George (1862-), 104
George (1876-), 143
George (1892-), 251,
  332
George (1917-1978),
  184, 273
George A (1836-
  1846), 135
George A (1837-),
  140, 232
George A (1873-),
  224, 306
George Alden, 396,
  421
George Burton (1844-
  1912), 54, 115
George C (1833-
  1915), 57, 118
George C (1895-
  1962), 250
George E (1834-), 72,
  143
George E (1841-
  1901), 84, 160
George E (1902-
  1984), 200
George Earl (1895-
  1972), 304, 373
George Edmond
  (1857-), 137, 229

George F (1873-),
  165, 257
George Franklin
  (1853-1856), 113
George Frederick
  (1874-1879), 125
George Gregg (1875-
  ), 116, 200
George Henry (1908-
  1975), 308, 376
George Jr, 273
George Kenneth
  (1928-1931), 255
George Lester (1884-
  ), 179
George Lewis (1879-
  1963), 122, 207
George M (1862-
  1893), 159, 251
George M (1898-),
  206
George M (1903-),
  181
George Mathew
  (1828-), 45
George McClellan
  (1864-), 113
George Melvin (1895-
  1960), 241, 320
George Melvin Jr
  (1919-1919), 321
George Nicholas
  (1852-1853), 94
George Otto (1876-
  1910), 120
George Raymond,
  333, 389
George W (1829-), 64
George W (1868-
  1925), 148, 239
George Walker (1866-
  1964), 56, 117
George Washington
  (1819-1865), 51,
  112
George Washington
  (1853-1862), 154
George Watson
  (1904-1956), 187
George White (1888-
  1965), 197, 286
George Willard (1853-
  1944), 102, 183

George William (1868-
  1934), 121, 206
George Y (1843-), 149
Georgia (Rose) (1892-
  ), 230, 309
Georgia Anna (1850-
  1850), 154
Georgia V (Cooper)
  (1875-1973), 157,
  249
Georgiana, 313
Georgie (1854-1854),
  59
Gerald, 324
Gerald (1915-1989),
  241
Gerald (1918-1986),
  243, 323
Gerald Arthur (1928-),
  320, 382
Gerald K, 362, 406
Gerald L (1951-1998),
  323
Gerald Nelson (1939-
  2002), 335, 389
Gerald P (1915-1990),
  127, 214
Geraldine (1843-), 45
Geraldine (1915-), 278
Geraldine (1919-), 208
Geraldine (Predmore),
  206, 293
Gerrit (1716-1716), 1
Gerrit (1722-), 1
Gerrit (1730-1804), 3,
  4, 10
Gerrit (1792-1879),
  29, 80
Gertrude, 7, 313, 319
Gertrude (1741-), 4
Gertrude (1766-), 11,
  31
Gertrude (1795-), 12
Gertrude (1800-), 12
Gertrude (1882-), 240
Gertrude (-1940), 249
Gertrude (Longhurst),
  220
Gertrude (Vanden
  Berg) (1736-), 2, 5
Gertrude Caroline
  (Fitzpatrick), 126,
  211

27

Gertrude Frances (1918-), 208
Gertrude Grace (1877-), 116, 201
Gertrude L ((---)), 236
Gertrude L (1878-1883), 172
Gertrude Louise (MacFarlane) (1911-1975), 310, 376
Gertrude Seton (Chapelle), 107, 190
Gilbert Humphrey (1862-), 88, 167
Gladys ((---)), 310, 340, 394
Gladys (1895-1929), 227
Gladys (1914-), 210
Gladys (1922-), 195
Gladys (Cook), 213
Gladys (Paquette), 272
Gladys Elizabeth (1899-), 235, 316
Gladys Gertrude (1890-1935), 177
Gladys I (Ralph), 243, 323
Gladys Leota (1913-1985), 184, 274
Gladys Lorette, 244
Glen David, 411
Glen Howard (1898-1971), 186, 276
Glen Roy (1878-1913), 62
Glen Wesley (1912-1912), 278
Glenda Carol, 347, 400
Glendon Charles (1917-), 310, 376
Glenetta Mae (Lemons), 203, 289
Glenn Arthur (1940-1989), 216
Glenn Dexter (1873-1959), 224, 305
Glenn Harold (1918-1919), 267

Glenn M, 341
Glenn M (1917-), 342, 396
Glenn Nelson (1911-1972), 254, 335
Glenn Peter (1888-1956), 177, 267
Glenn S (1919-1996), 272, 351
Glenn S (1924-), 291, 362
Glenn Thaddeus (1906-1984), 252, 333
Glennie (1917-1917), 332
Gloria L (1929-), 257, 339
Gordon H (1870-1928), 132
Gordon J, 366
Gordon L (1924-), 206
Gordon Lester (1905-1979), 207, 295
Gordon Olan, 284
Gordon W (1928-), 296, 366
Grace, 249
Grace ((---)), 116, 201
Grace (1886-), 160
Grace (1887-), 168
Grace (1894-), 174
Grace (Denison), 162
Grace (DeWitt) (1874-), 233, 312
Grace (Donnelly) (1900-1989), 246, 325
Grace B, 326, 384
Grace Edna (1919-), 250
Grace Ellen (Hanson), 257, 340
Grace Evelyn (1879-), 127, 212
Grace Gertrude (1868-1909), 115, 197
Grace Gertrude (1905-1948), 200
Grace L, 277
Grace Lavina (Oberst) (1879-), 172, 262
Grace M (1879-1916),

101, 182
Grace M (1912-), 254
Grace M (Walrath) (1874-1903), 102, 185
Grace May (1890-), 247, 329
Grant, 392
Grant Craig, 342
Gregory, 411
Gregory Joe, 280, 357
Gregory Lee, 354, 396, 403
Gregory Preston, 390, 420
Gregory Rene, 345
Gregory Richard (1955-1985), 343
Gregory Scott, 355
Gretchen (1898-1981), 177
Griffin Wesley, 400
Grosvenor A (1871-), 104, 186
Grosvenor D (1839-), 47, 106
Grover (1883-), 233, 313
Guy A (1875-1916), 231, 309
Guy Clinton (1877-1934), 227, 307
Guy Harrison (1889-1964), 152, 245
Guy LaMont, 325
Guy Patterson (1881-1883), 116
Gwendalyn Jean (1916-1981), 168
Halbert L (1902-1987), 178
Hallie May (1898-1984), 175
Halsey L (1841-1904), 138
Halsey Wood (1831-1879), 41, 97
Halsey Wood (1863-1918), 98
Hamilton (1840-1919), 48, 108
Hannah, 69
Hannah ((---)), 28, 77

28

Hannah ((---)) (1794-1866), 26, 70
Hannah (1790-1868), 14
Hannah (1814-1856), 39, 92
Hannah (1826-1914), 81, 155
Hannah (1852-), 59
Hannah (1856-1923), 130, 217
Hannah (Dolph) (1800-1865), 24, 62
Hannah (Hewitt) (1787-1864), 14, 33, 52
Hannah (Wigant) (1794-1868), 29, 80
Hannah A (Hays) (1812-1903), 27, 76
Hannah June, 357
Hannah M (Pettis) (1844-1927), 87, 165
Hannah Marie (1837-1918), 135, 225
Hannah Waitstill (1833-), 40
Hardy R (1895-1981), 171
Harland (1896-1963), 188, 277
Harland Ford (1911-1991), 182
Harley (1896-1932), 244
Harley Howard (1918-), 344, 397
Harley Ray (1913-), 264, 346
Harlow (1885-1951), 109, 193
Harmon (1825-1898), 67, 137
Harmon E (1847-1910), 135, 226
Harold, 286, 316, 360
Harold (1901-1983), 240
Harold (1903-1976), 242, 321
Harold (1910-1986), 196, 286

Harold (1914-1949), 265
Harold (1917-1985), 258, 340
Harold B (1902-1994), 230
Harold Burgit (1892-1986), 180
Harold E (1930-), 291, 362
Harold Ezra (1900-), 269, 348
Harold L (1896-1948), 250
Harold L (1900-1953), 111, 195
Harold L (1912-1975), 184, 274
Harold Leslie (1910-), 262
Harold Lloyd (1922-1999), 275, 353
Harold Mark (1903-1924), 232, 311
Harold Samuel (1907-1999), 235
Harold Vernon (1924-), 294
Harold Vincent (1914-), 181, 271
Harold Worden (1923-1943), 330
Harper (1793-1852), 24, 67
Harper Jr (1827-), 67, 137
Harper R (1812-1893), 65, 135
Harper W (1832-1916), 135, 224
Harriet, 263
Harriet ((---)), 317, 379
Harriet (1813-), 21
Harriet (1835-), 45, 102, 134
Harriet (1841-), 44
Harriet (1842-), 83
Harriet (1844-), 71
Harriet (1854-), 50
Harriet (1856-), 89, 169
Harriet (1865-1865), 149

Harriet (Dodd), 79
Harriet (Kellogg) (1805-1874), 16, 36
Harriet (Steele) (-1957), 183, 272
Harriet (Wood) (1869-), 48, 111
Harriet Angeline (1891-1895), 219
Harriet Augusta (1845-1925), 135, 226
Harriet G (Groves) (1839-), 63, 130
Harriet J (1897-1921), 240
Harriet Lucetta (Mugg) (1841-1914), 141, 234
Harriet Lucinda (Warren) (1842-1905), 47, 107
Harriet M (1858-), 153
Harriet M (1874-1964), 224, 305
Harriet M (Ludington) (1837-1898), 77, 148, 238
Harriet Minerva (1835-1927), 42
Harriet T (1821-1883), 73, 144
Harriett Victoria (1888-), 234, 314
Harrison C (1854-), 50, 111
Harry A (1867-), 140
Harry Carl (1875-1943), 237, 317
Harry F (1887-1970), 172, 263
Harry L (1888-1969), 227
Harry Raymond (1892-1969), 240
Harry Raymond (1907-), 317
Harry S, 375, 411
Harry Spencer (1924-), 306, 375
Harry W (1884-1959), 159, 252
Hartson (1908-1997), 250, 330

Henry DeLoss (1851-1856), 61
Henry Frederick, 324, 384
Henry Gordon (1894-1973), 126
Henry Harrison (1888-), 150, 241
Henry Hopkins (1869-1950), 173, 263
Henry Hopkins Jr (1915-1994), 264, 345
Henry Jacob (1837-1924), 75, 146
Henry Joseph (1854-1903), 78, 100, 152
Henry Jr. (1815-1872), 33, 84
Henry L (1859-1928), 149, 240
Henry M (1847-1901), 58, 120
Henry M (1862-1942), 157, 249
Henry M (1879-), 120
Henry Orgo (1867-1938), 156, 248
Henry Russell (1926-), 301, 371
Herbert Ezra (1909-1910), 235
Herbert H (1891-1957), 123
Herbert O, 155
Herbert Stephen (1863-), 98, 180
Herbert Warren (1867-1936), 107, 190
Herman (1840-), 84, 160
Herriet Eliza (1834-1916), 76
Hervey (1871-1875), 108
Hester A (Estice), 81, 155
Hewitt (1817-1900), 33
Hilda M (Harris) (1903-), 213, 299
Hilma (Kimes), 219, 300

Hiram (1814-1881), 22, 60
Hiram (1831-1902), 46, 104
Hiram (1845-), 140
Hiram (1851-1919), 141, 234
Hiram (1854-1854), 104
Hiram (1855-1900), 149, 240
Hiram (-1860), 105
Hiram C (Harry) (1901-1960), 186, 276
Hiram C (Harry) Jr (1924-1997), 276, 354
Hiram David (1866-1944), 102, 184
Hiram Nelson (1882-1946), 165, 258
Hiroyuki Nicholas, 400
Holly Elizabeth, 337
Homer Charles (1917-2004), 250, 331
Homer Myron (1878-1891), 109
Homer Thomas (1889-1965), 251, 331
Hope, 397, 421
Hope ((---)), 362, 406
Horace M (1839-1864), 64
Hortentia Dianna (1823-1897), 79
Howard Edward (1924-), 276, 354
Howard Francis (1917-1978), 265, 346
Howard L (1869-), 139, 230
Howard Norman (1898-1974), 123, 208
Howard Parker (1920-), 305
Howard W (1919-), 208
Hubert I (1895-1902), 180
Hugh Archibald (1912-

), 263, 345
Hulbert (1871-), 90
Hulda ((---)) (1815-), 65, 136
Hulda (1848-1936), 48, 109
Hye (Kyong), 340
Ida (1858-), 119
Ida (Gilles), 168, 259
Ida (M), 225
Ida A (1855-1905), 88
Ida A (1863-1924), 105, 187
Ida Ann (1855-1942), 93, 174
Ida Bell (1871-1943), 93
Ida Bell (1873-1875), 172
Ida E (1887-1957), 224, 306
Ida M (Camp) (1857-1886), 156, 247
Ida M (Houghton) (1858-), 139, 231
Ida May (Juby), 102, 183
Ida May (Stewart) (1876-1952), 151, 244
Ida May Bartlett (Shibley) (1865-1899), 147, 238
Ida P (Merritt), 232
Ila Beryl, (Obert) (1921-), 344, 397
Ila Kathryn, 397
Ila Mae, 346, 399
Ilene Marie (1922-), 317, 380
Ina ((---)), 220, 301
Ina Mae (1870-), 61
Ina Vera (1913-), 128
Inez (1874-), 131
Inez (1893-), 232
Inez Ford (Neiswonger) (1923-), 326, 385
Inez Mae (Brainard), 156, 248
Ingeborg (Meyer), 320, 382
Iola Anne (1913-), 213

35

Lyman George (1878-
), 127, 213
Lyman S (1879-1973),
224
Lynda (Berry), 398,
422
Lynda Karen, 338, 392
Lynell DeJon, 333
Lynn (Swanson), 389,
418
Lynn Albert (1889-
1963), 304, 374
Lynn Eleanor
(McCartney), 389,
419
Lynn Ernest, 378
Lynn Irl, 410, 424
Lynne Elizabeth, 358
Lynwood Wayne, 345,
398
Mabel, 113, 206
Mabel ((---)) (1895-),
116, 201
Mabel (1879-1880),
234
Mabel (1908-), 128
Mabel (1909-), 304
Mabel (Chart), 120
Mabel (Gilman) (1868-
), 98, 180
Mabel (Keyser) (1887-
1981), 231, 310
Mabel (Lewis), 220
Mabel A (Mallory)
(1883-), 122, 207
Mabel Arlene
(Vandevanter)
(1914-1991), 197
Mabel C (Hayes)
(1881-1958), 159,
252
Mabel Eliza (1897-
1898), 232
Mabel J (Gould)
(1884-1945), 123,
209
Mabel Maria (Cook)
(1872-1949), 223,
304
Mabel Melvina (1888-
1962), 120, 205
Mabel Pearle (1894-),
162

Mable (Darling) (1893-
), 134, 222
Mable (Tissue), 151,
245
Mable M (1889-), 237
Mac Henry (1903-
1951), 152, 245
Machelle ((---)), 361,
405
Machtelt (Van
Vranken) (1712-),
1, 4
Mack (1913-1913),
222
Madelime R (1916-
1983), 208
Madeline (Brockway),
321
Madeline (Crawford),
395
Madeline Judith
(Labree), 387, 416
Madeline Margaret
(1923-), 213, 298
Madelyn (1915-1997),
311
Madelyn Lucille
(Johnson) (1918-
1941), 302, 372
Madison, 416
Madison Riley, 428
Mae ((---)), 180
Maezene Belle
(Wamsley) (1924-),
192, 280
Magdelena
(Schermerhorn), 8,
19
Maggie (Alyea), 63
Malinda A (1848-),
149
Malona A ((---)) (1845-
1888), 146, 237,
238
Mamie ((---)) (1899-),
152, 245
Mamie (1878-1888),
173
Manfred (1858-), 130,
219
Manley Glenn (1884-
1953), 162, 254
Manley S (1869-),

144, 236
Manley W (1849-
1919), 97, 179
Mararet (Robinson)
(1858-1943), 96,
179
Mararetha Ann
(Martin) (1859-
1922), 58, 122
Marbara Muriel (1919-
1978), 332
Marci Rae, 418
Marcus Sherman
(1899-1977), 240,
320
Marcus Trevor, 320,
382
Marcus Trevor Jr, 382
Margaret, 203, 297
Margaret ((---)), 245,
254, 325, 334, 379,
414
Margaret (1725-), 2
Margaret (1829-1872),
80
Margaret (1839-), 38
Margaret (1844-), 134
Margaret (1870-1870),
118
Margaret (1903-), 250
Margaret (1910-1912),
245
Margaret (1918-), 292,
362
Margaret (1927-1940),
243
Margaret (Critchfield)
(1847-1919), 92,
172
Margaret (Cromwell),
278
Margaret (Hall) (1927-
), 276, 353
Margaret (Helmer)
(1817-1880), 22, 57
Margaret (Long), 322,
383
Margaret (McLeron),
30, 81, 83
Margaret (Mosier),
252
Margaret (Scott)
(1839-), 72, 143

Mary (Clark), 26, 63, 72, 130

Mary (Cromwell) (1830-1888), 68, 139

Mary (Crowell) (1824-1906), 63, 129

Mary (Geddes), 140, 232

Mary (Harris) (1857-), 61, 127

Mary (Hindman) (-1860), 87, 165

Mary (Jalet) (1911-), 241

Mary (Jay) (1827-1880), 39, 92

Mary (McFetridge) (1872-1956), 107, 190

Mary (Meyer) (1881-), 164

Mary (Millens) (1823-), 20, 50

Mary (Murphy) (1922-), 184, 273

Mary (Noonan) (1855-1904), 149, 240

Mary (Packard) (1855-1922), 45, 103

Mary (Palmer) (1808-1888), 16, 37

Mary (Springer), 15, 35

Mary (Taylor), 393, 420

Mary (Thompson), 12, 33

Mary (Van Dyke) (1803-1842), 26, 71

Mary (Van Vorst) (1838-1914), 74, 145

Mary A ((---)) (1888-), 150, 241

Mary A (1854-), 113

Mary A (1897-), 161

Mary A (Corrigan) (1857-1928), 58, 123

Mary A (Lasher) (1834-1915), 71, 142

Mary A (Margeson) (1872-1947), 99, 181

Mary A (Mastin) (1891-1973), 203, 290

Mary A (Ouderkerk) (1843-1925), 83

Mary A (Welch) (1836-1917), 63, 131

Mary A (Wells) (1888-), 166, 259

Mary Ada (1870-), 158

Mary Adelaide (1914-), 330

Mary Alice, 185

Mary Alice (Douglas), 280

Mary Alice (Russell), 272

Mary America (Lee), 264

Mary Ann (1813-1902), 74, 145

Mary Ann (1817-1908), 51

Mary Ann (1833-), 45

Mary Ann (1842-), 81

Mary Ann (1860-), 146

Mary Ann (Carpenter) (1812-1890), 20, 52

Mary Ann (Needham) (1851-1923), 86, 162

Mary Ann (Scoville) (1830-1908), 78, 149

Mary Ann (Stanton), 20, 52

Mary Ardell (1875-1959), 151, 243

Mary Arminda (1852-), 130

Mary Arnold (1840-1891), 43, 100, 152

Mary E ((---)), 65, 134

Mary E ((---)) (1838-1909), 81, 156

Mary E (1831-), 71

Mary E (1838-), 135

Mary E (Strator) (1865-), 136, 228

Mary Elizabeth, 274,

351

Mary Elizabeth (1840-), 50, 111

Mary Elizabeth (1850-1901), 94, 172, 176

Mary Elizabeth (1898-1978), 199, 288

Mary Elizabeth (Leathart) (1847-1913), 59, 124

Mary Elizabeth (Norton) (1875-1960), 61, 127

Mary Elizabeth (Osbourne) (1856-1918), 78, 152

Mary Elizabeth (Shutt) (1875-1957), 179, 269

Mary Ellen, 377

Mary Ellen (1849-), 141

Mary Ellen (1938-1938), 348

Mary Ellen (Story), 92

Mary Ethel, 195

Mary Ethel (Mayfield), 48, 111

Mary Etta (Young) (1859-), 141, 234

Mary Florence (1890-1890), 123

Mary Florine (1901-), 175

Mary Gertrude (Nelson) (1884-1967), 168, 259

Mary H (Brooks), 45

Mary H (Hall) (1834-1872), 80, 154

Mary Helen, 296, 368

Mary Helen (-2000), 127, 214

Mary Henrietta (Kinder), 41, 98

Mary Irene (Williams), 342, 395

Mary Isabel (Fillipe) (1900-1988), 152, 245

Mary Isabella (1876-), 56

Mary J (1838-), 144

Mary J (1853-), 139
Mary J (Franck)
(1920-), 344, 398
Mary J (Hubbard)
(1859-), 78, 100,
152
Mary Jane, 245, 277,
324
Mary Jane (1830-
1861), 135, 224
Mary Jane (1874-
1874), 151
Mary Jane (Ovitt),
381, 415
Mary Jane
(Parkhouse), 128,
214
Mary Jane
(Spearman) (1900-
), 162, 256
Mary Jane (Swart)
(1860-1905), 151,
244
Mary Jane (Wells)
(1861-), 53, 114
Mary Jean, 301
Mary Jennie (Heron)
(1838-1915), 92,
173
Mary Jo ((---)), 377
Mary Josephine
(1850-1925), 88,
167
Mary K (1903-), 184
Mary Katheryn
(Campbell), 258,
342
Mary L (Ward) (-
1987), 373, 409
Mary Lee, 295, 297
Mary Lois (1926-), 332
Mary Lou, 271
Mary Lou (Kaufman),
272
Mary Lou (Livermore),
301, 370
Mary Louisa (Bruyette)
(1847-1891), 58,
121
Mary Louise, 272, 350
Mary Louise (Berger)
(1890-1967), 305,
374

Mary Lucy (1883-
1947), 189, 277
Mary M, 397, 421
Mary Marcel (1920-
1992), 252
Mary Nell (Johnson),
339, 393
Mary Philena (1883-),
234, 313
Mary Rose, 395
Mary Roselia (1856-),
61
Mary S ((---)) (1880-),
230, 309
Mary S (1875-), 159
Mary S (Perkins), 96
Mary Selina (1849-
1869), 82
Mary Susan (1854-
1884), 93
Mary W ((---)) (1872-),
144, 236
Maryanne Margaret,
421
Marytie (1747-), 4, 6,
12, 30
Marytie (Huyck)
(1727-), 2, 7
Masayuki (1976-
1976), 400
Mathew, 350, 401
Mathew (1738-), 4, 11
Mathew (1765-), 5
Mathew (1768-), 5, 12
Mathew (1784-), 25
Mathew (1794-1846),
17, 40
Mathew (1803-1879),
19, 46, 104
Mathew (1814-), 73
Mathew J (1799-
1863), 19, 44
Mathew J (1823-
1882), 68, 139
Mathew Jacob (1844-
1905), 96
Mathew Raymond,
355
Mathew Scott, 383,
416
Mathias Jacob (1793-
1872), 18, 26, 41
Mathieu (-1720), 1

Mathieu Jr (1688-), 1
Matilda ((---)) (1879-
1921), 148, 239
Matilda (1795-), 21
Matilda (1818-), 51
Matilda E (1854-
1936), 60, 126
Matt, 359
Matthew (1725-), 2, 7,
25
Matthew (1739-), 4,
10, 13
Matthew (1765-), 8, 21
Matthew (1765-1830),
9, 27
Matthew Wamsley,
281, 357
Mattie (McIvor), 102,
183
Mattie Bovea, 405
Mattie Elaine (1910-),
277
Mattie Gleen
(Dulaney) (1888-),
172, 263
Maud Delilah (Love)
(1881-), 116, 200
Maude, 97, 179
Maude (1872-), 158
Maude (1877-), 237,
318
Maude (1881-), 121,
207
Maude (Fair) (1887-
1940), 108, 191
Maude (Loveless),
189, 278
Maude (McMillen),
179
Maude Jeanette
(Wright) (1884-
1961), 247, 327
Maureen Gray (Mello),
287
Maurice T (1923-
1968), 321, 382
Mavis Irena, 303, 372
Max L (1905-1924),
184
Max Nelson (1906-
1963), 222, 302
Maxine (Babcock),
265, 346

48

Vern Wheeler (1877-), 62
Verna (1862-1884), 93
Verna M ((---)) (1858-), 137, 229
Vernon Eugene (1915-1930), 211
Vernon Harold (1895-1972), 206, 294
Veronica, 421
Verus Carl (1893-1914), 199
Vesta Ruth (1909-), 317
Veva Fern, 278
Vianna Dawn (1910-), 314
Vicki (Corner), 398, 423
Vickie (Haykin), 325, 384
Vicky Lynn, 424
Victor (1867-1922), 119
Victor David (1891-1961), 203, 290
Victoria (1870-1964), 48
Victoria (Potter) (1845-1930), 86
Victoria Lee (Vogel), 387, 417
Vida (1874-1933), 225
Vida A (1884-1964), 131, 219
Viginia Mary (1913-), 208
Vina Irene (Sauter) (1890-1973), 177, 267
Vincent (1907-1907), 252
Viola (1854-1929), 136, 227
Viola Charlotta (1891-1891), 220
Viola E (Boren) (1868-), 104, 186
Viola F (1895-1926), 206, 293
Viola May (1898-), 187
Virgil Albert (1861-1943), 107, 189

Virginia, 268, 319, 380
Virginia Alberta (1924-1966), 321
Virginia Carol (Jackson), 389, 418
Virginia Dorothy (1919-), 255
Virginia Irene (1924-), 276
Virginia Ora, 270, 349
Vivian, 268
Vivian (Harger), 302, 372
Vivian G (1893-), 168
Vivian May (1921-), 294, 364
Vonnie, 222
W, 277
Waitstill (Hill) (-1841), 17, 40
Waity (Brundige) (1835-), 35, 88, 166
Wallace (1840-1907), 78, 151
Wallace (1868-), 150
Wallace (1872-1872), 150
Wallace M (1897-1961), 269, 348
Walter, 113
Walter (1790-), 28, 77
Walter (1819-), 77, 149
Walter (1871-1890), 115
Walter (1888-), 176, 267
Walter (1892-1968), 219
Walter (1909-1969), 202
Walter C (-1925), 156
Walter D (1910-1985), 257
Walter G (1903-1960), 171
Walter Haywood (1853-), 54, 116
Walter James (1913-1988), 197, 287
Walter Richard (1885-1929), 165, 256
Walter Vicary, 388

Walter W (1890-), 240, 320
Wanda Harriet, 194, 284
Ward (1885-1885), 111
Ward (1887-1967), 233, 312
Ward L (1881-1944), 183
Warren, 338
Warren (1862-), 106
Warren (1892-1957), 241, 321
Warren A (1889-1970), 168
Warren Everett (1921-1971), 258
Warren Franklin, 321
Warren Henry (1858-1922), 60, 126
Warren Polaski (1830-1906), 79
Warren Thomas, 402
Wava (1913-1988), 196, 286
Wayland Henry (1860-1919), 147, 238
Wayne, 268, 383, 409
Wayne Aaron (1918-), 211
Wayne Andrew, 258, 342
Wayne E (1914-), 329
Wayne Hunter (1905-1982), 190, 279
Wayne Marion (1926-), 278
Weltha Marie (Gooding) (1813-1887), 20, 52
Wendie Lynn (Cartright), 390, 420
Wendy, 403
Wendy Ann, 338, 393
Wendy Lynn, 413
Wendy Sue, 418
Wesley (1821-1905), 39, 93
Weston, 392
Wilbert Lemuel (1869-1938), 99, 181

57

Jack, 319
Brewer
  Maxine Amanda, 342
Briaske
  Marlene, 285
Bridenbaker
  Bonnibel Margaret,
    206
  Clyde G (1887-1978),
    121, 205
  Edith Mildred (Bovee)
    (1894-1948), 121,
    205
  Gilbert, 205
  Glen (1913-1971), 205
  Henry (1917-1993),
    206
  Lyle (1912-), 205
  Neil (1914-), 206
Bridger
  Caroline (Eddy), 220
  Elsie L (1857-1946),
    132, 220
  William, 220
Brimmer
  Anna Maria (Bovee)
    (1852-), 113
  Betsy (1791-1862), 8,
    22
  John J, 113
Brink
  Sarah (1848-1911),
    140, 233
Brock
  Bert, 158
  Mary Ada (Bovee)
    (1870-), 158
Brockway
  Madeline, 321
Brodie
  Christine (Campbell),
    238
  Jennie M, 238
  Peter, 238
Broerman
  Frances Marie
    (Bovee) (1929-),
    195
  Harold John (1923-),
    195
Brokaw
  Emma M (1862-1918),
    98

Bronson
  Charles Dempsey IV,
    422, 427
  Cienne Guobao, 427
  Makisa Xiaoli, 427
  Stephanie Chelene
    (Bovee), 422, 427
Brooks
  (---), 18, 41
  Charlotte (Bovee)
    (1842-), 54
  Jane (1815-), 41
  Mary Ann (1814-), 41
  Mary H, 45
  Selia (Bovee) (1791-),
    18, 41
  William Harlan, 54
Brosius
  Anna Margaret
    (Bovee) (1921-),
    275, 353
  Donald, 275, 353
  Eunice Ethel (Bovee)
    (1919-2002), 275
  Joseph, 275
Brouwer
  Anna (1724-), 3
  Ariantje (1737-1818),
    3, 4, 10
  Catarina (1740-), 3
  Catryna (1717-), 3
  Cornelia (1691-), 1, 2
  Jacob (1694-), 1, 2, 10
  Lena (1729-), 3
  Lena (1731-), 3
  Maria (1733-), 3
  Maria (Bovee) (1699-),
    1, 2, 10
  Mathew (1727-), 3
  Mathew (1743-), 3
  Neeltje (1719-), 3
  Peternelle Uldricks
    (Kleyn), 2
  Petrus (1722-), 3
  Pieter Adam, 2
Brown
  (---), 200, 289
  Alicia (Bovee) (1846-),
    141
  Alta (Frank) (1885-),
    248
  Carl, 141
  Donald Edward, 386

Ernest, 248
Floyde Paul, 186
Frank, 301, 371
Hannah, 223
Helen (Bovee) (1904-
  ), 200, 289
James Douglas (1927-
  ), 371
Jean, 320, 382
Jennie M, 231, 310
Joyce Eileen
  (Wagner), 386
Kathleen Sandra, 331,
  388
Lillian Adelia, 165, 258
Lillian Leone (Bovee)
  (1895-), 186
Linda, 289
Muriel Ferne (Bovee)
  (1908-1991), 301,
  371
Permilla Mildred, 94
Brownell
  Cornelius (1857-), 118
  Danita, 382, 416
  Dellu (1855-), 118
  Ellen (1860-), 154
  James (1860-), 118
  Jane (Bovee) (1831-
    1895), 80, 154
  Jefferson L (1864-),
    154
  Jennie (1868-), 154
  Joseph A, 80, 154
  Lucinda (Bovee)
    (1835-), 57, 118
  Perry A (1855-), 154
  Porter, 321
  Solomon, 57, 118
  Virginia Alberta
    (Bovee) (1924-
    1966), 321
Bruett
  Helen Isabel (Bovee)
    (1867-1899), 158
  Henry, 158
Bruinn
  (---), 254
  Althea Marie (Bovee)
    (1904-), 254
Brumhall
  Anna Maria (Bovee)
    (1822-), 33

61

Leona (Bovee) (1907-
), 208
Christian
Barbara Beth, 423
Christianson
Carol Louise, 376
Chester L, 308, 375
David L, 375
Esther (Bovee) (1906-
), 308, 375
Chun
John, 322
Lorraine (Bovee), 322
Churning
Myrtle Ethel (1895-
1973), 251, 332
Clark
Arthur George, 94
Benjamin, 218
Cora May (Bovee)
(1874-1959), 94
Dorothy (Bovee)
(1925-), 269
Elizabeth, 56
Emily Melvina (Bovee)
(1859-1930), 130,
218
Estella E (1893-1943),
218
Florence (1884-1898),
218
Hattie May (Bovee)
(1863-), 61
Josephine (1879-
1967), 218
Lela Alice (1887-
1960), 218
Maria (Baxter), 218
Mary, 26, 63, 72, 130
Mercy Maria (1806-
1869), 16, 37
Minnie Otilla (1876-
1958), 218
Oscar R (1881-1969),
218
Steve, 377
William, 61
William F, 269
William Moss (1848-),
130, 218
Yvonne Elicia (Bovee),
377
Claude

William, 381
Claycomb
Alida Lovina (Bovee)
(1850-), 144
George, 144
Clayton
Elizabeth (Bovee)
(1894-), 190, 279
Robert (1927-), 279
Thomas Stanford
(1894-), 190, 279
Thomas Stanford Jr
(1922-), 279
Clemons
Edna E (Bovee)
(1858-1919), 97
Elnora (Pittman)
(1846-), 96
Ezra, 97
Harvey, 96
Cleveland
Elizabeth (Bessey),
108
Henry, 108
Jane Elizabeth (1853-
1897), 48, 108
Clingingpeel
Myrtle (1916-), 222,
303
Closs
Sara Maysee, 180
Clove
Am (1830-1921), 81
Clute
Annatie (1788-), 31
Bata (Bovee) (1761-),
11, 30
Catherine (1793-), 31
Charles (1804-), 31
Frederick, 31
Frederick (1798-), 31
Gerrit (1761-), 11, 30
Gertrude (1785-), 31
Helena, 9
Hendrick (1801-), 31
Maria (1783-), 31
Maria (De Ridder), 31
Mathew (1795-), 31
Rachel (1799-), 31
Sarah Jane (1842-
1916), 78, 151
William (1790-), 31
Coan

Caroline (Bovee)
(1842-), 58
Lorenzo D, 58
Coates
Kevan Lance, 334
Lynell DeJon (Bovee),
333
Cody
Louisa, 240, 320
Cole
(---), 228
Anna, 2, 7, 9
Cornelia ((---)), 228
Flora (1847-), 136,
228
Maria (1734-), 2, 7, 25
Colegrove
(Mary) Harriet (1832-),
36
Alanson, 15, 36
Benjamin (1840-), 36
Child (1840-), 36
Christopher, 36
Ellen (Lewis), 36
Joshua (1820-), 36
Lewis (1819-), 36
Louisa (1824-), 36
Lucretia Ellen (1827-),
36
Maria (1835-), 36
Mary (Bovee) (1796-
1877), 15, 36
Richard (1829-), 36
Sarah (1822-), 36
Coleman
Calvin C (1847-1871),
141
Daniel, 119
Joanna Corsine
(Bovee) (1848-),
141
Orvilla (Bovee) (1874-
), 119
Collins
Anna Jenee, 362
Clarissa Eliza (Bovee)
(1844-), 76
Gerald Stephen, 289,
361
Henry W, 76
Jenne Ann (Bovee),
289, 361

72

Margaret Olive
(Bovee) (1864-
1955), 94, 177
Mary E (Leper), 177
Philip J, 177
Richard Kelly, 178
Wayne Theodore, 178
Gould
Mabel J (1884-1945),
123, 209
Goulette
Edwin, 368
Jeffrey, 368
Kristi Lee, 368
Marie ((---)), 368
Melissa Gail (Bovee),
296, 368
Paul (-1994), 296, 368
Grace
E (1881-1947), 176
Graff
Charles Amiel (1906-),
313
Elizabeth (Knosf), 313
Elsie Josephine
(1912-), 313
Frances Myrtle (1914-
), 313
Frederick Charles
Victor, 234, 313
Gertrude Juanita
(1919-), 313
Joseph, 313
Louis Kenwood (1908-
1971), 313
Mary Philena (Bovee)
(1883-), 234, 313
Merl Willard (1916-),
313
Worthie Lee (1911-),
313
Grange
Margery R, 329
Grant
Almon Henry (1853-),
105
Byron Mathias (1854-
), 105
Darius S, 47, 105
John C, 105
Lora Adelia (1857-),
105

Minerva (Bovee)
(1833-1905), 47,
105
Phebe (Covert), 105
Grattan
Betsey ((---)), 50
Jason, 50
Sarah (1817-), 20, 50
Graupman
Elizabeth Mae, 339
Iva Lee (Bovee), 257,
339
Jane Alice, 339
John Louis, 339
John William, 257, 339
Mary Lee, 339
Patrick Caryl, 339
Tim John, 339
Gravelle
Davon, 214
Elizabeth, 214
Lucille Monica (Bovee)
(1910-), 127, 213
Oswald Ronald, 127,
214
Stephen, 214
Graves
Ava (1877-1974), 101,
182
Brian L, 421
Burret, 50
Eliza Jane (Bovee)
(1840-), 50
George A (1854-), 89,
169
Harriet (Bovee) (1856-
), 89, 169
John, 397, 421
Mary M (Bovee), 397,
421
Nancy B ((---)), 169
Nathan J, 421
William, 169
Gray
Marian F, 52, 113
Robert, 377
Sally, 67, 138
Susan Louise (Bovee),
377
Grebe
Dorothy (1921-), 209,
297
Green

Addie S (1843-), 137,
228
Benjamin (1846-), 85
Benjamin R, 34, 85
Charlotte, 88
Ethan, 87
Maria Antoinette
(Bovee) (1819-
1848), 34, 85
Marilyn, 310
Mercy (Chase), 87
Niles C (1839-), 85
Orinda (1815-), 35, 87,
88
Warren C (1841-), 85
Greene
Cora (1880-), 225
Greenlee
Hazel Ellen, 108, 191
Griffin
Fidellia, 130, 217
Griffith
Rose, 59, 125
Grimes
Barbara, 324, 383
Grimsley
Elsie May (1888-),
116, 201
Grinnell
Fedelia, 307
Griswold
Andrew Eli (1875-
1961), 173, 265
Carrie Agnes (Bovee)
(1876-1947), 173,
265
Harlan Benham (1903-
1997), 265
Melba W (1905-1968),
265
Groesbeck
Cornelius (1817-), 38
David (1811-), 38
Hannah (1813-), 38
Harmon Bogardus, 16,
38
James, 38
Maria (1815-), 38
Maria (Bovee) (1786-
1873), 16, 38
Nicholas Harmon
(1819-), 38
Nicholas W, 38

Jean Patricia (Bovee), 378, 413
Richard Alan, 413
Robert Deane, 413
Hancock
Clara Dulceina (1861-), 94, 176
Howard C (1867-1932), 94
Minnie Luella (Bovee) (1872-1962), 94
Hand
Denise Kathleen, 372
Handy
Anna, 151
Frances ((---)), 151
George, 151
Hankins
(---), 168
Margaret Irene (Bovee) (1903-), 168
Hannon
Alicia Jolene, 412
Debbie Dawn, 412
Donna Lee (Bovee), 376, 412
Lincoln Todd, 412
Ronald J, 376, 412
Hansen
Curtis, 369
Edith (Bovee), 298, 369
Harriett Victoria (Bovee) (1888-), 234, 314
James William (1915-), 314
Melanie, 370
Minnie Amelia (1909-1988), 207, 295
Neil, 370
Philip, 298, 369
Sam, 234, 314
Timothy, 370
Hanson
Brian Timothy, 350
Bruce E (1929-), 272, 350
Christine Ann, 350
Grace Ellen, 257, 340
Mary Louise (Bovee), 272, 350

Mildred Louise, 208, 296
Paul Kevin, 350
Philip, 350
Harbin
(---), 227
Lulu (Bovee) (1890-), 227
Harding
Henry, 250
Margaret (Bovee) (1903-), 250
Hardy
Don, 301
Mary Jean (Bovee), 301
Harger
Vivian, 302, 372
Harlan
John, 91
Mary (Dunn), 92
Sarah (1812-1896), 39, 91
Harland
Helen Ione, 100, 182
Harmon
Beatrice Irene (1922-), 223, 303
Harold
Margaret ((---)), 323
Ralph Jr., 323
Harper
James J, 377
Louise (Acker), 377
Louise May, (1925-), 311, 377
Harrington
Anna, 179
Mary, 204
Harris
Dianna (1896-), 308
Elisha, 127
Emily (1812-1870), 19, 44
Hattie (Bovee) (1869-), 228, 308
Hilda M (1903-), 213, 299
Janice Irene (Bovee), 347, 400
Jessie W (1862-1899), 102, 183
John Ray, 347, 400

Kelly Lorene, 400
Mary (1857-), 61, 127
Mary (Lelly), 127
Raymond (1872-), 228, 308
Russell, 319
Virginia (Bovee), 319
Harrison
Daisy Leone (Bovee) (1914-), 205
Ethel Paulina (1875-1958), 56, 118
Rev John Frederick G, 205
Hart
Asa, 46
Charity (Bovee) (1801-1824), 19, 46
Ester, 46
William, 19, 46
Hartman
Sylvia (-1940), 227, 308
Hartzberg
Ethel (1920-), 257, 338
Haselweidt
Janet A, 310, 376
Hassenzahl
Caroll (John) (-1977), 279, 356
Carroll Jeff, 356
Dean, 356
Doug, 356
Jack, 356
Janice Laurene (Bovee) (1930-2001), 279, 356
Jennifer, 356
Joel, 356
Hassinger
Beatrice, 329
Haswell
(---), 26, 71
Annatje (Bovee) (1797-), 26, 71
Ida, 71
Lizzie, 71
William, 71
Hathaway
Ella May (1876-), 109
Ester (Bovee) (1847-1932), 48, 109

William Eugene (1868-
), 100
Huddleston
Ellen, 334
Frances H (Bovee)
(1911-), 254, 334
Gaylord, 254, 334
LeRoy, 334
Huerion
Alice Mabel (Bovee)
(1916-), 209
Courtland, 209
Hughes
Belva Marie (Bovee)
(1917-), 258, 341
Kenneth Taylor, 258,
341
Lucille Louise, 341
Hugo
Natasha, 418
Hull
Charles J (1856-
1939), 131
Jane (Bovee) (1818-),
35
John, 35
Mary (Bovee) (1860-
1934), 131
Humble
Effie, 134, 222
Hume
Cara Louise, 397
David Dylan, 397
Emmett, 344, 397
Sally Renee (Bovie),
344, 397
Hungerford
Henry, 223
Maria (1848-), 134,
223
Nancy ((---)), 223
Hunn
Charles C, 63
Julia Jane (Bovee)
(1827-), 63
Hunt
Addie Bell (Bovee)
(1870-), 228
Alice J, 374
Frank Hubert (1859-),
157
Lydia (Bovee) (1839-),
81, 157

Moses F, 81, 157
Ward, 228
Hunter
Diane Marie (Bovee),
342, 394
Edna Lelia (1919-
1998), 263, 345
Elias, 394
Mark, 342, 394
Huntley
Francis M, 153
Katie Ann, 404
Linnie K (Bovee)
(1857-), 153
Ratmond Allen, 404
Sandra Lynn (Bovee),
355, 404
Scott Aron, 404
Stacey Lynn, 404
Theron Milo, 355, 404
Hurd
Bertha (Bovee) (1868-
1929), 115
Rollin Judson, 115
Hurst
Helen (1907-1988),
252, 333
Huskins
Rachel Anna (1841-
1907), 63, 132
Hussey
Joanne, 346, 399
Johanna (1833-1913),
82, 157
Hutchins
Ardin, 150
Charlotte L (Bovee)
(1892-), 150
Hutson
(---), 280
Natalie Morgan
(Bovee), 280
Huyck
Andries (1744-), 6
Andries Cornelius
(1713-), 2, 4, 6
Anthony (1770-), 13
Catharine (Bovee)
(1718-), 2, 6
Catherine (1752-), 6
Catherine (1767-), 11,
13, 30
Cornelia (1746-), 6

Cornelia (1752-), 6
Cornelius, 6, 7
Cornelius A (1747-), 6,
13, 22
Cornelius J (1740-), 6
Eleanor (1779-), 8, 13,
22
Elizabeth (1756-), 6
Garrit (1774-), 13
Gertrude (1751-), 6
Gertrude (Vosburgh),
6, 7
Hendrick (1751-1828),
6
Hester (Gardinier), 6,
13, 22
Isaac (1748-), 6
Jane (1791-), 13
Johannes (1757-), 6
John Cornelius, 2, 6
Jurgen (1765-1819),
13
Maria (1764-), 6
Marytie (1727-), 2, 7
Marytie (Bovee)
(1747-), 4, 6, 12, 30
Neeltje (Bovee) (1716-
), 2, 4, 6
Nicholas (1741-), 6
Nicholas (1743-), 4, 6,
12, 30
Peter (1740-), 6
Peter (1761-), 7
Hyatt
Arthur (1860-), 111
Edward, 50, 111
Mary Elizabeth
(Bovee) (1840-),
50, 111
Ibbotson
Alison, 281, 357
Ingalllina
Bernadette, 289
Ingerson
Jane L (Bovee) (1827-
), 82
Rufus, 82
Ingham
Avis Christina (Bovee)
(1910-), 192
Robert Francis, 193
IOne
Elizabeth, 120

84

Manchester
  Abraham, 71
  Eliza C (Bovee) (1838-1907), 71
Maness
  Fay, 303, 373
Mann
  Erwin, 129, 216
  Ethel May (Bovee) (1918-), 128, 216
Manning
  Adah, 320
Manville
  Christopher William, 361
  Judith (Columbia), 361
  Lisa Marie (Bovee), 361
  William, 361
Manwaring
  Myrtle L, 179, 269
Marburger
  Laverna M (1920-), 294, 363
Marcellus
  Anna (Van Antwerp), 23
  Effie, 241, 321
  Jacomyntje (1771-), 9, 23
  John T, 23
Marciniak
  Albert, 208
  Frances (1892-1963), 123, 208
  Josephine (Bonczyk), 208
Margeson
  Mary A (1872-1947), 99, 181
Marianno
  Catherine (Tierman), 390
  Frank A, 390
  James Robert, 390
  Michael Alan, 335, 390
  Michael Alan Jr., 390
  Sharon Ann (Bovee), 335, 390
Markey
  Dr. Frank, 101, 182

Grace M (Bovee) (1879-1916), 101, 182
John, 182
Marlatt
  Angeline (1840-), 47
  Anna (Bovee) (1805-1879), 20, 47
  Anna (Sutphin), 46, 47
  Benjamin T, 20, 47
  Child, 47
  Eli (1828-), 47
  Eliza Ann (1824-), 47
  Enoch, 46, 47
  Ester (1808-1856), 20, 47
  Maria Louisa (1810-1887), 20, 46, 104
  Obediah H, 20, 47
  Salome (1847-), 47
  Silas (1826-), 47
Marsh
  Albert, 153
  Berthana Melinda (Bovee) (-1954), 153
Marshall
  Harriet R, 206
Marston
  Hannah Pearl, 175
Martin
  Cynthia, 163
  Elbert, 301, 371
  Hannah, 34
  John, 122
  Maggie ((---)), 122
  Mararetha Ann (1859-1922), 58, 122
  Muriel Ferne (Bovee) (1908-1991), 301, 371
  Ralph, 371
Marty
  Fern A (1895-1990), 179, 269
Martz
  Gary (-1945), 342, 396
  Pearl Rose (Bovee) (1923-), 342, 396
Marvell
  (---), 237, 318
  Mabel (1897-), 318
  Maude (Bovee) (1877-

), 237, 318
Marvin
  James E, 104, 186
  Jennie (Bovee) (1867-), 104, 186
  William Claude (1886-), 186
Masaitie
  (---), 242
  Ethyl (Bovee) (1906-), 242
Mason
  John, 288
  Lucy Ann (1897-1981), 199, 287
  Regina ((---)), 288
Masters
  Joseph A, 388
  Michelle Kent (Bovee), 388
Mastin
  Mary A (1891-1973), 203, 290
Matacle
  David, 363
  Mary, 363
  Robert, 293, 363
  Sherry May (Bovee), 293, 363
  Steven, 363
Matthew
  Mary Marcel (Bovee) (1920-1992), 252
  Robert, 252
Matthews
  Alinos (1780-1859), 24, 66
  Alinus Curtis (1832-), 66
  Catherine (Bovee) (1787-1842), 24, 66
  Eliada, 66
  Elvira (1829-), 66
  James M (1827-), 66
  Lucy (Curtis), 66
  Octavia R (1823-), 66
  Ruth Foote (1821-), 66
Mattrau
  Kimberly, 415, 426
Mawhinney
  James, 375, 411
  Sandra (Bovee), 375, 411

93

Phelina (1838-1904),
47, 106
Philena (Baker), 106,
107
Raymond John (1914-
), 198
Raymond Uriah (1879-
), 115, 198
Meys
Sandra, 303, 373
Michalski
Minnie, 207, 294
Migliore
Frank, 398
Joan Marie (Bovee),
398
Leonard, 398
Rose (Carbone), 398
Millar
Bertha Antionete
(Bovee) (1872-
1971), 125, 210
Daniel J, 210
George Harvey (1892-
), 210
Luca A ((---)), 210
Mildred Lucille (1897-
), 210
Olive Catherine (1893-
), 210
Ruth Muriel (1902-
1994), 210
Warren Bruce (1864-),
125, 210
Millens
Jacob, 50
Mary (1823-), 20, 50
Polly (Ries), 50
Miller
Amelia (1838-1887),
45, 103
Anne Marie, 390, 420
Barbara Louise, 282,
358
Bessie Blanch (Bovee)
(1900-), 317
Betty Jane (Bovee)
(1925-), 251
Child, 155
Clyde William, 420
David R, 377, 413
David Stephen, 413

Dorothy (1929-), 342,
396
Elise ((---)), 396
Fayette, 155
George, 396
Hannah (Bovee)
(1826-1914), 81,
155
Jacqueline (Bovee)
(1928-2005), 377,
413
Joseph, 189, 278
Kathryn Lee
(Randolph), 420
Kenneth Darrell, 268,
348
Maria, 177
Mary Lucy (Bovee)
(1883-1947), 189,
277
Mary S (Bovee) (1875-
), 159
Reta Eunice (Bovee),
268, 347
Richard, 251
Roy Edward, 317
Rueben J (1827-
1877), 81, 155
Susan Louise (Bovee),
377
Walter, 377
Will, 159
Millett
Shirley Arline (1924-
1986), 328
Mills
Carvella (1923-), 255
Chester, 287
Clifford O (1910-
1990), 198, 287
David Chester, 287
Fannie Mae (Yandell),
255
Gary, 336, 391
Jesse Walker, 255
Luray (Bovee), 198,
287
Mabel (Dennis), 287
Maureen Lee, 287
Melody Layne
(Bovee), 336, 391
Rachel Ann, 392
Robert Joseph, 287

Tamera Michelle, 392
Miner
Clyde Dennison
(1871-1959), 216
Delila Sarah (Bovee)
(1853-1926), 129,
216
Fred Jacob (1876-
1952), 216
Henry D (1835-1921),
129, 216
Mary Isabelle (1891-
1973), 217
Rollin H (Ralph Henry)
(1883-1885), 217
Minerta
Pauline M (1866-
1952), 93, 174
Minor
Alice Louise, 263
Frances ((---)), 125
John, 125
Sophia (1842-1885),
60, 125
Misenhelder
Addie Elizabeth
(Bovee) (1882-
1965), 109, 193
Carol Onalee (1919-),
193
Charles (1881-1967),
109, 193
Charles Dale (1921-),
193
Christian, 193
Katherine ((---)), 193
Katherine Irene (1911-
), 193
Othel Christian (1909-
), 193
Rhea Elizabeth (1904-
), 193
Mladenovic
Angie ((---)), 398
John Lewis, 398
Louis, 398
Therese Marie
(Bovee), 398
Modisett
Nancy Rose, 333, 389
Moffatt
Barbara Catherine,
378

94

Wanda Harriet (Bovee), 194, 284
Nichols
  James, 64
  Kathryn (1897-1992), 240, 320
  Lydia (1793-1879), 24, 67
  Margaret C (Bovee) (1826-1907), 64
  Roby (Kinnecut), 67
  Rosetta Diane, 302, 372
  Stephen, 67
Nicholson
  Malcom, 377
  Theresa Irene (Bovee), 377
Nightingale
  (---), 254
  Lois E (Bovee) (1908-), 254
Nixon
  Ann (1923-), 319, 380
  Erwin, 380
  Helen (Owens), 380
  Mary Jane, 259
Noble
  Donald J (1921-1981), 291
  James (1895-1979), 203, 291
  James Morton (1934-1943), 291
  John Murray (1928-), 291
  Sarah (Bovee) (1899-1975), 203, 291
  Sarah Jean (1926-), 291
Noonan
  Mary (1855-1904), 149, 240
Norman
  Ruby Iva, 332
Norris
  Cynthia Kay (Bovee), 339, 393
  Ethel Agatha (1871-1956), 236
  Frank Leslie (1865-), 236
  Grace (1869-), 236

James J (1834-), 144, 236
Kieth, 339, 393
Selinda H (Bovee) (1847-), 144, 236
Northrup
  George, 60
  Lucy Ann, 23, 60
  Wealthy (Tracy), 60
Norton
  Barbara Jean, 293
  Charlotte Huskins (Bovee) (1863-1931), 132
  Clair William, 205, 293
  Gary William, 293
  George S, 132
  Jacquelyn Sue, 293
  Margaret Helene (Bovee) (1917-), 205, 293
  Mary Elizabeth (1875-1960), 61, 127
  Richard Clair, 293
  Sandra Lee, 293
Nottier
  Dona Irene, 410, 424
Novotney
  Mildred Beatrice (1909-1988), 248, 329

O
  Frances, 143
Oberst
  Grace Lavina (1879-), 172, 262
Obert
  Beryl (Patrick), 397
  Ila Beryl, (1921-), 344, 397
  Leslie Ernest, 397
O'Brien
  Amanda (1829-1917), 23, 60
  Edith (Bovee) (1881-1971), 152
  George (1878-), 152
O'Dell
  Agnes, 240
O'Donnell
  Jane (1921-2004), 242, 322
Ogden

Phebe, 63
Ogura
  Kingo, 400
  Reiko, 347, 400
  Tsurue ((---)), 400
O'Hare
  Barbara, 303, 373
Older
  Martha (1857-1934), 107, 189
Oliver
  Charles, 350
  Janet, 350
  Joan, 350
  Lena (Bovee) (1910-1987), 272, 350
  Myron, 272, 350
  Roger, 350
Olmstead
  Florence Edna (1911-1975), 187, 277
Olson
  Betty Jean (Bovee), 321
  John, 321
  Marion, 252, 333
Olsson
  David C, 386
  Dr John M, 386
  Elizabeth Lorrain (Bovee) (1926-1997), 326, 385
  Eric T, 386
  John Olof, 386
  Karen L, 386
  Margit Elleretsen (Morbekk), 386
  Miriam E (Wildeman), 386
  Otto J (1924-), 326, 385
Olver
  Annie Malvina (Bovee) (1843-), 87, 166
  Elizabeth (Castle), 166
  Florence, 167
  Frank, 166
  Henry, 88, 167
  John, 166
  Joseph, 87, 166
  Mary Josephine (Bovee) (1850-1925), 88, 167

115

116

117

Unplaced Bovee Individuals and Families

Not Indexed

1. Abraham BOVEE (of Durlock) born abt 1776. He married on 19 Feb 1797 in DRC, Schenectady, Schenectady Co., NY, **Lydia PEEK** born abt 1779, baptized 6 Jun 1779 in DRC, Schenectady, Schenectady Co., NY.
Children
 2. i. **George Adam Smith**.
 ii. **John** born 2 Jul 1809, baptized in DRC, Glen, Montgomery Co., NY.
 iii. **Peter** born 23 Apr 1810, baptized in Fonda, Montgomery Co., NY.
 iv. **Eva Starenberg** born Oct 1812, baptized in Fonda, Montgomery Co., NY.
 v. **Abraham** born 12 Sep 1815, baptized in Fonda, Montgomery Co., NY.

2. George Adam Smith BOVEE [2] (Abraham [1]), born 15 Sep 1807, baptized in DRC, Glen, Montgomery Co., NY. He married **Maria YEARDON**.
children
 3. i. **Frank**.
 4. ii. **Daniel B**.
 iii. **Melvin** born 1837, died in Gettysburg, Adams Co., PA. Civil War.
 5. iv. **George Irvin**.
 v. **Almira** born abt 1841, died 30 Mar 1842, buried in Riverside cem, Grogham, Lewis co., NY.
 6. vi. **Abraham**.

3. Frank BOVEE [3] (George Adam Smith [2] Abraham [1]), born abt 1830, died 1870 in Jefferson Co., NY. He married **Jeanette TIFFT** born Nov 1843.
children
 7. i. **George**.
 ii. **Minnie E** (1942: res Belleville, Jefferson Co., NY) born Dec 1863. She married abt 1888 **Lewis DUTCHER** born Mar 1853.
  children
  i. **Mabel H** born Aug 1888.
 8. iii. **Melvin F**.

4. Daniel B BOVEE [3] (George Adam Smith [2] Abraham [1]), born 17 Feb 1836 in Syracuse, Onondaga Co., NY, died 13 Jan 1918 in Redfield, Oswego Co., NY. He married on 9 Sep 1859 in Barnes Corners, Lewis Co., NY, **Elizabeth YARDON** born Apr 1843 in NY, died 1 Mar 1915 in Redfield, Oswego Co., NY.
children
 i. **Melvin** born 6 Jul 1866, died 11 Mar 1867 in NY.
 ii. **Jannett M** born 20 Apr 1869 in South Rutland, Jefferson Co., NY. She married **ACKLEY**.
 9. iii. **Franklin A**.
 iv. **Frances A** born 6 Apr 1871 in South Rutland, Jefferson Co., NY. She married **Laflam**.

v. **Etta May** born 5 Aug 1879 in Redfield, Oswego Co., NY. She married **Cowles**.

vi. **Florence E** born 29 May 1883 in Redfield, Oswego Co., NY., died 10 Jan 1909 in Redfield, Oswego Co., NY.

5. George Irvin BOVEE [3] (George Adam Smith [2] Abraham [1]) (1960-1900: res Rutland Town, Jefferson Co., NY), born Sep 1838 in NY. He married **Ellen** born Oct 1856 in NY.
children
i. **Marion** born Dec 1885 in NY.

6. Abraham BOVEE [3] (George Adam Smith [2] Abraham [1]) (1880: res Rodman, Jefferson Co., NY. 1900: Henderson, Jefferson Co., NY). He married **Addie E BROOKS**, born Apr 1846 in NY.
children
i. **Joel B** born 1871 in NY.
ii. **Edith** born 1874 in NY. She married **Henry SMITH**.

7. George BOVEE [4] (Frank [3] George Adam Smith [2] Abraham [1]) (1900: res Alta, Buena Vista Co., IA) born 16 Apr 1862 in Belleville, Jefferson Co., NY., died 12 Mar 1927 in Alta, Buena Vista Co., IA. he married on 20 Feb 1894 in Philadelphia, Jefferson Co., PA, **Anna HOLMES** born 14 Nov 1864 in Toulon, Stark Co., ID, died 28 Sep 1951 in Alta, Buena Vista Co., IA, buried in Woodlawn cem, Alta, Buena Vista Co., IA.
children
10. i. **Earl Franklin**.
ii. **Glenn** born 27 Jul 1902 in Alta, Buena Vista Co., IA, died 12 Oct 1970 in Modesto, Stanislaus Co., CA.

8. Melvin F BOVEE. [4] (Frank [3] George Adam Smith [2] Abraham [1]), (1900: res Sandy Creek, Oswego Co., NY) born 22 Mar 1868 in Tylerville, Jefferson Co., NY, died 7 Mar 1942. He married on 12 Nov 1895 in Bellville, Jefferson Co., NY, **Kate Josephine HOWARD** born 1 Aug 1872 in Ellisburg, Jefferson Co., NY, died 8 Jun 1957.
children
i. **Gladys** (1942: res Pierrepont Manor, Jefferson Co., NY   1957: Syracuse, Onondaga Co., NY   1984: Yulee, Nassau Co., FL) born Feb 1897 in Jefferson Co., NY. She married **Ora BARNES**.
children
i. **Douglas**.
11. ii. **Glenn H**.
iii. **Arly W** (1942: res Syracuse, Onondaga Co., NY   1957: Central Square, Oswego Co., NY) died bef 1984. She married **Clark PHILLIPS**.

9. Franklin A BOVEE [4] (Daniel B [3] George Adam Smith [2] Abraham [1]), (1900: res Redfield, Oswego Co., NY   1915: Henderson, Jefferson Co., NY) born 6 Apr 1871 in South Rutland, Jefferson Co., NY. He married **Eva**, born Apr 1879 in NY.
children
12. i. **Melvin**.
ii. **George** born 22 Apr 1901, died Apr 1959. He married **Florence**.
iii. **Daniel** born 7 Oct 1902, died Jul 1980.

      iv. **Dorotha.**
13. v. **Elwin**.
14. vi. **Gilbert**.

10. Earl Franklin BOVEE [5] (George [4] Frank [3] George Adam Smith [2] Abraham [1]), born 29 Sep 1899 in Alta, Buena Vista Co., IA. He married on 23 Aug 1922 in Alta, Buena Vista Co., IA, **Harriet Katherine ANDERSON** born 28 Nov 1902, Alta, Buena Vista Co., IA.
children
15. i. **Rodney**.

11. Glenn H BOVEE [5] (Melvin F.[4] Frank [3] George Adam Smith [2] Abraham [1]), (of Pierrepont Manor, Jefferson Co., NY 1957: res Adams, Jefferson Co., NY) born 13 Sep 1901, died 26 May 1984 in Watertown, Jefferson Co., NY.. He married 1st on 7 Feb 1925, **Hilda BALCH** born 16 Sep 1906, died 20 Nov 1956 in Watertown, Jefferson Co., NY.
children
16. i. **Robert Glenn**.

He married 2nd on 8 Jul 1957 **Barbara HATHWAY** born 28 Oct 1915, died 24 May 1994 in Adams, Jefferson Co., NY.
children
    ii. **William**, born abt 1958.

12. Melvin BOVEE [5] (Franklin A [4] Daniel B [3] George Adam Smith [2] Abraham [1]), born 5 Dec 1899 in NY. He married **?--?**.
children
17. i. **Melvin (Max)**.

13. Elwin BOVEE [5] (Franklin A [4] Daniel B [3] George Adam Smith [2] Abraham [1]), born 27 Jan 1911 in Belleville, Jefferson Co., NY, died 1972. He married **?--?**.
children
    i. **Donald**.
    ii. **Frank**..

14. Gilbert BOVEE [5] (Franklin A [4] Daniel B [3] George Adam Smith [2] Abraham [1]). He married **?--?**.
children
    i. **Maria**.. She married **GUNDERSON**.

15. Rodney BOVEE [6] (Earl Franklin [5] George [4] Frank [3] George Adam Smith [2] Abraham [1]), born 23 Apr 1930 in Sioux Rapids, Buena Vista Co., IA. He married on 11 Jun 1950 **Beverly DONALDSON** born 18 Jan 1931 in Webb, Clay Co., IA.
children
    i. **Kal A** born 21 Dec 1954 in Storm Lake, Buena Vista Co., IA. He married on 6 Jun 1976 **Barbara ROBB**.

16. Robert Glenn BOVEE [6] (Glenn H [5] Melvin F.[4] Frank [3] George Adam Smith [2] Abraham [1]) (1956: res Potsdam, Saint Lawrence Co., NY 1984: Pierrepont Manor, Jefferson Co., NY), born Aug 1925. He married **?--?**.
children

    i. **Thomas.**

18. ii. **James Robert.**

    iii. **Kathy.** She married **Larry Lavere.**

    iv. **David** born aft 1956.

17. Melvin (Max) BOVEE [6] (Melvin [5] Franklin A [4] Daniel B [3] George Adam Smith [2] Abraham [1]) born 24 Feb 1940. He married **Joyce P.**

children

    i. **Michael** born 6 May 1962.

    ii. **Stephen** born 3 Dec 1966.

    iii. **Karl** born 17 Feb 1970.

18. James Robert BOVEE [7] (Robert Glenn [6] Glenn H [5] Melvin F.[4] Frank [3] George Adam Smith [2] Abraham [1]). He married 1st **Kathy M SLADE.**

children

    i. **Joel.**

    ii. **?--?.**

He married 2nd on 6 Aug 1977 in Pierrepont Manor, Jefferson Co., NY, **Sue M DRAKE.**

children 2 children.

---

1. William BOVEE (abt 1844 moved to IL, 1850-1860: res Viola Twp., Mercer Co., IL) born abt 1806 in NY, died 18 Apr 1867 in Viola, Mercer Co., IL. Buried there. He married 1st **Loretta MOOREHOUSE** born 1817, died 1853.

Children

2. i. **William H.**

    ii. **Sarah.**, born 1838 in NY. She married on 6 Aug 1858 in Mercer Co., IL, William **E WOOD** (1860 ; res Viola, Mercer Co., IL) born abt 1833 In PA.

        children

        i. **William** born 1859 in Mercer Co., IL

    iii. **Walter** (1870: res Boone Co., IA) born 1842 in NY. He married on 14 Jan 1863 in Mercer Co., IL, **Jane Eliza Wright WILHITE.**

      i. **Huldah** born 1844 in IL. She married bef 1867, **Andrew J WRIGHT.** (1880: res Des Moines Twp, Mahaska Co., IA).

        children

        i. **Lydia J** born abt1866 in IA.

        ii. **Henry O** born abt 1871 in IL.

        iii. **Geraldia** born abt 1874 in IL.

        iv. **Hannah G** born abt 1879 in IL.

    iv. **Loren L** (1900: res Creek Nation, IN) born Jul 1848 in IL. He married **Sarah A.**

3. v. **James Wallace.**

    vi. **Francis** born 1863 in Mercer Co., IL. He married 2nd on 28 Nov 1860, **Mary WILHITE** born 16 Apr 1814 in Jefferson Co., IN, died 2 Apr 1905 in Viola, Mercer Co., IL

2. William H BOVEE [2] (William [1]) (1900: res Newton Twp., Carroll Co., IA) born 6

Aug 1836 in NY, died 22 Oct 1912 in Dedham, Carroll Co., IA. Civil War. He married on 22 Jun 1865, **Ellen SHERLOCK** born 21 Feb 1846 in Derbyshire, England.
children

4.   i.   **William M.**
5.   ii.   **Charles F.**
    iii.   **Lillie C** born 29 Aug 1881 in IA.
6.   iv.   **James Walter.**

3. **James Wallace BOVEE** [2] (William [1]) (1880: res Dakota Territory, 1900 Turner, SD) born 17 Nov 1850 in Viola, Mercer Co., IL, died 5 Jul 1936 in Parker, Turner Co., SD, buried there. He married on 14 Jul 1877, **Ida Amelia PRUDEN** born 1 Jan 1856, died 16 Jun 1942.
children

7.   i.   **Paul J.**
    ii.   **Achye** born 18 Dec 1880, died Sep 1948 in Sioux Falls, Minnehaha Co., SD. She married on 21 Nov 1900, **Herbert BEAUMONT.**
    iii.   **Clara Belle** born 6 Aug 1882 in Turner Co., SD, died 14 Mar 1971 in Windom, Cottonwood Co., MN. She married 23 Dec 1903, **Herbert MORFITT** born 12 Apr 1878, died 24 Mar 1950.
> *children*
>   i.   **Harold** born 1908.
>   ii.   **Wendell** born 16 Oct 1919. He married on 28 Nov 1948, **Betty KRAFT** born 6 Oct 1926.

    iv.   **Ethel** born Jun 1884, died 1908.
    v.   **Della Rose** born 22 Feb 1885 in Turner Co., SD, died 24 Dec 1974 in Tea, Lincoln Co., SD. She married 1st on 12 Jun 1905, **Herman BENSON** died 1942 in Parker, Turner Co., SD. She married 2nd in 1943,**Bert ALGER**. She married 3rd **George PATNAUDE.**

> *children*
>   i.   **Wayne** born 31 Mar 1907 in Sioux Falls, Minnehaha Co., SD died 1974. He married 1st on 4 Apr 1927, **Edith UGLAND** born 31 Mar 1907, died 6 Jan 1964. He married 2nd on 23 Apr 1966, **Tillie WISEMAN.**
>   ii.   **Dale** born 1908, died 1 Feb 1967 in Sioux Falls, Minnehaha Co., SD.
>   iii.   **Ida** She married **Ed JORGENSEN.**
>   iv.   **Coral** born 27 Dec 1914. She married on 13 Apr 1935, **Elmer KASTINE.**
>   v.   **Luella.** She married **Bill PARKER.**
>   vi.   **Lorena.**
>   vii.   **Verna.** She married on Oct 4 1940, **George RUNYAN.**

8.   vi.   **Clyde Mitchell.**
9.   vii.   **Archibald Wallace.**
10. viii.   **Earl Eugene.**
11.   ix.   **Claude Arnold.**

4. **William M BOVEE** [3] (William H [2] William [1]). (1900: res Newton Twp., Carroll Co., IA) born 9 Aug 1867 in Carroll Co., IA, died 5 Jan 1934. He married abt 1898, **Nettie,** born Jul 1875 in IA.
children

     i. **Celia M**, born Apr 1899 in IA.

5. Charles F BOVEE [3] (William H [2] William [1]) (1920: res Wayne Twp., Minnehaha Co., SD) born 15 Dec 1875 in Carroll Co., IA. He married abt 1899, **Emma A** born Sep 1881 in IA.
children
     i. **Jessie** born abt 1913 in SD.

6. James Walter BOVEE [3] (William H [2] William [1]) born 9 Dec 1885 in IA., died Mar 1969 in SD. He married on 18 Jun 1909, **Anna Marie** born 30 Jan 1890, died Oct 1984 in Sioux Falls, Minnehaha Co., SD.
children
     i. **Ethel D** born abt 1910. She married on 8 Jul 1930, **Louis VOELSCH**.
12. ii. **Harold James**.
     iii. **Florence.** She married on 19 Dec 1933, **John OBESLO**.
         children.
         i. **Ruth** born 4 Jan 1946.
13. iv. **Dale**.

7. Paul J BOVEE [3] (James Wallace [2] William [1]) born 23 Nov 1877 in Rapids City, Rock Island Co., IL, died 31 Dec 1971 in Byron, Olmstead Co., MN. He married on 6 Mar 1904 in Bristow, Creek Co., OK, **Mae MCINTOSH** born 23 Oct 1886, died 13 Aug 1966 in Byron, Olmstead Co., MN.
children
14. i. **Guy Wallace,**
     ii. **Clarence R** born 3 Dec 1908, died 19 Dec1988 in Byron, Olmstead Co., MN. He married on 16 Oct 1945, **Emma BOLLINGER**.
     iii. Madeline born 27 Oct 1915. She married on 29 Oct 1939, **Donald Hart** born 8 May 1914, died 31 Jul 1985 in Elgin Wabasha Co., MN.
         children
         i. **Reginald.** born 23 Nov 1940. He married He married on 30 Dec 1960, **Marie Teresa ROBINSON,**
         ii. **Ralph Myron** born 3 May 1943. He married on 20 Jul 1962, **Dianne Kay SCHEUNEMAN**, born 12 May 1944.
         iii. **Luana Aldene** born 12 Jun 1945. She married on 6 Jul 1969, **Edwin Allen HARLAN**, born 14 Nov 1946.
         iv. **LaDonna** born 30 Sep 1953.
     iv. **Irelene** born 26 Nov 1917. She married on 29 Oct 1939,**Elmer Schauer** (res Rochester, Olmstead Co., MN) born 25 Jan 1917.
         children
         i. **Keith** born 22 Jun 1940. He married on 17 May 1964 ,**Gayle CHAFFE**, born 4 Aug 1943.
         ii. **Bruce** born 27 Mar 1943.
         iii. **Juanita** born 23 Jul 1947. She married on 7 Apr 1969, **Michael DEAN**, born 4 Jun 1939.
         iv. **Myra Jean** born 10 Jun 1949. She married on 7 Sep 1969, **Marty EKREM**.
         v. **Paulette Elmyra** born 7 May 1957.
         vi. **Patrice** born 31 Mar 1960.
     v. **Harriet** born 23 Feb 1920. She married on 28 Sep 1940, **Lyle BOWERS** (1971: res Loma Linda, San Bernardino Co., CA) born 18 Aug 1919, died 12 Dec 1988 in Loma Linda, San Bernardino Co., CA.
         children

     i.   **Darlene Margaret** born 1 Feb 1942. She married on Jun 30 1957, **LeRoy WRIGHT** born 21 Jul 1940.

     ii. **Dianne Shirley** born 2 Mar 1943. She married on 12 Jun 1966, **Dan POOLER** born 11 Oct 1942.

     iii. **Dave Lyle** born 2 Jan 1947.

     iv. **Dan Paul** born 17 Jan 1951.

     v.   **Denise Pamela** born 3 Jul 1954.

  vi. **Mildred** born 28 Mar 1921. She married on 26 Sep 1942, **Bill LOGAN** born 21 Jan 1917.

      children

     i.   **Patrick** born 8 Mar 1946. He married on 8 Apr 1972, **Veda May PLATTE** born 8 Oct 1952.

8. Clyde Mitchell BOVEE [3] (James Wallace [2] William [1]) born 27 Feb 1887 in Turner Co., SD, died Jul 1953 in Sioux Falls, Minnehaha Co., SD. He married on 16 Feb 1916, **Cecelia Maude SLETTIN** born 22 Sep 1896.

children

15. i. **Vernon Marvin**.

    ii. **Irene Maxine** (1975: res Viborb, Turner Co., SD) born 12 Feb 1918. She married on 30 Jun 1939, **Orval BERTHELSON** born 20 May 1919, died Aug 1965 in Viborg, Turner Co., SD.

      children

     i.   **Robert Eugene** born 31 Aug 1941. He married on 15 July 1961 **Mary BERENS**, born 19 Aug 1940.

     ii. **Shirley Mae** born 1 Sep 1943. She married on 9 Sep 1961 **Wesley PLUCKER**.

     iii. **Karen Faye** born 19 Feb 1949. She married on 15 Jul 1966 **Joseph LUKE**.

   iii. **Dorothy Belle** (1971: res Marion, Turner Co., SD), born 4 Mar 1922. She married on 21 Feb 1944, **Hubert LUKE** born 22 Apr 1912.

      children

     i.   **Lames Hubert** born 4 Mar 1945. He married on 14 Aug 1970 **Laurel Jean HINSETH**.

     ii. **Duane Arthur** born 27 Dec 1946. He married on 4 Sep 1965 **Joy CHRISTIANSON**.

     iii. **Charles Allen** born 18 Oct 1951. He married on 29 Apr 1974 **Linda Louise LARSEN**.

     iv. **Richard Clyde** born 12 Jan 1953.

     v.   **Ronald William** born 8 Oct 1959.

     vi. **Timothy John** born 21 May 1961.

   iv. **Marjorie Ann** born 3 Feb 1924. She married on 15 Oct 1944, **Anthony Raymond ALBERTY** (1971: res Middlesex, Middlesex Co., NJ) born 6 Oct 19??.

      children

     i.   **Allen Raymond** born 18 Nov 1948. He married on 8 Feb 1969, **Margaret WALES**.

     ii. **Steven Albert** born 18 Jun 1952.

     iii. **Michael Duane** born 27 Dec 1953.

     iv. **Sharon Marie** born 10 Apr 1956. She married on 12 Jul 1975 **Milton OLKESON**.

     v.   **Raymond Anthony** born 9 Sep 1964.

9. Archibald Wallace BOVEE [3] (James Wallace [2] William [1]) born 12 Jun 1892 in

Turner Co., SD, died 3 Dec 1971 in Silverton Marion Co., OR. He married 1st on 3 Mar 1914, **Leta Minerva FOGELMAN** born 6 Mar 1896, died 15 Jun 1965 in Silverton, Marion Co., OR.

children

16.   i.   **Luverne Oliver**.
17.   ii.   **Orval James**.
    iii.   **Genevieve Marie** (1971: res Roseburg, Douglas Co., OR. 1998 Salem, Marion Co., OR) born 28 Nov 1918 in Parker Turner Co., SD. She married 1st on 8 May 1940, **William Chester ALDEN** born 19 Oct 1918 in Portland Multnomah Co., OR, died 26 May 1988 in Fellows, Kern Co., CA. son of Walter Simon Alden and Goldie Nora Rice.

> *children*
> i.   **William Chester Jr**. born 31 Jan 1941 in Portland, Multnomah Co., OR, died 19 Jul 1944 in Silverton, Marion Co., OR.
> ii.   **Marie Elizabeth** born 13 Dec 1941 in Portland, Multnomah Co., OR, died 15 Nov 1973 in Emporia, Lyon Co., KS. She married on 30 Jun 1961 in Emporia, KS, **Lawrence Edward GETZ**, son of Wesley Getz and Helen Berrie, born 13 Mar 1942 in Emporia, KS, died 15 Nov 1973 in Emporia, KS.
> iii.   **David John** born 15 Dec 1943 in Silverton, Marion Co., OR. He married 1st on 24 May 1963, **Carol Ann KING** in Cottage Grove, Lane Co., OR. He married 2nd **Ellen**.
> iv.   **Geraldine Maurine** born 22 May 1945 in Portland, Multnomah Co, OR. She married 1st **Stanley Robert KUBORN**, born 5 Feb 1944 in Portland OR, son of Vincent Kuborn and Elsie Clark. She married 2nd on 14 Feb 1970, in Reno, Washoe Co., NV, **Melburn Hugh LINGENFELTER**, son of Elmer Lingenfelter and Leona Quave.
> v.   **William Curtis** born 14 Oct 1946 in Coos Bay Coos Co., OR. He married 1st on 1 Apr 1967 in Yakima, Yakima Co., WA, **Janis BLOCK**. He married 2nd on 22 Nov 1972, **Luella RICHARDSON**.

She married 2nd on 26 Jun 1955 **Walter Vernon ROWE** born 23 Aug 1915 in Silverton, Marion Co., OR, died 1 May 1972 in Silverton Marion Co., OR., son of Alfred B Rowe and Emily Cecelia ?.

> *children*
> i.   **Valeta Cecelia** born 26 Mar 1956.

    iv.   **Thelma Leona** (1971: res Pendleton, Umatilla Co., OR) born 12 Oct 1920 in Turner Co., SD, died 23 Aug 1990 in Pendleton, Umatilla Co., OR. She married on 1 Sep 1940, **Stanley Alden VESTERLYDE** born 1 May 1917 in Portland Multnomah Co., OR, died 8 Mar 1997 in Pendleton, Umatilla Co., OR. son of Walter Simon Alden and Goldie Nora Rice

> *children*
> i.   **Leona Jean** born 20 Aug 1941 in Portland, Multnomah Co., OR, died 30 Dec 1941 in Portland OR.
> ii.   **Paul Stanley** born 17 Jan 1943 in McMinnville, Yamhill Co., OR, died 4 Apr 1999 in Portland, OR. He married on 13 Sep 1974 in Pendleton, Umatilla Co., OR, **Phyllis Kay SHILLING**
> iii.   **Betty Faith** born 26 May 1944 in Silverton, Marion Co., OR. She married on 12 Jun 1972 in Post Falls, Kootenai Co., ID, **Grinnell Benn FOSNAUGH**.
> iv.   **Daniel James** born 29 Aug 1946 in Silverton, Marion Co., OR.

He married 1st on 30 Sep 1972, **Paulette DAVIS**. He married 2nd **Treva CHENNY**. He married 3rd **Janice**.

    v.   **Timothy Lee** born 28 Nov 1954 in Baker, Baker Co., OR. He married on 10 Jan 1995 in Barrow, Northwestern, AK, **Royce Ilene BERGLUND**.

    vi. **Carolyn Joy** born 15 Oct 1956 in Roseburg, Douglas Co., OR. She married on 23 Jul 1995 in Silver Creek St Park, Marion Co., OR, **Delmer Paul AYERS**.

v. **Evelyn Louise** (1971: res Salem, Marion Co., OR), born 18 Mar 1923. She married on 9 Jun 1945, **Kenneth Raymond HARMON** born 23 Aug 1924.

    children

    i.   **Raymond LeRoy** born 1 Apr 1946. He married 1st on 3 Sep 1966, **Claudia Ann BOWER**, born 24 Apr 1947. He married 2nd in summer of 1998, **Linda**.

    ii. **Barbara Jean** born 7 Jan 1948. She married on 9 Nov 1968, **Anthony Calvin CARBOUGH**.

vi. **Naomi Minerva** (1991: res Salem, Marion Co., OR), born 27 Jul 1925, died 21 Dec 1984. She married on 24 Aug 1945, **Earnest Leland HARMON** born 14 Dec 1922.

    children

    i.   **Colleen Marie** born 23 Dec 1947. She married on 1 Jun 1964, **William JOHNSON** born 24 Oct 1943.

    ii. **Kathleen Louise** born 4 May 1950. She married 1st on 24 Dec 1970, **Arthur Ray SELF** born 3 Jun 1949. She married 2nd **Mike ALLEN**.

vii. **Ester Joy** born 1 Oct 1930, died 3 Sep 1954 in OR. She married on 2 Jun 1952, **Raymond BROWN**.

    children

    i.   **Michael Ray** born 29 apr 1953, die Aug 1974 in OR. He married on 4 Sep 1972, **Marilyn Ruth BRIGGS**.

viii. **Lavonne Lois**, (1971: res Peten, Guatemala), born 14 Jul1932. She married on 11 Feb 1951, **James BECHTEL** born 24 Sep 1931.

    children

    i.   **Lyden Jay** born 26 Oct 1953. He married on 31 Dec 1978 **Barbara Joann ROSE.**

    ii. **Marlin Laray** born 7 Jun 1956. He married on 13 Nov 1977, **Carmel Rae WEST** born 4 Oct 1957.

    iii. **Kerri Rene** born 22 Sep 1957. She married on 5 Oct 1980, **Isaac Elden LOPEZ**, born 9 Sep 1953.

    iv. **Stanley Ray** born 25 Oct 1959. He married on 9 Aug 1981, **Twyla Lynn LEISKE**, born 21 Nov 1981.

ix. **Shirley Mae**, (1971: res Portland, Multnomah Co., OR), born 19 May 1937. She married on 18 May 1957 in Coeur D'Alene, Kootenai Co., ID, **Roy Harold BROWN** (1998: res Portland, Multnomah Co., OR), born 11 Feb 1937.

    children

    i.   **Marilyn Kay** born 28 Nov 1956. She married on 31 Dec 1982, **Stan WHITE**, born Jun 1952.

    ii. **Cheryl Marie** born 25 Feb 1958. She married **Ty LERUD**.

    iii. **Donna Denise** born 12 Mar 1960. She married on 2 May 1982, **Richard Earl CLARKE Jr.**, born 4 Mar 1951.

    iv. **Rose Ann Elizabeth** born 21 Jul 1964. She married on 24 Sep

10. Earl Eugene BOVEE [3] (James Wallace [2] William [1]) born 2 Dec 1898 in Turner Co., SD, died 19 Apr 1972 in Portland, Multnomah Co., OR. He married on 24 Dec 1921, **Leda BERTSCH** born 11 Mar 1901, died Oct 1980 in Portland, Multnomah Co., OR.

children

18. i. **Arlie**.
19. ii. **Lynn Eugene**.
  iii. **Norma** (1971: res Holly Hill, Daytona Beach Co., FL) Born 18 Apr 1927. She married on 9 Feb 1946, **Todd LESTER** born 4 Nov 1918.

> *children*
> i. **Monte Lee** born 26 Jun 1949. He married on 4 Oct 1969 **Joy LUNDEEN**.
> ii. **Debra Jo**. Born 15 Sep 1950. She married on 18 Oct 1969, **Randy HOMESLEY**.
> iii. **Roxanne** born 19 Oct 1953. She married on 27 Dec 1975, **Michael ELIOTT**.
> iv. **Jackie Lee** born 12 Jun 1956.
> v. **Mark Steve** born 9 Sep 1965.

11. Claude Arnold BOVEE [3] (James Wallace [2] William [1]) (1998; res Parker, Turner Co., SD) born 16 Mar 1900 in Turner Co., SD. He married on 18 Oct 1924, **Louise DICE**, born 26 Feb 1907.

children

20. i. **Arnold Eugene**.

12. Harold James BOVEE [4] (James Walter [3] William H [2] William [1]) born 28 Jan 1920. He married **Betty Jean JORENBY** born 7 Jan 1929.

children

  i. **Michael A** born 7 Jun 1954.
  ii. **James Patrick** born 6 Jun 1955.

13. Dale BOVEE [4] (James Walter [3] William H [2] William [1]) born 4 Jan 1925. He married **Ruth RASMUSSEN** born 27 Feb 1926.

children

  i. **Barbara** born7 Oct 1948.
  ii. **Toni R** born 26 Jan 1954.
  iii. **Jo Ann** born 11 Sep 1957.

14. Guy Wallace BOVEE [4] (Paul J [3] James Wallace [2] William [1]) born 18 Aug 1906, died 28 Jan 1989 in San Diego, San Diego Co., CA. He married 1st on 8 Feb 1931, **WINIFRED WOOD** died 11 Apr 1944.

children

  i. **Elaine Louise** born 27 Feb 1932. She married 1st **Gene NORTHWAY**. She married 2nd **Tom HINSHEY**. She married 3rd **Don SIEBERT**. (res Southland, KY.)
21. ii. **Warren Richard**.

He married 2nd on 21 Aug 1947, **Ruth SANDUSKY** born1 Dec 1899 in KY, died 5 Apr 1985 in San Diego, San Diego Co., CA.

15. Vernon Marvin BOVEE [4] (Clyde Mitchell [3] James Wallace [2] William [1]) (1971: res Sioux Falls, Minnehaha Co., SD) born 1 Sep 1916. He married **Neva Ruth DAVEY** born 13 Jan 1919.

children

  i.   **Dennis Marvin** born 24 Jan 1945. He married on 6 Jun 1964, **Janice Ann PEDERSON**.

  ii. **Vernette Ruth**, born 29 Apr 1948. She married on 6 Sep 1969, Ray **Kenneth RIECK**.

16. Luverne Oliver BOVEE [4] (Archibald Wallace [3] James Wallace [2] William [1]) born 5 Jun 1915, died 26 Jan 1933 in Solano Beach, San Diego Co., CA. He married on 2 May 1965, **Ann Mae GOODALL** born Nov 1945.

children

  i.   **April Mae** born 5 Apr 1965.

  ii. **Luverne Jr.** (ADPTD) born 22 Jun 1971.

  iii. **Betsy Jewel** born 4 Jul 1979.

17. Orval James BOVEE [4] (Archibald Wallace [3] James Wallace [2] William [1]) born 13 Jan 1917, died 9 Dec 1984 in Roseburg, Douglas Co., OR. He married on 6 Jun 1939, **Eleanor ROWE** born 19 Mar 1921.

children

  22. i.   **Donald LeRoy.**

  23. ii. **Harold Vernon.**

  24. iii. **Leslie Wallace.**

  25. iv. **James Cecil.**

18. Arlie BOVEE [4] (Earl Eugene [3] James Wallace [2] William [1]) (1970: res IL) He married 1st **unknown**.

children

  26. i.   **Barry Lynn.**

  ii. **Trent Marvin** born 2 Feb 1954.

  iii. **Kevin Earl** born 28 Oct 1955. He married on 21 Sep 1975, **Bertha CRAIG**.

He married 2nd, on 2 Jul 1962, **Betty CULLISON**.

children

  iv. **Michele Rae** born 12 Mar 1963.

  v.   **Robbie** born Apr 1964.

19. Lynn Eugene BOVEE [4] (Earl Eugene [3] James Wallace [2] William [1]) (1971: res Portland, Multnomah Co., OR) Born 20 May 1923 in SD. died 22 Jun 1987 in Portland, Multnomah Co., OR, buried in Willamette, Multnomah Co., OR. He married **Alyce** born 14 Dec 1926. died Aug 1988, buried same place.

children

  i.   **May Jane** born 1 May 1945.

  ii. **James Wallace** born 15 Oct 1949.

20. Arnold Eugene BOVEE [4] (Claude Arnold [3] James Wallace [2] William [1]) (1971: res Parker, Turner Co., SD) born 29 May 1925 in Turner Co., SD, died bef 1998. He married on 10 Sep 1948, **Fern Laurene NELSON** born 31 Dec 1926.

children

  27. i.   **Alan Lee.**

  ii. **Gwen Renae**, born 10 Aug 1952. She married on 25 Jul 1975, **James VANGERPEN**.

iii.   **Suzanne Kay** born 1 Sep 1967.

21. Warren Richard BOVEE [5] (Guy Wallace [4] Paul J [3] James Wallace [2] William [1]) (1990: res Seattle, King Co., WA) born 10 Feb 1937 In Dodge Center, Dodge Co., MN. He married on Feb 1967, **Donna CARPMAIL** born 25 Oct 1929.
children
   i.   **Lee Arthur** born, 4 Dec 1967 in San Mateo, San Mateo Co., CA.
   ii. **Jay Arthur** born 6 N0c 1969 in Redwood City, San Mateo Co., CA.

22. Donald LeRoy BOVEE [5] (Orval James [4] Archibald Wallace [3] James Wallace [2] William [1]) (1993: res Days Creek, Douglas Co., OR) born 21 Jun 1941 in Portland, Multnomah Co., OR.. He married on 20 Aug 1961, **Joan Margaret BRINK** born 28 Dec 1939.
children
28.   i.   **LeRoy Earnest.**
29.   ii. **Randall Scott.**
      iii. **Joseph Lee** (1993: res Springfield, Lane Co., OR) born 13 Sep 1966. He married on 10 Aug 1986, **Tamara Mccutcheon.**
30.   iv. **Jeffrey Allen.**

23. Harold Vernon BOVEE [5] (Orval James [4] Archibald Wallace [3] James Wallace [2] William [1]) (1993: res Roseburg, Douglas Co., OR) born 23 Oct 1942 in Dallas, Polk Co., OR. He married 1st on 21 Jun 1964, **Sharon Marie TRENHOLM** born 8 Mar 1947.
children
   i.   **Michelle Renae** born 12 May 1965. She married on 6 Sep 1986, **Keith Allan Knittle.**
        children
           i.   **Kristfer Warren** born 15 Jun 1988.
   ii. **Tammy Sue** born 26 Sep 1966. She married 1st on 5 Sep 1986, **Paul REID**.
        children
           i.   **Lashley Diane** born 5 Mar1988.
           ii. **Shawna Rea** born 1 Oct 1989.

        She married 2nd on 21 Jun 1997, **Jamie WATKINS**

   iii. **Evelyn Louise** born 5 Aug 1968. She married on 14 Mar 1992, **Shaun DRIVER.**
        children
           i.   **Nicole Danielle** born 1 Oct 1989.
           ii. **Brittany Ann** born 7 Mar 1995.
31.   iv. **James Garland**
      v.   **Annette Marie** born 19 Dec 1973.
           children
              i.   **Jessica Rose** born 30 Jun 1933.

24. Leslie Wallace BOVEE [5] (Orval James [4] Archibald Wallace [3] James Wallace [2] William [1]), born 2 Apr 1944 in Dallas, Polk Co., OR. He married on 27 Dec 1975, **Christine GREYEYES** born 3 Apr 1945.
children
   i.   **Catherine Audine** born 31 Oct 1976.
   ii. **Angela Ethyl** born 12 May 1978.

25. James Cecil BOVEE [5] (Orval James [4] Archibald Wallace [3] James Wallace [2] William [1]), born 26 May 1945 in Dallas, Polk Co., OQ, died 17 Nov 1997. He married 1st on 29 Aug 1965, **Sharon Lee CASTLE** born 27 Oct 1745.
children
  i. **Douglas James** born 21 Sep 1968, died 22 Sep 1968 in Eugene, Lane Co., OR.
  ii. **Brian James** (ADPTD) born 9 Feb 1971.
  iii. **Lisa** (ADPTD) born 11 Nov 1976.

He married 2nd on 2 Nov 1980, **Sharon NORRIS**.

26. Barry Lynn BOVEE [5] (Arlie [4] Earl Eugene [3] James Wallace [2] William [1]) (1990: res Beloit, Rock Co., WI) born 31 Jan 1953. He married on 31 May 1975, **Rebecca F BENNET**.
children
  i. Benjamin **Aaron** born 27 Sep 1976.

27. Alan Lee BOVEE [5] (Arnold Eugene [4] Claude Arnold [3] James Wallace [2] William [1]) (1971: res Omaha, Douglas Co., NE) born 2 Jan 1950. He married on 12 Oct 1974, **Mary Caryl NEVINS**.
children
  i. **Joshua James** born 3 Nov 1976.
  ii. **Nathan Alan** born 3 Nov 1976.

28. LeRoy Earnest BOVEE [6] (Donald Le Roy [5] Orval James [4] Archibald Wallace [3] James Wallace [2] William [1]) (2001: res Juneau, Southeastern Co., AK) born 5 Sep 1962. He married on 15 Aug 1982, **Gayle L SOERENSEN**.
children
  i. **Kaysey Lee** born 17 Feb 1984 In Roseburg, Douglas Co., OR.
  ii. **Jennifer Joan** born 30 Jun 1999 in Juneau, Southeastern Co., AK.

29. Randall Scott BOVEE [6] (Donald Le Roy [5] Orval James [4] Archibald Wallace [3] James Wallace [2] William [1]) (1993: res White Salmon, Klickitat Co., WA). born 5 Dec 1963 in Roseburg, Douglas Co., WA. He married on 7 Aug 1988 **Carol BENNETT**.
children
  i. **Karissa Nicole** born 28 Apr 1995.
  ii. **Karina Donielle** born 3 Feb 1998.
  iii. **Andrew Scott** born 19 Jun 2000.

30. Jeffrey Alen BOVEE [6] (Donald Le Roy [5] Orval James [4] Archibald Wallace [3] James Wallace [2] William [1]) (1993: res Days Creek, Douglas Co., OR) born 15 Mar 1969 in Vancouver, Clark Co., WA. He married on 3 Sep 1989, **Marianne** (of Taiwan) in Taiwan.
children
  i. **Kristie En-hui** born 5 Mar 1991 in Eugene, Lane Co., OR.
  ii. **Ryan Yao-zhu** born 17 Apr 1995 in Los Angeles, Los Angeles Co., CA.

31. James Garland BOVEE [6] (Harold Vernon [5] Orval James [4] Archibald Wallace [3] James Wallace [2] William [1]) born 12 Apr 1971. He married 1st on 11 Oct 1991, **Leila SCHWAN**.

children

    i. **Gabrielle Monique** born 17 Oct 1990.

    ii. **James Garland Jr.** born 22 Jun 1992.

He married 2nd on 25 May 1996, **Wanda K Pearson ANDERSON.**.

---

1. **William Arthur BOVEE** (1850–60: NY, 1865-85: IA, 1885-97: MN) born 21 Jan 1824 in Washington Co., NY, died 21 Jan 1897 in Minneapolis, Hennepin Co., MN., buried in Crystal Lake cem, Minneapolis, Hennepin Co., MN. He married **Hester Ann PIERCE** born 15 Oct 1826 in White Plains, Westchester Co., NY.
   children
       i. **Lois Jeannette** born abt 1846 in Sherman, Chautauqua Co., NY.
   2. ii. **John Wesley.**
   3. iii. **Alfred D.**
   4. iv. **Orlando William.**
       v. **Juliet** born abt 1856 in Sherman, Chautauqua Co., NY.
       vi. **Marvin Leslie** born abt 1859 in Sherman, Chautauqua Co., NY.
   5. vii. **Frank Devillo.**
       viii. **Carrie A** born 2 Feb 1869 in IA. She married James A BARRIE.

2. **John Wesley BOVEE** [2] (William Arthur [1]) (1880: res Humboldt, Richardson Co., NE 1900: Holdridge, Phelps Co., NE) born 16 Oct 1848 in Sherman, Chautauqua Co., NY, died 1918, buried in Greenwood cem, Renton, King Co., WA. He married on 6 Dec 1873 in Butler Co., IA, **Hattie E MOORE** born Oct 1854 in IA, died 12 May 1940, buried in Greenwood cem, Renton, King Co., WA.
   children
   6. i. **Charles Wesley.**
       ii. **Ethel** born Jul 1881 in NE. She married **Robert GIBB.**
           children
           i. **Collins.**
           ii. **Genevieve.** She married 1st **Claude HORNING,** She married 2nd **WHITE.**
       iii. **William Everett** born Oct 1883 in NE, died Mar 1910 in King Co., WA.

3. **Alfred D BOVEE** [2] (William Arthur [1]), (1880: res Cedar Falls, Black Hawk Co., IA) born abt 1850 in Sherman, Chautauqua Co., NY. He married on 18 Sep 1872 in Black Hawk Co., IA, **Mary E SHUPE.**
   children
       i. **Myrtle L** born Mar 1875 in MN. She married abt 1895 , **Edward T KERSTON**, born Sep 1872.
           children
           i. **Roland E** born Nov 1899.
       ii. **Ernest** born Oct 1876 in Cedar Falls, Black Hawk Co., IA.
       iii. **Nellie** born abt 1877 in Cedar Falls, Black Hawk Co., IA.
       iv. **Bessie B** born Dec 1879 in Cedar Falls, Black Hawk Co., IA.

4. **Orlando William BOVEE** [2] (William Arthur [1]) (1920: res Santa Cruz, Santa Cruz Co., CA) born 26 Mar 1854 in Sherman, Chautauqua Co., NY, died 9 Jan 1938 in Santa Cruz, Santa Cruz Co., CA. He married abt 1874 in Santa Cruz, Santa Cruz

Co., CA, **Nancy HUNTER** born abt 1853 died 19 Mar 1919 in Santa Cruz, Santa Cruz Co., CA.

children

    i. **William H** born June 1875 in Cedar Falls, Black Hawk Co., IA. Resided: 1920 Lincoln, Tama Co., IA.

7. ii. **Fred Orlando**.

   iii. **Eleanor** born Aug 1881 in Cedar Falls, Black Hawk Co., IA.

   iv. **Nannie H** born Dec 1883 in Cedar Falls, Black Hawk Co., IA.

   v. **James Jackson** born 24 Feb 1886 in Cedar Falls, Black Hawk Co., IA, died Dec 1978 in Dade City, Pasco Co., FL.

   vi. **Emmett** born 26 Mar 1889, died Oct 1969 in Oskaloosa, Mahaska Co., IA.

  vii. **Leslie** born 6 May 1894 in Anoka, Anoka Co., MN, died Mar 1978 in Sonoma, Sonoma Co., CA.

5. Frank Devillo BOVEE [2] (William Arthur [1]) (1900: res Minneapolis, Hennepin Co., MN) born 9 Sep 1861 in Sherman, Chautauqua Co., NY, died 27 Oct 1922 in Minneapolis, Hennepin Co., MN, he married 1st in Black Hawk Co., IA, **Alice M MOORE**.

children

    i. **Roy Devillo** born 18 Apr 1884 in Cedar Falls, Black Hawk Co., IA, died Aug 1962 in Longview, Cowlitz Co., WA, buried in Minneapolis, Hennepin Co., MN.

He married 2nd on 28 Oct 1886 in Minneapolis, Hennepin Co., MN, **Emily Frances KING** born20 Oct 1858 in Williamstown, Lewis Co., MO, died 9 Jan 1946 in Minneapolis, Hennepin Co., MN.

children

    i. **Lucy K**, born Aug 1887 in MN, died 9 Jul 1910 in Anoka Co., MN.

    ii. **Mabel L** born Jul 1892 in MN, died 1964 in Longview, Cowlitz Co., WA. She married **EDGECOMB**.

8. iii. **Willis Elmer**.

9. iv. **Howard Kingsley**.

6. Charles Wesley BOVEE [3] (John Wesley [2], William Arthur [1]) (1900: res Seattle, King Co., WA 1st mayor of Bellevue, King Co., WA.) born 1 Jun 1875 in Black Hawk Co., IA., died Nov 1961 in Ephrata, Grant Co., WA, buried in Ephrata cem, Ephrata, Grant Co., WA. He married on 3 Jun 1905 in Seattle, King Co., WA, **Jennie Ethel BEBE** born 30 Dec 1884 in Denver, Denver Co., CO, died 1970.

children

    i. **Marjorie** (1980s: res Centralia, Lewis Co., WA) born 8 May 1910 in Seattle, King Co., WA, died 1 Mar 1987 in Olympia, Thurston Co., WA, buried in Castle Rock, Cowlitz Co., WA. She married 1st **Alfred VEDDER**

       children

        i. **June**.

        ii. **Louis**.

    She married 2nd **Edgar OLSONRE**.

       children

        i. **Sharon Janet**. She married **DAVIDSON**.

        ii. **Eugene**.

She married 3rd **Volne DELO**

10. ii. **Charles Wesley Jr**.

7. Fred Orlando BOVEE ^{3} (Orlando William ^{2}, William Arthur ^{1}) (1900: res Minneapolis, Hennepin Co., MN 1920: res Santa Cruz, Santa Cruz Co., CA) born 25 Oct 1877 in Cedar Rapids, Linn Co., IA, died 8 Mar 1950 in Napa, Napa Co., CA. He married **Eva Lena KIRK** born 5 Nov 1880 in IA, died 15 Jun in Santa Clara, Santa Clara Co., CA.
children
    i. **Carroll F** born 11 Jan 1905, died 15 Jun 1964 in Santa Clara, Santa Clara Co., CA.
    ii. **Dorothy Lillian** born abt 1908 in CA. She married **PROFFITT**.
11. iii. **Eugene Victor**.

8. Willis Elmer BOVEE ^{3} (Frank Divillo ^{2} William Arthur ^{1}) born 6 Jul 1894 in Minneapolis, Hennepin Co., MN, died 7 Feb 1969 in Coon Rapids, Hennepin Co., MN. He married on 28 Sep 1917 in Champlin, Hennepin Co., MN, **Louise A MAGG** born 31 Aug 1894 in Champlin, Hennepin Co., MN, died 24 Aug 1982.
children
12. i. **Glenroy J**.
    ii. **Laurie**.
    iii. **Joseph M** born 16 Jul 1921, died 10 Jan 1991, buried in Fort Snelling National cem, Hennepin Co., MN.
    iv. **Margurite**.
13. v. **Lee**.
    vi. **Lou**.
    vii. **Darlin**.
    viii. **Elliot**.

9. Howard Kingsley BOVEE ^{3} (Frank Devillo ^{2}, William Arthur ^{1}), born 13 Jun 1897 in MN, died 11 May 1962. He married on 12 Sep 1920, **Mildred OLSEN** born 21 Sep 1900 in Omaha, Douglas Co/. NE, died 5 Feb 1995 in Hamel, Hennepin Co., MN,
children
    i. **Lu Ellen Frances** born 13 Jun 1929.
    ii. **Gail Jennette** born 22 Sep 1937. She married **Jack ROBINSON**.

10. Charles Wesley BOVEE, Jr. ^{4} (Charles Wesley ^{3}, John Wesley ^{2}, William Arthur ^{1}) (1990-2000: res Ephrata, Grant Co., WA) born 26 Mar 1913 in Seattle, King Co., WA. He married 1st on 22 Sep 1934 in Port Orchard, Kitsap Co., WA, **June BRONSON** born 26 Jun 1918, died 14 Jan 1985.
children
    i. **Marylyn Gail** born16 Jan 1936 in Renton, King Co., WA. She married **LUDDINGTON**.
        children
        i. **Janise** born in Ephrata, Grant Co., WA.
        ii. **Mark** born in Ephrata, Grant Co., WA.
        iii. **Lori** born in Ephrata, Grant Co., WA.
        iv. **Mike** born in Ephrata, Grant Co., WA.
14. ii. **Leland Burt**.

11. Eugene Victor BOVEE [4] Fred Orlando [3], Orlando William [2], (William Arthur [1]) born 30 May 1912 in CA, died 14 May 1995 in Monterey, Monterey Co., CA. He married **Isabel HULQUIST**.

children

  i. **Joyce** born abt 1937, She married in 1956 **Michael G PETERSON**.

12. Glenroy J BOVEE [4] (Willis Elmer [3] Frank Divillo [2] William Arthur [1]) born 2 Jan 1919 in Champlin, Hennepin Co., MN, died 22 Jul 1980 in Robbinsdale, Hennepin Co., MN. He married 3 Oct 1940 in in Minneapolis, Hennepin Co., MN, **Lovina LAUGENESS** born5 Aug 1919 in Fargo, Cass Co., ND.

children

  i. **Joy**.

  ii. **Bonnie**. She married **Larry SCHROEDER**.

15. iii. **Terry G**.

13. Lee BOVEE [4] (Willis Elmer [3] Frank Divillo [2] William Arthur [1]) He married 1st **Louise**.

children

  i. **Robert**. He married **JoAnn**.

  ii. **Stanley**.

  iii. **Gordon**.

  iv. **Pam**. (twin of Penny).

  v. **Penny**. (twin of Pam).

He married 2nd **Barbara RYMAN**.

14. Leland Burt BOVEE [5] (Charles Wesley Jr., [4] Charles Wesley [3], John Wesley [2], William Arthur [1])born 19 Dec 1940. He married in Los Angeles, Los Angeles Co., CA, **Betty Sawyer**.

children

  i. **Brenda June** born in Los Angeles, Los Angeles Co., CA.

  ii. **Becky** born in Los Angeles, Los Angeles Co., CA.

  iii. **Brian** born in Los Angeles, Los Angeles Co., CA.

  iv. **Beth** born in Medford, Jackson Co., OR.

He married 2nd on 17 Jan 1986 **Frances P PENCE** born 8 Dec 1921.

  i. **Marinn Virginia** (2001: res Fairbanks, Central Co., AK) born 27 Apr 1938 in Seattle, King Co., WA.

    children

    i. **Patti** born in Ephrata, Grant Co., WA.

    ii. **Diana** born in Ephrata, Grant Co., WA.

    iii. **Twilla** born in . Fairbanks, AK

    iv. **Mike** born 1 Aug 1982 in Fairbanks, AK.

15. Terry G BOVEE [5] (Glenroy J [4] Willis Elmer [3] Frank Divillo [2] William Arthur [1]), (2001: res Champlin, Hennepin Co., MN) born 20 Aug 1948 in Minneapolis, Hennepin Co., MN. He married **Deborah Conner**.

children

  i. **Cheriee**.

  ii. **Wendy**.

16. iii. **Jacques.**
    iv. **Mayke** born abt 1979.

16. Jacques BOVEE [6], (Terry G [5] Glenroy J [4] Willis Elmer [3] Roy Divillo [2] William Arthur [1]) (2000: res San Diego, San Diego Co., CA) born abt 1977. He married **Christy**.
children
    i. **Dayton.**

---

1. William BOVEE (1855: res Salina, Onondaga Co., NY 1880: res Hastings, Oswego Co., NY) born abt 1804 in Rensselaer Co., NY, died bef 1889. He married on 10 May 1849 in Washington Co., NY, **Rebecca TRIPP** born abt 1823 in Washington Co., NY, died Sep 1893.
children
2. i. **Henry.**

2. Henry BOVEE [2] (William [1]) (1880: Hastings, Oswego Co., NY) born 1850 in Washington Co., NY, died bef 1900. He married abt 1871 in NY, **Mary Ann GEORGE** born Jul 1842 in France.
children
    i. **Elmer** born abt 1867 in NY.
    ii. **Lena** J born abt 1868. (Niece)
    iii. **Emma May** born abt 1872 in Oswego Co., NY.
3. iv. **Charles Henry.**
    v. **Florida M**, born abt 1876 in Hastings, Oswego Co., NY. She married **GARDNER**.
4. vi. **William H.**
    vii. **Stella** born May 1883 in Oswego Co., NY. She married **GORDON**.
    viii. **Rebecca** born May 1884 in Oswego Co., NY. She married 1st **LASSIN**. She married 2nd **John MURDOCK**.
    ix. **Thomas** born 1892 in Hastings, Oswego Co., NE, died abt 1911.

3. Charles Henry BOVEE [3] (Henry [2], William [1]) (1900-1910: res Constantia, Oswego Co., NY) born Apr 1874 in Hastings, Oswego Co., NE, died 1935. He married **Christina GREELEY** born Apr 1878 in NY.
children
5. i. **Charles Elmer.**
    ii. **Leon T** born Oct 1897 in Oswego Co., NY, died abt 1902.
    iii. **Kathleen** born in NY. She married **Homer GEORGE Sr.**
        children
        i. **Homer Jr.**

4. William H BOVEE [3] (Henry [2], William [1]) (1920: res Oswego, Oswego Co., NY) born Feb 1880 in Hastings, Oswego Co., NY. He married 1st **Kate GEORGE.**
children
    i. **Dale.** (ADPTD)

He married 2nd **Margaret** born abt 1883 in NY.

children
    i. **Francis** born 24 Apr 1909.

5. Charles Elmer BOVEE [4] (Charles Henry [3], Henry [2], William [1]) (1922-23: res Rochester, Monroe Co., NY) born 12 Mar 1896 in Bernards Bay, Oswego Co., NY, died Apr 1974 in Addison, Steuben Co., NY, buried in Cath Cem, Addison, Steuben Co., NY. He married **Melissa Ann SHANNON** born 5 Mar 1898 in NY, died Aug 1978 in Addison, Steuben Co., NY.
    children
  6. i. **Charles Eugene Sr.**
  7. ii. **Shannon M.**
     iii. **Elmer William** born abt 1925 in NY. He married **Betty Lou CROUT** in NY.
  8. iv. **Eugene Leon.**
     v. **John M** born in NY.

6. Charles Eugene BOVEE, Sr. [5] (Charles Elmer [4], Charles Henry [3], Henry [2], William [1]) (res Rush, and Penfield< Monroe Co., NY), born 27 May 1921 in NY, died 5 Sep 1992, buried in Bath National cem, Bath, Steuben Co., NY. He married in NY **Wilma PHILLIPS** born in NY.

    children
  9. i. **William Charles** born 2 Nov 1942 in Corning, Steuben Co., NY.
  10. ii. **Charles Eugene Jr.** born 6 Sep 1949 in Lincoln, Lancaster Co., NE, died 17 Aug 2001 in NY.
     iii. **Charlene** born 26 Oct 1955 in NY.

7. Shannon M BOVEE [5] (Charles Elmer [4], Charles Henry [3], Henry [2], William [1]) born 12 Oct 1922 in NY, died Apr 1982 in NY, buried in Rural cem, Addison, Steuben Co., NY. He married in NY **Louise WATKINS** born 30 Apr 1921 in Addison, Steuben Co., NY, died 2 Mar 1997 in Addison, Steuben Co., NY.
    children
  11. i. **Michael.**
     ii. **Greg** born in NY.
     iii. **Christina** born in NY, She married **Bryan J DRINKWATER** in NY.
         children
         i. **Thomas** born in NY.
         ii. **Sean.**
         iii. **Julie.**
     iv. **Sharon** born in NY, She married **William RUDE** (1992: res Woodhull, Steuben Co., NY) in NY.
         children
         i. **Shane** born in NY.
         ii. **Danny** born in NY.

8. Eugene Leon BOVEE [5] (Charles Elmer [4], Charles Henry [3], Henry [2], William [1]) (res: Addison, Steuben Co., NY) born in NY, died bef 1992. He married in NY **Doris ABEL**.
    children
    i. **Eugene** Jr. born in NY, died bef 1992.
    ii. **John** born in NY.

9. William Charles BOVEE [6] (Charles Eugene Sr.[5], Charles Elmer [4], Charles Henry [3], Henry [2], William [1]) born 2 Nov 1942 in Corning, Steuben Co., NY. He married 1st **Carol E DALRYMPLE**.
children
   i. **Wendy**. She married **Joseph ARIENO**.

He married 2nd in 1995, **Kristine S SORTINO**.

10. Charles Eugene BOVEE, Jr. [6] (Charles Eugene Sr.[5], Charles Elmer [4], Charles Henry [3], Henry [2], William [1]) born 6 Sep 1949 in Lincoln, Lancaster Co., NE, died 17 Aug 2001. He married **Bonnie HOUSE**.
children
   i. **Charles W**.
   ii. **Clark**.
   iii. **Keri**.

11. Michael BOVEE [6] (Shannon M [5], Charles Elmer [4], Charles Henry [3], Henry [2], William [1]) (res: Addison, Steuben Co., NY) born 1948 in NY. He married on 31 Aug 1968 in Addison, Steuben Co., NY **Sharon POTTER** born 30 Apr 1950.
children
   i. **Michael** born 31 Dec 1968 in Addison, Steuben Co., NY.
   ii. **Michelle** born 21 mar 1970 in NY. She married on 8 Feb 1991 in Warren Co., NY **Lorne HULTZ**.
      children
       i. **Alexis** born 4 Aug 1991.
   iii. **Jeremy** born 27 Sep 1976 in Addison, Steuben Co., NY.
   iv. **Renee** born 3 Jun 1977 In NY.
   v. **Lacey** born 3 Dec 1981 In NY.

---

1. Matthias S BOVEE (1840: res Montgomery Co., IN 1850: res Weston Twp., Platte Co., MO) born abt 1800 in VT. He married 1st on 9 Sep 1824 in Rush Co., IN, **Nancy NIPP** born abt 1804 in IN. He married 2nd **Mary** born abt 1810.
children
2.   i. **James E**.
3.   ii. **Charles**.
   iii. **Ersley Jane** born 16 Mar 1837 in IN, died 12 Jul 1900 in Tarkio, Atchison Co., MO. She married on 1 Jan 1855 in Lindon, Atchison Co., MO **Abner Carpenter SMITH** born 26 Jun 1835 in Overton Co., TN, died 10 Sep 1906 in Tarkio, Atchison Co., MO.
      children
      i. **Ellen** born 4 Sep 1856 in NE., died 5 Aug 1905. She married in Dec 1875 **George JACKSON** born 2 Aug 1824, died 27 Apr 1916.
      ii. **Nancy J** born 21Apr 1859 in NE. She married **Philburt PAYNE**.
      iii. **Mary Isadore** born 14 Jul 1859 in NE. She married on 26 Feb 1882 **Joseph M JACKSON,** born 3 Mar 1858 in KS, died 19 Dec 1946.
      iv. **William Franklin** born 18 Mar 1863 in MO, died 9 Oct 1926 in Tarkio, Atchison Co., MO.

v.   **Matilda May** born 17 Apr 1865 in IA, died 15 Aug 1930 in Shenandoah, Page Co., IA. She married on 20 Sep 1882 **Alford Worthington MUTCHLER.**

vi. **Laura** born 2 Jul 1868. She married **William BAKER.**

vii. **Clara** born 16 Feb 1870 in MO. She married abt 1888 in MO **Thomas R REYNOLDS**, born Apr 1866 in IL.

viii. **Tully William** born 1 Jan 1873 in Phelps, Atchison Co., MO, died 6 Mar 1926 in Tarkio, Atchison Co., MO. He married 1st on 2 Mar 1897 **Emma Malissa ROBERTSON**, born 19 1871Apr in Rock Port, Atchison Co., MO., died 14 Oct 1923 in Tarkio, Atchison Co., MO. He married 2nd on 9 Apr 1924 in Rock Port, Atchison Co., MO **Bytha C MILLICAN,** born May 1890 in Franklin Co., AR., died abt 1945 in Higginsville, Lafayette Co., MO.

ix. **Thomas** born Jun 1877 in Tarkio, Atchison Co., MO., died 20 Jun 1877 in Tarkio, Atchison Co., MO.

x.   **Minnie May** born 17 Nov 1879. She married **Alonzo Enoch Van Deusen,** born 22 Dec 1870 in St. Joseph Co., IN, son of Henry Harvey Van Deusen and Artemisia Jane Field.

iv. **Mary** born abt 1840 in IN. She married on 20 Dec 1856 in Omaha Co., NE. **Harrison ADAMS.**

v.   **Elliot** born abt 1842 in IN.

vi. **Amelia** born abt 1843 in IN. She married on 11 Feb 1858 in Nemaha Co., NE. **D M RHODES.**

2. **James E BOVEE** [2] (Matthias S [1]) (1880: res Blair, Washington Co., NE) born Sep 1834 in Montgomery Co., IN. (1880: Blair, Washington Co., NE, 1900: Omaha, Douglas co., NE). He married 1st **Elizabeth C SMITH** born 24 Sep 1839 in Overton Co., TN.

children

i.   **Mathias E** born 3 Mar 1858, died Mar 1882, buried in Blair Cem Washington Co., NE.

ii. **Mary C** born 1863 in IA. She married on 7 Jul 1883 in Blair Washington Co., NE, **Charles H AVERY.**

iii. **Rosa Bovee** born abt 1864. She married 1st on 12 Jan 1884 in Douglas Co., NE, **Henry JOHNSON.**

   children

   i.   **Nellie**. She married **Thomas Adams.**

   She married 2nd **Charles MCCOY.**
   children

   i.   **Kenneth** born abt 1905. (Adopted)

iv. **Charles N** born 1869 in NE. He married on 12 May 1889 in Blair, Washington Co., NE **Gusta LUMAN.**

v.   **Martha Henrietta Jane Bovee** born 31 Mar 1870 in Mondamin, Harrison Co., IA, died 23 May 1927 in Greeley, Weld Co., CO. She married on 31 Jan 1863 in Blair, Washington Co., NE, **Eli Monroe AVERY** born 1 Jan 18763 in Woodbury Co., IA, died 2 Dec 1940 in Greybull, Bighorn Co., WY.

   children

   i.   **James Robert** born 20 May 1887 in Blair, Washington Co., NE, died 29 Aug 1953.

   ii. **Lillie May** born 12 May 1889 in Blair, Washington Co., NE, died

22 Sep 1954 in Torrington, Goshen Co., WY. She married on 12 Jun 1906 **John Robert Hardesty**.

    iii. **Samuel Ray** born 4 Mar 1892 in Blair, Washington Co., NE, died 1953. He married abt 1912 Corra May Pepper.

    iv. **Blanche** born May 1894 in Blair, Washington Co., NE, died 1908.

    v. **Josephina** born Sep 1896 in AR.

    vi. **Gladys** born Nov 1898 in NE.

    vii. **Lola** born 1900, died 1902.

    viii. **Francis Leonard** born 5 Oct 1900, died 10 Feb 1923.

    ix. **Doris Fern** born 18 Jun 1906 in Elwell, Weld Co., CO, died 4 Mar 1976.

    x. **Stewart** born 20 Feb 1909 in Elwell, Ward Co., CO., died 24 Feb 1924.

    xi. **Kenneth Grover** born 9 Nov 1911 in Elwell, Ward Co., CO., died 24 Sep 1974.

  vi. **Lydia E** born 1873 in MO. She married on 6 May 1889 in Blair, Washington Co., NE **Charles A KING**.

4. vii. **Samuel Francis**.

  viii. **Susan** born abt 1877 in IA. She married Charles **LEWIS**.

    children

    i. **Mabel**

  ix. **James** born 20 Jan 1882, died 15 May 1882, buried in Blair Cem, Blair, Washington Co., NE.

He married 2nd Rachael, born Nov 1836 in IN.

3. Charles BOVEE [2] (Matthias S [1]) (1900: rcs Omaha, Douglas Co., NE) born Feb 1835 in IN. (1900: Omaha, Douglas Co., NE) He married abt 1865 **Elizabeth A** born Feb 1847 in OH.

children

  i. **Clarence B** born May 1877 in IA. (1920: Omaha, Douglas Co., NE. He married **Elizabeth C** aft 1902.

  ii. **Grave N** born Jul 1884 in NE.

4. Samuel Francis BOVEE [3] (James E [2], Matthias S [1]) (1920: res Rosalie, Thurston Co., NE) born 10 Aug 1876, died 21 May 1960 in Sioux City, Woodbury Co., IA., buried in Lyons, Burt Co., NE. He married on 4 Mar 1803 in Blair, Washington Co., NE, **Myrlie DIXON** born 4 Mar 1885 in NE, died 24 Sep 1945 in Rosalie, Thurston Co., NE.

children

  i. **Vera Frances** born 15 Oct 1905 in NE. She married 1st on 15 Oct 1923 in Council Bluffs, Pottawattamie Co., IA, **Howard Andrew HARVEY** born 11 Jan 1901 in Decatur, Burt Co., NE, died 5 Jan 1975.

    children

    i. Lois Lorene born 10 Oct 1924 in Lyons, Burt Co., NE. She married 1st on 1 Sep 1946 Ezra Drew Morgan. She married 2nd on 17 Oct 1981 Wayne Birch Larsen in Boise, Ada Co., ID.

    ii. Duane Howard born 14 Jan 1926 in Lyons, Burt Co., NE. He married Irene Welch.

    iii. Ronald Dwight

    iv. Frances May born 24 Sep 1930 in Hardin, Big Horn Co., MT. She married 1st **James Lee White**. She married 2nd **William Charles**

She married 2nd on 9 Aug 1972 **Kenneth D HANNON**.

5. ii. **James Russell**.
6. iii. **Carroll Francis**.

5. James Russell BOVEE [4] (Samuel Francis [3], James E [2], Matthias S [1]) born 30 Nov 1915 in Rosalie, Thurston Co., NE, died 1989. He married on 5 Oct 1941 **Viola MARTIN** born 16 Jun 1911, died 11 Jul 1992 in Rosalie, Thurston Co., NE.
children
7. i. **Gail**
ii. **Lyle** born abt 1945. (1997: Rosalie, Thurston Co., NE).
8. iii. **Dallas D**.

6. Carroll Francis BOVEE [4] (Samuel Francis [3], James E [2], Matthias S [1]) born 5 Jul 1925 in Rosalie, Thurston Co., NE, died 23 Sep 1989 in Orleans, Harlan Co, NE, buried in Lyons, Burt Co., NE. He married on 18 Jun 1946 in Sioux City, Woodbury Co., IA **Lillian PHIPPS** born 11 Nov 1927 in Decatur, Burt Co., NE.
children
9. i. **Dana Francis**.
10. ii. **Sterling Francis**.
11. iii. **James Harrison**.
iv. **Suella Frances** (of Omaha, Douglas Co., NE) born 12 Sep 1953. She married on 19 Feb in Fremont, Dodge Co., NE, **William MAUDLIN**.
> *children*
> i. **Peter Charles** born 12 Mar 1976.
> ii. **Paul William** born 9 Apr 1977.
v. **Melody Fay** born 5 Aug 1955 in Omaha, Douglas Co., NE. She married on 23 Feb 1976 **Michael MAYS**.
> *children*
> i. **Rheanna Lynn** born 2 Feb 1980.
> ii. **Joselyn Sue** born 16 Oct 1983.
> iii. **David Willie** born 24 Mar 1986.

7. Gail BOVEE [5] (James Russell [4], Samuel Francis [3], James E [2], Matthias S [1]) born 11 Nov 1943. (1996: Lyons, NE) He married **Lyle BREHMER**.
children
i. **Rochelle** born 18 Oct 1972. She married **Stephen NELSON**.
ii. **Randi** born 29 Jun 1982.

8. Dallas D BOVEE [5] (James Russell [4], Samuel Francis [3], James E [2], Matthias S [1]) (1997: res Walthill, Thurston Co., NE) born 14 Dec 1950 in Oakland, Burt Co., NE. (1997: Walthill, NE). He married **Kristy WASHBURN** born 16 Jul 1948 in Sioux City, Woodbury Co., IA.
children
i. **Christopher** born 3 Oct 1977 in Sioux City, Woodbury Co., IA.
ii. **Kimberly** born 23 Jul 1982 in Sioux City, Woodbury Co., IA.

9. Dana Francis BOVEE [5] (Carroll Francis [4], Samuel Francis [3], James E [2], Matthias S [1]) (res: Anchorage, Southcentral Co., AK) born 22 Aug 1947 in Walthill, Thurston Co., NE. He married on 21 Jul 1971 in Valley, Douglas Co., NE **Judith**

KEISER.
children
i. **Jennifer Renee** born 13 Mar 1973 in NE. She married on 7 Jul 1995 **Dennie MICKEL**.
>   *children*
>   i.   **Jonathan Ray** born 27 Jul 1991.
>   ii. **Devon Cole** born 1 Jun 1994.

10. **Sterling Francis BOVEE** [5] (Carroll Francis [4], Samuel Francis [3], James E [2], Matthias S [1])born 18 Aug 1949 in Sioux City, Woodbury Co., IA. He married on 14 Feb 1971 in Fremont, Dodge Co., NE **Janet KEISER**.
children
i.   **Dustin** born 8 Dec 1995.
ii. **Cory Francis** born 7 Apr 1997.

11. **James Harrison BOVEE** [5] (Carroll Francis [4], Samuel Francis [3], James E [2], Matthias S [1]) (res: Alliance, Box Butte Co., NE) born 11 May 1952. He married on 1 Jun 1981 in Omaha, Douglas Co., NE **Susan THOMPSON**.
children
i.   **Kerri Sue** born 1 Dec 1981.
ii. **Jeffrey James** born 10 Apr 1985.

---

1. **Philip BOVEE** (1820: res Charleston, Montgomery Co., NY., 1850-1870: res NY.) born 27 May 1794, died 24 Oct 1880, buried in Old cem, Fultonville, Montgomery Co., NY. He married **Charlotte GOFF** born 17 Jul 1786, died 7 Sep 1857, buried same place.
Children
2.   i.   **Abraham J**.
3.   ii. **Lydia**
iii. **Peter** (1850-1870: Glen, NY, 1911: res Angola, Steuben Co., IN), born 1832 in Glen, Montgomery Co., NY, died aft 1911.
iv. **Charlotte**, born abt 1833 in Glen Montgomery Co., NY.

2. **Abraham J BOVEE** [2] (Philip [1]) (1855: res Glen, NY., 1860: res Veteran, Chemung Co., NY.)born 15 Mar 1820 in Fultonville, Montgomery Co., NY, died 19 Nov 1911 in Richland Twp, Ogemaw Co., MI. He married on 22 Jan 1848 in Fultonville, Montgomery Co., NY., **Elizabeth ROWE** born 15 Sep 1829 in Dutchess Co., MI, died 30 Mar 1912 in West Branch, Ogemaw Co., MI.
children
4.   i.   **Charles Henry**.
5.   ii. **George A**.
iii. **Charlotte Helen** born 23 May 1855 in Glen, Montgomery Co., NY, died 23 Jan 1951 in Churchill Twp., Ogemaw Co., MI. She married abt 1878 in NY, **George William PETERSON** born 28 Sep 1859 in NY., died 12 may 1947 in Churchill Twp., Ogemaw Co., MI.
>   *children*
>   i.   **James** born Sep 1881
>   ii. **Charles Abraham** born Sep 1883 in MI.
>   iii. **Gracie Ann** born 11 Sep 1885 in Miles Twp., Ogemaw Co., MI.

iv. **George** born 5 Sep 1886 in Au Gres, Arenac Co., MI, died 27 Jul 1971 in Twining, Arenac Co., MI.

v. **Leo** born Nov 1889 in MI.

vi. **Belle** born Aug 1891 in MI.

vii. **Gladys Charlotte** born 11 Aug 1893 in West Branch, Ogemaw Co., MI, died 28 Feb 1977 in Litchfield, Hillsdale Co., MI. She married in 1911, **Edwin VAN BUSKIRK**, who died 9 Mar 1946. On 18 Apr 1950 she married **Ransom MAY** who died 15 Apr 1961.

viii. **Grant** born Jun 1896 in MI.

iv. **Miranda** born 28 Apr 1857 in Montgomery Co., NY. She married **BRAGG**.

v. **Ida E.** born 26 Mar 1859 in Montgomery Co., NY

3. Lydia born 18 Oct 1824, died 9 Apr 1902, buried in same place. She married on 18 Mar 1847 in Fultonville, Montgomery Co., NY, **William GRIFFITH**

children

i. **Philip P** born abt 1852.

ii. **William** born abt 1853

4. Charles Henry BOVEE [3] (Abraham J [2] Philip [1]) (1900: res Saginaw, Saginaw Co., MI), born 23 Mar 1849 in Glen Montgomery Co., NY. He married **Esther D TYLER** born Aug 1858 In NY.

Children

i. **Minnie M.** born Oct 1883 in MI.

6. ii. **William Lanson**

5. George A BOVEE [3] (Abraham J [2] Philip [1]) (1920: res West Branch, Ogemaw Co., MI) born 6 Oct 1853 in Montgomery Co., NY. He married **Orilla LAPOINTE** born abt 1876 in Canada.

Children

i. **Fred** born abt 1900.

ii. **Mary** born 1903, died May 1980. She married **IRLAND**.

iii. **Edna** born 1906.

iv. **Matilda** born 1909

7. v. **.Vernon**.

vi. **Nellie** born abt 1915.

vii. **Herbert** born 4 Nov 1917, died Jun 1970.

6. William Lanson BOVEE [4] (Charles Henry [3] Abraham J [2] Philip [1]) born 20 Nov 1885 in Bridgewater Twp., Saginaw Co., MI, died 21 Jun 1954. He married **Sophia HINTZ** born 15 May 1887, died 9 Sep 1964.

Children

i. **Minnie Eleanor**, born 15 Sep 1908, died 16 Oct 1942. She married **Russell TRAVER**.

8. ii. **Albert Charles**.

iii. **Frank Richard** (1984: res Saginaw, Saginaw Co., MI) born 11 Sep 1924, died 4 Sep 1993 in Saginaw, Saginaw Co., MI.

iv. **Esther**.

v. **Clarence William**,born 12 May 1916, died Apr 1981 in Saginaw, Saginaw Co., MI.

vi. **Kenneth Leo** (1984: res Saginaw, Saginaw Co., MI.)

25

     vii. **Edward George** born 16 Nov 1919, died 1 Nov 1994 in Frankenmuth, Saginaw Co., MI.

    viii. **Helen Leona**. She married **ZUNIGA**.

     ix. **Edith Loraine**. She married **TRUCKNER**.

9.   x. **Donald Michael**.

7. Vernon BOVEE [4] (George A [3] Abraham J [2] Philip [1]), born 9 Jul 1911, died Jul 1962. He married ?--?.

Children

    i. **Shirley** born 4 Aug 1949 in Flint, Genesee Co., MI. She married **Ted SCHRAMM**.

        children

        i. **Karen Lynn**.

        ii. **Kevin Lee**.

8. Albert Charles BOVEE [5] (William Lanson [4] Charles Henry [3] Abraham J [2] Philip [1]) (1984: res Saginaw, Saginaw Co., MI), born 19 Oct 1910, died Jun 1984 in Birch Run, Saginaw Co., MI. He married **Lucille LENTZ**.

Children

    i. **Charles** born 26 May 1938.

10 ii. **James**

9. Donald Michael BOVEE [5] (William Lanson [4] Charles Henry [3] Abraham J [2] Philip [1]), born 20 Mar 1927, died Mar 1989 in Birch Run, Saginaw Co., MI. He married **Dorothy Louis FELTOR** born 15 Nov 1926 in Warwick, Orange Co., NY.

Children

    i. **Shad Craig** born 25 Aug 1950.

    ii. **Michelle Louise** born 29 Sep 1953.

   iii. **Melda Marie** born 2 Oct 1958.

10. James BOVEE [5] (Albert Charles [4] William Lanson [3] Charles Henry [2] Abraham J [1] Philip [1]) born 14 Jul 1939, He married **Marilyn ANSCENT**.

Children

    i. **Susanna** born 2 Aug 1965.

---

1. Eldert BOVEE (1880: res Queensbury, Warren Co., NY) born abt 1845 in NY, died 14 Apr 1900. He married **Mary Ann SHEARS** born Apr 1843 in NY.

children

    i. **Betsey** born abt 1865.

2. ii. **John H.**.

   iii. **Effie** born abt 1873. She married **John H HALL**.

        children

        i. **Myrtle**. She married **CODNER**.

        ii. **Eva May** born 15 Sep 1901, died 10 Oct 1975. She married **Arthur L JARVIS**.

3. iv. **George E.**

4. v. **Charles**.

   vi. **Frank P.** born Nov 1881 He married on 11 Apr 1903 in W Glens Falls, Warren Co., NY., **Mary E.**

2. John H BOVEE [2] (Eldert [1]) born abt 1869. He married 1st on 4 Sep 1892 in Queensbury, Warren Co., NY., **Margaret M** born 1875, died 1934 in W Glens Falls, Warren Co., NY
children
- i. **Evelyn** born abt 1893.
- ii. **Richard F**, born 5 May 1904, died 9 May 1911, buried in Glens Falls, Warren Co., NY.

He married 2nd aft 1934, **Hattie E.**

3. Effie born abt 1873. She married **John H HALL**.
children
- i. **Myrtle** , she married **CODNER**
- ii. **Eva May**

4. George E BOVEE [2] (Eldert [1]) (1900: res Queensbury, Warren Co., NY) born 27 Dec 1874, died 28 Dec 1951 in Sacramento, Sacramento Co., CA. He married on 3 Jul 1899 in Glens Falls, Warren Co., NY, **Bessie KIGSLEV** born 15 Jan 1880 in NY died 1 Feb 1957 in Sacramento, Sacramento Co., CA.
children
- i. **Howard E** born 14 Feb 1905 in Glens Falls, Warren Co., NY, died 22 Dec 1970 in Sacramento, Sacramento Co., CA. He married **Frances C CARPENTER**.

5. Charles BOVEE [2] (Eldert [1]) born Oct 1879, died 18 Apr 1942, buried in Bay st. cem, Glens Falls, Warren Co., NY. He married **Caroline LASHAWAY** born abt 1882, died 6 Jan 1932, buried in Bay st. cem, Glens Falls, Warren Co., NY.
children
- i. **Eldert Charles** born abt 1908, died 6 Jan 1932, buried in Bay st. cem, Glens Falls, Warren Co., NY. He married **Leona WAITE.**
- 6. ii. **James Emerson**.

6. James Emerson BOVEE [3] (Charles [2] Eldert [1]),. born 25 Jan 1912, died 31 Oct 1981, buried in St Mary's cem, Fort Edward, Washington Co., NY. He married on 30 Jun 1943, **Florence Victory BOWE** born 20 May 1911 in Fort Edward, Washington Co., NY, died 5 Jan 1999 in Argyle, Washington Co., NY.
children
- i. **Mary Helena** born 16 Dec 1944. She married **James PARKER**.
  children
  - i. **Katherine L** born 1 Dec 1972
- ii. **Joan Carol** born 25 Dec 1946. She married **Earnest V STEVES**.
- 7. iii. **James Dennis**.
- iv. **Lois ann**.
- v. **Barbara** born and died in Dec. aft 1955.

7. James Dennis BOVEE [4] (James Emerson [3] Charles [2] Eldert [1]) born 13 Jun 1951. He married 1st **Cynthia HOWARD**.
children
- i. **Angel Spowitz** born 20 Feb 1972, died 10 Jan 1993.

   ii. **James Douglas** born 21 Feb 1978, died 26 Mar 1978.

   iii. **Jennifer Lynn** born 3 Mar 1980.

He married 2nd **Barbara KLOTZ**.

---

1. James BOVEE (Capt) (1828 NYC, NY ref: The National Cyclopedia, V 16) born abt 1779 in PA, died 31 Jul 1828., He married on 30 Mar 1816, **Belphamer SCRIBNER** in Trinity Church, New York, New York Co., NY, born abt 1800, died aft 1870.

children

  2. i. **Christian Nestell.**

  3. ii. **William Henry.**

     iii. **Maria G** born abt 1826. She married **Leonard B GORHAM.**

  4. iv. **James S.**

     v. **Joseph Arthur** born abt 1828, bap 2 May 1831 in Presb Church, Queens Co., NY, died abt 1858. He married on 12 Oct 1852. **Rebecca Ann PARKER.**

2. Christian Nestell BOVEE [2] (James [1]) (1870: res Essex Co., NJ) born 18 Feb 1820 in NY, died 18 Jan 1904 in Philadelphia, Philadelphia Co., PA. He married on 2 Jul 1849 in New York, New York Co., NY., **Mary M DOUBLEDAY.**

children

     i. **Belle** born Jun 1855.

  5. ii. **Christian Nestell** Jr.

     iii. **Kate** died abt 1924.

     iv. **Eleanor** born Jun 1865 in NJ.

     v. **Stella** She married on 26 Oct 1875 in NJ. **Richard Morris POPHAM.**

3. William Henry BOVEE [2] (James [1]) (1849: res San Francisco, San Francisco Co., CA) born abt 1824 in NY. He married on 11 Jul 1842 in NY., **Elizabeth W MARSHALL.**

children

     i. **Belphamer** born abt 1843. She married **Henry P SONNTAG.**

     ii. **N C** born abt 1845.

     iii. **William** born abt 1847.

  6. iv. **Lillie.**

4. James S BOVEE [2] (James [1]) (1880: res San Francisco, San Francisco Co., CA) born 1827, He married **Helen A KIRBY** born abt 1838 in Ireland, died 16 Feb 1920 in San Francisco, San Francisco Co., CA.

children

     i. **Lillie Kay** born 8 Oct 1865 in CA, died 8 Jun 1948 in Contra Costa Co., CA. She married **Keith.**

         children

         i. **James D** born4 Dec 1887, died 14 Apr 1962 in Santa Cruz, San Francisco Co., CA

     ii. **Grace A** born abt 1874 in CA.

5. Christian Nestell BOVEE Jr. [3] (Christian Nestell [2], James [1]) (1900: res

Manhattanville, New York Co., NY) born Oct 1858 in Brooklyn, Kings Co., NY, died 4 Mar 1913 in Marion Co., PA. He married **Kate D HOWELL.**

children

   i.   **Gertrude H** born Aug 1888 in Manhattan, New York Co., NY. She married 1st **MACKAY,** She married 2nd abt 1920 **John A LEBOUTILLER.**

   ii.   **Mary Isabel** born Jun 1891. She married in Dec 1913 **Bertrand Leroy TAYLOR.**

6. Lillie Bovee born Mar 1856. She married **George D Toy** born Apr 1854 in CA.

children

   i.   **Mable** born Apr 1881.

   ii.   **Harvey M** born 27 Jun 1883 in CA, died 1 Mar 1960 in San Francisco, San Francisco Co., CA

---

1. George W BOVEE (1880–1890: Blair, Washington Co., NE, 1920 Omaha, NE). He married **Nancy CAMPBELL** born Dec 1860 in MO.

children

   i.   **Edward** born Dec 1876 in IA.

   ii.   **Lizzie** born Jan 1883 in NE.

2. iii.   **Eugene Taylor.**

   iv.   **May** born Apr 1888 in NE. She married **Ted WARD.**

   v.   **George Frank** born 22 Nov 1891 in NE, died Dec 1976 in Long Beach, Los Angeles Co., CA. He married **Katie.**

2. Eugene Taylor BOVEE [2], (George W [1]) born 26 Feb 1886 in NE, died 22 Jan 1958 in Los Angeles, Los Angeles Co., CA, buried in Ft Rosecrans Nat Cem, San Diego, San Diego Co., CA. He married 1st abt 1916. He married 2nd on 30 Jan 1918 **Naomi Elva ALLEMAN** born 17 Jan 1918 in Rochester, Beaver Co., PA.

children

   i.   **Nancy V** born abt 1920. She married 1st **Donald GARDNER** and 2nd **Fred LEWIS.**

       children

       i.   **James.**

       ii.   **Pam.**

3. ii.   **Eugene Taylor Jr.**

3. Eugene Taylor BOVEE Jr. [3] (Eugene Taylor [2], George W [1]) (res: Bishop, Inyo Co., CA.) born 11 Feb 1923 in Falling Springs, IL, died 1 May 1989 in Orange Co., CA. He married on 30 May 1942 in Las Vegas, San Miguel Co., NM, **Jeanette Mildred KOLB** born 7 Apr 1921 in Evansville, Vanderburgh Co., IN.

children

   i.   **Dianne Karen** born 23 Jun 1944. She married **Thomas Francis PRADO.**

   ii.   **John Kris** born 22 Sep 1956.

   iii.   **James Keith** born 28 Nov 1957.

---

1 Peter L BOVEE born abt 1810 in Montgomery Co., NY,(1840-1856: res Oneida Co., NY, He married **Catherine** born abt 1811 in Ireland.
children
2.   i.   **Elizabeth**.
     ii.   **John D** born 1839 in Oneida Co., NY.
3.   iii.   **William Cole**.
     iv.   **Unknown** born 1845, died 15 Apr 1850, buried in Potter cem, Utica, Oneida Co., NY.
     v.   **Jarret Willis** born abt 1849 in Oneida Co., NY.
     vi.   **Edward L.** born abt 1851 in Oneida Co., NY.

2. Elizabeth born abt 1837 in Montgomery Co., NY. She married **Jonathan MOSIER**.
children
     i.   **George A** born abt 1861.
     ii.   **Edwina M** born abt 1865

3. William Cole BOVEE [2] (Peter L [1]) born Nov 1842 in NY. (1880-1900: res Utica, Oneida Co., NY) He married abt 1868, **Harriet Samantha LATHAM** born Apr 1845 in NY.
children
     i.   **Harriet Mae** born Sep 1870 in NY.
4.   ii.   **William Cole Jr.**
     iii.   **Frank Alfred** born Feb 1878.
     iv.   **Ada Florence** born abt 1878.

4. William Cole BOVEE Jr.[3] (William Cole [2] Peter L [1]) (1925: res Utica, Oneida Co., NY) born 7 Jan 1873 in Utica, Oneida Co., NY. He married **Katherine Minnie NICKEL**.
children
     i.   **Harriet Lizetta** born abt 1906, died 23 Aug 1927 in Utica, Oneida Co., NY.
     ii.   **Louise Helena**.
     iii.   **Ada Katherine**.
     iv.   **William Cole III**. died bef 1927.

---

1. Unknown BOVEE.
children
2.   i.   **Richard J**.
3.   ii.   **Unknown**.

2. Richard J BOVEE [2] (Unknown [1]) born 8 Sep 1904 in Kalamazoo, Kalamazoo Co., MI, died 23 Feb 1990 in Tampa, Hillsborough Co., FL.
children
4.   i.   **Dale**.

3. Unknown BOVEE [2] (Unknown [1])
children

i. **James L** (1999 Tampa, Hillsborough Co., FL.) born abt 1934.

4. Dale BOVEE [3] (Richard J [2] Unknown [1]) (1999: res Tampa, Hillsborough Co., FL) born abt 1934. He married **Lois**.
children
  i. **Bruce** born abt 1953.
  ii. **Robert** born abt 1954. He married **Sandra**.

---

1. Charles BOVEE (1900: res: Omaha, Douglas Co., NE 1920: North Bend, Dodge Co. ,NE) (F born OH abt 1840, M born TN.) born Jan 1870 in MO. He married 1st **Alna M WADLING** born Jan 1869 in IA.
children
  i. **Victor J** born 1879.

He married 2nd **Alpha Mae WADLING** born 1879.
children
2. ii. **James**.
  iii. **Clifford** born 1 Aug 1908 in NE, died 1 Feb 1971 in Carson, Los Angeles Co., CA.
  iv. **Ronald** born 18 Jun 1911 in NE, died Jan 1986 in Omaha, Douglas Co., NE.
  v. **Ruth** born 18 Jun 1911 in NE, died 22 Jan 1993 in Tehama, Co., CA. She married **THODE**.
3. vi. **Bruce Jay**.
  vii. **Clayton** born 9 Jan 1915 in NE, died Dec 1976 in Bellevue, Sarpy Co., NE.
  viii. **Lewis A**, born 2 Feb 1918 in NE, died 27 Jun 1963 in Sierra Madre, Los Angeles Co., CA.
  ix. **Betty** born 1920. She married **PICKMYER**.

2. James BOVEE [2] (Charles [1]) born 14 Oct 1905 in NE, died 20 Oct 1972 in Lynwood, Los Angeles Co., CA. He married on 30 May 1927, **Goldie Thelma GABRIEL** born 11 May 1906, in Omaha, Douglas Co., NE, baptized 22 Jan 1922 in Omaha, Douglas Co., NE, died 21 Sep 1989.
children
  i. **Dorothy Irene** born 12 Oct 1931 in NE, died 7 Feb 1981 in Los Angeles, Los Angeles Co., CA. She married **WINSKILL**.

3. Bruce Jay BOVEE [2] (Charles [1]) (1940: res Los Angeles, Los Angeles Co., CA 1967: res Las Vegas, Clark Co., NV) born 16 May 1913 in NE, died 11 Jan 1993 in Las Vegas, Clark Co., NV. He married on 4 Jun 1934 in Omaha, Douglas Co., NE, **Mildred Lucille FURST** born 8 Mar 1917 in Omaha, Douglas Co., NE, baptized 21 Jun 1925 in Omaha, Douglas Co., NE, died 3 Jul 1942 in Los Angeles, Los Angeles Co., CA.
children
  i. **Marlene**.
  ii. **Darrel Bruce** born 4 Jul 1937 in Omaha, Douglas Co., NE. He married **Patricia M**.

---

1. **James BOVEE** (1880: Sierra Co., CA) born abt 1832 in VT. He married **Nelly** born abt 1842 in MN.

   children
   - i. **Lillian** born abt 1866 in CA.
   - ii. **Leon** (1900: Forest twp, Sierra Co., CA) born Jan 1867 in CA.
   - iii. **Clarence** born abt 1868 in CA.
   - iv. **Bertram L** born Oct 1869 in CA.
   - v. **Adel** born abt 1871 in CA.
   - vi. **Nelly** born abt 1873 in CA.
   - 2. vii. **James Francis**.
   - viii. **Daniel Forest** born abt 1877 in CA, died 17 May 1910 in Sierra Co., CA.

2. **James Francis BOVEE** [2], (James [1]) (1900: Forest twp, Sierra Co., CA. 1920 -1940: Los Angeles, Los Angeles Co., CA.) born 6 Mar 1874 in CA, died 7 Apr 1946, in Los Angeles, Los Angeles Co., CA. He married **Marguerite THOMAS** born 11 Mar 1865 in CA, died 13 May 1943 in Los Angeles Co., CA.

   children
   - i. **Frances Irma** born 25 Mar 1903 in CA, died 17 Nov 1958 in Los Angeles Co., CA. She married **VESSELLS**.
   - ii. **Claire Ida** born 9 Oct 1906 in CA, died 21 May 1986 in Placer Co., CA. She Married **KINRADE**.

---

1. **Unknown BOVEE**. He married ?--?.

   children
   - 2. i. **Stuart**.
   - 3. ii. **Chris D**.

2. **Stuart BOVEE** [2] (unknown [1]), born abt 1910 in PA. He married ?--?.

   children
   - i. **Stuart** (2000: res in MI), born abt 1938.

3. **Chris D BOVEE** [2] (unknown [1]), (1991 res: Redford, Wayne Co., MI, 1996 Detroit, MI), born abt 1918 in Pittsburg, Allegheny Co., PA. He married ?--?.

   Children
   - i. **Bruce** (1991-1996; res Redford, Wayne Co., MI).

---

1. **David BOVEE** (1938: res North Star Twp Gratiot Co., MI 47 Yrs.) born 9 Apr 1852 in Wood Co., OH, died 25 Jul 1938 in North Star Twp, Gratiot Co., MI. He married on 19 Dec 1880, **Jennie Minerva CLAY** died 1908.

   children
   - i. **Mertie** born 5 Jun 1881. She married **John PARLING**.
   - 2. ii. **Ralph**.

2. **Ralph BOVEE** [2] (David [1]) (1917: res Ashley, Washington Twp., Gratiot Co., MI) born 1884. He married **Violet**.

children

i. **Wayne** born 1907.
ii. **Lela** born 1917.

One generation families sorted alpha

Abraham BOVEE He married Hannah.
children

i. **Gilis** born 1 Jul 1791, bap 8 Feb 1795 in Evangelical Lutheran Ch, Guilderland, Albany Co., NY.
ii. **Elizabeth** born 28 Jan 1792, bap 8 Feb 1795 in Evangelical Lutheran Ch, Guilderland, Albany Co., NY.
iii. **Philip** born 24 Jul 1793, bap 8 Feb 1795 in Evangelical Lutheran Ch, Guilderland, Albany Co., NY.

Albert BOVEE (1900: res Fillmore Twp., Allegan Co., MI) born Sep 1869 in MI. He married **Siena** born Apr 1875 in MI.
children

i. **Gertrude.** born Oct 1896 in MI.
ii. **William McKinley.** born 1 Oct 1899 in MI, died Oct 1978 in Conneaut, Ashtabula Co., OH.

Alexander BOVEE Jr. born abt 1840, died 9 Aug 1877 in Utica, Oneida Co., NY. Civil War. He married on 30 Jan 1864, in St Mary's ch, Potsdam, St Lawrence Co., NY, **Miranda DELONGE** born 1842.
children

i. **John** born 28 Jan 1864, died 29 May 1865.
ii. **Henry** born 2 Sep 1866. died aft 1902.
iii. **William** born 28 Jul 1869, die aft 1902.
iv. **Alexander III** born 8 Mar 1872. died aft 1902.
v. **Julia** born 28 Sep 1876. died aft 1928. She married **Charles BABCOCK**. (1903: res Point Rock, NY, 1928 Syracuse, Onandaga Co., NY).

Andrew BOVEE born 1887, died 1929, buried in Riverside cem, Ladysmith, Rusk Co., WI. He married **Nora E**, born 1890, died 1965.
children

i. **Viola** born 1909, died 1943, buried same place,. She married **ELLINGSEN**.
ii. **Holman A** born 23 Jul 1915, died 5 Jun 1916, buried same place.

Burton N BOVEE born abt 1820 in NY. He married **Margaret** born abt 1823 in OH.
children

i. **James**, born abt 1847 In OH.

Clara A BOVEE She married abt 1847, **Alonzo BURRILL** born abt 1816, died 1854, son of Eaton Burrill and Minerva Fox.
Children

i. **Clara M** born 1848, she married **Fayette GETMAN**, son of Jeremiah Getman and Elizabeth Skinner.
  children
  i. **Ina Clara** born 1871.

Cyrus Burdett BOVEE (1900: res Luther, Lake Co., MI.) born 5 Mar 1857 in NY. He married on 19 Mar 1883 in Lake Co., MI, **Blanche MCCREADY**, born 22 Jan 1858 In PA.

children

    i.   **Meredith Dale** (1941: res Los Angeles, Los Angeles Co., CA), born Jan 1892 in Luther, Lake Co., MI.

    ii.   **Milton P**. born Aug 1893 in MI.

    iii.   **Freda B**. born Jul 1898 in MI.

Edwin Orville BOVEE (1870: res Parkersburg, Butler Co., IA) born Jan 1844 in MI. He married on 21 Sep 1867 in Albion, Butler Co., IA, **Almira R EGGLESTON.**

children

    i.   **Delia Minerva** born 8 Sep 1868 in Parkersburg, Butler Co., IA. She married **Frank Huron LOOMIS**.

        children

        i.   Gladys

Eliza BOVEE born abt 1804 in Rensselaer Co., NY. daughter of (mother) Mary, born 1769 in RI, died 12 May 1855. She married 1ˢᵗ **TOOGOOD**.

children

    i.   Daniel C born abt 1830

She married 2ⁿᵈ **William COON** born abt 1802 in Montgomery Co., NY.

children

    i.   **Lansing P** born abt 1837 in Onondaga Co., NY.

    ii.   **Celestia A** born abt 1840 in Onondaga Co., NY.

    iii.   **Caroline** born abt 1843 in Onondaga Co., NY.

    iv.   **Mary E** born abt 1847.

Flip BOVEE He married **Kint SILVESTER**.

children

    i.   **Cornelia** born 16 Dec 1749, baptized in DRC, 2ⁿᵈ River, Bellville, Essex Co., NJ.

Hannah BOVEE born abt 1820. She married 11 Jun 1839 in Stillwater, Saratoga Co., NY **Simon A VANPATTEN** born 27 Mar 1809, died 19 May 1908, buried in Old Reformed Dutch Cem, Scotia, Schenectady Co., NY.

children

    i.   **Lorenzo D** born 6 Jun 1864, died 10 May 1929. He married **Mary A Tatlor.**

Henry Hopkins BOVEE Jr. He married Ruth **CONKLIN**

Children

    i.   **William Roscoe** born 19 Jan 1938, died 16 Feb 1981 in Los Angeles Co., CA.

James H BOVEE (1880: res Guilderland, Albany Co., NY.) born abt 1831. He married Hester, born abt 1832.

children

    i.   **James**.

    ii.   **Lillian**.

Jane M BOVEE born 30 Aug 1817, died 28 Mar 1856, buried in Moses cem, Petersburg, Rensselaer Co., NY. She married on 14 Jun 1835 **John B HEWITT** born 12 May 1810 in Petersburg, Rensselaer Co., NY, died 8 Jun 1879. buried

same place.
children
  i.   **John H** born 21 Jul 1835, died 29 Nov 1890. He married 1st on 5 Dec 1857 **Mary M Taylor**, daughter of Hiram Taylor and Maria Jones. He married 2nd **Celestia Brown**, daughter of Martin Brown and Susan H Gardner.
  ii. **Sterry B** born 3 Apr 1833, died 3 Dec 1903. He married 1st **Carrie A Sweet.** He married 2nd on 2 Mar 1872 **Lois M Banker**, daughter of Henry Banker and Lois Hewitt.
  iii. **Betsey J** born 5 Jan 1841, died 17 Feb 1893. She married **Gilbert Ziba Scriven**, son of Ziba H Scriven and Lydia Smith.
  iv. **Infant** died 5 Jan 1841.
  v.   **Hannah M** born 19 Aug 1843, died 5 Oct 1906. She married on 24 Aug 1864 Hiram S Jones.

1. **John S BOVEE** (1840-1851: res Geddes, Onondaga Co., NY) born 4 Jul 1800, He married **Sarah (Sallie)Ann** born 3 May 1810.
   children
   i.   **Catherine** born 1831.
   ii. **S Elizabeth** born abt 1833.
   iii. **Margaret A** born abt 1835.
   iv. **Jennie Mahala** born 9 Oct 1842, died 11 Nov 1885. She married **Eric Wilson (Warren) LONGBOTHUM.**
        children
        i.   **Nora Belle** born 18 Aug 1875 in Lansing, Ingham Co., MI., She married **HOLLEY**.

   v.   **Alexander** born abt 1844.
   vi. **Amelia** born abt 1849.

Marvin BOVEE (1900: res Tacoma, Pierce Co., WA, 1920: Los Angeles, Los Angeles Co., CA) born Dec 1850 in NY. He married **Anna** born 1 Oct 1960 in MO, died 15 Feb 1951 in Los Angeles, Los Angeles Co., CA.
children
   i.   **Hattie** born Apr 1893 in WA.

Sarah BOVEE born abt 1799. She married in Canandaigya, Ontario, Co., NY **Birdsey WOODRUFF** born 2 Mar 1796, son of Charles Woodruff and Eleanor Orton
Children
   i.   **Margaret Jane** born 19 Jan 1822 in Clarkson, Monroe Co., NY
   ii.   **Seymour E** born 22 Aug 1824 in Clarkson, Monroe Co., NY.
   iii. **Jacob Franklin** born May 1828 in Clarkson, Monroe Co., NY.
   iv.   **James Byron** born 2 Mar 1830 in Clarkson, Monroe Co., NY.
   v.   **Sarah Rebecca** born 12 Aug 1834 in Clarkson, Monroe Co., NY.
   vi.   **Louisa Marie** born 12 Jul 1836 in Clarkson, Monroe Co., NY.
   vii. **Nelson Pomeroy** born 7 Dec 1838 in Clarkson, Monroe Co., NY.
   viii. **William B** born 5 Apr 1846 in Clarkson, Monroe Co., NY.

Unknown BOVEE.
children
   i.   **Almira** born abt 1823. She married **Benjamin HALLENBECK,** son of Anthony Hallenbeck.
   ii. **Mary E** born abt 1831, died 1904 in Kingfisher, Kingfisher Co., OK. She

married 1st **Anthony HALLENBECK**, born 1823 in Amsterdam, Montgomery Co., NY, died 1881, son of Anthony Hallenbeck.

children
- i. **William B** born abt 1851.
- ii. **Benjamin** born abt 1852, died 1921 in KS.
- iii. **Mary A** born abt 1854.
- iv. **Melissa** born abt 1855, died abt 1855.
- v. **Emily** born 1857.
- vi. **Anthony** born 1862.
- vii. **Melissa** born 1862.

She married 2nd **Levi PHELPS**.

William BOVEE (1850 census: res Orleans Co., NY 1855: res Mina, Chautauqua Co., NY) born 1815 in Montgomery Co., NY. He married **Abigail**, born 1821 in Montgomery Co., NY.

children
- i. **Hester Ann** born abt 1838 in Montgomery Co., NY.
- ii. **Malvina** born abt 1842 in Montgomery Co., NY.
- iii. **William Mathias** born abt 1845 in Orleans Co., NY.
- iv. **Mary** born 1847 in Orleans Co., NY.
- v. **Emma** born 1850 in Orleans Co., NY.
- vi. **Helen** born abt 1853 in Mina, Chautauqua Co., NY.

William BOVEE (1855: res Salina, Onondaga Co., NY) born abt 1807 in Albany Co., NY. He married **Freelove** born abt 1847 in Onondaga Co., NY.

children
- i. **Mary** born abt 1847 in Onondaga Co., NY.

Made in the USA
Lexington, KY
24 June 2011